MEDIEVAL FOUNDATIONS OF THE WESTERN INTELLECTUAL TRADITION 400–1400

The Yale Intellectual History of the West

General Editors:
John W. Burrow (University of Oxford)
William J. Bouwsma (University of California, Berkeley)
Frank M. Turner (Yale University)

Executive Editor:
Robert Baldock

This book inaugurates a major new series that seeks to provide a chronological account of the intellectual life and the development of ideas in Western Europe from the early medieval period to the present day.

Forthcoming:

The Intellectual Renaissance, 1400–1550 by Ronald Witt

The Harvest of the Renaissance, 1550–1640 by William J. Bouwsma

The World of Knowledge, 1640–1720 by Peter N. Miller

Reason's Empire: The European Enlightenment, 1710–1790
by Anthony Pagden

Intellectuals in a Revolutionary Age, 1750–1860 by Frank M. Turner

The Crisis of Reason, 1848–1920 by John W. Burrow

Medieval Foundations of the Western Intellectual Tradition 400–1400

Marcia L. Colish

Yale University Press
New Haven and London

Set in Ehrhardt by Best-set Typesetter Ltd., Hong Kong
Printed in Great Britain by Redwood Books, Wiltshire

Library of Congress Cataloging-in-Publication Data

Colish, Marcia L.
    Medieval foundations of the western intellectual tradition/by Marcia L. Colish.
    Includes bibliographical references and index.
    ISBN 0–300–07142–6
    1. Europe—Intellectual life.   2. Learning and scholarship—History—Medieval, 400–1400.   3. Comparative civilization.   I. Title.
    CB351.C54   1997   97–24370
    940—dc21   CIP

A catalogue record for this book is available from the British Library.

Permission to quote from copyrighted material is here gratefully acknowledged: extracts from 'Elene' and 'The Dream of the Rood,' trans. Charles W. Kennedy, copyright © 1963 by Charles W. Kennedy, reproduced by permission of Oxford University Press; 'Proverbs,' trans. Edward Westermark and L. P. Elwell-Sutton, and extracts from Ibn Sara, 'Pool with Turtles,' trans. Harold Moreland and Ibn Wahbun, and 'On Hearing Al-Mutanabbi Praised,' trans. Harold Moreland, both from *Anthology of Islamic Literature from the Rise of Islam to Modern Times*, edited by James Kritzeck, © 1962 by James Kritzeck, reproduced by permission of Henry Holt & Co., Inc.; extract from 'Sir Penny,' trans. George Whicher, from George Whicher, *The Goliard Poets*, copyright © 1949 by George Whicher, reproduced by permission of New Directions Pub. Corp.; extracts from Medieval Latin Lyrics (1951), trans. Helen Wadell, reproduced by permission of Constable Publishers.

10 9 8 7 6 5 4 3 2 1

Contents

Illustrations

Acknowledgments

It is my welcome duty to express my gratitude for the support and assistance I have received in writing this book. First of all, I would like to thank the general editors of the series in which it appears, especially William J. Bouwsma and Frank Turner, for inviting me to participate in that larger enterprise and for helping me to shape and focus my own contribution to it. A sabbatical leave from Oberlin College, a fellowship at the Woodrow Wilson Center in Washington, and a writing residency at the Rockefeller Foundation's Study and Conference Center at the Villa Serbelloni in Bellagio enabled me to put the book in its final form, and in ideal scholarly and physical settings. Several colleagues have lent me their expertise in specialized areas, giving me bibliographical leads and helpful reactions to my ideas, notably Jonathan Berkey, Steven Plank, Yasser Tabbaa, Natalia Teteriatnikov, and Nancy Van Deusen. Arjo Vanderjagt and Suzanne Nelis have kindly permitted me to use their unpublished findings on Anselm of Canterbury's description of God in *Proslogion* 2 and on his access to Boethius' logical curriculum, respectively. John P. Fanning read the manuscript in its entirety, catching errors as well as offering helpful suggestions for how to make it as accessible as possible to non-specialists. An anonymous reader for the press also flagged some errors, enabling me to correct them. The technical assistance of Thelma Roush and Terri Mitchell has been invaluable.

On a personal and scholarly level, the people who have helped me the most in my visions and revisions of medieval intellectual history have been the students to whom it has been my privilege to teach this subject at Oberlin College for over thirty years. I am happy to note in particular the contributions of Derek Churchill on Carolingian monasticism, Michael Bastedo on the status of women in early Germanic law codes, and Laura Gobbi on Hroswita of Gandersheim's use of her hagiographical sources, which I have folded into my account of those subjects. More than merely an audience, my students have been my true collaborators. Their enthusiasm, eagerness to learn, incisive intelligence, and responsiveness have been a continuing source of inspiration. Above all, they have shown me, as I hope to show the reader, that with good will and imagination we can enter a world of thought and sensibility remote from our own and understand that past world in its own terms. I dedicate this book to my students, with affection and my deepest thanks.

Introduction

Some readers of this book may be surprised by its claim that the foundations of western intellectual history were laid in the Middle Ages and not in classical Greece and Rome or the Judeo-Christian tradition. In defense of that claim we argue that the thought of western Europe acquired its particular character not only as a result of the cultural components that flowed into it. Equally important were the attitudes that western thinkers took to their sources and the uses to which they put them. It is certainly true that medieval thinkers expressed concerns, tastes, tolerances, and sensibilities that distinguish this period from other chapters of the western intellectual experience. At the same time, they developed institutions, viewpoints, and methods that mark them as specifically western and that help to explain why medieval Europe is the only traditional society known to history to modernize itself from within, intellectually no less than economically and technologically, enabling Europe to impose its cultural as well as political stamp on much of the non-European world as the Middle Ages drew to a close.

Both the uniqueness of the western medieval achievement and its shared history with its neighbors can best be grasped by comparing medieval Europe with the other contemporary civilizations that joined it in acquiring the lands of the former Roman empire. These sister civilizations, Byzantium and Islam, including the Jewish thinkers who were part of the Arabic-speaking intellectual community, had much in common with western Europe. All three were religious cultures, grounded in a revealed faith handed down in a sacred text interpreted authoritatively by the religious leaders and institutions that each society invested with this right and responsibility. All three were complex civilizations made up of a mix of peoples of differing ethnicity, language, and culture, owing to the fortunes of war and the migrations of peoples from the Asian section of the Eurasian land-mass. All three, as well, inherited the legacy of Greece and Rome. In each case there was an official culture combining these diverse elements to a greater or lesser degree and a culture that was not official. Each of these medieval societies created systems for the patronage of religion, learning, and the arts, systems that have some parallels with each other.

Yet, despite these similarities, faithful adherence to tradition and the creative use of it varied from one of these civilizations to another. Of the three, Byzantine culture made the most brilliant early start, only to crystallize fairly early. Apart from new developments in law and the visual arts, and military technology, Byzantine intellectual life after the eleventh century, despite a brief rally just before its demise in 1453, lapsed into a mode of conservatism in which the veneration of canonical authorities and the imitation of past models became a substitute for experimentation and change. Islam rose swiftly to the challenge of absorbing oriental as well as classical culture as the caliphate expanded into the Near East and Persia, becoming the most dynamic and original of the three sister civilizations in the early Middle Ages. Its scholars made creative and important contributions to the natural sciences, medicine, mathematics, philosophy, art, and literature, as well as elaborating Muslim theology and religious law. None the less, both in their Spanish outpost conquered in the eighth century and in the Near East, the Muslims failed to capitalize on their commanding lead in speculative thought after the twelfth century. For its part, western Europe made a painfully slow start. At the beginning of the Middle Ages its intellectual leaders were concerned with preserving the essentials of the Latin Christian culture of the late Roman empire and with spreading it to the Celtic and Germanic conquerers of western Europe. The institutions and values of the latter two peoples contributed a critical ingredient to the mix. Successive waves of invaders from Asia, from the Muslim world to the south, and from the Viking north repeatedly put at risk their gains and accomplishments. Compared with Islam and Byzantium, early medieval Europe was definitely bringing up the rear.

Such is the assessment that a hypothetical traveler would probably have made, fresh from a tour of the cultural capitals of the Mediterranean world and northern Europe in the year 1100. Had such a traveller been asked to predict which of these societies would produce a scientific revolution in the seventeenth century and an Enlightenment in the eighteenth, chances are that he or she would have bet on Islam. Yet, despite its apparently lackluster start, its need to reacquire much of its own classical heritage from its neighbors, and its long latency, it was western Europe that shot ahead, starting in the twelfth century. Western medieval thinkers developed the means and methods that enabled them to outpace the Byzantines and Muslims decisively in the high Middle Ages, creating new forms of thought and art that achieved Europe's intellectual modernization by the end of the period. In so doing, they produced a culture with its own, distinctively medieval qualities. They also produced institutions and attitudes, ways of dealing with their sources and their own new ideas that emerge as distinctively western and that connect the Middle Ages with subsequent chapters of European intellectual history.

The body of the book that follows is divided into two parts treating the early and the high Middle Ages respectively. Part I will cover the period from the late Roman world up through the eleventh century. Here we will consider the transition from Roman Christianity to the Latin Christian culture of the early Middle Ages in several stages, ending with the revival of speculative thought in the eleventh century. We will also investigate the vernacular cultures of the period in order to grasp their character and to see how, and how much, they interacted with Latin Christian culture. Part I will conclude with an extended comparison among western

Europe, Byzantium, and Islam. In Part II we will abandon the largely chronological organization of Part I in favor of a thematic approach. After grounding the thought of the high Middle Ages in the Renaissance of the twelfth century and its educational reforms, we will consider literature both vernacular and Latin, religious culture both clerical and lay and both orthodox and heterodox, scholastic philosophy and theology, and the impact of scholasticism on science, law, economic theory, and political theory including ecclesiology. The conclusion to Part II and to the book as a whole will raise and seek to answer the question, 'When did the Middle Ages end?' as a heuristic device for flagging those developments that are typically medieval and that do not survive the period as well as those that link medieval thought to the periods following it or that serve as foundations of the western intellectual tradition more generally.

PART I

FROM ROMAN CHRISTIANITY TO THE LATIN CHRISTIAN CULTURE OF THE EARLY MIDDLE AGES

CHAPTER 1

From Apology to the Constantinian Establishment

In charting the development of Christian thought in its Roman environment and in understanding the ways in which Christian intellectuals addressed the classical tradition we must first note that both the classical tradition and Christianity itself had undergone significant change before the earliest Latin Christian writers took up their pens. From a small Palestinian sect whose first converts were mostly Jews, the Christian church had expanded widely in the Mediterranean world by the third century and now drew most of its new members from pagan religions. In addition to adhering to the Roman state cult and to personal and family gods, many of these converts had been educated in the Roman schools and were familiar with philosophy as well as the liberal arts. As they knew it, the classical tradition was the legacy of Greek thought as it had been appropriated by Romans, who emphasized some aspects of it, downplayed others, and added their own perspective to the materials on which they drew. Thinkers in the Latin-speaking early Middle Ages were largely dependent on the Roman version of the classical tradition, unlike the Byzantines, who possessed that tradition fully in both its ancient languages, and unlike the Muslims, who made use of only some aspects of Greek thought once their conquests put them in possession of formerly Byzantine territories and subjects.

The Classical Background

The areas of Greek thought of least interest to the Romans were its most speculative and theoretical subjects, natural science and philosophy. Where the Greeks sought a systematic understanding of the essential natures of things, of being, truth, and goodness, of the world order and the interconnections of its phenomena, and where they developed methods for testing answers to scientific and philosophical questions and for predicting outcomes on the basis of existing patterns, the Romans were content to accept the findings of the Greeks, anthologizing their science in handbooks and applying it to technological problems. In philosophy they focused on ethics, its most practical aspect. In legal and political theory, they cared less for the Greeks' speculations on constitutional dynamics, their rationales for the best state, and their abstract definitions of law and justice, concentrating instead on the creation of institutions capable of governing a large and complex empire and on the development of a legal system whose principles and procedures proved applicable not only to ancient Rome but to later entities as diverse from it and from each other as the medieval church and modern France, Germany, and Italy.

Religion, literature, and art were areas where the Roman approach was closer to the Greek, although the Romans sometimes altered these fields to suit themselves. Both societies shared the same polytheistic religion. The Romans simply gave Latin names to the Greek gods. Like the Greeks, they practiced the public cult of the gods at temples and at natural sites where deities were held to be especially present. They believed in divination, in portents and oracles, and in the apotheosis of rulers and heroes. They also offered personal devotion to deities chosen by the individual. The same range of opinions about the afterlife can be found in Greece and Rome. The Romans added the practice of ancestor worship, the idea of cultic celibacy in the order of Vestal Virgins, and, as their conquests brought them into contact with a wide number of Near Eastern and western Asian religions, mysticism and mystery cults became popular. The Romans freely expanded their pantheon to include the gods of their new provincials. So long as they performed the state cult and venerated the emperor as the embodiment of the state, they could continue to practice their existing religions, a sticking point only for Jews and Christians in the Roman empire.

All the genres of literature produced by Roman writers originated with the Greeks. Roman authors were well aware of their dependence on Greek models and sometimes deliberately imitated them. In some areas they nuanced these genres, importing, for example, a nostalgic coloration into the pastoral poetry celebrating nymphs and shepherds in their sylvan glades and urbanizing the epic hero, giving him more subtle moral qualities beyond his standard military prowess and courage. Some forms of Greek literature did not draw much attention fom Roman writers because the social or religious contexts for their production in Greece did not exist in Rome. Tragedy, to be performed at state expense as part of a communal religious celebration after an open competition designed to obtain the best plays, is a case in point, as are the odes praising the victors in athletic contests such as the Olympian games. In Rome, while there was little incentive to write tragedy, comedy served the same function of satirizing a range of social stereotypes as it had in Greece. But the Romans developed a new and extremely vulgar type of comedy not found in Greece, commissioned by the state for performance to the masses as part of the emperors' bread and circuses policy.

The Romans also took over major Greek art forms. In architecture, the temple with an open colonnade, a triangular pediment, and an inner room housing the cult statue preserves the same form in Greek and Roman art. But, while the Greeks sited temples on high places, designed to be seen in relation to the landscape and to be approached from an angle and appreciated as freestanding art objects in their own right, the Romans placed temples in the middle of the forum, to be approached frontally as the worshipper entered and paid his respects to the god in between the political, economic, and social activities that brought him to the forum. The Romans achieved major architectural innovations of their own by using brick as a building material. Their large domed buildings and triumphal arches are salient examples. In the representation of the human figure in art, Roman painters and sculptors had a series of Greek models to consider, from the abstract archaic style to the idealized classical style to Hellenistic naturalism and expressionism. Their own taste led them to emphasize naturalistic portraiture, warts and all. Panel paintings, portrait statues, and busts of emperors and ancestors that really resembled their subjects also proliferated as a function of the cult of these personages in Roman religion.

The areas in which there was the most consistency between the Greeks and Romans lie in the field of literature and in the theory and practice of education. Along with literary genres that the Romans modified there were many they did not, notably satire, love poetry, philosophical poetry, historiography, and rhetoric. Indeed, rhetoric was the subject emphasized by the educational systems of both Greece and Rome. Initially there were two theories of education advocated in ancient Greece, Platonic and Isocratean. For Plato (*c.* 427–348 BC), the goal of education was a theoretical grasp of truth. All other subjects and stages of the student's career were designed to lead him to that end. On the other hand, Isocrates (436–338 BC) emphasized a literary education culminating in rhetoric, to prepare the student to take part in public life. Even after the city-state democracy presupposed by Isocrates as the context for his program was replaced by imperial bureaucracy in the age of Alexander the Great (*fl.* 356–23 BC), the essentially literary education he promoted won the day, as a means of forming good taste. The Romans took over the Isocratean system as it had been formalized in the late Hellenistic era. They agreed that education should include the study of standard liberal arts in the same sequence by each student. By the first century BC these arts were seven in number: grammar, logic, rhetoric, arithmetic, geometry, astronomy, and music. Grammar meant language study in both Greek and Latin as well as poetry. Roman rhetoric focused on prose and on eloquence in the Latin tongue. It embraced forensic oratory, both judicial and deliberative, and epideictic oratory, or all other forms of prose and public speaking. Logic was largely subordinated to rhetoric and seen as a source of arguments on which an orator might draw. Music meant music theory, music in its relationship to mathematics or rhetoric, rather than composition, performance, or music appreciation. Although other scientific subjects such as arithmetic, geometry, and astronomy were studied after the language arts, rhetoric was the crown of the curriculum. Following grammar school, the student completed his education at the school of the rhetor, a prestigious and state-supported position in Rome. Whether in the republican era or the age of the principate and whether or not Roman citizens could actually play a meaningful role in public life, the Romans agreed with the Isocratean emphasis on a literary culture based on canonical authors: through their imitation and appreciation, the student's taste would be formed. It would be a taste he shared with the community of learned men, living and dead. Literally, the liberal arts were designed for the aesthetic and intellectual formation of students who were both legally free and male. While some women were educated at home, they played no role in the Roman school system. Any professional training beyond the schools of rhetoric, outside of that provided by the state law schools in the later Roman empire, was arranged at the individual's own initiative and expense, with the architect, jurisconsult, physician, or philosopher with whom he studied on an apprenticeship basis. Romans studied scientific and philosophical subjects in Greek, using the standard texts in that language. Typically, Romans seeking advanced training in these fields went to Athens or Alexandria, or to another of the Greek-speaking parts of their empire where these studies were concentrated, or sought tuition from a learned Greek slave at home.

Heresy

The Greco-Roman world of learning, as characterized above, was the environment into which the Christian movement increasingly made its way. Its progress was impeded by the official persecution of Christians for failing to participate in the state cult. At the same time, the church in the Roman empire faced massive intellectual challenges. It is the response to these challenges that shaped the agenda of Roman Christian thinkers and that provided their Latin Christian successors in the early Middle Ages with their intellectual self-definition. While the language, rhetoric, and Old Testament references in the New Testament may have spoken meaningfully to converts from Judaism, they were often obstacles to classically educated pagans. As early as the Acts of the Apostles, St. Paul was shown underlining the parallels between pagan thought and Christianity in his mission to the Gentiles, and the Pauline Epistles to them did not shrink from using classical rhetoric. The Old Testament had already been translated into Greek by the Jews of Alexandria; translating both Testaments into Latin was a necessity and it was done. But this was only a partial solution to the problem of explaining Christian doctrines in terminology that pagans could understand. In the eyes of many Roman Christians, recasting these doctrines in classical literary and conceptual forms was a missionary strategy needed to win pagan hearts and minds. At the same time, they were acutely conscious of the fact that this very process might lead to the debasement or perversion of the Christian message. Some new Christians, it emerged, had indeed misinterpreted Christian doctrines precisely because they had applied classical ideas or criteria to them. The period between the second and the fourth centuries thus witnessed both a meeting of minds between the Christian and classical traditions and the misconstruction of Christianity in some quarters because of it. Side by side with state persecution and the criticisms of non-Christians, the church found itself beset by heresies within the fold resulting from the tendency of pagan converts to try Christian ideas on for size and to tailor them to fit pagan assumptions, whether religious or philosophical.

This emergence of heresy is a phenomenon important to intellectual historians for several reasons. First, it points to the difficulty of re-expressing Christianity in classical terms in the Roman era. Second, the kinds of heresies that proliferated at this time are highly indicative of the mentality of the pagan converts and the kind of stumbling block that they found in the new faith. The key point is that the heretics of this period focused immediately on inherently speculative issues and on doctrines central to Christianity, doctrines that distinguish it from other religions. Analytical minds capable of distinguishing essential teachings from their corollaries were clearly at work here. In particular, the doctrine of the Trinity, the nature of Christ, and the problem of evil were the most troublesome. A third, more general point must be made about heresy. Over time, the nexus of doctrine comprising the consensus of what Christians have thought defines orthodoxy has shifted even as the vocabulary in which the doctrines are articulated has changed. What counts as heresy in this book is what the majority of Christians in the centuries it covers thought was unacceptable. Their very effort to grapple with heresy and to explain why it constituted error led them to state the orthodox consensus position more clearly. In this sense, heresies are important historical markers telling us what the perceived problems in Christianity were at particular times and they also served as catalysts in the development of orthodox doctrine.

A large number of the heresies in the late Roman world reflect the difficulties some new Christians had with the idea that Christ, as the second person of the Trinity, is the metaphysical equal of God the Father, and with the idea that the incarnate Christ can be fully God and fully man at the same time. The first of these doctrines, indeed, the doctrine of the Trinity as such, seemed inconsistent with the principle of monotheism. On the other hand, a series of three deities arranged in a hierarchical order made sense to people familiar with Neoplatonism, which held that there is a supreme being, the One, from which emanates Mind, from which emanates the World Soul, the latter two subordinate to their predecessors. The same notion appealed to pagan religionists whose pantheons included first-order gods and second-order gods. For its part, the idea that a single individual could be fully divine and fully human at the same time flew in the face of logic and metaphysics alike. On this latter point, the Christological heresies can be divided into two groups, illustrated by the Nestorians and the Adoptionists, although their positions in no sense exhaust the possibilities. The Nestorians emphasized Christ's divinity at the expense of His humanity, arguing that His incarnation, life in the body, passion, and resurrection were illusory, not real. The Adoptionists emphasized Christ's humanity at the expense of His divinity, arguing that Jesus was a human being and no more, although He had been 'adopted' by God and given special powers, along the lines of Old Testament prophets or wonder-working saints who were, nevertheless, only human. The most elaborate and popular Christological heresy of the time was Arianism. Part of its appeal lay in its grounding in biblical exegesis as well as in norms palatable to the philosophical mind and to the mind of the pagan religionist alike. Culling passages from the New Testament which they held supported this view, the Arians taught that, even before His incarnation, God the Son was metaphysically inferior to God the Father. This subordination, they held, could only increase in the incarnation. And, since the sum total of any compound being must add up to 100 percent, the Arians concluded that the incarnate Christ was 50 percent human and 50 percent divine. Aside from its neat resolution of the logical and metaphysical anomaly in the orthodox view of Christ's nature, this Arian position also made sense to people comfortable with the notion of demigods, persons born of unions between gods and mortals, and of human beings apotheosized fully or in part, both of which are found in Greco-Roman religion.

For the Arians, the Son is subordinate to the Father; but an alternative way of dealing with the paradox of one God with three equal persons was to reverse that relationship. One prominent attempt to do so was Montanism, which applied chronological distinctions to the persons of the Trinity. In the first age in Montanist chronology, extending from the creation of the universe to the eve of the incarnation, God the Father, the creator, was the only God. The Old Testament and its rules of conduct were His normative revelation to mankind and the Jews were His chosen people. In the second age, initiated by the incarnation, God the Son, the redeemer, was the only God. Christ made God the Father obsolete; likewise, the New Testament and the Christian church made the Old Testament and the Jewish community obsolete. In turn, this second age would be followed by the third, in which the Holy Spirit, the sanctifier, would replace God the Son as the only God. His direct inspiration of His chosen people would replace the entire Bible and He would teach them how to behave without any formal rules or any institutionalized religious community. Most Montanists thought that the third age was imminent; some thought that Montanus (*c.* 135–75), their leader, was ushering it in. Before leaving Montanism, another version of which we will encounter later, it is worth noting that, despite the antinomianism that the Montanists thought would prevail in the age of the Holy Spirit, they led lives of strict asceticism, which they felt was their duty as heralds of the new dispensation.

A heresy unique at the time for its capacity to touch so many bases and to address virtually all the theological problems reflected by other heresies was Gnosticism. The Gnostics developed not only a theory concerning Christ's nature and His relationship to God the Father but also a theory of human nature and of the human dilemma and a cosmological scenario that offered a metaphysical answer to the problem of evil. This sect was extremely syncretistic, with a marked propensity for borrowing from diverse traditions. It existed in a purely pagan form and in a Jewish form in addition to attaching itself to Christianity. The most minimalist version of Gnostic doctrine will be presented here. A central principle of Gnosticism, the one that provides its name, is the idea that *gnosis*, or knowledge in Greek, is the essence of salvation, and that all saving knowledge can be known by reason, at least for adepts in the sect. This notion harks back to the Greek scientific and philosophical assumption that the human mind is adequate to the universe, which is intrinsically knowable. It also reflects the spiritual inegalitarianism of some of the mystery cults. It is an outlook at odds with the Christian grounding of the religious life on a faith that all can possess but that can yield only partial knowledge in this life.

The Gnostics' saving knowledge begins with a version of the creation that also fails to square with the account in Genesis. Like the Neoplatonists, they start with a creator deity, the One, a purely spiritual being from whom being flows, or emanates, into a series of subordinate spiritual beings, called *aeons*. As with all versions of emanationist metaphysics, the Gnostics' supreme being is held to create out of the superabundance of being in His own nature. In effect, He cannot refrain from creating. According to the Gnostics, the transition from the spiritual to the physical order is effected by two *aeons* quite low on the hierarchy of *aeons*. The phenomenal world first issues from the womb of an earth-mother *aeon* in a form-less state. Order is imposed on it by another low-status *aeon*, conceived of in masculine terms and equated with the creator God of the Old Testament.

Within the created order as envisioned by the Gnostics human beings are faced with a dilemma, the problem of evil, stemming from their very nature and not from anything they have chosen or done. Since the Gnostics saw spirit as good and matter as evil, intrinsically, and since the essence of a person, the soul, is trapped in a material body, the very situation of mankind makes redemption necessary. The Gnostics shared with the Stoics the idea that the human soul is, metaphysically, a spark of the divine. This belief makes even more hateful its entrapment in an evil body. Redemption in this theology is redemption of the soul from the body. But, not all can achieve it. The Gnostics divided mankind into three categories with inborn traits, the carnal, psychical, and spiritual, in the light of a person's prevail-ing temperament. Some Gnostics equated the three categories with pagans, Jews, and Christians, respectively. Either way, and despite the challenge to this theory represented by the fact of frequent conversion from one of these religions to another in late antiquity, they held that a person's capacity for salvation was rigidly determined by the accident of birth, and was unchangeable. The carnal, hopelessly enslaved by the body, would never be saved. The psychical had a better chance. But salvation was guaranteed only to the spiritual, who alone could be initiated fully into saving knowledge. This knowledge, the Gnostics held, was made available by Christ, Who imparts it to them. The Gnostics' Christology departed as radically from orthodox Christianity as their view of creation and human nature. Christ, they held, was an *aeon*, a purely spiritual being higher up on the hierarchy than the creator *aeon* and His earth-mother collaborator. Christ's incarnation, they agreed with the Nestorians, was really an illusion, undertaken to facilitate the communi-cation of saving knowledge, a communication emphasizing the definition of evil as matter and the Gnostics' view of the proper response to it. The ethics flowing from this position did not see moral agents as responsible for their actions since one's moral aptitudes and options were deemed to be givens over which one has no control.

For the spirituals, at least, there was one area in which they could exercise free will, in deciding whether to reunite the soul with God swiftly, by asceticism, or more slowly, by doing whatever they wanted with their bodies. In either path, the body was not seen by the Gnostics as part of our essential humanity. They privi-leged the ascetic route and downgraded social institutions, such as marriage and the family, that cater to life in the body. Gnostic ecclesiology also parted company with that of the orthodox church, since their church numbered as true members only the spirituals who could be full initiates.

Gnostic metaphysics, cosmogenesis, Christology, anthropology, ethics, and eccle-siology all presented serious problems for Christian leaders, especially since this heresy offered a far more comprehensive world view than was true of other early heresies, while at the same time it included elements attractive to philosophically trained minds as well as to adherents of mystery cults. In addition, Gnosticism had its own interpretation of Scripture and its own gospels and it accorded to women wider leadership opportunities than were available in post-biblical Christianity. It shared with another heresy of the time, Manicheism, the principle of metaphysical dualism, resolving the problem of evil that arises in any monotheistic theology by proposing that spirit and matter, identified as good and evil, had been created by different deities. It is easy to see why Gnosticism, along with Arianism, had a widespread appeal to new Christians and why they, and other heresies, no less than the pagan alternatives to Christianity, demanded a response from orthodox Christian thinkers.

The Latin Apologists: Tertullian, Minucius Felix, Lactantius

Even the briefest consideration of heresies in the early church indicates that classical philosophy and religion, if applied to Christian doctrine, could misrepresent it; at the same time, Christian leaders were convinced that classical thought could and should be used to clarify and defend the Christian message. On one level, they took collective action by defining the canon of Holy Scripture, ruling out the apocrypha to which some heretics appealed. Another major collective policy was the formulation of creeds stating the essentials of Christian belief in language philosophers could understand, an action taken by ecumenical church councils, which thus became the highest locus of ecclesiastical authority for the articulation of theological truth. The creed defined by the council fathers at Nicaea in 325 is the single most important case in point. A comparison of its terminology with that of the earlier Apostles' Creed reflects the shift to a more precise philosophical vocabulary. Yet another collective effort of churchmen was to institute catechetical schools for new Christians and for children. From the standpoint of intellectual history, the most notable of the anti-heresy policies was the defense of orthodoxy and the attack on heresy and paganism by individual writers, the apologists. Their strategies of argument are diverse, ranging from hostility to conciliation. Nor do they all target the same issues in classical thought as the likeliest source of theological error for Christians. The three Latin apologists considered next were familiar with the work of their Greek opposite numbers and took some cues from them. But all are interesting for the decidedly Roman approach they take to the task of apology and for their courage as well, since they wrote at a time when Christianity was illegal in the Roman world and they invited sanctions by calling attention to themselves in their writings. Three other generalizations may be made about them. Tertullian, Minucius Felix, and Lactantius all received an excellent classical education and held important professional posts, which in turn reflects the fact that they came from the upper ranks of society. All three were converts and sometimes suffered persecution on that account. And, all hailed from the north African province of the church, a region to whose vibrant intellectual and ecclesiastical life their works testify.

The first Latin apologist and the first Latin Christian writer altogether was Tertullian (*c.* 155–220). Trained in rhetoric and law, he was an advocate by profession, a fact which is clearly evident in some of his writings. His apologetic style is one of invective and denunciation. He aims at the complete demolition of his opponent, not his persuasion. Reveling in flamboyant rhetorical excess, his weapon of choice is the bludgeon not the scalpel. Alternatives, as Tertullian presents them, are black and white absolutes, with no shades of gray. This penchant for extremism in stating positions appears to have been a reflection of Tertullian's personality as well as a rhetorical stance he deliberately assumed. For, after defending Christian orthodoxy for decades he became a Montanist. The ethical rigor of that sect seems to have been its attraction for him.

The enemies Tertullian targets, both inside and outside the Christian fold, are pagans and heretics, especially Gnostics. His two most famous attacks on them are his *Apology* and his *Prescription against Heretics*. The arguments in these two works have much in common, both drawing on forensic oratory and legal procedures. The *Apology*, addressed to the governors of all provinces of the Roman empire, is framed as a lawyer's speech to the prosecutor, the Roman state, on behalf of Christianity, the defendant, explaining why the charges against him should be dropped. Tertullian first argues that there is no evidence to support the pagans' claim that Christians are immoral. Next, he tries to cast doubt on the credibility of the pagan accusers, attacking not only the substance of their criticism but also their good faith. Having done so, he then urges the prosecution to drop the case for yet another reason. The policy of persecution, he observes, simply does not work. It just produces martyrs, and 'The blood of martyrs is the seed of new Christians,'[1] one of his most oft-quoted lines.

Equally forensic is the rhetoric of the *Prescription*. The title itself denotes a term of art in Roman law, a procedure enabling a defendant to reject the plaintiff's charge, in effect throwing the case out of court. In this work, heretics are the plaintiff. In addition to invoking this legal ploy, the *Prescription* is of interest because in it Tertullian states the criteria distinguishing true doctrine from heresy, criteria that proved influential. First, he notes, the apostles received true doctrine from Christ Himself. Then, they handed it down to the bishops ruling the local churches they founded. In turn, these bishops handed it down to their successors, up to the present day. The norm of orthodoxy, for Tertullian, is thus twofold: the unbroken apostolic succession of bishops, and the consensus of those bishops. We should note here, in considering Tertullian's understanding of the locus of doctrinal authority in the church, that he wrote before the first ecumenical councils provided an institutional forum for the articulation of episcopal consensus. His criteria were later combined with the legislative authority of such councils. Tertullian's norms of orthodoxy were influentially recast in the fifth century by Vincent of Lérins, whose formula states that doctrines are true if they have been held 'always, everywhere, by everyone.'[2]

In the works just discussed, Tertullian devotes more attention to the forensic tactics of the apology's form than to the defense of particular doctrines; at most, in the *Apology*, his goal is to exculpate Christians from alleged immorality. Tertullian also wrote apologies framed as attacks on specific figures, most of whom he charges with Gnosticism. In developing his case against them he states some substantive theological points, both positive and negative. His main argument against the Gnostics is that, in refusing to submit to the rule of faith and in rejecting the principle that, in this life, our knowledge of theological truth is, perforce, partial, they are guilty of the primordial sin, intellectual pride. It is in this context of anti-Gnostic apology that Tertullian's famous lines, 'I believe because it is absurd,'[3] and 'What has Athens to do with Jerusalem?'[4] appear. What he criticizes here in attacking Gnosticism, under the heading of 'Athens,' is the philosophical mentality as such, the idea that reason alone is sufficient. While in other works he draws selectively and knowledgeably on particular philosophical teachings that he regards as compatible with particular Christian doctrines, and while he acknowledges a real continuity between reason and faith, arguing that the human soul is naturally Christian, he clearly sees in philosophy as a comprehensive method and world view the most serious threat to Christian orthodoxy. And, as for rhetoric, his apologies show with equal clarity his view that Christianity has nothing to fear from the classical literary tradition.

Our second Latin apologist, Minucius Felix (late second century), likewise a lawyer, could not be more different from Tertullian in his approach. In *Octavius*, his only known work, Minucius accents the similarity between paganism and Christianity. And, while he makes some lawyer's points, the genre of literature he draws on is not forensic rhetoric but the philosophical dialogue. This genre, invented by Plato, had a more recent Roman exponent in Cicero (106–43 BC). In particular, Minucius draws on Cicero's *On the Nature of the Gods* as his model. Both his and Cicero's dialogues feature interlocutors who are lawyers and friends, cultivated men who admire and respect each other even when they disagree. In both dialogues the speakers are discussing religion while taking a stroll on a holiday when the courts are closed. The tone of voice throughout the *Octavius* is urbane, gracious, and eloquent, a style Minucius chooses deliberately. For his chief argument is that pagans and Christians are much alike. Conversion to Christianity will not be an intellectual, ethical, or aesthetic disruption for the pagan, since Christianity will enable him to attain the highest and purest aspirations toward wisdom and goodness that his own background has given him.

Minucius makes some other deliberate, and telling, choices in providing Caecilius, the pagan interlocutor, with his lines. He does not present Caecilius as a follower of Platonism, Aristotelianism, Stoicism, or Epicureanism, philosophical schools with positive and systematic positions. Rather, he presents Caecilius as a Skeptic. Some Skeptics held that it was impossible to possess certitude of any kind. Others held that one could arrive at probable truth and that this norm was a sufficient basis for practical ethical decisions. As a defender of pagan philosophy, then, Caecilius professes no positive position. Minucius makes a similarly strategic decision in depicting Caecilius as a pagan religionist. Far from being a hot-eyed fanatic or a member of an ecstatic mystery cult, he is a devotee of the state cult which, he says, should be observed on probabilist grounds and as a matter of convention, good form, and civic spirit. He has two objections to Christianity. One is the alleged improprieties occurring at Eucharistic celebrations and the low social status of most Christians, which undermines their credibility in his eyes. He also expresses discomfort with the doctrines of God's unity and ubiquity and the resurrection of the body.

As the Christian interlocutor, Octavius, takes the floor, he opens with a lawyer's argument against Caecilius' moral critique of Christians. Noting that Caecilius, on his own testimony, has never attended a Eucharistic service himself, Octavius points out that the charge of impropriety he submits is based on hearsay, and hence inadmissible. Further, he observes, on Caecilius' own evidence, Christians, irrespective of their social status, lead exemplary lives, to the point of martyrdom. Here, Octavius appeals to Caecilius' sense of fair play and his knowledge of the legal rules of evidence. In dealing with his doctrinal objections, Octavius' strategy is to show the continuities between classical philosophy, especially Stoicism, and the Christian beliefs in question. Fully as important as the doctrinal issues that Minucius includes are those he omits. He is careful not to refer to Christian doctrines that have no parallels or analogies in classical philosophy. This pre-selected assortment of points on which he can argue for the similarities between paganism and Christianity is thoroughly in line with the graceful and elegant literary style of the dialogue, designed to persuade pagans that they will not have to give anything up in becoming Christians.

Our final apologist displays a temperament and a set of arguments different from those of Tertullian and Minucius Felix, as well as a response to the altered historical circumstances in which he wrote. Lactantius (*c.* 250–*c.* 326) lived through a momentous change in the official Roman policy toward Christianity, marked by the Edict of Milan issued in 312 by the Emperor Constantine (306–37), which made the church a legitimate corporation within the Roman state. The same emperor was the first Roman ruler to convert to Christianity. This new situation required Lactantius, and other Latin Christian writers of the fourth century, to regroup in decisive ways. Lactantius wrote apology both before and after 312. He experienced persecution for his faith at the hands of Constantine's predecessors and later enjoyed Constantine's patronage. Thanks to his support, Lactantius was able to write the first positive exposition of Christian doctrine in Latin after the legitimization of the church. His works thus are a valuable index of how that transition was internalized by Lactantius and his contemporaries.

Lactantius was a professional rhetorician, holding a public chair in Nicomedia until anti-Christian legislation in 303 forced him to resign. After years of difficulty, he sprang back when Constantine appointed him tutor to his son in 317. Although that prince was later executed for treason, Lactantius remained Constantine's protégé for the rest of his life. It is easy to see why he regarded Constantine as a personal hero as well as a hero in Christian history more generally.

Although the arguments offered in Lactantius' three major works, *On God's Handiwork* (*c.* 303–4), *On the Deaths of the Persecutors* (before 321), and the *Institutes* (completed after 313 and dedicated to Constantine), differ given his changing personal situation and the changing status of the church when he wrote, all three display stylistic traits that are his hallmarks. Cicero is Lactantius' stylistic model and he attains remarkable success in emulating him. His Latin is lucid and elegant. His aim is appropriateness, restraint, the avoidance of exaggeration, colloquialism, and idiosyncrasy. The extremely high literary polish of his work led Lactantius later to be dubbed 'the Christian Cicero.' For him, as for Tertullian and Minucius, the classical literary tradition held no dangers and he saw no problem in adapting it to Christian purposes.

Turning from form to content, Lactantius' apologies reveal another facet of his mind, his rather sketchy grasp of Christian theology. In *On God's Handiwork*, framed as a theodicy, the issues he targets do not really address the doctrinal difficulties that pagans found in Christianity. While he demonstrates a respectable acquaintance with Platonism and Stoicism, he lacks Tertullian's sense of the nature and rational claims of the philosophical enterprise as such. His approach is not systematic but random, selecting individual philosophical ideas with which he agrees or disagrees. It is true that the schools and thinkers he cites support the view that the rational order of the cosmos points to the existence of a rational and benevolent creator ruling it providentially. Unlike them, however, Lactantius glides right by the pendant problem of evil, despite the fact that the Gnostics and Manichees had made it a burning issue, and one for which the Bible and the Stoics, to whom he refers, had offered non-dualistic answers. With Minucius, he is extremely selective, accenting the parallels between carefully chosen classical ideas and their Christian counterparts, and letting the rest go by the board.

The *Institutes*, however, is apology in a new key. In addition to attacking paganism, this is also the first Latin effort to expound Christian doctrine positively. In the first section of the work, aimed against paganism now that the cause of the church has been vindicated, Lactantius departs from the conciliatory tone he had taken in his first apology and argues that pagan thought has no redeeming features whatsoever. His technique is to beat the pagans with their own stick, citing pagan philosophical and religious texts that criticize pagan cult practices, that advocate monotheism, and that allegedly foretell the coming of Christ. Another line of attack, and a weak one given his use of philosophy elsewhere in the work, is the claim that, since the philosophical schools disagree, philosophy as such is an unreliable source of truth. Here, Lactantius makes no effort to refute any particular philosophical position. Still, having disposed of the philosophers, at least to his own satisfaction, he turns to the positive exposition of Christianity. In this section of the *Institutes*, he shows little interest in basic dogma and the teachings he presents are not always handled impeccably. Ethics is his main focus. Lactantius presents Christ as a sage, an ethical teacher and example, Whose chief index of heroic virtue is His patient endurance of suffering. This emphasis may reflect Lactantius' personal experience of persecution. But, oddly enough, in the light of his wholesale dismissal of the philosophers, his Christ ends by resembling a Stoic sage, marked more by equanimity than by charity. In sum, Lactantius' *Institutes* presents Christianity as valuable less for the truths it proclaims than for the ethical corollaries he derives from them. If the use of rhetoric is thoroughly unproblematic for him, his use of philosophy reveals notable inconsistencies, some of which can be explained as debaters' points and some not.

On the Deaths of the Persecutors rings a final, and significant, change on Latin Christian apology as a genre. Even more than Lactantius' *Institutes*, it could not have been written before the reign of Constantine. An important subtext is the author's defense of Constantine's policy and critique of his detractors. The classical literary model on which Lactantius draws here is the didactic biography, part of the canon of classical historiography, which praises or blames leaders for their virtues or vices. In appealing to the ancient historians, Lactantius ignores their scrupulous regard for the verification of evidence. For he wilfully distorts the historical record in trying to prove that emperors who had persecuted Christians in the age just past had also been terrible rulers in general, betrayers of the Roman political ethos, and that they had met gruesome deaths as requital for their sins. Conversely, he argues that emperors who had not persecuted Christians had been model rulers in all respects. Like all polemical distortions of history, this work can be read as a quest for a relevant past. At the same time, it reflects the emergence of a new relationship between the Christian church and the Roman state. Earlier, the martyrs had had to defy Roman law and order in adhering to Christian values. Now, Christians could adhere to their own values while identifying them with the Roman political order. This synthesis, on Lactantius' part, is fully as important as the defense of Christianity, by him and by earlier apologists, by means of classical philosophy or rhetoric. The work of Lactantius thus brings to a conclusion the age of apology and ushers us to the new terrain to be mapped by the next group of Latin Christian writers, the church fathers.

CHAPTER 2

The Latin Church Fathers, I:
Ambrose and Jerome

The next stage of our story takes us to the church fathers. During their time (fourth to sixth centuries), the major change in the relations between the Christian church and the Roman state heralded by the writings of Lactantius created a new context for the development of Latin Christian thought. Yet another factor was the increasing entry of the Germanic peoples from central Asia into Europe, at first peaceably and then aggressively. Despite a 'pagan reaction' during the reign of the Emperor Julian (332–63), Christianity became the official religion of Rome in the fourth century. The church became a bureau of state, fitting itself into the imperial subdivisions of province, diocese, and parish, each governed from an urban hub, and adopting Roman law as the basis for canon or ecclesiastical law. And the bishop of Rome took on the title of supreme pontiff formerly held by the high priest of pagan Rome.

While its move out of the catacombs and its new face as a part of the Roman establishment gave the church a position of advantage, the same condition brought many new problems which the works of the church fathers reflect. Paganism remained a viable option for some Romans, and Christians still faced criticism from pagan religionists as well as philosophers. Dualistic heresy in its Manichean form was widespread and Arianism remained rampant, receiving support from some emperors. To the extent that the Germanic peoples in the Roman world embraced Christianity at this time, it was Arian Christology that appealed to them, since their own religion included the belief in human beings descended from the gods or raised to superhuman status after death and there were first- and second-order deities in their pantheon.

While older heresies persisted, newer ones arose, notably Pelagianism and Donatism. These sects reflected the difficulties of working out the ethical and ecclesiological corollaries of basic Christian doctrines. Donatism, which flourished in north Africa, was also deeply embedded in its social, economic, and political tensions. Like their opponents, the Donatists sought validation for their position in the earlier church history of this province. And, within the community of the faithful, the numerous adherents of the now official church included many whose grasp of its theological and behavioral norms was hazy. In contrast to the church of the martyrs, confined to the zealous, the church in the patristic age had to develop rules and institutions to minister to its vastly increased if often conventionally devout membership.

As the patristic period continued into the fifth and sixth centuries, another massive change in the historical setting confronted Christian leaders with additional problems. The Germanic peoples' shift from a policy of accommodation to one of all-out military attack on the Roman empire and their defeat of that empire made the church virtually the only public institution of ancient Rome to survive the transition to the Germanic successor states. When the Roman empire had been in existence in western Europe, Christians could and did rely on its social welfare system and state-supported schools. Indeed, the four western church fathers were all outstanding products of that school system. In most cases the new Germanic rulers had little interest in funding classical education. Yet, Latin Christianity depended on literacy. The educational emergency resulting from the collapse of the Roman empire is visible most clearly in the career of the last church father, Gregory the Great, in the next chapter, and in the work of the transmitters. In the case of each of the fathers, the particular stage in the political and cultural shift from Roman to German rule during which he lived, no less than his personal proclivities, interests, and professional responsibilities, helped to specify his sense of his intellectual mission. It is also worth noting that, unlike the apologists, the fathers were all raised as Christians. This is also true of Augustine, the only one of them who was a convert. Of equal importance is the fact that, except for Jerome, they were all bishops. They had congregations to serve, and much more to do than merely to indulge their own intellectual tastes. In his own way, each of them took a conscious position on the classical tradition and the Christian uses to which it should be put. Historically, these decisions are more important than those made by the apologists. For the fathers' range of views on the interaction of classicism and Christianity, visible in their careers and writings, became far more authoritative for their medieval successors.

Ambrose

Ambrose (339/40–97) served as bishop of his native city of Milan and saw as his chief goal the defense of freedom of worship for orthodox Christians and the destruction of the Arianism favored by the imperial court in residence in his diocesan capital. Quite early in his clerical career he decided that he needed to advance these goals by political action as well as by pastoral work, participation in church councils, and writings. Allying the church with the state and elaborating, in theory and practice, the role of bishops in both institutions that is one of his major contributions, Ambrose brought to his chosen role a social, political, and educational background and a personality that were decided assets.

Ambrose came from a high rank of late Roman society and from a pious Christian family. Like many men of his class, he received a thorough classical education, gaining renown as a fluent public speaker, and applied his training to a career in public service. Ambrose's ability and dedication earned him high political office.

He was serving as provincial governor of Milan at the time of his impromptu election as bishop by popular acclamation. Ambrose at once turned his administrative skills to the task of ruling a diocese in which orthodoxy was beleaguered. In so doing, he was well served by the general respect he had won before his consecration. He was already a leader whom his people were used to following. His learning and eloquence, his knowledge of the inner circles of government, his self-confidence, and his imperturbable spirit lent weight to his pronouncements. He made his views known straightforwardly and, however controversial the stands he took, he was never accused of ambition or selfishness. Ambrose was keenly aware of the value of symbolic actions. When Symmachus, a pagan aristocrat, urged that the altar of the goddess Victory be reinstalled in the forum, he refused politely but firmly. 'It is no disgrace,' he said, 'to pass on to better things.'[1] His first step after assuming episcopal office was to bring back the remains of a former bishop of Milan, who had suffered death in exile for his defense of the Nicene Creed, to be buried in the basilica with fitting pomp. He also kept on most of the staff of his immediate predecessor, a bishop notoriously soft on Arianism. He thereby made his own position on Arianism perfectly plain while winning the loyalty of his staff by letting them prove themselves rather than dismissing them on a guilt by association basis.

Ambrose took direct political action against Arianism and on behalf of orthodoxy in the 380s, leading his people in a passive resistance strike in the teeth of the queen mother's attempt to install Arian clergymen in the diocese, even when his basilica was besieged by imperial troops. When the emperor was assassinated in 383 and replaced by a usurper, Ambrose, working with several army officers, took the rightful heir under his own protection and was instrumental in recovering his throne for him. Later he served as a counselor to this emperor. Ambrose's rationale for his political activism was that a Christian, and especially a bishop, has a civic duty to support and serve the lawful ruler. Also, by so doing, he would be able to influence the ruler to promote peace, justice, good moral behavior, and the protection of the orthodox faith. The basic principle underlying this position is that the church should be the conscience of the state. For Ambrose, this theory also meant that bishops have the right and duty to chastise rulers for wrongdoing. He did not hesitate to excommunicate an emperor for bloody reprisals he took in crushing a revolt in Thessalonica. The Ambrosian conception of the bishop requires him to perform a delicate balancing act. On the one hand, he must be an obedient citizen and servant of the state. On the other hand, the state may not silence him; he must remain free to exhort and correct wayward rulers. Ambrose himself does not seem to have seen or experienced the latent tension between these two potentially conflicting duties. But his theory of church–state relations could and did place that tension in high relief for leaders with more ambition and less integrity.

When Ambrose turned to writing as a means of advancing his agenda, he was likewise concerned with results. His aim was to edify and inspire his people and to show Arians why they were wrong. There is nothing of the speculative thinker in Ambrose, no love of the play of ideas for its own sake. All his writings have immediate practical ends. Ambrose brings to their composition a well-stocked mind, conversant with Greek Christian literature as well as classical literature and philosophy. For him, none of the adaptations he makes of this material is problematic. He simply rolls up his sleeves and draws on what he knows in order to get the job done, just as he transfers his skills as a secular politician to ecclesiastical statesmanship without missing a beat.

Ambrose's writings fall under four main headings: biblical exegesis, dogmatic works, liturgical poetry, and ethical treatises. As is the case with all the church fathers, he devoted much attention to biblical exegesis. His output here reflects his preaching on particular biblical texts and themes, an area in which he made an untroubled transition from forensic to homiletic and hortatory rhetoric. Ambrose introduced into Latin exegesis two ideas that were to have great influence in the Middle Ages. Both were derived from Greek Christian models. From Basil the Great (*c.* 330–79) he took the idea of describing cosmogenesis following the creation account in Genesis in a work entitled *Hexaemeron*. He also expressed in Latin the idea that the Bible contains four levels of meaning. First it yields a literal or historical meaning. Then, it can be read for its moral or tropological significance. The Old Testament can also be read allegorically or typologically, as forecasting events in the New Testament. Finally, the text can be read anagogically, for the light it sheds on the next life and on eternal truths. The idea that canonical texts have several levels of meaning came originally from classical literary criticism. Greek grammarians had applied it to Homer (ninth century BC) and Roman grammarians to Vergil (79–19 BC). The first exegete to apply it to the Bible was Philo Judaeus (*c.* 13–45/50 BC), who used it to show how earlier parts of the Old Testament pointed to events later in that Testament. The first Christian author to apply the method to both parts of the Bible was Origen (*c.* 185–*c.* 254). He strongly influenced Greek exegesis, and through Ambrose, Latin exegesis as well.

Ambrose's dogmatic works all target areas of dispute with the Arians, whether they are addressed directly to Arians or aim at strengthening the faith of the orthodox. In these works he frequently appeals to the arguments of contemporary Greek theologians and he uses a philosophical vocabulary, drawn largely from Platonism. Ambrose is not trying to be original or to make a theoretical statement on the relations between theology and philosophy. He uses other thinkers' ideas because he finds them persuasive. He uses philosophical terminology because he thinks that the first necessity in proving the Arians wrong and in explaining orthodox doctrine is a vocabulary rigorous enough to address speculative doctrines such as the Trinity and Christology, a vocabulary that is clear, precise, and understood in the same way by all contestants. His approach is utilitarian. As he sees it, philosophical terminology enables us to state the essentials of doctrine unambiguously and to reduce them to the fewest possible number of formulae, making it easier to teach and defend them.

Both the anti-heretical and pedagogical aims of Ambrose as an exegete and as a controversialist can also be seen in his work as a liturgical poet, writing hymns stressing orthodox doctrines contested by the Arians for use in congregational singing. There were other Latin Christian poets at work during the patristic period. Ambrose was scarcely alone in thinking that it was perfectly appropriate to use classical meters, poetic genres, and subjects as vehicles for poems with a Christian content. Latin Christian poets of the time include Dracontius (*c.* 450–after 496), writing on the theme of theodicy; Prudentius (348–after 404), who versified saints' lives and treated the battle of the vices and virtues, and, perhaps more startlingly, the learned matron Proba (fourth century), who retold the creation account in Genesis in a poem whose lines are all quotations from Vergil. Nor was Ambrose the only author of lyrics expressing religious ideas and emotions. But he transformed religious lyric poetry, expanding its range beyond the expression of the speaker's personal feelings, making it the statement of a communal faith, articulated by the congregation it is designed to teach and inspire. Ambrose also sought to make the liturgy more enjoyable by including congregational singing of these hymns, enhancing his flock's participation in church services and, not incidentally, encouraging them to attend them more frequently so that other parts of the service, such as the sermon, could instruct them as well.

As a moral theologian, Ambrose addressed himself to his congregation at large and also to certain sub-sets of Christians within it. The moral exegesis that was part of his fourfold method of biblical interpretation and a series of works on Old Testament patriarchs, each exemplifying a particular virtue, speak to the first part of this assignment. There were two groups of people in his flock whose ethical needs Ambrose thought required special attention: celibate women and clergymen. Along with many theologians of the day, he praised celibacy and practiced it himself, although there was no official ban on clerical marriage at this time. Ambrose's personal life gives no indication that he found celibacy stressful or especially difficult. For him, the subject is not personally fraught. In letters and treatises directed to women following the lifestyle of consecrated virgin or celibate widow, Ambrose, as a pastor, seeks to advise and support them, by accenting the advantages of their calling. He emphasizes that, although Roman law accords to the male guardians of women the power to arrange their marriages, Christians should respect the wishes of such virgins and widows and not force them into unwanted marriages. Ambrose manages to make his encouragement of virginity and widowhood clear, and the right of women to self-determination irrespective of the legal system, without denigrating marriage for the majority of Christians. His moderation on this topic is noteworthy. In Ambrose's day, monastic communities for women had not yet come into being. He envisions celibate women as living at home and as playing two roles. On a personal level, he thinks they should seek their own spiritual development through prayer, the reading of the Bible, and the contemplation of its message, activities suggesting that these widows and virgins came from the upper classes in which women were likely to be literate. Ambrose also thinks that they have a public function. Aside from inspiring others through their moral example, they, like the deaconesses of the New Testament, can aid the clergy in distributing poor relief and in instructing female catechumens.

The second group of Christians whose ethical needs Ambrose addresses are the priests of his diocese. To instruct them how to fulfill their clerical functions he wrote his most influential and widely read work, *On the Duties of Ministers*. This treatise is an excellent index of Ambrose as a Christian intellectual more generally, drawing with ease, and also with independence, on the resources of the classical tradition. His express literary model for this work, Cicero's *On Duties*, had been written for the edification of future statesmen. In turn, Cicero had modeled his work on one with the same title in Greek by the Stoic Panaetius (second century BC), which had a less specifically political focus. Given Ambrose's own career, it is not surprising that he thought Cicero's advice on political morality would be useful to priests. With Cicero and Panaetius, he distinguishes between what is good in itself and what is useful. With them he appeals to the classical cardinal virtues of wisdom, temperance, courage, and justice. The schools of Greek philosophy had defined these virtues differently and had disagreed on which was paramount. Panaetius takes the Stoic line that prudence, or practical wisdom, is supreme; Cicero departs from him, following Aristotle (384–22 BC) in making justice the supreme virtue, and repeating Aristotle's definition of it.

Ambrose appropriates these sources his own way. For him, the paramount virtue is temperance. He draws this conclusion because he approaches ethics from a developmental standpoint, not from a normative or teleological one, as Panaetius and Cicero do. As he observes, children can be taught to control their impulses before they are old enough to grasp why some types of behavior are appropriate and some are not. At the same time, he joins Cicero and Aristotle in invoking the golden mean as an ethical standard. In contrast with Aristotle, Panaetius, and Cicero alike, he defines the good in terms of eternal life. He also uses examples of virtue drawn from the Bible. And, more in accord with Stoicism on this point than Cicero, he defines virtue as life in accordance with reason and nature. As he puts it, 'A virtuous life is in accordance with nature, for God made all things very good,'[2] a statement reinforcing and Christianizing Stoic natural law ethics. While Ambrose sees the good life as eternal felicity, in practice his advice to clerics on the exercise of the cardinal virtues would not require behavior modification from a Ciceronian. But the cardinal virtues are not enough. The Christian virtues of faith, hope, and charity must also be practiced to attain the good life. Ambrose presents the theological virtues as fully compatible with the cardinal virtues. Indeed, he argues that the possession of the theological virtues is what gives the moral subject the psychic energy to practice the cardinal virtues. Just as he sees no discrepancies between the Roman statesman and the Christian priest, between the bishop as servant of the state and as simultaneously its conscience, so here, as elsewhere, he appeals freely to classical literary and philosophical genres, ideas, and arguments, adding his own emphasis and projecting throughout this treatise, as throughout his writings and policies as a whole, the assurance of a man comfortable with the idea that he can make full use of his intellectual endowment for the pursuit of his pastoral and polemical objectives.

Jerome

Jerome (*c.* 340–419), like Ambrose, received a thoroughly literary education and loved the same classical authors, especially Cicero. But it would otherwise be difficult to find two contemporary Latin Christian thinkers whose personalities, aims, and work were more different. Where Ambrose attacked heresy systematically as a statesman and polemicist, Jerome rarely took up his pen against it although he spent most of his life in the Near East, where heresy was rampant. A private scholar, he tended to view heresy personally, not institutionally, ignoring it unless he wanted to express his animosity toward a particular opponent. Jerome certainly lacked the civic spirit, the serenity, the self-confidence, and the self-forgetfulness of Ambrose. He was quite vain and proud of his achievements, although the recognition he won never enabled him to lower his guard. Jerome was adroit at making enemies and at stabbing former friends in the back and he could display a nasty sense of humor. He had a flair for making himself obnoxious to others and then felt genuine dismay when they disliked him. At the same time, Jerome was capable of forging strong and durable friendships. Typically, they were relationships in which he played the role of mentor or spiritual advisor, rather than relationships between equals.

After studies in his native Rome with Donatus (mid-fourth century), the foremost Latin philologist of the day, the young Jerome tried to establish a monastic community, a venture that failed because of a falling-out with his associates. After some years in the Near East honing his Greek and learning Hebrew, he was called back to Rome in 377 by Pope Damasus I (305–84), to serve as his secretary. It was Damasus who gave Jerome the commission, a Latin translation of the Book of Psalms, that led to his life's work, a Latin translation of the entire Bible. Thanks to the financial and emotional support of a circle of extremely wealthy and ascetic women he had met and befriended in Rome, he was able to build a monastery and research institute at Bethlehem. It was here that he spent the rest of his life, producing the Vulgate Bible, which supplanted the earlier Latin translations of parts of the Bible collectively called the Itala and which became the standard Latin Bible of the Christian west. Jerome accompanied the Vulgate with extensive commentaries on individual books of the Bible and guides, glossaries, and handbooks for resolving linguistic and exegetical problems. In these works, he was less concerned with extracting a theology from the biblical text than with ascertaining and stating what the text said. In addition, Jerome carried on an extensive correspondence, advising and exhorting addressees whether they had requested his guidance or not, expressing acrimonious complaints against other scholars who disagreed with his readings of Scripture, and satirizing society priests and hypocritical lay Christians whom he thought needed taking down a peg. Jerome also wrote some polemical works aimed against individuals, treatises and letters advocating celibacy and asceticism, saints' lives upholding the same values, and a collection of potted biographies of men noted for their contributions to Christian literature, starting with St. Peter and ending with Jerome himself. But the Vulgate Bible is his most important and enduring monument.

In establishing the text of the Bible and in deciding how to translate it, Jerome emerges as the most outstanding classical philologist of his day, able to call upon the full resources of linguistic and literary scholarship. He also made a principled choice in deciding on the tone of voice he would use in his translation. Eschewing the grand style, he chose the Latin of everyday speech, in order to make the Bible more accessible. Yet, the same literary culture without which Jerome's work is inconceivable was a source of profound concern to him. In one of his letters, he speaks of a nightmare in which he is called before the judgment seat and asked by God whether he was a Christian or a Ciceronian. The internal conflict posed by this question awakened him with a start, he relates, and he vowed to purge his writings of references to the classics. For, as he observes, 'What has Horace to do with the Psalter?'[3] Despite this traumatic experience and despite his vow, Jerome was unable to detach himself from the classical literature with which he was imbued. After the Ciceronian dream, his writings reflect it as much as those he had composed earlier. The rhetorical question Jerome places in God's mouth in his letter is worth comparing with Tertullian's 'What has Athens to do with Jerusalem?' Clearly, for Jerome, it is not philosophy but the beauties of classical literature that are likely to lead Christians astray. Toward the end of his life, Jerome arrived at a resolution of his dilemma, expressed in an analogy telling in its imagery. He compares the classics to the captive pagan woman whom the Old Testament Jew is forbidden to marry, unless she is ritually purified by having her hair and nails cut. Once purified, she may be espoused. Jerome thus presents classical literary culture as a prize of war which the Christian has won, as a sexually desirable woman. The resultant marriage following her purification preserves the subordination of wife to husband normal both in the Old Testament and in the late Roman society of which Jerome was a part.

This erotic image is also of interest in the light of Jerome's harsh strictures on life in the body. He expressed an intense discomfort with his own body, from early manhood onward. He followed a rigorous ascetic regime, which evidently did not bring him the detachment and spiritual equipoise he sought. It is no accident that the temptations of Jerome became a popular subject in Christian art or that the saints he chose to immortalize in his hagiographical works fled to the desert to lead lives of great austerity. Jerome sees food and physical cleanliness, no less than human sexuality, as temptations to sin. The advice he gives to friends and correspondents seeking instruction in the ascetic life is so extreme that one devout female friend is thought to have met an untimely death by following his instructions. Jerome's writings on virginity, widowhood, and celibacy reflect none of the moderation and concern for the ascetic's role in the wider Christian community and none of the respect for other callings found in Ambrose. For Jerome, the institution of marriage is merely a concession to human weakness and has no redeeming features except the procreation of new virgins who, he hopes, can be persuaded to remain in that state. Jerome does not think that the propagation of the human race sexually was a condition of the original creation. Rather, he sees it as a punishment for the fall. Had the primal parents not sinned, he claims, they would have been able to reproduce by non-sexual means, although he declines to explain how.

At the same time, Jerome's letters to his female friends and to parents requesting his guidance on the education of their daughters display another side of his anthropology. If the body must be seen as the enemy and subjected to harsh discipline by men and women alike, the minds and souls of women as well as men are to be appreciated and cultivated. Jerome regards women as capable of serious intellectual pursuits, the mastery of difficult subjects, and the making of independent contri·· utions to theology and biblical exegesis. He frequently discusses highly technical exegetical points in his letters to his female friends and holds up these learned women as examples to be emulated in letters to women he wants to draw to the same activities. The educational program he outlines for girls, although it substitutes the Psalms for classical poetry in the teaching of grammar, is otherwise based point for point on the educational scheme laid down for boys by the Roman rhetorician Quintilian (*c.* 35–*c.* 95). While it is common for patristic writers to praise virtuous women, especially if they are celibate, the attention Jerome calls to women's intellectual abilities is unusual. He evidently thinks that this idea needs defending and does so in the remark, 'We judge not by sex but by soul.'[4] In this respect, Jerome made an important contribution to Christian feminism as well as to the extremist side of Christian asceticism.

All told, Jerome's major legacy to medieval intellectual history and to the western Christian tradition more generally is his Vulgate Bible. Whatever doubts he may have had about the seductions of classical literature, it was this aspect of the classical tradition on which he drew the most heavily. He not only used it as a philological tool in making his biblical translations and commentaries but also appropriated classical literary genres such as satire, the edifying biography, and the epistle as a vehicle of moral instruction. He was able to take over these literary forms and fill them with a Christian content with great success. There is only one salient case in which Jerome's expertise as a philologist failed him. He regarded as genuine a spurious fourth-century correspondence between St. Paul and the Roman statesman and Stoic philosopher Seneca (4 BC–AD 65), despite the differences between first-century and fourth-century Latin. He also believed on the basis of this forged text that Seneca had converted to Christianity and included him in his *Lives of Famous Men* on that account. This error aside, and despite his worry that Horace was incompatible with the Psalter, Jerome brought a rich store of classicism, essentially literary in character, to the tasks he set for himself as a Christian scholar. But the single church father who includes and goes beyond the address of both Jerome and Ambrose to the classical tradition is the towering peak in the western patristic landscape, Augustine.

CHAPTER 3

The Latin Church Fathers, II:
Augustine and Gregory the Great

Augustine

Augustine (354–430) is the single most important of the Latin church fathers. His works range widely over an enormous number of subjects. In them he puts his own personal stamp on Christian theology, on church–state relations, on the classical tradition, and on Rome as a historical phenomenon. He draws on classical literature and philosophy alike, applying them to his work as a pastor, a controversialist, an exegete, an ethicist, and a speculative thinker more broadly. He is the only Latin church father with a truly philosophical mind, who enjoys thinking as an activity in its own right. He frequently goes farther than he needs to in an argument out of the sheer pleasure he takes in intellectual inquiry. The selections from his vast output discussed here have been chosen because they reveal how his mind worked; his approach, stated or not, to the classical tradition; themes of enduring importance to him throughout his career; topics on which his opinion shifted over time; and works and positions that made him the single greatest authority, after the Bible, in western Christian thought.

Although he was raised in a household with a Christian mother, Augustine was a convert, entering the church in 387 after the long intellectual odyssey related in his *Confessions*, a work that draws on classical autobiography and moves the genre to a new stage of development. For this is a spiritual autobiography. Facts Augustine thinks have no bearing on his inner life he omits, and those he includes he manipulates with great artifice. Events in his pre-Christian days foreshadow analogous events on his road to conversion, and his frequent allusions to Vergil's *Aeneid* and to himself as the epic's hero reflect his deliberate arrangement of his material and the connection between pagan and Christian Rome he is forging in himself as the work's central character. After Augustine has reached safe harbor at the baptismal font, he discusses time and memory in the *Confessions*. The ostensible function of this passage is to show, by analogy with the human experience of time, why the question of what God was doing before the creation is a non-question. The future, says Augustine, is the soul's present expectation. The present is the soul's present attention. The past is not whatever has happened, but the soul's present memory. This reduction of all times to the present in human psychology helps explain the point that God lives in the eternal present. But it can also be read as a rationale for Augustine's selective memory in the *Confessions*, written as it was about a decade after his conversion and recalling to him, from his current position as bishop of Hippo in his native north Africa, faced with many pastoral and polemical problems, what he wanted to reaffirm about his past. The work's gripping subject is enhanced by Augustine's vivid Latin style. Interlarded with prayers, the text is addressed to the deity and decorated with many plays on words and euphonious syntactical inversions. Augustine is remarkably successful in combining a style and subject matter that convey the personal immediacy of his story, involving the reader in his own concrete, lived experience and his intellectual struggles.

As the *Confessions* relate, Augustine came from a comfortable but not an aristocratic family. He had great gifts of both heart and mind. Anything he wanted, including wisdom and truth, he wanted passionately. Augustine received the standard education in the liberal arts, culminating in a rhetoric which he describes, from his later perspective, as sophistic, a value-free technique for manipulating an audience. He became a professional rhetorician of this sort after studying in Carthage, his talent winning him state chairs in Rome and Milan.

Augustine depicts his youth as misguided morally as well as intellectually, marked by selfishness, and by lack of proportion and civic spirit. This self-description reveals some of his fundamental personality traits and psychological convictions. First, Augustine always sees himself in relation to others, not as an isolated individual. He is gregarious by nature, capable of deep love and friendship. Even when he is engaged in introspection, he presents this activity as an interior dialogue, either with himself or with an author he is reading. He seeks and finds mentors and role models and they exercise a powerful influence on him. Second, Augustine sees love and knowledge as interconnected. Vices such as pride or selfishness can impede the quest for truth, as they did in his youth; while a correct moral attitude to one's object of knowledge is needed to attain it.

Uninspired by the dull style of the Itala, the Latin Bible as Augustine first encountered it, and by the closed minds and authoritarian views of the north African Christians, he looked elsewhere for enlightenment. While still a student he read the *Hortensius*, ascribed to Cicero, a conventional exhortation to the study of philosophy, and took it seriously. He also congratulated himself on mastering Aristotle's *Categories*, a logical classic, on his own. But the first school of thought with which he experimented was Skepticism. The version of this philosophy he took up claimed a Platonic heritage, although Plato would not have recognized his offspring in the Skeptics' probabilism or claim that truth cannot be known with certitude. Cicero had dabbled in this school, which may have attracted Augustine to it, but by Cicero's day the emphasis had shifted from Skepticism as an epistemology to the question of whether probabilism yielded an adequate foundation for moral decisions. Augustine's Skepticism shared this ethical focus. He did not find Skepticism appealing for long and later wrote a dialogue refuting it. The positive epistemology he eventually developed shares with most schools of Greek philosophy the conviction that a real world exists outside the thinker's mind and Plato's view that pure intellection is a surer guide to truth than sense data. In the realm of religious knowledge he borrows a Neoplatonic metaphor, analogizing God as the supreme truth to light, needed for us to see light itself or anything else.

Augustine's major attachment for most of his youth was to Manicheism, which attracted him by giving a clear answer to the problem of evil, an issue that was to remain a major theme in his thought. The Manichees saw matter as evil and spirit as good, each with its own divine creator. With the Gnostics, they saw mankind as in need of salvation by the very fact that the soul, the essence of a human being, is trapped in an evil material body. Since they did not see the body as an integral part of human nature, it could be indulged or disciplined, depending on whether one wanted to liberate the soul from it slowly or swiftly. As a Manichee, Augustine was neither an ascetic nor a hedonist. He installed a concubine in his household, with whom he lived in amity and fidelity for fourteen years and by whom he had a son. As Augustine presents Manicheism in the *Confessions*, the version of its doctrine that he held had departed from strict metaphysical dualism and was trying to account for evil, still seen as matter, as the creation of a good, spiritual deity. His inability to resolve this anomaly provoked disillusionment with Manicheism. When he had the opportunity to hear Faustus, a leader of the sect, Augustine seized it, hoping for clarification. The encounter was a disappointment. He found Faustus a pompous fraud with no answers, another case of the interrelation of moral character and wisdom. Augustine thus looked elsewhere for a solution to the problem of evil. For some years he thought he had found it in Neoplatonism.

Sharing with Plato the view that the eternal, immutable world of spirit is metaphysically and morally superior to the changeable world of matter, the Neoplatonists expressed this notion in an emanationist cosmology in which the supreme being, the One, does not engender the material world directly but delegates the task to subordinate spiritual beings. The material order, despite its limits, they held, does mirror the spiritual order more or less clearly, depending on the place a being occupies in the material chain of being. Properly used, the material hierarchy can serve as a ladder of ascent to the world of spirit. It thus has an instrumental value. Evil, therefore, is not located in matter as such. For the Neoplatonists, evil is nonbeing, the absence or privation of being. It has no metaphysical reality.

In the *Confessions* and elsewhere Augustine gives Neoplatonism high marks as a philosophy and states that it helped detach him from Manicheism, even though traces of his earlier Manicheism can be detected in his later attitude to the human body and human sexuality. Yet, while he could grasp the privative theory of evil intellectually, he found it ultimately unsatisfying. It might be possible to define evil out of existence this way, but, evil still exists as a felt psychological reality. This point, made as Augustine reviews the soul-searching that led him to isolate his overweening vices—the desire for pleasure, status, and wealth—and his simultaneous inability to abandon them in his classic analysis of the divided self in Book 8 of the *Confessions*, states another key theme in his thought, a preference for arguments that resonate with his own psychological experience.

In the end, it was this dilemma, immortalized in his famous line, 'Oh Lord, make me chaste—but not yet,'[1] that inspired Augustine to turn to St. Paul for the answer that spoke directly to his condition and that gave him the moral power to act on his convictions. As he sat brooding in his garden, some children playing a game in the street piped the phrase, 'Take up and read.'[2] Augustine flipped open his copy of the Epistle to the Romans and his eye fell on the text that sealed his conversion. In understanding the way Augustine appropriates this event in the *Confessions*, it must be noted that he cites as role models both Anthony (250–356), who did the same with the Bible and found the passage which he internalized as a call to asceticism as a desert monk, and Marius Victorinus (late third century after 363), a pagan rhetorician who took his courage in both hands in becoming a Christian. Since Victorinus lived during the pagan reaction, this meant the loss of his chair. Victorinus is also important to Augustine as the translator of the *Enneads* of Plotinus (205–70), founder of Neoplatonism, who then devoted his learning and eloquence to biblical exegesis and the defense of orthodoxy against Arianism. Augustine presents these role models as critical in showing him what he had to do. And the notion of opening the Bible at random to find a solution to a personal problem, a Christian carryover of the use of Homer and Vergil for the same purpose in classical circles, is another point at which Augustine marks continuity and transition between the classical and Christian traditions.

A second important feature of the role of St. Paul in Augustine's conversion is his acceptance of Paul's understanding of the problem of evil and his re-expression of it in terms of the idea of order, a key concept in his thought. He agrees with Paul that everything in the creation is good. But all things, spiritual or material, can be misused. We use things badly when we use them without proper reference to God. And, as a consequence of original sin, we are likely to misuse things in ways harmful to ourselves and others. Evil thus lies in the abuse of human free will. In reformulating this Pauline doctrine, Augustine invokes the concept of order found in two philosophical schools, Neoplatonism and Stoicism, using the resulting amalgam to recast the free will position into a description of human psychic drives understood under the heading of love, another of his central ideas. The Neoplatonists saw order as hierarchy, in which the moral value of a thing is a function of its position in the chain of being, an order in which eternal beings are better than transient beings. For the Stoics, the universe in general and human beings as part of the natural order are governed by a rational, fixed, law of nature from which nothing is exempt. But it lies within our power to make correct judgments about the value of what we experience and correct moral responses to it. The Stoics maintained that we can educate our minds and hearts to understand the place of any event in the larger cosmic order and we can train ourselves to judge things compatible with reason as good, things incompatible with reason as evil, and everything else as morally indifferent. As Augustine combines St. Paul with the Neoplatonic and Stoic concepts of order, he agrees that we have the power to evaluate the moral worth of things and the power to order our desires so that we desire the best things most, the good things less, and the bad things not at all. The norm of goodness, for him, is how much a thing conduces to the love and knowledge of God, the only end that can satisfy our craving for a good that is supreme and that can never be lost. Created goods may be loved rightly if they are loved ordinately.

This means both that they are not loved too much or too little and also that they are ordered appropriately to God.

There is a third critical aspect of the particular passage of Scripture on which Augustine's eyes fell when he took up and read St. Paul. The text, Romans 13:13–14, states, 'not in rioting and drunkenness, not in chambering and wantonness, not in strife and envying. But put on the Lord Jesus Christ, and make no provision for the flesh.' Augustine internalized these lines as an interdiction of ambition as well as sensuality. He resigned from his chair with the intention of sharing the contemplative life with a group of friends and he decided, after some hesitation, to give up not only the socially advantageous marriage planned for him but also all sexual activity. Aside from reading this text as a commandment concerning his lifestyle, his acceptance of Christ had two other fundamental implications for Augustine. The doctrine of Christ's incarnation resolved for him a problem that his Neoplatonism could not resolve. How can the human soul, united as it is with a body subject to time, change, and mortality, make contact with its divine spiritual source, the One? The Neoplatonists advised contemplation or mysticism, 'the flight of the alone to the Alone.'[3] But those capable of achieving such contacts with the One reported that they were brief and irregular. On the other hand, Augustine saw that sustained contact with God was possible in Christ. For, in His incarnation, the timeless, spiritual God had taken on a human nature, making Himself subject to birth, suffering, and death, the mutabilities of the human condition, while remaining the eternal and immutable deity. Through prayer and the sacraments of the church, and not just through mysticism, Augustine held, Christians can remain in touch with God on a sustained basis. Certainly, the doctrine of the incarnation is central to any Christian theology, but the Augustinian interpretation of that doctrine presents it as closing the gap between time and eternity in the Neoplatonic system. The incarnation of the Word and His physical resurrection also meant, for Augustine, that human language could be redeemed. With Victorinus he too could convert his eloquence to the service of theology and to the pastoral and polemical tasks he inherited when he was drafted into the priesthood and then into the episcopate on his return to north Africa soon after his baptism.

In the final books of the *Confessions*, Augustine provides a sampler of the theological issues he had addressed during his first decade as a cleric. As we move on to consider some of his most typical and influential works it must be noted that, in some areas, his ideas changed over time, conditioned by the need to defend orthodoxy against various heresies. Even in cases where his opinions did not shift, his rhetorical strategy often differs when he addresses different opponents. In Augustine we have a thinker who was highly conscious of his own shifting views and arguments. Toward the end of his career he wrote a work, a gold mine for the intellectual historian, the *Retractations*, listing his writings to date, what he had thought at the time, and his current position. The three major heresies inspiring many of these developments were Manicheism, Donatism, and Pelagianism. Aside from the needs of polemic, Augustine treated the same subjects differently depending on his audience. Thus, he could praise marriage and the sexual mode of procreation as ordained by God in the original creation in pastoral works aimed at people preparing for marriage. He could also denigrate marriage and state that the sexual relations of spouses, even with procreative intentions, were always tainted by sin, when he was opposing clerics who, unlike himself, were or had been married and who saw marriage and celibacy as equally worthy. In this area, Augustine's personal history and sensibilities colored his outlook.

A good index of the mentality Augustine took with him into his new career as a clergyman is one of his earliest works, *On Order*. In the months prior to his baptism, he and several friends and relatives stayed at a villa in Cassiciacum, outside Milan, conducting discussions which Augustine redacted in dialogue form. *On Order* is one of them. Cicero's philosophical dialogues are his immediate models. Like Plato, the ultimate source of this philosophical genre, Augustine uses it to underscore the importance of the interpersonal setting in which wisdom is sought and found. *On Order* deals with the problem of evil, a topic that had preoccupied Augustine for many years. As a Christian, he now frames the issue differently. In opening the work, he observes that we know, because the Christian faith teaches us, that God is good and just, that He is omnipotent, and that He oversees His creation. These are theological givens that cannot be denied; nor can any of these divine attributes or functions be limited in any way. We also know that the universe is subject to an orderly, rational law of nature in which nothing happens arbitrarily. Augustine does not indicate the source of this second axiom, but a good answer would be classical science and most classical philosophy, in which this notion is a self-evident principle. Now the goal of the dialogue, he notes, is to account for the presence of evil in the universe in the light of both sets of givens. That is, the interlocutors are not going to use rational analysis to attack ideas regarded as givens, whether theological or philosophical. The role of reason is to explore the corollaries of these givens and to try to grasp how they relate to each other. This statement articulates a methodological principle applied widely in Augustine's writings.

The dialogue has a brief curtain-raiser that is likewise designed to make a larger point. Augustine and another member of the group have stayed up later than the others. Suddenly, they notice that the sound of water flowing through the pipe serving the villa's bath house has become noisier. On investigation, they find that a mass of autumn leaves which had clogged the stream feeding the plumbing system had been dislodged, allowing the water to flow through the pipe faster and hence more noisily. The point drawn from this discovery is that all events have causes and are part of the wider law of nature. With this idea in place, Augustine proceeds to the argument that God is the creator of this universal order. This foray into natural theology is designed not so much to validate a scientific understanding of the natural world for its own sake as to argue that such knowledge is valuable because it helps us to know God. It is much more typical of Augustine to focus on one creature in particular, the human soul, as a source of information about the deity. After making the point that the world order is identical with God's governance of His creation and that, like all His activities and attributes, it is one with His nature and not superior or subordinate to Him, an argument criticizing Platonism and Neoplatonism alike, Augustine proceeds to tackle the problem of evil by subdividing it into two types, natural and moral.

Natural evils he describes as events such as earthquakes and volcanic eruptions in which innocent people suffer. In addressing this kind of evil Augustine calls on Stoic theodicy, along the lines of Lactantius' first apology. If we look at the big picture, he argues, we will see that these events are not evil but neutral or good. Some organisms must die so that others can live. The volcanic eruption that destroy's one's farm in the long run increases the fertility of the soil. In the face of such events, then, the rational response is to adjust one's attitude to the universal perspective. If one does so, natural evil can be defined out of existence.

Moral evil is a tougher nut to crack. Augustine's first line of attack is to rationalize some behaviors which, while admittedly evil, are acceptable because they forestall or requite still greater evils. The taking of human life is evil, he agrees. But the legal system permits the execution of criminals convicted of capital crimes so that they can no longer prey on the community. Another example, in which the yoking of the items that leap to Augustine's mind suggests how difficult it was for him to divest himself of Manicheism, is the presence of sewers and prostitutes within the city. Both are unattractive, but the city is better off with them than without them. This still leaves unexplained moral evils that cannot be so justified. Confronted with them, Augustine frankly admits that he cannot resolve the problem they present. None the less, he observes, the discussion thus far has helped to clarify the issue and rational analysis of it should be continued.

Both the notion that rational reflection can untie knotty theological and philosophical problems and the shifting contexts of his own later consideration of the question of evil can be seen in Augustine's subsequent works. In *On Order*, his emphasis is on theodicy. Free will as the source of human misbehavior is mentioned but it draws little attention. At the start of Augustine's career as a bishop, debate with the Manichees was a consuming activity. In the anti-Manichean context, both in commentaries on Genesis contesting the Manichean account of the creation and the fall and in treatises on ethics and the nature of the soul, Augustine stresses free will as the sole source of evil in the world. In opposition to Manichean dualism, he argues that it is not matter and certainly not God's own action that causes sin but the misuse of human free will. Later, in his *On Free Will*, the relationship between divine providence and human free will takes the center of the stage. In mid-career, Augustine argues that divine providence does not limit human free will. For providence means foresight, not causation. God knows, from all eternity, what will happen. Some events will occur because they are the effects of natural laws. Others, including the choices made by moral agents, are contingent. So, the fact that God knows ahead of time how a moral agent will exercise free will does not alter the freedom of its exercise. Nor does this freedom limit God's power, since it was His own free decision to create beings possessing free will.

At the end of his career the major problem Augustine faced was the Pelagian heresy, which, in his view, gave too much credit to mankind and not enough credit to God in its account of salvation. In opposition to the Pelagians, he developed a highly pessimistic view of the effects of original sin, even in the redeemed, and his doctrine of grace and predestination undercuts free will considerably. According to this late Augustinian position, in the state of sin we are free to will evil only. In order to will the good, we are dependent on divine grace. There is the grace of pre-destination, by which God aids those He has decided to save. To them He grants prevenient grace, that is, grace that comes before anything they can do. Further, the anti-Pelagian Augustine holds that prevenient grace is irresistible. Those to whom it is given have no choice but to accept it. Once they do, grace frees their wills so that they can collaborate with God in choosing the good and developing virtues, a process in which grace remains continuously necessary. This whole topic is an excellent indicator of the fact that, in ascertaining what Augustine taught, we first have to ask 'When?' and 'In reaction to what or whom?' It also shows why Augustine could be cited as an authority by later Christian thinkers who stood in sharp opposition to each other.

In the foregoing example, the shift from anti-Manichean to anti-Pelagian polemic explains Augustine's restriction of free will and his articulation of a very influential position on predestination and grace. The third heresy that served as a catalyst for several other major doctrinal contributions he made was Donatism. Given the embedding of this sect in north African society and the bloodshed and disruption it provoked, the Donatists were not open to reasoned discussion alone and Augustine's overestimation of its likely impact is a measure of him as an intellectual. The central Donatist doctrine is that the church should be composed of saints only. With orthodox Christians, they agreed that baptism washes away all sins. But what of sins committed after baptism? Since the Donatist church could contain only the sinless, two alternatives were open. A sinner could leave the church or be excommunicated. Or the sinner could be rebaptized, as often as necessary. Against this position Augustine restates firmly the proposition on baptism in the Nicene Creed: there is one baptism in remission of sins. He also argues that the church should not be understood as a narrow conventicle of saints but as a broad community of all the faithful. After all, only God knows whom He has predestined to salvation. It is God's prerogative to separate the sheep from the goats at the last judgment and presumptuous for us to arrogate that prerogative to ourselves. On the matter of post-baptismal sin, Augustine maintains that the sacrament of penance is the proper way to deal with it. As he envisions it, penance has three stages: contrition, in which the penitent acknowledges his sin and sincere sorrow for it; confession, the penitent's admission of his sins and absolution by a priest; and satisfaction, imposed by the priest, which might be prayer, almsgiving, fasting, making restitution to anyone injured by the sins, and which typically, in this period, involved a conspicuous separation of those completing satisfaction from the rest of the Christian community.

It was also in the context of anti-Donatist polemic that Augustine made one of his most influential statements on church–state relations. At one point in the dispute, the Donatists succeeded in getting a pro-Donatist provincial governor appointed, who used the power of his office to take political reprisals against the orthodox. Augustine followed suit, urging the government to enforce orthodoxy by political means. It is true that the Donatists had been the first to advocate religious persecution by the state, but Augustine's repayment of the Donatists in their own coin had a far more durable effect, given his continuing authority in the western church. His stand on this subject is a peculiar legacy indeed for a person who had come through the experience he recounts in his *Confessions* and who believed, early and late, that faith is a gift of God that cannot be coerced.

In addition to forging doctrines on the anvil of controversy, Augustine also worked out many of his positions in his extensive exegetical works and sermons, in letters taking the form of philosophical epistles, and in straightforward dogmatic and moral works. His continuing need to refute the Manichees led him to comment on Genesis repeatedly. In addition, the scientific anomalies in the hexaemeral account of creation piqued his speculative interest, well beyond his anti-Manichean agenda. Two other parts of the Bible that were favorites of his were the Book of Psalms, on which he wrote his lengthiest commentary, mining the text for ethical, Christological, and ecclesiological doctrine, and the Gospel of St. John, which yields the richest harvest of Augustine's doctrine of love. Like Ambrose, he read the Bible polysemously, although he took an increasingly more literal approach to the text toward the end of his career. Also like Ambrose, he inherited the classical cardinal virtues, expounding them in a largely Ciceronian vein early in his career. By the time he came to his commentary on St. John, he had redefined these virtues as modes of charity.

One of Augustine's most important dogmatic works is *On the Trinity*. There are traces of anti-Arian argument here. But what is more noteworthy is the replacement of that agenda with Augustine's desire to think about the Trinity as such, apart from any manifestation that God has made of Himself in the order of creation or the order of grace. The first and least interesting part of the treatise assembles data on the Trinity found in the Bible. The second part presents Augustine's extended orchestration of a note struck early in *On Order*, the use of rational reflection to shed light on a profound mystery of the faith. Augustine looks at the created order for analogies of the Trinity on the warrant of St. Paul: God can be known through the things He has made. The best natural analogies Augustine finds are in the human soul, made in God's image and likeness. He develops four analogies. There is the lover, the beloved, and the love that unites them, three and yet one. There is the self, its own self-love, which, rightly ordered, is good, and its own self-knowledge, knowledge and love being functional correlatives. The third analogy can be seen as a refinement on the second. It involves three faculties of the soul, memory, intellect, and will. Each has its own distinct function and each works in and through the others. Finally, there is memory of God, knowledge of God, and love of God, with a similar interaction of the soul's faculties, now aimed at its highest object. In the last book of *On the Trinity*, Augustine reminds the reader that these analogies are analogies; they are not identical with the divine analogate. He then points out the areas in which the human soul inevitably falls short of its divine prototype. Both for its sheer virtuosity as a piece of theological speculation and for the human psychology it elaborates, this work is unparalleled in western patristic thought. It certainly develops many themes on which Augustine touches elsewhere, from his confidence that reason can illuminate faith to the interconnection of love and knowledge to the preference for arguments that can be tested in psychological experience to the idea that, in order to find God, we should look within our own souls.

In most of the material already considered, we have seen Augustine making use of the classical tradition, sometimes critically and often constructively and independently, without always mentioning his sources or acknowledging the fact that he is combining ideas from different quarters or using arguments in ways that would have astonished their authors. There are also two works in which he takes an overt stand on the classical tradition, *On Christian Doctrine* and the *City of God*. Both were extremely influential. In some respects the first of them can be compared with Ambrose's *On the Duties of Ministers*, since Augustine wrote it to educate the clergy in his diocese. The focus, however, is a different one: the training of biblical exegetes and preachers. While Cicero is the muse of both works, it is Cicero the rhetorician, not the ethicist, to whom Augustine appeals. He agrees with Cicero that there are two parts to the orator's task, finding what one wants to say and expressing it persuasively. He shares Cicero's anti-sophistic approach to rhetoric, holding that the speaker must join eloquence with wisdom and virtue, using his art to edify his hearers.

Before tackling his main assignment, Augustine discusses use and enjoyment, signs and things. The first distinction, derived from Cicero's *On Duties*, contrasts enjoyment, the attitude proper to goods that are ends in themselves, with use, the attitude proper to things that help us attain those goods. For Augustine, the supreme object of enjoyment is God, the supreme good. The Bible is to be used as a means to the knowledge and love of God. In turn, biblical exegesis is to be used to understand the Bible's message. The knowledge and skills discussed in *On Christian Doctrine* are also useful because they enable the exegete to interpret the Bible correctly and to preach it effectively. The first three books of the work rehearse the full content of the classical school curriculum as they apply to the utilitarian goal of finding what is in the biblical text. The linguistic arts are essential, and in two ways, which harks back to the second distinction with which Augustine prefaces the work, the distinction between signs and things. A thing, he notes, is merely itself and does not stand for anything else. A sign is a thing which also signifies something else. While he acknowledges the existence of non-verbal signs, it is verbal signs that the reader of the Bible needs to understand. Augustine notes that some events in the Bible are things; that is, they are to be interpreted literally or historically. Other events or passages are signs; they involve figurative language with a transferred meaning or the typological or anagogical foreshadowing of something that will happen later. Philology enables us to read the Bible and to understand its literal language. Rhetoric teaches us to grasp the meaning of passages that involve figures of speech. The knowledge provided by all the other arts will also be useful here. For example, in interpreting a passage such as 'I am the good shepherd,' an understanding of how metaphor works and a knowledge of animal husbandry will both aid the exegete.

In the last book of *On Christian Doctrine*, Augustine turns to preaching. Like Ambrose, he makes an untroubled transition from classical rhetoric to homiletics.

Augustine does ring one change on Cicero here. Where classical rhetoric prescribes levels of style in relation to particular kinds of subject matter, Augustine notes that the Christian orator will be dealing with the same type of subject matter whenever he preaches. He advises the speaker to adjust his style to his audience, using whatever will facilitate communication with a particular group. In this connection, he observes, we should not use a golden key if it cannot open the door that stands between speaker and hearer and we should not shun a wooden key if it will open the door. What is important is that what was closed should be opened.

In summing up his advocacy of the use of the classics in *On Christian Doctrine*, Augustine makes an assumption as well as a major point. His assumption is that the men he addresses in this work already possess a thorough classical education and that all they require from him is guidance on what to think about it and how to use it. In describing the attitude they should take toward classical learning, a curriculum in which language and literature are fundamental but in which they scarcely exhaust the syllabus, he adverts to a biblical anecdote worthy of comparison with Jerome's view of classical literature as a pagan woman. When the Israelites were about to escape from slavery in Egypt, they asked Moses what they could take with them. Moses referred the question to God, Who ruled that, since they had worked for no pay as slaves, they should spoil the Egyptians of their gold and silver. The contents of the classical tradition, in virtually all fields, constitute this gold and silver, for Augustine. They are intrinsically valuable and they are goods that Christians have earned by their labor. These goods, however, are to be removed from their original habitat and carried into the promised land, applied to the needs of Christian thought and education.

The move from the forum to the pulpit and the revaluation of the classical tradition in its broadest sense can be seen in Augustine's *City of God*, where he deals not only with the intellectual and religious legacy of the ancient world but also with the Roman empire as its political embodiment. The immediate inspiration for this work was the first sack of Rome by the Visigoths in 410. The imperial capital was later to suffer repeated assaults and Augustine was to experience the Germanic invasions closer to home, dying with the Vandals at the gates of Hippo. But for him and for other Romans no political disaster of this period was as shattering as the first sack of Rome. It was a calamity challenging their belief that Rome was eternal and that her rise and imperial expansion constituted the meaning of human history. One of the reasons why Augustine wrote the *City of God* was to refute the pagan charge that Christianity was responsible for the defeat of Rome. But, in larger terms, Augustine wanted to develop a philosophy of history that could include and transcend the history of Rome. For classical historians, history repeats itself. Drawing on the biblical view of time, Augustine substitutes a linear conception of history in which God, the lord of history, uses human events to manifest His revelation and express His will. Further, and this is an insight Augustine also derived from the Bible, God uses other nations, as well as His chosen people, as instruments for accomplishing His historical objectives. From this standpoint, history begins with the creation. Its major turning points are the moments when God specifies His relationship with His chosen people through His covenants with the Old

Testament patriarchs, above all Moses, and finally through the incarnation of Christ and His creation of the church. The end of history will occur at the last judgment, when all will be assigned their posthumous habitations and time itself will cease. It is this trajectory, and not the fortunes of any nation, that describes the scope and direction of human history. God may give particular nations their roles to play in the larger story. He wills that various civilizations come into being, rise, and fall, including Rome. The specific role of Rome has been twofold, according to Augustine. First, the Romans were rewarded with empire and prosperity by God for their virtues, their moderation, their sense of duty, and commitment to public service. Rome has especially manifested the virtue of justice, a sanction for the coercive power of the state. For kingdoms without justice, Augustine remarks, are great robberies. Second, God allowed Roman expansion to unify the then-known world because He had decided that Christ's incarnation would take place within the Roman empire at its territorial height. This political setting had facilitated the dissemination of the Christian message to the uttermost parts of the Roman empire. The empire had adopted Christianity as its state religion, expediting that process. But, since the Christianization of the empire has been accomplished, Rome has fulfilled her historical mission and her continued political existence is no longer needed.

In denying that Rome and, indeed, any other civilization, is the key to the meaning of history, while still giving it a privileged place in the story line he substitutes, Augustine adds another important dimension to his philosophy of history. The real meaning of history, he argues, is the conflict between two human tendencies writ large, which he calls the city of God and the city of man. These are inner, psychic drives. They are intermingled in all human institutions and cannot be equated with any particular institutions. On a collective, social level they represent the conflicting inclinations of the divided self within the individual soul, the inclination toward rightly ordered love and the inclination toward inordinate love. For, as Augustine puts it, two loves have made two cities. Love of God to the exclusion of self makes the city of God while love of self to the exclusion of God makes the earthly city. Each city is a community defined by its loves, its moral priorities. The two cities will remain in tension with each other throughout human history. The true citizens of each will not be fully known until the end of time, when the city of God will be eternalized as heaven and the earthly city as hell. People will be assigned to one or the other depending on the type of love that has predominated in their lives. As Augustine sees it, there is a seamless connection between the individual and society. Both have the same motivations and both are caught in the opposing and overlapping gravitational fields defined by love.

In arguing his case for this new social theory and philosophy of history, Augustine has some other points to make as well, which can be seen in his disposition of material in the twenty-two books of the *City of God*. In the first ten, he turns defense into offense by arguing that, despite the virtues of the Romans, paganism did not save Rome. In the course of making this case, he gives a full relation of Roman history drawn from the standard historians and reviews the beliefs of the pagan religions of Rome, which he presents as having no intimations of truth or positive features. He also reprises the schools of ancient philosophy, apportioning praise and blame as he sees fit, reserving most of his compliments for the Neoplatonists and Stoics. Later readers could and did extract a concise history of Rome and of ancient religion and philosophy from this portion of the *City of God*, making it a valuable indirect source for this material. Books 11 to 14 treat the origins of the two cities, which go back to Cain and Abel, while Books 15 to 18 recount their development in both secular and sacred history up to the early fifth century. The last three books describe the ends of the two cities in heaven and hell.

In a narrow sense, the *City of God* transmits a great deal of information about ancient Rome, classical paganism, and philosophy. In a broad sense, it puts the message of Augustine's *On Christian Doctrine* on a wider canvas. In both works he takes a deliberate position on the classical tradition and on the theme of rightly ordered knowledge and love, as well as the theme of use and enjoyment. Just as he advocates the warm embrace and creative use of classical learning for the exegetical and homiletic needs of Christian education in *On Christian Doctrine*, so, in the *City of God*, he values the ethos, achievements, and history of Rome, the embodiment of the ancient ideal of the city-state, and at the same time annexes that ideal to a Christian view of history and society, seen as a means to eternal life and not as an end. This larger message was there for the taking long after the immediate historical circumstances that prompted the writing of the *City of God*, as was the broad, profound, and sometimes contradictory legacy of Augustine's larger contribution to western Christian thought.

Gregory the Great

By the time of Gregory the Great (540–604), the new political realities signaled by the Germanic conquest of the western Roman empire in Augustine's day had thoroughly altered the political and religious map of Europe. The last of the Latin church fathers can be compared with both Augustine and Ambrose. Like Ambrose, he was a statesman who applied his administrative skills to ecclesiastical government as Pope Gregory I; and he drew much of his spiritual doctrine from Augustine. But he lived in circumstances that would have beggared the imagination of both of these predecessors. By the sixth century the Ostrogoths, who had conquered Italy some seventy years earlier, had been defeated by the Lombards, another Germanic group, and the Emperor Justinian in the east hoped to reclaim the entire Roman world. The absence of the western emperors and the entrenchment of Germanic successor states in Europe meant the devolution of many functions of the Roman civil service onto the shoulders of bishops, the sole remaining members of the bureaucracy. Not just the governance of the church but also education, the administration of poor relief and social welfare, and such basic matters as food supply and water supply became episcopal duties. Titular head of the church as well as bishop of Rome, Gregory asserted an active and energetic style of leadership in all these areas. Mediating between the Lombards and the eastern emperor in the quest for peace and the religious liberty of his people, ministering to their pressing practical needs as well as to their souls, and taking wide oversight of the western church, Gregory created a model for future popes that parallels and expands upon Ambrose's conception of the bishop. Gregory's correspondence, which details his handling of these manifold responsibilities and policies, is the single best source for his extraordinary career.

Public office in the church had been far from Gregory's thoughts in his early years. A member of the aristocracy, he received the best education available in Italy in his day, which included Greek, an increasing rarity in Europe in the sixth century. Like Ambrose, he first entered the civil service, becoming the chief magistrate of Rome in around 573. But Gregory was drawn to the contemplative life. Using his personal fortune, he founded a monastery in Rome, dedicated to St. Andrew, to which he retired and which he led. The current pontiff thought that Gregory was hiding his light under a bushel at St. Andrew's. He also needed a man on his staff with Gregory's education and political skills. Calling him back into public life, he sent Gregory to Constantinople as a papal ambassador. After carrying out this duty, Gregory returned to St. Andrew's, but in 589 he was called into the limelight again, this time to be elected pope. Gregory felt keenly the tension between his public duties and the lure of contemplation. He wrote about it frequently, especially in letters to other prelates who had been called from the cloister to high ecclesiastical office. Remarkably, he managed to preserve, in the midst of public life, a spirit of recollection and perspective. In his own spirituality, the theme of the inner life, beset by the demands of the outer life, speaks to his concern that the cloister within might be lost in the fragmentation of time and attention occasioned by his papal duties.

The turbulent times in which he lived, his temperament, and his high profile as a pastor and ecclesiastical statesman are reflected clearly in Gregory's writings. In striking contrast with earlier Latin fathers, he does not have heresy on his agenda as a doctrinal problem. Church–state relations definitely are on that agenda, the issue being the liberty of the church and of orthodox worship in the face of the Lombards, who were either Arians or pagans, and the effort to dominate the church by the eastern emperor. Beset by these threats, Gregory thought that his people should have their faith reinforced with a liturgy embellished by music. Although it was not invented by him, Gregorian chant was the result of this idea. With respect to the Germans, Gregory saw as his duty not only the defense of orthodoxy but also its propagation through an active missionary policy. He was the first Latin Christian prelate to promote and organize the evangelization of the Germanic peoples north of the Alps. This missionary policy was linked to his support of monasticism. Gregory used monks as missionaries. They could supply both educational and spiritual services to converts and their group solidarity would also serve them well in the mission field, where it would present a model of Christian society to the Germans. Like Jerome, Gregory sought to promote monasticism in his saints' lives, although he focused not on ascetics who fled to the desert but on figures like Benedict of Nursia (*c.* 480–550), his favorite saint and author of the monastic *Rule* most influential in the western church. The education of his clergy and people was another of Gregory's concerns. His strategies for accomplishing it reveal just how much the conditions of labor and the cultural assumptions of ecclesiastical leaders had changed between the age of Ambrose and Augustine and his own time.

Before leaving the topic of his missionary enterprise, it is worth noting that Gregory was capable of combining centralized direction of this endeavor with flexibility in the light of local conditions, a mark of his policy in other areas as well. He advised his missionary to England to adopt 'go slow' tactics and not to try to jettison local traditions overnight. Similarly, when a newly elected Spanish bishop discovered that baptism by both single and triple immersion was in use in his diocese and requested a ruling from Gregory, he replied that there were good symbolic warrants for both practices and that local tastes could prevail, observing that the unity of the faith would not be undermined by diversities in sacramental practice. This respect for diversity within the orthodox consensus and the belief that unity does not require uniformity is a Gregorian insight that bore rich fruit in the intellectual history of medieval Europe as well as in medieval theology.

Aside from his letters, Gregory's writings fall under the headings of hagiography, sacramental theology especially as concerns penance, spiritual writings, biblical exegesis, and advice to his clergy. Regardless of the genre in which he writes, Gregory uses plain and simple language. His style is extremely repetitive, and deliberately so. He is never abstract, constantly hammering in his points with multiple concrete examples. Gregory's chosen style indicates that he does not expect his audience to get the message on first hearing, or to be able to work out the corollaries of general principles on their own. Gregory's saints' lives are presented in his *Dialogues*. Far from being philosophical or theological discussions, his dialogues convey biographical data and accounts of saintly miracles in brief, lively speeches that will not tax a reader or hearer with a short attention span. The genre of hagiography had already undergone several stages in its development before Gregory wrote. The first saints' lives glorified the heroic virtue of the martyrs, whose miracles even included the translation of the dead from hell to heaven. Next came lives of the ascetic desert hermits, of the sort Jerome wrote; their chief virtues were self-denial and the victory over carnal temptation. Following them came saints' lives celebrating founding fathers, clerics who had established local churches, evangelized their regions, or defended their people with their pastoral and organizational skills. Their miracles were often set in the context of proving the superior power of the Christian God in stand-offs with pagan magic. In addition to being exponents of monastic community, Gregory's heroes are wonder-working saints. Their miracles are designed not to prove the superiority of Christianity to paganism but to provide practical and spiritual help to people in the world around them. These are the ideal Christians to whom Gregory was devoted and whom he holds up as examples to his flock.

Yet another objective of Gregory's hagiography is his vigorous advocacy of the doctrine of the communion of saints, stated in the Nicene Creed. The communion of saints, as he understands it, includes the living faithful as well as the dead. The departed saints pray for the living, interceding with God on their behalf, just as living Christians can and should pray for each other and for the repose of the dead.

This belief that Christians can assist fellow Christians with their prayers, after death as well as in this life, is one of the principles informing Gregory's treatment of penance. He takes the basic doctrine of the anti-Donatist Augustine, giving his three-part scheme crisper definition, and perceives an anomaly which he then rectifies. The problem, as he sees it, lies in the third, or satisfaction, stage of the sacrament. Let us suppose that a penitent, sincerely sorry for his sin, confesses to a priest and receives absolution. With a firm purpose of amendment, he undertakes the satisfaction that the priest imposes, satisfaction that Gregory is more likely than Augustine to envision as good works or pious practices. But what if the penitent dies before he completes the satisfaction? In Gregory's view, it would be unfair to condemn him to hell, since he was following the church's rules on penance with a good will and was prevented from completing his satisfaction only by the accident of death. At the same time, it would not be right to assign the penitent to heaven, along with people who had completed their satisfactions while still alive. Gregory's solution is to posit a third posthumous destination, purgatory. Unlike heaven and hell, which are timeless realms, purgatory is temporal. Persons sent there can work off any satisfaction remaining on their account by enduring punishments that have a term. The prayers, masses, and almsgiving of their fellow Christians on earth as well as the prayers of the saints in heaven can speed them on their way to their eventual heavenly abode. In addition to serving as a concrete application of the doctrine of the communion of saints, Gregory's teaching on purgatory reflects a neat, and just, administrative treatment of a group of souls who do not fit into other existing pigeonholes. It is also a teaching that has analogies in some versions of ancient pagan religion and philosophy. In all respects, it is an excellent index of the generous, practical, and bureaucratic mentality that Gregory brought to Christian doctrine no less than to church governance.

While it is by no means his only exegetical work, Gregory's *Moralia* illustrates that genre and his spiritual writing at the same time. This work uses a commentary on the Book of Job as the springboard for Gregory's analysis of the spiritual life. He does not use biblical exegesis for polemical purposes. Nor does he use it to extrapolate dogma or to reflect on fundamental doctrines of the church. Rather, his focus is ethical and contemplative. He chooses Job for his intended purpose because Job's story raises the ever-popular question of why the just man suffers. Gregory is not interested in treating the problem of evil in metaphysical terms. For him, God's permission of evil and His infliction of suffering on Job are ultimately mysteries, designed to test and strengthen the faith of believers, as they do for Job. If Job, an Old Testament figure who lived outside of God's covenant with the Jews, could endure his afflictions with an unswerving love and trust in God, how much more should Christians do so, profiting from his example. The ethical analysis in this work includes a Gregorian theme that was to become a standard idea in the Christian west, the seven deadly sins, moving, in order of increasing seriousness, from lust to gluttony to avarice to sloth to wrath to envy to pride. This sequence treats sins of the flesh as less serious than sins of the intellect. Gregory's other exegetical works, such as his commentary on Ezekiel, share with his *Moralia* a penchant for allegory and a concern with the moral message of the Bible above all.

Easily Gregory's best-known work is his *Pastoral Care*, written to instruct his clergy. Observing that the cure of souls is the art of arts, Gregory produces a manual worthy of comparison both with Ambrose's *On the Duties of Ministers* and Augustine's *On Christian Doctrine*. With Ambrose, Gregory accents moderation, decorum, and workable solutions. Even more than in Ambrose's day, clerics have to be prepared to take on major practical duties on behalf of their people. They will also have to preach. With Augustine, Gregory advises preachers to adjust their style to their audience, even if that means omitting literary niceties, a point suggesting the declining educational level of the average congregation. Gregory also assumes that the men now becoming priests have weaker educational backgrounds than those for whom Augustine wrote. In explaining how to preach to a congregation made up of diverse people, damping down the vices of some without inflaming the opposing vices of others, he makes several telling points both in substance and in style. First, he classifies people according to their prevailing moral traits, not by age, sex, class, or occupation. Starting where the members of his flock actually are, the preacher can educate them morally by showing them how to temper their excesses. A scale of values is to be preserved in which lesser goods are not discarded even as one strives for the highest, one in which the preaching of the good does not give incidental help to what is bad. Balance, practicality, and realism are Gregory's counsels. And, although he addresses the best-educated members of his diocese in this work, his style reflects the fact that he cannot expect them to grasp abstract ideas and make their own applications of them. So, he reiterates his advice, citing example after example and using but two variants on the same sentence structure throughout the lengthy passage in question.

These writings and policies accurately portray Gregory's self-definition as a church father. Although Augustine is a doctrinal authority for him, Gregory does not share his enthusiasm for speculation or controversy. Nor is he a sparkling stylist like Jerome. He resembles Ambrose more than any other of the Latin fathers, in his active application of the skills of the Roman statesman to church governance, although his engagement with contemplation is something that Ambrose lacked. Given Gregory's spiritual inclinations, his ability to simplify, clarify, and make accessible the heritage of earlier patristic thought in a practical and applicable manner is all the more striking in a Europe gripped by the political and educational crises that his works faithfully reflect. These same crises were confronted in a more immediate way by the group of thinkers called the transmitters, whose self-proclaimed task was to fill the intellectual vacuum left by the collapse of the Roman school system in western Europe.

CHAPTER 4

Hanging by a Thread:
The Transmitters and Monasticism

The Transmitters

The age of the transmitters (fourth to seventh centuries) overlaps the age of the church fathers and spans the period marked by Augustine's educational assumptions on the one side and Gregory the Great's on the other. Some transmitters were Christian; others were pagan, and there are still others whose religion is unknown. Some of these figures regarded themselves quite consciously as transmitters, assuming a personal responsibility to preserve classical or Christian culture or both. Other transmitters lacked this sense of mission but their work had the same ultimate importance for early medieval scholars.

The first three authors we will consider can be described as inadvertent transmitters whose works and biographies give no inkling of their religion. The same works do give a clear idea of how the literary disciplines were taught in the late Roman and post-Roman schools. Two of these writers, Donatus and Priscian (sixth century) produced standard textbooks on Latin grammar and rhetoric, while Macrobius (fourth century) was a literary critic, particularly influential for the philosophical gloss he gave to Vergil and Cicero. Methodologically, Donatus and Priscian have much in common, although Priscian's work is fuller and more precise. Both present grammar and rhetoric deductively, defining their terms, stating a series of rules, and then quoting passages from canonical authors to illustrate them. They treat literary texts more as examples of grammatical and rhetorical usage than as works of art. The goal of the education in the verbal arts provided by Donatus and Priscian is to teach the student to write by the rules, so he can understand their application by classical authors, and to imitate those authors rather than developing his own personal style. In approaching language itself as a system of signs, both Donatus and Priscian are descriptive, not theoretical; for them, what words mean is governed by usage, in conformity to the rules and conventions of Latin as it is actually spoken and written. By contrast, the literary criticism of Macrobius is quite theoretical. In annotating Vergil's *Aeneid* in four of the books of his *Saturnalia*, and in commenting on the dream of Scipio, an otherworldly journey made by Scipio Africanus (*c.* 185–129 BC) as a character in the last book of Cicero's *On the Commonwealth*, Macrobius brings philosophy, especially Neoplatonism, to bear on both texts. Each of these works drew the careful attention of medieval readers. With the help of Macrobius, they could acquire an indirect knowledge of the philosophical ideas he presents. Along with Book 6 of the *Aeneid*, his *Commentary on the Dream of Scipio* gave them a fund of information about the duties and rewards of the statesman and served as a classical source for the hero's trip to the other world where he converses with an ancestor about his future.

Donatus, Priscian, and Macrobius, whatever their religion, were inadvertent transmitters of the verbal arts, classical literature, and philosophy, playing this role in the course of conducting their professional activities in their writings. Another exponent of classicism in this period, Martianus Capella (fifth century), was a deliberate transmitter. Nothing is known about his life, profession, or religion, but his only known work, *The Marriage of Mercury and Philology*, makes it clear that he thought all seven of the liberal arts needed defense and preservation. Martianus' goal is to package them in a manner attractive to contemporary readers and to help perpetuate their study by prefacing the main body of his work with an allegorical fable, written in alternating sections of prose and verse. The scene is set on Mount Olympus. The chief character is Mercury, who had a number of functions in classical mythology. The ones Martianus accents are his quickness of intellect and fleetness of foot. The latter trait leads the other gods to make him their messenger in their amatory affairs, matrimonial and otherwise. Mercury's familiarity with these matters inspires him to seek a wife. After receiving Jupiter's permission, he interviews a series of allegorical candidates including Psyche, or soul, and Sophia, or wisdom, all of whom he finds wanting. Finally, assisted by Virtue, who asks the advice of Apollo, leader of the Muses, Mercury is introduced to Philology, the language arts. They hit it off at once. Ushered by Apollo and the Muses, they arrive at Jupiter's court and are received by his consort, Juno, who instructs Philology on Olympian etiquette and introduces her to the rest of the pantheon. The other gods, assembled by Jupiter, agree to confer divinity upon her. Apollo is the master of ceremonies at the wedding. Philology is attended by her mother, Phronesis, or practical wisdom, and Jupiter ties the knot. This wedding is the social event of the season on Mount Olympus. The entire pantheon and all the very best abstractions are present.

After the couple have exchanged vows, Apollo announces that Mercury will present his bride with a wedding gift: seven servants. These servants turn out to be none other than the seven liberal arts. As a dévotée of learning, Philology is thrilled by the gift. Each art now advances and gives a comprehensive account of herself in one book. The arts differ in age and appearance. Grammar, for instance, is a gray-haired old woman carrying a knife and a file, with which she excises barbarisms and smoothes the rough edges off awkward phrases. Rhetoric is a tall and beautiful young woman whose colorful dress displays the flowers of rhetoric, the figures of speech that embellish orations; she carries weapons with which she attacks opponents, and so on. What we have here, in short, is a handbook on the liberal arts, conveying their content and not just the uses to which they may be put, introduced by an entertaining story that grabs readers by the lapels and gets them involved.

In the summaries of the arts given by each of these allegorical figures, Martianus draws on the school texts standard in the educational practice of his time. Donatus and Priscian are the authorities for grammar. Rhetoric is based on Cicero's *On Invention*, and, to a lesser extent, the same author's *On Oratory*, as well as the *Rhetoric Dedicated to Herrenium* ascribed to Cicero. Together, these works cover the rules for constructing speeches, for selecting the appropriate style for particular subjects, for decorating speeches with figures of speech, for memorizing them, and for delivering them. Martianus' logic draws on the elementary logic of Aristotle found in his *Categories* and *On Interpretation*. These works treat the construction of arguments through the use of inductive, deductive, and categorical syllogisms, the analysis of necessity and probability as logical concepts, future contingents, and fallacies. The chief authority for arithmetic is Nicomachus (first century AD), whose approach emphasizes number theory, ratio, and proportion, rather than the technique of calculating. Martianus' geometry is based on the *Elements* of Euclid (third century BC); his astronomy follows that of Ptolemy (second century BC), and his music, with its typical focus on music theory, associated with mathematics, and not music appreciation or performance, draws on Aristoxenus (third century BC), who combines the mathematical approach to music derived ultimately from Pythagoreanism with a sensitivity to its acoustic qualities reflecting Aristotelian empiricism. In this attractively packaged form, Martianus' work gave late classical and early medieval students and educators exactly what they wanted, a fact attested by the frequent commentary and pedagogical use that the *Marriage* attracted, the comforting feeling that the essentials of what they needed to know about the liberal arts were here between the covers of a single book. His depictions of the personified liberal arts also became a source for medieval artists.

The lack of evidence about the religion of the transmitters just discussed suggests that the imperative of summing up and preserving classical culture in an age when the Roman state was no longer there to fund it was acknowledged by intellectual leaders irrespective of their beliefs. The next three transmitters, on the other hand, were Christians who saw their role quite consciously as the preservation of both the Christian and the classical traditions. Boethius (480–525/6), Cassiodorus (*c.* 480–575), and Isidore of Seville (*c.* 560–636) lived and held office in the age of the Germanic successor states. They were all too painfully aware of the fact that the schools were in a parlous state and not likely to improve under current leadership. None of them was a professional educator and each offers his personal response to the contemporary situation. While they all wrote to address the concrete problems of their own times, their works, like those of the other transmitters, cast a long shadow. For early medieval readers they were lifelines to the traditions the transmitters had sought to preserve.

The event that makes the career of Boethius comprehensible was the defeat of the last Roman emperor of the west in 476 and the establishment of the Ostrogothic kingdom in Italy by Theodoric (454/5–526). This ruler posed as the lieutenant in the west of the eastern Roman emperor. In line with that policy, he picked up the reins of Roman government and the patronage of art and culture to a degree unparalleled by the rulers of other Germanic kingdoms, encouraging the collaboration of his Roman aristocratic subjects. This policy had its benefits for Theodoric. Since he wanted to maintain diplomatic contact with Constantinople, he needed the services of men who knew Greek, court etiquette, and the operation of the late Roman bureaucracy. He found one such man in Boethius.

Born into a distinguished aristocratic family, Boethius was educated in the manner befitting his class. He then undertook the study of philosophy, probably in Athens. On his return to Italy he entered the service of Theodoric, attaining the post of master of the offices, or prime minister, which he discharged with probity and distinction. None the less, in 524 he came under suspicion of conspiring with the emperor in Constantinople to unseat Theodoric. He was imprisoned in Pavia and put to death in 525 or 526 without a trial or the opportunity to exculpate himself. The grounds for Theodoric's suspicion are unclear and it is possible that his hostility to Boethius reflects religious bias, since he was an Arian and Boethius an orthodox Christian. It is also possible that it unnerved Theodoric to have on his staff a man whose intellectual projects he found incomprehensible. In any event, his treatment of Boethius reveals the limits of his tolerance of the old order.

The writings of Boethius fall into three categories and enjoyed varying levels and types of influence later in the Middle Ages. Although interest in them did not begin until the ninth century and they received careful study only from the twelfth century onward, his five theological treatises were of urgent contemporary importance to Boethius. They aim at refuting Trinitarian and Christological heresies, indicating the continuing interest in these speculative doctrines in the Greek part of the church. They also reflect the continuing refinement of heretical objections to the Nicene Creed, especially in the form given to it at the council of Chalcedon in 451. For all involved it had become increasingly important to articulate theological propositions in precise philosophical language. Boethius entered the debate not only because, as a Christian intellectual, he felt a responsibility to refute heresy, but also because heresy created misunderstandings that impeded relations between the Ostrogothic court and Constantinople. His own philosophical education and his application of it to theological polemics are indices of the eclecticism with which philosophy was taught in late antiquity. Boethius uses both Platonic and Aristotelian terminology, choosing from these lexicons whatever he thinks will work best in a particular argument. The legacy his theological treatises left to the Middle Ages is thus a double one. On the one hand, these works mark a notable advance in the development of a technical philosophical vocabulary in Latin and its use in the explanation and defense of Christianity. On the other hand, the lack of univocity in Boethius' use of philosophical terms was capable of causing confusion when his theological works started receiving serious study.

Besides theology, Boethius had a larger project in view with respect to the classical tradition, which also derived from his philosophical culture. Boethius had been educated bilingually, and, like all interested Romans before him, he had studied Greek philosophy in its original tongue. Despite Theodoric's cultural patronage, the continued existence of Roman education as Boethius had known it was growing increasingly precarious. How, then, would people knowing no Greek be able to study philosophy? It is true that Cicero had translated one of Plato's dialogues and had presented the positions of a number of schools in his own dialogues, and Marius Victorinus had translated Plotinus and some Aristotelian and Stoic logical texts. But no one had translated the complete works of Plato and Aristotle, the greatest philosophers of ancient Greece. Boethius undertook to do so. He also wanted to show that their philosophies were compatible, despite Aristotle's departures from Plato. The very idea that this translation was needed is eloquent testimony both to Boethius' conviction of the importance of philosophy in the intellectual lives of Christians and to the waning of instruction in Greek in the west.

Strange to say, he decided to begin with Aristotle, although Plato had written first. Equally strange, while Aristotle had laid down a program of philosophical education beginning with metaphysics, Boethius began with logic, translating Aristotle's elementary logical texts, the *Categories* and *On Interpretation*. Before he got very far, Boethius concluded that readers tackling even these introductory works would need assistance. To provide it, he translated the *Isagoge*, or commentary on the *Categories*, by the Neoplatonist Porphyry (233–301); he commented on Cicero's logical works, derived from both the Aristotelian and Stoic traditions, and he wrote his own commentaries on Aristotle's elementary logic. A comparison of Boethius' translations and commentaries shows that he was more faithful to the letter and spirit of Aristotle in the former. In the latter, he does not hesitate to substitute examples and arguments of his own, which frequently reflect a preference for Stoic logic, with its purely formal criteria for verifying arguments and its use of hypothetical syllogisms, for an Aristotelian logic that structures our knowledge of extramental reality and whose arguments are verifiable empirically as well as formally. Whether Boethius was aware of his Stoic sources or not, his appeal to Stoic logic proved to be immensely influential in the later history of medieval philosophy. It provided his successors with a post-Aristotelian alternative that eventually helped them to develop a post-classical logic of their own. Thus, it was not merely the Latinizing of Aristotle's logic and the improvement on Victorinus' translations of it that are important consequences of Boethius' work.

Yet another contribution he made in his philosophical translations was to flag the problem of universals, which he found in Porphyry's *Isagoge*. Boethius did not take a stand on the matter himself but it proved to be of keen interest to later medieval thinkers. The debate centers on the logical status of universals, or abstract ideas, in relation to concepts standing for individual things. Some held that what we know first, and what we can verify by comparing them to the phenomena from which they are derived, are the concepts representing individual things. We can compare such concepts with others of the same kind, noting similarities, and develop abstract general concepts that can be attributed to all the particular members of the genus. The universal or general idea arises at a secondary stage of reasoning. Others held that universals are what we know first and that we can grasp the significance of an idea representing an individual thing only in the light of the universal of which it is a specific case. The first of these positions is compatible with Aristotelianism and its emphasis on sense data as the source of our knowledge; the second is compatible with the Platonic belief in innate ideas and in the superiority of the abstract over the concrete. The ups and downs of this debate, its extension by some medieval thinkers from logic to metaphysics, and the shifting applications made by defenders of both positions to theological argument were, initially, made possible because Boethius had brought the problem of universals to his readers' attention.

Indeed, in the Middle Ages, Boethius was often thought of and depicted in art as a musician as well as a logician, since another pedagogical detour he made, coupled with his untimely death, prevented him from going beyond logic in his philosophical translations. Just as he thought that readers of Aristotle's elementary logic would need help in understanding the texts from Porphyry, Cicero, and himself, so, he decided, they would need still more basic background, drawn from the scientific and mathematical subjects of the school tradition. Like philosophy, the standard texts in arithmetic, geometry, astronomy, and music had been written by Greeks and had been studied in Greek in the Roman schools. Labeling them the quadrivium, Boethius put these texts, already noted for their use by Martianus Capella, into Latin. Side by side with Donatus and Priscian for grammar, the Ciceronian and pseudo-Ciceronian texts for rhetoric coupled with a work Boethius wrote on topics, or rhetorical commonplaces, and his translation of Aristotle's logic, Boethius' quadrivium translations provided medieval students with their introductions to the liberal arts in Latin for many centuries. The role of Boethius as a transmitter and his contribution to the history of medieval education were thus fundamental.

As central texts in the school tradition, Boethius' translations and commentaries were required reading, but equally famous was his last work, a bestseller read by choice. This was his *Consolation of Philosophy*, written in prison while he awaited execution. Both its style, an elegant dialogue between Boethius and Lady Philosophy in which each prose book is headed by a poem, and its subject, why the just man suffers, made it an immediate and durable classic. In writing the *Consolation* Boethius had no library and drew on the contents of his well-stocked mind. Unlike Gregory the Great in his *Moralia*, which treats the same theme, Boethius does not base his reflections on the Bible and he does not treat the sufferings of the just as a divine mystery designed to test and strengthen the believer's faith. Rather, Boethius treats the question as one yielding a rational answer. He bases his arguments on philosophy, with Stoic theodicy contributing to an understanding and solution of a problem that he frames in largely Neoplatonic terms. Boethius' Lady Philosophy, a figure whose head touches the clouds and whose dress has the Greek letters beginning the words 'practical' and 'theoretical' at its hem and top, carries books and a scepter, suggesting that philosophy is the ruling discipline. She opens the dialogue by chasing away the Muses with whom Boethius had first sought consolation. She had a long career ahead of her in medieval literature and art. So did another personified abstraction in the *Consolation*, the goddess Fortune. Boethius appropriates her from classical mythology and endows her with his own attributes, a band covering her eyes to suggest that fortune is blind and a wheel suggesting her capriciousness. Like Augustine's dialogues, the *Consolation* appeals to the tradition of Socratic argument. The exchange between the interlocutors is the means by which Lady Philosophy helps Boethius correct his errors and discover truth. But, unlike Augustine's *On Order* and Lactantius' *On God's Handiwork*, its theme is not theodicy in the sense of rationalizing the cosmic order but the effort to find meaning in man's inhumanity to man.

Accepting Philosophy's assertion that he is suffering because he has lost a true sense of who he is and what the world is really like, Boethius the interlocutor adjusts his outlook accordingly, starting with the deity. He describes God both as the Aristotelian unmoved mover and as light, a Platonic and Neoplatonic metaphor, the supreme being Who is also supreme goodness and truth. Boethius sees the universe ordered in a Neoplatonic chain of being, an order that, he holds with the Stoics, is fully rational and has nothing arbitrary about it. Fortune, who seems capricious, is not an independent force, he argues, but one who executes God's rational providence. The vicissitudes of life, including the sufferings inflicted on Boethius, are thus part of the rational divine plan, however distressing or apparently irrational they may seem. In particular, fame, wealth, rank, honor, and respect, even life itself, whose withdrawal constitutes Boethius' personal dilemma, are transitory and inferior goods by nature. The lasting good of union between our immortal soul and God can never be withdrawn, and it must be recognized as the true good that Boethius can attain once he accepts it as such through correct judgment and the exercise of free will. Boethius adds the Neoplatonic privative theory of evil to this analysis in order to define as apparent rather than real the misfortunes he suffers. On this point, as well as on the point that Fortune is an agent of divine providence, he parts company with Augustine. But they agree that providence is foresight, not causation, and that it does not limit choices made by free will. For Boethius, this conclusion reinforces the necessity and possibility of choosing to alter his attitude and of making peace with himself before his unjust imprisonment is terminated by his still more unjust summary execution. The sense of the author's pressing need to come to meaningful terms with his situation, the personal immediacy of the *Consolation*, no less than its attractive literary form, the perennial interest of the question it poses, and the rich store of classical ideas from varied sources that Boethius weaves together, do much to explain its lasting popularity.

As his dates indicate, Cassiodorus was born a contemporary of Boethius, although he lived to a ripe old age. Both the years and energy at his disposal and the state of Italian politics in the later sixth century gave him his project and the opportunity to implement it. Cassiodorus came from the same social class as Boethius and was also one of the educated aristocrats co-opted by the Ostrogothic kings. He held a series of high offices. His duties included drafting state papers and diplomatic correspondence, an activity reflected in his *Variae*. Other works he wrote that fall outside the category of transmission are his *History of the Goths*, a good source for the history of his times, a long and much-quoted commentary on the Psalms, and a treatise *On the Soul*, documenting a continuing debate among Christian thinkers on whether or not the soul is material. Cassiodorus also translated the works of some Greek church fathers into Latin, sharing Boethius' concern about the decline of Greek studies in the west. By this time, the Ostrogoths had been replaced by the Lombards, a people uninterested in the sponsorship of classical education. The situation in the schools had grown exponentially worse since the time of Boethius. Cassiodorus' first idea was that classical and Christian education alike should be supported institutionally in a systematic and centralized manner. Since the rulers were a vain hope, he turned to the pope, broaching the idea of a Christian academy located in Rome and subsidized by the papacy to the current pontiff, Agapetus (ruled 535–36). Given the political problems on his own plate, Agapetus was unable to respond, so Cassiodorus decided to take his own initiative. Having retired from the civil service in 538 or 540, he drew on his own personal wealth and created a model school at Vivarium in southern Italy, in a monastery he founded. He served as the head of this school for the rest of his life, devoting himself to building up a library of manuscripts on both secular and theological subjects. And it was here that he produced his major work as a transmitter, the *Institutes concerning Divine and Human Readings*.

The *Institutes* can best be described as an extremely detailed annotated bibliography, in which Cassiodorus covers both theology and the liberal arts. In each area, he is concerned not only with indicating what titles a good library should have. He also summarizes the historical development of each discipline, discussing the authors who have played important roles in that development, even if their views are no longer current. This historical account of the subjects he covers is more broadly conceived than Martianus Capella's summary of the liberal arts as taught in his own day, both because Cassiodorus includes Christian literature as well as the liberal arts and because he enables us to reconstruct a tradition of doctrinal and educational thought that, in some cases, would be otherwise irretrievable, since the works of some of the authors he comments on have not survived.

In addition, in the preface to the first book of the *Institutes*, which deals with the liberal arts, Cassiodorus offers an explanation for their inclusion and for the way he treats them that bears comparison with Augustine's *On Christian Doctrine* and also, stylistically, with Gregory's *Pastoral Care*. Like Gregory, Cassiodorus relies heavily on the repetition of his chosen phraseology, and instead of simply referring to the liberal arts he names them specifically, suggesting that his readers' knowledge of what they are cannot be assumed. He offers an essentially Augustinian rationale for their study by Christians. These arts, he agrees, are essential for understanding the Bible and for equipping students to read and contribute to Christian literature more generally. At the same time, he does not expect all his readers to be well grounded in the arts. Some, he observes, may indeed have such knowledge. For them, his extended commentary on the disciplines will provide a brief review. But, he acknowledges, there are others who lack a liberal arts education. For them—and he envisions readers as falling increasingly into this second group—his elaborate annotations will introduce them to the history and content of the liberal arts. Another major difference from Augustine is that Cassiodorus sees it as incumbent upon Christians to provide instruction in the liberal arts as well as in religious subjects. 'Let the task of the ancients be our task,'[1] he exclaims. It is Christians like himself, operating out of monastic centers at the grass-roots level, not leaders in the upper echelons of the church or state, who must shoulder the burden, with commitment, enthusiasm, and good will. Otherwise, the *Institutes* intimates, both the classical and Christian legacies will be lost irretrievably.

Cassiodorus' location of his model school in a monastery was a fateful conjunction, to which we will return later in this chapter in considering monasticism as an agency for the transmission of the Christian and classical traditions in early medieval Europe. Cassiodorus also wrote a *Rule* for his monastery. But his final work, intimately related to his grounding of education in good library collections and likewise deeply illustrative of changing times, was a book on spelling. As we have noted, he made translations to address the decline of Greek literacy in the west. His handbook on spelling reflects the decline of Latin literacy as well. Cassiodorus clearly recognizes that correct Latin is necessary if the manuscripts schools depend on are to be accurate, without the introduction of textual errors stemming from scribal illiteracy. The works Cassiodorus considered essential in this connection remained the norm for early medieval teachers and librarians. No school worthy of the name was without a copy of his *Institutes* and all librarians in that period used it as the indispensable guide to what their collections should contain.

If the early medieval scholar wanted to go beyond the basics provided by the transmitters already mentioned, our final transmitter, Isidore of Seville, was the author of choice. Unlike all the other transmitters who, to the best of our knowledge, were Italians, Isidore came from Spain. But, like them, he spoke Latin as his native language and he was one of a shrinking number of people in his country, which had been one of the most intensively Romanized provinces of the former Roman empire, who knew Greek. Isidore served as bishop of Seville. Like Gregory the Great, he lived in a politically turbulent age. In his day the Iberian peninsula was overrun, successively, by Visigoths, Vandals, Alans, Suevi, and other Germanic groups whose treatment of their conquered subjects was diametrically opposed to the Ostrogothic policy of relative toleration of classical culture and orthodox Christianity. Like Cassiodorus, he wrote a history of his times charting the comings and goings of these conquerors. Isidore also contributed to biblical exegesis. But here he and Cassiodorus part company. Isidore's *Questions on the Old Testament* tackles those passages most replete with multiple meanings. The various readings he provides are not his own, but excerpts from patristic exegesis. Isidore's self-appointed task is to cull what he thinks are the best interpretations of the fathers and to anthologize them. He compares this activity to the assembling of a mixed bouquet of flowers plucked from diverse fields whose editor thereby spares a reader with a short attention span or a distaste for prolixity the chore of doing the research himself. As a genre, then, this work takes the form called the *florilegium*. It won favor in the early Middle Ages and beyond with readers either too busy or too unprovided with educational opportunities or research facilities to expand on the pre-selected quotations of the anthologist. Also helpful to the reader of the Bible who is pressed for time or unable to make use of the more extensive reference works provided by Jerome are Isidore's handbooks, which list in chronological order the birthplace, life span, place of burial, and notable traits of biblical personages, as well as a compendium of all the allegorical meanings that patristic exegetes had attached to them.

The same need to distill the essentials for the same kind of audience is clearly visible in Isidore's chief contribution as a transmitter, the *Etymologies*. This work could be described as a *florilegium* on an encyclopedic scale, reflecting Isidore's view that if he did not save culture, armed with his own extensive knowledge and the weapons of scissors and paste, no one else would. The easiest way to convey Isidore's notion of the knowledge worth preserving is to recapitulate the table of contents. The *Etymologies* has twenty books. Books 1 to 3 cover the seven liberal arts. Book 4 treats medicine. Book 5 covers civil law, days, nights, seasons, months, years, and equinoxes. Book 6 deals with canon law. In Book 7 Isidore considers God, the angels, and the saints. Book 8 is devoted to the church and the various heretical sects. In Book 9 Isidore discusses languages, peoples, and kingdoms. Book 10 treats the etymological derivations of words. Book 11 deals with man as a natural phenomenon, the human body and its parts, and fabulous monsters. Book 12 covers zoology. In Book 13 Isidore turns to cosmology, the universe and its parts, including elements, atoms, winds, and waters. Book 14 presents geography. Book 15 deals with cities, architecture, and fields. Book 16 treats stones and metals, their properties curious and otherwise. Book 17 is devoted to botany. Book 18 treats war, games, and pastimes. Book 19 considers ships and their parts, buildings and their decoration, clothing and its ornaments. Book 20 concludes the *Etymologies* with furniture, food and drink, and the best receptacles in which to keep leftovers.

Isidore's aim in the *Etymologies* is clearly to include everything he can think of, up to and including the kitchen sink. His encyclopedia certainly made an enormous amount of information available. What is less obvious is the rationale for his arrangement of his material. Unlike encyclopedias produced in other periods, Isidore's is neither alphabetical nor, apparently, topical in its organization. He does actually have a principle in mind, the one that gives the work its title. Isidore believes—and the idea has a reputable ancestry going back to Plato—that words deriving from the same etymological roots denote things that are somehow related to each other in real life. His application of this principle to his subject matter produces the results just noted because many of his etymologies are incorrect, fantastic, or arbitrary. None the less, Isidore's *Etymologies* became a standard reference work in the early Middle Ages, for classical and Christian subjects alike. And Isidore's very name conveyed such authority that it was attached to a forged document in the ninth century purporting to enlarge the scope of papal power, to give it greater credibility.

Monasticism

The transmitters, whether pagan, Christian, or of no known religious affiliation, and whether inadvertent or deliberate, produced the texts that connected early medieval thinkers to the classical and Christian traditions. The places where these texts were taught, studied, commented on, and copied became, in this period, monasteries, a locus for schooling already acceptable to Cassiodorus. Monasticism also became, increasingly, the vehicle for the Christianization of the Germanic and

Celtic peoples, a development that Gregory the Great took steps to reinforce. Our earlier references to monasticism have noted that it came into being as a Christian institution, with parallels in pagan asceticism and intertestamental Jewish sects, in the fourth century. Its earliest stage featured the flight to the desert, a life of extreme austerity, and very little organization, as in the lives of saints praised by Jerome. Women also participated in this early desert monasticism, or stayed at home as virgins and widows of the sort to whom Jerome and Ambrose gave advice. Later in the fourth century, settled monastic communities began to emerge. Augustine had occasion to write sternly to monastic houses in his diocese whose members were living obstreperously, and his letter of advice to a woman seeking to found a convent became the basis for what later would become the Augustinian *Rule*. The popularity of community-style monasticism, for both sexes, and the idealization of the Benedictine version of this idea seen in Gregory the Great's *Dialogues*, leads us to a wider discussion of monasticism and its impact on early medieval intellectual history. Along with its perceived value as an ideal form of Christian life, Benedictine monasticism was also the sponsor of education, music, and the visual arts and the model used later in the Middle Ages for monastic reform and the foundation of new monastic orders.

Benedictine monasticism needs to be understood as one of the options available to Christians called to the monastic life in the age of Benedict of Nursia. As early as the mid-fourth century, critics had begun to object to desert monasticism as antisocial and too disorganized. Some critics thought that the extreme asceticism of the desert fathers and mothers might be masking or reinforcing a Gnostic or Manichean loathing of the flesh as evil. While the anchorite or hermit mode of monastic life always remained an option, constructive reactions against it took the form of proposals for community monasticism which replaced ascetic individualism with moderation and a stress on social ethics. The first two monastic reformers to develop rules reflecting these principles, Pachomius (*c.* 287–346) and Basil the Great, wrote in Greek. Since their *Rules* were immediately translated into Latin, they were widely known in western monastic thought and Benedict was thoroughly familiar with them, as well as with the *Rule* of an anonymous Latin author more or less a contemporary, with whom he has much in common. The contrast between Pachomian, Basilian, and Benedictine monasticism is an important index of the different intellectual and social roles played by medieval monasticism east and west.

In urging that community should replace the solitary life, Pachomius places much emphasis on coherent organization, with a clear chain of command along military lines, the strict enforcement of obedience, and a stress on manual labor, all of which are designed to undercut individualism and to inculcate group spirit. Pachomius also emphasizes labor in order to make the monastery economically independent. He assumes that those drawn to the cloister will be contemplatives. Requiring them to do manual labor, he thinks, will instill humility in them. His view of work as having a positive moral value for the individual and the group reflects Pachomius' conscious departure from the understanding of work in the biblical and classical traditions as a punishment for sin or the consequence of a fall from the golden age. In his *Rule*, discipline is to be enforced with admonitions and chastisements, including corporal punishment and expulsion. At the same time, he provides lavish care for the sick. Still, the prevailing tone of Pachomian monasticism is that of the army camp.

This positive stress on work and community is emphasized even more in Basil's *Rule*. In a striking shift away from Pachomius, the institutional model Basil chooses is not the army camp but the family. Given the patriarchal structure of fourth-century law and society, the family model means hierarchy and the subordination of monks to the abbot, or head of the community, who governs it with the authority of a Roman paterfamilias over his dependants. Still, the family model suggests affective ties among its members. Aside from its importance economically and as a means of individual self-discipline, work, for Basil, is valuable socially, for two reasons: not only will it build and express fraternal charity within the monastery, it will also be a means by which it can serve the wider community outside its walls. Basil prescribes that monasteries be built near towns, so that any surplus produced by the monks' labor can be used for poor relief. He de-emphasizes asceticism, as does Pachomius, setting definite limits to the austerities he allows his monks. He accents not physical asceticism but a spiritual appropriation of self-mortification, seen as the sacrifice of things that are not evil in themselves but that are encumbrances in the monk's moral development. His example is that of an athlete stripping down to a minimum of clothing not because there is anything wrong with clothing but because it gets in his way. Another new feature of Basil's *Rule* is his emphasis on poverty. For him, poverty does not require the renunciation of all personal property on the part of the brethren, or on the part of the community as a whole, but the use of wealth in a spirit of detachment, stewardship, and charity.

Basil's *Rule* was regarded as a distinct improvement on the Pachomian *Rule*. It was adapted to convents of women as well as men; it was approved by the council of Chalcedon and incorporated into Roman law in the sixth century. It served as the foundation for most of the monastic life in the Greek church in the Middle Ages and beyond and found some adherents in the west in southern France and Italy. Yet there were features of Basilian monasticism, given the situation in western Europe in the post-Roman era, that limited its appeal there and that explain why Benedict's *Rule* was preferred. Basil's *Rule* is quite precise on food, clothing, and work assignments and it conceives of them in terms of the sub-tropical climate of the Mediterranean world. These prescriptions were not practical in other climates, such as northern Europe. Also, like Pachomius, Basil sees the contemplative life as the real aim of the brethren and sisters. He makes no provisions for people who might be drawn to the ordered life of the cloister but who are not mystics. In the light of the retention of the Roman school system in the east, Basil also assumes that members of his communities will already have been educated, by the state. He makes no provision for educational or other cultural activities sponsored by the monastery itself.

It is precisely these perceived deficiencies in the Basilian *Rule* that Benedict's *Rule* sought to correct and it is these corrections that account for its wide popularity in the west. It is not clear whether Benedict intended Monte Cassino to be the flagship monastery in a Europe-wide movement when he founded his first convent there in 529. But such was the result of the flexibility, adaptability, and administrative workability of his *Rule*, written with the Roman bureaucrat's keen eye for the creation of an organization that could meet the needs of many kinds of people in widely different settings. In striking contrast with Pachomius and Basil, Benedict lays down a minimum of specific regulations. He leaves a great deal to the discretion of the abbot or abbess, particularly with respect to the enforcement of discipline, work tasks, clothing, and food.

There are also some areas in which Benedict borrows from and refines Basilian monasticism. He shares Basil's dislike of hermits, wanderers, and extreme asceticism, counseling moderation and a focus on community life as the alternative. Benedict adds to the vows of poverty, chastity, and obedience taken when the monk or nun makes his or her formal profession the vow of stability, the agreement to stay put physically unless the individual is required to travel on the community's business. Benedict finds Basil's model of family life attractive but modifies it, in an extremely important way, combining the stress on the affective relations binding members of the community with the conception of the monastery as a legal corporation. The abbot or abbess is the chief executive officer. He or she is elected by the members and must discuss policy with the professed brothers or sisters before making major decisions. As we will see, this legal structure had a critical impact on the social and intellectual functions of western monasticism. On the subject of work and poverty, Benedict goes farther than Basil. He rules that monks and nuns may own no personal property, with two telling exceptions, a pen and a pen-knife. Sharing the positive moral revaluation of work for the individual and the community, Benedict does not hesitate to describe it as prayer in his motto, 'To work is to pray,' suggesting that, whatever kind of work one does, it should be done with integrity and offered to God as well as to one's fellow man. Another major change in the organization of the monastery in Benedict's *Rule* is the inclusion of a procedure for the admission of would-be monks and nuns. These candidates are to serve a novitiate for one year, living in the monastery and following its routine of prayer and work, so that both the novices and the community can test their vocation and suitability. Only after the novitiate has been completed successfully can the novice take final vows and become a professed member of the community.

These vows specify the main duties and the moral responsibilities of Benedictines. Members of the order were expected to be guided by the Ten Commandments and the Sermon on the Mount and to make humility the foundation of their other virtues. The moral outlook envisioned by Benedict could certainly accommodate people with mystical temperaments, and some of the greatest contemplatives of the Middle Ages were nurtured in the Benedictine tradition. But this aptitude was not an entrance requirement. Many other kinds of people could find a home in Benedictine monasticism and could develop their own kind of spirituality, especially in the free time Benedict allotted to each member along with the common round of liturgical prayer eight times daily, in addition to the mass. Work, too, could be individualized depending on the intelligence and ability of the people in a particular community. It is here that Benedict made one of his most influential contributions to medieval intellectual history. In order to read their service books, liturgical texts, and the spiritual texts they were required to digest privately, Benedictine monks and nuns had to be literate. Given the age in which he lived, Benedict was well aware of the fact that he could not expect this literacy at the time when candidates were admitted to the convent. So the monastery had to have a school, and the education it provided should be made available not only to the monks or nuns but to people from the region who wanted to send their children to the convent to study, whether they intended to enter monastic life or not. Benedict puts the provision of education in the same class as the convent's sharing of its medical knowledge and its mandate to offer hospitality as a major service to the wider Christian society. Teaching in the school, scholarship in the liberal arts or in theology and exegesis, the copying and embellishment of manuscripts, the production and performance of music for the liturgy, were all as acceptable to Benedict as manual labor in fulfilling the obligation to work. These unique features of the Benedictine *Rule*, in comparison with the other forms of monasticism available to early medieval Christians, made it a prime locus for the teaching of the classical liberal arts no less than for the dissemination of Christianity. The Benedictine approach to education, artistic production, and patronage of the arts applied to nuns as well as monks, providing an institutionalized framework in which women could pursue learning and the arts and in which they could exercise leadership roles as heads of corporate bodies that often attained great wealth and political prominence.

In addition to providing for the sharing of authority between the members and the head, and even a legal means of redress if the head violated the *Rule* or proved deficient for some other serious reason, the structure of the convent as a legal corporation enabled individual Benedictine communities to make their own collective policy decisions on what to emphasize, be it in estate management, liturgical music, a certain style of manuscript illumination, or a particular scholarly emphasis, based on the members it produced or attracted and the patronage it might draw from donors wishing to associate themselves with the community and be remembered in its prayers. The accident of location, coupled with its freedom to act as a legal person, also played a role in the specific emphasis found in the culture of individual Benedictine convents, making for intellectual, spiritual, and artistic diversity within the same order. The very flexibility of the *Rule* itself also made possible a wide array of applications of the order's mission. That mission, in learning, evangelization, and the arts, fairly entitles the Benedictines to share with the transmitters the honor of serving as an intellectual lifeline between early medieval thinkers and their classical and patristic heritage. For, to a large extent, they were the schoolmasters who conveyed the works of the church fathers and transmitters to their students in the early Middle Ages.

CHAPTER 5

Europe's New Schoolmasters: Franks, Celts, and Anglo-Saxons

As we move to the next phase of our story we encounter a striking shift in the dynamics of cultural interaction. For, unlike the transmitters and early Benedictines, who came from Italy and Spain, heartland regions of the former Roman empire in the west, most of Europe's new schoolmasters in the period immediately following were Celts from Ireland or members of the Germanic groups who settled in northern Europe and England. The Celts, apparently indigenous to Europe, left their first traces in southwestern Germany in *c*. 2000 BC. Between *c*. 800 and *c*. 200 BC they had expanded into Gaul, Spain, eastern Europe, western Asia, and the British Isles. They were conquered on the continent by the Romans, except in Ireland and Scotland, which the Romans never penetrated. Similar in material culture wherever their remains are found, the Celts used two related languages, one prevailing in Ireland, Scotland, and the Isle of Man and the other in Cornwall, Wales, and Brittany. The Germanic peoples, of central Asian origin, moved westward into Europe, where they were noted by classical ethnographers, by the first century AD. They continued to move, crossing into Roman territory, first peacefully but eventually invading and defeating the western Roman empire, from the late fourth century until their final victory over Rome in the late fifth century.

Whether conquered or conquerors, the Celts and Germans accepted the language and religion of Christian Rome; although Germans usually embraced Arianism before converting to orthodoxy and Celtic Christianity had features of its own. Unlike Byzantine missionaries, who translated the Bible and the liturgy into a tongue understood by the Slavic conquerors of their European lands, western churchmen who evangelized Celts and Germans kept the liturgy in Latin. Wholesale translations of the Bible into the German vernacular, such as that of Ulfilas in the fourth century, are atypical, even though baptismal vows, confessional formulae, popular sermons, catechetical materials, the creed, and the Lord's Prayer survive in Old High German. There is evidence of the deliberate semantic manipulation of German by missionaries so as to give pagan terms a Christian sense. The noun *Heil* and its adjective *heilig*, which originally denoted the charisma surrounding a pagan king, were first reinterpreted to mean healing, as in recovery from an illness, which could occur through the power of a Christian saint or the saint's relics. From political and physical well-being and protection, these terms came to mean salvation. Such examples do indicate that emissaries of Latin Christian culture were willing to make use of the German vernacular in their program of evangelization. There is no evidence of any analogous use of Old Irish or Old French. For the most part, Celtic and Germanic thinkers had to learn Latin before they could open the seals of the sacred books, the liberal arts, the church fathers, and the transmitters. Yet, it was they who became the chief authors of Latin literature, sacred and secular, and leaders in the Christian missions. They lived in two worlds intellectually, maintaining the vernacular culture originating in their pre-Christian past even as they took on the task of propagating Latin Christian education. Typically, these Celtic and Germanic thinkers were monks, teaching in monastic schools in their own countries and in those they founded in foreign lands, pushing back the boundaries of western Christendom to the north and east and reactivating religious and intellectual life in some parts of Europe where its earlier flowering had waned after the fifth century. Most of these new monastic schoolmasters acted on their own initiative, on the basis of whatever patronage they, as individuals or small groups, could draw to their endeavors. While their vision of what was needed was a common one—the evangelization of Europe and the provision of basic education in the liberal arts—their efforts were rarely coordinated or directed from above.

In understanding the internalization of the Christian and classical traditions by Celtic and Germanic thinkers only recently exposed to them, a sense of what they brought to these traditions as well as how they were presented to the Celts and Germans is as vital as understanding the enculturation of Christianity in the Roman world. Just as Christianity took on the coloration of classical literature and philosophy and an institutional shape based on the bureaucratic and legal system of Rome, so church leaders made adjustments to the Celtic and Gemanic mentalities and value systems in their effort to evangelize these peoples, a process that intensified when thinkers from these very groups became the leaders who took charge of the schoolrooms and pulpits.

The ideas and institutions critical for assessing the Irish in this connection must be gleaned largely from archeology, since Old Irish was not written down until the fifth century. Redaction began before, but was hastened by, Ireland's first contacts with Christian missionaries. Ireland had never been part of the Roman empire. In the early Middle Ages, the country had no cities and no professional merchant class. Its economy was largely pastoral, with livestock as the principal index of wealth, along with seafaring and fishing. Ireland was organized politically into tribes, both patrilinear and matrilinear. Compared with other contemporary societies, there was little difference in the legal status and social roles of early Irish men and women. Several forms of marriage were regarded as legal. More than one form could coincide in the same household, and the legitimacy of a child was determined by the parents' recognition of the child, whether born in one version of wedlock or not. Each tribe had its own ruler, with a high king over all the tribes. Tribal chiefs also served as religious leaders. The religion of the pagan Celts included deities representing the forces of nature, a host of sub-divine otherworldly beings, both malevolent and benevolent, and a lively belief in their frequent and active intervention in human affairs. The pagan Celts also believed that human souls could inhabit the bodies of animals and that there was a good other world on an island across the sea, which some people might visit while still alive.

For the Germanic peoples the archeological record is supplemented by the observations of Hellenistic and Roman ethnographers and historians, of whom the most famous is Tacitus (*c*. 65–*c*. 117). In his *Germania*, Tacitus may have drawn on earlier ethnographers as well as on the personal contact with Germans he made during his military service in northern Europe. His testimony is extremely valuable. But Tacitus must be used with caution. Germanic institutions developed over time and did not always match his findings several centuries later, when Germanic thinkers were taking on the mantle of Latin Christian culture. In addition, Tacitus wants to criticize Rome as corrupt and effete by contrasting it with Germanic society. This motive leads him to omit Germanic institutions and practices, aside from drunkenness, that do not support his agenda. His reference point is always Rome. He considers the Germans in terms of their differences from or similarities to the Romans, not in their own terms. The greatest similarity he sees is in the field of religion. The Germans, Tacitus notes, are polytheists and their gods have the same functions as those in the Roman pantheon, whose names he attaches to them. The Germans also believe that some deities dwell especially in certain groves, which are sacred shrines. Exponents of heroic virtue are believed to enjoy a pleasant afterlife and are elevated to demigod status; in this life they can obtain advantages through descent from or patronage of a god. The only contrast Tacitus notes with Roman religion is the absence of temples as sites for worship among the Germans.

The reason for this lack of temples is the semi-migratory nature of the Germanic economy, which combines herding with agriculture and raiding. Germanic law and society, Tacitus observes, are patrilinear, as is the case with Rome. Germanic institutions are otherwise quite un-Roman. For the Germans, political relations are personal relations, since, in their tribal society, the political leader is the head of the lineage and is related by blood to all its members. Family loyalty is the main legal and social cement. It entails a strict obligation to avenge injuries against one's kin, leading to blood feuds; although crimes against persons, even as serious as murder, can be resolved by the payment of a fine, or *Wergeld*, to the injured party or his or her family. The rules for assessing the *Wergeld*, and for everything else, are customary, not written. Legislation means not the making of new laws but the recalling and applying of traditional custom, which, the Germans hold, travels with the tribe wherever it is and is not attached to a fixed territorial jurisdiction. All free men in the tribe have the right to ratify the tribal leader's decisions. Although all members of the tribe are bound to the leader by family loyalty, in the conduct of war he has a band of warriors, the *comitatus*, who swear a special oath of loyalty, vowing to fight to the death and not to survive him if he is slain. In return, the leader rewards *comitatus* members with booty after successful battles.

Marriage and the status of women also attract Tacitus' interest. Here, we can assess his emphasis and omissions or, perhaps, developments subsequent to his account, by comparing what he says with the first Germanic law codes written down in Latin on the model of the Theodosian Code (of 438) starting in the early sixth century. Tacitus claims that German women enjoy legal and social rights far greater than those of Roman women and that marriage vows are respected, in contrast to the sexual immorality and easy divorce prevalent in Rome. In fact, while Roman matrons could escape the legal tutelage of male relatives if they had borne three children (or four, for freedwomen), German women in the early law codes remained under such tutelage for life. While Tacitus does note the institution of bride-price and the morning-gift a Germanic husband gives his wife in contrast to the dowry given by the Roman bride's family as the economic foundation of a marriage and the source of support for a widow, he omits the fact that some Germanic groups practiced polygyny. Also, in deference to the Romans' horror of rape as a heinous crime meriting the death penalty, he omits the Germanic practice of raiding other tribes for their women and the establishment of a marital claim to a female captive by rape.

While Christianity found its way to Ireland in a more or less haphazard manner, from Roman Britain, from contacts between Irish mariners and monastic centers in southern France, and eventually by a mission sent by Pope Celestine I in 431, first in the person of Palladius and, on his death, by Patrick (*c.* 389–*c.* 461), the missions which popes sent from south to north dealt mostly with Germans. Good indices of the problems faced by these representatives of Roman order and Latin Christian culture in their encounter with the Germans, and their responses to these problems, are the books of penitentials, written between the fifth and seventh centuries for the aid of pastors administering penance to new converts, and other strategies and adaptations church leaders made. The penitentials instruct pastors to be on the alert for sins reflecting pagan survivals. They also suggest ways to reconceptualize Christian doctrines and practices that conflict with Germanic sensibilities. Parallel with the building of churches on the sites of pagan temples in Rome, missionaries had to address the Germanic veneration of sacred trees and groves and the importance for them of fertility rites occurring at the winter solstice. The result was the 'baptism' of the sacred tree as the Christmas tree or Yule log and the promotion of Christmas as a holiday, given much more attention than it had drawn in the liturgy of the early church. Just as the penitentials reflect the persistence of pagan worship among Germanic converts, they also show conflict and accommodation in the realm of morals. Penance had to be adapted in its administration to assuage the Germanic sense of honor. Instead of confessing before the whole congregation, the penitent now confessed privately to a priest. Roman Christian pastors also faced major difficulties with abduction and rape as establishing a marriage and with the blood feud. Their response was to assimilate the notion of bride-price to the satisfaction owed to the parents of an unmarried woman whom a man acquired as a wife by rape. They also promoted the use of the *Wergeld* as a means of settling personal injuries without bloodshed. In hagiography, Latin Christian writers in Germanic lands capitulated to the warrior ethos that enshrined violence as a means of conflict resolution. While earlier, being a soldier had been seen as a disqualification for sanctity, in the sixth century the warrior saint starts to make his appearance in Europe, sparked by 'sightings' of Michael the Archangel, defender in battle, who added patronage and pilgrimage sites in Rome, Normandy, and Italy to this hagiographical turn. In all these ways, Christianity as taught by the Roman missionaries was modified to meet Germanic requirements. This fact should not be surprising given the accommodations Christianity had earlier made to Roman institutions and values, not only in terms of the intellectual tradition and governance, but also by its retention of a legal system in which concubinage and prostitution and the right of the male head of a family to expose unwanted infants remained on the books well after Christianity became the official religion of Rome.

Given the evidence of superficial Christianization and of the carry-over of pre-Christian attitudes among the Celts and Germans, it is remarkable that they should have wanted to absorb, teach, and contribute to Latin Christian culture in the first place. Yet such was the case. Between the sixth and eighth centuries, and after the transmitters, the leading exponents of that culture came from Merovingian Gaul, Celtic Ireland, and Anglo-Saxon England.

Franks

While the Franks were the most powerful Germanic group on the European continent, conquering most of the other Germanic peoples in what is now France and Germany and creating a multi-tribal empire under Clovis (*c.* 465–511), they were the least successful of these three groups in perpetuating and adding to Latin Christian culture. In some respects this outcome is strange, since the province of Gaul, especially south of the Loire, had been a vibrant cultural center in the fourth and fifth centuries, boasting an impressive array of schools and many Latin writers working in genres as varied as theology, exegesis, speculative thought, hagiography, history, rhetoric, poetry, and even comedy. Monastic life flourished, with convents following the Basilian rule as well as the foundations of John Cassian (*c.* 360–*c.* 435), whose writings earned him the recommendation of Benedict of Nursia. Theologians such as Hilary of Poitiers (*c.* 310–68) staunchly defended Nicene orthodoxy against the Arians; while Faustus of Riez (*c.* 400–92) and Claudianus Mamertus (*c.* 400–79) debated the materiality of the human soul. Poets such as Ausonius (310–393/4) wrote on religious and secular subjects, as did prose writers such as Sidonius Apollinaris (430–79/80).

That this speculative and literary activity did not appeal either to the Germanic invaders of Gaul in the fourth and fifth centuries or to the Merovingian Franks when they first seized control in the early sixth century can be seen by the fact that the chief writers contributing to Latin Christian literature in sixth-century Gaul came not from the Frankish community but from the increasingly vestigial Gallo-Roman elite which it had conquered. Their work shrank in quantity and plummeted in quality in comparison with their fourth- and fifth-century forebears. Two figures will serve as illustrations, Caesarius of Arles (*c.* 470–543) and Gregory of Tours (534–94). Their careers span the sixth century and show a changing relationship between these emissaries of elite Christian Latin culture and their Frankish masters.

Caesarius, bishop of Arles, was in office when the Franks conquered Gaul and converted to Christianity. Like the authors of the books of penitentials, he labored to instill Christian values in a population for whom the new religious allegiance was rarely accompanied by attitudinal change. Caesarius' sermons repeatedly stress basic doctrines. We can gain a keen sense of his understanding of the pastoral problem he faces and how he addresses it in a sermon explaining the moral meaning of the haircut Delilah gave to Samson. Traditional exegesis of this story portrayed Samson as a man undone by lust who received his due punishment, the loss of his physical strength when the temptress cut his unshorn locks. Had Caesarius followed this interpretation, however, it might seem as if he were putting his stamp of approval on a pagan survival, the myth of the long-haired kings. Male Franks wore their hair long, and members of the royal family were regarded as ineligible to rule if their hair were ever cut. Caesarius handles his tricky exegetical assignment by distinguishing between two kinds of razor, Christ's razor, which cuts off vices, and the devil's razor, which cuts off virtues. Samson's haircut thus points the standard moral without reinforcing the myth of the long-haired kings.

Here Caesarius clearly shows that he sees a gap between his own religious and cultural values and those of the Franks to whom he ministers; in the case of Gregory of Tours, the sense of such a gap diminishes to the vanishing point. Gregory, bishop of Tours, wrote his most important work, the *History of the Franks*, to criticize the vicious and quarrelsome descendants of Clovis and to hold up Clovis and his wife Clotild as model Christian rulers. Gregory begins his history with the creation, proceeding through biblical history, the Romans' persecution of the Christians, the Christianization of the Roman empire, and the evangelization of Gaul up to the present. Despite his idealization of Clovis and Clotild, and his combination of sacred and secular history, both the values Gregory displays and his style of writing show little that is either Christian or classical.

An incident marking a real contrast with Caesarius on Samson and Delilah is one Gregory relates after the death of Clovis. Clotild has secluded herself, devoting herself to prayer and good works and raising two grandsons, children of one of her sons, now deceased. Her other two sons seek to remove these nephews as possible contenders for the throne. Having seized custody of the young princes, they send an envoy to Clotild bearing, in one hand, a naked sword, and, in the other, a pair of scissors. The envoy tells her that the fate of her grandsons is up to her. She can either have their hair cut, or she can have them put to death. Without hesitation, Clotild chooses the sword. Both the sainted Clotild and Gregory himself are clearly animated more by the myth of the long-haired kings than by Christian or classical ethics.

Yet, this same Clotild plays a key role in Gregory's account of Clovis' conversion. Prior to that event, he portrays Clovis as a brutal, crafty, and bloodthirsty leader, ruling his men by violence and fear. His wife, already Christian, preaches to Clovis in speeches full of theological and literary lore that Gregory puts in her mouth, enjoining him to abandon his pagan gods. She insists on the baptism of their first two children and Clovis is enraged when the elder dies, blaming his death on the Christian God. Clovis is moved to take that God seriously only when, hard-pressed on the battlefield, he invokes his own gods to no avail. So he decides to appeal to Christ, on a strictly quid pro quo basis: if this deity grants him the victory, he will convert. Such is the outcome, and neither Clovis nor Gregory sees the new religious affiliation as entailing more than a formal shift of allegiance. Indeed, Gregory makes much of the parallels between Clovis' conversion and that of Constantine. As reported by Eusebius (*c.* 263–*c.* 340), the historian of his reign, Constantine also regarded Christ as the God of battles, converting when other gods failed him on receipt of a vision of the cross and a heavenly message that he would conquer in this sign. Despite the parallelism, Gregory does not expect his readers to pick up the Eusebian allusion, and nails it down himself by describing Clovis at the baptismal font as a new Constantine. In chronicling Clovis' career after his baptism, Gregory shows him applying the same policies he had used before becoming a Christian. Gregory also praises his ferocity and duplicity, describing the kingdoms he annexed thereby as rewards God gave Clovis for his orthodoxy and upright life. Although Clovis was unusual among Germanic leaders in converting to orthodox Christianity directly, rather than to Arianism, the attitude to him and his wife displayed by Gregory, a prelate in the Frankish church and easily the best-educated man of his time and place, suggests why continental Europe in his day was regarded as a missionary field for both religion and the liberal arts by thinkers from the British Isles.

Celts

It was the Irish who were the first British missionaries. Not only were they the earliest and the most far-flung emissaries of the Christian and classical traditions between the fifth and seventh centuries; they also internalized the Christian and classical legacies more successfully than any of the newly converted peoples, while placing their own construction on this inheritance. This fact is the more striking given the absence of a Roman chapter in early Irish history. The Christian and classical traditions entered Ireland by way of England and southern France. Irish contacts with southern France are important for two reasons: the absorption of pre-Benedictine monasticism and the acquisition of Greek and some Hebrew as well as Latin, both of which gave Irish intellectual and religious life a temper all its own. Also distinctive was the attachment of Irish Christianity to the tribal structure of Irish society. While episcopal functions existed, a diocesan organization based on city life did not. Typically, each tribe had a religious leader who was an abbot. In addition to governing his monks, he also exercised episcopal authority and served as pastor to the lay people in his tribe. Irish monasticism was much more ascetic than Benedictine monasticism. But, unlike the Basilian-style models on which they drew, Irish monasteries were artistic and educational centers. At the same time, Irish Christianity differed from Roman Christianity in its liturgy, the dating of movable feasts like Easter, and the shape of the tonsure, the part of the head shaved when a man became a cleric.

Other traits characteristic of Irish Christian culture are the fact that the Irish wrote their own penitentials and that they took the initiative in the missions, founding monasteries and schools first in England and Scotland and then on the continent. These missions had little formal organization. A monastic leader with twelve followers, in honor of the number of Christ's disciples, would simply get into a boat, vowing to spread the gospel wherever it landed. Part of their success lay in the fact that the prevailing winds were in their favor. Often the evangelizing of the people on whose shores they arrived was a secondary interest. The monks' initial goal was to live as pilgrims and strangers, imitating the description of the Christian life in the Epistle to the Hebrews physically as well as spiritually. The austere morality and devotion of the Irish earned them a reputation as holy men and inspired others to emulate them. Rulers sometimes invited them to preach to their people. The two most important leaders in this movement were Columba (sixth century), who founded monasteries in Britain such as Lindisfarne and Iona, and Columbanus (sixth to turn of the seventh century), whose foundations on the continent include Corbie, St. Gall, and Bobbio. This last-mentioned site, in northern Italy, indicates how dramatically cultural leadership had shifted from south to north. In all these monastic centers, the Irish provided bilingual education in Greek and Latin and produced a substantial secular as well as Christian literature, in connection with the teaching of the liberal arts, the writing of hagiography, and an extremely allegorical form of biblical exegesis. Both at home and abroad, the Irish also developed a distinctive style of handwriting and manuscript illumination (Plate 1).

Anglo-Saxons

During the fourth and fifth centuries, Roman emperors pulled troops out of England to address military problems closer to home, leaving the country virtually undefended when the Angles, Saxons, and Jutes decided to invade it. Organizing themselves by the sixth century into seven kingdoms whose pre-eminence constantly shifted, these peoples were evangelized first by the Irish and then, starting in 597 with Gregory the Great's sending of Augustine (d. 604/5), from Rome. After Augustine's establishment of the archbishopric of Canterbury, Pope Vitalian (ruled 657–72) sent Theodore of Tarsus (*c.* 602–90) as his successor in 669. As his toponym indicates, Theodore came from a Greek-speaking part of Asia Minor. The monastic schools he founded at Canterbury, York, Jarrow, and Wearmouth taught Greek as well as Latin, a curriculum they shared with the Irish schools. The two forms of Christianity existed side by side until the Anglo-Saxons decided to affiliate with the Roman church at the synod of Whitby (664). None the less, the educational and artistic impact of the Irish foundations continued to be felt, reinforcing the work of Theodore's Benedictine schools.

The first Anglo-Saxon writer to reflect the confluence of the Irish and Roman traditions was Aldhelm (seventh century). Educated at Malmesbury and then at Canterbury, he returned to Malmesbury, becoming its abbot and writing widely, on exegesis, theology, and Roman law as well as grammar, arithmetic, and astronomy. He produced some fine Latin poetry as well. His literary style reflects Celtic tastes, especially in his fondness for allegory, alliteration, florid imagery, and the frequent use of Greek terms. Aldhelm was probably the best-read person in Europe in his day after Isidore of Seville.

Another sign of the Anglo-Saxon ability to continue the work of the Irish and to mesh it with their own Roman connections can be seen in their entry into the mission field in the early eighth century. The most outstanding figure in this movement was Boniface (*c.* 675–754). While the educational effects of his work were similar to those of Columbanus in the schools he founded east of the Rhine, most notably Fulda, his strategy was quite different. Before leaving England, Boniface gained the pope's support. He held the portfolio of roving archbishop. Where his evangelization was successful, he had the authority to ordain clergy and to establish diocesan and parish structures along Roman lines. Boniface also sought the backing of the kings whose people he aimed at converting. Some rulers were cooperative, but some obstructed his work and objected to his insistence that they observe the same moral standards as their subjects. Aside from the political support Boniface received from lay and ecclesiastical rulers, he also gained intellectual and religious support from monastic colleagues in England. His letters show him appealing to them frequently for new blood and for books.

The fact that Anglo-Saxon England had replaced Ireland at the cutting edge of Latin Christian culture by the eighth century can be seen clearly in the work of Bede (672/3–735). Educatéd at Wearmouth and Jarrow, he was a monastic scholar with broad interests. He lists his writings in his best-known work, the *Ecclesiastical History of England*, enabling us to reconstruct his contributions, some of which have not survived. In this latter category is a translation of the Bible into Old English, indicating an important shift in policy. The vernacularization of the Christian message made sense to Bede although he was the best Latin writer of his time. Bede's surviving works fall under four headings. The largest subdivision is biblical exegesis. Like Ambrose, Gregory the Great, and the Irish exegetes, he is interested in allegorical exegesis and his exegetical works were influential later in the Middle Ages. In the second category fall Bede's educational writings, reflecting the critical need for school texts. He wrote on poetry, rhetoric, and on the scientific subjects of the quadrivium. In the latter area, he made some scientific observations of his own, discovering the correlation between the tides and the phases of the moon, and establishing, in his chronology, the distinction between BC and AD. Bede also wrote a work on spelling. In contrast with Cassiodorus, who did the same, the task he addresses in this work is teaching Latin to students with a Germanic native language. In the third category of Bede's works are writings reflecting his calling: martyrologies, lives of local saints, and chronicles of his abbey.

Finally there is Bede's *History*, which takes its story to the year 731. It is worth comparing this work with Gregory of Tours' *History*. Although Gregory belonged to the old Gallo-Roman Christian elite and Bede came from the newly evangelized population in his society, Bede's history is both more Christian and more classical than Gregory's. It is also far better written despite the complexities of a narrative line that has to juggle events in the seven Anglo-Saxon kingdoms at once.

Along with classical historians, Bede shows a scrupulous regard for the critical evaluation of his sources and takes pains to explain how he has documented the period before his own time. Also, like some classical historians introducing readers to an unfamiliar country, he opens his *History* with a description of England's geography, topography, flora, fauna, and natural resources. His conceptual framework is not that of universal history. Rather, he begins the history of England in 55 BC when Julius Caesar (*c.* 100–44 BC) added it to the Roman empire. Bede thus places England's political and religious history in a firmly Roman context. For him, the Roman and the Christian mission in world history and in England are identical. Bede is as interested as Gregory in the climactic conversion of key leaders on whose action and conviction the evangelization of their people depends. Of centrality to him is the conversion of Edwin, king of Northumbria, in 627. Like Clovis, Edwin has a Christian wife, whose influence is important, along with that of her father, the king of Kent. But even more important is the role of a Roman missionary, Paulinus, and the personal epistolary intervention of the pope. For Edwin, as for Clovis, political and military successes or setbacks condition his willingness to give Christianity a hearing. At the same time, Bede's Edwin thinks that he has to understand Christian doctrine and what it entails before making a commitment. Before taking such a major step, Edwin finds it necessary to consult his advisors and to receive their consent. In the ensuing conversation, the high priest of pagan Northumbria takes a pragmatic line, similar to the one Gregory's Clovis follows. But it is the reasoning of another counselor that prevails. He compares human life to the cold, dark, snowy night, from which a bird flies into a warm and brightly lit banquet hall, remaining there briefly before flying out again into the night. If Christianity can shed some light on what human experience means, he says, we ought to give it a try. Bede's characters, and Bede himself, show a greater sensitivity to the metaphysical and moral content of the Christian faith; their God is more than a God of battles. And Bede is far more successful than Gregory in delineating characters through their speeches as well as through his descriptions of them; they emerge as individual personalities with inner lives.

Once converted, Anglo-Saxon kings like Edwin could and did bestow royal patronage on the existing network of Irish and Benedictine monastic schools. Communities that remained out of the line of fire as the wars among the Anglo-Saxon kings continued could build on the achievements of Bede and his predecessors up to the early ninth century. It was, therefore, to Anglo-Saxon England that the Carolingian Franks turned in seeking intellectual leadership for medieval Europe's first coordinated imperial cultural program, the Carolingian Renaissance.

CHAPTER 6

The Carolingian Renaissance

The Carolingian Renaissance is a major chapter in the intellectual history of early medieval Europe. Two central developments converge in this movement. One is the shift of the main centers of learning from the British Isles to the continent, especially the Rhineland, the heartland of a series of rulers from Charlemagne (742–814) to Charles the Bald (823–76), who made significant patronage and cultural initiatives. For this was a legislated renaissance, launched by royal edict in 789 and continued by the policy of Charlemagne's successors. But while these rulers maintained court schools staffed by scholars from many lands as vital nerve centers for educational and religious reform, the activation of their programs depended on the revitalization of monastic and cathedral schools throughout their domains. These schools also benefited from their own local patrons and from the fame of the masters they attracted or produced. As corporate bodies, they could decide which studies to emphasize and which styles of manuscript illumination to produce (Plates 2, 3, 4 and 5). The rulers were not always troubled by the fact that some masters they supported disagreed with each other. Consequently, imperial initiatives and directives did not produce uniform or monolithic results. Thus, while the rulers accented a pragmatic revival of learning and the return to first principles in religion, the Carolingian Renaissance was more than a mere salvage operation or a merging of the cultural traditions on which its masters drew. It produced new ideas and new artistic and musical styles and genres as well.

Basic to the reform of education was the reform of the church and the upgrading of the moral and intellectual qualifications of the clergy, both monastic and secular. By the late eighth century, the Franks' superficial adherence to Christianity reflected by Gregory of Tours had given way to a deeper religious commitment on the part of the rulers and a sense of responsibility for the religious lives of their people and the evangelization or conversion to orthodoxy of pagan or heretical groups in their empire. This attitude also led to the alliance with the papacy that had helped Charlemagne's father take over the Merovingian throne in 751 in exchange for subduing the Lombards and granting to the pope the lands in central Italy that henceforth made up the papal states. These religious and political changes help to explain the strategies and priorities in the Carolingians' cultural policy, since more was at stake than their recognition of the fact that educational reform would have to begin with the clergy.

The rulers launched a number of programs for the educational and religious improvement of their subjects. Children and converts were to be catechized and preaching made more effective. Charlemagne thought that, in order to disseminate Christian doctrine, all churches and monasteries should have a copy of the Vulgate Bible, a Bible whose text was purified of the scribal errors that had crept into it between the fourth and eighth centuries. This stress on the correction, recopying, and distribution of basic texts, both religious and secular, is a recurrent theme in the Carolingian Renaissance and one of its most central services to European intellectual history. In many cases, the Carolingian rescensions are the earliest copies to survive and provide the bases for modern critical editions of works fundamental to the classical and Christian traditions. Charlemagne looked first to Anglo-Saxon England for a scholar to head his court school, finding him in Alcuin (*c.* 730–804). He assigned to Alcuin the correction of the Vulgate. In conjunction with this project, and later in his career when he became abbot of Tours, Alcuin invented a new style of handwriting, the Caroline minuscule (Plate 6). This script was far more legible than earlier medieval hands and an improvement on Roman book hands, since it provided spaces between the words, more extensive punctuation, and a hierarchy of hands, with capitals used for titles, a mix of capitals and lower-case letters for subtitles or chapter headings, and lower case for the body of the text. With the newly corrected Bible, pastors would be able to base their teaching and preaching on what it actually said. Charlemagne provided another aid, commissioning Paul the Deacon (*c.* 720–*c.* 799) to compile sermons for all the feast days from the church fathers. Ideally, these sermons would serve as models for pastors. At a less than ideal level, a pastor could simply use one of the patristic sermons instead of composing his own.

Charlemagne also saw the liturgy as an important vehicle of Christian education. He imported the Roman liturgy and with it Gregorian chant and congregational hymn singing. He agreed with Ambrose and Gregory the Great that the musical embellishment of the liturgy could raise church attendance and that hymn texts could be used to inculcate correct doctrine. He also sought to impose liturgical uniformity within his empire by means of this policy. This goal was not achieved. As the emperor noted with annoyance, although he had sent Roman monks who knew Gregorian chant throughout his domains, he found on his travels that the liturgy was sung differently in different churches. Far from merely receiving the Roman musical tradition, Carolingian musicians retained Gallican chant, produced compositions reflecting the cross-fertilization of the two liturgies, and invented several new systems of musical notation. Two new musical genres, the trope and the sequence, also made their first known appearance in Carolingian manuscripts.

Carolingian policy emphasized monastic reform as well, with the original goal being the elimination of abuses and the enforcement of the Benedictine *Rule*. As with the Vulgate Bible, the first step was to secure an accurate text of the *Rule*, which was obtained from Monte Cassino, and to duplicate it so that every convent possessed a copy. The reform agenda that began under Charlemagne was continued by Louis the Pious (778–840) with the aid of Benedict of Aniane (*c.* 750–821). If we compare Benedict's proposals and the manuscript blueprint for an ideal monastery drawn up at St. Gall, although never built, with the original Benedictine *Rule*, it is clear that adaptation had replaced simple revival (Plate 7). By the Carolingian age monasticism had acquired economic, social, and political functions not envisioned by Benedict of Nursia. Child oblation, while permitted by the *Rule*, had become and remained a major source of monastic recruitment, often undercutting its stress on the mature commitment of adult novices. Royal and noble appointment of abbots and abbesses from prominent families, who were not elected by their communities and who sometimes remained in the lay state, also remained the order of the day. As persons of great prestige and influence, abbots and abbesses lived and entertained in their own quarters. These departures from the Benedictine *Rule* are reflected both in the St. Gall plan and in Benedict of Aniane's reform proposals.

When it came to the monastic schools, Carolingian legislation stressed two points: an essentially Augustinian rationale for the study of the liberal arts and greater attention to education both for monastic personnel and for externs, or students not destined for the cloister. Sometimes externs undertook the same studies as the incipient monks or nuns and sometimes followed a system that took account of their differing educational needs. The effect of this policy can be seen in the rise of Latin literacy among Carolingian lay people. In addition to devoting more time to education than the Benedictine *Rule* provides for, Carolingian monastic schools developed their own academic specialties, some of which can be reconstructed from extant library catalogues. Thus, Laon and Fulda accented biblical exegesis; St. Wandrille stressed music; Tours and Reichenau focused on the copying and editing of manuscripts; Ferrières emphasized classical literature, and so on.

We can get a good sense of the degree to which Carolingian masters followed imperial mandates in considering what they actually wrote, whether at the court school or at local monastic and episcopal centers. Textbooks in the liberal arts, especially the verbal disciplines of the trivium, make up the largest subdivision of their literary output. Alcuin's textbooks are excellent illustrations of the Carolingian approach. He frames them as dialogues, but we are at a far remove from the philosophical dialogues of a Boethius, Augustine, or Minucius Felix. Rather, Alcuin's approach is catechetical. His dialogues on the arts typically have two interlocutors, a member of the royal house, who asks questions, and Alcuin as master, who answers them. As adjuncts to the teaching of the arts Carolingian masters wrote dictionaries, glossaries, bilingual word lists, handbooks on spelling, commentaries, compilations, and summaries of the transmitters' works. The first group of pedagogical tools indicates that the students' native languages were Old High German or Old French, not Latin. A good example of the Carolingian reworking and simplification of the transmitters is *On the Universe* by Rabanus Maurus (*c.* 780–856), an encyclopedia based on Isidore of Seville's *Etymologies* which abbreviates and reorganizes it thematically. Texts like this speak to the need that was felt for user-friendly reference works. A series of commentaries on Martianus Capella begun by the Irish master John Scottus (d. *c.* 877/9) and carried on by his pupils at the school of Auxerre reflects the same assessment of the Carolingian educational mission.

Some of the products of Carolingian writers refer directly to their society's ecclesiastical and political concerns. Substantial amounts of exegetical and homiletical literature were produced, with Alcuin and Haimo of Auxerre (d. *c.* 875) taking the honors in the first area and Agobard of Lyons (769–840) providing a good example of popular preaching. A leading author of liturgical hymns was Theodulph (*c.* 760–821), a Spanish Visigoth brought to France and made bishop of Orléans by Charlemagne. Carolingian authors also wrote many saints' lives. While they continue to emphasize the miracles of the saints, the hagiographers import some new features into their work. They concentrate on recent and local saints, the missionaries, abbots, or bishops who had evangelized their regions. Outside of the localization of the cult of saints, which parallels the contemporary localization of institutions more generally, some of these works also recast the saint's life as popular romance, with narrow escapes, trials and tribulations of the protagonist, deeds of high emprise in foreign lands, and the like. Treatises and other sources that take a stand on ecclesiastical and political controversies of the day will be discussed below. In literature, the Carolingian age saw the revival of political panegyric in both prose and poetry, glorifying rulers along classical lines. The most famous prose example is the *Life of Charlemagne* by Einhard (*c.* 770–840). Other histories directly connected to Carolingian politics include other emperor biographies and works acquainting readers with newly conquered parts of the empire, such as Paul the Deacon's *History of the Lombards*.

At the same time, and without any imperial reproofs, Carolingian masters produced large amounts of literature, primarily poetic, that was not composed for utilitarian purposes. Some verses were written as occasion pieces, as is the case with a poem by Walafrid Strabo (*c.* 808–99) on a statue of Theodoric that Charlemagne stole and transferred to his court at Aachen, or Theodulph's gently ironic group portrait of the members of the court school. But most Carolingian poetry, religious or secular, was written simply to express the poet's personal feelings and interests. Theodulph wrote several lyrics marked by delicacy of touch and a classicizing style on the beauties of nature and the charm of human society. Walafrid too celebrates the pleasures of the countryside, including his love of gardening and his enjoyment of the quiet life of the cloister. His most distinctive contribution to Carolingian literature is the poetry of friendship, in which he freely adapts the erotic vocabulary of classical love lyrics to express his affection for friends and his sadness when he is separated from them. Easily the most versatile of the Carolingian poets is Sedulius Scottus (*fl.* 848–58/74), who uses the widest variety of poetic meters and who tackles all subjects with inventive freshness and the capacity for appropriate utterance on any theme. Most of these poets were also pedagogues; Sedulius, for instance, was a grammarian and wrote a didactic poem showing how to decline the name 'Robert' in Latin. But they show quite clearly that Carolingian masters enjoyed and produced literature as an end in itself. A similar point is made by Lupus of Ferrières (*c.* 805–*c.* 862), the leading classical philologist of the Carolingian Renaissance. His letters reveal his abiding love of the classical authors and his concern with editing their manuscripts to obtain the most accurate texts. His efforts yielded the earliest surviving manuscripts of the philosophical works of Cicero, as well as improved texts of Vergil, Macrobius, and the Roman historians. His easy familiarity with the classics is also reflected in the elegance of his prose style. The overall attitude to the liberal arts, especially those of the trivium, conveyed by Carolingian authors shows them going well beyond the utilitarian application of them to biblical exegesis and Christian education, as ordered by Charlemagne, to a personal appreciation of the arts. The non-utilitarian and the utilitarian approach to the classics can sometimes by found side by side in the work of the same master.

Just as Carolingian masters could mix the didactic and the non-didactic in their literary works, so many of the same thinkers contributed to more speculative subjects. As writers of philosophy, theology, and political theory they sometimes pursued personal reflections and sometimes fulfilled royal commissions or took a stand on debated questions. They embraced the revival of logic as a trivium subject and Boethius' translations and commentaries, along with his theological treatises, as sources for philosophical concepts. Using a version of Aristotle's *Categories* ascribed to Augustine, they succeeded, over the course of the ninth century, in reclaiming subject matter for logic that had been annexed to rhetoric or grammar by earlier authorities. The commentaries on Martianus Capella noted above also provided a context for elaborating on the philosophical aspects of the quadrivium along with logic.

Philosophical speculation as such had a major exponent in John Scottus. John had been brought to the court of Charles the Bald for his knowledge of Greek, which enabled him to translate Greek patristic authors who had been heavily influenced by Neoplatonism. The most important of these, Dionysius the Pseudo-Areopagite (480–510), was regarded as a great authority in the Carolingian age and later owing to a double confusion of his identity with the Dionysius mentioned in the Acts of the Apostles, who heard St. Paul preach in Athens and became its first bishop, and the martyred evangelist of France, Dionysius or Denis, the country's patron saint. The royal abbey of St. Denis near Paris had been endowed in the latter's honor and it was here that Louis the Pious lodged the copy of the Pseudo-Areopagite's works given to him by the Byzantine emperor. Hilduin, prior of St. Denis (c. 775–855), had translated them into Latin, and badly. John's new translation put the works of the Pseudo-Areopagite in circulation. They were to have an extensive influence on medieval mystics as well as on speculative theologians and philosophers. John also translated the Greek Christian writers Gregory of Nyssa (c. 335–c. 394) and Maximus the Confessor (c. 580–622). Drawing on these sources, as well as on Latin philosophy and theology, he developed his own highly Neoplatonic system in his *Periphyseon*, based on that school's view of a cosmic process in which all beings proceed from the deity and return to Him.

As John recasts this notion, he views nature, understood as everything that has being, as divided into four parts. The first part is the creative and uncreated, or God as the first cause of the universe. Next comes the created and creative. For John, the entities in this group are archetypes or exemplary causes. They are created and hence not identical with the deity. God uses them as models for the creatures lower on the chain of being. In that sense they participate in His creative activity. Next comes the created and uncreative. This subdivision includes angels arranged in a ninefold order following the Pseudo-Areopagite's *Celestial Hierarchy*, human beings, and the subhuman world. Finally, there is the uncreated and uncreative, or God as the final cause of the universe, to which all created beings seek to return.

There are a number of problems in John's system which he does not resolve. Some are terminological. John's vocabulary is sometimes vague or used inconsistently or idiosyncratically. A good case in point is his theological language. On one reading of John, the deity is part of nature as an existing being, describable positively as a cause. On the other hand, following the Neoplatonist Proclus (410/12–85), John calls God the superessential One beyond being, describable only by negative theology, that is, by formulae such as 'God is not unjust,' deemed to be less inaccurate than positive statements about the deity based necessarily on concepts derived from the speaker's finite human experience and hence inapposite to an utterly transcendent deity. From a theological standpoint, John's anthropology and Christology raise some questions. He thinks that, in the original creation, human bodies were not sexually differentiated; the body was a pure spiritual body like the one promised in the resurrection. The body as we know it and our need to reproduce sexually are punishments for original sin. Nor is it clear that John thinks the body is saved along with the soul. In the *Periphyseon* he does not indicate Christ's role in the return of mankind to its divine source. He has more to say about Christ as the supreme archetype in the creation. But, given the created status of the archetypes in John's second division of nature, he has difficulty preserving the principle that, as a member of the Trinity, Christ is not subordinate to God the Father. These and other difficulties limited the appeal of the *Periphyseon* among John's contemporaries, although it received considerable attention later in the Middle Ages. It must be said that his speculative enterprise is more important for the fact of its existence than for John's ability to resolve the problems his world view raises.

On balance, speculative thought for its own sake is far less typical of the Carolingian Renaissance than theories addressing practical concerns of church or state. Carolingian theology is generally controversial not systematic theology. With one exception, it is a response to heresy, the evangelization of pagans, and Carolingian policy toward the Muslims and Byzantines. There were two theological debates with the Byzantines that converged: the iconoclastic controversy and the *filioque*. The former deals with the propriety of representing the deity and the saints in art and the latter is the code word for the relationship of the Holy Spirit to the other persons of the Trinity. The iconoclastic controversy broke out in the Greek church in the mid-eighth century. After several decades of debate, the defenders of icons won over their opponents and outlined a rationale for religious art as well as norms for its execution at the council of Nicaea in 787. Although papal legates were present, no representatives of the Frankish clergy had been invited to this conclave, a point that rankled. And, although the council had settled the matter theologically to the clergy's satisfaction, some Byzantine emperors continued to oppose icons and rode roughshod over the clergy. From the perspective of western churchmen, their Greek colleagues were spineless. Further, between 797 and 800, diplomatic relations between the Carolingians and Byzantines reached their nadir. In 797, the Byzantine emperor died and his widow, Irene (*c.* 752–803), sought to rule in her own right, in defiance of Byzantine constitutional law. Both Charlemagne and the pope decided that the Byzantine throne was legally vacant. They also agreed that it could be assumed by Charlemagne, although, as we will see, the issue of who had the authority to transfer title to the throne was contested. In 800, Charlemagne was crowned emperor by the pope, an act totally unacceptable even to those Byzantines most eager to depose Irene. The two empires severed diplomatic relations. In the early years of the ninth century, Charlemagne allied with the Muslim caliph Haroun al-Raschid (*c.* 760/70–809), the Byzantines' major enemy. The Byzantines retaliated in 809 by attacking lands in the papal states. In turn, the Carolingians convened a council of their own and affirmed the value of icons, but with a rationale for the cognitive value of visual art derived from Gregory the Great different from that of Nicaea. They also held a council at Aix in 809 defining the western doctrine of the Holy Spirit and added it to the creed. The pope lent this action his support and ruled that the amended creed be recited at mass wherever the Roman liturgy was used.

The issue in Trinitarian theology exacerbated by these political circumstances was whether the Holy Spirit proceeds from the Father through the Son, as the Greeks taught, or whether He proceeds from the Father and the Son equally, as the Carolingians held. The western position certainly had both theological and conciliar precedents. Augustine's analogy of the Trinity as the lover, the beloved, and the love passing between them had been an authoritative reference point since his writing of *On the Trinity*. In 589, the council of Toledo, convened in the effort to convert Arian Visigoths to orthodoxy, ruled that the Holy Spirit proceeds from the Father and the Son. No Greek clerics were present at this council. The Toledan formula was added to the creed in Gaul, against a backdrop of converting Arian Germanic groups there. On this matter, as well as on iconoclasm, both western and eastern churches could validly claim that they had been excluded from councils that made decisions on important matters, and that the other church had put itself in a state of schism thereby. While some modern theologians think that the eastern and western formulae on the Holy Spirit are not incompatible, the political situation at the time led to an irreconcilable theological breach between the two churches.

Another political development explains the Carolingians' interest in refuting the Adoptionist heresy present in Spain. The Muslims had invaded Spain in 711 and were the possessor power there. Charlemagne had conquered the northern part of the country and felt responsible for defending and monitoring the orthodoxy of his Spanish Christian subjects. In Carolingian eyes, Adoptionist Christology looked alarmingly similar to the Muslim view of Christ as a holy man with prophetic gifts, miraculous powers, and wise teachings, but purely human. Charlemagne set Alcuin and Paulinus of Aquileia (before 750–802) the task of writing anti-Adoptionist polemics.

A third theological controversy, on free will and predestination, racked the Car-

olingian empire from within, owing to the fact that its protagonist, Gottschalk
(*c.* 803–867/9) repeatedly broke ecclesiastical rules in an age when reformers were
seeking to enforce them, in addition to articulating a controversial position. His
biography reflects the perdurance of child oblation in Carolingian monasticism and
the problems to which it could lead. Given as a child to the abbey of Fulda,
Gottschalk took his vows before he realized that he lacked a monastic calling. He
sought release from his vows but his abbot denied him. Fleeing Fulda, he tried to
live the monastic life at Corbie and then at Orbais. There he encountered the same
difficulties as at Fulda. Having violated the vow of obedience and stability to three
abbots and abbeys, Gottschalk moved to Italy. Although he was ordained, he began
preaching without an episcopal license, another breach of canon law. It was in his
preaching that he developed the doctrine of double predestination, adding what he
saw as a logical corollary of the position of the anti-Pelagian Augustine. As he reasoned, if God predestines some people to salvation from all eternity, and if we sub-
tract that group from the rest of mankind, it follows that the rest of mankind, who
can never be saved, must be predestined to damnation. Nothing we can do can alter
the divine decree for either group. This being the case, free will is non-existent, for
both groups. Further, we cannot say that Christ came into the world to save all
mankind. His mission, and by extension, that of the church, is irrelevant to the
damned.

Having taken this position, Gottschalk made the mistake of returning to
Germany in 848, where he was promptly arrested and tried by Hincmar of Rheims
(*c.* 806–82), primate of the Carolingian church, in the presence of Charles the Bald.
Condemned for his various breaches of canon law as well as for his theology, he
was unfrocked, forced to destroy his works, forbidden to preach or to publish,
beaten, and imprisoned for the rest of his life. The controversy over Gottschalk
erupted only after he was silenced. It drew leading thinkers on both sides, concerned as much with the harshness of Hincmar's sentence as with Gottschalk's theology. Some, like John Scottus and Ratramnus of Corbie (*fl.* 844–68), defended
Gottschalk on that account although they rejected double predestination. In 860,
the Carolingian church formally affirmed the Augustinian doctrine of single
predestination.

The only notable Carolingian theological debate that lacked a political dimension was one also deemed to have no practical implications either, even though it
focused on the Eucharist, a sacrament central to Christian belief and practice. The
issue was whether Christ is corporeally present in the sacrament or present in a
symbolic sense. It is true that, in 838, Amalrius of Metz (*c.* 775–*c.* 850) was condemned by the council of Quierzy for maintaining the symbolic interpretation. Yet,
in the reign of Charles the Bald the matter was treated as an open question. Two
monks of Corbie, Ratramnus and Paschasius Radbertus (*c.* 790–*c.* 860) debated the
matter, at the emperor's invitation, the former defending the real presence doctrine
and the latter the symbolic view of Christ's Eucharistic presence. Neither the
emperor nor anyone else in authority at that time seems to have felt a need to
support one of these positions to the exclusion of the other.

On this last debate, then, no formal action was taken, except in the sense that imperial and ecclesiastical inaction could be seen as overturning the judgment of the council of Quierzy; on Adoptionism, the Carolingians reaffirmed Nicene Christology; on predestination, they reaffirmed Augustine. But on the *filioque* and in the defense of religious art they made their own contribution to the development of doctrine in the western church.

We can see development, and innovation, in a final area of Carolingian speculation, political theory, which includes church–state relations. Here, political iconography and ritual round out the more obvious written sources. Carolingian political theory draws on elements from the Germanic, the Roman, and the Christian traditions, producing not one but several competing positions. This diversity was accompanied by new institutions, animated by political conceptions not found in pre–existing traditions. Another signal Carolingian contribution was to delineate, on the widest canvas, Europe's first general understanding of itself as a political community in the idea of the Holy Roman Empire.

Turning to law as an index of the Carolingian understanding of political authority, we can see rulers and theorists drawing on Germanic and Roman law and going beyond both systems. The emperors ruled a number of Germanic peoples, applying to them the Germanic principle of personality of law. Bavarian law applied to the Bavarians, Frankish law to the Franks, and so on. The ruler was seen to be under the law, the enforcer of inherited custom. At the same time, the emperors issued edicts or capitularies, reflecting the Roman concept that the ruler has the authority to make new laws that bind all his subjects. Here the ruler stands above the law, as its source. Carolingian rulers also placed themselves below the law in the new, non-customary institution of feudalism, in the contracts they made with vassals, a means of organizing political and military power which they helped to foster. In this institution, lord and vassal have specific rights and duties *vis-à-vis* each other and the relationship is bilateral and mutually enforceable.

We can see a mixture of traditions and a combination of tradition and innovation in Carolingian notions of what sanctions a ruler's exercise of power. Germanic kinship ties, right of blood, and membership in the royal family were deemed to be necessary. So was divine right, expressed in the coronation of the ruler by a clergyman in a ceremony similar to a bishop's consecration. This same coronation liturgy also institutionalized the Germanic notion that the ruler's acts must be ratified by his followers. The acclamation 'Long live the king,' made by those of his subjects present at the ceremony, was taken to represent the election of the ruler by his people at large, a principle acknowledged specifically in the way that some Carolingian rulers styled themselves in prefaces to their official documents.

Diversity is also present in Carolingian theories on church–state relations, which embrace the ruler's relationship to the church within his empire as well as his relationship to the papacy. Three positions on these issues emerged, the royalist, the clericalist, and the Romanist. The royalist view was held by Charlemagne and other rulers and defended by masters such as Sedulius Scottus. The royalist understanding of the ruler's coronation by a cleric was that it recognized the ruler's existing divine right, rather than transferring it to him. This was the interpretation given by the royalists to Charlemagne's coronation as emperor in 800. He, himself, had restored the Roman empire; the pope's role in the transaction had been merely ceremonial. For the royalists, the church was one among other institutions in the empire that the ruler governed and for which he was responsible. They saw him as the arbiter of many of its administrative decisions, the judge of clergymen accused of crimes, the one who appointed and transferred bishops, presided over synods, and enforced their rulings. He was also held to be in charge of the religious life of the community, patronizing the Christian faith, propagating it to pagans, repressing heresy, and reforming the church and its liturgy, correcting the Bible, and establishing norms for Christian education and preaching. While the royalists preserved a distinction between civil and canon law and did not grant priestly functions to the ruler, they conceded to him extensive control over the church and saw him as the senior partner in the alliance with the papacy.

Many Carolingian clergymen supported the clericalist position. A good example is Hincmar of Rheims. The clericalists saw the church, led by the bishops, as largely independent, in the administration of church property, the appointment of bishops, and the judgment of clerics accused of crimes. Reflecting the Ambrosian notion of the church as the conscience of the state, they agreed that the church had the right and duty to correct the ruler's moral behavior.

The Romanist view, which elevated the pope over both the emperor and the Carolingian clergy, owes its origins to the theory of pope Gelasius I (ruled 492–6) as reformulated by masters such as Einhard and the ninth-century forgers of the Pseudo-Isidorian Decretals and Donation of Constantine. With respect to the clergy, the Romanists held that as many ecclesiastical matters as possible should be referred to the papacy, rather than being settled in the Frankish empire by its clergy. The Romanists' view of the relationship between pope and emperor can be seen in their interpretation of Charlemagne's coronation. All power, secular as well as spiritual, they held, is given by God to the pope. He delegates secular authority to the emperor. He also judges the exercise of that power. If it is wielded illegitimately or immorally, the pope can transfer secular power to another ruler, as was done when the crown was shifted from Irene to Charlemagne. This theory makes the papacy a major player in secular as well as ecclesiastical politics.

All three theories were current in the Carolingian age as the brainchildren of Carolingian thinkers. In practice, the royalist view prevailed, since the emperors held all the high cards. Carolingian emperors actually did everything that their theory said they could do. Despite the noteworthy diversities in Carolingian political theory, diversities we can add to the mix of doctrinal positions, artistic, musical, literary, and scholarly emphases that mark Carolingian culture, the greatest common legacy it left was the idea later to be called the Holy Roman Empire, the conception of Europe as a Christian commonwealth whose supreme secular leader parallels the pope as its supreme spiritual leader. This notion, created in the Carolingian Renaissance, was to characterize Christian Europe's understanding of itself as a civilization for the rest of the Middle Ages, long after the personalities and political circumstances that gave rise to it were gone.

PART II
VERNACULAR CULTURE

CHAPTER 7

Celtic and Old French Literature

In the light of the Irish and Frankish contributions to Latin Christian culture in the early Middle Ages, one might expect to find that culture strongly represented at an early stage in Irish vernacular literature and visible increasingly in Old French once the Carolingian Renaissance had done its work. In actuality, there was little carry-over of either classical or Christian thought in the vernacular literature of these two languages even though it was composed or redacted in monastic scriptoria by the same people engaged in producing and promoting Latin Christian literature. Their desire to preserve their communities' indigenous culture is a remarkable gauge of the capacity of early medieval authors, redactors, and audiences to retain a non-classical and non-Christian world view and literary aesthetic while simultaneously participating in and perpetuating elite culture.

Celtic Literature

Among Celtic peoples, vernacular literature was produced in the early Middle Ages primarily by the Irish and the Welsh. The major contribution of the Welsh to medieval literature was the figure of King Arthur and the personalities, themes, and exploits relating to him. While this material surfaced early, the texts in which it is found were not redacted until the later Middle Ages and it first became generally available in the twelfth century, in Latin not Welsh. Consideration of its impact will thus be deferred to the history of that period. Here we will focus on Old Irish literature. The Irish produced both lyric poetry and prose, composed and redacted before the eleventh century. Greater chronological precision is impossible, and in most cases authorship is unknown. Irish prose treats a range of subjects in various forms: from epics on the semi-divine and allegedly Trojan origins of the Irish and their emigration and settlement, to epic cycles featuring famous heroes, accounts of ancient kings, visionary trips to the other world, and miscellaneous subjects. Apart from the myth of Trojan ancestry there is nothing either classical or Christian in the content of Old Irish prose. Stylistically, it is also thoroughly unclassical. It is often vague in its grammar and syntax. Run-on sentences abound; verbs are sometimes omitted, and parenthetical digressions sometimes fail to return to

the main story line. The sequence of events is also somewhat random and haphazard. Irish prose authors and their audiences clearly preferred the sensuous play
of words, images, and highly colored synaesthetic effects to tight formal construction and coherent narrative. On the other hand, Irish lyric poetry borrows rhythm,
meter, and the placement of accent from classical Latin lyrics. The Irish lyricists
combine these classical formal values with aesthetic criteria of their own, especially
alliteration and assonance. The combination yields a poetry distinctive in its ability
to present a coherent progression of ideas or emotions and to create a sustained
mood, rendered with luscious sound-effects.

References to Christianity occur only in the lyric poetry and they are rarely its
central subject. *The Desire for Hermitage, The Hermit and the King*, and *The Monk
and His Cat* speak of monasticism. The first poem praises the eremitic calling
because the speaker has a temperamental preference for solitude. In the second, a
dialogue poem, the monastic speaker extols his vocation mainly in terms of the
natural beauties of his sylvan retreat. The monk in the third poem is a scholar; it
is the learning of his chosen lifestyle that he enjoys. In all cases, monasticism provides the speaker with the chance to indulge other tastes; prayer and the contemplative life are not the goal. There are also a few lyrics in which Christian themes
such as penance, last things, and pilgrimage to a site called St. Patrick's Purgatory
are addressed less marginally. Two religious lyrics are attributed to women. In one
the recluse Ita has a vision in which the infant Jesus is placed in her care. *The Vision
of Ita* appears to be the earliest evidence of devotion to the infant Jesus, which
gained in popularity in the later Middle Ages. The nun Brigid is the putative author
of *The Heavenly Banquet*, which gives a good sense of the quality of the religious
sentiment found in Old Irish lyrics treating Christian subjects:

> I would like to have the men of Heaven
> in my own house,
> with vats of good cheer
> laid out for them.
>
> I would like to have the three Marys;
> their fame is so great.
> I would like people
> from every corner of Heaven.
>
> I would like them to be cheerful
> in their drinking.
> I would like to have Jesus, too
> here amongst them.
>
> I would like a great lake of beer
> for the King of Kings.
> I would like to be watching Heaven's family
> drinking it for all eternity.[1]

The only Irish lyric that approaches Christianity with anything resembling theological sophistication is *The Icebound Swans*. The poet compares the swans caught in the ice with sinners hardened by pride and prays that both may be liberated. He is the exception who proves the rule.

Much more typical as subjects in Irish literature are the love of conversation, the love of nature, sensuous description, and a sense of the easy permeation of this world by inhabitants of the other world. As for conversation, Old Irish authors and characters are the most loquacious of any in early medieval literature. Authors make the same point over and over again, not because they despair of the audience's grasp of the message but out of the sheer delight in ringing verbal changes on a topic. Their characters have all kissed the Blarney Stone: they chatter on for pages and pages. They regard conversation as an art form, a means of entertainment, and even as a virtue. Conversations are used to reveal character and to motivate action in narrative literature. Plots are triggered and developed as much by what people say as by what they do. Feuds arise from sallies of wit, arguments between husbands and wives, and verbal jokes that backfire. And while in Old Irish epic heroes certainly do battle, contests can also be settled by verbal rejoinders, fully as honorable as bloodshed and more amusing. The verbalism of this literature is also reflected in a love of word-play, exaggeration, hyperbole, the telling of tall tales, and a sense of humor. And the inhabitants of the other world encountered in Old Irish literature are just as articulate as the human beings.

Authors also describe everything in detail, appealing to the senses of sight and hearing alike. People, clothing, personal accoutrements and weapons, chariots, furniture, buildings, animals, plants, landscapes, the clash of weapons, and war cries are all rendered vividly to a degree unrivaled by any other medieval vernacular literature. Several lyric poems speak eloquently of the joys and sorrows of the changing seasons and of the poets' delight in nature, their close and sympathetic observation of it, and of their feeling of being in harmony with it. The most magnificent example is *May Day*; the translation cited also conveys beautifully the sound effects created by rhyme, assonance, and alliteration in the original:

> May day! delightful day!
> Bright colours play the vale along.
> Now wakes at morning's slender ray
> Wild and gay the blackbird's song.
>
> Now comes the bird of dusty hue
> The loud cuckoo, the summer-lover;
> Branchy trees are thick with leaves,
> The bitter, evil time is over.
>
> Swift horses gather nigh
> Where half dry the river goes;
> Tufted heather clothes the height;
> Weak and white the bogdown blows.

Corncrake sings from eve to morn,
Deep in corn a strenuous bard!
Sings the virgin waterfall, white and tall
Her one sweet word.

Loaded bees with puny power
Goodly flower-harvest win;
Cattle roam with muddy flanks;
Busy ants go out and in.

Through the wild harp of the wood
Making music roars the gale;
Now it settles without motion;
On the ocean sleeps the sail.

Men grow mighty in the May;
Proud and gay the maidens grow;
Fair is every wooded height;
Fair and bright the plain below.

A bright shaft has smit the streams;
With gold gleams the water-flag;
Leaps the fish and on the hills
Ardor thrills the leaping stag.

Loudly carols the lark on high,
Small and shy his tireless lay,
Singing in wildest, merriest mood,
Delicate-hued, delightful May.[2]

The same sympathetic observation of nature and the same sense that
human beings are in tune with it expressed so broadly in *May Day* is concentrated
on two creatures, the cat Pangur Ban and his monastic master, in *The Monk and
His Cat*:

Pangur Ban and I,
each at his own craft
his mind is intent on mice
and mine at my own trade.

Better than any fame I love ease
and deep study in my little book.
Pangur Ban bears me no envy;
he loves his own childish play.

When we are alone in our house—
it is a tale I never weary of telling—
we each have—and what endless sport it is!—
something against which we test our wits.

Now and again, after daring foray,
a mouse catches in his net;
meanwhile there falls into my net
some difficult rule of subtle sense.

He directs against the wall-boards
his eye, full of obscurity;
while I direct against the ramparts of knowledge
my bright, if ageing, eye.

He rejoices, swiftly racing,
until his sharp nails catch a mouse;
and if I have grasped a difficult, dear problem,
I too rejoice.

And though we are always so
neither hinders the other;
each loves his own craft
and pleases himself in his own way.

He is master of the trade
he follows every day;
so am I in mine
when I put my finger on an answer.[3]

A combination of sensuous description, repetition, and a stress on the importance of wealthy patrons for the production of poetry can be seen in *The Court Poet in Trouble*. The speaker is threatened by the loss of his patron's support. He stands to lose not only his livelihood but, even more important to him, his place in a court populated by ladies whose physical charms he catalogues enthusiastically, using the same sentence structure in each case. He ends by addressing the patron directly, asserting that his deeds will be forgotten unless they are immortalized by poets, to underscore the importance of his services.

The frequent, and unpredictable, irruption of otherworldly beings into human life is another topic that appears frequently in Old Irish literature, especially in prose. Epic heroes interact with benevolent fairies and leprechauns as well as with malevolent dwarfs. So does the rest of society. In *The Wooing of Etain*, Eochaid Airem, a high king, discovers that his wife, whom he thought was a human being and a virgin when he married her, is actually a fairy with a fairy husband. This husband arrives, in human form, claiming her by defeating Eochaid Airem in a chess match, a standard metaphor for erotic competition in Irish literature. The fairy couple depart in the form of birds, folding into this story the theme of shape-changing and the idea that animals can be inhabited by human or presumed human souls. In cases where the fairy wife bears a son to her human husband before mysteriously vanishing, the chance is excellent that the son will grow up to be a hero. Otherworldly beings also arrive to conduct living persons to Hy Brasail. In addition to being located on an island across the sea, the other world is typically described in terms of the negative formula, as a place with no pain, no want, no extremes of temperature. In some works it is also envisioned as a city or fortress containing a series of palaces. A talisman, a silver branch, with or without golden apples, is needed to enter it. While getting there or identifying its emissary the voyager often sees or is enveloped by a mist, always a sign of encounter with someone or something otherworldly in Old Irish. In some cases, the voyager remains in the other world; in others, he either never gets there or arrives and then returns to this life, with otherworldly keepsakes, to relate his experience.

This theme in Irish literature had considerable influence on other medieval vernacular traditions. Another is the theme of the falsely accused wife, who endures unjust punishment and is vindicated in the end. There is the jealous stepmother, the nagging wife, and wives envious of each other who sometimes provoke their husbands to action. There is the king whose death by his grandson's hand is prophesied and who tries to avert this outcome by forbidding his children to marry. His ban is circumvented and a grandson does unwittingly kill him. There is the theme of animals aiding human beings, an idea closely allied with the belief in shape-changing. There is the hero as a child prodigy, undergoing phenomenal growth as a youth. Heroes also undergo trials for the hand of the beloved, not only physical tests but also tests of wit, such as guessing the answers to three riddles. Three wishes and triads in general abound. There is also what we might call the Miles Standish motif, whereby a shy man delegates his wooing to a friend. Finally, there is the theme of adulterous love declared orally but deliberately frustrated in its consummation. Some of these themes, like the motif of the cuckoo heralding spring and the negative formula noted above, have analogies in classical and other world literatures, eastern as well as western. It is difficult to prove whether their incidence in Old Irish literature reflects pre-classical or classical influences or whether it is merely parallel.

Perhaps the most unusual feature of Old Irish is that its epics, unlike most other epic traditions in world literature, are in prose, not poetry. There are two main epic cycles, the Leinster cycle featuring Finn, who actually lived in the third century, and the Ulster cycle featuring Cuchulainn. There are many versions of Finn's story but all agree that he was a great warlord who led a national Irish militia. After contending with various human and otherworldly adversaries and conducting an active, complex, and sometimes bigamous love-life, he dies, through treachery, in a major battle defending his country against the Vikings.

Cuchulainn appears to be an entirely fictitious hero. As a child prodigy, he is endowed with eloquence, wit, and prudence along with athletic and martial prowess. Reflecting the Irish penchant for exaggeration, he has seven pupils in each eye and seven digits on each hand and foot. In his youth, Cuchulainn woos and wins a maiden by performing feats and guessing riddles. Although he has passed the stipulated tests, his fiancée's father imposes another qualification which he must meet before claiming her, an education in arms, which he must obtain from a fairy woman in the other world. The hero overcomes the obstacles that separate him from the other world and arrives there with the aid of a lion-like animal, a youth who gives him the necessary talisman, and his own athletic skill. After gaining his education in arms, he helps a maiden in distress *en route* back to this world. They pledge their troth, Cuchulainn and the author evidently having forgotten that he is already engaged and that the whole point of his education in arms is to enhance his image in the eyes of his prospective father-in-law. This episode is a good example of the digressiveness of Old Irish prose. The hero and his new fiancée agree that he will precede her to Ireland, which he does, there forgetting her entirely and marrying his first fiancée. The second lady arrives, in the form of a bird, and Cuchulainn kills her inadvertently while hunting, a weak device but one that enables the author to extricate the hero from the compromising situation in which he has embroiled him.

Following the resolution of the hero's marital affairs, he engages in many exploits. The most dramatic is a war provoked by a cattle-rustling incident triggered in turn by a marital argument. At one point during this war, a young girl is stationed in a tower, charged with alerting her people to the arrival of Cuchulainn and his army. When she does sight them, she, and the author, are so entranced by the beauty and splendor of their weapons, chariots, clothing, and personal appearance that all involved forget her duty to report the invasion. The special flavor of Irish epic and of Old Irish literature in general can be tasted in this scene. While it is weak in consistent or logical narrative force, devoid of character development, and lacking in subtlety, it is extremely rich in color, fresh and sensuous description and imagery, a delight in nature, and a delight in the play of language. These are the qualities that give Old Irish its special place in medieval vernacular literature.

Old French Literature

Like their compeers who settled in Spain and Italy, the Germanic peoples who remained in France abandoned Old High German in preference for a Romance language, Old French, as their vernacular. The first documentary evidence for the existence of Old French dates to the late ninth century. The one genre of literature it produced in the early Middle Ages is a type of epic poem called the *chanson de geste*. It deals with two subjects, saints' lives and the exploits of military heroes such as William of Orange or, more famously, Charlemagne and his associates. The presence of vernacular saints' lives certainly indicates some meeting of minds between Old French authors and Christianity. And, while it has to be said that Christianity shares the honors with other motivations in the heroic epics, these poems are set in a world where Christians are fighting non-Christians, whether Muslims in Spain or pagan Vikings in France. Thus, despite the fact that France had become a missionary field profiting from the labors of Irish and Anglo–Saxon monks during the period when these epics were composed, Old French literature exudes a stronger sense of community identification with Christianity than contemporary Irish literature does. At the same time, the *chanson de geste* is formally devoid of classical influence. These poems are composed in stanzas containing verses of ten syllables. They use end–rhyme, but assonance is the main stylistic cement. The meter relies on accent, not on quantity as in classical Latin verse. Unlike classical epics, *chansons de geste* do not have a continuous narrative line; they are made up of small units or events relatively independent of each other. Another non-classical convention is the use of verbs in the present tense to heighten the immediacy of the action.

There are other literary conventions associated with *chansons de geste*. They are not as visually oriented as Irish literature, confining description to the personal appearance, clothing, weapons, and accoutrements of the heroes. No attention is paid to the back-up troops or the social context in which heroes function as leaders, and there is no description of landscape, cities, or the physical stage on which action takes place. What interest the authors and audiences of this literature are the concrete details of action—the wonder-workings of the saint or the military strategy of the warrior, exactly how one character killed another and with what weapon. Characters are needed, essentially, as the agents of events, but they tend to be flat, two-dimensional stereotypes. In the *Song of Roland*, for instance, Roland is the hero of great prowess, loyal to his lord unto death. Ganelon is the traitor who betrays his lord and brings disaster to his expedition. Charlemagne is the ideal king. All are psychologically quite uncomplicated. Characters are capable of strong emotions, but they are liable to lapse from one emotional state to another abruptly and without nuance. It is the events themselves that are the focus.

When the events are miracles, the saints who perform them tend to be home-grown; when they are military exploits, the warriors, while they often have heavenly assistance and advantages, are treated as human beings and not as quasi-divine. Their battles or saintly lives are actual historical events. The poems are thought to have been composed fairly soon after the lives of their protagonists and transmitted orally until their later redaction. Saints' lives, such as the *Song of St. Eulalia*, were redacted as early as *c*. 900. Some Old French heroic material was retold in Latin; the feats of William of Orange appear in a Latin emperor panegyric poem by Ermoldus Nigellus (d. *c*. 835) and the *Fragment of La Haye*, which also deals with William and other characters in his vernacular epic, was redacted in Latin prose between 980 and 1030, probably in Normandy.

The *Song of Roland*, the acknowledged masterpiece among Old French epics, is one of a group whose heroes are Merovingian and Carolingian leaders, above all Charlemagne. Over a hundred epics about these heroes survive. They lived between the sixth and the ninth centuries, but the first redactions of heroic epics date to the eleventh century. We can test the historicity of the *Song of Roland* by comparing it with a contemporary account of the events it relates, the *Life of Charlemagne* by

Einhard, who was an eyewitness. According to Einhard, in 777 certain Spanish Muslims offered to secede from the caliphate of Córdoba and to accept Charlemagne as their ruler. The next year, Charlemagne went to Spain to make good this transference of allegiance. After besieging, conquering, and destroying Pamplona, he proceeded to Saragossa, where he received hostages as pledges of his new subjects' good faith. He then turned north to go home. While crossing the Pyrenees, his army was attacked from the rear by the Basques and suffered a serious defeat at Roncesvalles, at which many members of his host were killed, including Roland, count of Brittany. On the heels of this defeat, Charlemagne withdrew into France.

Between these events and the first redactions of the *Song of Roland* in the late eleventh century, the story was retold many times, in Latin as well as Old French. Local versions emerged, easily detectable since a hero from the region is given prominence or even invented and inserted into the action. In Brittany, Roland was emphasized and he became the leading hero. The initial redactor, whose version provides the foundation for the modern editions, came from Normandy, which had just succeeded in absorbing Brittany. He drew on different versions but gave pride of place to the Breton one. We are told that Norman troops in the late eleventh century chanted this epic as they marched into battle. The resultant text is conservative in some respects and innovative in others. The single largest area of continuity lies in the ethos which the redactor ascribes to the heroes. Martial valor, male bonding, and loyalty to the leader are their central virtues, while disloyalty to the leader is the most despicable vice. Women are virtually absent as characters, except for a Muslim princess who is a prize of war and Roland's fiancée. Her role in the plot is to drop dead when she is told of Roland's death, mainly to display Charlemagne's pity on that occasion. Christianity certainly makes its appearance in the poem. One of the characters, Turpin, an archbishop, sheds blood just as energetically as his lay confrères and when he falls in battle he is mourned by them not as a pastor or holy man but as a good fighter. Roland worries briefly about his salvation, asking God to forgive his sins before he dies. But Christianity is treated as an essentially political concept in the epic. Fighting the Muslims represents the spread of Christianity by the sword. Religion is seen as an allegiance to which people can be forcibly reduced. Conversion does not require theological understanding or behavioral change. The main force driving the action is the hero's support of the warlord and his desire to win fame for his military prowess. The conservatism of the values manifested by the *Song of Roland* is impressive, especially when we note that its redaction coincided with the First Crusade and the beginnings of the Christian reconquest of Spain.

As for the new elements in the epic, in contrast with Einhard's account and in response to the redactor's regional emphasis, Roland becomes its central character. Not only is he the outstanding exemplar of loyalty and prowess, with almost superhuman strength—the blasts he blows on his horn can be heard for thirty miles, although he is wounded at the time—but his social status and accomplishments are upgraded. He is not merely the count of Brittany; he is Charlemagne's nephew as well. He has already conquered lands far and wide and reduced them to his uncle's rule, including Constantinople. And, although Charlemagne was actually thirty-five at the ːme of the battle of Roncesvalles, the redactor depicts him as an old man with a white beard, full of years and honors. Considering these last two points, it may not be surprising to find that history-as-it-should-have-been elbows real facts off the stage. As Einhard reports it, the Franks lost the battle of Roncesvalles because of the superior strategy of their enemies, and then beat an ignominious retreat. The *Song of Roland* alters the facts so as to bestow more honor on the Franks. A major way this is done is by introducing the character Ganelon, a sheer literary invention. As a traitor, he serves as an excellent foil to Roland as the loyal liege-man. Ganelon also provides a more palatable explanation of the Franks' defeat, which in the poem is a result of his treachery. And, while in actuality the Franks retreated after that defeat, in the *Song of Roland* they regroup instantly, pursuing and destroying the Basques. The sun obligingly stands still in the heavens for over a day to facilitate this exploit, a nice biblical allusion. Then, the Franks penetrate farther south, returning to Saragossa where they defeat a large army of Muslims. The result is that Charlemagne becomes the ruler of all of Spain. Clearly, these plot changes constitute wish-fulfillment on the part of all who transmitted the epic in this form as well as the Norman-Breton desire to inflate the importance of Roland.

Just as Celtic literature was to make its mark on later medieval literature, so new incarnations were in store for Roland and his companions. The *Song of Roland* also appears in art, not only in illuminated manuscripts of the epic but also in the stained glass of Chartres cathedral, the sculpted archivolt over the main door of Verona cathedral, and the mosaic floor of Brindisi cathedral. In the case of both of these early medieval vernacular literatures, later tastes and interests worked their transformations, re-expressing their themes in a new key. In part, this is because the Latinization of these vernacular materials made them available to writers in other parts of Europe. As we have noted, Latin retellings of Old French epics began in the early Middle Ages; the Latinization of Celtic materials began in the twelfth century. The causeway connecting Latin literacy to the redaction of these vernacular literatures was thus a two-way street. This fact is eloquent testimony to the intellectual and aesthetic flexibility of the scribes who kept them in circulation.

CHAPTER 8

Varieties of Germanic Literature: Old Norse, Old High German, and Old English

If Celtic and Old French literatures are diverse in their genres and stylistic strategies, the ethos they reflect, and their address to the Christian and classical traditions, the same is true of the early Germanic vernaculars. Old Norse, the largest subdivision of this literature, is the least affected by classicism and Christianity, a function of the conversion of the Scandinavians only in 1000 or after. Germanic peoples on the continent who retained German as their vernacular were exposed to Latin Christian culture much earlier, even if most of them had to be won from Arianism to orthodoxy. They profited from the educational reforms of the Carolingian Renaissance east of the Rhine. Their literature combines classical, Christian, and Germanic elements more than Old Norse does. Of all the early Germanic literatures, Old English reflects the widest range of attitudes toward its available sources. As is the case with Celtic and Old French, all three Germanic literatures depended on monastic personnel for their composition or redaction, authors who were capable of preserving pre-Christian and non-classical values as well as mixing them with Latin Christian materials.

Old Norse Literature

Their late conversion and their location on the fringes of Europe made the authors of Old Norse literature the most hyper-Germanic of the early Middle Ages. Even after their official conversion their absorption of Christian attitudes was slow. It is this vernacular tradition that provides our richest literary source for Germanic paganism. Old Norse also has literary conventions and genres unique to itself, as well as ones it shares with Old High German and Old English.

The earliest works in Old Norse are the Eddas, episodic poetry stanzaic in structure. The first known manuscript of the Eddas dates to the tenth century, but internal evidence shows that they were composed before 600 and transmitted orally until their redaction. Germanic philologists have established that a Great Vowel Shift, which changed the pronunciation of vowels in these languages, occurred in c. 600. Since Eddic poetry has elaborate metrical rules and makes heavy use of alliteration, it must have been composed before 600: the verse would not scan with the post–600 vowel sounds. Stylistically complex, the Eddas are also difficult to read because their subject matter was thoroughly familiar to the audience and the poets freely omit or only allude to important events. Redactors sometimes add prose passages to smooth out the story line, but narrative gaps remain. In the thirteenth century the Eddas were rewritten in prose. The prose redactors were certainly Christian but they preserved faithfully the Eddas' pagan content.

Whether in verse or prose, the Eddas treat pagan mythology and heroic epic. The mythological Eddas deal with cosmogenesis, the gods and other supernatural beings, and the end of the world. The characters in the heroic epics are leaders of the Germanic tribes in the age of migrations. Some, like Theodoric and Attila the Hun (*fl.* 435–54) are historical figures, while others appear to be literary inventions. The heroes often have otherworldly connections and advantages and may have to overcome superhuman as well as human adversaries.

The *Voluspa* or *Sybil's Song* is the Eddic text that gives the fullest account of pagan mythology. Central to this account is Yggdrasil, a creative world tree. It is rooted in the three parts of the universe, Asgard, the home of the gods; Midgard, the home of mankind engendered by the tree; and Utgard, the home of giants, trolls, elves, and dwarfs, malevolent supernatural beings. These three regions are arranged in concentric circles, with Asgard at the center, each separated from its neighbor by a body of water. A bridge, Bifrost, connects Asgard and Midgard and must be crossed by the heroes ushered to Valhalla, the good other world, by Valkyries or warrior maidens. A serpent with its tail in its mouth swims in the water separating Midgard from Utgard. There is also a bad other world, underground and in the north, presided over by the goddess Hel, who lent her name to the Christian hell.

The pantheon is divided into first-order and second-order deities. Initially, their major achievement was to defeat the giants who first ruled the universe, a victory representing the triumph of order over chaos. Still, harmony within their ranks is relative. Odin, the king of the gods, is also the god of death, the master of the Valkyries, the god of poetry, which he stole from the giants, and the god of knowledge and runes, which he gained by struggle and sacrifice. Odin is also an oathbreaker. This is a curious and even unsettling collection of divine attributes. Other first-order gods are Thor, god of thunder and lightning and mankind's most powerful protector against the giants, trolls, elves, and dwarfs; and Frey and his sister Freya, fertility gods. The second-order gods include Frigg, Odin's consort and a sun goddess; Aegir, god of the sea; Idun, who guards the golden apples that give the gods eternal youth; Volund, the smith and artificer, who sometimes forges swords for heroes; and Balder, a god of purity and innocence whose death and return to life symbolize the cycle of the seasons. Balder is invulnerable except to weapons made of mistletoe. Being good-natured, he offers himself to the gods as a dartboard and is inadvertently killed by his blind brother with a mistletoe wand. It is understood, even as the gods mourn his death, that Balder will return, bringing spring and fraternal pacification.

The worm in the apple of Asgard is Loki, called a mischief-maker but better understood as the embodiment of unmotivated hostility. It is he who arranges

Balder's death. Odin accepts him as a blood-brother although he is of giants' parentage. This decision should probably not be understood as a choice on Odin's part. For fate rules the gods along with everything else. Fate is represented by the Norns, three sisters with spindles spinning the past, the present, and the future. The gods' eventual fate is a calamity called Ragnarok. Their own feuds, Loki's malice, and Odin's oath-breaking provoke a revolt of the giants and all-out war. Although the heroes ally with the gods, they are defeated. The outcome, apparently, is a return to primal chaos. Even considering the hope signified by Balder's return, this is a difficult religion to believe in since the gods the Germans worshipped are doomed to defeat. There are certainly some parallels between Germanic and Greco-Roman mythology. As with some of the motifs in Celtic literature, it cannot be proved whether we are dealing with cross-cultural influence here or the harking back to a common Indo-European tradition.

The heroic Eddas, both in poetry and in the prose *Volsunga Saga*, center on Sigurd, the chief member of the Volsung family, his ancestors, in-laws, and descendants. The Old Norse version of his story was known to other Germanic groups. It is quoted in the Old English *Beowulf* and *Deor's Lament* and there is an Old High German version of the tale, the *Nibelungenlied*. The Edda relates the Volsungs' descent from Odin who also fructifies the barren marriage of Sigurd's grandparents. Sigurd's horse is descended from Odin's horse and Volund forged the sword he inherits from his father. Sigurd's father is king of the Franks and his mother is a Danish princess. The first part of the story deals with Sigurd's ancestors, his youth, and his acquisition of a treasure gained by killing the dragon guarding it. As he does so, the hero tastes the dragon's blood, which enables him to understand the birds, who warn him of an attempt on his life, which he forestalls.

The next section of the story treats Sigurd's relations with the warrior-maiden Brynhild, sister of Atli or Attila the Hun. There are some narrative inconsistencies here. Brynhild vows to marry only a fearless man. She meets Sigurd twice and both times they pledge their troth. On the second occasion Brynhild prophesies that, none the less, he will marry Gudrun, sister of Gunnar, king of the Burgundians, and that the marriage will be brief and tragic. She gives the same prophecy to Gudrun, adding that Gudrun will later marry Atli. Two conventions of Old Norse epic come together here, the epic denial of suspense and the idea that some people have second sight. No reason is given for the failure of Sigurd and Brynhild to act on their vows and marry.

The marriage between Sigurd and Gudrun duly takes place, the Burgundian queen mother having given Sigurd a potion causing him to forget Brynhild, and the hero becomes the blood-brother of Gunnar and his younger brother Hogni. Sigurd helps Gunnar win Brynhild's hand. She has been placed in a ring of fire by Odin. Using his gift of shape-changing, Sigurd overcomes this obstacle in Gunnar's form. After agreeing on Brynhild's marriage settlement he shares a bed with her for three nights with his sword placed between them. He also takes back a ring he had given her on the occasion of their earlier vows. If Sigurd has forgotten these vows, Brynhild has not. She is torn between her earlier commitment to Sigurd and the belief that Gunnar has truly won her. She decides to marry Gunnar. There is some confusion in the text about her premarital chastity, because, the sword in the bed notwithstanding, she tells her brother-in-law and foster-father that she is pregnant by Sigurd and that she will give him the child to rear.

This lack of clarity about the true state of the relations between Brynhild and Sigurd before her marriage surfaces and provokes a quarrel between Brynhild and Gudrun, who accuses her of having had a premarital affair with Sigurd. It was then, Gudrun asserts, that he took from her the ring that Gudrun now wears. Brynhild counters with the charge that the Burgundians knew she had promised herself to Sigurd and that they had manipulated matters, causing her inadvertently to forswear herself. Her former love for Sigurd now turns to hate and she urges his murder to avenge her honor, dissociating herself from Gunnar for the same reason. Gunnar's youngest brother, Guttorm, who had not been involved in the blood-brotherhood pact, is suborned to do the deed, his brothers giving him a potion that suppresses his scruples. Sigurd's death, in the Edda account, is extremely gory. Guttorm bursts into the bedroom of Gudrun and Sigurd and murders him before he can seize a weapon, and Gudrun awakes to see her husband dead in a welter of blood. Brynhild laughs when she hears of the murder. Repudiating the Burgundians' charge and her own earlier remarks to her foster-father, she insists that her premarital chastity was preserved by the sword in the bed and then commits suicide after requesting that she and Sigurd be burned on the same pyre with the sword between them.

It is Gudrun's motivations that now move to center stage. After seven years of widowhood, she is persuaded by her relatives to accept Atli's marriage proposal. Her mother gives her a potion of forgetfulness and compensation for Sigurd's death. But Gudrun remembers revenge. Her chief grievance is her brothers' seizure of Sigurd's treasure, hers by right of inheritance. Like the Burgundians, Atli lusts after the treasure, which he hopes to secure through this marriage. The Edda presents him as treacherous as well. He invites his in-laws to a feast intending to trick them out of the treasure. Gudrun remains loyal to her kin and warns them not to accept the invitation. They do so none the less, hoping to take over Atli's kingdom. Their greed for power matches the avarice that has cheated their sister out of her inheritance. When the Burgundians arrive, hostilities erupt and Gudrun's brothers are killed. To avenge them, Gudrun kills her two children by Atli, cooks their hearts, and feeds them to him, telling him what he has eaten before killing Atli with the aid of Hogni's son. Then Gudrun sets fire to Atli's hall and destroys everyone in it except herself. The following passage, close to the end of the tale, portrays Gudrun well as the implacable executrix of vengeance and also conveys the meter and the literary texture of the poetic Eddas:

> Clamour arose from the benches, wild the cry of warriors;
> Beneath the damask hangings, the Huns lamented loud,
> All save Gudrun who wept not ever.[1]

The Volsungs' story continues into the next generation but, even without the addenda, it is clear that two themes predominate, the lust for the treasure and the curse that falls on anyone possessing it, and the duty to avenge kinsmen or one's own honor, which transcends all other human loyalties. The vice of treachery is evenly divided between male and female characters, who are equally cruel in getting what they want and in upholding the commitments that bind them. According to the Norse code of values, it is easy to see why places in Valhalla were reserved for Brynhild and Gudrun, and the thirteenth-century redactor of the *Volsunga Saga* shows no discomfort in preserving these essentially pagan values. The Sigurd story exercised so powerful a hold on the Scandinavian imagination that it was also represented visually in Christian artistic settings, on stone crosses, baptismal fonts, and church portals, where it mingles with biblical events and personages. The dragon-slaying pagan hero also made his contribution to the warrior-saints of this period and to the cult of the Archangel Michael.

The next type of Old Norse literature to emerge after the Eddas was skaldic poetry, *skald* being the generic term for poet. This genre reached its peak in the ninth century. Skaldic poems are short, emotion-packed statements about some person or event. They have extremely complex literary rules. Like the haiku poet, the skaldic poet is limited to a fixed number of syllables. He achieves his effect with alliteration, internal rhyme, assonance, and elaborate sound patterns. He also uses kennings, or circumlocutionary metaphors to refer to ordinary things, like 'stallion of the sea' for ship. The highly developed and even recherché character of skaldic poetry suggests that a professional cadre of poets produced it. Yet, given the survival of most skaldic poems as quotations in the sagas, in the mouths of people who are not professional poets, it appears that the ability to express one's feelings in skaldic form was widespread.

This brings us to the sagas, the largest subdivision of Old Norse literature. 'Saga' means prose narrative as such. The term is applied to straightforward historical works, and later to saints' lives, as well as to heroic epics. Old Norse shares with Old Irish the unusual genre of prose epic. Most of the heroic sagas were composed in Iceland and deal with people who lived there between 870 and 1025, soon after their protagonists' lives. They were transmitted orally and redacted in the twelfth and thirteenth centuries. As with the Eddas, the redactors of sagas report faithfully the beliefs and attitudes of their characters, most of whom are pagan. On the rare occasion when a redactor inserts an anachronistic reference to Christianity in pagan times, it stands out as an obvious error for its failure to harmonize with the sagas' prevailing world view. Such accretions can be excised mentally by the reader without doing violence either to saga plots or to characterizations.

Not only are the sagas concrete in their temporal and geographical setting and in the historicity of their characters, they are also highly specific in other ways. The author always states where and when the action takes place, who the rulers of neighboring countries were at the time, the kinship ties of characters and their relationship to Iceland's original settlers, and even when a character is no longer in the story. The political, economic, social, and legal institutions of Iceland are integral to saga plots and to the attitudes of saga characters. In turn, the sagas are an important source for these institutions. Iceland was settled in 875 by a group of Norwegian families unwilling to give up their tribal autonomy in the face of the centralizing drive of the Norwegian kings. They enshrined in their institutions the liberties for which they had emigrated. Authority was vested in regional tribal chieftains who were also religious leaders and the country was divided into four quarters, each with its *Thing*, or assembly. Every summer a general assembly, the *Althing*, convened. All free Icelanders could attend these assemblies, which functioned as deliberative and legislative bodies and as courts of law. Icelandic legal procedures were extremely elaborate and law men, learned in the law, advised litigants and the court while the chiefs served as judges. The complexities of the legal system fuel the plots of some sagas. A clearly just case may be dismissed because a litigant fails to comply with a procedural technicality, inspiring him to seek redress illegally. The main weakness of the Icelandic constitution was its lack of an executive branch, to ensure that defendants appeared in court and to enforce legislation and the court's judicial decisions. Consequently, saga characters often resort to violence even though they have gone through the process of peaceful litigation, arbitration, or compensation, and despite the fact that defiance of the law made one an outlaw, excluded from the normal networks of support and protection. The spirit of the law is a palpable presence in many sagas. Law men, such as Njal in *Njal's Saga*, constantly plead for recourse to law instead of force. As he puts it, 'With laws shall our land be built up, but with lawlessness laid waste.'[2] In writing that line, the redactor may well have been giving a nostalgic backward look to an earlier Iceland, where blood feuds of the type Njal fails to avert had weakened the country so decisively that, in the thirteenth century, it was annexed by Norway and lost its liberties.

Aside from the fact that the legal system is deeply ingrained in saga characters' behavior, the *Althing* is also important in saga plots as the single biggest social event of the year. After the long winter when travel is difficult, friends and relatives meet at the *Althing* and exchange news. Bargains are struck; marriages are arranged and also dissolved; offense is given and taken, and fights break out, quite apart from the grievances of litigants whose cases receive adverse judgments. Major policy decisions were made at the *Althing*, such as the adoption of Christianity by vote in 1000, an event related in *Njal's Saga*.

Several other features of Icelandic society must be noted to explain their function in the sagas. The economy of the country combined agriculture, fishing, manufacturing, and commerce. But Viking raiders were still present. Sometimes they were ordinary citizens adding booty to their balance sheet in a slow season. But the berserkers, so called because they fall into a frenzy of rape, pillage, and slaughter, are feared by other saga characters as throwbacks to a less civilized age. Kinship, marrriage, friendship, and the host–guest relationship created strong social bonds and obligations. So did foster-parenting. Parents entrusted their children to foster-parents not because they were unable to raise them but to enlarge the circle of people on whom their children could rely for help. Although women needed the consent of their male kin when they married, especially for the first time, they could inherit and manage their own property independently and could initiate divorce and other legal actions. The sagas show that in Scandinavia, by the ninth century, bride-price had given way to a bilateral foundation for a marriage combining a dowry from the wife's family and a marriage settlement from the husband's. The sagas present women as characters with strong personalities. They are often vital movers of the action. The virtues prized in women are the same as those valued in men: executive ability, good judgment, and courage. They share with men the vices of greed, vindictiveness, lust, and malice. Both men and women can have second sight. Another feature of the social environment reflected in the sagas is the fact that the heroes, while socially prominent, are not presented in isolation from other classes; they are shown interacting with their followers, servants, and slaves. Part of what makes them heroic is the community's judgment of their worth.

The sagas have literary conventions that distinguish them both from classical epics and from epics in other medieval vernaculars. The sagas know nothing of the flashback or of the omniscient author: they present events in the order in which they occurred. Since the author cannot defer mention of a character who does not enter the story until later, he introduces his characters early, always giving them a brief genealogy and a description of their leading character traits. They are then on hand when needed to move the plot forward. The author also maintains the convention that he knows no more about a character than his or her contemporaries in the saga can observe. He does not step into his protagonists' minds. Nor does he present them as at all introspective.

Polar opposites of their counterparts in Irish epics, the characters in Norse sagas are the least loquacious in medieval literature. They sometimes manifest their personalities and general outlook in their speeches, which are always short. The hero of *The Saga of Grettir the Strong* is a good example. Grettir is a murderer and an outlaw. He has also suffered unjustly and has helped other people, including families with daughters threatened by berserkers. His longest outlawry arises from a misunderstanding when he tries to bring fire to some people whose fire has gone out and who will otherwise die. At one point, his brother Thorsteinn observes, 'You would be handy at many things . . . if misfortune did not follow you.' Grettir's never-complain, never-explain rejoinder is, 'Men will tell of deeds that are done.'[3] Brusque as they are, saga characters sometimes express themselves in the form of skaldic poems. An illustration, also from *The Saga of Grettir the Strong*, shows the treatment of female characters and the importance of public opinion in defining a character's reputation. Angle, Grettir's enemy, has killed him and his brother Illugi, not fair and square but by means of pagan witchcraft. Adding insult to injury, he brings Grettir's severed head to his mother:

> Angle's party entered the room with the head and set it on the floor. The mistress of the house was there and several others; no greeting passed between them. Angle spoke a verse:
> 'Grettir's head I bring thee here.
> Weep for the red-haired hero, lady.
> On the floor it lies; t'were rotten by this,
> but I laid it in salt. Great glory is mine.'
> She sat silent while he spoke his verse; then she said:

'The swine would have fled like sheep from the fox
if Grettir had stood there hearty and strong.
Shame on the deeds that were done in the North!
Little the glory you gain from my lay.'
Many said it was small wonder that she had brave sons, so brave was she herself
before the insults which she had received.[4]

Saga characters are less likely to manifest themselves in speech than in action,
and also in what they fail to do. Their personalities are treated as givens, undergoing no development and requiring no explanation. In rare cases, characters are
introduced as children. When this is so they always play a central role in the saga.
A good example is Hallgerd, wife of Njal's friend Gunnar in *Njal's Saga*. She is
easily the nastiest female character in medieval literature, greedy, extravagant,
selfish, overbearing, spiteful, and manipulative. Directly or indirectly, she is responsible for many deaths, including those of her first two husbands, and for the feud
that overtakes Njal and Gunnar and destroys them both. We are alerted to the fact
that Hallgerd will be a major figure in *Njal's Saga* on its first page, where we are
shown why and how. Her father, Hoskuld, is hosting a feast and enthusing to his
kinsman, Hrut, about the beauty of his little daughter, with her silky blonde hair
down to her waist. He asks her to come over to him. She does; he tips up her chin
and plants an affectionate kiss on her cheek. He then turns to Hrut and invites
comment. Hrut remains silent. When pressed, Hrut, who usually tells the truth,
says, 'The child is beautiful enough, and many will suffer for her beauty; but I
cannot imagine how thief's eyes have come into our kin.'[5]

Aside from illustrating Hrut's second sight as a means of effecting the epic denial
of suspense, two other features of this passage are telling. Hallgerd does not return
her father's kiss. Although she is only a child, she has already discovered that men
are drawn to her because of her beauty and that she can thereby get what she wants
from them. She is a taker of homage and affection, not a giver. When she matures
she will also be a taker and manipulator of sexual love. But maturity merely enlarges
the stage on which she enacts the psychology she already possesses as a child. Her
long blonde hair is mentioned whenever Hallgerd is described in the saga. It yields
one of the few motifs Old Norse shares with classical literature in the scene where
Gunnar, besieged by his enemies, snaps his bowstring and makes the following
appeal:

He said to Hallgerd, 'Let me have two locks of your hair, and help my mother
plait them into a bowstring for me.'
'Does anything depend on it?' asked Hallgerd.
'My life depends on it,' replied Gunnar, 'for they will never overcome me
so long as I can use my bow.'
'In that case,' said Hallgerd, 'I shall now remind you of the slap you once
gave me. I do not care in the least whether you hold out a long time or not.'
'To each his own way of earning fame,' said Gunnar. 'You will not be asked
again.'[6]

It is clear that infamy is what Hallgerd earns, virtually condemning Gunnar to death for a slap he administered in punishment for Hallgerd's ordering a servant to steal food from neighbors and to burn down their dairy. The function of the author's repeated and atypically detailed descriptions of her beauty is to explain why Gunnar, introduced as a man of prudence and sound judgment, marries a woman of such evil character, paying with his life for his infatuation.

Just as action, or inaction, is more important than speech in revealing character in the sagas, so the characters' moral and intellectual traits outweigh their physical features except in cases, such as Hallgerd's, where there is a salient reason for describing a person's appearance in non-generic terms. We learn less about how people, clothing, accessories, and natural background look in Old Norse literature than in any other medieval vernacular. When a saga author does give a colorful description, it is almost shocking in its departure from usual practice. Nature is rarely described. When it is mentioned, it is usually presented as a hostile environment, as in a scene in *The Saga of Grettir the Strong* where a character fording a stream in winter finds, on reaching the other side, that a toe has become frostbitten. He stops, cuts off the toe, binds up his foot, and continues his journey without comment.

All the sagas focus on people of heroic stature, whose stories involve a small number of themes. Some, like *The Saga of Grettir the Strong*, *Gisli's Saga*, and *Egil's Saga*, are biographies of the eponymous hero. Some, like *Njal's Saga*, are family sagas, taking the action into the next generation of the major families involved. There are also expedition sagas, like the *Vinland Saga*, which relates the voyage of Erik the Red and his son Leif Erikson across the Atlantic in search of a wine-producing land. After landfall at Newfoundland and then Cape Cod, where all they find are cranberries, they return to Iceland greatly annoyed. Other sagas, like the *Laxdaela Saga*, are regional. They may include elements of the family saga and, as in this case, the theme of the love-triangle. But the main bond among the episodes is the fact that the characters all hail from the same part of Iceland. In all kinds of sagas, conflicts of loyalty, the conflict of duty and passion, oath-breaking, the machinations of malicious spoilers who enjoy stirring up trouble, the avenging of wrongs, envy and greed, and the winning of honor and repute, motivate the characters. Brooding over all is fate, not just in the sense that actions once taken unleash ineluctable outcomes but also in the larger sense that all human beings have destinies they cannot avoid. The measure of a hero, or a heroine, lies not in overcoming misfortune but in accepting his or her fate, facing doom unflinchingly, with full knowledge and sometimes foreknowledge of it. This fatalistic outlook is shared by saga characters whether they are pagan or ostensibly Christian. Either way, they defy their fate by accepting it, and in that very acceptance they manifest the invincibility of their spirits. It is not a posthumous reward in Valhalla or in the Christian heaven that moves these characters, but the desire for fame in the memories of men.

Saga characters are portrayed starkly and vividly. As personalities they can be quite multifaceted and complex. Grettir, the self-sufficient and violent outlaw, is still a benefactor to his fellow man, unresentful of injustices done to him, and afraid of the dark. Egil, a drunkard from the age of three, who commits his first murder as a child and who disgustingly violates the laws of hospitality as a guest, is not a mere sociopath but also a great poet and a father so grieved by his son's death that he tries to commit suicide, evoking the love, understanding, and shrewd compassion of the daughter who draws him back into life. To a large extent, the unexplained personalities of saga characters are the destinies they act out; and their actions, and the reactions of others to them, are designed to illuminate character. Saga characters are strong-willed. They can be crushed but not bent. They are capable of passionate feelings but they are never sentimental. The golden mean is not in their moral lexicon. Saga characters are super-real, but at the same time fully human. Ultimately, whatever their plots may be, the theme of the Old Norse sagas is character. What the reader remembers are the protagonists of the sagas, as people, not the story line.

Old High German Literature

The literature produced by German-speakers on the continent is more diverse than that of Germanic peoples speaking Old French. Compared with both Old French and Old Norse, it reflects a more conscious desire to combine Germanic subjects and Germanic ethical and literary values with the Christian and classical traditions. Side by side with works aiming at this blending of cultures are works conventionally German, whose authors or redactors show scant interest in other viewpoints. In the first category are biblical rewrites and saints' lives. The second category contains heroic epic poetry alone.

Two kinds of borrowing appear in the Old High German literature that deliberately draws on Christian or classical materials. In some cases, authors combine literary form from one tradition with content from another, juxtaposing these elements without really synthesizing them. In other cases, they achieve a coherent fusion of their sources. The works falling into the first of these two sub-sets are Germanic in form, date mostly to the ninth century, use biblical material or saints' lives, and recast their subjects according to the conventions of Germanic epic poetry. The authors of the biblical rewrites, who do not hesitate to include apocryphal material, deal with the creation, the last judgment, and the life of Christ. The first two topics provided replacements for the pagan theology of the Eddas. The biblical message sometimes caused intellectual indigestion, as can be seen in the *Heiland*, a version of Christ's life whose title reflects the semantic shift that the noun *Heil* and its cognates had by now undergone. In this poem Christ becomes a *comitatus* leader and his disciples his military followers. The desert becomes a forest and the scene shifts from Palestine to Saxony. Given the military preoccupations of Germanic epic, the author is stymied by the lack of warfare in Christ's life. He makes the most of the scene in which St. Peter severs the ear of the high priest's servant, but he is puzzled by Christ's turn-the-other-cheek doctrine. He is also alarmed by Peter's denial of Christ, another baffling departure from the warrior ethos and the retainer's duty of loyalty to his leader. Eventually he abandons the effort to explain Peter's action, declaring that it must have been fated. A fine example of a saint's life recast as heroic epic is the *Ludwigslied*, a panegyric on the eponymous emperor portraying him as a warrior-saint fighting against pagan Vikings as well as working miracles.

There are other Old High German works that achieve a smoother integration of the traditions on which the author draws. A good contrast to biblical rewrites like the *Heiland* is the *Evangelienbuch* of the ninth-century monk Otfrid of Weissenberg. We know his name and calling from the elegant Latin preface to his Old High German gospel poem. The preface also reflects his Latin Christian learning; he urges that the fourfold method of patristic exegesis be applied to the text. Even more noteworthy as an original contribution, Otfrid has noticed the grammatical similarities between Latin and German. Both are highly inflected languages in which nouns and the adjectives modifying them have different endings depending on their syntactical functions, yielding many words with isomorphic endings. Classical Latin poetic meters capitalize on this fact. And so, for Otfrid, can German poetry. He thus abandons rhyme, alliteration, and assonance, the building blocks of Germanic poetic metrics, and uses an iambic meter, which works quite well in his poem without sounding contrived.

The same sub-set of works which the *Evangelienbuch* inhabits contains epics on non-biblical subjects. The *Ruodlieb*, dating to the eleventh century, relates the exploits of an epic hero. It devotes far more attention to his love-life than is the case with *chanson de geste* heroes. Like Otfrid, the author has discovered that German is grammatically hospitable to classical meters and uses the hexameter to good effect. An even more striking convergence of classical form and Germanic content, admittedly a joker in the deck in a chapter on vernacular literature, is the ninth-century Latin epic *Waltharius*. It tells of two Germanic characters, Walter of Aquitaine and Hildigund, who are raised as hostages at the court of Attila the Hun. They fall in love, make good their escape, and, after many adventures including Walter's severe wounding, return to Aquitaine, where they marry and he gains his rightful throne. On one level, this work is a conventional account of epic deeds in the age of migrations, colored by the continental German interest in a love story. On another level, the author wants to make the point that free will, not fatalism, determines events and that forgiveness is a virtue. Christian ethics thus modifies the epic outlook. The Latin of the poem is thoroughly classical, using dactylic hexameters and modeling itself largely on Vergil's *Aeneid*.

We also find Old High Germanic literature in this period that conveys a more unadulterated Germanic viewpoint in both form and content. In this category are epic poems about heroes from the age of migrations closer in spirit to the heroic Eddas than to the *Waltharius*. Many survive only in fragmentary form. One cycle centers on Attila, here called Etzel, Theodoric, here called Dietrich of Bern, and his fellow-Ostrogoth Odoacer. Another deals with Hildebrand, Dietrich's faithful retainer. As with the Eddas, these poems are made up of stanzas of four lines, each line divided by a caesura and each with a fixed number of stressed syllables. Alliteration, internal rhyme, and end rhyme are used heavily. Here too, philological evidence indicates composition before the Great Vowel Shift, although the first of these epics to be redacted was written down in the ninth century and some were redacted as late as the thirteenth. Later redactors do intrude their attitudes into the story in a manner more difficult to excise than is the case with the Norse sagas. Still, a remarkable carry-over of traditional Germanic literary strategies and pre-Christian values remains. As in Old Norse epic, some characters have second sight, which they use to provide the epic denial of suspense, although premonitory dreams and authorial comment also play that role. While Old High German epic characters are more talkative than their Norse opposite numbers, they still manifest themselves primarily through action. Fate remains a major element in the plot, along with the unexplained malevolence of some characters, and loyalty and vengeance are key motivations. The Old High German author likewise maintains the convention that he cannot look into his characters' souls. At the same time, in contrast with Norse epics, these epics make use of the flashback and the device of understatement. Tears flow freely and gore is less in evidence. Persons, clothing, and accoutrements are described in colorful detail. Another contrast with Old Norse, particularly in Old High German epics of late redaction, is that the heroes are not shown in relation to other social groups but are presented as members of a knightly class associating only with each other, with sufficient leisure to engage in elaborate festivals and athletic contests as well as in martial and amatory exploits.

Just as *chanson de geste* material attracted the interest of Latin authors in France and Walter of Aquitaine's story the interest of the author of the *Waltharius*, so the *Hildebrandslied* drew the attention of the Carolingian Latin author Walafrid Strabo. This latter epic can also be compared with the *Song of Roland* in that both rewrite history. In actuality, Theodoric triumphed over his rival Odoacer through brutality and guile, but in the *Hildebrandslied* Dietrich of Bern is exiled unjustly by a usurper and regains his throne by honorable combat. In this battle, Hildebrand, who has followed him into exile, is trapped in a classic and insoluble Germanic conflict of loyalties when he faces a warrior on the other side who turns out to be his son.

This last-mentioned theme, as well as some of the characters in the *Hildebrandslied*, are found in the single most important Old High German epic, and the only complete one, the *Nibelungenlied*. Redacted in Austria in the thirteenth century, it treats the same subject as the *Volsunga Saga*, although with notable shifts in emphasis. Gunnar, king of the Burgundians, becomes Gunther and his two brothers become Gernot and Giselher. His sister becomes Kriemhild and his mother, while she interprets dreams, has no other role in the plot. Sigurd becomes Siegfried. The past history of his family is omitted, as is an account of his acquisition of the treasure, an event referred to only after the fact. Brynhild becomes Brunhild. Instead of being the sister of the king of the Huns, she is an Icelandic queen in her own right. Her sister and brother-in-law are omitted. In becoming Etzel, Atli also becomes a far more upright and sympathetic character. Along with Hildebrand and Dietrich of Bern, other new faces include Rudegar of Bechlaren, a retainer of Etzel, and Hagen, a kinsman of Gunther and a central figure in the plot. All the characters are presented as being of exclusively human descent. Siegfried's parents are the king and queen of the Netherlands. But he does have otherworldly advantages, notably a cloak of invisibility and virtual invulnerability as a result of bathing in the dragon's blood after he had dispatched him.

The action of the *Nibelungenlied* begins with Siegfried's arrival at the Burgundian court to seek Kriemhild's hand. They marry and he becomes Gunther's comrade-at-arms as well as an affectionate husband. Siegfried assists Gunther in wooing Brunhild not by assuming his shape and going through a ring of fire but by using his cloak of invisibility to help Gunther overcome the athletic and martial tests she imposes on suitors. Although she thinks that Gunther has won her truly, Brunhild inexplicably refuses to let him consummate their marriage. Once again, using his cloak of invisibility, Siegfried aids Gunther by physically chastising Brunhild. But the text makes it clear that it is Gunther to whom she submits sexually.

Other major changes occur in the sequence of events culminating in Siegfried's murder. Brunhild plays less of a role and the Burgundians, especially Hagen and Kriemhild, more of a role than in the Sigurd story. The Burgundians envy Siegfried's prowess, even as they benefit from it, as well as lusting after his treasure. The redactor indicates that Kriemhild shares her relatives' greed. It is she who provokes the quarrel with Brunhild and she who charges that Brunhild had a premarital affair with Siegfried, which Brunhild hotly denies. Brunhild claims that her ring and belt, which Kriemhild wears, were stolen from her and not given to a friend or lover. Like the *Volsunga Saga*, the *Nibelungenlied* never settles the true facts of this matter. In response to Gunther's query, Siegfried merely states that he never told his wife whether such an affair had taken place, evading the issue of what really happened, and Gunther pursues the inquiry no farther. The veracity of Kriemhild, Brunhild, and Siegfried alike is unresolved.

Instead of murder by a brother-in-law in his own bed, Siegfried's death is orchestrated at the conclusion of a vividly described hunt. The evil genius responsible is Hagen, with Kriemhild's unwitting collaboration. Under the pretext of protecting Siegfried, Hagen asks whether his invulnerability is complete. Kriemhild replies that there is a spot between his shoulderblades where a leaf fell when he bathed in the dragon's blood; there he can be wounded. Her premonitory dream the night before the hunt, in which she sees flowers wet with blood, is borne out when Hagen stabs Siegfried in the back and his own blood falls upon the flowers. This motif may also be an echo of Vergil's description of warriors cut down in the flower of youth in the *Aeneid*. In any event, the appeal to pathos made in the *Nibelungenlied* contrasts sharply with the grim slaughter of Sigurd.

As with the widowed Gudrun, Kriemhild now moves to the fore as a motivator of the plot. She is portrayed as a devout Christian, weeping and praying and making pious donations to the abbey of Lorsch founded several centuries after the age in which the epic is set. Yet, after Siegfried's death, her real motivation is a dual obsession, her desire for the treasure which her brothers have appropriated and her desire to avenge her beloved husband. In her case, marital love transcends loyalty to her kin; although Kriemhild is not above using her second husband as a means of accomplishing her goals. In this section of the story, we see Kriemhild develop from a naive and credulous bride into a virago who marinates in her own bile for thirteen years waiting for the opportunity presented by Etzel's marriage proposal, brought by Rudegar of Bechlaren. Her brothers welcome the match as a means of ridding themselves of a sister whom they have cheated and whose mourning is a constant reproach. Kriemhild's own initial misgivings about marrying a pagan quickly cede to her decision to make Etzel an instrument of vengeance against her brothers. For his part, Etzel is portrayed as an honest and honorable man. Attila the Hun clearly enjoyed a better reputation among the continental Germans than he did in Scandinavia. Another thirteen years go by and a son is born to Kriemhild and Etzel. But she continues to nurse her grief over Siegfried's death and her desire to avenge it and to gain his treasure. It is she who prevails on Etzel to invite the Burgundians to a feast where she can treacherously achieve these goals.

When the invitation comes, Hagen has a premonition of doom and sinks the treasure in the Rhine for safe keeping, but the Burgundians do not take his advice and travel to Etzel's court. *En route*, they are entertained by Rudegar, who had earlier pledged his loyalty to Kriemhild and who now strengthens his host–guest bond with the Burgundians by marrying his daughter and only child to Giselher. When her brothers arrive, Kriemhild provokes hostilities. Rudegar faces an insoluble conflict of loyalties. He ends by fighting on the side of the Huns and falls in battle immediately, almost as if a death wish were extricating him from an impossible situation. Gunther and Hagen are captured and Kriemhild personally beheads Hagen. Then, although he fights on Etzel's side, Hildebrand kills Kriemhild. His rationale is that it is an insult to a warrior, however despicable, to be killed by a woman. Both sides are destroyed, with no protagonists surviving and no sequels. There is no slaughter of children, no cannibalism, and no torching of Etzel's hall. The closing passage of the *Nibelungenlied* conveys well its difference in tonality from the *Volsunga Saga*:

> There lay the bodies of all that were doomed to die. The noble lady was hewn to pieces. Dietrich and Etzel began to weep, and deeply lamented their kinsmen and vassals.
>
> Their great pride lay dead there. The people, one and all, were given up to grief and mourning. The king's high festival had ended in sorrow, as joy must ever turn to sorrow in the end.
>
> I cannot tell you what happened after this, except that knights and ladies, yes, and noble squires too, were seen weeping for the death of dear friends.
>
> The story ends here: Such was the Nibelungs' Last Stand.[7]

Both the free flow of tears and the philosophical turn of this passage would have grated on Norse sensibilities. But the audience of the *Volsunga Saga* would have agreed wholeheartedly that fate controls human events, particularly fate as manifested in protagonists whose character is their destiny. The fleeting references to Christian worship and to classical literature in the *Nibelungenlied* do not, fundamentally, alter the values the characters express. The major shift in motivation, Kriemhild's placing of her love for Siegfried over her loyalty to her kin or to her second husband, may well reflect the courtly romance perspective which the redactor brings to the tale. At the same time, it is consistent with the attention given to marital love in other Old High German epics written or redacted centuries earlier. A major achievement of the *Nibelungenlied* is its portrayal of characters, even minor ones, in a three-dimensional manner. While their characters are givens, they are also subject to development and their later behavior is never inconsistent with the moral traits shown early in the text. The most central cases in point are Kriemhild and Hagen. For the redactor of the *Nibelungenlied*, plot and characters are equally important and he gives his characters a more finely nuanced psychology than anything we find in other early medieval vernacular epic traditions. The inevitabilities attached to the treasure combine with actions to which the characters are driven to make the aesthetics of the *Nibelungenlied* more human and less stark than the dark and bitter beauty of the *Volsunga Saga*.

Old English Literature

Old English is both the smallest and the most diverse body of Germanic literature in its approaches to its constituent traditions. This literature dates from the seventh century, when the language was first committed to text, to the eleventh, when the Norman conquest of England (1066) brought more words with Latin roots into English and when the language began to be uninflected. The texts we have date mostly to the first three centuries of written Old English but a later date does not necessarily reflect change or development. Old English shares many linguistic and literary features with Old Norse and Old High German. As with these sister literatures, some works in its corpus were composed before the Great Vowel Shift and redacted later. Other family resemblances, in the epic branches of these literatures, are warriors with otherworldly connections who battle superhuman as well as human foes, the setting of epics in the age of migrations in which historical characters or events are joined by fictitious ones, a heavy reliance on fate as the motivator of action, the epic denial of suspense, and understatement, often expressed ironically. Other literary conventions that old English poetry shares with Old Norse and Old High German, regardless of genre, are a poetic line with a fixed number of stressed syllables divided by a caesura, the use of kennings, and a great dependence on alliteration, although with only incidental use of rhyme.

Old English also has qualities that distinguish it from other Germanic literatures, some reflecting Celtic or classical influences and some unique to it. Old English epic protagonists are extremely verbal and their speeches express character to a notable extent. Old English is the only early medieval vernacular literature in which characters, superhuman and human alike, are introspective and in which the author explores their inner thoughts, fears, and desires. But Old English characters are not drawn with as much psychological complexity as their Old Norse or Old High German counterparts. Accounts of their physical activities predominate in their delineation; they rarely face inner struggles or conflicts of loyalty. Female characters play less prominent roles in Old English epics. When present at all, they are introduced as hostesses welcoming guests and then recede into the background. The Old English poet is less interested than his Old Norse or Old High German compeer in describing the appearance, clothing, or moral traits of his characters.

But he pays far more attention to the natural setting, both landscape and seascape. While this focus on nature may bespeak classical or Celtic influence, or both, the interest in the sea is distinctive of Old English literature. Another trait possibly derived from the Celts is the use of run-on sentences and a delight in riddles, puns, and other plays on words. Among the classical devices found widely in Old English are the personification of inanimate objects which then express their feelings, and the idea that nature mirrors the speaker's mood or, conversely, contrasts ironically with it. When this latter motif is used, the poet sometimes invokes the classical *locus amoenus*, or pleasing place, a woodland glade with flowers, birds, and a babbling brook. The concept of the other world in Old English literature combines Christian eschatology with elements drawn from classical, Germanic, and Celtic paganism. The good other world, an island across the sea, is described frequently as a *locus amoenus* or in terms of the negative formula. The bad other world, which combines Nordic ice with the fire envisioned by authors from Mediterranean climates, also involves passage over or under water. The presence of someone or something otherworldly is sometimes signified by Celtic mist. The otherworldly beings encountered in middle-earth, the home of mankind, are the exclusively malevolent trolls, giants, and dragons of Germanic and Celtic paganism.

Before discussing the main canon of Old English literature it is worth noting that the Anglo-Saxons went farther than any other early medieval people in using the vernacular in public documents such as law codes, writs, wills, charters, treaties, and monastic chronicles as well as in vernacularizing Christian and classical texts. Bede's translation of the Bible has already been mentioned. Another major initiative was made by Alfred the Great, king of Wessex (849–99), through his personal example and patronage, which carried over into the tenth century. Alfred himself translated Boethius' *Consolation of Philosophy*, Augustine's *Soliloquies*, the *History against the Pagans* by Orosius (early fourth century), Bede's *Ecclesiastical History*, Gregory's *Pastoral Care*, and some of his *Dialogues*. He insisted that men working in his royal administration be literate at least in their native tongue. Aelfric (*c.* 955–1010/5) continued the project, translating sermons of Augustine, Jerome, Gregory, and Bede and Priscian's *Grammar* as well as writing his own vernacular sermons. The success of some Anglo-Saxon writers in synthesizing the Germanic, Christian, and classical traditions can be ascribed, in part, to the availability of classical and Christian materials in their own language. At the same time, some of the most thoroughgoing syntheses were made by Old English authors relying on Latin texts.

Leaving aside translations and minor works such as riddle poems, gnomic poems encapsulating generic nuggets of folk wisdom, and occasional didactic poems like the *Address of the Soul to the Body*, a dialogue in which the soul castigates the body for the sins that have landed them both in hell, the principal genres of Old English are epic and lyric poetry. Within each of these genres there are sub-sets defined by subject matter and sensibility.

Whether written or redacted earlier or later, Old English epics run the gamut from purely Germanic to synthetic. In the earliest epic known, *Widsith*, the eponymous speaker is a bard who tells of the princes he has known and of whom he has sung in his wanderings, from Persia to Greece to Israel to the courts of the Anglo-Saxon kings of the day. This survey clearly reflects the catalogue of heroes, classical, biblical, and current, with whom a bard needed to be conversant in exercising his craft. It is also an index of the range of the audience's interests. On the other hand, three later and fragmentary epics, the *Fight at Finnesburgh*, the *Battle of Maldon*, and the *Battle of Brunanburgh*, are purely Germanic battle poems commemorating historical clashes between human armies. They are forthright and sanguinary, focusing on the details of military action and the prowess and loyalty of the heroes. There is also an Old English version of the *Waltharius*, *Waldere*, which tells the same tale and which is unusual in this epic tradition for its interest in the protagonists' love story.

The most important Old English epic and the only one to survive in relative completeness is *Beowulf*, first redacted in *c*. 975/1025 although the action takes place centuries earlier. Comparable to a biography saga, it features a hero different from his Celtic opposite numbers. Far from being a child prodigy, Beowulf is a slow learner. But he matures into a great warrior and athlete, particularly good at swimming. Unlike those of heroes in other vernacular epics, his opponents are exclusively otherworldly, monsters who menace the human community. Beowulf's first exploit aids Hrothgar, king of the Danes, whose people are plagued by the monster Grendel and his mother. It is hard to say whether responsibility should be assigned to the author, the transmitters, or the redactor, but the epic makes a signal effort to reconceptualize these monsters, legacies from the pagan past, in Christian terms, presenting Grendel and his ilk as descendants of Cain and foes of God who bear His anger for their gratuitous attacks on mankind. Grendel and his mother live on a moor marked by cliffs surrounded by a Celtic mist. After besting Grendel, Beowulf must track his mother to a lake from which noxious vapors rise, swimming underwater for a full day without coming up for air, before he finds and overcomes her. The passage in *Beowulf* describing the Grendel homestead is rightly regarded as one of the finest scenic descriptions in Old English literature. It also fuses successfully elements drawn from the Bible, Celtic paganism, and the entry to the other world in *Aeneid*, Book 6. In the second half of the epic, Beowulf's chief antagonist is a fire-breathing dragon. Aside from these military exploits, he demonstrates his aquatic prowess by swimming from the mouth of the Rhine to Sweden without stopping, in a tempest and wearing multiple coats of chain mail, as well as in the episode with Grendel's mother. In the metaphysical background of *Beowulf* we certainly find Christianity. The poet or redactor chides Hrothgar for trying to exorcize Grendel and his mother by appealing to the pagan gods, a point indicating the perpetuation of that practice and the need that Christians felt to attack it. Both the characters and the Anglo-Saxons who composed and transmitted the epic firmly believe in the existence of trolls, giants, and dragons, however much they may be biblicized as heirs of Cain. In the event, fate outpaces any other force, metaphysical or moral, in propelling the epic's action.

Notwithstanding their references to Christian or pagan beliefs and despite the nature of the foes confronted by Beowulf, the epics just discussed can be viewed as essentially secular in their subject matter. Old English poets also wrote epics which, while thoroughly Germanic in literary conventions and attitudes, have an expressly Christian content. This sub-set of epic includes biblical rewrites and saints' lives that have Old High German parallels. They were written by Caedmon (*fl. c.* 675), Cynewulf (ninth century), and their followers up to the tenth century. Poets in both schools used earlier Latin Christian works, both patristic and Anglo-Saxon. The Cynewulfians are more learned and achieve a more thoroughgoing integration of Christian content and Germanic form, enhanced by Celtic and classical devices. The Caedmonians reflect a more conservative Germanic viewpoint.

The epics *Genesis, Exodus, Daniel, Christ and Satan*, and *Judith* were written by Caedmonians. Their choice of these biblical subjects and their treatment of them reflects the poets' desire to write about warfare, in tune with the military ethos of Germanic epic. The battle between the Israelites and Egyptians is the high point in *Exodus*. Christ leads an army against Satan to liberate mankind in *Christ and Satan*, and the protagonist of *Judith* is all but turned into a Valkyrie. The author of *Genesis* is so intent on recasting Satan's fall as the military rebellion of a rival warlord that he does not hesitate to depart from the biblical account. His Satan tempts Adam before Eve, a plausible idea for a commander recruiting troops. As with the authors of Old High German biblical rewrites of this type, the Caedmonians shift the scene, setting their epics amid the cliffs and moors of England and converting Palestinian deserts into heaths.

The Cynewulfians are far more successful in merging Christian content with Germanic form, showing that they have internalized Christianity and that they can draw on it as part of their mental and emotional equipment. The Cynewulfian biblical rewrites include *Christ, Doomsday*, and *The Fates of the Apostles*, subjects indicating an ability to appreciate non-martial events. *Christ* draws on the liturgy of Advent and on Gregory the Great's Ascension sermon as well as the Bible. It achieves dramatic force in the speeches of the Virgin Mary and St. Joseph expressing their feelings as they await Christ's birth, as well as in Christ's speeches, which present His sufferings and His love for mankind and which plead with His audience not to recrucify Him for its sins. *Doomsday* reflects a spiritual and not merely physical understanding of posthumous rewards and punishments and uses the negative formula in portraying heaven.

Among the saints' lives in the Cynewulfian school are *Andreas*, on St. Andrew the Apostle, *Juliana*, on an early Christian martyr, and *Elene*, on Helena, mother of Constantine, whose fame as a saint rests on her discovery of that relic of relics, the true cross. The *Elene* poet, revealing a careful study of Eusebius, recounts with epic realism the battle scene where Constantine's conversion occurs. The emperor then asks his mother to go to the Holy Land to seek the true cross. In the following passage, her expedition is launched in one of the most outstanding descriptions of seafaring in Old English literature. To be noted are the use of kennings, the reference to Anglo-Saxon noble titles and armor, the use of alliteration, and the overall literary qualities which the translation preserves:

> Then a host of eorls made haste to the shore;
> Sea-horses stood ready at the ocean's rim,

Bridled sea-stallions breasting the waves.
The lady's departure was plain to see
As she moved with her train to the tumbling breakers.
Many a stately man stood on the shore
Of the Wendel-sea. Swiftly they hurried
Over the border-paths, band after band.
They loaded the vessels with buckler and lance,
With men in byrnies, with battle-sarks,
With man and maid. O'er the sea-monster's home
They drove their foaming deep-flanked ships.
Oft on the waves the stout wood stood
The blow of the billows. The ocean roared.
Never learned I early or late
Of lady who led on the ocean-lanes
Fairer band o'er the path of the flood.
There he might see who beheld that sailing
Sea-wood scud under swelling sails,
Sea-steeds plunge and break through the billows,
Wave-ships skim. The warriors bold
Were blithe, and the queen had joy of the journey.[8]

On arrival, Helena completes her mission, the presence of the true cross on Golgotha indicated by a Celtic mist arising from the site. Altogether, *Elene*'s fine blend of Latin learning, Christian religious sentiment, Old English literary techniques and interests, and this Celtic grace-note make it an excellent example of Cynewulfian poetry.

The lyric subdivision of Old English literature is much smaller than the epic although it shares the same literary strategies, except for the use of a repeated refrain in some cases. Lyric poets, too, display a wide range of attitudes toward their materials. Most of these lyrics are written in a minor key, expressing loss, grief, or sadness. Sometimes the speaker's suffering is unrelieved. In other poems, speakers seek consolation by placing their woes in a larger philosophical or religious framework. The poems in which the speakers' suffering is the most intense and the most unredeemed are love lyrics bemoaning the pain of separation from the beloved. In *The Wife's Lament* and *The Husband's Message*, regarded as companion pieces, the wife laments the exile, or captivity, that separates her from her husband, ruing her loneliness and cursing her captors. The husband's response, an epistolary poem sent from afar, tries to reassure the wife by telling her that he will return to her when the cuckoo sings, this last motif a classical allusion to spring. The most passionate and elegiac lyric in this group is *Wulf and Eadwacer*. The speaker is a woman who is in love with Wulf but married to Eadwacer. Her ambivalent attitude toward her husband may be an evocation of the combination of love and hate that Catullus (*c.* 84–*c.* 54 BC) immortalizes in one of his odes. Another classicizing feature is the device of nature mirroring the speaker's mood:

I waited for Wulf with far-ranging desire,
When it was raining and I sat weeping.
When the warlike man wound his arms around me,
It was pleasure to me, but it was also pain.
O Wulf, my Wulf, my yearning for you
Has made me sick: You come so seldom
My heart is starved . . .[9]

In another group of lyrics the speakers move from their personal sorrow to a broader understanding of its meaning. *Deor's Lament* features a poet who has lost his lord's patronage. He laments the loss of livelihood and protection but then considers the fates of various heroic and mythical figures who also suffered. After each stanza the repeated refrain states that their sorrows passed away and so may his. The poet thus universalizes the speaker's dilemma, urging philosophical detachment; also, like the Psalmist, he is comforted by his singing. *The Wanderer* presents a different solution to a similar problem. Its speaker is also bereft of his lord's protection, alone and friendless. But, after stating his predicament, he moves directly to the theme of fate and divine providence, seeking consolation in the theological principle that all earthly events are controlled by higher powers and that security rests in God alone. Less philosophical or theological than vocational in contextualizing the speaker's lament, *The Seafarer* also reflects the Anglo-Saxon fascination with the sea. The speaker sadly describes the dangers and hardships of the sailor's lot. Yet, the same calling which the sea makes so hazardous draws him to it irresistibly.

In the lyrics just discussed, poets sometimes appeal to Christianity to assuage their speakers' woes and sometimes not, but there is a final sub-set of Old English lyrics whose Christian content is profoundly felt and eloquently expressed. The most superb example is *The Dream of the Rood*, a vision poem of great freshness and deep religious sensibility, written in a dramatic and pathos-ridden style. It achieves its effect through the device of personification. The poem opens with the speaker meditating before a large bejewelled cross. Then, the decorations fall away as he sees the crude, bloodstained cross on which Christ died. The cross now speaks, telling of how it was fashioned, how it bore the suffering Christ, and how it felt, thereby drawing inanimate nature into the crucifixion and making it a cosmic event:

'Long years ago (well yet I remember)
They hewed me down on the edge of the holt,
Severed my trunk; strong foemen took me,
For a spectacle wrought me, a gallows for rogues.
High on their shoulders they bore me to hilltop,
Fastened me firmly, an army of foes!
   'Then I saw the King of all mankind
In brave mood hasting to mount upon me.
Refuse I dared not, nor bow nor break,
Though I felt earth's confines shudder in fear;

All foes I might fell, yet still I stood fast . . .
Those sinners pierced me; the prints are clear,
The open wounds. I dared injure none.
They mocked us both. I was wet with blood
From the Hero's side when He sent forth His spirit.
    'Many a bale I bore on that hill–side
Seeing the Lord in agony outstretched.
Black darkness covered with clouds God's body,
That radiant splendour. Shadow went forth
Wan under heaven; all creation wept
Bewailing the King's death. Christ was on the cross.[10]

After the cross has spoken, the speaker tells of his sorrows, his old age, his loss of friends, his loneliness, his longing for death, and his hope that, through the cross of Christ he may abide in heaven with God and the saints. Thoroughly Germanic in its meter, its presentation of Christ as an epic hero staunchly accepting His fate, and in the understatement of the last line quoted, the poem's personification of the cross and its religious pathos combine to produce a lyric that is not only brilliantly realized but an original combination of the classical, Christian, and Germanic traditions. This poem, and others in Old English, are masterpieces of early medieval vernacular literature. They are also indices of how Latin Christian and vernacular cultures interacted in the formation of a new literary and religious sensibility in the medieval west, an interaction that distinguishes it from the literary and religious culture of the Christian east.

PART III
EARLY MEDIEVAL
CIVILIZATIONS COMPARED

CHAPTER 9

Imperial Culture: Byzantium

Originally the eastern part of the Roman empire with its capital in Constantinople, Byzantium could draw on Christianity, the classical tradition in Greek and Latin, and the cultures of its subject peoples and those who conquered Byzantine terrain and entered its ecclesiastical fold. The single most important factor accounting for the unique uses which Byzantium made of these resources is the unbroken continuity of central imperial rule. Although from the seventh century onwards the Byzantine empire underwent administrative reforms designed to facilitate taxation and military recruitment at the local level, reforms with a decentralizing potential politically, its intellectual leadership came increasingly from the capital and the imperial court, which determined the character of cultural patronage. Habituated to directives and funding from above, Byzantine thinkers developed a mindset that precluded the establishment of autonomous institutions for the creation and dissemination of ideas independent of imperial policy. The ups and downs of Byzantine cultural life parallel the court's decision to support it or not. When military priorities were uppermost, emperors diverted funds to defense and severely undercut intellectual activity.

A second feature of Byzantine intellectual history differentiating it sharply from the west is the lack of interplay among the languages used in the empire. Demotic Greek was spoken by everyone, including subject peoples with other mother tongues, as the language of everyday life. In the early Byzantine centuries, emperors continued the policy of supporting at public expense the liberal arts as they had been taught in ancient Rome, with a rhetorical emphasis, in Latin and Greek. A significant number of Byzantines attained literacy thanks to the public school system. After the sixth century, the government cut back funding for primary and secondary education. Those who sought it had to pay private teachers, reducing the number of Byzantines able to participate in elite culture. At the same time, instruction in Latin waned and fewer Byzantines knew it except for students in the imperial law schools. Formal education increasingly centered on the canonical Attic Greek authors. The tiny class of mandarins who could read and write Attic Greek had no interest in updating it and making it a living language, as Latin remained in the medieval west. Nor did they draw on the languages and literatures of non-Greek-speakers in the empire: they displayed the ancient Greek prejudice that they were barbarians from whom there was nothing to learn. The producers and consumers of elite culture did not use demotic Greek either, except in technological treatises for which the lexicon of Periclean Athens was useless. Literature in vernacular Greek was late in developing. Thus, even within the ranks of Greek-speakers, a gulf soon opened between the few users of Attic Greek and other Byzantines, less elaborately educated, to whom that language gradually grew more incomprehensible. Far from seeking to expand the availability of Attic Greek culture, the intellectual leaders restricted it to themselves, shielding themselves from other influences, and used it, as a definition of their own cultural identity, to create the illusion of stability and continuity with the classical past in the face of Byzantium's losses to her enemies and her internal tensions. In defining themselves in terms of the Attic Greek canon, elite writers also privileged the least innovative aspect of the classical tradition: the veneration of past models and the belief that they could not be improved on or criticized. Isolated in other respects from the masses, their major bond with other Byzantines was the cult of saints, their relics, and their icons. But even here, intellectual, literary, and artistic standardization reflected the imperatives of high culture and its aristocratic and imperial patrons.

The issue of language also presents a striking difference between Byzantium and western Europe in relation to the Christianization of invaders who occupied imperial lands or those adjacent to them. Aside from the fact that the Byzantine missions were always initiated and directed from the capital, the missionaries saw their role exclusively as bearing the gospel to the peoples to whom they were sent and not as purveying the liberal arts as well. They recognized the fact that some of their new converts were not native Greek-speakers and translated the Bible and the liturgy into languages spoken in the Near Eastern part of the empire, such as Syriac, Coptic, Armenian, and Georgian. Since the Christians in these churches later split with the orthodox church on doctrinal issues or were conquered by the Muslims, this translation policy was ultimately less important than the missionaries' linguistic policy toward the Slavic peoples who conquered the Balkans or who bordered the empire to the north. What they did was to invent an artificial language, Old Church Slavonic, when they began to evangelize the Slavs in the late ninth century. This language was designed to be generically Slavonic and to make the Bible and the liturgy comprehensible to any Slav. But, while providing an alphabet permitting the redaction of Slavic vernaculars, it was not identical with any spoken Slavic language. In this sense, the use of Old Church Slavonic as the language of prayer and catechesis is not comparable to the use of Old English or Old High German for those purposes in the west. Clerics who wrote in Old Church Slavonic showed little interest in drawing on the literary traditions of the spoken Slavic languages. They also made Slavophones in their daughter churches dependent on translations of classical Greek and Greek Christian works into Slavonic. The clergy had little enthusiasm for translating these materials. Few people in these Christianized Slavic societies learned Greek, so their evangelization did not give them simultaneous access to classical and patristic Greek works. And the static, artificial language in which they prayed grew increasingly remote from the developing languages they spoke. What seems at first to have been a bold venture at conveying the Christian message in the vernacular, then, ended by barring the Slavic daughter churches of Byzantium from the more speculative side of its Greek Christian tradition.

One of the major reasons why missionaries did not bring the liberal arts along with the Bible and the liturgy is that the church, and monasticism, played a different social, political, and intellectual role in Byzantium than they did in the west. Since education in the liberal arts remained available through teachers who were laymen, whether state supported or directly paid by students, churchmen never saw the task of liberal education as devolving on them. Imperial patronage of higher education, starting in the mid-eleventh century, focused on law and philosophy. Theology never became a university discipline in which intellectual jockeying with colleagues in other fields was a normal educational process. Bishops ran seminaries for the theological training of the clergy. Monasteries educated their own members, and those who sought them out, in basic doctrine and the art of prayer. Parish priests catechized their flocks. Thus, although the Greek apologists and church fathers, all thoroughly educated in classical rhetoric and philosophy, recast theology in classical form with no difficulty, a separation between secular and religious thought, carried out by laymen and clerics respectively, developed in the post-patristic period, along with the polarization of the Atticism that defined elite culture and the Christianity of clerical and popular culture.

The institutional as well as the educational context in which Byzantine monks and secular clerics operated also affected their cultural roles. Monasticism was a vibrant aspect of church life in eastern Christendom. Whether in Basilian communities or in hermitages, it accented austerity and contemplation. Hagiographers praised monks who scorned book-learning as worldly and irrelevant, beyond the Bible and the liturgy. The charismatic, the ascetic, the mystic, and the holy fool were seen as better exemplars of the monastic ideal than the scholar-monk of the west. And, while ecclesiastical corporations in the early medieval west were absorbed into feudal and manorial institutions, giving them significant political and economic functions, the localization of fiscal and military institutions in Byzantium did not have an analogous effect on the church there. Clerics were exempted from the fiscal and military responsibilities of lay people. Monasteries flourished on a highly individual basis, often loosely knit into the social fabric and unconnected with each other or with the bishops in whose sees they were located. Bishops themselves were under the control of the emperor. This arrangement, inherited from the church in the Roman empire, developed into Caesaropapism by the sixth century. In this system, the emperor appointed, transferred, and dismissed bishops. He supervised the legal and fiscal side of church life and its social welfare agencies. He called and presided over church councils and gave their decisions the force of law. He enforced orthodoxy, determining which doctrines were acceptable, the forms of liturgical prayer, and ecclesiastical policy more generally, irrespective of what the clergy thought. The larger importance of more than one doctrinal controversy in Byzantium is its demonstration of the power of the emperors, rather than that of the bishops, theologians, and church councils, to choose the directions taken by the Byzantine church.

The fact that neither monks nor bishops were encouraged by the structure of the Byzantine church to accent the administrative or the practical helps to account for the emphasis on the speculative and the mystical in their theology. This fact is well illustrated by the Greek apologists and church fathers and by other Christian intellectuals to the end of the sixth century. Altogether, the Greek apologists have more in common with Minucius Felix than with any of their other Latin opposite numbers. Like him, they reflect an enthusiasm for classical rhetoric and the view that pagan philosophy has much in common with Christian revelation. Unlike Minucius, however, they do not confine themselves to refuting Skepticism or allegations of Christian misbehavior. Rather, they focus squarely on the metaphysical and moral teachings of the philosophies they find compatible with Christianity. It is also true that Origen points out a significant difference between the philosophical mentality and Christianity. As he notes, the first causes of the philosophers are, as with the Stoics, reducible to the laws of nature or, as with the Platonists, creative by emanation out of the necessity of their own nature. By contrast, the Christian God is a personal being Who creates freely. While Origen's point is well taken, and while it reflects a sense of the limits of the philosophical enterprise analogous to Tertullian's, Origen's critics thought he had erred by using too much philosophy in his theology, not too little.

The Age of the Church Fathers

The careers and writings of the four theologians regarded as fathers of the Greek church indicate the availability and the appeal to Christians of high-quality instruction in the liberal arts and philosophy, the draw of monasticism, and the fact that men with speculative minds rather than administrative ability were seen as prime candidates for high ecclesiastical office in the fourth century. All four came from wealthy and distinguished families and received a thorough classical education. All found ways of re-expressing Christian theology in classical terms that were fresh, creative, and influential. All would have found Tertullian's 'What has Athens to do with Jerusalem?' absurd, Jerome's Ciceronian dream peculiar, and the need to justify the classics to Christian scholars pointless. Three of the Greek fathers came from Cappadocia, whose major city was Caesarea. The fourth came from Antioch.

We have met two of the Greek fathers before in the context of western intellectual history, the brothers Basil the Great and Gregory of Nyssa. As noted, Basil's major monastic *Rule* was adopted widely in eastern Christendom and he was the first Christian author of a creation account in his *Hexaemeron* that follows the opening chapters of Genesis. After an interlude as a monk and monastic reformer, Basil was ordained a priest and became bishop of Caesarea in 370. As a bishop he energetically combated heresy and schism, writing anti-Arian polemics, biblical exegesis, sermons, letters, works of consolation and advice, and a liturgy. In all these writings he reflects the position on the relationship between the classics and Christianity that he summarizes in his *Admonitions to Young Men on the Profitable Use of*

Pagan Literature. This work bears comparison with Augustine's *On Christian Doctrine*. While Basil agrees that pagan errors should be rejected, he offers a far more positive assessment of the classics than Augustine, seeing them as valuable for their own sake. Literary study enables us to form our aesthetic sensibility. Philosophy is valuable for the ethical wisdom it imparts. For Basil, there is more to be gained from these studies than mere information and techniques that can be applied to biblical exegesis and preaching. Basil's view on this matter was seconded by the other Greek fathers.

Gregory of Nyssa, Basil's brother, who also lived for a time as a monk until called to the see of Nyssa in 371, was the most outstanding speculative thinker among the Greek fathers. His original combination of Greek philosophy and Christian doctrine draws independently on the Neoplatonic, Stoic, and Aristotelian traditions. He wrote the obligatory polemics against heresy and paganism, orations and sermons, personal letters, and works on ascetic moral themes. But his most important writings fall under two headings, systematic philosophical theology and mystical theology. The fact that he produced works of both types indicates his view that we can attain a knowledge of God both through rational study of the natural world, which reflects its creator, and through suprarational mystical experience.

In the first category of philosophical theology we can place Gregory's *Hexaemeron* and *On the Creation of Man*. He follows Basil's model in the *Hexaemeron*. While he draws most heavily on Neoplatonism, he also calls on other schools and on consensus positions in Greek natural philosophy, such as the existence of four prime material elements, earth, water, air, and fire. In Gregory's creation account, God gives each being in the universe its matter, made up of these elements, along with its powers, its intelligible essence, and its capacity to serve as a cause in its own right. Since all beings have an intelligible aspect, the natural world, for Gregory, is intrinsically knowable by the human mind. Calling on a metaphor used by both Neoplatonists and Stoics and giving it a Stoic turn, Gregory sees light, in the sense of creative fire, as the medium through which God creates. After creating the universe, the deity withdraws into a heaven which is material, although made of highly rarefied matter akin to fire. Gregory also holds that God creates purely spiritual beings analogous to Plato's archetypes.

Gregory gives more detailed attention to human nature in *On the Creation of Man*. We are created, he begins, in God's image, visible mainly in the human soul, which, like God, has free will, is granted rulership over creation, and has a capacity for beatitude. Despite this stress on the human soul, Gregory does not identify human nature with the soul or define human nature as a soul using a body, as do many Platonizing theologians. Rather, he follows Aristotle in defining human nature as an integral union of body and soul. This hylemorphic constitution is what gives us our distinctive place in the creation, at the crossroads of the material and spiritual orders which we unite in our own being. At the same time, the psychological operations that distinguish us from the subhuman world display the interaction of body and soul. Gregory analyzes three such faculties. The first, called the flesh, is the faculty that leads us to pursue sinful pleasures. The body contributes heavily to this faculty. But so does the mind: sin is the conscious decision of the will to capitulate to temptation. For Gregory, as for the Stoics, this is an intellectual choice. The second faculty, called intellect or soul, enables us to acquire rational knowledge. The mind is heavily involved here. But so too is the body, since we depend on sense data as sources of knowledge. Finally there is spirit, the faculty that makes possible the moral life, whose positive exercise is rewarded with beatitude. The function of this faculty involves the mind making moral choices. But it also requires the collaboration of our infrarational emotions. Aside from this integration of mind, heart, and body in our makeup and psychological operations, Gregory's anthropology stresses another theme. We have obscured the image of God in our souls through original sin. None the less, he argues, we can initiate positive action in turning away from sin on the basis of the moral and intellectual capacities that remain in fallen humanity. In sharp contrast with the anti-Pelagian Augustine, Gregory thinks that sinful mankind can take the first step back to God on its own. His view of the relations between divine grace and human effort in salvation is altogether more synergistic and less territorial than Augustine's. Gregory here articulates a position that became standard in Byzantine theology.

Gregory of Nyssa devotes two treatises to his mystical theology, using a biblical source as his point of departure in each case. In his *Life of Moses* he treats that patriarch's biography as an allegorical account of the mystic's progress to the vision of God. Gregory's *Commentary on the Song of Songs* draws on Origen's interpretation of that book of the Bible as an allegory of the soul's intimate love of God. Gregory adds his own twist to this doctrine. In his view, the mystic must begin by practicing the virtues of faith and charity, mobilizing the intellectual and affective sides of the personality. Moral self-discipline, love of one's fellow man, and the acquisition of self-knowledge are required to purify the image of God in the soul. Then, from the self, the mystic mounts up to God. This functional interaction of love and knowledge and the stress on introspection as the way to the mystical union reflect a pattern similar to Augustine's spirituality. The translation of Gregory's works into Latin in the ninth century, along with the still earlier translation of Basil's *Rule* and the adaptation of his *Hexaemeron* by Ambrose, made them the Greek fathers best known to Latin readers in the medieval west before the twelfth century.

The third Cappadocian, Gregory Nazianzus (*c.* 329/30–90), was a friend of Gregory of Nyssa and Basil, whom he met while completing his education at Athens. He shared their taste for monasticism, writing his *Apology* to justify his flight to the desert in disobedience of his father's wishes. He, too, became a bishop, elected although not consecrated to the see of Sasima and patriarch of Constantinople (379–81). Gregory never seems to have made his peace with the forced abandonment of his monastic lifestyle. As a result, he could be hypersensitive, nervous, and irritable. Gregory's writings, all very solid doctrinally, reflect his thorough philosophical education, but his theology is bound more closely to the biblical text than Gregory of Nyssa's and he sees less need to recast it in philosophical terms. More than philosophy, rhetoric was the air he breathed. In a field heavily populated by superlative orators, Gregory won the palm as the most eloquent preacher in the fourth-century Greek world, unrivalled for the beauty of his style and his literary breadth. His nickname, 'the Christian Demosthenes,' bespeaks the appreciation of his contemporaries. Among his works are letters and personal documents such as his *Apology* and a versified autobiography as well as other religious verses treating theological and devotional themes. Chief among his writings are his forty-five *Orations* devoted to oratory of all kinds, from the homiletic to the exegetical to the topical.

The Antiochene church father, John Chrysostom (344/54–407), bears close comparison with both Gregory Nazianzus and Gregory of Nyssa. As with the former, his greatest contribution lies in his sermons and, like the latter, he was dragooned into high ecclesiastical office, being made patriarch of Constantinople in 398. His administrative ineptitude and the antagonism he aroused in other clerics inspired the emperor to banish him from the capital for a spell for fear of his life. John's real legacy lies in the sermons he preached in the church of Antioch between 386 and 398, after ill health forced him to give up the monastic life. The pulpit eloquence that won him his cognomen, which means 'golden mouth,' reflects his thorough classical education and the literal approach to biblical exegesis favored in Antioch. Most of John's sermons work systematically through whole books of the Bible, covering Genesis, the Psalms, Isaiah, the Gospels of Luke, Matthew, and John, and the Pauline Epistles. He felt a particular affinity with St. Paul. John's sermons are marked by profundity of content, beauty of form, and effective rhetorical presentation. Although he sometimes spoke for two hours at a time, he kept his congregation spellbound by his imagery, his parables, and his apt references to current events. He accents both personal holiness and social ethics, frequently depicting with pathos and vividness the sufferings of the poor and contrasting them with the senseless luxury of the rich, as he seeks to instill a spirit of charity and social responsibility in his hearers. The hundreds of sermons left by John are his major testament; although another enduring contribution is the liturgy he composed, used widely in eastern Christendom.

Individually and collectively, the church fathers reflect the ease with which theologians highly educated in the liberal arts and philosophy in this period put their education to use. Other Byzantine thinkers of the time were equally eager to conceptualize their Christianity in classical terms. This tendency can be seen in the rich store of Greek Christian prose and poetry written in a classicizing style and in the thought of the period's leading philosopher, Dionysius the Pseudo–Areopagite, whom we met earlier as a source translated and used by John Scottus. In his native context, he is important for his dependence on Proclus, his authority for the view of God as the superessential One beyond being that sets the stage for the semantic theory and epistemology he develops in *On the Divine Names* and *On Mystical Theology*. In the first treatise, he develops the negative theology which he puts into practice in the second. *On Mystical Theology* is structured as a series of negations, and then negations of the negations, designed to show that God transcends both affirmation and negation, and that He can be known directly in this life only by mystical union, albeit briefly and intermittently. The Psuedo-Areopagite outlines three stages in the mystic's itinerary, derived directly from Proclus: purgation, illumination, and union. Purgation involves moral self-discipline, the removal of vices, and the cultivation of virtues, in a mode more ascetic than Gregory of Nyssa's program. The Pseudo-Areopagite shares Gregory's view that Christians can take the first step in disposing themselves toward God through self-improvement. In the illuminative stage, God progressively enlightens the mystic; here the action of divine grace is expressed in terms of Neoplatonic light imagery. Finally, there is mystic union, transitory, but a foretaste of the soul's eternal communion with God in heaven. This three-stage model was widely followed by contemplatives in both eastern and western churches.

Since the first two Dionysian treatises conclude that we can know and say very little about God directly unless we are mystics, the *Celestial Hierarchy* and *Ecclesiastical Hierarchy* turn to our indirect knowledge of God through the creation and the ministry of the church. In both treatises the Pseudo-Areopagite invokes the emanationist, participatory, and hierarchical cosmology of Neoplatonism. A chain of being emanates from God, descending from spiritual beings to human beings to the subhuman world. Angels, in nine ranks divided into sub-sets of three analogized to union, illumination, and purgation, receive detailed analysis. As a cosmologist, the Pseudo-Areopagite is concerned with how creatures are related metaphysically to each other, and to God, and how the human soul can use them to return to its maker. He is not interested in how the world system or the creatures in it function scientifically. When it comes to human nature, he departs from Gregory of Nyssa's hylemorphic anthropology in favor of the Platonic view that the soul is our prime identity; although, with the Neoplatonists, he thinks that the material chain of being can be used, if ultimately transcended, as our ladder of ascent to God.

Aside from a cosmogenesis and anthropology that depart from those of the Bible, there are other points in the *Celestial Hierarchy* that some Christian readers found problematic. One, a feature of Neoplatonizing theologies noted early by Origen, is that the Pseudo-Areopagite's emanationist cosmology makes creation necessary to the creator and deprives Him of freedom. Another is his understanding of evil as non-being. Two difficulties flow from this theory. One is that it effectively removes free will from spiritual beings as moral agents, since a being's goodness is a function of its fixed location in the chain of being. It is instructive to note in this connection that the Pseudo-Areopagite's elaborate angelology omits the topic of fallen angels and where they fit into the scheme of things. Second, as Augustine had noted, we may be able to conceptualize evil as the privation of good but it remains a datum of our psychological experience. A final difficulty readers found with the *Celestial Hierarchy* is the absence of Christ, whether as the archetype of the creation or as the means of our return to God. Despite these problems, the Pseudo-Areopagite remained the most influential Byzantine philosopher, east and west.

Another approach to the return to God, and one less fraught with difficulties, is offered in the *Ecclesiastical Hierarchy*. Here, in outlining the grades of holy orders, the sacramental ministry of the church, and the uses of religious music and art, the Pseudo-Areopagite presents clerics as participating in Christ's own ministry and as extending it to the laity. He treats both the sacraments and religious music and art as vehicles of grace through which believers, by using their physical senses, can make contact with spiritual reality. This doctrine, which offers a firm philosophical rationale for these devotions, make this treatise more than a pendant to the *Celestial Hierarchy*.

While the Pseudo–Areopagite could thus adduce Neoplatonic support both for Christian mysticism and for the religious practices of ordinary believers, in some areas his philosophy could be seen as deforming as well as informing Christian theology. The fear that philosophy would lead Christians astray, an apologetic commonplace, resurfaced in Byzantium in the patristic period and after. For, despite the constructive use of philosophy by the church fathers and some later thinkers, its use by heretics opened a wedge between philosophy and orthodox theology that eventually set Byzantine Christianity on a course quite different from that of western Christianity. Between the fourth and seventh centuries, the eastern church remained beset by speculative Christological heresies that drew on philosophy to frame their doctrines. The most important is Monophysitism and its offshoots, which drew many followers. The Monophysites understood the co-inherence of the divine and human natures of the incarnate Christ in terms of Aristotle's doctrine of substance. In Aristotle's view, all creatures are substances that are composites of matter and form. The matter is the particular mix of the four elements in the creature's makeup and the form is the creature's principle of individuation and its intelligible aspect. If we regard Christ as a substance, His matter is clearly His human body. In the case of other human beings, their souls are their forms. But, the Monophysites argued, Christ's form is His divine nature. Orthodox Christians rejected this conclusion. For, in denying that Christ had a human soul, the Monophysites denied that He was fully human. The council of Chalcedon (451) ruled Monophysitism heretical but conciliar action and polemical theology failed to crush it, largely for political reasons. During the next two centuries, emperors often took a soft line on the Monophysites, most of whom lived in the Near East. Locked in an age-old war with Persia, the emperors wanted to avoid alienating subjects in that region. Another factor was the resistance of the patriarchs of Jerusalem, Alexandria, and Antioch to the simultaneous effort of the emperors to subject them to the patriarch of Constantinople. In the seventh century, Monothelite Christology arose as a would-be compromise doctrine. The Monothelites agreed with the orthodox that Christ had a fully human nature. But they held that He had a single will, a divine one. This position was also judged heretical and anathematized by councils in Rome (649) and Constantinople (680–1). In the end it was not conciliar decrees or imperial policy that resolved the problem, but the Muslim conquest of the Near East in the seventh century. The Monophysite and Monothelite churches were removed from Byzantine control and their members either maintained their own Christologies under Muslim protection or converted to Islam.

The Age of Justinian

It is not only the history of heresy but intellectual life more generally that reflects the increasing politicization of Byzantine culture after the age of the church fathers.

This is certainly the case during the reign of Justinian (*c.* 482–565), regarded as a golden age because of both the quality and the quantity of the work it produced. The imperial court now made the decisions on which fields of culture to support. The consensus at court was that the church fathers could not be improved on and speculative theology and philosophy received no official patronage. Indeed, Justinian closed the schools of philosophy in Athens in 529. Nor was scientific thought of great interest. John Philponius (d. *c.* 570) commented on several of Aristotle's works in natural philosophy and thought he had erred in distinguishing matter and motion in the sublunar and supralunar worlds, on the local motion of bodies on earth, and on the eternity of the universe. But these criticisms did not inspire a general re-evaluation of Aristotelian science. Instead, it was Atticizing prose and poetry and liturgical verse and music that flourished during Justinian's reign. The latter art forms were quite innovative. Liturgical musicians rejected the ancient Greek musical modes and invented new modes of their own along with a sophisticated system of musical notation indicating the phrasing and dynamics the composer wanted. Liturgical verse adopted a rhythmic meter remote from classical metrics, reflecting the sound patterns of the Psalms and the prophetic books of the Septuagint, the Greek translation of the Old Testament, and the liturgical chants of Jewish converts to Christianity in Palestine and Syria. Other major areas of imperial patronage were law and art.

Justinian ordered the fullest and most influential compilation of Roman law in history, the *Corpus of Civil Law*. It is divided into four parts. In the *Code*, his editors screened the laws of his predecessors and codified those he wished to keep, providing a historical conspectus of Roman law as well as an expression of the emperor's authority to decide unilaterally which laws remained in force. The *Novels* codify Justinian's own legislation and also show the emperor as the sole source of law. Together, these two sections of the *Corpus* illustrate Justinian's administrative priorities as well as the growing autocracy of Byzantine government. The *Institutes* and the *Digest* were designed to shape legal education and jurisprudence. The *Institutes* presents current law organized topically, as it pertains to things, persons, and actions. The *Digest* uses the same scheme. In each section, Justinian's editors collected those opinions of the jurisconsults across the ages that the emperor wanted to preserve. After the *Digest* was completed, he ordered the destruction of the original texts to prevent criticism of the interpretive agenda reflected in his editors' choices. This *Corpus* was to exert a massive influence on law and political theory in Byzantium and also in western Europe after its rediscovery in Bologna in the eleventh century.

The patronage of art also bears a decidedly imperial stamp in the age of Justinian, reflecting his control and support of the church and his use of art and architecture to give visual expression to his theology and political theory. One of Justinian's main goals was the reconquest of the former Roman empire in the west. His general, Belisarius, did manage to retake parts of north Africa and southern Italy. Most of these conquests, later lost to the Muslims, were impossible for the Byzantines to retain in the face of the military pressure of Slavs, Avars, and Persians closer to home. But the Byzantines managed to maintain an ecclesiastical presence in Italy for some centuries, with an exarchate in Ravenna. As a statement of the Caesaropapism rejected by the western church, Justinian rebuilt S. Vitale at Ravenna. Its iconographic program combines a statement of imperial patronage with one of divine right. In the apse dome, Christ enthroned accepts a model of the church and blesses its patron saint. Directly below, Justinian appears, accompanied by courtiers and the current archbishop, as Christ's vicar on earth, presenting gifts to the church in the vessel used to offer the Eucharistic bread at mass, thus also symbolically participating in the church's liturgy (Plate 8). Another classic example of Justinianic art is Haghia Sophia, the imperial cathedral in Constantinople (Plates 9 and 10). A fire that destroyed much of the city center in 532 enabled the emperor to reorganize civic space and to connect the palace to the cathedral with a broad boulevard that facilitated processions and other imperial ceremonies. Haghia Sophia is a much more complex and innovative building than S. Vitale, involving a Greek cross with four arms of equal length on which a series of domes and semi-domes is superimposed. An intricate use of light at different levels of the building suggests that it has been poured down from above, creating a heavenly environment in which light, as a symbol of the deity, irradiates and articulates its parts. Also prominent at Haghia Sophia is an imperial gallery where the court sat while attending services, adequate space for processions and coronations, and an iconographic scheme that, in addition to presenting central mysteries of the Christian faith in an awesome, majestic, and timeless manner, underscores imperial activities such as the dispensing of alms.

From the Seventh Century to the Early Comnenian Age

The dominance of Byzantine intellectual life by imperial patronage is visible not only in the age of Justinian but even more strikingly in the next two centuries, when the fiscal demands of fighting, and losing, wars on all fronts inspired the emperors to replace civilians with military men at the court, the chief producer and consumer of elite culture. Constant warfare also engendered the cult of warrior-saints and their icons, including the conversion of the Virgin Mary into a warrior-maiden thought to have saved Constantinople from the Avars in 626. Then, in the ninth century, after the empire had stabilized its shrunken borders and had reorganized what remained so as to exploit its reduced tax base effectively, another period of flowering emerged under imperial control, which continued until the Seljuk Turks posed a military threat so acute that the emperors appealed to the west for help. The response to that appeal, the Crusades, weakened Byzantium so decisively after the early thirteenth century that her eventual conquest by the Ottoman Turks in 1453 was entirely predictable.

During the period of intellectual decline between the seventh and ninth centuries, cultural production of all kinds shrank, indicating that Byzantine scholars and writers had not found ways of carrying on their activities by means of grassroots organizations. The fact that Byzantium was now on the defensive can be seen in the work of the only notable speculative thinkers of the time, Maximus the

Confessor and John of Damascus (*c.* 675–*c.* 750) and in the major debate of the period, the iconoclastic controversy. All three manifest a mood of retrenchment and of heightened Caesaropapism in one way or another.

Although Maximus began his career as secretary to the emperor, he saw his main task as defending orthodoxy in north Africa and Italy against the latest stage of post-Monophysite Christology, Monoergism. The Monoergists agreed with the orthodox that Christ had a fully human body, soul, and will, but asserted that He had a single energy, a divine one. In attacking this doctrine and all earlier Christologies that limited Christ's humanity in any respect, Maximus draws on Origen, Gregory Nazianzus, and the Pseudo-Areopagite purged of his questionable views. Maximus expresses both a thoroughly orthodox theology and the idea that synthesizing the teachings of his predecessors rather than developing new arguments defines the theologian's role. In 648, the emperor issued an edict banning further discussion of the will, or energy, of Christ. Maximus, then in Italy, was arrested by the exarch in Ravenna in 662 for continuing to defend orthodox Christology. He was condemned and silenced, although his position was later vindicated.

As for John, his toponym indicates that he did not live in Byzantine territory and his work shows that no one there felt the imperative he did to defend Christianity against Islam. As with Maximus, he draws on previous patristic thought, especially Gregory Nazianzus. He focuses on the Trinity and Christology, the chief Christian doctrines rejected by the Muslims. John also wrote a history of heresy and studied philosophy, emphasizing Aristotelian logic. He was one of the greatest hymnographers in Byzantine history, to the point where liturgical poets and musicians after his time felt that there was nothing more to say. The leading speculative mind writing in Greek in his century, John illustrates even more clearly than Maximus the fact that the enterprises he was engaged in were not receiving imperial support, despite the authority and esteem they were later granted.

John also opposed iconoclasm, the major controversy of the period. In understanding its seriousness to Byzantines, several points need to be kept in mind. First, from an early date, religious art had been central to the devotional lives of Byzantine Christians. More recently, the rationale for its function provided by the Pseudo-Areopagite, the veneration of miraculous icons invoked in times of crisis, and changes in the liturgy and in church architecture had heightened its appeal. At issue in the last case was the erection of a screen decorated with icons separating the congregation from the celebrant. The decline of preaching or its recasting into an Attic Greek meaningless to the congregation led worshippers to relate to the sacred mysteries primarily through visual images and music. Another issue was the place of monasticism in Byzantine society. Many monasteries had acquired extensive land and wealth in an age when emperors, faced with territorial losses, demographic decline, and a shrinking tax base combined with relentless military needs, eyed these riches and sought to integrate monks and nuns into the civil society they controlled. Monasteries were also great repositories of icons. Finally, like John of Damascus, the Near Eastern patriarchs defended icons because they were living under Muslim rulers who regarded figural art as idolatry. These were the same patriarchates that had objected to the emperors' centralizing of the Byzantine church at their expense.

Launched in the mid-eighth century, the debate over icons drew theologians on both sides, but its dynamics were controlled by imperial policy, which was often iconoclastic. At the council of Nicaea (787), the iconodule or pro-icon theologians won over the iconoclasts on the basis of the rationale for religious art developed by earlier Byzantine thinkers. They also agreed on clear norms for the portrayal of Christ and the saints, especially in church decoration, with particular parts of the building assigned to particular personages, presented in three-quarter or frontal view and accompanied by standard iconographic accoutrements and inscriptions. These norms affected Byzantine pictorial art for the rest of its history. But, despite the theological resolution of the conflict, the presence of iconoclast rulers on the throne after 787 prolonged it and continued the destruction of religious art objects, whose production was interdicted. The ending of the controversy in 843 and the reinvigoration of religious art in Byzantium are results of the fact that the ruler at the time was an iconodule who decided when, and how, it would end. The entire course of the debate, and its outcome, illustrate both the ingrained devotion to icons, which could not be uprooted, and the emperors' strong grip on the church.

While officially sponsored Atticizing literature waned between the seventh and ninth centuries, this period produced the first surviving example of popular literature in Byzantium, the epic *Barlaam and Josaphat*. Its chief interest, outside of its very existence, is that one of its characters is Buddha, suggesting that Byzantium's breaking of ties with the west and closing in on herself was combined with an opening to the east. Borrowings from the Muslims noticeable in this period include the use of prayer rugs, the wearing of turbans by men, the sequestering of women in their own domestic quarters, and their veiling in public. More centrally, the imperial court increasingly adopted an etiquette reflecting a fusion of oriental despotism with the imperial autocracy derived from ancient Rome.

A new imperial dynasty, the Macedonians, inaugurated a new golden age in the ninth and tenth centuries, during which Byzantine intellectual history took the form it was to retain, for the most part, for the rest of its history. With the exception of local styles of art, the keynote of intellectual activity was its response to imperial directives and the fact that what was wanted by the patrons was the summation of work already done rather than innovation. There are important exceptions to this rule. In law, changes in local government and in the norms governing marriage added new legislation to the books and new topics for jurisprudential discussion. In art, the ninth century displayed a classicizing taste that can be contrasted with both earlier and later transcendental and non-narrative art in that figures were presented three-dimensionally and naturalistically in relation to landscapes or architectural settings. There is also evidence of some scientific and technological developments. In medicine, autopsies were used both to teach anatomy and to ascertain causes of death. Grudgingly, but eventually, Byzantine mathematicians accepted algebra and Arabic numerals, but not the concept of zero, from the Muslims. They also adopted the Muslims' astronomy and, like them, applied mathematics to it. Greek fire, or naphtha, a flammable liquid that floats on water, was developed as an adjunct to naval warfare. Leo the Philosopher (*c.* 790–869) invented beacon lights as an early warning system alerting commanders to the arrival of enemies and new siegecraft emerged both in terms of tactics and technology. But, these areas aside, the trend prevailing from the ninth century to the eleventh, when the Macedonians were replaced by the Comnenians, was to consolidate what was already known, to discourage creativity, and to encourage the production of encyclopedias and standard reference works in all fields of endeavor.

A figure well illustrating this turn is Photius (*c.* 819–93), patriarch of Constantinople, civil servant, controversialist with the Carolingians, and his century's leading classicist. His chief work, the *Myriobiblion*, is an encyclopedia summarizing over 300 works of ancient Greek literature in every genre except poetry. It displays learning and wide reading but no original insight into the authors presented. Similar are two tenth-century classical literary summations, the compendium of Emperor Constantine VII (913–59) and the anonymous *Souda* produced later in the century. Constantine's encyclopedia is vast, ranging over an enormous number of types of ancient literature. The *Souda* proved to be more popular, if that is not a misnomer given the very small number of people conversant with Attic Greek. In comparing the two compendia, one can see why they preferred the *Souda*: it confines itself exclusively to canonical authors in the school tradition and includes a lexicon of Attic Greek helpful to those studying it. Among readers interested in the ancient literary heritage, then, the choice of the *Souda* shows the narrowness of their literary taste. Compendia of the same type, collecting works deemed canonical in science, philosophy, liturgical music, and hymnography were also produced, likewise conveying the message that the task of culture is to venerate past models, not to depart from them. Earlier hagiographies catering to demotic tastes were rewritten in Attic Greek. It is striking that the musicians never went beyond the monophony that Byzantine liturgical chant began with and that the Atticists never used their philological expertise as a critical tool for the correction and edition of classical texts or for their placement in historical context.

The eleventh century witnessed the emergence of a vernacular literature that shows little connection to the classical tradition. References may be made to ancient heroes such as Alexander and Achilles and to the fables of Aesop (sixth century BC), but in substance and form, vernacular texts are largely unclassical. The epic *Digenes Akrites*, which refers to tenth-century events and which was first redacted in the late eleventh century, uses the fifteen-syllable metrical system of vernacular Greek folk song and features a hero of mixed Muslim and Christian parentage who lives on the fringes of the empire. He is a two-dimensional stereotype of athletic and military prowess, with no otherworldly connections, whose adventures include besting human opponents and winning the hand of his beloved. His heroism attracts the attention of the emperor, who seeks and receives Digenes' advice, banal advice at that, to be just and generous to the poor and to put down heretics. The hero has the demeanor and attributes thought desirable in Byzantine public figures. He is decorous, grave, and erudite. The palace he and his wife inhabit is richly decorated with silk carpets, contains a private chapel dedicated to the warrior saint Theodore, and mosaics depicting biblical and classical heroes. He plays the cithara while his wife sings. If Digenes thus manifests a refinement as an epic hero not seen in his western opposite numbers, they would take exception to his treatment of women. At one point he rescues a girl who had been seduced, robbed, and abandoned and himself takes sexual advantage of her. In the century when this epic was redacted, Symeon Seth wrote a Greek version of an Arabic beast fable, the *Kalila and Dimna* of Ibn al-Muqaffa (eighth century), a Zoroastrian convert to Islam. The two chief characters are jackals and the world they come from is India by way of Persia. The gap between vernacular literature and the Atticizing literature of the elite codified in contemporary compendia is quite wide.

Also increasingly bifurcated are theology and the subjects studied in the higher educational system developed in Byzantium in the eleventh century. In the mid-1040s, the higher schools of Constantinople were reformed by imperial order. Two subjects, law and philosophy, were taught. Both the curricula and the teaching staff were subject to imperial scrutiny. The law school had its own buildings, including a library, and offered free tuition, making law the chief career open to men of talent. Those who wanted to practice law or to work in the imperial administration had to complete its course of study and receive its certificate. Philosophical education did require tuition fees and appears to have been less centrally organized, but it was equally under official control. Both Aristotelian and Platonic philosophy were taught, the former seen as propaedeutic to the latter. Although each had its advocates, most philosophers made an eclectic blend of these traditions. Students were required to hold philosophical disputations in the presence of the patriarch, who was charged with reporting ideological deviants to the emperor. Leading philosophers, like Michael Psellus (*c.* 1018–78), were subject to disciplinary action for their views. A proponent of the position that philosophy has much to contribute to theology, he was a Neoplatonist heavily influenced by Iamblichus (*c.* 250–325). With him, Psellus argued that there were many spiritual intermediaries between God and the material creation and sought to show that this doctrine was compatible with Christianity. He also drew on Iamblichus' theurgy, the stimulation of spiritual experience by herbs and incantations. Psellus' view that Neoplatonism has a religious dimension and that it can be seen as a positive forerunner of Christianity and an adjunct to it, a notion that earlier apologists and church fathers would have found unexceptionable, provoked his dismissal from the faculty. By this time, Byzantines had come to regard philosophy as an alien science: not as a part of the Greek heritage that served the true, Christian wisdom but as a discipline exterior and even as irrelevant to it. Psellus' successor as chief philosopher in Constantinople, John Italos (*fl.* 1055), also lost his post for seeking to express Christian theology in terms of Aristotelian logic. Aside from their efforts to combine philosophy and theology, not in itself a new idea but one now unwelcome in Byzantium, the main work of Psellus and Italos lay in summarizing and commenting on their chosen philosophical sources. Like the philologists, they did not see their task as criticizing or going beyond them.

It is emblematic of the gulf between east and west that, following the schism between the Greek and Roman churches in 1054, Byzantine theologians showed little interest in the work of their western compeers and that translations of their writings into Greek were rare and were made late. Those of Thomas Aquinas (1224/5–74) were translated in the first place as an aid to critics of Hesychiasm, a late-blooming mystical movement that gave reason no role in theology or religious experience. The post-patristic continuation or revival of speculative Christian thought and its positive association with mysticism was the work of western theologians, often, paradoxically, inspired by the Byzantine authors available to them. And Greek science and philosophy were bequeathed to the Muslims, a legacy they embraced with far more enthusiasm and creativity than it received in Byzantium.

CHAPTER 10

Peoples of the Book:
Muslim and Jewish Thought

Of the sister civilizations considered in this book, only Islam, while linked to Judaism and Christianity, lacked roots in the classical tradition, since it arose in the seventh century after the old Rome had disappeared. During its first half-millennium, Islam conquered the Near East, north Africa, and Spain. The caliphs, or successors of Muhammad (*c.* 570–632), became the rulers of Jewish and Christian subjects whom they offered protection and religious toleration as 'Peoples of the Book.' The bishops and rabbis heading these religious communities were given a measure of civil jurisdiction over them, since Muslim law did not govern non-Muslims. The Muslims regarded their faith as the full, and final, expression of a religious tradition that had begun with Judaism and Christianity, sharing the belief that God reveals His will and moral law in history through His prophets. Islam joined Judaism and Christianity in professing monotheism, the belief in divine creation out of nothing, and a way of life combining public and private prayer, almsgiving, fasting, and social as well as personal ethics. Islam also shared with Judaism the circumcision of males to signify their membership in the religious community, and dietary restrictions, in this case abstention from pork and alcoholic beverages. Islam parted company with Judaism in believing that God had continued to reveal Himself through prophets after the Old Testament age. With Christianity Islam shared the idea that its message was universal and that its spread to all mankind should be promoted by vigorous missionary activity. The Muslims also thought it acceptable to spread Islam by the sword. Another point of agreement with Christianity was the belief in physical resurrection in the next life; although for Muslims the resurrected body is much like the earthly one. But they thought that Christianity had departed from strict monotheism in its doctrines of the Trinity and the incarnation of Christ. Other teachings of Christ, viewed as a uniquely privileged prophet of God, they deemed worthy of respect.

Pre-Islamic paganism also made its contribution to Islam. While decisively rejecting its polytheism, Islam retained its patriarchy and the practice of polygyny, as well as the idea of pilgrimage. Mecca, the city where Islam was first preached, was a pre-Islamic pilgrimage center and the Muslims maintained the rite of travel to its shrine, the Ka'aba, as a pillar of their faith. Another carry over from their pagan past was a strongly fatalistic outlook.

The early conquests of the Muslims made them masters of the Persian empire as well as of lands formerly ruled by Byzantium and the Germanic successor states in Spain and north Africa. Arabic, the language of the first Muslims and of their holy scripture, the Koran, became the official language of theology, prayer, law, and administration throughout the caliphate. A vigorous literary tradition already existed in Arabic before the rise of Islam, and Arabic literature continued to flourish, patronized by Muslim rulers more consistently than any other form of culture. Persian became another important literary language, especially in the Near Eastern part of the Muslim world. Persian writers sometimes borrowed Arabic literary forms and the reverse is also the case. Literature was a fruitful area of interchange between rulers and the ruled. In the field of religious practice, the Muslims borrowed mysticism, called Sufism, from their Persian and Asian subjects, along with spiritual techniques for inducing contemplation and ecstasy. From the same subjects they also took over the idea of oriental despotism and the notion of an empire whose constituent parts could be related to the central government in various ways.

Their Hellenized subjects in the previously Byzantine part of the caliphate provided the Muslims with the classical tradition. This was a legacy they appropriated selectively. Given their existing Arabic literary tradition and the linguistic differences dividing Arabic from Latin and Greek, classical literature had no appeal. Nor did Roman law or Greek political theory. Muslim law, based on the Koran and the sayings of Muhammad and the early caliphs, drew on its own criteria, developing four orthodox schools of legal interpretation essentially from within. On the other hand, Greek science and philosophy were of great interest to Muslim thinkers and to the Jews who participated freely in Arabic intellectual life. These disciplines received official sponsorship in the Near East up to the middle of the ninth century and, in Spain, through the end of the tenth. After that time, the rulers' scientific patronage was patchy. Along with other wealthy patrons, some supported observatories and hospitals because of the practical utility of astronomy and medicine. The patronage of hospitals also subsidized medical education and provided care for the needy. Philosophy, unable to inspire similar charitable intentions, fared less well as a field for official support. Of all three early medieval civilizations, Islam produced the most original work in science and philosophy. Thinkers in these fields grasped their principles and used them to make new and creative discoveries. At the same time, neither they nor the community at large found these subjects central to the religious culture. Unlike literature, science and philosophy were often treated with criticism or indifference by the theological establishment and by fundamentalist rulers who invaded the Near East and Muslim Spain in the eleventh century and after and who lacked interest in speculative thought. As a result, despite the brilliant work of thinkers in the golden age of Muslim science and philosophy, few scientific advances were made after the eleventh century and philosophy was regarded as an alien discipline after the twelfth. Aside from the medical students in hospitals, most thinkers who wanted to work in these fields were thrust back on their personal resources and had to rely on private tutors and informal networks.

The structure of schooling in Muslim lands first advanced and then took its toll on speculative thought. The Near Eastern caliphs supported an academy in the late eighth and early ninth centuries, the House of Wisdom, for the translation and study of Greek science and philosophy, parallel with their sponsorship of mosque schools for the study of the Koran and religious law. But they withdrew funding from the first enterprise in the mid-ninth century, as did the Spanish caliphs after the tenth century. Thereafter, scientists and philosophers usually had to earn a living some other way, pursuing research in their free time. Starting in the eleventh century, rulers and wealthy patrons making charitable donations established *madrasas*, centers for the advanced study of the religious sciences whose teachers gave formal accreditation to students demonstrating mastery of these subjects. Whether the patrons of *madrasas* were public or private, the legal structure of their foundation charters gave them control over the theological and legal interpretations taught there and over academic personnel. These schools and their faculties had no collective authority, in part because Muslim law lacked the concept of the legal corporation. Academic freedom was thus non-existent. Students were expected to accept the views of their teachers and teachers were required to profess the views of the founders. The educational process rarely included the interaction of proponents of differing positions face to face. Typically, students were taught to refute opponents in the abstract. Unlike the educational systems of Byzantium and western Europe, where the liberal arts including logic and the scientific subjects of the quadrivium preceded higher learning in theology and all other fields, the Muslim schools purveyed literacy through rote memorization of the Koran and the use of grammars written to help students learn classical Arabic. If they moved on to a *madrasa*, they might encounter some philosophy at the end of their course of study. It was not presented as a mode of inquiry or as a means of structuring knowledge that informed theology or religious law. While the House of Wisdom and analogous patronage in Muslim Spain still existed, the double educational track ensured that scientists knew philosophy, and vice versa. As believers, they might have a personal interest in integrating their learning in the secular sciences with Islam, but that was not part of their professional mandate. Scholars in the *madrasas* might also want to apply philosophical ideas to theology, but they were not systematically trained in science and philosophy. And, in parts of the Muslim world where official patronage of these subjects ceased, their perceived relevance to the religious culture declined. Thus, the extraordinary advances in speculative thought initially fostered by the patronage of Muslim rulers came to a halt after the twelfth century. In the sequel, it was western Europe rather than Islam that capitalized on this achievement once it was translated into Latin.

Muslim Literature

Literature was the form of Muslim culture best able to weather political ups and downs, the replacement of one ruling dynasty by another, and the eventual disintegration of the caliphate into small and mutually hostile units. For, whatever their political and religious positions might be, all Muslim rulers thought it important to support literature, which brought luster and entertainment to their courts. Political change and fragmentation had the effect of multiplying the centers of literary patronage. Writers built on the strong foundations of pre-Islamic literature with a notable cross-fertilization of the Arabic and Persian traditions.

The baseline for the flowering of Muslim literature is pre-Islamic literature, which includes epic, lyric, and proverbial poetry. As with early medieval vernacular literatures in Europe, it was composed and transmitted orally and redacted later, starting in the eighth and ninth centuries. All genres of pre-Islamic Arabic poetry are formally and metrically complex. They use elaborate imagery and vivid, sensuous descriptions of people, scenery, and animals. They reflect the tribal, semi-nomadic society of Arabia, whose economy combined herding with long-distance trade along established trade routes with cities as commercial and pilgrimage centers. The epics relate the many inter-tribal feuds and the genealogies of the protagonists, enabling the current audience to make connections with its ancestors. Martial prowess and adherence to a code of honor requiring the avenging of injuries are values linking these epics to other early medieval epic traditions. The lyrics are odes, sometimes lengthy, treating a range of subjects. They celebrate or comment dolefully on the natural environment, especially the desert, which holds a place in pre-Islamic lyric analogous to the sea in Old English poetry. Wine and love are popular themes, the latter treated at times with graphic eroticism and at times with delicacy. Sometimes the loss of love is the subject, as in an anonymous ode in which the speaker seeks his beloved and finds, literally, that her tribe has folded its tents and moved on. Lyric poets are as likely to praise their trusty camels as their ladies. The proverbial poems, unlike the one-line gnomic poems in Old English, string a series of proverbs together. They range from the banal to the witty and ironic. Our personal favorite is, 'Lower your voice and strengthen your argument;'[1] the one cited in all anthologies is, 'Trust in God, but tie your camel.'[2]

The first literary work of the Islamic age, the Koran, is also the first work of Arabic prose, albeit a highly rhythmical and alliterative prose. The Koran is not a narrative as so much of the Bible is. Nor is it presented as Muhammad's synthetic or pastoral interpretation of the revelation he received. Rather, the Koran is regarded as the word of God spoken to Muhammad, which he repeated literally in a series of individual verses stating divine revelation on specific topics. When the text was redacted, these statements were not organized thematically or in the chronological order in which Muhammad articulated them: the longer verses were put in the front of the book and the shorter ones in the back. A reader interested in charting the course of Muhammad's prophecy over time needs to read the Koran back to front, since the revelations in the shorter verses came first. One interested in collecting the Koran's teachings on particular topics needs to use an edition with a detailed subject index. The absolute centrality of the Koran to the religious life of Muslims and its use in the teaching of basic literacy ensured its literary no less than theological influence on all subsequent Muslim authors.

The Ummayads (632–750) who first ruled after Muhammad's death fostered epics and lyrics along pre-Islamic lines as well as prose history and fable, genres new to Arabic literature derived from Persia. Prose histories drew on the ruler-panegyric and the edifying life of the holy man, delineating the lives, virtues, and achievements of Muhammad and his early followers. History later expanded to include political and military narrative, personal memoirs, and travelogues. The fable made its way into Arabic from India via Persia. Unlike the fables of Aesop, in which animal characters allegorize human vices, Arabic beast-fables, a good example of which is Ibn al-Muqaffa's *Kalilah and Dimnah*, show animals behaving like human beings in positive ways as well. This idea may derive from the belief, in some Asian religions, that human souls can inhabit the bodies of animals. In any event, fables, like edifying biographies, make a didactic point.

The Abbasids (750–1258), who replaced the Ummayads in the Near East and who moved the capital from Damascus to Baghdad to reflect the eastward spread of Islam, continued the lavish patronage of literature, as did the local rulers who broke away from Abbasid rule starting in the tenth century. Arabic literature in this period shows increasing Persian influence, not only with respect to literary genres and themes but also in a literary sensibility emphasizing refinement, courtliness, luxury, effusiveness, and urbanity. These traits are also visible in the most famous work of Persian literature from the Abbasid period, the twelfth-century *Rubaiyat* of Omar Khayyam. A second feature of Abbasid literature is that writers chose their subjects with an eye to the tolerances of the current ruler. If he was open-minded or lax, he might support poets exalting wine or expressing religious skepticism; if not, not. Haroun al-Rashid was one caliph who gave poets much latitude. Two he patronized were Abu Nuwas (*fl.* early ninth century), a thoroughgoing sybarite whose verses praise wine as well as love, and Abu al-Atahiyah (d. 828), a philosophical poet who stresses the transience of earthly pleasures and who freely addresses a poem, *Vanity*, to the caliph himself, telling him that his wealth and power are ultimately meaningless. Both of these poets use a new form of lyric shorter than the pre-Islamic ode and both manifest an urban sensibility. Al-Mutanabbi (915–65) reflects the political situation of his day. He was first patronized by the Hamdanid dynasty in Syria and then by an Abyssinian ruler of Egypt who later dropped him and who, in the poet's estimation, is anything but an ornament to Islam. He lashes out at his erstwhile patron with vicious and bitter satire. The most cynical poet of the Abbasid Near East is Al-Maari (d. 1057). He is an exception who proves the rule, a poet so famous that he attracted hundreds of pupils and auditors and was able to function professionally without official patronage. This independence allowed him to assert that Judaism, Christianity, and Islam are equally superstitious and that he has abandoned all three faiths for the religion of love.

A second center of Arabic literary patronage and production was Muslim Spain, initially under an Ummayad caliph with his capital at Córdoba and later in the *taifas*, or smaller units into which this caliphate disintegrated. The arrival of the fundamentalist Almoravids (1091–1145) and Almohads (1145–1223) from north Africa did not hinder official support of poetry, the writing of which itself became a subject for lyricists along with love, invective, satire, self-defense, description, and the evocation of a mood. Spanish Muslim poets excelled at the deft use of figures of speech. In Al-Husri's *The Tress*, his speaker laments rejection by his faithless beloved and compares a lock of her hair to a mallet with which she batters his wounded heart. His tenth-century contemporary, Ibn Sara, packs two charming similes into his brief poem, 'Pool with Turtles':

> Deep is the pool whose overflow
>   In the cool bright showers
> Is like an eye weeping below
> Lashes of quivering flowers
>
> Look—the merry turtles sport
>   Like Christians in the field
> That sidle, frolic, and cavort
> Bearing a casual shield.[3]

The poets of Muslim Spain also developed new genres, including two forms of lyric poetry with refrains. Prose also had its adherents. A leading prose author, Ibn Hazm (994–1064), received support from several rulers. He takes the theme of love and the sensuous, erotic, and descriptive tradition of the lyricists and expresses it in *The Dove's Necklace*, a treatise analyzing and celebrating love, which he sees as combining physical, moral, and spiritual union with the beloved. Ibn Hazm also wrote an essay, 'A Philosophy of Character and Conduct', revealing his psychological astuteness, in which he argues that the chief motive of all human action is the desire to avoid anxiety. Whether writing prose or poetry, the vast majority of Spanish and Near Eastern authors operated under court patronage, a point summed up in one of the verses of 'On Hearing Al-Mutanabbi Praised' by Ibn Wahbun (tenth century):

> Ibnul Husain wrote verses eloquent:
> Of course: but princely gifts most excellent
> Results achieve, and offerings open throats
> To make delivery of their sweetest notes.[4]

The same level of support, however, cannot be found in other areas of Muslim culture.

Science

The vagaries of official patronage and the inability of scholars to find or to create institutionalized agencies for the support of their work in its absence, except for hospitals and observatories, can be seen with startling clarity in the case of science, the field in which early medieval Muslims decisively outpaced both Byzantium and western Europe but in which growth waned after the eleventh century. The first step that made possible the achievements of the golden age of Muslim science was the translation of Greek scientific texts into Arabic, made by way of Syriac by the caliphs' Christian subjects starting in the late eighth century, an evident benefit of their toleration of this 'People of the Book.' The leading translator, Hunayn ibn-Ishaq (809–73), headed the House of Wisdom and established a school of translators who continued his work, adding new translations and refining earlier ones. Since many Greek philosophers had written on natural philosophy they were included in the project. By the tenth century the entire corpus of Greek science and most of Greek philosophy, except for some of Plato's dialogues, were available in Arabic.

Well before that time, scholars had seized on these materials and had begun to make important contributions to particular sciences. In some areas they drew on the scholarship of India as well. Al-Kwarizmi (780–*c*. 850), the most creative mathematician in medieval Islam, is a good case in point. He appropriated the concepts of zero and Arabic numerals from India, replacing Roman numerals and the use of letters of the alphabet for numbers in Greek mathematics. The combination revolutionized arithmetic. Al-Kwarizmi also made many discoveries in algebra, including algorithms, a term derived from the Latinization of his name. When his work was translated into Latin it became the chief authority on algebra for the next four centuries. Musicology was another field of great interest to Muslim scientists, who, like the Greeks, treated it from a theoretical standpoint, as a branch of mathematics. Al-Farabi (*c*. 870–950) contributed most notably to this field. Mathematics was also applied to astronomy by Muslim scientists; like all medieval astronomers, they connected astronomy with astrology just as they joined mineralogy with the quest for the philosopher's stone. The natural scientist most original and profound in all these areas was Al-Biruni (973–1048).

The very association of astronomy with astrology and of mineralogy with white magic that raises modern eyebrows explains what made these sciences seem practical in medieval Islam. Astronomy was also deemed useful because it enabled Muslims to predict the occurrence of the movable religious feasts and fasts in their lunar calendar. The penchant for sciences with clear technological applications is nowhere so visible as in medicine, accounting for its great popularity in early medieval Islam and the patronage hospitals received well after the age of important medical discoveries. The two main stages in the history of Muslim medicine can be documented in the careers of Al-Razi (865–925) and Avicenna (980–1037). Al-Razi, the most original of Muslim physicians, was chief of surgery at the Baghdad hospital funded by the caliphs, which was also a research institute. Many of his discoveries resulted from his clinical practice. These include new surgical instruments and procedures, the etiology of measles, and the first clinical description of smallpox in world history. Al-Razi's voluminous writings include treatises on individual diseases and a medical encyclopedia summing up Persian, Greek, Hindu, and Muslim medicine to date. Clearly, he profited from the official support his work received. On the other hand, Avicenna lived and worked in Bukhara where he earned his living as a civil servant, not as a scientist paid to do research in a clinical setting. His accomplishments in medicine, as in philosophy, were achieved in his spare time. He acquired his education in these fields from private tutors, there being no school system in the secular sciences. His birth into a family wealthy enough to gratify his voracious intellectual appetite acounts for the breadth of his learning. While Al-Razi summed up his own and other physicians' clinical findings as a means of guiding readers through the contemporary explosion of knowledge, Avicenna's main innovation was his extensive, and, as events were to prove, final, codification of Greco-Arabic medicine, which replaced earlier encyclopedias on the subject and which integrated medicine with philosophy. His own discoveries, in the area of contagious diseases and diagnosis, are dwarfed by the magnitude of his systematic survey of the field and by his correlation of it with philosophy. The speculative dimension of Avicenna's work distinguishes his encyclopedia from the compilations in all fields that contemporary Byzantines were making. But the effect was the same: the production of standard works from which subsequent divergence was not envisioned or encouraged. While some Muslim scientists after Avicenna persuaded rulers to subsidize observatories and hospitals, the authorities they relied on were Avicenna and his predecessors. None of these institutions produced significant scientific discoveries after his time.

There is another dimension to Muslim science that must be noted along with the indubitable creative achievements of its golden age. The Muslims were interested in selected scientific fields, those noted above, or in particular scientific problems, like optics. In each case, the subject was appealing because it had practical applications. Pure scientific theory, the lure of scientific knowledge for its own sake that had animated the ancient Greeks, was not. Nor were Muslim scientists concerned with using science to develop a coherent world view based on reason or a universally applicable method of testing ideas. They certainly internalized the principles of those Greek sciences that interested them and added to what was known in them. But, aside from noting the departures of Ptolemy from Aristotle's astronomy and John Philponius' criticisms of Aristotle, they did not question any of the basic premises of Greek science or the Greeks' explanations of the phenomena they had studied. The ability to amplify Greek scientific knowledge along its own lines did not go hand in hand with the desire to forge connections among all the sciences or to contemplate the possibility of alternative scientific paradigms.

The Religious Culture

While astronomy and medicine could be seen as ancillary to the religious values and needs of Islam, philosophy proved to be more problematic in its interaction with the religious culture. In contrast with Byzantium, where a disjunction between philosophy and theology occurred at the end of the early Middle Ages, reinforced by the different institutional settings where these subjects were taught and despite the ease with which earlier apologetic and patristic writers had framed their theology in philosophical terms, the tension between these disciplines in medieval Islam stemmed not only from the gulf between theological and philosophical education but also from the fact that important developments in Muslim theology occurred before Greek philosophy became available. Some of the doctrinal debates arising in the first centuries of Muslim history were later thought to be arguable in philosophical terms. But others were not.

The earliest conflict to emerge and one that split the religious community into two camps that survive to this day was the question of Muhammad's successor. On this subject the Koran states only that the leader of the Muslim community should be the strongest male member of his tribe. In the event, the succession was contested between Umar, father of the prophet's favorite wife, and Ali, husband of his daughter Fatima. Umar won, giving his name to the first dynasty of caliphs. The Alids, or Fatimids, remained unreconciled. The Ummayads regarded them as sectarians, giving them the label Shi'ites, in contrast to the label Sunni, or orthodox, which they applied to themselves. While the issue was initially one of leadership, the Shi'ites later developed a theological rationale for their oppositionist stance, both to the Ummayads and later to the Abbasids, and their movement produced a number of doctrinal offshoots and its own schools of legal interpretation.

A second purely intra-Islamic debate that escalated with the Muslims' spreading conquests and one related to the issue of succession was the very conception of the religious community. Side by side with the Koranic statement that the caliph should come from Muhammad's tribe, and hence be Arabic, are verses asserting the universality of the message of Islam and the idea that the bond of faith transcends race, tribe, ethnicity, and nation. From the first perspective, a leader who is not Arabic is illegitimate. Since non-Arabs ruled the Muslim world after the eleventh century, Sunni proponents of the Arabist position could justify passive obedience to them, at best, so long as they were orthodox Muslims and defenders of the faith. But this raised problems for Shi'ites whose definitions of orthodoxy varied from that norm. From the universalist perspective, the faith required a broad rather than an ethnically based understanding of the religious community. The missionary principle meant that newcomers were welcome, as was leadership from whatever group could best protect and serve the religious community as as whole. This Arabist–universalist debate about the nature of the religious community was heavily conditioned not only by the ways in which the contestants privileged one Koranic injunction over another but also by the *de facto* power struggles in the Muslim world.

A third theological issue in the first century of Muslim history is a likely carryover from pre-Islamic paganism: the question of whether women have souls. Those asserting the affirmative eventually won over their opponents. But the fact that the issue was raised at all and the status of women as it emerged in Muslim law and theology reflects a consensus view, among men, of female inferiority. While permitted to inherit and to manage property, women were socially segregated from men and veiled in public. As noted, Islam retained polygyny and also the legitimacy of concubinage. Husbands had the right to divorce wives at will, but not the reverse. The religious duty of attending public prayer meetings on Friday, the Muslim day of rest, did not apply to women, and their bliss in the next life was held to lack the sensory pleasure enjoyed by men.

Another theological debate that was joined and settled early, also on an intra-Islamic basis, was the authority of the various traditions on which Muslim law was based. In addition to the substance of the sayings of an early follower of Muhammad, a key point was the impeccability of his lineage as a witness of a witness of a witness, going back to the prophet himself. Legal scholars formulated methods for evaluating the credibility of the traditions and for applying interpretive techniques to Muslim law without external influence, with the differing weights assigned to these matters by different scholars yielding four major schools of Sunni jurisprudence.

The only major theological debate to arise in early Islam that was later judged amenable to philosophical treatment was the problem of free will and predestination. In part, defenders of predestination can be seen as continuing pre-Islamic fatalism. But here, as in the debates on the nature of the religious community, the issue was joined in the light of verses of the Koran that support each position. The predestinarians emphasized verses referring to God's omnipotence and control over everything. The proponents of free will pointed to Koranic passages stating that the righteous will be rewarded and the reprobate punished in the next life, rewards and punishments the Koran describes as just. They concluded that God would not be just in making these judgments unless we have freedom to obey His law or not. The most striking feature of this debate is that partisans on both sides approached it from the standpoint of the divine nature. The question was which divine attribute to defend at all costs, omnipotence or justice.

Kalam

In the Abbasid period, as peoples with infidel doctrines new to Islam were conquered and converted and as Greek philosophy became available in Arabic, the movement called *mutikallimun* theology emerged. Derived from the term *kalam*, or reasoned argument, its proponents applied philosophy to Islam for two purposes, polemics against competing theologies and debates within the fold. The apologists' chief concern was defending radical monotheism against polytheists, members of mystery cults, Neoplatonists, and Christians. In Muslim eyes, all these positions departed from radical monotheism or saw the deity as sharing His creative and governing power with subordinate spiritual beings, or as too immanent in the universe. In attacking these views, thinkers from the Mu'tazilite school of *mutikallimun* drew on Aristotle's argument that God is radically one, with no distinction between His essence and His attributes. At the same time, they called on Neoplatonic negative theology to accent God's transcendence. Here, we see a key operative principle of *kalam*, its eclectic use of individual philosophical ideas at points where they were useful, rather than the systematic reformulation of theology in philosophical terms.

The Mu'tazilites also took on another group of *mutikallimun* thinkers, the Ash'arites, on a range of issues, especially free will and predestination. The Ash'arites stressed divine omnipotence and denied human free will. Their tactic was to borrow the Stoic theory of natural law as a universal rational law identifiable with the deity, governing everything with no exemptions. So too, they argued, we are controlled by laws external to ourselves and by divine actions. The

Mu'tazilites defended free will. They recast in syllogistic terms the argument of their predecessors who had emphasized God's justice. Given that God is just, it follows that we must have free will; otherwise God would punish or reward us unfairly, a conclusion fallacious because it fails to square with the major premise. The Mu'tazilites also invoked a teaching of the Atomists and Epicureans, the idea that the universe is ruled by chance, so as to rule out predestination. They appealed as well to an argument similar to the one used by the anti-Manichean Augustine in attacking dualists along with Ash'arites: we must have free will in order to make the human will, and not God, the cause of evil in the universe. While neither *mutikallimun* position defeated the other, the caliph who stopped supporting the House of Wisdom in the mid-ninth century is thought to have done so because of his opposition to Mu'tazilite *kalam*. But, in so far as there were challenges to mainstream theology from other quarters, it was not so much *kalam* as Sufism and *falsafah*, philosophy studied apart from theology, that raised a red flag for Muslims.

Sufism

Mysticism, as distinct from prophetic inspiration, had not originally been a feature of Islam. The Muslims encountered this religious practice as the caliphate spread eastward and most of them at first regarded it with suspicion, as likely to conflict with the theological consensus and as a source of heresy or political dissent. The Sufis, whether operating in brotherhoods or as individuals, drew heavily on the mysticism of the Near and Far East as well as basing their meditations on the life of Muhammad and other Muslim holy men. Some of them were ascetics or used mood-altering drugs, breathing exercises, and prayers repeating a single syllable, to promote contemplation. These practices seemed bizarre to mainstream Muslims. From a theological perspective, the very notion of mystic union with God seemed at odds with the doctrine of divine transcendence. The claim that God was immanent in some way in the mystic's consciousness, or that mystic experience was a participation in the divine nature, was offensive. Not without relevance was the fact that some Shi'ite leaders, apparently inspired by Sufism, did claim that they were divine theophanies. Another point of friction was the Sufis' allegorical reading of the Koran, an approach to the sacred text unacceptable to orthodox Muslims. Also, in emphasizing the salvific effect of their personal religious experience, the Sufis appeared to downgrade the moral and religious law that defined the practice of Islam. Given the fact that the Muslim religious community was coterminous with the Muslim political community, such antinomianism looked like an attack on the caliphate itself. The weakening and fragmentation of the Abbasid caliphate made these fears lively. The eventual eclipse of the Abbasids altogether and the conquest of the Near East by successive waves of Turks, some of whom had been converted to Islam by Sufi missionaries, as well as the guidelines for moderating Sufi practice offered by Al-Ghazzali (1058–1111), helped to normalize Sufism and to make it an acceptable and popular approach to religious life after the eleventh century. From that point onward, Sufi academies were added to the *madrasas* as centers of religious education.

Falsafah

Falsafah fared less well in medieval Islam despite the fundamental role it was to play in European intellectual history. Its leading proponents have several points in common. First, while each appeals primarily to one school of Greek philosophy, they are all eclectic to a greater or lesser degree. Second, all had a scientific education and are equally well known for their contributions to medicine, musicology, or mathematics. Third, aside from Al-Kindi (*c.* 800–*c.* 866), who lived before the caliphs closed the House of Wisdom and who received official patronage as tutor to the son of Al-Mu'tasim (835–42) in addition to teaching his own circle of students, they all made their livings as court physicians or as civil servants, not as philosophers. Among them, Al-Ghazzali is unusual for his knowledge of the religious sciences and Sufism and for his systematic effort to integrate them with philosophy.

The figure who initiated *falsafah* is Al-Kindi. He agrees with the Mu'tazilites' emphasis on the unity, simplicity, and transcendence of God but objects to the piecemeal use of philosophy characteristic of *kalam*. He substitutes for it a more thoroughgoing philosophy based largely on Plotinus and Porphyry with some Aristotelian elements. Al-Kindi's research into optics and the operation of light rays fuses his scientific interests with Neoplatonic light metaphysics. From Aristotle he takes the idea of quintessence, a type of matter more rarefied than the four elements, not subject to change and decay once created, which constitutes the heavenly bodies. One of Al-Kindi's most influential ideas, derived from Aristotle but given a Neoplatonic interpretation, concerns the agent intellect, the faculty of the human mind that enables us to formulate abstract ideas and to understand the causes of things. He regards it as a separate spiritual entity or intelligence in the chain of being above mankind, whose participation in our minds enables them to conduct these intellectual functions. For him, the agent intellect has no other role. Perhaps most striking, as an act of throwing down the philosophical gauntlet, is Al-Kindi's assertion that philosophical monotheists are saying the same thing as the Koran.

If Al-Kindi launched *falsafah*, the next two thinkers continued the enterprise, developing some independent arguments of their own. Al-Farabi cuts a wider swath than Al-Kindi. He draws on Plato in his political theory, Neoplatonism in his metaphysics and cosmology, and Aristotle in his logic, which he studied with Christian teachers, and in his analysis of intellection. Al-Farabi puts his own stamp on the distinction between essence and existence, which he takes from Aristotelian logic and moves in a new direction. According to Aristotle, we may consider a being's essence, its intrinsic definition, and its existence, its actual behavior. We can make this distinction in logic for the purpose of thinking about these two aspects of a being, one by one. But, in actuality, they are equally real and present inseparably in the being. Al-Farabi first argues that essence is logically prior to existence. In his view, we have to grasp a being's essence before we can understand its existence. He also transports the essence–existence distinction from the realm of logic to the realm of metaphysics. Not only is a being's essence known first, it is also a higher and more real mode of being than its existence. In effect, what Al-Farabi does here is to Platonize Aristotle's distinction by granting logical and metaphysical priority to the abstract aspect of being at the expense of its concrete aspect.

Al-Farabi's analysis of human intellection comes from the same sources as Al-Kindi's: Aristotle's *On the Soul* as interpreted by Hellenistic commentators. Although both impart a Neoplatonic coloration to Aristotle's psychology, Al-Farabi handles the question in his own way. He distinguishes four faculties in the human mind. The potential intellect is our capacity to master a body of knowledge we have not yet begun to study. The actual intellect is the mind engaged in that study and hence actualizing its potential. The acquired intellect, and this definition is Al-Farabi's own, is the mind considered as having already mastered the knowledge it is in the process of acquiring. Finally, there is the agent intellect. Al-Farabi agrees with Al-Kindi's understanding of its intellectual function and his view of its nature as a separate intelligence. He departs both from Al-Kindi and from Aristotle by giving the agent intellect another role, that of the Platonic Demiurge, imposing form on matter in the creation of the phenomenal world. The notion of God sharing His creative power with any other being is incompatible with Muslim theology. The fact that Al-Farabi maintains this view of the agent intellect none the less reflects his interest in philosophizing as such, rather than in tailoring his philosophy to fit theology.

At the same time, Al-Farabi speculates on the caliphate as a political system and seeks to reconceptualize it philosophically. He does so in two ways, first by recasting the caliph as the philosopher-king of Plato's *Republic*, and then by correlating the hierarchy of offices in the caliph's bureaucracy with the Neoplatonic chain of being. This accomplished, he argues that the caliphate, understood as the microcosm, corresponds to the universal macrocosm. Original as this political theory is, it had no influence on later Muslim philosophy or statecraft. In neither quarter did other Muslims think the caliphate needed the help of Greek philosophy. But Al-Farabi's views on essence and existence and the agent intellect drew considerable comment, positive and negative.

Easily the most original philosopher in early medieval Islam is Avicenna. Whether he sought to unite philosophy and theology or practiced pure *falsafah* with a compartmentalized mind has inspired debate since his own day, for there are positions he takes that support both interpretations of his work. Here, we will address areas in his thought that best display the texture of his mind and his chief emphases, as well as his major innovations. Unsurprisingly, given his scientific interests, Avicenna agrees with the Aristotelian idea that we derive valid information from sense data which the mind then forms into concepts and propositions enabling us to correlate causes with effects. He adds to this process a step drawn from Stoic epistemology, the judgment of the truth or falsity of our concepts and propositions. For Avicenna, certitude involves more than having an idea of something in our minds. It also requires the judgment that our ideas correspond with extra-mental reality. This desire to make the world outside the mind the norm of objective certitude informs Avicenna's acceptance of Al-Farabi's metaphysical understanding of the essence–existence distinction. The fact that we can think about essence as different from existence is based on the distinction of essence and existence in reality as well as in logic. Avicenna's handling of this subject reveals one of his most typical traits as a philosopher. He is primarily a metaphysician, a thinker who holds that the essences of things can be known correctly, and directly, by the human mind. This Platonic conviction is even more fundamental than the sense-based epistemology he takes from Aristotle.

The primacy of metaphysics in Avicenna's thought underlies some of his most original ideas. One is our certitude of our own existence and identity, which, he asserts, we know immediately, apart from sense knowledge, memory, or ratiocination. In presenting this claim he asks us to imagine a man suspended in space, brought into being as an adult, so that he has mature intellectual capacities but no memory as a source of personal identity. Leaving aside the question of what keeps him floating in space, we are asked to envision him as blindfolded, with his nose and ears stopped up, with his arms, legs, fingers, and toes spread out, so that no part of his body touches another. Deprived of sense knowledge as well as memory, Avicenna argues, this man would none the less know, with complete certitude, the fact of his existence and identity. His being, as a metaphysical fact, would be immediately accessible to his mind. This argument has sometimes been compared to the 'I think, therefore I am' of René Descartes (1596–1650). It is more radical in its claims, since Descartes' proof rests on the certitude of mathematical reasoning while Avicenna's involves no ratiocination at all.

Another highly original application of Avicenna's view that we can know metaphysical ideas directly is the analysis of the concepts of being, necessity, and possibility basic to his proof of God's existence. As he sees it, once these notions are presented to us, their meaning is self-evident. We can see at once that some beings are necessary. They have to exist and they have to be the way they are. We can also see that other beings are possible. They do exist and they exist in a certain way. But they do not have to exist and they could exist in other ways. Having noted that this distinction between necessary and possible being is intrinsically intelligible, Avicenna annexes the idea of causation to it. A necessary being is its own cause, while a possible being must be caused by another being, which is not obliged to be its cause. Avicenna then argues that a necessary being, which exists in and of itself, exists necessarily, while a possible being, while it actually exists, does not exist necessarily: the possible being requires a cause to bring it into being. And, if that cause ceased to cause it, the possible being would cease to be. With this reasoning in place, Avicenna concludes that God, the first cause, is the only being we can call a necessary being. Here, Avicenna develops a proof based entirely on his analysis of metaphysical concepts. He makes no appeal to the natural world, sensory experience, or psychological data. His proof of God's existence was to be one of his most influential contributions to medieval speculative thought.

Related to it is Avicenna's analysis of efficient causation. He starts with Aristotle's theory of causation and adds to it an innovation, the idea of metaphysical efficient causation. Avicenna agrees with Aristotle that, in the natural world, there are first and final causes as well as the material and formal causes accounting for the makeup of substances. There is also the physical efficient cause that accounts for their behavior. This physical efficient cause has three features. Directly or indirectly, it has physical contact with the phenomenon it effects. Its causal efficacy is finite. And its causal role is transitory. Once it has given the phenomenon its causal push, its efficacy ends. Thus, the physical efficient cause of the flight of an arrow is the contact between the bowstring, the arrow, and the archer's fingers. Once he has shot the arrow, the bowstring and his fingers stop affecting its trajectory. What Avicenna adds to this Aristotelian account of efficient causation is the idea that a metaphysical efficient cause is needed along with the physical efficient cause. This metaphysical efficient cause can be understood as the phenomenon's ground of being. Its action does not involve physical contact with the phenomenon. It is not finite or transitory. It remains necessary once the phenomenon has come into being for as long as the phenomenon remains in being. While, in the physical world, each phenomenon has its own particular physical efficient causes, depending on the physical processes of which it is capable, all phenomena have the same metaphysical efficient cause, God, Who undergirds and sustains all things. This function of the deity, as well as His role as the first and final cause, in no way alters the agency of physical efficient causes or the need for them. But, after they have set phenomena in train and have ceased to affect them, God maintains them in being.

Taken together, Avicenna's proof of God's existence and his doctrine of metaphysical efficient causation lend support to the Muslim view of an utterly transcendent God Who is radically different from creatures and Who is needed to sustain their existence. They are also creative contributions to philosophy. At the same time, Avicenna freely takes stands that either have nothing to do with Islam or that conflict with some of its tenets.

As a purely philosophical innovation, Avicenna's doctrine of the form of corporeity is an original addition to Aristotle's account of the makeup of created beings. Avicenna agrees that each substance is a combination of matter and form, the matter making it similar to other beings in the same genus and the form being the principle of individuation that makes it uniquely itself. In addition, Avicenna holds that corporeal beings have another form, one identical in all of them, the form of corporeity. This is an abstract form that gives bodies their capacity for three-dimensional extension in space. Avicenna's desire to take a more abstract look at Aristotelian substances reflects his willingness to Platonize Aristotelianism, a trait notable elsewhere in his philosophy.

We can see this Platonizing tendency in Avicenna's cosmology and psychology. He maintains an emanationist view of creation as well as the privative theory of evil, despite the objections that Muslim theology could raise to both doctrines. With the Platonists, and against Aristotle, he defines the human soul as the human essence, rather than the union of body and soul. In support of his position he recalls his argument for our direct intellection of our own existence and identity, without benefit of sense data, and the ability of the soul to live without the body, as it does after the body's death. He therefore sees no reason to accept the Muslim doctrine of the resurrection of the body in the life to come.

As for the activity of the agent intellect in our mental operations, Avicenna sides with Al-Kindi, although he makes three and not four subdivisions of our mental faculties and defines them in his own way. Avicenna's material intellect corresponds with Al-Farabi's potential intellect. His habitual intellect is the mind viewed as possessing a knowledge which it has not yet put to use, a definition unique to Avicenna. He agrees with Al-Kindi and Al-Farabi alike that the agent intellect is a separate intelligence above mankind in the chain of being. He joins Al-Kindi and opposes Al-Farabi in assigning no cosmic role to it. But, unlike both predecessors, Avicenna sees the agent intellect doctrine as a problem, on philosophical grounds. Aristotelians see the soul as the formal, individuating principle in each person's nature. Platonists see the soul as immortal. Yet, the agent intellect, which enables us to actualize our intellectual potential, is not an inborn personal attribute of any individual human mind. It is an external intelligence, existing independent of any individual human being, even as it participates in all human minds and enables them to function fully. Yet, the perfection of the intellect through the agent intellect's operations in individual minds must also yield the perfection of their intellects which they take with them into the next life, otherwise the doctrine of personal immortality would be compromised. Now, the defense of personal immortality would be a theological desideratum for Muslims, although Avicenna raises the question in philosophical terms as a function of his conflation of Platonic and Aristotelian psychology. He presents a solution to the problem that found both supporters and detractors. Although the agent intellect that enables us to perfect our intellects is a separate, superhuman intelligence, he argues, thanks to its activity in our minds we acquire a knowledge that becomes our own personal intellectual possession, which we can take with us into the next life without compromising our individuality. The way in which Avicenna frames his solution suggests that he was stimulated more by the parallels and disjunctions between the Platonic and Aristotelian traditions than by the wish to coordinate philosophy with theology, even though his conclusion is congruent with Islam. And while certainly eclectic, he gives more space to Aristotelianism than his predecessors, despite the creative changes he rings on it.

Avicenna is known to have been a contemplative in his personal religious life although this fact never emerges in his philosophy, but the desire to integrate that dimension of Islam with theology and philosophy found a major exponent in Al-Ghazzali. His goal was to moderate what he found excessive in all three approaches and to encourage practitioners in each to welcome insights from the others. This harmonization is the aim of his chief work, the *Incoherence of the Philosophers*. This project resulted from a profound spiritual crisis he underwent when he was fifty-seven. A teacher of the religious sciences at the *madrasa* of Baghdad, Al-Ghazzali was beset by doubt and made the long intellectual pilgrimage through philosophy and Sufism grippingly recorded in his *Deliverance from Error*. After years of study, prayer, and asceticism, he resolved his personal dilemma. He found that theology, philosophy, and Sufism all merited criticism. Philosophy, especially the Neoplatonic sort, he argues, produces teachings that conflict with Islam. In Al-Ghazzali's view, these teachings are also weak philosophically and do not stand up to Aristotelian objections, which he advocates as a corrective. He criticizes the orthodox theologians for being all too often obscurantist and authoritarian. And, he notes, the Sufis sometimes succumb to doctrinal extravaganzas, extreme subjectivism, and neglect of the moral laws of Islam. For the philosophers he urges not only greater recourse to Aristotelianism but also a willingness to recognize that, while philosophy yields a true knowledge of the natural world, it is reductionistic to apply its criteria to all forms of knowledge. The theological tradition is basic, he holds. The truths of faith are supreme in their own realm. At the same time, Al-Ghazzali observes that believers are intelligent people with inquiring minds. Theologians must thus stand ready to give intelligent and intelligible explanations of the faith. Finally, the Sufis, as mystics, accent the highest form of religious knowledge we can possess in this life. Even though mystical experience is not available to everyone, its very possibility for some reminds us that the essence of religion is the believer's personal encounter with God. Those not capable of mystic transports can still infuse their obedience of the moral law with a grasp of its inner meaning. At the same time, Al-Ghazzali urges the Sufis to recognize that they are bound by the rule of faith and by the moral law.

In principle, Al-Ghazzali holds out the possibility of integrating the intellectual and the experiential in religion, of synthesizing reason and authority. Although he maps this path with originality and with hard-won insight, it was not the road taken by most subsequent Muslim thinkers. The theologians generally saw *kalam* as the farthest they were willing to take philosophical speculation. The proponents of *falsafah* saw no reason to accept Al-Ghazzali's retrenchment of their enterprise. In the immediate sequel, the one call made by Al-Ghazzali that did have some resonance in the philosophers' ears was his advice to Aristotelianize their thinking. The twelfth-century Muslim who heard that call and who embraced it with the greatest rigor, Averroes (1126–98), is at once one of the most brilliant proponents of *falsafah* in medieval Islam and an index of why it became marginalized in Muslim culture after his time.

Averroes represents the high tide of rationalism in medieval Islam. He is a proponent of *falsafah* in its purest form. He views Aristotle as reason incarnate and his own project as the promotion of a correct and systematic understanding of the master. Averroes achieved the most thorough grasp of Aristotle of anyone up to his time. His conviction that Aristotelianism was the one true philosophy led him to take a stand that was deliberately provocative and at odds with Muslim theology. He had unusual intellectual breadth, encompassing not only philosophy but also the religious sciences, Muslim law, and medicine. An education producing this range was possible in the Spain of his youth. But, during his adulthood, the Almohads invaded. While he served as a judge and as court physician to some members of that dynasty, one ruler's hostility to his philosophy led to Averroes' fall from grace for a period of years during the 1170s and the destruction of some of his writings. This loss was a token of things to come. At issue was the fact that Averroes saw philosophy as offering a world view independent of theology. He studied the entire Aristotelian corpus, although logic, natural philosophy, cosmology, psychology, and metaphysics are the chief areas in which his works survive. Averroes commented on all of Aristotle with the aim of disengaging his ideas from those of Neoplatonic interpreters, producing three sets of commentaries addressed to the needs of beginning, intermediate, and advanced students. One limit on Averroes' commentaries is that he knew no Greek, and so was dependent on earlier Arabic translators who often reflected the very Neoplatonism he wanted to purge from the Aristotelian tradition. Given his reliance on these sources, his own interpretations were tinctured with Neoplatonism at some points. None the less, Averroes' commentaries gained instant recognition as the most accurate and authoritative access to Aristotle available. When they were translated into Latin, they earned him the cognomen 'the Commentator.'

Although Averroes' goal was to resurrect and profess pure Aristotelianism, there are some areas where he develops his own positions, largely as criticisms of Al-Ghazzali and Avicenna. Writing his *Incoherence of the Incoherence* against Al-Ghazzali, he rejects any limitation of the scope of philosophy and the desirability of synthesizing it with theology. He portrays Al-Ghazzali as little more than a practitioner of *kalam* and one with an inaccurate grasp of philosophy at that. In opposition to him, Averroes outlines his own view of the relation between reason and revelation. Referring to the three modes of proof described in Aristotle's *Rhetoric*, exhortation, dialectic, and demonstration, Averroes states that exhortation, which revelation provides and which faith accepts, is appropriate for the uneducated masses. For them, adherence to the moral law of the Koran by faith leads to the truth. Dialectical argument, which rests on premises that are probabilities and which yields conclusions that are likewise probable, not certain, is the method of the theologians, who combine faith and reason. Theology conduces the educated to the truth. The third and most rigorous type of argument is demonstration, which uses proofs that are entirely rational, proofs verifiable deductively and empirically, proofs that yield scientific certitude. This is the method of the philosophers. It is suited only to the most highly trained minds and it leads them to the truth. Now, according to Averroes, truth is the terminus of all three approaches and truth is one. In principle, it is inconceivable that the conclusions of revelation, theology, and philosophy should disagree. If they appear to disagree, he argues, the inconsistency is apparent, not real. In such a case, Averroes offers two prescriptions. First, logical analysis will show that apparent discrepancies are just that. And second, since the Koran is written in metaphorical language, one can always read it allegorically if it seems to conflict with philosophy. This position proved to be one of Averroes' most controversial teachings. He is sometimes described as the proponent of a double truth, or as opening the door to theological skepticism. Actually, he thinks that there are three paths to a single truth. At the same time, he does privilege philosophy as the means of resolving perceived conflicts among them and he recommends for the same purpose a mode of Koranic exegesis abhorrent to orthodox Muslims.

In the case of Avicenna, Averroes' criticisms target points where he thinks Avicenna is too Neoplatonic. These include some of Avicenna's most original ideas. With respect to the essence–existence distinction, Averroes argues for a strict Aristotelian understanding of these aspects of being as equally real and as distinguishable only in logic. His attack on Avicenna's distinction between necessary and possible being as a means of distinguishing between God and creatures substitutes an Aristotelian alternative Averroes prefers, the distinction between potency and act. God alone, he states, can be seen as pure act, a perfectly realized being from all eternity. On the other hand, creatures are in the process of actualizing their potentialities. Even when they complete this operation, they will still be distinguishable from God since, unlike Him, they have had to go through a process in becoming actualized. Also, consistent with Aristotle, Averroes sees creatures as endowed with the capacity to actualize their potentialities from within. They can act as their own causes in that connection, without the need for God to act on or through them. God remains as the first and the final causes in Averroes' universe and he develops a posteriori proofs of God's existence based on the need of natural phenomena to have these causes. But creatures, for him, are not dependent on God to sustain them in being or to activate their operations. Averroes also rejects the emanationist model of creation. In his view, its proponents support it so as to assign to subordinate intelligences the task of uniting matter and form, sparing the deity from direct contact with matter. But, Averroes points out, matter is just as eternal as God and it is not inferior to spirit. Basing his position on Aristotle's *Physics*, he argues that both the four elements and the forms of all things, forms that exist in the mind of God, are eternal. When God creates, He simply imposes the forms of particular creatures on their existing material components. To be sure, when creatures die their matter becomes available for recycling and is used in the generation of new creatures. There is an economy of matter. While creatures are constantly undergoing change, in contrast with the unmoved mover, matter as such neither comes into being nor passes away. On one level this last argument might be seen as offering a doctrine advantageous to Islam by eliminating two problems central to the emanationist cosmology, the sharing of God's creative activity with other beings and the idea that He has to create as a necessity of His own being, notions that undercut God's freedom and omnipotence. But the Averroist alternative inspired voluble opposition from Muslim theologians because it dismisses the principle that God creates the universe out of nothing.

A final area in which Averroes criticizes Avicenna for being too Neoplatonic is the doctrine of the agent intellect. In this area, however, he reveals his own debt to the very Neoplatonism that he wants to eliminate from Aristotle's psychology. Given Averroes' objections to chain of being cosmology and his defense of the Aristotelian claim that creatures are endowed by nature with the capacities they need to actualize their potentialities, a reader unfamiliar with his agent intellect doctrine might think that he would simply sweep away all Neoplatonic versions of that idea as unnecessary. But, partly because of Aristotle's lack of clarity in his *On the Soul* and partly because of Averroes' dependence on Neoplatonizing translations and commentaries on it, he does not do so. As he sees it, the human mind has two faculties. There is the passive intellect, our potential disposition toward knowledge, which is also a person's substantial form. It is integrally related to the body to which it is united. There is also the agent intellect, Averroes agrees, which enables the mind to actualize its intellectual potential. But, while he sees the passive intellect as a natural human endowment, each person's principle of individuation, he regards the agent intellect as a separate intelligence, originating in the heaven of the moon. It participates in each person's mind in the same way and for the same purposes but it is no one's personal possession. Further, Averroes argues that, since the passive intellect dies with the body, there is no personal immortality of the human soul. In addition to departing from his predecessors from Al-Kindi through Avicenna, this argument shows Averroes retaining a Neoplatonic understanding of the agent intellect. For mankind, Averroes concedes at most a collective intellectual immortality in the agent intellect, although, strictly speaking, the immortality at issue is that of a superhuman intelligence, not of the human race in general. Averroes' handling of the agent intellect is problematic in its own right, philosophically. It also clashes head-on with the Muslim belief in personal immortality.

In sum, if *falsafah* as conducted by largely Neoplatonic thinkers from Al-Kindi to Avicenna and as criticized by Al-Ghazzali and Averroes was deemed to produce unacceptable teachings by Muslim theologians, they saw *falsafah* as conducted by Averroes as even more threatening. While Averroes was immediately hailed as providing the most accurate introduction to Aristotle in his day by Jewish, Christian, and Muslim philosophers alike and while he had considerable influence, positive and negative, on the thought of Jews and Christians in the sequel, in Islam he represented everything that was most to be feared from philosophy. In his own community his doctrinal innovations were rejected as incompatible with the Muslim faith. In later centuries, *kalam* and Sufism charted the course of Muslim theology and defined the limits of speculative thought. Those philosophers who remained active had to produce exoteric versions of their positions for public consumption, hiding their real opinions, which they shared only within their own increasingly disempowered circles. It was left to the other 'Peoples of the Book' to develop and to apply the contributions of the greatest philosophers of medieval Islam.

Jewish Thought

Jewish thinkers up to the end of the twelfth century lived largely in lands governed by Muslims. Conversant with Arabic along with Hebrew, Aramaic, and local vernaculars, as a 'People of the Book' they participated actively in the intellectual life of the Muslim Near East and Spain. We find parallels to and influences from Muslim intellectual movements in their work as well as concerns specific to Judaism. In early medieval Judaism we likewise find traditional theology based on Holy Scripture and the interpretation of the religious law by the rabbis. We also find mysticism and pietism, which have similarities to and differences from Sufism and Christian analogies. And we find as well the desire to rationalize Jewish theology, both along the lines of *kalam* and in a more wholesale way, along with philosophy practiced as an end in itself unconnected to theology. Judaism was the first of the three revealed religions to produce philosophical theology, in the person of Philo. His thoroughly Hellenized world view, based on Neoplatonism and Stoicism, was, he believed, perfectly compatible with revealed truth. His work failed to appeal to his co-religionists and had much more influence on Christianity. Up to the time of the Greco-Arabic translations that made philosophy available to Jewish thinkers in the Muslim world, the key developments in Jewish thought lay rather in Talmudism and mysticism.

Talmudism

The commentaries on the moral and religious law known as Talmud, and the commentaries on the Talmud known as Mishnah, became increasingly important as a basis of religious identity for Jews after the destruction of the second temple of Jerusalem in AD 70 and the diaspora. The rabbis were the interpreters who produced these texts, which coalesced by the sixth century. The texts present issues in dialogue form. The interlocutors are all respected rabbis giving their opinions on debated matters. The redactor may suggest which opinion he favors by his stage-managing of the debates. Theological authority is presented in a much more fluid and open-ended manner in Talmudic Judaism than in Christianity or Islam. Orthodoxy is not viewed as a position determined by clerical consensus institutionalized by ecumenical councils or by the fiat of a religious leadership co-extensive with political authority. True, in order to participate in Talmudic theology one had to be a rabbi and one had to offer one's opinions as an extension of the debates already redacted. But the doctrinal parameters of the theological establishment represented by Talmudism were comparatively flexible. They were also permeable by ideas from extra-Jewish traditions. As cases in point, the immortality of the soul and its superiority to the body receive more attention in Talmudic literature than they do in the Old Testament, and the Talmudists show more interest in eschatology, although without decentering the Jew's moral responsibilities in this life as the chief focus of religious belief and practice.

Mysticism

Jewish mysticism took two main forms in the Middle Ages, Gnosticism and cabbalism, with cabbalism becoming more dominant in the later medieval centuries. Jewish Gnosticism emerged at the same time as pagan and Christian Gnosticism and emphasized the same key ideas, the belief in a human condition from which we need to be saved and the quest for an esoteric saving wisdom available to a spiritual elite. As Jewish Gnosticism developed between the fourth and the sixth centuries, its adherents felt a need to modify some Gnostic doctrines and the conception of mystical experience itself to make them conform with their belief in God's unity and transcendence. They achieved the latter goal with the doctrine of the 'throne room,' a supernatural world composed of seven palaces, in the last of which is God's throne. After ascetic discipline and the use of assorted occult techniques to alter mental states and after negotiating the obstacles in the throne world, the successful Gnostic would have a mystical experience of God's throne, avoiding actual union with the deity Himself. In sharp contrast both with pagan and Christian Gnosticism and with traditional Judaism, Jewish Gnosticism elaborated no ethical teachings whatever. In order to avoid the conflict with God's unity and transcendence represented by the emanationist cosmology adopted by other Gnostics, the Jewish Gnostics avoided cosmological speculation. They thus declined to explain why human salvation is needed and offered no advice on how, or whether, the created universe can be used as a ladder of reascent to its source.

The cabbalists, on the other hand, did speculate on cosmology. From what is known about the beginnings of this movement, it emerged between the third and sixth centuries. After that, cabbalism was quiescent, or perhaps underground, until it resurfaced in Babylonia in the tenth century. Most of the texts documenting this movement date to the twelfth century and after, the classic summary being the *Zohar* of Moses of Léon (*c.* 1240–*c.* 1305). The cabbalists share with the Gnostics the use of occult techniques to stimulate contemplation and an elitist membership, in their case excluding women. But they depart from Jewish Gnosticism in presenting an elaborate account of creation reflecting their willingness to compromise God's unity and transcendence and in their use of numerology as an exegetical and mystic strategy. For the cabbalists, the universe was created by emanation, with ten emanations between God and the phenomenal world. The first three they call Words, the next seven Voices. They see the Words as links in the chain of being and the Voices as symbolic of divine functions. The exact metaphysical status of the Voices is unclear. The cabbalists describe the deity in physical terms and hold that each emanation corresponds to a part of God's body. Since mankind is the microcosm of the divine macrocosm, the cabbalists also see correspondences between the human and divine anatomies. In their view, the creation of the phenomenal world resulted from a union between God, envisioned as masculine, and God's Glory, a divine hypostasis envisioned as feminine. Both the ditheism and the anthropomorphism of cabbalism were profoundly offensive to mainstream Jews. So was their numerology, based on the idea that three, four, seven, and ten are mystical numbers. They used the letters of the Hebrew alphabet as numbers. With this principle in mind, biblical or liturgical texts that produced numerical equivalents or multiples of the mystic numbers were thought to have rich mystical content: meditation on such texts was held to expedite ecstatic religious experience. Moses of Léon adds Neoplatonic light metaphysics to the brew, along with negative theology. As he sees it, human nature combines a body with a soul that shares the nature of the supralunar spiritual world and God. Our goal is to cast off the body and to reunite the soul, which pre-exists it, with God, a possibility about which the cabbalists are more sanguine than the Gnostics. According to Moses, those who fail to attain mystic union are condemned to the transmigration of their souls into new bodies. Moses also thinks that the human exercise of free will has cosmic as well as moral effects. Our sins can keep God and God's Glory apart and our virtues help Them stay together. Human choices thus affect the coherence of the cosmos and the activities of the deity. All of these positions inspired hearty suspicion from orthodox Jews, as did the fact that some cabbalists in the thirteenth century claimed direct inspiration by God and the same authority as Old Testament prophets, or even identity with the Messiah. Unlike Sufism, which Al-Ghazzali more or less normalized in Islam, cabbalism never attained official status as an orthodox form of religious life, despite its increasing popularity among Jews throughout the Middle Ages.

Pietism

On the other hand, pietism, as a reaction against the perceived legalism of the Talmudists and as an effort to stress inner religious experience, was regarded as orthodox by medieval Jews and claimed numerous supporters. The two most important medieval pietists, Bahya ibn Pakuda (1059–1111) and Judah Halevi (*c.* 1080–1141) both lived in Muslim Spain and wrote their pietistic works in Arabic. As a token of the dawn of a new and more repressive era, Halevi fled from the Almohads and ended his life in the Near East. In *The Duties of the Heart*, Ibn Pakuda argues that the ethical applications of the Jewish faith are central, not speculation on it. He distinguishes the 'duties of the limbs,' the external moral law, ritual, and ceremony, observed by Jews because God prescribes them and He must be obeyed, from the 'duties of the heart,' or inner piety, moral and ceremonial acts performed because they resonate meaningfully in the believer's inner life. In Ibn Pakuda's eyes, the aim of pietism is to transform all the duties of the limbs into duties of the heart, so that inner understanding, subjective commitment, and piety will inform our obedience to all the prescriptions of the law. When that goal is reached, the believer will be inspired to act out of the love of God, Who has revealed His wonderful law to mankind. For Ibn Pakuda, love of God is not mystic rapture but inner joy, certitude, and tranquillity.

Halevi's approach to pietism reflects not only the deep sensibility expressed as well in his Hebrew religious poetry but also two things not found in Ibn Pakuda, the desire to react against philosophy, especially Aristotelianism, seen as a threat to religion, and the need he felt to defend Judaism against Christianity and Islam. He manifests these concerns by stating flatly that the God of the philosophers is an abstract idea and not a personal God of love. He also argues that the capacity to know God and to appropriate His revelation correctly requires a special, suprarational religious faculty, possessed uniquely by the Jews as His chosen people. Their lack of this special faculty explains why the other 'Peoples of the Book' profess erroneous teachings.

Halevi develops this argument anecdotally in his *Kuzari*, drawing on a tradition concerning the Khazars, a nomadic Asian people who settled in the Crimea and converted to Judaism in the eighth century. The region also had many Christian and Muslim inhabitants. According to Khazar tradition, their king entertained three sages representing Judaism, Christianity, and Islam, inviting them to debate in his presence with the idea that he would commit himself and his people to the faith of the winner. The debate was a draw, each sage proving equal to the other two. So the king tried another gambit. Taking aside the sages in turn, he asked them which of the other two faiths he would profess if he could not profess his own. The sequencing of these interviews, needless to say, is controlled by Halevi's desired outcome. The Christian sage, questioned first, said that he would profess Judaism, since the Jews had been the earliest chosen people. The Muslim sage, questioned next, also preferred Judaism, because the Jews had not abrogated any of the laws of the Old Testament, as the Christians had. Given the odds thus far, the king thought it unnecessary to question the Jewish sage; he converted to

Judaism and took his people with him. Having thus set the stage, Halevi presents the rest of the *Kuzari* as a catechetical dialogue between the Jewish sage and the king prior to his admission to the fold.

Engaging as this curtain-raiser is, it also creates problems given the thesis Halevi wants to defend. If only participants in the Jewish gene pool possess the religious faculty that enables them to know God accurately and to profess the one true faith, why should anyone try to convert to Judaism? Indeed, how could such a conversion even be possible? Halevi recognizes this objection and responds with the argument that there are varying degrees of the religious faculty. The prophets possess it to the highest degree; ordinary Jews possess it to the degree necessary for salvation; converts possess it to a lesser but still sufficient degree; infidels lack it. This softening of his doctrine helps somewhat, but it still fails to explain how an infidel could become a convert. A second problem with Halevi's argument that he neither recognizes nor addresses is the tension between his group definition of Jews as true believers and his emphasis on piety as the definition of true religion. For, in agreement with Ibn Pakuda and the whole pietistic tradition, he sees religion as the believer's personal relation to God and as the loving response to God that takes place within the individual soul. This inconsistency remains. It derives from the polemical stance Halevi takes in defending Judaism, and his interpretation of it, against rival faiths in an environment growing less tolerant of other 'Peoples of the Book' and increasingly given over to rationalism.

Jewish Kalam *and* Falsafah

Like their Muslim compeers, Jews drawn to speculative thought in the early Middle Ages wrote in Arabic and followed two approaches, *kalam* and *falsafah*. The leading proponent of Jewish *mutakallimun* theology, Saadia Gaon (882–942) is an energetic partisan of Mu'tazilite *kalam*. But he also needs to be understood in the context of the first post-Philonic effort to rationalize Judaism, the Kara'ite movement of the eighth century, centered in Egypt and Iraq. Thinkers rallied to Kara'ite banners for various reasons. They were united only in their criticism of the exilarch, the chief rabbi who governed them, the rabbinical establishment, and the Talmudic tradition buttressing rabbinical authority. Some Kara'ites rejected Talmudism because they regarded the Old Testament as the only admissible source of religious truth, a striking anticipation of the *Scriptura sola* position of some high medieval Christian sectarians and later Protestants. These Kara'ites objected to the Talmudic tradition not just on principle but because, they charged, the Talmudists advocated the Scripture-and-tradition view for selfish reasons, since they controlled the interpretation of tradition. Other Kara'ites objected to Talmudism because they disagreed with particular interpretations given to the religious law by the rabbis. Within this group, some found the rabbis too legalistic; others found them too lax. Some criticized the Talmudic tradition as full of inconsistencies and contradictions; others attacked it for including legendary and superstitious material that distorted the purity of Judaism. Other Kara'ites had largely political grievances. Some opposed the exilarchy as a system; others opposed the policies of specific exilarchs and the exclusiveness of the rabbis who led the Jewish community; still others wanted to substitute themselves for the existing rabbinical establishment in place. Testifying to the presence of an articulate anti-rabbinical party in Near Eastern Judaism and to the stresses and strains within that society, the Kara'ite movement drew on philosophical arguments, since philosophy was now becoming more available in Arabic, for *ad hoc* polemical purposes. But there were orthodox Jews who did not find fault with Talmudism and who thought that the Kara'ites themselves merited criticism. They sought to provide it by taking over the strategies of the Muslim *mutakallimun*. Chief among them was Saadia. The swiftness with which the Kara'ites collapsed once he took to the field against them is indicative not only of the contradictions within the Kara'ite movement but also of Saadia's thorough grasp of the Bible and the Talmud and his ability to develop arguments of genuine philosophical interest that outlasted the immediate passions of the age in which he wrote his major work, *The Book of Beliefs and Opinions*.

Heavily involved in the politics of the exilarchy and a respected rabbinical teacher, as his cognomen attests, Saadia wrote in Arabic to address a wide audience, also translating the Old Testament into Arabic. There was much to draw philosophers from other faiths to his book in addition to the arguments he frames to address intra-Jewish problems. Saadia's work is divided into three parts treating God's unity, God's justice, and ethics, including human nature and eschatology. He devotes more space to the moral law, as the main way mankind comes into contact with God, than to any other topic, and his chief authorities are biblical, Talmudic, and philosophical, in declining order of importance. He prefaces the main part of the work with a proof of God's existence and proofs that the universe was created out of nothing. In both cases he offers a posteriori proofs, moving from features of the observable universe to their cause. His proof of God's existence is the argument from design to the rational orderer of the cosmos as its first cause. Saadia is even more interested in proving that the universe was created and draws on Platonic and Aristotelian principles in so doing. Everything limited by time and space, he argues, must be maintained by powers also limited by time and space. Thus, everything in the universe is finite. Thus, it must have been created. As a variant on this proof, he adds that all bodies in the universe have accidental traits conditioned by time. The attributes are thus created, and so are the bodies in which they inhere. Attributes conditioning creatures, Saadia stresses, differ from divine attributes, which are eternal, uncreated, and identical with God's being. Hence, when we refer to divine attributes using terms that also apply to creatures, we use the terms metaphorically, since the divine mode of being transcends the created mode of being. These proofs and arguments that open the *Book of Beliefs and Opinions* swiftly lay down positions on which later thinkers drew and reflect Saadia's sensitivity to the problem of theological language as well as his confidence that philosophy is compatible with these key Jewish beliefs about God and the creation.

But, asks Saadia as he warms to his central subject, why does God create at all? He does so to endow creatures with the gift of existence and, in the case of human beings, with the means of attaining eternal happiness by obeying God's law. Saadia accents two main points here. First, it is not speculation about God's nature that leads to human felicity and it is not as the creator that we best know God, even though reason helps confirm those beliefs. Rather, God is known to us and is related to us primarily as the giver of the moral law, obedience to which is the path to bliss. Second, obeying God's law requires human effort and entails the free will needed to exercise it. God so arranges matters, knowing that those who attain happiness by freely choosing obedience will enjoy their happiness all the more, having worked for it. God may foreknow what choices we will make, but this foreknowledge is not causative. Here Saadia aligns himself with the position of the Mu'tazilites on free will. But he does not appeal to occasionalism and he views this issue both from the perspective of God's justice and from the perspective of human needs.

One of Saadia's goals is to remove doubt concerning how we should obey the law, which inspires him to develop an epistemology all his own. He begins by observing that both sense data and reasoning lead to truth. Both can also lead to error if we are sloppy and lacking in thoroughness. But, with persistence and application, they will bring us to a knowledge of objective truth. Desirable as that acquisition may be, it does not constitute real knowledge which, for Saadia, combines objective knowledge with the state of subjective certitude that he calls belief. This definition of belief is Saadia's own. It can be contrasted with St. Paul's definition of faith as the certain, but partial, knowledge of religious truths that we will know more fully in the next life. It can also be contrasted with Plato's conception of faith as the least reliable form of knowledge, since it is based on hearsay. What Saadia means by belief is the subjective appropriation as true of an idea we know to be true objectively. His definition is shaped by his focus on the Jewish moral law. For Saadia, the Jew starts with a body of information that he holds to be objectively correct, the moral law. In acquiring belief, the Jew then appropriates this external truth with subjective conviction, embracing it as the law of his own being. In effect, Saadia provides here a psychological and epistemological analysis of the internalizing of the duties of the limbs as duties of the heart described by Ibn Pakuda. Before leaving this subject, Saadia adds that, along with sense data and reasoning, there is another authentic source of truth, biblical revelation as passed on by the religious tradition. Saadia argues that it is not unreasonable to accept the ideas transmitted by an authoritative religious tradition. For, in all areas of learning, he notes, we reasonably rely on what other people tell us. Otherwise, each person in each generation would have to reinvent the wheel and try to learn in a single lifetime what it has taken the human race millennia to learn. What Saadia does here is to place acceptance of the Bible and the Talmudic tradition on the same plane as our acceptance of the word of any trustworthy teacher from whom we learn something we have not experienced ourselves. At the same time, Saadia accords to the religious truths so obtained a privilege not extended to other bodies of knowledge received indirectly. For, he argues, reason cannot criticize them. With respect to religious truths, the role of reason is to substantiate what we know by revelation and tradition and to refute opponents. Here, Saadia's position approximates Augustine's. But Saadia is living in a pluralistic society in which he wants to defend not only the reasonableness of Talmudism against the Kara'ites but also the truth of Judaism against other revealed religions. In addressing the latter issue, he hits a snag. If revelation as such can be regarded as reasonable, this principle does not provide a criterion for determining which revelation is admissible and which is not. In arguing for the unique authority of the Jewish revelation, Saadia falls back on two weak arguments, both of which beg the question: the trustworthiness of the prophets attested by their miracles, and general consent. The first is a tautology because the authority of the text relating the prophets' miracles is what he is trying to prove by means of the miracles. Also, Christians and Muslims share the Jews' belief in these miracles but not their views on when the age of revelation ended. And general consent fails because it did not in fact exist, whether among the three 'Peoples of the Book' or between the Kara'ites and other Jews. Despite these problems, Saadia's epistemology testifies to his conviction that the results of rational inquiry will tally with the data of revelation and tradition.

Moving to the central theme of the internalizing of revelation and tradition, understood as providing objectively true guidance on the moral law, Saadia offers some general rationales for obeying the law and then considers the two headings under which he thinks it can be rationalized. On a general plane, he argues that it is reasonable to obey a deity Who is our benefactor, as manifested in laws showing that He knows what is good for us better than we do. These benefits promote social harmony and deter us from injuring others, which are rational desiderata. This general rule understood, there are two types of precept. The first includes the Ten Commandments. These are laws that reason would counsel even if God had not ordained them. Their rationale is concrete and practical, making for healthy social relations. Saadia accents social utility, not conformity to abstract rational principles, in making this case. The second category of precepts is a harder nut to crack. It includes the host of dietary, ritual, and ceremonial laws that do not, in themselves, inspire the approval or disapproval of reason. Still, Saadia tries to rationalize them as best he can, ending here as well with a utilitarian justification. Even precepts that are totally a-rational are useful because they remind us that we are governed by a deity Whose mind is ultimately inscrutable and Who has the authority to legislate for the universe He created. Hence, they inculcate in us a fitting attitude of humility. This final part of Saadia's effort to rationalize the moral law suggested to subsequent Jewish speculative thinkers that further work was needed here.

If Saadia's approach to the rationalizing of Judaism can be seen as the opening salvo of Jewish *kalam*, pure *falsafah* also drew some early medieval Jewish thinkers. Like their Muslim confrères up to the twelfth century, they tend to be Neoplatonists. This is certainly the case with Solomon ibn Gabirol (1021/22–58), whose *Fountain of Life* tries to resolve a problem in that philosophical tradition, springing from the issue of the one and the many. Why would a creator radically one want to generate a multiform creation, given that unity is better than multiplicity? And, how does the creator, being pure spirit, engender a world that contains matter, given that spirit is better than matter? As we have seen, medieval philosophers with a Neoplatonic bent appealed to creation by emanation to answer these questions. The created intelligences below God in the chain of being spare Him the need to come into direct contact with matter. He creates because He wishes to diffuse His own being and goodness. Still, the difficulty Ibn Gabirol sees and wants to resolve remains, the nature of the created intelligences. Since they are not God, he reasons, here reflecting a somewhat Aristotelianized Neoplatonism, they cannot be pure spirit. Nor can they be unitary beings, since unity is attributable to the deity alone. Thus, like all other created beings, the intelligences must be composites of matter and spirit. But, if they have matter, it must be a kind of matter different from the matter making up creatures in the sublunar world. Let us recall that there was more than one way to tackle this issue. One could adopt Aristotle's concept of quintessence and extend it from the heavenly bodies to the intelligences. Or, if one wanted to regard the intelligences as purely spiritual beings, one could invoke either Aristotle's potency–act distinction or Plato's distinction between mutable creatures and an immutable deity. Or, irrespective of the constitution of the intelligences, one could apply Avicenna's distinction between necessary and possible beings to explain their difference from God.

These modes of addressing the problem were all available to Ibn Gabirol. But his handling of it is his own. He draws on Proclus, Aristotle, and the concept of abstract matter, which Ibn Gabirol invents on the analogy of Avicenna's form of corporeity. Following Aristotle, he argues that all beings are composites of matter and form. As for God, He is not to be understood as a being but as the One beyond being. He therefore lacks these attributes, which in God's case is a perfection. This Proclan description of the deity, also found in John Scottus, gives Ibn Gabirol a way of distinguishing God adequately from the intelligences. But how is the material aspect of the intelligences to be understood? Ibn Gabirol transfers to matter the central concept underlying the form of corporeity, the idea that a corporeal being, in addition to its specific individual form, also has an abstract, generic form. As he sees it, creatures possess matter in two ways as well. There is the particular combination of the four elements present in their constitution. And there is abstract matter, a universal, generic material principle that is the same in all creatures. As for the intelligences, they are made up neither of the four elements nor of quintessence. Their material aspect and the only matter they contain is abstract universal matter, more rarefied than quintessence. This conclusion, which some of Ibn Gabirol's successors found persuasive and some did not, reflects his desire to resolve a difficulty within the Neoplatonic tradition in strictly philosophical terms. It could be argued that his theory has implications for Jewish theology. If so, the possibility never occurred to him. He never adverts to religious sources and he sees no need to appeal to anything but the philosophical sources on which he draws, and his own ingenuity.

The Maimonidean Synthesis

While Talmudism and *falsafah* can be found in Jewish thought after the eleventh century, *kalam* tends to give way to a more thoroughgoing application of philosophy to theology and the philosophy in question is Aristotelianism, not the Neoplatonism largely professed by Ibn Gabirol. The figure primarily responsible for this development is Moses Maimonides (1135–1204), whose goal was to synthesize

Aristotelianism with the Jewish religious tradition. A native of Córdoba, he was thoroughly educated in the Talmud and the natural sciences as well as philosophy. Like Judah Halevi, he found the intellectual climate in Spain inhospitable when the Almohads arrived and moved to Egypt, where he served the local ruler as court physician and his fellow Jews as their chief rabbi. Maimonides shares Averroes' profound admiration for Aristotle, agreeing that the apex of human reason had been attained in his philosophy. When he speaks of 'reason' he basically means Aristotelianism. He also agrees that Aristotle should be purged of Neoplatonic accretions and embraced systematically. That embrace, however, should include the Jewish theological tradition rather than ignoring it. Thus, while Maimonides rejects current and previous Neoplatonic thinkers in Judaism and Islam alike for the reasons Averroes does, he also takes a strongly critical position toward Jewish *kalam* and pietism. Against both he argues that the proper study of mankind and the essence of Judaism is a speculative understanding of God. He replaces *kalam* with its eclectic appeal to individual philosophical ideas applied *ad hoc* with a rigorous, thoroughgoing integration of Jewish theology and Aristotelianism in his chief work, the *Guide to the Perplexed*.

Maimonides' basic premise in the *Guide*, stated with more force and originality than is true of any other philosophical theologian in any of the three sister faiths, is twofold: revealed religious truth and philosophy are totally congruent, and revealed truths need to be recast in philosophical terms across the board. Any apparent discrepancies between these two bodies of thought he dismisses as the result of faulty reasoning and misperception. While stating the same truths as philosophy, Maimonides notes, revelation articulated them across the ages of biblical time, contextualizing them historically in a bygone society and expressing them in ancient thought patterns and rhetorical forms. On the other hand, while philosophical truths may have been stated initially centuries ago, they are eternally true and intrinsically more accessible to the human mind than are revealed truths appropriated through the filter of biblical narrative or exhortation. Maimonides therefore asserts that it is possible to reformulate Jewish theology in its entirety in Aristotelian terms, without fudging either the theology or the philosophy, and that it is eminently desirable to do so, in order to make theology more immediate and comprehensible to people living in the post-biblical age.

At the same time as he offers this bold and sweeping argument for the rationalizing of theology, Maimonides also maintains that philosophy does not have all the answers. A major area in which he thinks that no philosophical school has produced a solid demonstrative proof, understanding demonstration in Aristotle's sense as a proof that compels assent, is the question of how the universe was created. On this point, he thinks that Averroes erred in accepting Aristotle on the eternity of matter. Maimonides does not think that either Aristotle or Averroes demonstrates that claim. Nor has anyone clearly refuted it. Maimonides also takes issue with the Neoplatonic emanationist model of creation found in many of his predecessors. Since he rejects the Aristotelian account of creation as undemonstrated, he cannot use it against the Neoplatonists. But he finds the Neoplatonic account impossible to disprove as well. Neither school can prove its cosmogenetic thesis, and the accounts of both schools are problematic in the light of the doctrine of God and creation professed by all three 'Peoples of the Book.' The eternity of matter thesis denies that God created everything out of nothing. Emanationism makes creation neces- sary to God and denies His freedom, omnipotence, and transcendence. In this area, since no philosophy can validate its claims, Maimonides thinks it acceptable to hold religious beliefs on religious grounds alone.

On the other hand, Maimonides is confident that the human mind can demon- strate God's existence and find meaningful ways of speaking about the deity despite His transcendence. He holds that we derive a positive knowledge of God through both physics and metaphysics, offering three proofs of God's existence based on observable natural phenomena and on the nature of being. All had been articulated by earlier Muslim or Jewish thinkers and all are given crisp and clear recapitula- tion by Maimonides. One is Avicenna's proof that the existence of possible or con- tingent beings requires the existence of a necessary being. Another, similar to the first, maintains that finite beings require an infinite being as their cause. The third, derived from Aristotle, argues that the phenomenon of motion requires the exis- tence of a prime mover. These proofs yield several attributes of the deity as well as providing rationales for His existence. Beyond that, and this is his chief depar- ture from Aristotelianism, Maimonides thinks that we must resort to negative the- ology in commenting further on God's nature.

Ethics takes up less of his interest than the speculations just discussed. None the less, like Saadia, Maimonides aims at rationalizing the Jewish moral law. With Saadia, he divides it into two categories. He finds the general principles of conduct enjoined by the Ten Commandments intrinsically rational. Left to its own devices, the human mind would arrive at the same conclusions. No further justifications are necessary. When it comes to the ritual and dietary laws, Maimonides finds that they have no intrinsic rationale. He falls back on Saadia's social utility argument for laws in this group, but reformulates it. The ritual laws are reasonable, Maimonides main- tains, because they are conducive to the social cohesiveness of the Jewish commu- nity, not because they induce humility before an inscrutable God.

This last observation points to the changing historical circumstances within the Arabic intellectual community and particularly in Spain, as fundamentalist Muslim rulers took charge and as Christian kings increasingly conquered the Iberian penin- sula, circumstances that were to alter Jewish thought in Maimonides' day and beyond, in ways sometimes parallel to Muslim thought and sometimes not. Pietists, like Judah Halevi, became polemicists. Rationalizers, whether synthesizing phi- losophy with theology, like Maimonides, or engaging in pure *falsafah*, like Aver- roes, found themselves and their work at higher risk in Spain. As Spanish Muslims lost ground to Christian kings, the most learned and mobile among them heeded the advice of the school of Muslim law enforced in their homeland and emigrated to parts of the Near East governed by Muslim rulers, leaving their co-religionists in Spain leaderless in speculative thought. Muslims subject to Spanish Christians fell back increasingly on the religious law, the Koran, and Sufism, to reinforce a social and religious identity growing ever more precarious. In the Near East, the lack of support for speculative thought in the school system was coupled with the desire to reinforce religious identity when Sunni Muslims ruled Shi'ites or vice versa, when Turkish rulers imported new social or political institutions, or when rulers, like the Mongols, were initially not Muslims. Both sets of circumstances encouraged a focus on the religious sciences and Sufism and the belief that speculative thought was irrelevant.

Mobile Jewish scholars, like Maimonides and Halevi, also left Spain for the Near East. As a result of the Crusades, anti-Christian sentiment among Muslims there reduced their tolerance for Jews as well and, in any case, the scientific and philosophical community of which Jews had been a vital part was becoming vestigial. Jews remaining in Europe were not welcomed in Christian schools, and persecution, ghettoization, or expulsion further separated them from the European intellectual mainstream. Thrown back on their own resources, they no longer wrote in Arabic, translating the works of Jewish thinkers who had earlier done so into Hebrew and having to reappropriate them anew in that language. The circumstances of European Jews in the later Middle Ages also encouraged them to emphasize Talmudism, pietism, and cabbalism as sources of religious identity and consolation. Whether or not they followed the line of Maimonides, a figure who certainly supplied his successors with powerful weapons for the rational support of Judaism, they too became more defensive. When Maimonides' *Guide* was translated into Latin it was received with awe and respect, especially by thinkers in the Dominican school. He was cited simply as 'the Rabbi' or as 'Rabbi Moses' in the way that Averroes was cited as 'the Commentator.' Maimonides enjoyed a wider influence among all three 'Peoples of the Book' than any other medieval thinker. His biography, along with those of Judah Halevi and Averroes, is a boundary stone, marking the limits of the times and places in which fruitful interactions of thinkers from these sister faiths were possible in Muslim lands.

CHAPTER 11

Western European Thought in the Tenth and Eleventh Centuries

In the period when Muslim thought was reaching its apex and when Byzantine thought was entering its age of codification, western Europe went through an age that began in a state of confusion and regression but that ended on a note of intellectual and religious revival, with new art forms and bold speculative innovation. Beset by new Magyar, Viking, and Muslim invasions and the replacement of central by localized institutions, tenth-century intellectuals could do little but tread water until political and economic life became more stable. England endured successive waves of Danish conquerers, alternating with Anglo-Saxon kings. In the wake of the Carolingian empire, its German section took possession of the imperial title and lodged it in the dynasty of Otto I (912–73) and his successors, who also claimed northern Italy. The Byzantines and Muslims fought over southern Italy until it was conquered by the Norman Giuscard family in the mid-eleventh century. In the French section of the former Carolingian empire, Hugh Capet (ruled 987–96) and his dynasty gained recognition as kings but ruled directly only in Paris and the Île de France, with vassals individually and collectively more powerful than the crown. One of them, William of Normandy (1027/8–87), became a king in his own right with his conquest of England in 1066. Amid these political shifts, western Europe also launched an agrarian revolution based on newly invented or imported technology that, for the first time in its history, enabled it to produce an economy of agrarian surplus. In turn, this surplus stimulated the revival of trade and of urban life. As invasions subsided and travel became easier, long-distance commerce extended Europe's outreach to non-European areas and the interdependence of its parts. By the late eleventh century, the changing relations between western Europe and her neighbors could be seen in the related movements of Crusades to the Holy Land and the reconquest of the Iberian peninsula from the Muslims, as well as by the new Norman presence in the Mediterranean world. The intellectual life of Europe likewise revived, affected by all these developments. Royal courts rarely provided guidance except through indirect patronage. Bishops, monastic leaders, and the local noble supporters they attracted moved to the forefront as patrons of culture.

At the beginning of this period, monasteries were the leading centers of religious, artistic, and intellectual life. To persons eager to support these activities, the reform and support of monasticism was a natural response. While aiming at the restoration of older monastic rules, however, the monastic reforms of the tenth and eleventh centuries developed new features. In the effort to free monasticism from the interference of lay people or bishops lacking in zeal, the Burgundian nobleman who founded Cluny in 909 specified that the abbey and its dependencies would be exempt from such external control. Although its goal was to restore the Benedictine *Rule*, Cluny thus created a new governance structure for monasticism. The abbeys linked to Cluny were all ruled by Cluny's abbot, who appointed their priors. The frequent visits he made to daughter houses spread to all Cluniac convents common styles of liturgical music and art (Plates 11 and 12), the promotion of pilgrimage to Santiago de Compostela in northern Spain, and prayer for the dead on the feast of All Souls. This feast, created for the Cluniac liturgy by Abbot Odilo (994–1049), was then adopted by western Christendom generally. An earlier abbot, Odo (926–44), contributed to the growing hagiography of the lay warrior-saints in his *Life of Gerald*. By the end of the eleventh century, Cluny possessed an abbey church that was the largest structure in western Christendom and had produced a series of leaders who brought their vision and skills to the reform of the church at large from their positions as cardinals and popes. In all, the Cluniac movement is a good example of the capacity of Benedictine monasticism to reinvent itself, adapting to the needs and interests of the age.

Another, if less dramatic, illustration of the same theme is the reform of monasticism in England by Dunstan, archbishop of Canterbury (909–88). Eager to continue the translation of Latin works into Old English, to bring monastic life and learning back to the standing they had had in the reign of Alfred the Great, and to repair the damage wrought by the Danish invasions, Dunstan invented a new technique for monastic reform while still abbot of Glastonbury, which he enforced nationally when he became primate of the English church. He began with a single abbey. Once it had been reformed and was running smoothly, he sent a few of its brethren to an unreformed abbey with the charge of showing its members how to observe the Benedictine *Rule*. When this had been achieved, the process was repeated in other abbeys, one by one. This method, especially when ordained by Dunstan as archbishop, undercut the authority over his own community that the *Rule* gives to the abbot. Dunstan did likewise in legislating liturgical norms, on a national level, for all monasteries, incorporating specifically English usages that made English Benedictine observance different from that of their brethren elsewhere.

Adaptation, in the name of restoring past custom, can also be seen in Italian monasticism in the tenth and eleventh centuries. Here, owing to the Byzantine presence, Basilian-style monasticism and the hermitage were popular. New orders, such as Camaldoli and Vallombrosa, were launched by individual reformers to express the values of this type of monastic life, less interested in education and art patronage and more strictly ascetic and contemplative than the Benedictine model. A leading advocate of these reforms was Peter Damian (1007–72). In a striking reprise of Tertullian's position, Peter used his distinctive and eloquent Latin to denounce vain curiosity and, in *On Divine Omnipotence*, picking up on an observation made by Jerome, he opened what was to become a major speculative debate with his argument that God's power enables Him to undo the past. As monastic organizers, Peter and his associates brought something new to the Basilian and eremitic traditions. In orders like Vallombrosa, monasticism combined the eremitic experience with community life. Brethren lived, prayed, and worked in individual cells, coming together only for mass and a few other functions. This lifestyle required the reconceptualization of monastic architecture, providing an organization of space different from that required by monks who lived most of their lives in common. Moreover, Peter created 'congregations,' forging institutional links among individual monasteries or hermitages that undercut the complete autonomy they had earlier had.

To the extent that secular rulers patronized culture, the most visible force was the Ottonian court in imperial Germany. While ostensibly modeling their patronage on the Carolingians', the Ottonians' approach was actually different, partly because of the political structure of the German empire, which was extremely decentralized. The emperor could not legislate for the whole empire. He wielded direct authority only in his own duchy; the other dukes were independent. Otto succeeded in reconnecting his empire with Byzantium diplomatically, arranging a marriage between his son and a Byzantine princess. Ottonian culture, especially in art, was hence more open to Byzantine influence than had been true of the Carolingian Renaissance. It was largely through the bishops the emperor appointed, through individuals he patronized, and through the resources of monasteries with imperial and noble connections that the Ottonian Renaissance took shape. Totally absent was an imperially driven agenda. These traits can be seen in the four most outstanding figures linked in one way or another to the Ottonian Renaissance, Bernward of Hildesheim (ruled 993–1022), Hroswita of Gandersheim (*c.* 935– *c.* 1001/3), Liutprand of Cremona (*c.* 920–*c.* 972), and Gerbert of Aurillac (940–1003).

Bernward, bishop of Hildesheim, well illustrates the explosion in the visual arts sponsored by episcopal and monastic leaders like himself, engendering a distinctive Ottonian style of manuscript illumination, the new Romanesque style of architecture with local features typical of Germany (Plates 13, 14 and 15), and monumental sculpture, with large art objects cast in bronze on a scale not seen in the west since ancient Rome. Bernward built a new cathedral and underwrote the casting of its bronze doors as well as a baptismal font and an Easter column (Plate 16). It is still not entirely clear how Ottonian artists discovered the technology needed to move beyond the sculpting of small portable objects such as ivories and book covers to the production of these large-scale works.

Hroswita's connection to the Ottos stems from the fact that her convent was an imperial foundation. The abbess in Hroswita's day was a niece of the ruling emperor, with the status of an imperial prince and even the right to mint her own coinage. The wealth and privileges of Gandersheim made it a magnet for aristocratic women entering monastic life. In their case, the Benedictine *Rule* was relaxed, since they were not required to take the vow of poverty. The strength of the education of the Gandersheim nuns is reflected in Hroswita, the best Latin writer in

Europe in her day. She produced poetry and histories of her convent revealing a thorough mastery of the classical Latin authors in the school tradition. Her best-known works, and deservedly so, are her six plays. Aside from being the first expression of non-liturgical drama since late antiquity, Hroswita's plays show her ability to draw independently on literary sources not in the school curriculum and to use them her own way, developing a distinctive literary style and outlook. She has two sets of models. One is the collection of saints' lives celebrating the early Christian martyrs, the desert ascetics, and the sinners they had converted to a life of repentance and austerity. The second is the Roman comedian Terence (195/85–159 BC). Like all ancient comedians, he wrote plays quite racy in their language and situations. He is a surprising source for a nun whose protagonists are Christian martyrs, Magdalenes, and virgins. Hroswita chose Terence because he taught her how to write humorous dialogue and how to manage the flow of events from scene to scene. She ignores or allegorizes the racy passages. As for her hagiographical sources, they typically exalt the male saint who counsels virgins and martyrs or who converts harlots. In Hroswita's hands, the female characters become the protagonists and the role of their male mentors is downplayed or ignored. The result is a series of plays that are genuinely comic, that play very well on stage, and that have happy endings spiritually. They are entertaining and edifying at the same time. Hroswita's use of her sources as a springboard for her own innovations, in style and substance, is as noteworthy as the high literary finish of her plays.

If Hroswita is her century's major playwright, a leading indicator of Otto I's new policy toward Byzantium is Liutprand, whom Otto sent as his ambassador to Constantinople. Liutprand, bishop of Cremona, had performed similar services for several Italian rulers, who likewise chose him because he spoke Greek, attesting to the lingering presence of bilingual classical studies in Italy. Liutprand wrote historical works and political satire aimed in all directions, against the rulers of the north Italian cities, against personal opponents in the Italian church, and against the emperors, whose claims to northern Italy he contests and whom he presents as transalpine barbarians. Matters are otherwise, however, in his most famous work, the *Embassy to Constantinople*, which reports the failure of his first round of negotiations with the Byzantines in 968. Although Liutprand succeeded in gaining Otto's objectives in his second embassy of 971, the report given in the *Embassy* surrounds the German emperor with a radiant aura of uprightness, generosity, nobility, and wisely used authority while presenting the Byzantines as uncouth, perfidious, and hostile, as a means of explaining the failure of the mission it relates. In so doing, Liutprand displays a keen narrative and descriptive sense and a sinewy Latin style liberally besprinkled with classical allusions. He is a shrewd political observer, as is revealed in his analysis of the tensions among Byzantine leaders. But the chief pleasures of reading his *Embassy* derive from his intellectual and literary sophistication and his acerbic wit.

The tenth century produced, as its leading scientific thinker, Gerbert. Like Hroswita, he was a product of convent life. But he was an inveterate traveler, his quest for scientific knowledge indicating how hard it was to come by in Europe during his time. Gerbert's career depended on his good fortune in meeting wealthy and powerful people willing to point him in the right direction and to support him and his studies. Gerbert began as a monk in the French abbey of Aurillac. Thanks to a local noble who recognized his intellectual potential, he was able to transfer to Bobbio, becoming its abbot. But its school, resting on its original Irish foundations, proved inadequate to his needs. A visiting Spanish noble advised him to go to Muslim Spain to learn science, and made his trip possible. Gerbert studied in Auch, in Catalonia, obtaining the best scientific education of any non-Spanish European of his day. On his return, the emperor appointed him as tutor to his heir and then made him archbishop of Rheims, after further studies in Spain which the ruler subsidized. At Rheims, Gerbert reorganized the curriculum of the cathedral school, placing heavy emphasis on the quadrivium and introducing an expanded Boethian logical curriculum. It was during this phase of his career that he produced his own scientific writings, reflecting his use of empirical observation and instrumentation. He applied the abacus to calculation and the astrolabe in astronomy, and was one of the first Latin authors to use Arabic numerals. Gerbert ended his career as Pope Sylvester II. After becoming pope he lacked the time for further scientific studies. Although he was able to make Rheims a major center of scientific education during his years there, there were no successors with similar interests to continue his work. While Gerbert's life is certainly a success story, and while he received substantial aristocratic and imperial patronage, perhaps the most striking feature of his career is its accidental quality. He was lucky enough to impress patrons able and willing to forward his projects, but he neither found, nor was able to create on an enduring basis, schools that institutionalized the scientific studies dearest to him.

The same kind of accidental convergence, and divergence, of particular masters and schools is visible in France as well, although intellectual life in that country in the tenth and eleventh centuries enjoyed no patronage from the crown. Here, too, cathedral schools entered the ranks along with monastic schools, both showing evidence of high-quality instruction. Just as Gerbert could give Rheims a new look, scientifically, by his presence there, so too the cathedral schools in France reflect the scholarly and literary interests of the masters they attracted or produced. Similarly, the ability of a school to perpetuate a particular educational specialty beyond the liberal arts depended on whether masters stayed or left. The cathedral schools of Orléans and Chartres, for example, made a specialty of classical Latin literature. This subject, launched at Chartres by Fulbert (*c.* 970–1028), was studied along with astronomy and Boethian logic. Chartres succeeded in maintaining consistent leadership in literary studies until the middle of the twelfth century thanks to a succession of masters after Fulbert who shared his tastes. On the other hand, the cathedral school of Laon, which became a major center of biblical exegesis and theology under Anselm of Laon (*c.* 1050–1117), lost its momentum; in the next generation, Anselm's leading pupils moved to other schools such as Rheims, taking Laon's mantle and Anselm's method with them.

In Gerbert's case we see new material added to the curriculum thanks to his importation of scientific advances from Muslim Spain; in the case of the other figures and schools mentioned, what is involved is not new material but a deeper and more personalized use of materials already in the curriculum or of available authors who had not been pressed into service by earlier medieval thinkers. In moving to the revival of speculative thought that culminates in Anselm of Canterbury (1033–1109), the same keynote is struck. Ideas and authors already there for the taking were now being studied in new ways, with new questions put to them and innovative arguments inspired by them. And, while metaphysical questions arose, such as Peter Damian's consideration of divine omnipotence, the single development fueling the emergence of speculative thought in the eleventh century was the study of grammar and logic and the emergence of semantic theories that were to take medieval philosophy in creative post-classical directions and to give philosophers and theologians new tools with which to work.

There are strong indicators, both in commentaries on their works and in internal evidence found in logicians and speculative grammarians, that the works of Priscian and the logical curriculum found in Boethius' wider writings were receiving detailed scrutiny in the eleventh century, producing new debates. The *Rhetorimachia* of Anselm of Besate (*c.* 1020–67) points to one such controversy, on whether the denotations of words are natural or conventional. The first view sees language, in this case Latin, as mirroring the real world perfectly. The second maintains that speakers of a given language agree that certain words have certain meanings by common convention. Both positions had partisans in classical antiquity. Boethius reprises the debate and opts for the conventional denotation theory. He is the likely source for Anselm and Drogo, the contemporary whom Anselm attacks for making Latin grammar the criterion of truth. Anselm's claim, in the *Rhetorimachia*, that Drogo's teaching has infested Germany, Italy, and England is partly a justification for his own effort to refute it. But other developments suggest that Drogo and Anselm were far from unusual in their concerns.

Another important index of rising interest in logic and semantics is the emergence of the debate over universals, presented by Boethius although he does not take a stand on it. Two schools of thought emerged in the eleventh century, one defending the logical priority of universals or abstract ideas over ideas standing for individual things and the other defending the logical posteriority of universals. Taking this issue from the realm of logic to the realm of metaphysics, extreme exponents of these positions argued that the things signified by universals are either more, or less, real than the individual things that concepts standing for them signify. This move, an independent development not sanctioned by Boethius or his sources, attained notoriety in the later eleventh century because of its application to theology by Roscellinus (*c.* 1050–1125), who studied at the cathedral schools of Soissons and Rheims and who taught logic at a number of other schools, including Compiègne. Roscellinus argues that individual things and the concepts signifying them are more real than universal things and concepts and applies this idea to the Trinity. He concludes that the Father, Son, and Holy Spirit are truly deities and that Their names are truly meaningful. On the other hand, 'God' as a term signifying the divine nature possessed by all three Trinitarian persons is a meaningless abstraction. Roscellinus was charged with tritheism at the council of Soissons in 1092 and was criticized pointedly by Anselm of Canterbury. Whether or not he was convinced by his critics, Roscellinus retracted his argument and continued his career as a respected logician until his death.

Another high-profile controversialist whose arguments turned on semantic issues, the sign theory of Aristotle and Priscian, and on other features of Aristotelianism, was Berengarius of Tours (*c.* 1000–88), who applied these ideas to the Eucharist. His goal was to attack the consensus doctrine that Christ is corporeally present in the Eucharist after the officiating priest has spoken the words of consecration in the mass, 'For this is my body.' Drawing on the Aristotelian notion of substance modified by accidents, Berengarius argues against this doctrine by asserting that the accidents of bread and wine can inhere only in the substance of bread and wine. If bread and wine have ceased to exist on the altar, their accidents have nothing to subtend them; they cannot inhere in a different substantial substrate, the body of the resurrected Christ. This argument presented an enduring challenge to orthodox theologians defending the consensus position for the next several centuries. It was a powerful force inspiring a more general sense of the need to explain Eucharistic doctrine in Aristotelian terms.

A second issue raised by Berengarius concerns the ways in which parts of speech signify. His inspiration was the fact that Priscian and Aristotle were held to disagree on the semantic force of nouns. As a grammarian, Priscian simply describes the way the Latin language is used in citing his standard example: the nouns 'man,' 'tree,' and 'stone' can refer to individual men, trees, and stones or to men, trees, and stones in general. For his part, Aristotle is prescriptive. Looking at substances as beings that retain their identity despite the changes they undergo and the accidents that may or may not inhere in them, he states that a noun cannot properly signify both the substance and the accidents; it must signify either one or the other. Eleventh-century thinkers, including Berengarius, developed what they hoped was a compromise, conflating Aristotle with Priscian on nouns and applying the Aristotelian view to pronouns. Thus, they held that nouns signify their objects substantially and accidentally. Pronouns, although they stand for nouns in the sentences where they are used, signify their objects substantially but not accidentally as well. Approaching 'For this is my body' with the semantic weapons forged by this theory, Berengarius notes that 'body,' clearly a noun, signifies Christ's body. He also notes that 'this,' the subject of the sentence, is a pronoun, whose semantic force is weaker than that of a noun. In this sentence, the noun 'body' functions grammatically as a predicate nominative. As such, it must agree with the subject of the sentence which governs it. Now if, as his opponents claim, the substance of bread were turned into the substance of Christ's body when the priest says the words of consecration, the predicate nominative would be rising up and annulling the subject of the sentence, a manifest grammatical impossibility. Ingenious and novel as it is, this argument is literally incomprehensible unless one is conversant with eleventh-century developments in logic and grammar.

Indeed, Berengarius' analysis of the consecration formula was so ingenious and so in tune with current speculation in these fields that his major antagonist, Lanfranc (*c.* 1010–89) did not try to attack Berengarius on his own terrain but offered a flanking movement. A native of Pavia who had gone to the Norman monastery of Bec, a new foundation supported by rising noble families of the duchy, whose school he currently headed, Lanfranc later became abbot of St. Stephen's in Caen and then archbishop of Canterbury after the Norman conquest. His counteroffensive against Berengarius uses a technique of argument called equipollency, invented by a Platonic logician in the second century and now coming back into use. In equipollent argumentation, the debater starts with a proposition and redefines it, with his opponent's consent to the redefinition. He continues this process, with each redefinition bringing the original proposition closer to the one he wants to prove, until he arrives at that conclusion. Berengarius may or may not have found Lanfranc's argument responsive to all the questions he had raised. While his position on the Eucharist was condemned at the synod of Vercelli in 1050, the legacy of Berengarius continued to set the agenda for later Eucharistic theologians.

Both the increasing urge to frame theological issues in philosophical terms and the intense interest in logic, speculative grammar, and semantics which the foregoing episodes illustrate provide the historical context for Anselm of Canterbury, the greatest speculative mind of his century and one of the most original medieval thinkers, whose thought has not ceased to attract attention from his day to the present. Like his master Lanfranc, he came from northern Italy, traveling from his native Aosta to Bec, where he headed the school with distinction before becoming abbot and then succeeding Lanfranc as primate of England. As a logician, Anselm reveals his deep knowledge of the Boethian curriculum. Manuscript evidence indicates that Gerbert, when teaching at Rheims, had begun the study of the larger Boethian canon, a pedagogical legacy he passed on to pupils who later taught in France, such as Abbo of Fleury (*c.* 945–1004). The same materials were available at Chartres, but organized in such a way as to reflect an unawareness of the particular pedagogical order Boethius imposed on the subdivisions of logic. Bec also possessed a manuscript containing these materials, with the Boethian sequence in place. It was acquired most likely by Lanfranc through personal contacts. But it was Anselm who not only taught this logical curriculum at Bec but put it to use, as his own logical and theological works attest. Four indications of that fact are his familiarity with paronyms, modal propositions, hypothetical syllogisms, and negative formulations. In the last two cases, he draws on Stoicizing elements in Boethian logic that take the subject beyond Aristotle's *Categories* and *On Interpretation.* In the case of paronymy, Anselm also elaborates a logical distinction noted but not developed by Aristotle and Boethius, an innovation taken up by many later medieval logicians.

As Aristotle states in his *Categories,* paronyms can be distinguished from synonyms and homonyms in that they refer to the same thing, as an adjective derived from a noun, like 'strong' from 'strength' or as one noun derived from another, like 'grammarian' from 'grammar.' Anselm siezes on the second example in his *On the Grammarian.* Informed by the conflict between the semantic theories of Priscian and Aristotle noted above, he sees a problem here which neither Aristotle nor Boethius resolves. Both 'grammar' and 'grammarian' are nouns. But they do not denote what they signify in the same way. Anselm introduces a third term, 'man,' the individual who is a grammarian, in order to distinguish between signification and appellation and between direct, or proper signification and indirect, or oblique signification. 'Man' both signifies and names the person who is a grammarian and it does so directly. On the other hand, 'grammarian' names this person, but only indirectly. What 'grammarian' signifies directly is a quality, the grammatical knowledge this person possesses. Anselm's distinctions between signification and appellation and between proper and oblique signification are genuine post-Aristotelian additions to semantics. In developing them he goes beyond the sources alerting him to the problem raised by paronyms. And, aside from the conclusions he draws on paronymy, he sees that the semantic rules applying to logical signification are not necessarily the same as those applying to the Latin language as spoken, and seeks to place the whole subject of logical signification on a more technical plane.

Modal propositions are another logical issue Anselm considers, using arguments based on them in a number of works. These propositions, as Aristotle defines them, contain terms such as possible, impossible, necessary, and contingent. The terms function either as the predicates of the propositions in conjunction with the verb 'to be' or as adverbs modifying the verb. 'God's existence is necessary' illustrates the first type; 'God exists necessarily' illustrates the second. In turn, modal syllogisms are syllogisms whose premises or conclusions are modal propositions. When properly constructed, modal syllogisms yield conclusions that follow logically from their antecedents with a high degree of formal rigor. Anselm joins Boethius in adding to this received doctrine the post-Aristotelian distinction between antecedent and concomitant possibility. Antecedent possibility is a latent potentiality that has not yet been actualized. Concomitant possibility can be subdivided into necessary concomitant possibility, which applies to conditions that are always actual once created, such as the orderly movements of the planets, and nonnecessary concomitant possibility, which applies to conditions that may be actualized but that do not have to be, such as the seated position of a person who could be standing instead. These distinctions lend greater precision to modal arguments and are used by Anselm the theologian.

For Aristotle, syllogisms that are truly demonstrable have terms that refer to phenomena in the world outside the mind, against which our logical conclusions can be cross-checked; for the Stoics, on the other hand, logic is a purely formal art. They indicate this by using hypothetical syllogisms based on 'if–then' and 'either–or' formulations, and the like, whose conclusions are verifiable in terms of the formal relations of the premises comprising them, not in terms of their correspondence to extra-mental phenomena. Boethius had written about hypothetical syllogisms in a treatise devoted to them, also illustrating their forms in detail in his *Topics*. Anselm draws on Boethius and makes extensive use of this kind of argumentation.

Another post-Aristotelian notion Anselm derives from Boethius, as well as from earlier eleventh-century masters, is the Stoic distinction between negating a verb in a proposition and negating the entire proposition by placing a negative term in front of it. Thus, if we say 'It is not raining,' we deny that it is raining at present. If we say 'Not: it is raining,' we deny the existence of rain as such. In electing to use locutions such as 'Not: it is raining' to denote this more exhaustive mode of negation, Anselm highlights another point at which the desiderata of logical rigor take precedence over the grammatical conventions governing the spoken language.

All these concerns show that Anselm was a major player in the front-line debates on logic, speculative grammar, and semantics of his time. They arm him for the attack on the philosophical and theological issues he addresses, many of which raise fundamental questions not considered since the patristic period. The most celebrated cases in point are his proofs of God's existence in the *Monologion* and *Proslogion*. Also of great interest, in themselves and for the light they shed on these proofs, are the doctrine of truth as rectitude developed in Anselm's *On Truth* and the doctrine of necessary reasoning displayed not only in the proofs but also in his *Why Was God Made Man?*, where Anselm also develops his own explanation of Christ's saving work.

In *On Truth*, Anslem makes a distinction, original to him, between natural truth and truth properly speaking, or truth possessing rectitude. It has some parallels with Avicenna's treatment of the criterion of truth, although there is no way Anselm could have known of Avicenna's work. Natural truth is subjective certitude. It is what a person thinks is true. A proposition stating a natural truth accurately signifies the person's conviction. But it may be objectively untrue if the thinker's idea fails to correspond with actual fact. Like Avicenna, Anselm thinks that a real world exists independent of what we think about it and that we can judge the objective accuracy of our subjective certitudes by comparing them with the realities for which they stand. If they do correspond with extra-mental reality, our ideas possess rectitude, and rectitude, the criterion of truth, should be our goal in reasoning.

Another attribute of sound argumentation, for Anselm, is necessary reasoning, which he defines in *Why Was God Made Man?* Here, we should note that he does not mean by this term arguments that are Aristotelian demonstrative syllogisms, which compel consent as necessarily true. Rather, what he means are arguments based on reason alone, arguments making no appeal to authority. They are the most cogent arguments he can find; although he presents them with the proviso that they are subject to replacement if he or anyone else finds better ones. Anselm presents necessary reasons as ways of displaying the rectitude between objective realities or events and the true statements we frame about them. In this treatise, Anselm invokes the method to address a question basic to Christian theology that had not been aired since the days of the early church. Given that God is omnipotent and given that He decided to redeem fallen mankind, why did He choose Christ's incarnation and crucifixion as the mode of redemption, rather than accomplishing it some other way? Anselm offers his own rationale against those who argue that God could have redeemed mankind by direct divine fiat and, even more, against proponents of the 'rights of the devil' theory, those who view Christ's saving work as reclaiming the obedience which sinful mankind transferred from God to the devil, from whose sway sinners cannot extricate themselves, in terms of a military victory over the devil that liberates sinners and restores them to their proper allegiance to God. His own theory sees the need for some just recompense to be made to God, an infinite being infinitely offended by human sin. But, since human beings are finite, nothing they offer to God can make just reparation. Hence, Christ, as a God-man, is needed. As God, He is an infinite being and infinitely good. He can thus offer an infinitely worthy recompense to God for human sin. And as man, Christ can impute to other human beings the merits of his reconciliatory self-sacrifice. In keeping with the rules that Anslem lays down for necessary reasoning, nowhere in this treatise does he argue for the cogency of his conclusions by citing proof-texts from the Bible or the church fathers.

Even more basic, as a theological doctrine to which Anselm wants to apply necessary reasoning, is the existence of God. His first search for proofs of God's existence in the *Monologion* does invoke arguments drawn from Augustine. When this is the case, Anselm uses them because of their rational force, not on Augustine's authority. Proofs drawn from grammatical analysis and equipollency also abound. Anselm's initial proof is an Augustinian one, moving from degrees of goodness in the universe to a supreme good. Next, he equipollently redefines this supreme good as a being, next redefines it as the supreme being, and then redefines it as a unitary and self-existent being, the source of all being and goodness. Having established these features of the supreme being by equipollency, he also uses grammatical analysis to explore God's attributes. The relations between God's essence and mode of being can be analogized to the relations among 'light,' 'to light,' and 'shining.' The nominal, infinitive, and prepositional terms all refer to the same phenomenon. And, while God's essence and mode of being can be thought about individually, they are united in God's being, just as these grammatical terms all refer to the same phenomenon of light.

As he continued to reflect on the problem of proving God's existence, Anselm grew dissatisfied with his approach in the *Monologion*. He wanted a simpler and more elegant proof. He presents the one he found in the *Proslogion*. Three important points must be made before proceeding. First, Anselm describes what he is doing in his subtitle as 'faith seeking understanding.' The role of rational argument is to clarify the truth of what we believe, not to establish it in the first place. Second, like Augustine's *Confessions*, the *Proslogion* is interlarded with prayer and the author's addresses to the deity. Thus, while Anselm refrains from adducing arguments from authority, he makes it plain that his rational method is not opposed to a devotional relationship to his object of knowledge. Third, the statement in *Proslogion*, Book 2 in which he offers his description of the deity, a description which, in his view, enables us to grasp God's necessary existence, is not a proposition framed in the third person, as is true of propositions in syllogistic reasoning. Rather, the statement reads, 'We believe that You are that than which nothing greater can be conceived.'[1] Such a being must exist, and must exist necessarily, he argues, because, if it did not, we could conceive of a still greater being, and the description given would therefore be self-contradictory and lack rectitude with respect to God.

In the preface of the *Proslogion*, Anselm makes his point of departure the fool of the Book of Psalms who says there is no God. He asserts that his own description of God is shared by fools and unbelievers, who agree with believers on the nature of the deity Whose existence they deny. But a God so understood, he argues, must exist in reality as well as in thought. Anselm derives this conclusion from the idea that a being that exists both in the mind and in reality is greater than one that has intra-mental existence only. Thus, God must have extra-mental as well as intra-mental existence if the description given of Him in *Proslogion*, Book 2 is accurate. With these foundations laid, Anselm works out the other divine attributes by equipollency. Among these attributes is omnipotence. Here, he offers the same analysis of this topic as he gives in his treatises on divine omnipotence and on the devil's fall. In opposition to Peter Damian, Anselm maintains that God cannot undo the past. For doing what is unbecoming to a being is a weakness, not an expression of power, and undoing the past or destabilizing the natural order would be unbecoming of God. Here, as elsewhere, Anselm underlines the difference between theological and grammatical signification, showing how terms signifying apparent limitations actually display perfections in God's case.

One of Anselm's contemporaries, the monk Gaunilo of Marmoutiers (d. 1081) took issue with Anselm's *Proslogion* in a treatise *On Behalf of the Fool*. Gaunilo's central contention is that it is fallacious to say that because we have a certain idea of God in our minds we can leap from thought to reality by claiming that this God has extra-mental reality. For, he notes, we can think about fictitious beings, such as the most perfect island imaginable. But the fact that we have an idea of this perfect island in our minds does not prove that it exists extra-mentally. In his response to Gaunilo, Anselm makes three points. First, he reminds Gaunilo that the purpose of the *Proslogion* is faith seeking understanding. In particular, the *Proslogion* is a quest for a description of God that has rectitude, that corresponds with God as He is. Anselm observes that he is not moving from thought to reality, but the reverse. His second point reformulates the passage contrasting being in the intellect with being both in the intellect and in reality into a hypothetical 'if–then' syllogism. The aim of this gambit is to gain his opponent's assent to the conclusion he draws at least in formal terms. Finally, invoking the distinction between necessary beings and non-necessary possible beings, he notes that islands, however perfect, are not analogous to the deity. God is a necessary being Who exists in and of Himself. Like other changeable created beings, perfect islands are contingent. Their non-existence is entirely conceivable. Anselm concludes by repeating that, when we speak about God, the divine nature is the criterion of the rectitude of the statements we make about Him.

Aside from his *On Behalf of the Fool*, nothing is known about Gaunilo or the monastic school of Marmoutiers to which he was attached, but, no less than Anselm, he testifies to the revival of speculative thought in eleventh-century Europe and to the ways in which contemporaries framed their debates. The patronage supporting their respective abbeys came from local nobles, concerned with securing the prayers of the monks for their souls and those of their relatives and eager to associate themselves with the spiritual power of the abbeys' patron saints and the relics they might possess. Unlike patrons in Byzantium and Islam, they did not think it was their place to dictate which studies were appropriate, how they should be taught, and whether it was acceptable to ring changes on ancient sources and go beyond them. Nor did they enforce guidelines on the application of logic or grammar to theology. The monastic and episcopal corporations that nurtured the thinkers discussed in this chapter set their own guidelines under the leadership of their own members. Thin on the ground though they may have been, the writers, artists, and thinkers of the time are impressive for their creative exploitation of the sources available to them. Their resources were far more limited than those of contemporary Byzantines and Muslims. But they display a different outlook, one confidently reworking and rethinking the legacy of the past, posing afresh the big questions, and enlarging the scope of their philosophical, theological, literary, and artistic agendas. The resourcefulness that accompanied this outlook, and the eagerness to travel far from home to find the education they sought, would enable Europeans to make dramatic strides forward when the Greco-Arabic translations of the twelfth and thirteenth centuries enabled them to reclaim the Greek part of their ancient heritage as well as to reap the fruits of Muslim and Jewish philosophy and science. Figures such as Gerbert and Anselm indicate that their successors would know what to do with these materials when they became available, and also that innovation, although speeded up by their arrival, did not depend on them in all cases. The latency of the intellectual history of Europe in the early Middle Ages was long, and often marked by an independence forged in the crucible of adversity. By the end of the eleventh century, early medieval thought had come of age.

PART IV
LATIN AND VERNACULAR LITERATURE

CHAPTER 12

The Renaissance of the Twelfth Century

As witnessed in the work of such authors as Hroswita of Gandersheim and Gerbert of Aurillac and in the revival of speculative thought in the age of Anselm of Canterbury, a renewed interest in the liberal arts informed European thinkers by the eleventh century. Attached to monastic and cathedral schools, these concerns reflect both local patronage and the initiatives of individuals and small groups. In the twelfth century the study of the liberal arts continued to burgeon, now primarily in cathedral schools. The desire to make fuller use of available classical sources has given this period the name 'Renaissance.' The term accurately describes an age of educational reform paying closer attention to classical literature, in which the liberal arts were studied as professional disciplines in their own right as well as for their ability to mold character or to inform biblical exegesis, homiletics, and theology. At the same time, as in the Carolingian Renaissance, more was at issue than merely reviving and appreciating the classics. Educators and writers eagerly put their knowledge to new uses. In addition to improving the quality of Latin composition in all literary genres, they were open to an increasing two–way traffic between Latin and vernacular literature. This fact is a vital link connecting high medieval culture to the western intellectual tradition more generally. For, what began as a deliberate classical revival and as education in the classical and Christian traditions ended by empowering vernacular languages and literatures, enabling them to become the means by which late medieval writers and their audiences appropriated not only their Christian and classical inheritance but also their earlier vernacular legacies, achieving cultural self-definition by their own selection from and re-expression of these sources.

Basic to all these developments were educational reforms. Schools continued to reflect regional emphases and the tastes and talents of individual masters, but they drew on a more international clientele. The biographies of many learned figures of the day attest to the willingness of students to travel long distances for the education they sought. The same biographies reflect an increasingly prosperous society with marginal time and money available for protracted study, and the relative political stability that facilitated travel. Masters, too, moved frequently, their credentials consisting in the perceived authority of their teaching in their students' eyes. They made direct arrangements with their students for tuition fees, enabling scholars to make a significant impact whether or not they were on the staff of an existing cathedral school. Located in cities, the centers of the new Gothic style of art (Plates 17, 18 and 19) and of Europe's expanding commercial and industrial life, cathedral schools ceased to be princely courts grooming young men for careers in church and state and became full-time educational institutions purveying technical instruction in the arts, viewed as learned disciplines.

During the first half of the twelfth century, the trivium subjects received sustained attention. Logic, stimulated by eleventh-century developments, continued to draw students. We will defer consideration of the history of logic to the next part of this book, where it plays a major role. Regional emphases affected grammar and rhetoric, reflecting local political developments and institutional needs as well as differences in taste. This fact is clearly visible in rhetoric. While commentaries on Priscian, Cicero, and other standard rhetorical authorities abounded across Europe and while treatises on homiletics reflected the general view that rhetoric should be applied to preaching, Italy produced a revival of forensic oratory as a result of the rise of a city-state political culture and the need for the art of persuasion in the forum as well as the courtroom.

From Italy also came a new type of rhetoric called the *ars dictaminis*, oriented to written documents. Its name derives from the *dictatores*, or notaries who served as public officials. They kept official records of legal contracts, wills, and formal correspondence. The last of these duties reflects growing Latin literacy and the need to convey instructions, requests, and information in business and private life in epistolary form. The rhetorician most influential in developing the formal model used in *ars dictaminis* was a Benedictine monk, Alberic of Monte Cassino (d. 1105). His scheme has a rigid five-part form. First comes the salutation, reflecting the writer's status and relationship to the addressee. Next comes an exordium, a quotation or moral sentiment designed to put the addressee in a receptive mood for the exposition, which outlines the writer's situation and needs. The chief point of the letter, the request, follows, presented as a logical deduction from the circumstances related in the exposition. The letter concludes with a closing usually expressing thanks in advance for a favorable response to the request. The largest single subdivision of surviving letters of this type consists of those written by students at cathedral schools and universities to their parents or other patrons requesting an advance on their allowance. They bring student concerns vividly to life and testify to the fact that higher education appealed increasingly to lay people who had no intention of entering scholarly or ecclesiastical careers.

As a rhetorical innovation, the *ars dictaminis* stands beside more classicizing uses of the epistolary genre, as a medium for moral counsel or philosophical instruction and as a mode of self-expression and self-definition aimed at an audience wider than the stated recipient. In some cases, epistles of the latter type use pseudonymous persons as their ostensible addressees. Here, the classical authors who provided the models, such as Seneca, offered both generic and stylistic inspiration, applied to Latin epistolary prose on such unclassical subjects as monastic reform, theological exhortation, and polemic.

Masters in France who sought to improve liberal studies focused on literature

more generally and on curricular reform and the refinement of pedagogy. An outstanding case of curricular reform is the *Didascalicon* of Hugh of St. Victor (d.
1141). His convent, which we will encounter again as part of a new clerical movement, the Augustinian canons, was founded in 1108 on the outskirts of Paris by a
former master from the cathedral school of Notre Dame. It had a strong academic
program until the last quarter of the twelfth century. In his other writings as well
as in the *Didascalicon* Hugh explains how and why intellectual breadth should be
cultivated. His program begins with the seven liberal arts. Hugh shares with Augustine the view that they equip us to interpret the Bible, God's chief revelation of
Himself to mankind. But Hugh goes farther. He places the revealed knowledge of
God on an epistemological trajectory that includes knowledge of God through the
natural world attainable by reason and the knowledge of God that culminates in
contemplative vision. From this perspective, the liberal arts that equip us to interpret texts and to gain a rational understanding of the physical order are an integral
part of Christian education. In the actual teaching of the arts, Hugh departs from
early medieval educators. He rules out *florilegia*, watered-down summaries, and
similar aids. Instead of snippets of Vergil or Cicero illustrating their meter and
style, his students study a whole poem or oration, understanding it as a work of
art. Hugh's goal is to teach appreciation of literary works as literature and not just
as illustrations of grammatical or rhetorical rules. The liberal arts, so envisioned,
and what he calls the practical arts, or information on matters like seafaring or agriculture found in classical texts, do much more than arm students to understand the
Bible. They also provide enjoyment, aesthetic pleasure, the formation of good taste,
and intellectual enhancement. Thus, while he begins with Augustine's rationale for
classical education, Hugh ends by going beyond it, relating the arts curriculum to
the student's intellectual and aesthetic enrichment and to his own position on the
various, and compatible, ways we can learn about ourselves, the universe, and its
creator.

Another leading educational theorist writing later in the twelfth century was John
of Salisbury (1115/25–80). An Englishman who spent many years in the schools
of Paris and Chartres, who was a secretary at the papal court and a protégé both of
King Henry II (1133–89) and his martyred archbishop, Thomas Becket (1118–70),
John addresses the educational developments of a later generation, in which the
arts had become specialized academic disciplines carried out by professionals who,
from John's perspective, sometimes lacked interest in how their discipline related
to others. In his *Metalogicon*, he laments what he sees as runaway over-
specialization in liberal studies, in favor of a more integrative model of education,
one harking back to the Ciceronian notion that eloquence should be combined with
wisdom and virtue. In John's view, this Ciceronian ideal entails the application of
liberal studies to theology. It also entails moral as well as intellectual education
and the notion that the master teaches as much by his example as by his technical
expertise.

John's educational theory reflects nostalgia for the education he had received at
Chartres, a school specializing in Latin literature and Platonic philosophy and
guided by the principles of its leading master at the beginning of the century,

Bernard of Chartres (d. *c.* 1130). John praises Bernard warmly both for integrating literature and ethics and for a pedagogical method that gave students a fine-grained appreciation of how classical authors achieved their literary effects and created their personal styles. The Bernardian techniques John describes constitute a recovery of the way that classical literature was taught in antiquity, combining detailed textual analysis by the master with extensive memorization and oral and written exercises in all literary genres by the students. Bernard was a good educational psychologist, adjusting his lessons to the perceived ability of students to absorb them and grasping the fact that students learn more readily if they are given reasons for what they are doing. But there was more to Bernard's pedagogy than that. As John notes, Bernard was also alert to the dangers of passive imitation and even the plagiarism that might result from the mere veneration of past models. Bernard's goal was to show students how to internalize the techniques that make authors in the literary canon great and that give them their personal voices, so that students can develop styles that are correct, elegant, and their own. And, while canonical authors were the touchstones for this literary education, they were its beginning, not its end. John quotes Bernard as remarking that 'we [moderns] can see farther than the ancients, because we are dwarfs standing on the shoulders of giants.'[1] Not all authors connected to Chartrain pedagogy were as modest. Of Alan of Lille (*c.* 1120–1202/3), a writer in that tradition, the grammarian John of Garland (*c.* 1195–1272) could say that he was 'greater than Vergil and more consistent than Homer.'[2] Both John and Alan, not to mention other leading Latin authors of this century, took the Chartrain message to heart and developed excellent and highly personal literary styles. The enrichment of the arts curriculum and the improvement of teaching methods by masters such as those mentioned had a notable effect on Latin literature in the high Middle Ages. This period witnessed a marked efflorescence of Latin literature. Older genres were perpetuated and new genres created. The interaction of Latin and vernacular traditions expanded, as did the interaction of literature and music.

One of the most striking innovations in Latin literature is the production of texts, purporting to be classical, invented out of whole cloth by twelfth-century writers. The most impressive example is John of Salisbury's *Education of Trajan*, which he attributed to Plutarch (*c.* 46–after 129). John's subject, the education of the future statesman or ruler, uses the ancient genre of the mirror of princes. The content of the work is integrally related to his *Policraticus*, a treatise on political theory, where he holds up Trajan as a model ruler, capitalizing here on the belief, first articulated in an anonymous Anglo-Saxon monk's *Life* of Gregory the Great, that Gregory, moved by the emperor's virtues, had prayed the pagan Trajan out of hell and into heaven, a legend retold and embroidered many times up to John's day and beyond. John's confidence that he could pass off his own work as that of a classical Roman moralist was well founded; the *Education of Trajan* was not exposed as pseudonymous until the twentieth century.

On another level, a major innovation in twelfth-century Latin literature is the emergence of philosophical poetry, not seen in Europe since the verses launching each book of Boethius' *Consolation of Philosophy*. Several authors connected with

the Chartrain program, particularly the interest there in Plato's *Timaeus* and commentaries on it, harked back to the still earlier models of Lucretius (*c*. 99–*c*. 55 BC)
and Manilius (late first century BC). Like them, the Chartrains wrote long poems
on cosmogenesis. But unlike Lucretius and Manilius, inspired by Epicureanism and
Stoicism respectively, the Chartrains draw on Plato and the Neoplatonists and
borrow the dialogue form from Boethius. They reflect the strong appeal of allegorical characters typical of late ancient and early Christian Latin literature. A
leading example is Bernard Silvestris of Tours (*fl. c.* 1130–60). His *Cosmographia*,
a mixture of prose and verse, opens with Nature complaining to Providence on
behalf of Matter, who yearns for the impress of Form. Thanks to a series of theophanies in the chain of being, Matter and Form are brought together and produce
the phenomenal world. Separate theophanies, Physis and Urania, supply the human
body and soul. There are several features of this work that are quite original.
Bernard combines his largely Neoplatonic cosmogenesis with the Stoic idea of a
cyclical cosmology in which the universe is created, runs its course, self-destructs,
and is recreated eternally. The scenario he envisions as his work opens is simply
the current creation phase of the cycle, not a once-and-for-all creation. Second,
given the cast of characters already on the stage when the action begins, Bernard
is clearly comfortable with the idea that matter as such exists before the creation of
individual material beings. He does not address the question of whether unformed
matter is itself created, and, if so, when. Third, while theophanies different from
those that produce the subhuman order are needed to produce the human soul and
body, they are purely natural forces. No deity appears in Bernard's creation account,
whether directly or indirectly; the theophanies to which the task is delegated are
the only creative forces mentioned. There is much in the *Cosmographia* that a Christian reader, even one with Neoplatonic leanings, might find alarming, especially its
thoroughgoing naturalism and cyclical cosmology. Yet, there is no evidence that
anyone in authority taxed Bernard with ideological deviance. He lived out his years
as a respected master at the cathedral school of Tours.

Another approach to the Chartrain project was taken by Alan of Lille, who puts
his own contemporary and personal stamp on it in his two philosophical poems,
the *Anticlaudianus* and the *Complaint of Nature*. The first is directed against the
poet Claudian (*fl.* 395–404), whose *Rape of Proserpina* had, in Alan's opinion,
delineated the worst kind of man. In contrast, he outlines the creation of the best
kind of man. Unlike Bernard Silvestris, Alan is not a pure naturalist. His character Nature concludes that she cannot create mankind alone. She and the Virtues
agree that, while she can produce a perfect human body, she cannot make a perfect
human soul. Guided by Reason, Theology, and Faith, Prudence travels to heaven
and meets God, Who assents to her request on Nature's behalf and creates the
perfect human soul, which He unites with the perfect body created by Nature. God
then makes the perfect man the ruler of the universe. In the *Anticlaudianus*, clearly,
Alan finds a naturalistic understanding of human beings insufficient; although he
does not take the history of humankind beyond its creation to its fall and redemption. Still, within her own sphere, he argues, Nature's authority is wide and must
not be spurned. He elaborates on that theme in the *Complaint of Nature*, a

dialogue between himself as speaker and Nature. She enumerates her laws and berates people who disobey them, notably in the field of sexual behavior. Here, Alan reflects both a belief in the procreative teleology of human sexuality derived from Aristotelianism and the desire to attack the contemporary Catharist heresy. The Cathars thought matter was evil; they prohibited procreative sexual acts that trap pure souls in carnal bondage and regarded non-procreative sexuality as the only acceptable kind. Alan's strong anti-Cathar brief also informs the stand against homosexuality he takes in this work. While his version of the creation of mankind pays more lip service to theism than Bernard Silvestris' does, both authors, along with other colleagues who shared the project of exploring Platonic cosmogenesis in their works, poetic and otherwise, deal with classical materials already available, which they study more intensively and reformulate in their own ways.

Prior to the twelfth century, Europeans had written a good deal of history and biography. Both genres were highly didactic in emphasis, although Christian moral and theological lessons generally replaced the political advice of classical historians. Biographies had taken the form of saints' lives and ruler-panegyrics. These approaches continued in the high Middle Ages while newer treatments of these genres also appeared. Strikingly present is an interest in autobiography, which began to attract attention in the late eleventh century. The genre has a confessional or self-exculpatory flavor in authors such as Guibert of Nogent (*c.* 1064–*c.* 1125) or Othloh of St. Emmeran (*c.* 1100–*c.* 1170), monastic writers exploring the moral crises that brought them to deeper levels of spiritual insight. The combination of confession and self-vindication appears in the autobiographical letters of Peter Abelard (1079–1142), a leading philosopher and theologian, and Heloïse (*c.* 1099–1163/4), the woman he seduced, impregnated, married, and then forced into a convent. A good example of emperor-biography taking that genre in a new direction is the *Deeds of Frederick Barbarossa* by Frederick's uncle, Otto, bishop of Freising (*c.* 1114–58), who moves from straightforward political biography to the defense of a 'great man' theory of historical causation so compelling that it leads him to ignore Frederick's numerous miscalculations and failures. Otto takes historiography in another direction in his *The Two Cities*. Appealing directly to Augustine's *City of God*, Otto brings the account of the two cities into contemporary German history, while at the same time leaching most of the sophistication from Augustine's analysis of the conflicting moral drives found in all human institutions. For Otto, the inhabitants of the city of man are reducible to his enemies, while he places partisans of his own causes in the city of God. This yoking of the great church father's philosophy of history to the factional rivalries of twelfth-century Germany suggests how the patristic no less than the classical tradition could be harnessed to the agendas of high medieval authors in ways the original authors would have found startling. Another category of history, which includes descriptions, travelogues, pilgrims' guides, and bulletins from the front, reflects the widening horizons of Europeans, their interest in the strange and the wonderful in other parts of the world and in the human comedy at home, as well as practical advice to merchants, pilgrims, crusaders, or missionaries who may follow in their wake. These writers sometimes make use of descriptive and ethnographic material found in classical authors. But their own observations and sense of what is important and interesting are what characterize their work, from the luster of intellectual life in the schools of France and Italy in Alexander Neckham (1157–1217) to the personalities, political intrigues, and new recipies for ravioli in Salimbene (1221–after 1287). By the thirteenth century, Crusade chronicles and travel and descriptive literature had been taken over by vernacular authors, the *Travels* of Marco Polo (1254–1324) being the best-known contribution to this subdivision of the genre.

Another area in which Latin literature flourished and where it had important connections with vernacular literature as well as with music is religious poetry. The rich flow of religious lyrics and hymns also strikes new notes in popular devotion, especially an affective piety focusing on the Virgin Mary, the human Christ and His sufferings, the worship of the Holy Spirit, and the Eucharist. Learned Latin authors of poetry on these themes certainly share the devotional outlook of the less well educated, their emphasis sometimes reflecting styles of devotion associated with particular religious or monastic orders. The mobilization of the emotions to which Franciscan poets appeal in such works as *Stabat Mater*, where Mary's grief as she witnesses Christ's crucifixion is accented to stimulate the audience's identification with that event, can be contrasted with the metaphysical conceits and word-play of the Eucharistic hymns of the Dominican Thomas Aquinas, designed to promote intellectual contemplation of the mysteries embodied by the sacrament. The most notable form of religious verse is the sequence, the poetic text written to accompany sequences as liturgical music. Just as the sequence itself is a post-classical and post-patristic musical genre, so sequence texts, while written in Latin and while frequently making allusions to classical as well as biblical material, are post-classical in their metrics and literary strategies. In a reversal of the tactics of an Otfrid of Weissenberg, sequence authors take over the metrics of vernacular poetry, based on accent not quantity. Drawing heavily on the aesthetics of German poetry, regardless of the author's native language, they use both end-rhyme and internal rhyme, rhythms based on symmetrical constructions, the correspondence of word accents and verse accents, and alliteration. The emergence of rhymed and accented Latin poetry to be sung in the liturgy represents the arrival, and the confluence with the public worship of the church, of vernacular literary values.

Just as the literary values that informed vernacular poetry now informed the Latin poetry of the sequence, so another new development, polyphony, which began in the ninth century and which flourished in several forms from the eleventh and twelfth centuries until the end of the Middle Ages, produced music that accompanied both Latin and vernacular texts. Verses in the vernacular expressed sacred as well as secular subject matter. The same musical genres were deemed appropriate for both kinds of subject whatever the language of the texts. The freedom to combine material and genres from all registers of thought and feeling, with the vernaculars outpacing Latin in the later medieval centuries, is a clear index of the innovative character of religious verse and music alike and of the high medieval taste for uniting literary and musical categories more self-contained in other cultures.

This field is also one in which we can see, across the high Middle Ages, the growing role of royal and noble courts as centers of musical patronage, both religious and secular.

A final case in which the convergence of Latin and vernacular literatures is clearly visible is the epic. Twelfth-century Latin authors rewrote earlier classical epics, including the *Iliad*, the *Aeneid*, and the *Thebaid*, updating them by giving their characters recognizably medieval traits. They did the same with ancient heroes, such as Alexander the Great, about whom no epics had been written in antiquity, basing their work on historical accounts. Along with this 'matter of Troy,' as epics based on classical works and subjects were called, stood two other sources for Latin epic, the 'matter of Charlemagne,' and the 'matter of Brittany.' The first refers to the many epic cycles dealing with Charlemagne and his associates as well as other heroes whose stories were told in early medieval vernacular epics. Along with heroes in the 'matter of Troy,' their attributes were updated by Latin epic poets. The 'matter of Brittany' denotes Celtic material. It includes themes such as metempsychosis, the fairy wife, and the unjustly persecuted wife, and centers on the legend of King Arthur, the knights of the Round Table, the wizard Merlin, and associated characters. Some of this subject matter was treated in Latin by Gerald of Wales (1146–1223) in his *Itinerary of Wales*, but the chief author to make it available in Latin was the Oxford master and eventual bishop of St. Asaph, Geoffrey of Monmouth (*c.* 1100–55). He wrote for both episcopal and lay patrons in the hope of securing ecclesiastical preferment. At the request of the bishop of Lincoln he first wrote the *Prophecy of Merlin*, later expanding his account of Celtic legend presented as historical fact in his *History of the Kings of Britain*, dedicated to Robert, earl of Gloucester (d. 1147), illegitimate son of King Henry I (1068–1135) whose daughter Matilda (1102–67) he supported in her bid for the English throne. Some early versions of the *History* are rededicated to Stephen of Blois (*c.* 1097–1154), Matilda's cousin and successful rival. Claiming that Arthurian Britain combined Christian faith with Trojan origins, Geoffrey argues for a common heritage binding all the British Isles, whoever the ruler is. The octosyllabic couplets of the *History* show him taking over a Germanic poetic strategy even as he blends Celtic myth, ancient history, and Christianity. Although conditioned by the English historical setting to which Geoffrey speaks, his *History* was immensely popular. It made Arthurian material available to anyone who knew Latin and was swiftly and repeatedly translated into vernacular languages from French to Middle English to Welsh, with later translations into Spanish, Portuguese, and Dutch. In many ways, Geoffrey epitomizes the intersection and combination of traditions and languages that give high medieval literature its special quality. Informed by the vernacular, he makes Latin the medium through which other writers gained access to a vernacular tradition not originally their own, a tradition that served as a major inspiration for the vernacular literature of courtly love in a host of languages.

CHAPTER 13

Courtly Love Literature

One of the most striking developments in medieval literature, beginning in the late eleventh century and extending to the early thirteenth, and reappearing through the later Middle Ages and beyond, is vernacular literature dealing with love, especially the type called courtly love, linked with a chivalric code of manners. This theme, first aired in lyric poetry by Provençal troubadours and then by northern French trouvères, German Minnesingers and Italian practitioners of the *dolce stil nuovo*, was expressed in many languages. It moved from lyric to narrative poetry, both epic and romance. In addition to producing extensive literary treatments of courtly love, medieval authors also theorized about it, both in Latin and in the vernacular. Not all medieval writers on love followed the conventions of courtly lyric, epic, or romance, choosing other genres from whose vantage points they could criticize those conventions and offer other perspectives. At the same time—and it is a striking indication of the willingness of medieval writers working in courtly genres to eye their subject critically—some authors who made central contributions to courtly love literature and to the theories discussing it raise questions concerning its merits, freely subverting the very genres in which they write.

Medieval Definitions

This critical attitude to both the values articulated by courtly literature and to the classical and Celtic sources on which it drew can certainly be seen in theorists on love. Their most important classical source was Ovid (43 BC–AD 18). His long poem, the *Metamorphoses*, tells the stories of many lovers from classical mythology, as does his *Heroides*, which features the loves of female protagonists and speakers. Even more important were Ovid's *Art of Love* and *Remedies of Love*, companion pieces explaining how to win the beloved's favors and how to terminate an affair or recover from rejection if the beloved terminates it first. Ovid's attitude to love is witty, tongue-in-cheek, and frankly sensual. He sees love as a malady causing people to depart from reason and their normal pursuits, whose cure is physical consummation. Pleasure and the self-esteem gained from amorous conquest are what love is about. It does not involve the lovers' minds and souls, only their bodies. Ovid is a good example of a classical author available to medieval readers all along, whose works on love started to receive in-depth study only in the twelfth century, both in Latin and in the French translation made by Chrétien de Troyes (1159–91), himself a notable writer of courtly romances.

In addition to Ovid's advocacy of erotic love, writers in this period could draw on anti-erotic authorities. The dispraise as well as praise of women was part of the stock-in-trade of rhetoricians; satirists such as Horace (65/8–8 BC) and Juvenal (60/70–128) and the comedians wrote on this theme as well as exposing the foibles of men. The topos was adopted and Christianized in the early Middle Ages by clerical writers promoting celibacy and distancing themselves from women as daughters of Eve. They and a host of moralists, preachers, and authors of didactic and hortatory literature seized on classical anti-feminism and theologized it.

It was in the context of these classical and Christian approaches to love, pro and con, and the Arthurian materials made widely available by Geoffrey of Monmouth, not to mention the courtly literature already in circulation, that the major medieval theorists on courtly love produced their works. The first was Andreas Capellanus (*fl.* 1170–80), whose *Art of Loving Rightly* was written in Latin under the patronage of Marie, countess of Champagne (1145–98), daughter of Louis VII of France (1121–80) by his first wife, Eleanor of Aquitaine (*c.* 1122–1204). Both mother and daughter were noted patrons of literature. Andreas was a priest who served as Eleanor's court chaplain before becoming Marie's court poet. His work reflects a thorough knowledge of the pertinent classical and patristic sources and contemporary rhetoric. Indeed, rhetoric figures heavily in the *Art*, and in several ways. Persuasion is needed to win one's amorous objectives. Rhetoric also surfaces in a pseudo-forensic mode in the rules Andreas lays down for judging lovers' behavior, and it informs his whole treatise, which is written in the form of a debate, the first part presenting a positive view of courtly love and the second part attacking it. The style and structure no less than the content of the *Art* suggest that Andreas is presenting a send-up of both viewpoints, for the amusement of an audience thoroughly familiar with all sides of the question.

Andreas begins part I with a partly Ovidian definition of love. Love, he says, is a form of suffering, inspired by the beauty of a member of the opposite sex, which provokes the desire to unite sexually with that person. Love is not sexual consummation itself, or the pleasure attending it, but the yearning endured before consummation. Andreas states here that love is a response to physical beauty alone; although later in part I he contradicts himself. He also stresses that love is heterosexual only. In defending that claim, he contrasts erotic love with friendship between people of the same sex, typically men, on which there was an extensive classical tradition that had been Christianized by patristic and more recent monastic authors. According to Andreas, the distinction lies in the fact that friendship is a three-dimensional relationship while love is physical only. If lovers cannot be friends, neither can they be husband and wife. True love, according to Andreas, is adulterous. His reason is that love improves the lover, making him more courteous, humble, and graceful in the service of his lady. But these improving effects occur only if love is freely chosen and freely given. Such freedom is not present in marriage, in which the spouses' sexual relations are a matter of rights and duties. So insistent is Andreas on this point that he argues that if two lovers able to marry do so, marriage will destroy their love. While defining adulterous love as the only form of true love, Andreas acknowledges that society frowns on it, especially in the case of women. This fact, he notes, requires lovers to be devious and discreet so as to preserve the woman's reputation.

Before leaving Andreas' definition of love for the practical, or 'how to,' section of part I, we may note that, in addition to ruling out marital love, homosexual love, and the love of friends, he also excludes unconsummated love. And, while stimulated and assuaged by the beloved's body, love's effects are moral, improving and ennobling the lover's character and manners. What interests Andreas is the effect of love on the male partner. He does not discuss what effect, if any, love has on the female partner. Two reasons are possible for this asymmetry, both of which can be documented in Andreas' advice: the idea that the woman is essentially passive, unimportant except as a means of satisfying her male partner's needs, and the idea that she is intrinsically superior to him and thus able to confer benefits that she possesses and he lacks. Andreas does not take an unequivocal stand on this matter, but he does advise the male lover to address his beloved as if she were morally superior.

Andreas cites several disqualifications barring people from love in addition to those already noted. These include excessive youth or age, which prevent sexual consummation; excessive lust, which provokes indiscriminate and promiscuous sexual behavior; and blindness. Blindness makes love impossible because it is the beloved's physical beauty that arouses love. Certain professions also impede love. Andreas asserts that clerics make the best lovers, although bound by the rule of celibacy in place since the late eleventh century, a satirical reference to the lecherous priest, a stock character in medieval literature. Conversely, and illogically, he bars nuns sworn to celibacy from love categorically. Andreas makes no effort to justify this double standard. He also disqualifies three other groups of women: prostitutes, since they provide sex for money and not freely; peasant women, since the peasants' approach to sex is no better than animals' in the author's class-biased view; and women who give in too easily. This last group, distinguished by character not by class or calling, are to be avoided. For lovers should be faithful and, with an easy woman, the lover is never sure of her fidelity.

Following Ovid's *Art of Love* while updating his advice to accord with the mores of contemporary court society, Andreas next deals with how love may be gained. As he sees it, talk is the principal means of winning the lady. It is the lover's rhetoric, not his behavior, appearance, or personal attractiveness to her that gains the prize. Therefore, the lover's rhetoric should take account of the lady's social class and whether it is higher, lower, or the same as his. If he outranks her, he should argue that he pays her a social compliment by seeking her favors, contrasting this point artfully with the benefits to his character that she conveys. If the lady outranks him, he should exalt her still more by recasting her social superiority as moral superiority. In addition to describing these rhetorical strategies, Andreas includes sample dialogues illustrating them concretely. In all cases, he presents the lover's verbal claim that the lady improves his character ambiguously, both as a statement of fact and as a mere oratorical gambit.

Talk suffices to initiate the affair, but to retain and increase love, other tactics are needed. Andreas advises lovers to be courteous and discreet in public concerning the affair but to signal it by wearing some token of the lady, to pay attention to their grooming, to be prompt and attentive in the lady's service, to be generous, never to take the lady for granted, and to express their feelings with delicate sighs and groans. Love can be increased, he observes, by staging fights for the pleasure of making up and by inciting jealousy, which, he says, is essential to true love. Andreas also warns lovers as to what decreases love and ends an affair. Meeting too frequently should be avoided, since familiarity diminishes the affair's excitement. Inconsiderate or uncouth behavior on the lover's part weakens love, as does his discovery of character flaws in the lady, such as infidelity, irreligion, or blasphemy. Indeed, the major acts that end love, outside of marriage, are apostasy and sexual infidelity. Neither sin is forgivable in the forum of love. In particular, and here Andreas invokes the double standard once again, sexual infidelity is far worse in women than in men. Part I of the *Art* then concludes with a series of moot 'cases' posing questions about the proper conduct of love affairs and enabling the audience to test itself, determining whether it has internalized the rules Andreas outlines.

Before proceeding to the second part of the *Art*, it is worth noting that part I is full of self-contradictions, from the double standard to the importance of Christian belief in lovers flouting the church's teaching on extramarital sex to the issue of character improvement and whether it is a real goal of love or just a seducer's talking point. Likewise, if love is a purely physical relationship inspired by the beloved's appearance, her character or beliefs would seem to be irrelevant. Lovers are advised to be honorable and to wear their ladies' tokens and, at the same time, to be dishonest as they dissimulate the fact of their love to save the ladies' reputations. Well before he offers the opposing arguments in part II of the *Art*, Andreas thus highlights tensions intrinsic to courtly love even in his ostensibly positive delineation of it.

Much more disruptive is his rejection of adulterous love in part II. Here, he opens by observing that his reason for analyzing adulterous love with such care earlier in the work is to help the prudent avoid love's snares by exposing them in theory and practice. Andreas then rehearses the standard classical and Christian attacks on adultery and women. Adultery, he points out, is a mortal sin, a breach of God's law. It is also a sin against oneself, since it leads to enslavement to the senses and the distraction of one's attention from constructive pursuits. It is also a sin against one's neighbor, the husband whose wife one seduces. If discovered, it can lead to violence and murder. Oddly, Andreas omits under this heading the sin against the lady committed by leading her astray. Added to these moral and legal negatives are psychological ones. Adulterous love is evil, Andreas says, because it leads lovers into deceit, secrecy, fear, and the idolatrous attachment to transient pleasures. Further, love may be deleterious to one's health if one weakens the body through overindulgence in sex. It may also damage one's social reputation, branding the lover as frivolous, shallow, and unreliable. Finally, Andreas observes, notwithstanding all these theoretical and practical reasons for avoiding adulterous love, the love outlined in part I of the work is impossible in any case. For it presupposes the existence of women who can confer moral benefits on men. But women, as is well known, are repositories of all the vices, and here Andreas recites the standard classical and Christian anti-feminist clichés. Taken by itself, part II argues at cross purposes just as part I does, offering Christian virtue and self-interest as simultaneous rationales for avoiding love. The work as a whole is a superb illustration of the fact that audiences in the high Middle Ages were entertained by and felt comfortable with the presentation of conflicting viewpoints and with the criticism of authorities. Moralists from the classical and Christian traditions could be spoofed just as readily as writers advocating illicit affairs and claiming that they are morally improving.

Even more impressive as an indicator of high medieval tolerances on the subject of courtly love is the *Romance of the Rose*, written in French by Guillaume de Lorris (*c.* 1213–*c.* 1237) and Jean de Meun (*fl.* 1275–1305). Here, in addition to the contradictions found in each author's part of the work, their differing perspectives on love add another level of ambiguity. The *Romance* is a long allegorical poem, presented as a dream vision, written in rhymed couplets with four stressed syllables per line. Nothing is known about the patronage setting in which Guillaume wrote his part. Jean, who combined a career as a university scholar and possibly teacher at Paris with one as a writer and translator of classical and medieval Latin texts into French, dedicated to the king and various nobles, does not indicate a specific patron for his continuation. In each part, the *Romance* advances its argument both through narrative and through the speeches of its allegorical characters. A brief plot summary will reveal each author's outlook.

The poem opens with the Lover asleep. He dreams of a garden surrounded by a wall containing the Rose, the female love object. On the wall are ten figures depicting vices barring him from the Rose: Hate, Felony, Villainy, Greed, Covetousness, Envy, Sorrow, Old Age, Hypocrisy, and Poverty. In Guillaume's view, the Lover lacks these vices and can enter the garden. We should keep our eye on Villainy and Hypocrisy, however. Once inside, the Lover finds a fountain with an inscription warning him of the fate of Narcissus, told in Ovid's *Metamorphoses*, and he renounces egotism. He spies the Rose and, following Andreas' definition of love, falls in love with her beauty. His condition is also induced extrinsically by Cupid's arrows, Beauty, Simplicity, Courtesy, Companionship, and Fair Seeming, the latter of whom mingles the pleasures and pains of love. But among Cupid's other arrows are Pride, Villainy, Shame, Despair, and Faithlessness. This assortment of weapons in Cupid's quiver suggests love's self-contradictions, as does the inclusion of Villainy, earlier presented as a vice excluding lovers from the garden. Other characters there, including Idleness, Mirth, and Sweet Looks, welcome the Lover. Wealth and leisure are clearly needed to play the game. The Lover becomes a vassal of Cupid, who outlines the behavior that will make him acceptable to the Rose and the pains of love along with their remedies. Picking up on the homophobic theme addressed by Andreas and, in another context, Alan of Lille, Cupid includes in his advice the avoidance of cosmetics and homosexual love. Hard on the heels of this lesson, Shame and Danger drive away the Rose's Fair Welcome. Reason, the mother of Shame, intervenes. She advises the Lover to abandon Cupid, to shun both lust and unprocreative love, and stresses love's transience and the need to rise above its fickle fortunes. But a new arrival, the Lover's Friend, attacks Reason's arguments, urging him to remain in Cupid's allegiance. Franchise, Pity, and Venus intercede on the Lover's behalf and he gets to kiss the Rose. But, before the Lover can do more, Jealousy, Fear, and Shame rush in, building a castle in which the Rose and Fair Welcome are immured.

Here Guillaume's section ends. Before moving to Jean's continuation, we may note some of the central tensions in the first part. As we have seen, Villainy, one of the vices impeding love, is also one of Cupid's minions. Love is presented as opposed to Reason. Yet Reason in her speech, emerges less as an anti-eroticist than as a promoter of procreative heterosexual love, in an argument compatible with the strictures on effeminacy and homosexuality made by her arch-rival, Cupid. On the one hand, Shame is one of Cupid's arrows; on the other, Shame obstructs the Lover's access to the Rose. And the Lover forswears egotism; yet self-gratification is the essence of his quest.

Jean offers a different perspective on love in his part of the *Romance*. As his continuation opens, the Rose, locked in the castle, is given a new guardian, an Old Woman who, as events prove, is poorly suited to the task. None the less, the Lover despairs. Reason returns, recapitulating the argument made in Guillaume's part. Jean gives it two new notes. Taking her cue from Augustine and Boethius, Reason amplifies her critique of love as a transitory pleasure, advising the Lover to seek happiness in eternal goods. She also attaches the fickleness of women, drawn from the anti-feminist tradition, to the dispraise of love. The Lover's Friend reappears, with a plan of action. He advises the Lover to storm the castle and take the Rose by bribery, hypocrisy, and deceit. Here we see Hypocrisy, one of the vices that keeps lovers out of the garden, presented by Jean as a means of entering its recesses, while the wealth that equips the Lover to display the virtue of Largesse for Guillaume becomes the means of bribery. The Lover is offended by the Friend's advice. In support of his case, the Friend presents the Rose's Jealous Husband, who recites a litany of anti-feminist complaints against her. The Friend, observing that the Husband treats the Rose cruelly, disallows his claims and persuades the Lover to return to the fray. The Friend, too, is an anti-feminist; he depicts women as greedy, which is why he advocates bribery as a strategy of seduction. His speech gives both pro- and anti-feminist arguments, as well as a critique of husbands who treat their wives as chattels. Spurred on by the Friend, the Lover returns to Cupid, who forgives him for giving Reason a hearing. Cupid's followers, False Seeming and Forced Abstinence, are joined by Largesse and Courtesy. Together they succeed in liberating Fair Welcome from the castle.

Next, three speakers take the floor, at some length. The Old Woman presents her rules for love, counseling frivolity, manipulativeness, and infidelity. She sees love as the gratification of a natural urge, uncomplicated by moral considerations of any kind. Rather than protecting the Rose, her role is to induce Fair Welcome to accept the Lover. The other two speakers are Nature and Genius. Nature, echoing the argument of Alan of Lille's *Anticlaudianus*, notes that human beings, thanks to their possession of free will, can reject her laws, particularly those governing the procreative use of sexuality. She repeats Reason's earlier point here. Nature also agrees with Andreas' assertion that clerics make the best lovers. In her estimation, this fact absolves them of their vows of celibacy, which, by implication, she rejects as unnatural. Genius serves as an ambassador from Nature to Cupid. Conveying Nature's views on love to him, Genius says that Nature will agree to bless his campaign on the Lover's behalf on two conditions: he must dismiss False Seeming and Forced Abstinence and he must yoke the love that he and Venus inspire to fecundity. In her peroration, Genius observes that if we make this connection between sex as a natural inclination and its virtuous procreative use we can attain heaven on earth, which, she says, makes the garden of mirth described in part I of the work a deceptive illusion. Cupid and his forces agree to these terms. They take the castle and the Lover unites with the Rose. The dream ends and he awakens.

On one level, Jean tries to disentangle some of the ambiguities in Guillaume's section of the poem. The ultimate dismissal of False Seeming, or Hypocrisy, as an agent of Cupid restores this character to her role as a vice impeding love. Through the character of Nature, Jean effects a rapprochement between the positions of Reason on the one hand and Cupid and Venus on the other. But Jean adds his own complications. Both the pro- and anti-feminist positions are given a hearing. While neither side is privileged, no mention is made of the idea that the Rose can convey moral benefits to the Lover or, alternatively, that she cannot. While Nature agrees with Reason's defense of procreative love, what is striking in Nature's argument is her thoroughly naturalistic understanding of love and human sexuality and her connection of it with virtue. Her claim that rightly ordered sexual love produces heaven on earth in the natural order challenges Reason's relativizing of transient earthly love in comparison with eternal happiness. It is really Nature who is the victor, in Jean's section, winning against the Old Woman's egotism and irresponsibility, the Friend's underhanded tactics, Reason's otherworldliness, and Cupid's initial willingness to employ Hypocrisy. Cupid also has to dismiss Forced Abstinence, a helper more difficult to envision in Cupid's employ. Through the character of Nature, Jean simultaneously criticizes the courtliness of Guillaume, the transcendental claims of both classical and Christian ethics, the Ovidian notion of the pleasure principle as the only goal of love, and the rule of clerical celibacy as enforced by the church. While both authors of the *Romance of the Rose* subvert courtly love from within the genre of romance itself, Jean subverts much else as well. Both Guillaume and Jean show the interaction of classical, Christian, and earlier vernacular literature in their work. And, as with Andreas, there is a satirical subtext that runs through both parts of the poem. Each of these works remained quite popular during the remaining medieval centuries, being copied, translated, and commented on frequently.

If medieval literary audiences could find a range of conflicting ideas on love in

Andreas, Guillaume, and Jean, they could also find many of the same contradictions in the lyrics, epics, and romances dedicated to that subject. Although this literature features noble protagonists, it was produced by authors of varying social ranks and it reached a wide audience, assisted by the fact that it was written to be performed orally, the lyrics and romances sung or chanted to the accompaniment of a stringed instrument, and by its dissemination, starting in the twelfth century, through the book trade, which copied and sold courtly literature in both simple and de luxe editions for different segments of the book-buying public. Courtly literature thus entered the mainstream of high medieval culture and the breadth of its appeal is indicated by the existence of a medieval Hebrew version of the Arthurian romances. Its initial appearance, however, was usually tied to aristocratic patronage and the entertainment of noble courts.

Lyric

The first genres of courtly love literature were the lyrics of the Provençal troubadours, starting in the late eleventh century. Their work became fashionable immediately, spreading to northern France and Germany, where it flourished from the mid-twelfth to the early thirteenth century, and to the Iberian peninsula and Italy. These lyrics treat a small number of set themes: the plea to the lady, the dawn song in which the lover laments the coming of day which ends the rendezvous with his beloved, the pastoral or dialogue between a knight and a shepherdess, the debate poem, the satire, and the crusading song in which the speaker laments the military service that will part him from his lady. These themes rapidly became traditional, each acquiring its own literary conventions. The mark of successful lyricists lay less in the invention of new genres than in the freshness and vigor with which they handled the established conventions and used them to express a personal voice and a personal attitude toward love.

Differing attitudes there certainly were, even in the work of a single poet. The first troubadour, Duke William IX of Aquitaine (1071–1125) ranges from tenderness, the romantic pledging of love, to the speaker's locker-room boasts about his amorous conquests and sexual prowess. Some of his poems express the need for a love that involves more than the lady's body. William occasionally applies the rhetoric of religious devotion or of feudal service to the lady's praise; at other times he comments wryly on the lustfulness of women. His most typical stance is one of frank eroticism that neither sentimentalizes love nor ignores its physical pleasure. The example cited below also illustrates William's ability to shift from the delicate to the coarse within a single poem:

> In the sweetness of springtime
> Forest, flower, and the birds
> Sing—each in his native chant—
> Therefore a man stands well
> When he has what he most desires. . . .

Our love affair moves on
Like a flowering hawthorn branch
Standing above a trembling tree:
At night, only rain and frost;
But the next day's sunshine gleams
Through green branches and leaves.

I still remember that morning
When we pledged an end to our war,
And she gave me that great gift—
Her loving, and her ring:
Oh, God, let me live some more
To grope beneath her cloak! . . .
Let other gabbers brag about their love
We've got the meat and the knife.[1]

In sharp contrast with William stands Marcabru (*fl.* 1130–50). Where William was a major nobleman in the France of his day, Marcabru was a penniless itinerant poet, the child of an unwed mother who abandoned him. This misfortune may account for his thoroughgoing misogyny. In one of his poems he bitterly remarks that he has never loved, or been loved by, a woman. Marcabru often writes about the wretchedness of love. It is an indignity, he notes, to be emotionally dependent on someone in a position to make one suffer. For Marcabru, lovers are fools. He describes their folly with humor, malice, a brilliant use of language, and a fresh and dramatic style. He sometimes criticizes adulterous love, not only from the standpoint of Christian ethics but also because he thinks that marriage contributes more to honor and personal dignity than the deceit and dissimulation required by illicit affairs. He puts his opposition to adultery on a secular basis, which coincides with Christian teachings but which is grounded in psychology more than theology. Marcabru also wrote crusading songs promoting that venture, and pastoral dialogues. In the latter case he subverts the genre and the class-based notion of the girl's inferiority by making his shepherdesses wiser and more virtuous than his knights, and perfectly good candidates for courtly love. Marcabru is also credited with inventing *trobar clus*, an elaborate, sophisticated, allusive, and even recherché style that other troubadours, especially Arnaut Daniel (*fl.* 1170–1210), brought to a level of great virtuosity.

Another troubadour who introduced an important trope into courtly love lyric was Jaufré Rudel (*fl.* mid-twelfth century). This trope, which had a long career ahead of it, presents the speaker sighing for a faraway beloved, their physical separation combining with her social, moral, or personal inaccessibility. Since the lady is unattainable, the main emotion the speaker expresses is his yearning, rather than the joy of consummation. At one point in his career, Jaufré went on crusade, an event that marked a shift in his subject matter, inspiring him to transfer attention from human to divine love and to convey his religious feelings in a highly ecstatic style.

A different approach both to love and to politics is found in Bertran de Born (*c.* 1140–*c.* 1215). Dante Alighieri (1265–1321) places him in hell in his *Divine Comedy* as a sower of discord, a judgment plausible in the light of his career. A noble protégé of Eleanor of Aquitaine, Bertran figured in the conflicts between her second husband, Henry II of England, and his sons. Bertran's poems often deal with politics and warfare and show him as witty and irritable, a spoiler who enjoys stirring up trouble for the intellectual pleasure that intrigue provides. He relishes war for the color and movement of battle and is uninterested in its pain and suffering. He also criticizes current rulers, comparing them unfavorably with their upright and virtuous ancestors. Bertran wrote a small number of love poems. His treatment of love is vigorous, concrete, and unromantic. In his most famous love lyric, the speaker begins by castigating his lady for dropping him, as he says, without the slightest reason. Lamenting her loss, since her charms transcend those of other women, he notes that he will have to seek a composite of the best features of other ladies to approximate her. In so doing, he describes with a keen and lascivious eye the parts of these other ladies he would have to airbrush together, suggesting that he will be easily consoled for his loss. Bertran may also be alluding to the ancient Greek painter who said he would have to do the same to approximate the beauty of Helen of Troy.

Troubadour poetry also had its female voices. Some twenty-three female lyricists are known. Since this is a literature of convention, not one of sincerity, the vast majority of their poems, like those of their male colleagues, have male speakers who explore their feelings toward female love objects. But the best of these poets, Beatrice, countess of Dia (1150–*c.* 1200), circumvents some of the conventions and writes passionate, outspoken, and sensual poems in which female speakers take center stage and vent their emotions. In the following example, Beatrice's female speaker expresses, with sarcasm, invective, and concentrated force, the pain of erotic rejection:

> That wondrous virtue that with you dwells
> And your rich worth upset me totally,
> For I know there's not a woman near or far
> Wanting love who doesn't veer toward you;
> Ah, yes, my friend, you have the finest taste
> And out of all, I know you'll choose the best:
> And just remember too our secret pledge.
>
> My merit should help me, my lineage too,
> My beauty, and even more, my loyal heart;
> And so I'm sending over to your abode
> This little song to serve as my messenger;
> And please reply, my sweet and handsome lover,
> Why you're so harsh, so very cruel to me
> Tell me, is it arrogance or wicked will?[2]

Having launched courtly lyric, the troubadours passed the torch to the northern French trouvères and German Minnesingers in the mid-twelfth century. In the immediate sequel, the trouvères did little but imitate the troubadours in their own dialect. Their chief distinction was their maintenance of this poetic tradition, reinventing it vigorously up to the end of the Middle Ages. The leading authors of love lyrics in northern French lived in the fourteenth and fifteenth centuries. Writing with refinement and power, Christine de Pizan (1364–1429/34), Eustache Deschamps (*c*. 1346–*c*. 1406), Guillaume de Machaut (*c*. 1300–77), and Charles of Orléans (1394–1465) produced religious lyrics, poems of longing and suffering, and poems celebrating spring and love. Machaut was a leading composer as well. Charles, a member of the French royal family and a participant in the Hundred Years War (1337–1453) between France and England, was a prisoner of war for twenty-five years and also wrote about war and politics. All involved maintained the earlier tradition with vitality, delicacy, and a light touch.

On the other hand, the Minnesingers, in addition to treating standard themes like the praise of the lady, the yearning and sadness when the speaker is cut off from her, and the idea that love ennobles the lover, added ballast to the satirical and subversive tendencies of some troubadour lyrics. Hartmann von Aue (*fl.* 1180–1210) criticizes courtly convention in a poem in which the speaker asserts that he will not pay court to noble ladies. All one gets is tired feet from standing around in court all day and the likelihood of a supercilious refusal. Instead, he will spend his time with women lower on the social ladder who are less snobbish and more cooperative. Wolfram von Eschenbach (*c*. 1170–after 1217), agreeing here with Marcabru but elaborating the theme, contrasts favorably the enduring joys of marital love with the furtive and transient pleasure of illicit affairs. The Minnesinger who most drastically subverts the courtly ethos from within is Walther von der Vogelweide (*c*. 1170–*c*. 1230). In one of his poems, the speaker turns to a simple maiden as his love, defying the class-based distinction between courtly love and low love. In deciding how to approach love, he appeals to Lady Moderation, who proposes *ebene Minne*, love on an equal footing. According to this norm, the lover ennobles the lady and is concerned with making her happy in addition to receiving the same services from her. Walther thus presents the ideal of mutual love joined with friendship instead of the one-way adoration of the courtly lover.

Courtly lyric took a distinctive local form in the Italian *dolce stil nuovo* or sweet new style, which flourished in the late thirteenth and early fourteenth centuries. Its leading practitioners include Guido Guinizelli (*c*. 1230/40–*c*. 1276), Guido Cavalcanti (*c*. 1250–1300), and the young Dante. The Italians selected certain themes from the troubadours, treating with acute psychological penetration the feelings inspired in the lover by his lady. Orchestrating a note struck by William of Aquitaine, they transfer the rhetoric of devotion, particularly Marian devotion, to the praise of the lady and the benefits she confers, describing her agency in the secular ennoblement of the lover in religious language. Crossover of this type did not seem at all inappropriate to the poets or their audience. Other conventions typical of the Italian lyricists are a focus on the eyes and smile of the lady, as

indicators of her moral excellence and also as means by which she acknowledges
the lover's gentle heart and candidacy for her affections, and the mandatory physical description of the lady from the top of her head downward, with less attention
paid to features below the neck than a Bertran de Born would give.

Epic

A second major type of vernacular poetry serving as a vehicle for courtly love was
the epic. As with contemporary Latin epics, subjects were drawn from the matter
of Brittany, or Arthurian material, the matter of Troy, or classical material, and the
matter of Charlemagne, or earlier medieval heroic material. The taste for epic in
the high Middle Ages was broad and flexible. At the same time as early medieval
epics enshrining military and pre-Christian values were being redacted and enjoyed
and when classicizing Latin epics were being written, vernacular epic poets were
recasting the genre in the light of courtly love. Whether the hero is an ancient Greek
or Roman or an early medieval leader, they redefine him as a chivalric knight on
the battlefield, in the court, and in the boudoir. Current attitudes to Christianity
and its relations with rival faiths are projected onto the characters and their motivations. A good example of this courtly transformation of epic is the Spanish *Poem
of the Cid* and its sequels during the 150 years after it was first written. The Cid
was a historical personage, Rodrigo Díaz de Vivar (1043–99), a knight in the service
of Alfonso VI of Castille (ruled 1065–1109). The first version of the epic was
written in *c.* 1140, a generation after Rodrigo's death. As with earlier medieval epic
heroes, he has great military prowess, a special sword and horse, and, as his main
motivation, unswerving fidelity to his king even though Alfonso exiles the Cid
unjustly. He leaves home obediently, taking his family and followers. He thereupon
becomes a great conquerer, winning wide lands and much repute in the continuing
struggles among the Christian kings of Spain and between them and the Muslims.
The Cid sometimes allies with Muslims, sometimes with Christians, as the needs
of war and diplomacy require. Military and political desiderata, not conflicts of
religion, are the issue. The Cid has a close and trusted Muslim friend whom he
charges with escorting his daughters back to Castille to marry the husbands Alfonso
chooses for them. A loving and concerned father, who succeeds in improving his
daughters' situations when these marriages turn out badly, the Cid also has a
resourceful and respected partner in his wife. His daughters' problems provide the
occasion for the formal complaint against their husbands that enables the Cid to
regain Alfonso's favor. And, when he is killed in battle besieging Valencia, his
widow places his armored corpse astride his horse, demoralizing the enemy and
giving his troops the victory.

As we move from the original epic to its successive retellings through the late
fourteenth century, notable changes appear. The Cid's loyalty to his lord remains a
strong theme, but the amount of space devoted to battle scenes shrinks progressively and the poets show a declining interest in technical military details. Increasingly, they present the Cid as a chivalric courtier, a paragon of etiquette in the field

and court alike. No longer a practical, energetic helpmeet, his wife becomes a passive lady love whose contribution to the Cid's efforts is to smile encouragingly from her tower window, inspiring him to valiant deeds. The Cid's central mission also undergoes a major change. Instead of regaining Alfonso's good graces and winning territory and renown as a conqueror, his career now acquires a religious-political meaning. He becomes an agent of the reconquest, committed to purging the Muslims from the sacred soil of Spain. Similar courtly and religious transformations of other epic plots and characters could be cited in abundance.

Romance

The third literary vehicle for the expression, and sometimes the subversion, of courtly love is the romance. This genre also constitutes a new form of medieval vernacular literature. Written in octosyllabic rhymed couplets in a variety of languages, romances are narrative poems whose length ranges from that of the modern short story to the novel. Like love lyrics, they were performed with musical accompaniment, although the music in question had a less pronounced melodic structure. Five writers launched the romance in their respective languages, the northern French poets Marie de France (*fl.* 1170s–80s) and Chrétien de Troyes and the German poets Hartmann von Aue, Gottfried von Strassburg (*fl.* early thirteenth century), and Wolfram von Eschenbach. The French writers adhere to the short story length while the Germans often write full-blown novels. All draw on Arthurian and other Celtic materials as well as on classical sources. All put their own construction on courtly love. Some of their heroes are adulterers; some are husbands whose ladies are their wives. In one celebrated case, the hero is celibate. The weaving of Christian material into the Arthurian tradition can be seen, aside from incidental details, in the theme of the quest for the holy grail, associated by some authors with the lance that pierced Christ's side at the crucifixion, the chalice He used at the Last Supper, or a stone with curative powers.

Marie de France subscribes largely but not entirely to the praise of adulterous love. In her preface she asserts that she has deliberately adopted Breton sources, and she is known to have received patronage from the English royal court. Marie treats her characters with lightness and charm, if with little depth. In her *Lay of the Nightingale*, she presents an adulterous affair in which both parties exhibit courtliness and refinement. The woman is seen as justified in betraying her husband because he treats her with brutality and insensitivity. The trilling of the nightingale, the classical singer of love, is a poignant symbol of the destruction of the lovers' hopes. In Marie's *Lay of the Two Lovers*, the obstacle is not a jealous husband but a possessive father, who demands that a suitor undergo impossible trials for his daughter's hand. The suitor dies as a result and the girl commits suicide. There is some suggestion here that, had they lived, this couple's love might not have been destroyed by marriage. In Marie's *Lay of Eliduc*, the lovers get the best of both worlds. Although he is fond of his wife, Eliduc enters into an adulterous affair for courtly reasons, his wife obligingly stepping aside and entering a convent. After Eliduc and his mistress consummate their love, they suffer pangs of conscience, repent, and enter monastic life themselves. This is the only romance of Marie's reflecting any tension between courtly and Christian values.

Marie also wrote romances that put other Celtic themes into circulation. Her *Lay of Sir Launfal* introduces the fairy wife, who spirits Launfal away to Avalon. Shape-changing and metempsychosis appear in the *Lay of Yonec*. Yonec comes to his beloved, immured in a tower by her aged husband, in the form of a hawk. To assure her that he is a Christian, he assumes her own form and receives communion from her chaplain. Ringing another change on metempsychosis, Bisclavret, in the *Lay of the Werewolf*, periodically becomes a wolf. He wreaks revenge on his wife, who prevents him from resuming human form by removing his clothes, and who then remarries, by biting off her nose.

The Arthurian subdivision of the Celtic tradition is used by Marie's contemporary, Chrétien de Troyes, a protégé of Marie of Champagne. Most of his romances deal with knights of the Round Table, who are always chivalric in combat and in courtly conversation. Chrétien runs the gamut from adulterous to married to celibate heroes. He treats them all as ideal types. Two romances promoting the hero's wife as his lady love are *Erec and Enide* and *Yvain*, which can be read as companion pieces. In each case the hero leads an immoderate life. Initially, Erec is too uxorious, to the point of avoiding exploits. Enide pushes him back into the field and accompanies him, helping him to achieve a correct balance. This hero's virtues include Latin learning; when he inherits the duchy of Brittany his coronation robe is decorated with signs of the quadrivium. Yvain has married Laudine, the ruler of lands for which she needs an armed champion. Yet, he goes off to perform valiant deeds elsewhere, neglecting his duty to his wife and her people. In his case it is not his wife's direct action but the intervention of a lady in her service that brings him to his senses.

Chrétien's romance praising adultery is *Lancelot* or *The Knight of the Cart*. Lancelot is in love with Guinivere, Arthur's wife. In seeking to serve her, he disdains the use of a cart that would have speeded him to her side, as an ignoble vehicle. When he arrives, Guinivere instructs and chastises him for letting any consideration prevent him from reaching her as soon as possible. Here, Chrétien combines approval of adulterous love with the idea of the lady's moral as well as social superiority.

The romance featuring a celibate hero is Chrétien's *Perceval*, which introduces the quest for the holy grail as a theme. As Chrétien treats it, this quest requires the hero's total purity of heart. Perceval certainly has knightly prowess and good manners. But, in accordance with his calling as a grail knight, he must be celibate, a monk on horseback.

Chrétien also wrote a version of the Tristan and Isolde story that has not survived but to which a character in his *Cligès* refers. *Cligès* is also of interest for its claim that, just as there was a transfer of empire from Byzantium to the west and a transfer of classical studies, so also there has been a transfer of chivalry. Cligès and his father are Byzantine princes who travel to Arthur's court to perfect themselves in chivalry. The father marries his lady love but Cligès' lady, Fenice, is trapped in a May and December marriage to the Byzantine emperor. Unlike the typically passive lady of courtly literature, Fenice takes an active role in planning the deception of her husband by simulating her own death, enabling her to escape with Cligès. In advocating this plan, she asserts that she has no intention of being an Isolde, whom she regards as dishonorable for sleeping with a husband she does not love in addition to the Tristan she does love. According to Fenice's thoroughly sophistic argument, it is acceptable to commit adultery so long as a woman does not embrace an unloved husband. She turns St. Paul's remark that it is better to marry than to burn into the claim that it is better to commit adultery than to burn, so long as the lovers are discreet. Fenice and Cligès make good their escape and consummate their affair. But, after the emperor dies, they marry and preserve their love in so doing.

The multiplicity of approaches to love found in Marie de France and, even more, in Chrétien, does not characterize the German authors of romance, even though they depended directly on these French writers as sources. While they sometimes produced romances featuring the same subjects and characters, the Germans are united in rejecting implicitly or explicitly the praise of adulterous love, in glorifying married love, and in subjecting material borrowed from the French to a more penetrating psychological analysis.

The first German romance writer was Hartmann von Aue, who produced his own *Erec* and *Iwain* poems, with notable differences from Chrétien's. The particular combination of exploits and service to his lady achieved by each hero is not a mechanical balancing of two sets of activities expected of chivalric knights. For Hartmann, it is important that Erec bestir himself in the field because exploits are necessary for the service of others and for his own inner growth. In Iwain's case, the hero has to learn that his Round Table exploits have been meaningless because he has used them to escape from the duties attached to his marriage. In each story, Hartmann presents the adjustment of public and private life as a maturation process, an education in responsibility, and socially approved activities are seen as meaningless unless the hero can come to grips with his intentions and perform them for reasons that make sense in his inner life.

This concern with the ethical intentionalities that make outward acts meaningful, which certainly resonates in the theology of Hartmann's day, also finds expression in his *Gregory*, a saint's life, and in his romance, *Poor Henry*. *Poor Henry* turns a major courtly convention on its head. Henry is a nobleman afflicted by a serious illness. The doctors agree that the only cure is the blood of a virgin. A young peasant girl on Henry's estates decides to sacrifice herself to save his life. Just as the knife is about to fall, Henry stops the execution. God intervenes and cures him miraculously; he marries the girl and they live happily ever after. Here, Hartmann not only celebrates marriage and the efficacy of the girl's self-sacrificial intention; he also inverts the chivalric ethic by having a humble maiden save a knight in distress.

A similar exercise in internalizing the values motivating Arthurian characters is Wolfram von Eschenbach's *Parzival*. Wolfram converts the quest for the holy grail into an account of the education of the hero, described, in the subtitle, as 'the brave man slowly wise.' Parzival is raised by his mother without knowing his true identity. From his father he has inherited the right to be a knight of the Round Table and from his mother the right to be a grail knight. But he cannot activate either legacy until he attains self-knowledge and a grasp of what these callings mean. He does learn, slowly and painfully, making mistakes along the way, in both love idylls and exploits, in a narrative carefully constructed to span the seven years between the Pentecost when Parzival is knighted and the Pentecost when he becomes a knight in spirit. His grail mission is thus linked to Christ's gift of the Holy Spirit to His apostles as He commissions them to spread the gospel, commemorated by that feast. What Parzival learns by trial and error in his love life prepares him for marriage, which Wolfram treats as compatible with the grail knight's calling. He also departs from Chrétien by introducing Parzival's son, Lohengrin, at the end of the romance, presumably to move the reader on to the sequel. Wolfram's *Parzival* is an extremely successful fusion of Christian and Arthurian values, strong on character development in a manner reminiscent of the *Nibelungenlied*.

Authors like Hartmann and Wolfram present their own positive marital alternatives to adultery and celibacy alike. But the single most subversive romance is Gottfried von Strassburg's *Tristan and Isolde*. Gottfried explores the adulterous passion of the lovers from within and shows how it destroys them psychologically. In comparison with other treatments of this tale, in which the lovers are brought together by a love potion that they drink unwittingly, in Gottfried's version they have already committed themselves to betray Mark, Isolde's husband and Tristan's overlord, and seal that commitment by drinking the potion voluntarily. Their decision brings them suffering, for two reasons. First, they desire honor, which pulls them away from their affair even as their love pulls them toward it. Second, the man they betray is not the stock brutal or decrepit husband but a sympathetically drawn and thoroughly likeable character. Mark is magnanimous and generous. He postpones taking action against the lovers until well after he has discovered their affair and he is willing to forgive and forget. His goodness and uprightness contrast starkly with the lovers' lying and deceit. Their physical death at the end of the romance is the external manifestation of the spiritual death they acknowledge they have undergone, resulting from the irreconcilable conflict between love and honor that destroys them. Many authors of courtly lyric and romance raise basic questions about the value of adulterous love and present their own courtly alternatives. Gottfried criticizes adulterous love even more effectively by exposing the moral and psychological havoc it wreaks in the inner lives of his Tristan and Isolde.

None the less, Gottfried offers this devastating attack on courtly love from within the genre of romance. Romance continued to appeal to medieval audiences after its first flowering and, in this case, Middle English poems from the thirteenth-century *Sir Gawain and the Green Knight* to the *Morte d'Arthur* of Thomas Malory (1393/4–after 1470) take the prize for their authors' ability to reformulate Arthurian romance and to relate it to their country's political needs. Some of the authors of courtly romances, lyrics, and epics also wrote in other literary genres appreciated by the same audiences drawn to courtly literature. Some of these other genres also deal with love, but take a decidedly uncourtly approach to it. Side by side with the complex legacy of courtly love literature, the critical, the satiric, the classicizing, the humorous, and the ribald approaches to life and love receive attention in the non-courtly and anti-courtly genres to which we now turn.

CHAPTER 14

Goliardic Poetry, Fabliaux, Satire, and Drama

The genres of high medieval literature discussed in this chapter are quite different. At the same time, they are all non-courtly or anti-courtly. And, while they freely mix classical, Christian, and vernacular materials, they all reflect an increasingly popular literary enterprise, even as their modes of production and consumption witness a progressive vernacularization and laicization of literary culture during the high Middle Ages. Some of these genres also make express use of humor, whether as a means to an end or as an end in itself. All reflect the growing appeal of literary crossover in this period and the openness with which high medieval writers and audiences responded to the combination of different registers of thought and sensibility.

Goliardic Poetry

The earliest poetry in the goliardic canon, the *Cambridge Songs*, dates to the tenth century, but most of it was written between the late eleventh century and *c.* 1200 and preserved in a manuscript, from the Austrian abbey of Benediktbeuren, called the *Carmina Burana*. The goliards wrote in both Latin and the vernacular, in this case German, sometimes producing macaronic verse with alternating lines in the two languages. Their verse is organically related to the revival of classical studies in this period and they are familiar with the Vulgate Bible and the Latin liturgy, which they sometimes parody. The term 'goliard' was applied to this school of poets because one of its leading members, the Archpoet (*fl.* late twelfth century), acquired the cognomen 'Golias' and it was extended to the whole group. Socially, they can be described as marginal men, displaced persons, the underside of academia, drop-outs who wandered from school to school staying as long as their non-payment of tuition bills was tolerated, and then moving on. They lived loosely, traveled light, and were on the lookout for fun. Their marginal position gave them a jaundiced view of contemporary mores and institutions, which they eagerly criticize. But their learning is evident, not only in their use of literary and theological sources but in their scholarly vocabulary and their delight in scholastic word-play. From the classical poets they take their presiding deities and mythologies, the *locus amoenus* theme, the nightingales and cuckoos, the praise of spring, youth, love, wine, and the enjoyment of life, and their debates, satires, and burlesques. From the Bible and the Latin liturgy they borrow rhetoric and substance, parodying sequences, whose literary form they often use, organizing their verse in terms of accent, with extensive use of end and internal rhyme as well as alliteration. Like sequences and courtly lyrics, goliardic poems were performed to music with a strong rhythmic beat. The goliards' parodies of ecclesiastical literature, such as the *Gambler's Mass* and the *Gospel according to St. Marks-of-Silver*, reflect their own favored pursuits and their anti-establishment values.

There are few goliards whose biographies we know in any detail. The Archpoet was patronized by the archbishop of Rheims and studied in Paris. His autobiographical apologia, the *Confession of Golias*, is the main source for his life as well as a résumé of the outlook of the goliard movement. Another goliard, Hugh of Orléans (mid-twelfth century), nicknamed 'the Primate,' worked in Paris and is mentioned by several contemporaries, who give his poetry high marks. Walter of Châtillon (1135–76) is the best-documented goliard. After studies in Paris and Rheims, he held a post in the chancery of Henry II of England but left England because he sided with the archbishop in the Becket affair. He then studied law at Bologna, served as secretary to the archbishop of Rheims, and ended as a canon of Amiens cathedral. In addition to goliard verse, Walter produced a notable Latin epic on Alexander the Great.

Whether their authorship is known, or, as is more usual, unknown, goliardic poems treat a small repertoire of themes, all mentioned above, and do so with verve and technical skill. Three examples will illustrate some of these themes. *Sir Penny* typifies the goliards' critique of the powers that be:

> The hand that holds a heavy purse
> Makes right of wrong, better of worse.
> Sir Penny binds all bargains fast;
> Rough is smooth when he has passed.
> Who but Sir Penny settles wars?
> He is the prince of counselors.
>> Sir Penny's law no man can budge
>> In courts ecclesiastic;
>> Make room for Penny, ye who judge
>> With consciences elastic. . . .[1]

The themes of love, youth, and spring are frequently intertwined. Classicizing in its flippant allusion to the stern moralist, Cato, and in its evocative linking of spring and love is *Spring*:

> Behold, all things are springing
> With life come from the dead.
> The cold that wrought for evil
> Is routed now and fled.

> The lovely earth has brought to birth
>   All flow'rs, all fragrancy.
> Cato himself would soften
>   At such instancy.
>
> The woods are green with branches
>   And sweet with nightingales,
> With gold and blue and scarlet
>   All flowered are the dales.
> Sweet it is to wander
>   In a place of trees,
> Sweeter to pluck roses
>   And the fleur-de-lys;
> But dalliance with a lovely lass
>   Far surpasseth these. . . .[2]

Our last example, *Let's Away with Study*, accents youth:

> Let's away with study,
>   Folly's sweet.
> Treasure all the pleasure of our youth:
>   Time enough for age
> To think on Truth.
>
> So short a day,
> And life so quickly hasting
> And in study wasting
>   Youth that would be gay! . . .[3]

Altogether, the attitude to life and love displayed by the goliards has little to do with either the high seriousness or the subversiveness of courtly literature. Instead, their poems breathe an air of playfulness. They are characterized by gusto, a secular spirit, a virtuosity in the use of their sources, and a perfect willingness to thumb their collective nose at the very academic and ecclesiastical establishment that nurtured them.

Fabliaux

Vernacular fabliaux first flourished between the late twelfth and the mid-thirteenth centuries. Along with courtly lyric and romance, fabliaux enjoyed a broad social audience and, in some cases, such as Marie de France and Rutebeuf (*fl.* 1248–77), common authorship. They likewise drew on a wide range of sources, classical and vernacular. Their major Latin sources are Aesop, translated into French by Marie, the classical satirists and comedians, and earlier medieval Latin fables. Their vernacular sources are largely Celtic, although they also call on primordial folkloristic motifs, which surface in sermons and didactic works too, the same themes finding a comfortable berth in both religious literature and the decidedly secular fabliaux. Like romances, fabliaux are story-length tales in narrative verse, with octosyllabic rhymed couplets. Being short, they share the romances' economy of style; digressions are ruthlessly excluded. They also use stock characters, usually presented as two-dimensional types.

Another point that most fabliaux have in common with romances is the theme of love, especially seduction, the easily persuaded widow, adulterous affairs, and, above all, the love triangle, subjects comprising the vast majority of fabliaux plots. Other themes include vengeance, trickery, gourmandise, and coprophilia. As with romances, in fabliaux with erotic themes winning the love object is often accomplished deceitfully and by means of rhetorical gamesmanship. But here the similarity abruptly ends. For the speeches of fabliaux characters and, indeed, the entire vocabulary of the fabliaux is colloquial, not elevated. It is slangy, transparently carnal, scatological, and frequently obscene. In this sense, fabliaux can be read as a parody of the amorous verbal fencing and occasional sophistry of courtly speeches.

Also quite different from romances is the fabliards' attitude toward love. In some cases, fabliaux burlesque the courtly orientation. For, however authors of courtly literature treat love, they focus on the lovers. Obstructive husbands or fathers, if present, are vaguely menacing forces in the background. In fabliaux, the relations between husbands and wives occupy center stage. If an adulterous affair occurs, the introduction of the lover points up problems in the marriage: it may be a May and December union in which an elderly husband cannot satisfy the sexual needs of a vigorous young wife, or a marriage in which the husband cruelly abuses the wife, or one in which the wife is greedy, extravagant, untrustworthy, or sexually insatiable. In the fabliaux, love is reduced to sex, a carnal, even a gross if natural need, to be assuaged as quickly and frequently as possible. Marriage is treated as a burden, largely because so many couples are sexually mismatched. Generally both spouses are at fault, in failing to accept each other's needs and capacities. If the wife is lascivious, the husband lacks adequate virility. In this respect, fabliaux idealize neither women nor men. They invoke all the standard anti-feminist tropes against women and they present husbands as feeble, tyrannical, credulous, avaricious, and jealous. As for the lovers, not to put too fine a point on it, their sole virtue is that they are studs. All involved in the fabliaux plots receive their comeuppance. The satire of social types is not limited to characters in erotic plots, but extends to arrogant knights, layabout students, and ivory-tower intellectuals. The supreme example of the last theme is *Aristotle and Phyllis*, in which the old and presumably wise philosopher falls in love with a frivolous young girl who makes a complete fool of him.

Although the original intention of the fable, as a genre of classical literature, was to moralize or to make a didactic point by the use of humor, most medieval fabliaux are not didactic at all. Quite simply, the fabliards reinvent the fable as a literary genre. They have no 'message' to convey. They merely ridicule different types of people for the sake of a good story. They are never refined, always funny, and almost always bawdy.

There is also a special subdivision of fabliaux that shares these traits, the beast fable, starring Reynard the Fox, Isengrim the Wolf, Chanticleer the Cock, and the ineffectual lion king. Marie de France wrote the earliest vernacular beast fables, featuring the lion and the fox, but the authorship of most of them, anthologized under the title *Reynard the Fox*, is unknown. Each animal typifies a particular moral trait. Reynard stands for guile and wit, Isengrim for the arrogant abuse of power, Chanticleer for lust and domestic tyranny, the lion for ineptitude making a sham of authority, and so on. As with other fabliaux, beast fables are not concerned with pointing a moral. In so far as their plots, set in the contemporary medieval world, convey any consistent point of view besides the generically satirical intent of fabliaux as such, it is the triumph of wit and guile, in the person of Reynard, over the qualities embodied in other animals.

Just as courtly lyrics and romances continued to be written in the later medieval centuries, their authors sometimes recycling earlier themes with vigor and freshness, so the original fabliaux were retold in major European vernaculars. In some cases we find continuity that does not go beyond the hackneyed repetition of older tales, simply collected by the later author. Examples are the Spanish *Book of Good Love* by Juan Ruiz (*c.* 1283–*c.* 1350), archpriest of Hita, and the French *One Hundred New Tales* (1456–62), compiled for the duke of Burgundy, 'new' being a decided misnomer in this case. On the other hand, as the next chapter will note, two of the greatest masterpieces of later medieval literature made original, engaging, and highly personalized use of fabliaux themes. Thus, fabliaux, along with other medieval vernacular genres and the Latin classics, served as the inspiration for literary innovation.

Satire

Satire runs like a red thread through more than one medieval literary genre, often in the service of some other end, be it entertainment or the subversion of literary conventions. There are also many high medieval satires with no other purpose than social criticism. Whatever their preferred literary strategy, the professed satirists had a serious didactic purpose. They wrote in both Latin and the vernacular and their weapon of choice could be humor or allegory. In either case, satirists availed themselves of the social typologies found in fabliaux and goliardic verse. One specimen of each type will suggest the range of possibilities.

Our Latin, twelfth-century, and humorous entry is Nigel Wireker, his *Mirror of Fools* based on a classical work, the *Golden Ass* of Apuleius (*c.* 150–200). Nigel plays fast and loose with his model. In Apuleius' tale, a man is turned into an ass as punishment for his misdeeds. After many tribulations, he regains human form, expressing his gratitude by becoming a priest of Isis. Nigel's work relies on his audience's familiarity with both Apuleius and school logic, in which 'Brunellus' or 'Burnellus' was the conventional name given to the ass standing for the concept 'animal' in syllogistic arguments. His own protagonist is the ass Daun Burnel. Lest the message escape the reader, Nigel explains the work's didactic point in his dedicatory preface, an evident weakness, since it is clear enough from the action. Burnel is unsatisfied with his natural condition, especially the shortness of his tail, which compares unfavorably with the luxuriance of his ears. So, he escapes from his master and seeks ways to lengthen his tail. Burnel first goes to the famed medical school at Salerno, whose doctors he ridicules for their pomposity and ineffectual prescriptions. He shops for the medicines he needs among the London merchants, who swindle him and whose greed and duplicity he exposes. Burnel is then attacked by the dogs of a not-so-spiritual Cistercian monk, losing half of his tail in the fray. Too embarrassed to go home in this reduced condition, he decides to compensate for his loss by acquiring learning at the universities of Bologna and Paris, affording Nigel a rich opportunity to satirize academics. He presents them as pursuing higher education merely for the sake of degrees that are passports to high-status, lucrative careers. The teachers cannot teach and the students waste their time in amusements rather than studying. After seven years as a university student, during which time all he learns is how to say 'Heehaw,' Burnel receives a message in a dream, parodying the dream vision genre, telling him that he is destined for a bishopric. He is so flattered that he decides to accede to the office without simony, or ecclesiastical kick-backs. But an impediment prevents his preferment, and, shattered, Burnel leaves Paris, without even being able to remember the city's name. He decides to repent his sins and enter monastic life. Burnel surveys all the religious orders of the day, highlighting their salient faults, and concludes that none is worthy and that he will have to found his own order, drawing on the most worldly features of the existing ones. From the orders of nuns, he decides, he will take a wife. But, to get his new order approved, Burnel has to travel to Rome and appeal to the pope, occasioning Nigel's observations on the greed, corruption, and abuse of power of the leaders of church and state alike. In the end, Burnel's monastic plans are aborted. He is recaptured and returned in disgrace to his master.

No commentary is needed on the message of the *Mirror of Fools*; nor is it difficult to detect Nigel's satiric strategy. His style is lively and his episodes flow easily, one to the next. There are some digressions, but they contribute to the air of informality and improvisation conveyed by the work. Nigel is never heavy-handed. He displays a wide range of classical reading apart from his immediate source, and the conviction that the cure for the serious social ills he diagnoses begins by holding his *Mirror* up to the reader's face and provoking him to acknowledge his own foibles by laughing at them.

A second satirist, this one writing in Middle English in the fourteenth century, is William Langland (d. after 1388), to whom *Piers Plowman* is attributed. He eschews humor in favor of allegory. In this work we find some of the stock characters encountered in other medieval literary genres, such as the greedy merchant, the arrogant noble, the lascivious cleric, the irresponsible ruler, the corrupt civil servant, and more. We also meet a large number of personified abstractions, including the Seven Deadly Sins, the Vices, the Virtues, Reason, Conscience, and Holy Church. Langland places these characters in a poem presented as a four-part dream vision. The first is Will's vision of Piers Plowman, the speaker, who sees a field crowded with people. On closer inspection, they prove to be afflicted with major vices. They constitute an anti-society ruled by egotism and disharmony. The next three visions, entitled the Life of Do Well, the Life of Do Better, and the Life of Do Best, outline the progressive moral remedies for these vices.

Piers Plowman is a profoundly moral work whose author certainly invokes the rhetoric of high seriousness as his vehicle. His tone is that of a prophet, castigating his fellow men for their shortcomings and hoping to promote compunction and catharsis by his eloquence and pathos. In this sense, the various social stereotypes he presents go beyond the critique of the foibles of others for the sake of a good story. Langland highlights the generic vices of sinful humanity at their most depraved, as well as problems specific to late fourteenth-century England. He seeks to prick the conscience of his audience and to inspire them to seek salvation and the good life, which, for him, can be attained only by practicing social justice. Langland was an educated man in minor orders, an itinerant hymn singer who never became a priest officially charged with the task of preaching or Christian education. Yet his work speaks deeply of his conviction that he, and his vernacular poem, can be the bearers of serious religious instruction.

Drama

The notion that vernacular literature and non-clerical authors could purvey religious education and celebration is displayed with particular clarity in drama, easily the most popular genre of medieval literature and the one drawing on the widest range of sources, Christian and pre-Christian, classical and vernacular, elite and popular, literary and folkloric. Some works in the medieval dramatic canon, the mummers' plays, reflect a fusion of the lowbrow drama of the later Roman empire and indigenous folklore, a vernacular art form that always enjoyed a long and healthy life despite clerical opposition to it as a pagan survival. Other works, the farces, which were written in both Latin and the vernacular, were produced by learned authors who parodied other literary genres. The single largest subdivision of medieval drama is religious drama. Originating as an amplification of intrinsically dramatic moments in the Christian liturgy in Latin, within the church building and with clerics as actors, it rapidly became vernacularized, with the writing, production, and financing taken over by lay people, who did not hesitate to include their own secular viewpoints.

The classical background of medieval drama is twofold, highbrow and lowbrow. A significant part of highbrow classical drama was not appropriated as drama strictly speaking. The comedies of Plautus (*c.* 254–184 BC), a difficult read, were not in the school curriculum. The tragedies of Seneca were read as literature and commented on by grammarians from the thirteenth century onwards, but were not staged or used as models for medieval plays. Terence was the only Roman dramatist to serve as such a model, as we have seen in Hroswita's case. Hroswita excepted, the medieval tendency to treat classical drama as literature to be read or recited rather than staged was joined by an understanding of comedy and tragedy different from that held in antiquity. Medieval people extended these terms to any kind of narrative literature involving dialogue, in prose or verse, dramatic or not. For them, a tragedy is a story told in elevated style, about eminent people, that begins happily but ends sadly. A comedy is a story told in colloquial style, involving a broader range of social types, that begins sadly but ends happily.

In addition, the Middle Ages inherited a tradition of lowbrow drama, derived from the theater patronized by the late Roman emperors as part of their bread and circuses policy. Aimed at plebeian sensibilities, these plays combined burlesque, lewd pantomime, and spectacles of such dubious taste that 'theater' became synonymous with vulgarity both for cultivated Romans and for early Christian moralists. Once the imperial system and its dramatic patronage collapsed, the personnel who had earned their living thereby remained. They became nomadic jongleurs, merging with the Celtic and Germanic bards and minstrels who entertained early medieval audiences with their lyrics, epics, and *chansons de geste*. These performers were sometimes on the payroll of royal or noble patrons. Despite condemnation by many churchmen, they also entertained bishops in their courts, pilgrims on their travels, university scholars in their common rooms, and the urban public in city squares. These players served as mimes, acrobats, musicians, singers, poets, fools, and straight men. Their bag of tricks included tumbling, juggling, marionettes, animal shows, and a repertoire of songs to please the audience of the evening, ranging from the witty to the narrative, the racy to the semi-devout. They generally worked in teams composed of men and women and used costumes, masks, and props. When they had finished their act, if they did not hold court appointments, they collected the largesse of the audience, packed up their wagons, and moved on.

This legacy of lowbrow Roman drama combined with folkloric traditions to produce the mummers' plays derived from pre-Christian and even pre-Roman ceremonies associated with events in the agrarian calendar, like plowing, the vintage, and harvest, when the presiding gods were worshipped. These plays were popular throughout the Middle Ages, indicating the inability of ecclesiastical authorities to eliminate ingrained folk customs. The mummers' plays were communal, and local, involving everyone in the village. Although generic types can be distinguished, they all have local variations. They take the form not only of drama but also of songs, dances, feats of strength, the election of a ceremonial king and queen or community fool for a day, on a collective holiday from work. Although the earliest texts of mummers' plays date to the late thirteenth and fourteenth centuries, they record an elaborate and highly stylized dramatic genre that clearly had been in place for some time.

One prominent type can be illustrated by the play celebrating Plough Monday, the day when plowing was completed in the East Midlands in England. The standard cast of characters includes Tom the Fool, a Recruiting Sergeant, a Recruit, three farm hands called Threshing Blade, Hopper Joe, and the Plowman, the Doctor, Beelzebub, a Young Girl, and Old Dame Jane. The Fool opens the play with a prologue. The Recruit woos the Young Girl, and, when he is rejected, signs on with the Sergeant. The Girl is consoled by the Fool. Then the farm hands enter. Each describes his agrarian function, with much comic byplay. Next, Old Dame Jane tries to seduce the Fool. Beelzebub enters, knocks her down, and kills her. The Doctor arrives. After some comic business detailing his travels, his education and medical qualifications, his remedies, and his cure record, he examines Jane, announces that she is not dead but in a trance, and revives her. Then follow songs and dances and a quest, in which the village children take up a collection of cakes, eggs, or whatever from the audience.

A second type of mummers' play centers on a test of arms between two champions. One is invariably a local hero, a popular historical figure or patron saint. The other is a foreigner. He may be generic, in which case he has a name like Captain Slasher. Or, he may be specific, in which case he is typically cast as a Muslim, the Turkish Knight or Prince of Paradine, and made up in black-face. This latter variant indicates the spread, at this cultural register, of the understanding of medieval civilization as Christendom, over against other faiths. Sometimes the two champions fight with subordinate troops, sometimes in single combat. Either way, one or both heroes fall in battle and the comic Doctor arrives and restores the dead to life, after which a minor character takes up a collection in a frying pan or large ladle.

The mummers' plays, as pagan survivals, thus sometimes integrate Christian attitudes and beliefs. When this occurs, they can be compared with the Yule logs, Christmas trees, and Easter-egg hunts that were baptized by early medieval churchmen. But a much more extensive fusion of the ecclesiastical and vernacular traditions can be seen in liturgical drama, which produced the largest surviving number of medieval plays. The first step in their emergence was their use to accent moments in the liturgy of the mass that are naturally dramatic, especially in the season between Palm Sunday and Easter. The gospel readings for these seasonal feasts could be dramatized by having several clerics read the speeches of the biblical characters; a procession of clergy and laity could be inserted into the Palm Sunday service to commemorate Christ's entry into Jerusalem; His washing of the disciples' feet on Maundy Thursday could be acted out by the celebrant with the assistance of other clerics or lay people. During Easter week, sequences could be added to the liturgy dramatizing the discovery of Christ's empty tomb by His followers.

Indeed, it is this last-mentioned development that served as the springboard for the earliest liturgical plays, dating from the ninth century onward, the mystery plays called *Quem quaeritis*, or, 'Whom do you seek?' The Easter *Quem quaeritis* is a mini-play based on the gospel reading for the mass of Easter morning, performed in church as part of the service. The three Marys approach the altar where they find an actor playing the angel guarding Christ's empty tomb. 'Whom do you seek?' he asks them; when they say they are looking for the tomb of Jesus, he announces Christ's resurrection and tells them to inform the other disciples. Following the Easter *Quem quaeritis* plays similar mini-plays were introduced into the liturgy of Christmas and Ascension. In the case of Christmas, the question is addressed to the shepherds as they follow the star guiding them to Bethlehem; in the case of ascension, it is addressed to Christ's disciples, still looking for Him on earth although He has just ascended to heaven.

The earliest *Quem quaeritis* plays were so popular that congregations wanted them to be broadened and lengthened. They thus moved out of the church building and were staged on the church porch or square in front of the church, following the mass. These emerging full-length mystery plays, like the original mini-plays, were based on the biblical texts read at mass on particular feast days. But their authors went well beyond the gospel accounts of events in Christ's life in seeking sources for their scripts, turning to the Old Testament as well as the New. The rationale for the choice of plots was less their theological importance than their psychological tension and dramatic possibilities. Favorite Old Testament themes were Adam and Eve and the fall, Noah and the flood, Abraham and the sacrifice of Isaac, and David and Bathsheba. Key moments in the life of Christ continued to dominate the themes chosen from the New Testament. While the Bible supplied the ideas for the scripts, mystery plays also included chants and choruses drawn from the liturgical music of the day. The earliest mystery plays were written in Latin and performed by clerics, with choir boys playing female roles. Since singing was involved, parts were assigned according to the voice quality of the available clerical staff.

By the thirteenth century, the increasing popularity of mystery plays and the frequency of their staging led to their translation into the vernacular, and then to their composition in the vernacular ánd the laicization of their production. Numerous cycles of such plays survive from the later Middle Ages, their complexity indicated by their large casts, detailed stage directions, and set directions. More was now required than the clergy of a local church could supply. Producers employed minstrels, students, and local lay people recruited as amateur actors. Lay people took over the financing of mystery plays as well. Typically, the various guilds in late medieval towns assumed responsibility for the financing, staging, and acting of specific plays. In the York cycle, for instance, the cardmakers took on the creation, the fullers the garden of Eden, the coopers the fall, the butchers the crucifixion, the saddlers the harrowing of hell, and the tailors the ascension. Although church leaders feared that irreverent secular material would be introduced into mystery plays if lay people controlled them, the tide was irreversible. As a result, there is a certain amount of topical secular material and comic byplay in these dramas, and a lay and extra-biblical outlook sometimes surfaces. Thus, in the Wakefield *Shepherds' Play*, the scene is shifted to the English heath, where the shepherds complain about the bitter winter cold, as well as their grasping manorial lord, freely placing biblical events in the audience's time and place.

Mystery plays remain the predominant type of liturgically based drama of the Middle Ages, but in the fourteenth and fifteenth centuries they were joined by two other forms of religious drama, the miracle and the morality plays. Both were written in the vernacular and staged by the same lay groups that produced mystery plays. They were also performed in the open air, in church squares or other urban public spaces. Miracle plays deal with miracles of the saints, above all the Virgin Mary, testifying to the popularity of her cult and the general belief in her intercessory power. Although they are clearly religious in content, they are extraliturgical, since they are rarely based on the biblical texts read at church services.

Morality plays, the last on the scene, deal neither with biblical events nor with saintly persons. They are abstract, allegorical statements about the human condition and its ethical dilemmas. Popular themes are the crisis of moral temptation, the contest between personified vices and virtues, and, above all, the crisis of death, the best example of which is *Everyman*. The eponymous protagonist is summoned by Death and asked to render an account of his life. He is examined by God; the stage of action is the world. Things that Everyman loved in this world, like Fellowship, Riches, and Kinsmen, are brought forward to see if they can sustain him in his hour of need. Then Good Deeds, Knowledge, and Penitence take the stage. Predictably, they make a better showing, and usher Everyman to salvation. Next, Discretion, Strength, Beauty, and the Five Senses take formal leave of Everyman and Death returns to claim him. An alleluia chorus is sung and an angel welcomes him into heaven. Finally, the inevitable Doctor appears, in this case not to bring Everyman back to life, since he already enjoys life eternal, but to hammer in the moral, in case it has escaped the audience, and to close the play.

Didacticism and celebration, devotion and instruction are certainly the main stock-in-trade of medieval religious drama. At the same time, throughout the medieval centuries religious drama grew increasingly vernacular and secular in its authorship, financing, staging, audience, and outlook. It affords a striking example of the propensity of the medieval religious and literary imaginations to merge, of the multiplicity of the traditions flowing into high medieval culture, and its growing laicization.

The same can be said of the last genre of medieval drama to be considered, the farce. Farces drew on many of the same sources as religious drama, which they sometimes parody, as well as on classical comedy, satire, and pastoral, on earlier medieval fabliaux and goliardic poetry, and on the folk tradition enshrined in the mummers' plays. Farces are always humorous and written with a light touch. Their tone ranges from just plain fun to a ribaldry verging on obscenity to satire to slapstick. In farces treating religious subjects, what separates them from miracle or mystery plays is not theme or rhyme scheme but emphasis and vocabulary. Although straightforward religious dramas have comic and popular interludes, farces with religious themes give the comic material primary emphasis, and their language is much more colloquial.

The authorship of farces is better known than that of other forms of medieval drama. Also well known are the institutions responsible for their production in France and Flanders, where most of them were written and staged, in the *puy* and confraternity, respectively. These organizations were urban clubs whose members included professional writers, students, citizens, and interested amateurs. Unlike the lay confraternities that proliferated in late medieval towns for devotional and charitable purposes, they were literary and dramatic societies whose chief function was to produce plays. They arose to fund and stage farces, but they sometimes produced religious drama as well. One of the *puys* of Paris, for instance, held a monopoly on the performance of the *Passion Play* there. The two best-known authors of farces, Jean Bodel (1165–1202) and Adam de la Halle (d. 1287/8), both of whom also contributed to other literary genres and in Adam's case to music, were citizens of Arras and members of its dramatic society. The contrast between their careers reflects the transition from farce-writing by authors who made a living some other way to its emergence as a paid profession. Some of the principal farce types can be illustrated from these authors' works.

Bodel, clerk to the city council of Arras, composed his *Play of St. Nicholas* on his own time as a member of the Confraternity of the Holy Candle and in conjunction with the translation of its candle, believed to have saved Arras from the plague in the early twelfth century, from the chapel of St. Nicholas to a new location in 1200. This event accounts for Bodel's choice of subject. His farce draws on miracle plays about St. Nicholas of Bari. Although Nicholas lived in the fourth century, Bodel moves the action to the Crusade era and focuses on the conflict between Christians and emirs, their Muslim opponents. Interwoven into that theme is a series of comic interludes involving stock characters. There is a band of thieves who rob everyone blind, from a wine merchant to the royal treasury, in a succession of merry pranks. Nicholas, the ostensible protagonist, appears only in the final third of the play. His character displays human weaknesses: he throws temper tantrums, manifests fear, and undergoes moral improvement in the course of the action. Clearly, Bodel's intention is not to present Nicholas as an ideal type but to use his relocated story as the scaffolding for the humorous dramatic edifice he builds.

In addition to joining the Confraternity of the Holy Candle and being a political activist who participated in a local tax revolt against the French king, although he later pamphleteered in favor of the same king's Crusade, Adam secured appointments as court dramatist and musician first from the count of Artois and then from Charles of Anjou (1226–85), the French prince who became king of Naples and Sicily. Along with farces produced at Charles' court, Adam wrote an epic on the Sicilian Vespers, a revolt against Angevin rule in 1282. Two of his plays exemplify a major farce type, the revue consisting of a series of skits or 'turns' with minimal plot, the entertainment provided by the skill with which the author brings in one episode on the heels of another.

Adam's *Play of the Foliage* or *Play of the Canopy* is so named because it was performed in a branch-covered public space used for the production of plays in Arras. The series of skits that comprise it involve stock characters from widely scattered sources, ranging from Boethius' Dame Fortune with her wheel to the Celtic fairy Morgan le Fay to the village idiot and his despairing father, the town slut, the monk trading on his relic collection, and the comic doctor. The play's engaging effect is achieved by Adam's deft alternation of the turns of this grab bag of characters. Slightly more freighted with plot is his *Play of Robin and Marion*, which embroiders a theme found in fabliaux and some subversive courtly literature, linking it to the pastoral tradition. The play is set in a pastoral landscape. Into this idyll irrupts a selfish and arrogant knight, who presses his unwanted attentions on the shepherdess Marion, engaged to the shepherd Robin. She succeeds in evading him, demonstrating her superior virtue and wit despite her humble status. The threat to her honor removed, Marion joins Robin and their friends in the picnic, games, songs, and dances that make up the rest of the play.

While social satire abounds in these and other farces, some plays in this genre focus more singlemindedly on satire as such. This is true of most farces in Latin, which were written by the same kinds of author and for the same audiences as goliardic verse. Satirical vernacular farces are less classicizing and owe more to fabliaux. They are also of greater literary interest. A good example is the anonymous fourteenth-century French *Farce of Master Peter Pathelin*, which invokes satire on two levels. It is a comedy of character, exposing a central figure and scoring off him, while simultaneously satirizing other social types. The chief character, Pathelin, is the stereotypical pettifogging shyster lawyer. He constantly tricks others. In the play, he gets a dose of his own medicine. Other stock characters who also receive their comeuppance are the greedy merchant, the courtroom parasite, the pompous judge, and the hypercritical nagging wife. Like other medieval farces, this one is strong on comic situations and characters, relying more on them than on witty dialogue or elaborate plotting to achieve its effects.

Altogether, the various sub-genres of drama written and enjoyed in the Middle Ages, from the mummers' plays to the religious plays to the farces, display the breadth and variety of the literary traditions on which medieval writers drew, which they combined in their own ways and expressed in increasingly vernacular form under the auspices of increasingly lay patronage. In this sense, drama is emblematic of the larger history of medieval literature and of medieval literary sensibilities and tolerances, reflecting the capacity to blend the sublime and the ridiculous, the didactic and the entertaining, the sacred and the profane, without any sense of impropriety. These traits, along with the vernacular and lay appropriation of Europe's Christian, classical, and new medieval traditions, also characterize the masterpieces of Dante, Boccaccio (1313–75), and Chaucer (1344–90), who bring late medieval literature to its triumphant conclusion.

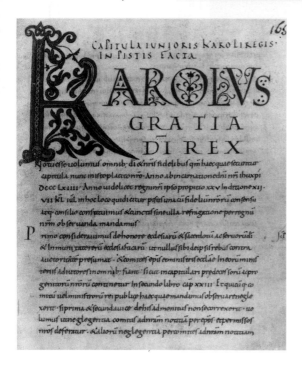

Insular illumination.

1. Initial page, Gospel of St. Matthew from the Book of Kells, late eighth-century to early ninth-century.

Carolingian miniscule

2. From the capitularies of Charlemagne, Louis the Pious, and Charles the Bald, *c.* 873.

Varieties of Carolingian illumination (*anti-clockwise from left*).

3. The initial Q from Polchard's Psalter, St. Gall, ninth-century.

4. Psalm 26 from the Utrecht Psalter, *c*. 832.

5. St. Matthew from the Gospels of Ebbo of Rheims, 816–35.

6. St. Luke from the Ada Gospels, *c*. 800.

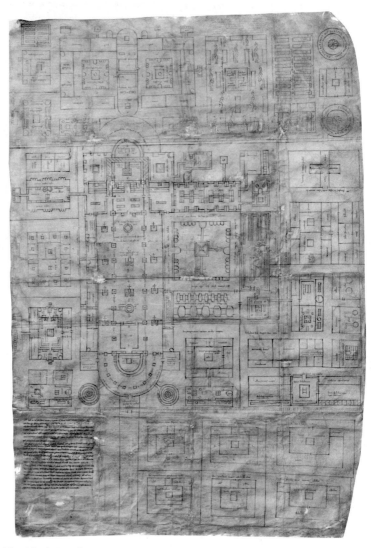

The ideal Carolingian monastery.

7. Plan of St. Gall, *c.* 820.

Justinian's Imperial cathedral: Hagia Sophia, Constantinople, 532–7.

8. (*above*) Exterior and 9. (*below*) interior views.

Imperial political theory in art.

10. Apse mosaic in San Vitale, Ravenna, sixth-century. Justinian bringing gifts to the consecration of the church.

Ottonian monumental sculpture.

11. St. Michael's, Hildesheim. (a, *left*) Easter Column, *c*. 1020 and (b) bronze doors of Bernward, *c*. 1015.

Clunaic architecture: Paray-le-Moniale Abbey.

12. (*above*) Exterior view, *c*. 1100 and 13. (*right*) nave interior.

Varieties of Romanesque architecture (*anti-clockwise from above*).

16. Maria-Laach Abbey Church, 1093–1156.

17. Modena Cathedral, begun 1099.

18. La Trinité Abbey Church, Caen, 1062–1140.

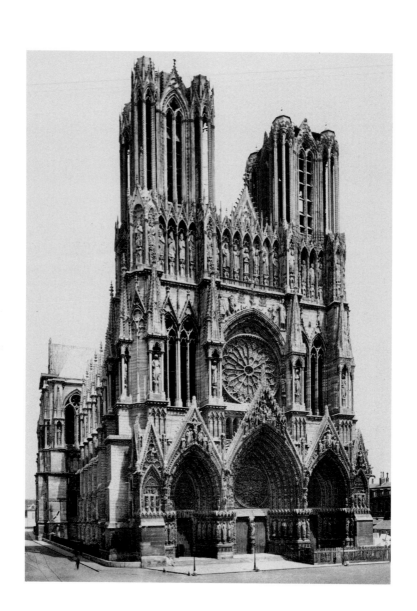

Varieties of Gothic Architecture.

19. (*left*) Rheims Cathedral, begun 1230s.
20. (*above*) Santa Croce, Florence, late thirteenth-century.
21. (*overleaf*) Lincoln Cathedral, lower porch eleventh-century, remainder thirteenth to fourteenth centuries.

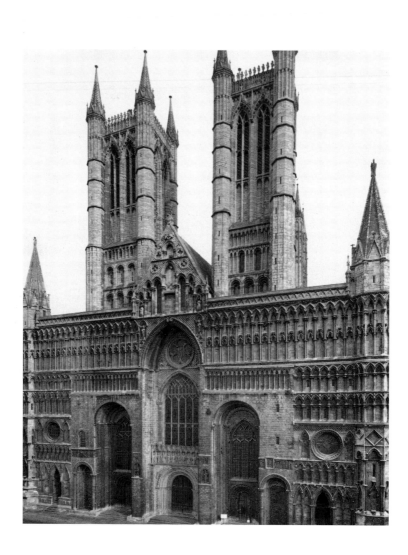

Later Medieval Literature

The triumph of the vernacular as a medium for expressing ideas on all levels of seriousness continued to define the enterprise of leading writers and literary theorists in the later medieval centuries. As the first chapter of the western intellectual tradition, the Middle Ages made a critical contribution to the successful appropriation of the Christian and classical heritage by vernacular authors and to their placement of the vernacular tradition on a par with the ancient literary canon. In the fourteenth and fifteenth centuries, vernacular literature itself became canonical. This development occurred diachronically in different countries, depending on when various languages gained the lexical and syntactical maturity enabling them to express abstract and sophisticated ideas, and on whether literary masterpieces were produced in them during these centuries. Neither condition applies to the Germanic and Iberian languages. Nor was a major masterpiece written in late medieval France. But Francophone writers did establish a new literary identity, largely in relation to the *Romance of the Rose* and other medieval French texts. A lively debate on the merits of the *Romance of the Rose*, especially Jean de Meun's part, engaged leading writers and thinkers of Paris at the turn of the fifteenth century. Two of them, Jean Gerson (1363–1429), scholastic theologian and chancellor of the university of Paris, and Christine de Pizan, who, in addition to lyrics wrote a feminist utopia and defended Joan of Arc (*c.* 1412–31) against her detractors, denounced Jean de Meun. Gerson attacked his erotic vocabulary and his denigration of marriage on Christian ethical grounds while Christine objected to his misogyny. Three other Parisian writers supported Jean. Jean de Montreuil (*c.* 1354–1418) took exception neither to his lexicon nor to his praise of procreative sex while the brothers Gontier (1350/2–1418) and Pierre (*fl. c.* 1402) Col argued that Jean was satirizing the anti-feminist, anti-matrimonial, and anti-celibacy positions alike, and that his naturalistic sexual terminology was as inoffensive as the clinical language of physicians.

What is instructive about this debate is that all participants recognized the hybrid nature of the rhetoric of the *Romance of the Rose*. They saw that this text had multiple interpretive possibilities and that it could and should be commented on in the same way as a classical text. The fact that the interpretation of their own medieval literature had become a means of national literary self-definition for French writers in this period is also evident in the anonymous *Rules of the Second Rhetoric* (1411/32). For its author and his audience, the first, or classical, rhetoric now gives way to French rhetoric, that is, medieval vernacular literature from Guillaume de Lorris up to contemporary authors, seen as the founders of a canonical French literary tradition.

In Middle English, a vernacular coming of age occurred in practice, not theory, thanks largely to Geoffrey Chaucer, and especially to his *Canterbury Tales*. In the case of Italian, a late-blooming vernacular, the language was catapulted into literary maturity by Dante Alighieri, both in theory and poetic practice, and in prose as well by Giovanni Boccaccio. The fact that both authors, being Florentines, wrote in Tuscan made that dialect literary Italian. Like the *Canterbury Tales*, their masterpieces, the *Divine Comedy* and the *Decameron*, are towering contributions to their national literature. The three works also reflect how freely high and late medieval writers drew on an exceptionally wide range of materials, classical, Christian, and vernacular alike, using them as inspiration for their own distinctive literary creations and for the articulation of their own authorial voices. In Boccaccio and Chaucer, those voices celebrate variety. In Dante's case, the poet puts the orchestration of his many characters' diverse uses of language to the service of a central, overarching vision.

Dante

Dante began his writing career as a *dolce stil nuovo* lyricist, addressing his verses to a girl named Beatrice, with whom he fell in love while still a child. Her untimely death in 1290 provoked a religious conversion in Dante and inspired the first major insight that led him to the literary theory undergirding his *Divine Comedy*. As he says in the *New Life*, after Beatrice's death he took literally the metaphorical *dolce stil nuovo* trope of the lady conveying divine grace to her lover. He now sees Beatrice in a religious, intercessory role. In the *Comedy*, Beatrice, along with St. Lucy and the Virgin Mary, initiates the events that allow Dante the traveler to visit hell, purgatory, and heaven while still alive. Beatrice also guides him through most of heaven. If a new understanding of Beatrice emerges in the *New Life*, Dante still adheres there to the idea that the vernacular has a limited scope and audience. It treats love poetry dedicated to women. But, in his next work, the *Convivio*, he broadens his range to encompass ethics and political theory, aimed at a wide Italophone audience. The *Convivio* also presents Dante's first statement of literary theory. Observing that poets, like biblical authors, use allegory, he contrasts the two kinds of allegory, concluding that theologians who read the Bible polysemously, extracting from the text the multiple meanings its authors wrote into it, perform a privileged kind of interpretation; the allegory of the poets he calls a 'beautiful lie.'[1]

An expanded statement on the vernacular followed in Dante's *On Vernacular Eloquence*, the first treatise ever written on Romance linguistics. Dante subdivides Romance languages into those that use 'si,' 'oui,' and 'oc,' for 'yes.' Then, focusing on Italian, he describes the fourteen dialects currently spoken, with several ends in view. First, he wants to promote a single, unified Italian language, a cultural unification that might lead to the political unification of a land split into warring city-states. Second, he understands the division of Italian dialects morally, seeing it as part of the larger problem of the division of tongues as punishment for human presumption in the building of the tower of Babel. Mankind has lost the language of Eden, a stable, unchanging language, replacing it with diverse vernaculars that impede translocal communication and whose usage constantly changes. Despite the mutability of the vernacular, Dante thinks it possible, and desirable, to elaborate rhetorical rules for its use, parallel to those governing Latin, so that Italian can be applied with propriety and effectiveness to every conceivable subject. The bulk of his treatise is devoted to specifying these rules.

The final theoretical step Dante needed to take to equip him for his unprecedented achievement in the *Comedy* was to close the gap opened in the *Convivio* between the allegory of theologians and the allegory of poets. This move was essential given his extensive use of allegory as a literary device in the *Comedy*. There is reason to think that Dante did take this step in the letter on this subject addressed to Can Grande della Scala (1290–1329), lord of Verona and one of his patrons after a partisan upheaval led to his exile from Florence. The letter, equating poetic with theological allegory, also shows how allegorical interpretation can be applied to the *Comedy*, which he was then completing.

Having developed a theory placing vernacular literature on a par with biblical and classical literature, Dante uses it in the *Comedy* to address the lofty theme of human salvation, thereby asserting that a layman writing in Italian is qualified to teach and inspire others by virtue of his poetic art. This claim is as innovative as the new verse form he created for the *Comedy*, *terza rima*, tercets in which the first line end-rhymes with the third line, the second with the fourth, and so on. Dante develops his theme by casting himself as a traveler to the other world. This being the case, he needed scientific, philosophical, and theological knowledge about the cosmos no less than literary data. Never a university student, he acquired the prodigious learning required through his own reading. He illustrates how a literate nonspecialist could gain expertise in these fields, in all of which he holds distinct opinions. Dante also brought to bear on the *Comedy* his equally firm political convictions. These ranged from partisanship in Florentine politics to opposition to Angevin rule in Italy and papal intervention in temporal affairs to his support of the German emperors, both as claimants to parts of Italy who might unify the country and as Europe-wide leaders. All these concerns converge in the *Comedy*, blending widely held views with Dante's personal opinions and sensibilities.

From a moral and theological standpoint, the topography of Dante's other world is largely unexceptional, but he gives the conventions his own coloration. Hell, envisioned as a pit starting at the earth's surface, is a series of circles organized in terms of Gregory the Great's doctrine of the seven deadly sins. The traveler moves from the carnal, or less serious, sins to the intellectual, or more serious, as he proceeds downward, ending with the worst sin, pride. In each circle, he meets condemned sinners whose punishment fits the crime and whose speeches reflect their desire to exculpate themselves, to shift responsibility, to complain, and to mislead the traveller. Here, and in purgatory and heaven as well, Dante's characters include well-known historical figures, literary characters taken to be historical, and names currently in the news. In all cases their identities and moral states would have been instantly recognizable to a contemporary audience. Dante does not hesitate to place in hell leaders of church or state whom he opposes. His hell is preceded by a limbo. With most current theologians, who had rejected Augustine's harsh teaching on the unconditional damnation of the unbaptized, Dante reserves a place here for unbaptized, innocent infants. More independently, he houses in limbo characters like Pope Celestine V (1215–96), whose resignation of the papal office in 1294 profoundly shocked Dante; he places Celestine among the terminally uncommitted. He also has a limbo of virtuous pagans. In addition to standard classical examples of virtue, he includes Muslim worthies such as Avicenna, Averroes, and Christendom's greatest enemy in the Crusades, Saladin (1137/8–93). Equally personal is Dante's treatment of the classical poets in this limbo and his own relationship to them. Led by Vergil, who introduces the traveler to the other poets, he receives a warm welcome from them. They greet him as a member of their company and he accepts this accolade as his due.

If the moral landscape of hell is defined by Gregory on sin, most of the actual landscape and superhuman denizens of this region derive from classical literature, with help from Celtic and Norse mythology. To enter hell one must cross the river Styx on a ferry piloted by Charon. Other classical figures who join Christian demons in tormenting sinners are centaurs, the minotaur, and the gorgon. The notion of a hero making a trip to the other world finds resonance in the biblical and classical as well as the vernacular traditions, especially, for Dante, *Aeneid* Book 6. But the lowest pit of hell combines biblical fire with Nordic ice, and Satan is given three heads, a reverse and perverse image of the Trinity.

Dante presents purgatory as a mountain located between the earth and the heavens, on whose ledges souls who repented their sins before death endure apposite, but finite, punishments, as they develop the countervailing virtues and prepare to graduate to heaven. Dante states the consensus view that their progress can be expedited by the prayers of fellow Christians. The effort of climbing the mountain signifies the labor involved in moral rehabilitation. Both Dante and the souls in purgatory find that less effort is needed the closer one gets to the summit. As in hell, where souls in the same circle speak in highly personalized ways, illustrating the idea that sins are not abstractions but concrete psychic states that affect people differently, so in purgatory the rhetoric of souls on the same ledge serves to individualize characters and the varying ways their moral attributes inhere in them. Where hell is dark, purgatory is increasingly light. Song, in the form of hymns chanted communally, reinforces gracious and forthcoming speech as an expression of community and of the moral optimism of purgatory's inhabitants.

At the top of the mountain of purgatory the traveller finds the earthly paradise and Vergil cedes his role as guide to Beatrice. Presented as a classical *locus amoenus*, this zone reflects the view that, once purged of sin, we recover the primal state of mankind in Eden. To enter it, the traveler must pass through two classical rivers, Lethe and Eunöe. The first passage enables him to forget past sin and the second gives him remembrance of his true, primal self. In Dante's case this process requires a recapitulation of his conversion from courtly to Christian love. Beatrice's eyes and smile mediate the grace helping him do so, and continue to instruct him as he proceeds through heaven, along with increasingly lengthy speeches of ravishing eloquence testifying to his growing ability to learn.

Dante's heaven is structured in terms of Aristotelian cosmology, with the earth at the center surrounded by seven planets from the moon to Saturn, including the sun. Heaven is populated by saints manifesting the virtues correlative to the sins of the damned, virtues in which the souls in purgatory are being perfected. Some souls are stationed on individual planets suggestive of their particular virtues. Thus, humility is displayed in the heaven of the moon, just rulership in the heaven of Jupiter, and the like. After the realm of the fixed stars, the orbit beyond Saturn on which, for Dante as for the classical astronomers, all the stars are located, equidistant from the earth, he finds the Empyrean. Here theology joins astronomy. The saintly host is presented arranged like the petals of a rose—another Dantean transmutation of a courtly love trope—where the Virgin Mary reigns as queen. Instead of Aristotle's unmoved mover as the universal cause, Dante substitutes the Christian God. He depicts God as three concentric circles of light with the figure of a man at the center and describes God as 'the love that moves the heavens and the other stars.'[2] Access to this deity requires the traveler to move beyond the discursive theology represented by Beatrice to mystical vision. And so, at the end of the *Comedy*, the Cistercian mystic Bernard of Clairvaux (1090–1153) becomes his guide. Bernard shared other positions with Dante, in the fields of monastic reform, church–state relations, crusading, and Mariology, which is why he, above other medieval mystics, receives this honor. The vision of God as concentric circles of light is the climax of a heaven increasingly brilliant with sparkling colors as well as light, where the communal song of purgatory is amplified by communal dancing. In canto 26 of the *Paradiso*, the angels stop chanting hymns in Latin and start singing in Italian. This development underscores Dante's last comment on the vernacular in the work. The traveler meets Adam, who tells him that even if he and Eve had not sinned and had remained in Eden, the language of Eden would have changed over time. There is no permanent, unchanging language governed by an immutable grammar. Latin is not privileged over Italian. Both in theory and practice, in the enormous range of diction Dante deploys and gives his characters in the *Comedy*, from the sublime to the sophistic to the homespun and even to babytalk, the poet magnificently vindicates these claims.

Boccaccio

The poet, for Dante, is a teacher; the allegory of poets is ultimately as efficacious as theology in conveying saving doctrine and inspiring moral reform. Indeed, poetry does so better than theology, thanks to its aesthetic power. Boccaccio agrees with and sharpens Dante's assessment of the power of poetry in a Latin work written to assist readers of classical literature, *On the Genealogy of the Gods*. But in most of his vernacular writings, the *Decameron* included, he does not take the high road of Dantean didacticism. Nor does he aim at the reader's salvation. His vision is naturalistic. And, while he is just as conversant with earlier vernacular and classical literature as Dante, he is inspired as much by fabliaux and satire as by lyric and romance. Boccaccio's development as a writer differed from Dante's. Instead of moving from a single literary genre he had thoroughly mastered to the creation of a new poetic form and meter, he experimented with a number of genres in his early works, sometimes less than successfully, frequently bending genres in the crossover manner of earlier medieval authors. It took him some time to discover that what he really excelled at was prose dialogue. He had a finely tuned ear and could render expressively the ways that different characters speak and convey their personalities. Boccaccio's narrative flair and gift for dialogue come together in the *Decameron*. While contributing to the short story as a genre, this work is innovative mainly as an illustration of how earlier tales from diverse sources could be recast and combined while avoiding the static anthology approach, by presenting them in a frame that invests them with fresh meaning and vigor.

Boccaccio's framing device is the epidemic of bubonic plague that struck Europe in 1348–9, with devastating demographic effects in many areas and attendant economic, social, and spiritual dislocations. He opens with a description of the impact of the plague on Florence, outlining with clinical precision both its medical symptoms and its social pathology, a hysterical fear of contagion leading Florentines to suspend normal rules of conduct. Boccaccio's source was literary, the description of a plague in Paul the Deacon's *History of the Lombards*, but he shows the plague's effects in the context of fourteenth-century institutions and mores. One Sunday, ten young Florentines, men and women, meet in church and decide to flee the city. Moving to a series of country houses owned by one or another of their families to escape contagion, they take along servants and provisions and decide to elect a leader for each day of their quarantine. The leaders lay down times for meals, recreation, bathing, holidays, churchgoing, fasting and, as the group's central activity, storytelling, with each member telling ten tales on the themes the leaders ordain. These arrangements are socially unconventional. All members of the group are single; several male members are officially courting several of the women, and they are unchaperoned. At the same time, the rationality, harmony, and decorum of the group's behavior, under the procedures they establish for themselves, contrast pointedly with the social and moral meltdown of plague-ridden Florence. And, since the leadership role is shared by everyone in the group, their mini-society offers an egalitarian alternative to the existing social hierarchies. It is actually the female members who first propose the project. They decide that they need male counterparts so that a full range of viewpoints will be represented in the storytelling and so that a natural and normal balance will obtain in their association and recreation. The *Decameron* thus posits an idealized society set over against real life, if only for a brief interlude.

Since the group is fleeing from the grim realities of plague, they decide to avoid depressing themes. Aside from two days on which the leaders decree that storytellers can address any subject, the theme of one day is met by an opposing theme the next day. Thus, the theme of fate as controlling human life is countered by adverse fortune turned to advantage; love as a destructive force is paired with the profitable use of love; language or rhetoric altering the course of events, especially in the deceptions of adulterous wives, is followed by inarticulateness as the cause of failure; liberality as a virtue is paired with liberality as a source of surprising outcomes. While fate is mentioned and while the members of the group are practicing Christians whose actual behavior on retreat gives no cause for scandal, metaphysics and theology are not so much satirized or contradicted as ignored. The stock character of the lecherous priest or monk puts in more than one appearance, joined by lecherous nuns. In *Decameron* 2.10, Boccaccio simultaneously scores off the juiceless intellectual who cannot satisfy his wife and the absurdity of the canonists' efforts to restrict the days in the calendar when married couples may have sexual relations. The tone of the work, whichever storyteller is speaking, is resolutely secular. Love, adulterous or otherwise, is neither theologized nor idealized but naturalized. While Boccaccio draws heavily on fabliaux, and while one of his storytellers invariably puts a ribald gloss on the stories he tells, his effect is less gross and more lighthearted. And, particularly on the days devoted to the theme of liberality, he offers support, if thoroughly uncourtly support, for the idea that love can be ennobling and can be joined with good moral character.

Each of the hundred tales in the *Decameron* is recycled, whether from classical, Byzantine, French, Spanish, Near Eastern, or Italian sources. In *Decameron* 5.1 and 10.8, Boccaccio places classical materials in classical settings. In all other cases, whatever his source, he sets the story in the mid-fourteenth-century Italian world, occasionally combining people who actually lived then with fictitious characters. Characters sometimes migrate from one story to another. Along with thematic connections, this device is another link among the tales. In addition to providing a compellingly good read, Boccaccio achieves a striking combination of unity and diversity in the *Decameron*. There is diversity in the tales, in the adroit stage-managing of themes and speakers, and in the personalizing of each storyteller. At the same time, the similar social status and outlook of the members of the company, the ordered and harmonious society they create, in which ribald tales, tales about illicit love, and tales about nasty trickery can be told without compromising anyone's reputation, and in which storytelling itself is balanced by other activities and bracketed by Boccaccio's introduction and conclusion, all create a structure giving a stable equilibrium to his collection of stories, while never undermining their narrative propulsion or their specific rhetorical features as individual tales told by individual speakers.

Chaucer

Boccaccio was one of Chaucer's sources, for earlier works as well as the *Canterbury Tales*. In some ways, Chaucer's achievement is the more remarkable. In his masterpiece and elsewhere, he made a major contribution to Middle English poetic style. Up until his time, Middle English poets wrote paratactic poetic lines, each ending with a full stop. Chaucer is the first to use enjambment, or the carry-over of a phrase and an idea from one line to the next. This practice frees his poetic diction and makes it a far more flexible instrument of expression. Chaucer's flowing poetic line also makes richer use of participial constructions and a wide vocabulary that includes more polysyllabic words and more words with French or Latin roots. Also, in a literary tradition rich in alliteration as a device but poor in rhyme, he makes brilliant use of rhyme, virtually creating a taste for it and a precedent for its later use by English authors. Altogether, comparing Chaucer's style with that of his immediate predecessors and contemporaries, his innovations made his poetry far more fluid, precise, and expressive. In these respects, his contribution to the history of the English language and to English poetry is more massive than Boccaccio's contribution to Italian prose.

Also more sophisticated is Chaucer's framing device and the mechanisms moving the *Canterbury Tales* from story to story. He assembles a band of pilgrims setting forth from London to the shrine of Thomas Becket at Canterbury. In his justly famous prologue, he observes that spring is in the air, along with travel fever, suggesting at the outset the mixture of secular and religious motivations in his pilgrims. On a deeper level, he also suggests the coexistence of various understandings of reality and authority, a theme he orchestrates in a number of ways in many individual tales. Chaucer also gives the reader thumbnail sketches of the pilgrims in the prologue, personalizing them thereby as well as through the stories they tell and the ways they tell them. In contrast with the decorous behavior of Boccaccio's company, Chaucer's pilgrims sometimes interrupt each other and comment unfavorably on each other's tales, individualizing them still further. As with Dante and Boccaccio, Chaucer excels at giving his characters their own voices. His innovations here are the more remarkable since he had no English model to point the way; in Chaucer's predecessors, each speaker sounds the same in poetic dialogue. While Boccaccio draws on classical, romance, and above all on fabliaux materials, Chaucer expands the number of genres he calls on, including the saint's life, the sermon, and the autobiography. He is much more likely than Boccaccio to bend genres, to hybridize them, and to parody and subvert them. Where Boccaccio's company is socially homogeneous, Chaucer's pilgrims cut a wide swath through fourteenth-century English society. They range from a knight to an Oxford scholar to a monk to two nuns to a much-married laywoman to clergymen to bureaucrats to merchants to craftsmen and to unskilled laborers. This diversification of social types contributes to the individualizing of the pilgrims' voices, their choice of subjects and genres, and their rhetoric. In Chaucer's case, no theme of the day is stipulated and there is a single master of ceremonies, the innkeeper at the hostelry where the pilgrims foregather, who decides to accompany them. He ushers the storytellers on and off the stage, sometimes editorializing on their tales or cutting them off if he finds them too longwinded.

A few comparisons between specific tales that are used both by Boccaccio and Chaucer will illustrate some of their similarities and differences. There are also parallels between Dante and Chaucer that are equally illuminating. Chaucer's *Monk's Tale* tells the story of Ugolino da Pisa recounted in *Inferno* 32–33, cantos in which

Dante consigns Ugolino to the bottom of hell as a traitor who also abused his parental authority to implicate his sons in his crime. The thoroughly sophistic speech Ugolino makes presents him and his sons as innocent deer stalked by callous hunters in the scene where the outraged Pisans come after them. He does not shrink from exculpating himself for sacrificing and cannibalizing one of his sons under the rubric of a father's duty to feed his children. The effect of this appalling presentation of self in the *Comedy* is, and is designed to be, revolting. Chaucer's Monk refers to Ugolino and to Dante by name. But, far from viewing Ugolino as a loathsome sinner, he treats him as a tragic figure, the victim of a frame-up. On the other hand, the Wife of Bath cites with approval a point made by Dante in the *Convivio* and seconded in *Decameron* 10.10, the idea that nobility is based on virtue, not lineage. At the conclusion of this story in the *Decameron*, which relates Griselda's endurance of her husband's cruel and unjust punishments, the storyteller adds that, in his opinion, such mistreatment would have justified adultery on Griselda's part. Chaucer's *Clerk's Tale*, which retells Griselda's story, omits this observation and treats the husband's behavior more as test of Griselda's virtue than as a manifestation of brutality or misogyny worthy of criticism.

In another comparison, *Decameron* 9.6 tells of two youths who make an overnight visit and abuse their host's hospitality, one seducing his wife and the other his daughter, the stratagem pulled off by changing the location of the baby's cradle in the bedroom they all occupy, the rearrangement of furniture confusing family members as to whose bed is whose. The theme illustrated is lust succeeding through trickery. Chaucer's *Reeve's Tale* turns the youths into Cambridge scholars, who play the same trick on a miller notorious for cheating his customers, including their college. They are motivated less by lust than by the desire to pay him back. In *Decameron* 8.1, a man borrows money from a merchant which he uses to bribe the merchant's wife into sleeping with him. He then tells the merchant that he has repaid the loan to his wife, from whom the merchant retrieves it unspent. The wife gets her comeuppance for betraying her husband and the lover's trickery is rewarded. In Chaucer's *Ship-man's Tale*, the lover is a monk, drawing that stock character into the plot, and the wife has the opportunity to spend the money on clothes for herself before her husband is told that the loan has been repaid to her. In *Decameron* 7.9, a wife and her lover, a household servant, trick her husband by claiming that a pear tree in their garden has unusual properties. Anyone who climbs the tree and observes activities elsewhere in the garden will be deluded into thinking that he sees the wife and the servant copulating, which they proceed to do with impunity by means of this ruse. Chaucer's version, in the *Merchant's Tale*, has the lovers copulating in the tree and the husband blinded, and then recovering his sight.

The same *Merchant's Tale* trades heavily on a theme used much more by Chaucer than by Boccaccio and for largely subversive reasons. All the characters in this tale make use of written documents, and sometimes sign language as well. Legal documents, such as the marriage contract that makes the wife, May, her husband's chattel, and the will in which the husband, January, makes his wife his heir, define and depersonalize the relations between the spouses. This is a specifically Chaucerian change the tale rings on the May and January union as artificial in any case. The lovers forward their affair through writing and signs, which subvert the marriage. Perhaps more than any other, the *Wife of Bath's Tale* raises questions about textual authority itself and the fact that diverse viewpoints on the same subject were rampant in the Middle Ages. One of her husbands, she relates, constantly quoted misogynistic doctrine. The Wife, regarding herself as a better authority on this topic, attacks the learned quotations and ripostes with her own destabilizing judgments. Descriptions of love and marriage would be different, she observes, if women wrote the books. The Wife is a lineal descendant of the Old Woman in Jean de Meun's part of the *Romance of the Rose*, crossed with Christine de Pizan *avant la lettre*.

In all, the manipulation of texts and genres, the transvaluation of authorities, and the ability to see and to feel unthreatened by the multiple valencies operating simultaneously in literary traditions express both Chaucer's self-conscious positioning of himself in those literary traditions, ancient and recent, and his authorial gloss on the act of storytelling itself. More than Boccaccio, he seeks to raise questions. His *Canterbury Tales* remained incomplete. Originally he planned to have thirty pilgrims, each telling one story *en route* to Canterbury and another on the return trip. He completed only a fraction of the intended sixty stories. Despite the programming of the innkeeper, the articulation of one perspective on life after another as the work progresses creates the impression of multiple realities. The *Parson's Tale* at the end of the text purports to summarize and to set in order what has gone before; it succeeds only in adding yet another opinion on the nature of reality, authority, and order to those of the other pilgrims. With an unfinished work, we can never know how, or if, Chaucer would have drawn conclusions and achieved closure. But the *Canterbury Tales*, as we have them, present a specifically Chaucerian outlook, a serene, playful, non-judgmental enjoyment of variety for its own sake. He takes people as they are, presenting them with verisimilitude and a delight in the particular. His masterpiece, like those of Dante and Boccaccio, is a virtuoso turn. Together they show brilliantly the medieval literary penchant for using conventional materials unconventionally and for empowering the vernacular, moving it to center stage as the eventual transmitter of Christian, classical and medieval literature to future ages.

PART V

MYSTICISM, DEVOTION, AND HERESY

CHAPTER 16

Cistercians and Victorines

We now move to spirituality, mysticism, and heresy, the religious views and practices of high medieval Christians, including lay people, monks, nuns, and secular clerics, and those who departed from the orthodox consensus. At first glance, it may seem strange to place under a single heading the beliefs of people in these diverse subdivisions of Christian society, embracing as they do various levels of education and different lifestyles. It is certainly true that clerics had a professional interest in religion and spirituality not shared by most lay people. It is also true that church leaders had a professional interest in distinguishing orthodoxy from heresy and in stigmatizing the latter. But there are more commonalities in the religious culture of the high Middle Ages than initially meet the eye. Despite the areas of life in which lay people dug in their heels and resisted the teachings of the clergy, sexual behavior and economic activity being the clearest examples, trickle-down, percolation up, and cross-fertilization of official and popular religion were normal in this period. The learned shared and promoted popular beliefs and devotions, while increasing access to theology, discursive, devotional, and mystical, was available to a wide audience through vernacular preaching and texts. Orthodox and heterodox thinkers often shared the same concerns, differing mainly in their capacity to articulate and institutionalize them in ways consistent with consensus Christianity. As with other forms of culture that proliferated in the twelfth and thirteenth centuries, so too religion underwent renewal, reflecting the desire of medieval people to appropriate the Christian tradition in personal ways and to develop their own innovative approaches to and applications of it.

The revival of spirituality and the emergence of new forms of religious association in the twelfth century are well illustrated by the Cistercian and Victorine movements. Each of these groups sought to revitalize a traditional form of religious life, Benedictine monasticism and the canonical life respectively, and each ended by reinventing rather than merely reviving a past model. The Cistercians and Victorines were not unique in this respect. As an alternative to Benedictine monasticism, the Carthusian order, founded by Bruno of Cologne (*c.* 1030–1101) in 1084, paralleled the earlier orders of Camaldoli and Vallombrosa, while adding to their semi-eremitism its own characteristic rule of silence. The most popular monastic reform of the twelfth century was the Cistercian order, founded to enforce observance of Benedict's *Rule*. As with the Cluniacs, the Cistercians produced their own reinterpretation of Benedictine monasticism, in organization, policy, and spiritual doctrine, while leaving some parts of the Benedictine world untouched.

Despite the Cistercian clamor for reform, there was no lack of vitality in twelfth-century Benedictine thought, especially in Germany. Not only did German Benedictinism produce leading theologians and reformers such as Honorius Augustodunensis (1075/80–*c*. 1156) and Rupert of Deutz (*c*. 1075/80–1129), who saw no need to found a new order, it also nourished a vibrant school of mystics, all nuns from the Rhineland. The leading figures are Hildegard of Bingen (1098–1179) and Elizabeth of Schönau (d. 1155). Hildegard was raised, educated, and served as abbess in Benedictine convents, attaining the latter post in 1136. This office made her a major player in German public life, quite apart from the learning and visionary gifts that won her contemporary renown. Hildegard travelled widely, adjudicated conflicts in church and state, and advised princes and prelates as well as fellow monks and nuns. She produced scientific and medical works, music and poetry, and a letter collection detailing her wide interests and associations, aside from writing the *Scivias*, her guide to mystical experience.

As a rule, medieval mystics tend to be either descriptive, reporting their experience in vivid sensory imagery, or analytical, subdividing their experience into distinct stages so as to guide others along the same path. Hildegard combines both approaches. Some medieval mystics also see their experience as producing a supra-rational knowledge not available elsewhere while others describe their experience as producing unearthly joy, an emotional reward, and a moral rebirth; still others see mystic union as combining cognitive and affective experience. Hildegard is in the first category. She tells us that her visions yielded a grasp of the mysteries of the Christian faith she would not have gained otherwise. She is quite specific about her psychic state during her visionary experiences. Her view on that subject is atypical. Her visions, which she reports with a full range of the sensory analogies on which mystics call, occurred when her soul was in its normal psychic condition, without the suspension of her ordinary sensory functions. She distinguishes this state from one of rapture or hallucination. On the basis of her personal experience, Hildegard maintains that it is not necessary to have a special mystic aptitude or to undergo special ascetic practices in order to be a visionary. Any serious believer can be one: all that is needed is an observance of the monastic rule, attentive reading of Scripture, and devout participation in the liturgy. Of particular importance—and here Hildegard manifests a devotion increasingly popular in the twelfth century—is the reception of the Eucharist at mass. It is Eucharistic communion that typically triggers her visionary experiences.

Elizabeth's public life as abbess of her convent was less extensive than Hildegard's and she influenced other people more by writings such as the *Way of God* than through personal contacts. She differs from Hildegard in other respects. Elizabeth is a classic example of a descriptive mystic. She lacks Hildegard's interest in analysis. Also, for Elizabeth, the insights derived from mysticism are moral rather than dogmatic. Her visions gave her ethical wisdom useful to people in all walks of life, and it was for their assistance that she committed them to writing. Another salient difference between Elizabeth and Hildegard is that Elizabeth's visions were less likely to be encounters with Christ or God the Father than with major saints or angels. But a central Benedictine trait they share is liturgical mysticism, the reception of the Eucharist as the catalyst for visionary experience.

Cistercians

Although the foregoing examples indicate that Benedictine spirituality was thriving in some quarters and that new monastic alternatives to it were available, the Cistercian reform, whose avowed goal was the restitution of Benedictine practice, remains the most dynamic religious movement of the twelfth century. Its founder, Robert of Molême (*c.* 1027–1110), launched it in 1098 as a reaction against Cluny, which, by his day, had lost its reforming zeal. Robert objected to the complexity of Cluniac art, architecture, and liturgy, which he thought had taken embellishment to the point of no return, detracting from worship rather than enhancing it. He proposed instead an austere lifestyle with hard physical labor, modest clothing, and a vegetarian diet. He located Cistercian abbeys on the fringes of civilization, remote from worldly temptation. Cistercian art and architecture featured a plain style devoid of ornamentation, relying on line and form for their aesthetic appeal (Plates 20 and 21). But if Robert's goal was the return to first principles, the result of his reform was a departure from the original Benedictine tradition even greater than Cluny's. While each Cistercian abbey elected its own head, the abbots all conferred on a regular basis, making the Cistercians more of a religious order with common practices than any other to date. An unanticipated result of the location of Cistercian communities in frontier areas was that they became instrumental in the period's economic revival, which involved the placement of more land under cultivation and the improvement of agrarian technology. Cistercian abbeys became models of efficient estate management and manual labor was relegated to lay brethren or to serfs contracted to abbeys as their manorial overlords, in a two–tier system not envisaged by Benedict.

If Cistercian reform led to a reinvention of Benedictine monasticism organizationally, the same can be said for its reformulation of Benedictine spirituality, largely in the work of Bernard of Clairvaux, the order's leading figure in the twelfth century. Bernard, the son of a nobleman in the service of the duke of Burgundy, received his monastic calling at the age of twenty-two. An important fact about the history of medieval education that emerges from his biography is that, while still a layman preparing for the range of secular careers open to a man of his class, he acquired the command of classical literature that enabled him to develop a distinctive Latin style and to win the cognomen 'the Mellifluous Doctor' for his eloquence. Bernard certainly put his learning to good use as a monastic leader. Shortly after he became a Cistercian his abilities were recognized and he was sent to found a new abbey at Clairvaux, whose abbot he became. In addition to the government and spiritual guidance of his own monks, the popularization of his order, and his preaching against heretics, Bernard served as an ecclesiastical statesman, advising several popes and counseling kings. He urged the calling of church councils where he attacked academics who, he thought, had strayed from orthodoxy; he promoted devotion to the Virgin Mary and the infant Jesus, preached the Second Crusade, and supported the Knights Templar, one of the new military orders arising to fight the Muslims in the Crusades and the Spanish reconquest. Indeed, of all the monastic reforms of the Middle Ages, the most original, and the greatest, departures from Benedict's conception of the monk as a man of peace who stays in one place are these military monastic orders. They also reflect the capitulation of the western church to the military ethos of the European nobility, a reinterpretation of Christianity in medieval terms of which Bernard was an enthusiastic proponent.

Bernard also wrote extensively. His exegetical, doctrinal, hortatory, and spiritual works all aim at evoking compunction and moral conversion in his audience. Himself a profound mystic, he sees visionary experience as the crown of the monastic life which provides its necessary preparation. His approach to mysticism draws heavily on Origen's reading of the Song of Songs as an allegory of the soul's mystical marriage to God. In his own lengthy commentary on the Song of Songs and throughout his works he analogizes the mystic's relationship to God to nuptial love. The love that the Virgin and the human Christ manifest and inspire are central to his argument. He puts his own personal stamp on both of these popular devotions. Bernard opposes the efforts of some contemporary theologians to define dogmatically the Virgin's exemption from original sin. For him, she is important for her humility and for her willingness to serve as the vehicle of Christ's incarnation. Bernard agrees with Benedict that humility is the mother of the virtues. In Mary's case it led her to accept the divine plan freely. Through her, God, Who could have accomplished our redemption any way He wanted, teaches us the importance of our voluntary collaboration with divine grace. Bernard develops this theme most fully in *On Grace and Free Will*, where he joins contemporaries in departing from the late Augustine on this subject. The affection inspired by the human Christ is essential to Bernard's understanding of the psychodynamics of conversion and of Christ's saving work. For it is our subjective appropriation of Christ's love for us that alone can free the human soul from enslavement to sin, enabling us to respond in love to God and neighbor. This recovery of the ability to love rightly is integrally related to the contemplative life, as Bernard sees it. The practice of virtue is the preparation for mystic vision, which, in turn, energizes the soul and enables us to serve God and neighbor even better.

This combination of the active and the contemplative life, exemplified by Bernard in his own career, is what he advocates in his spiritual doctrine, found most concisely in his *Degrees of Humility and Pride* and *On the Love of God*. The first treatise takes the Benedictine and Marian virtue of humility and develops it into a schematic summary of the moral preparation for contemplation. Bernard analyzes twelve vices, all stemming from pride, and the correlative virtues stemming from humility that are their correctives. He proceeds anecdotally, providing, with a keen eye and acute psychological penetration, a series of case studies of monastic misbehavior illustrating the moral pathologies that need healing. Once these vices have been replaced by their offsetting virtues, the monk is ready to approach his God, his abbot, his brethren, and himself with moral rectitude; he can then begin the mystic's journey.

Bernard details that journey in *On the Love of God*, outlining four stages in the mystic's progress. In the first, we love God for our own sake, because we recognize our need for His help and consolation. In the second, we love God because we have begun to taste His sweetness and are drawn to Him as the greatest good. In the third, having attained mystical union with God, our reason and will are restored and our souls are renewed and perfected. We are turned back to earth, loving God by loving our neighbors, extending to them the unselfish love that God has shown to us. Finally, in the fourth stage, we love God by loving our own souls rightly, that is, for God's sake, evaluating ourselves as God does, neither more nor less.

As these treatises show, for Bernard and for the Cistercian school of mysticism in general, the Augustinian theme of self-knowledge is coupled with an appraisal of human nature and of human free will more optimistic than Augustine's. Bernard sees original sin as blurring the image of God in the human soul but not as depriving us of the capacity to respond to God's love and to will the good in collaboration with divine grace. He sees mystical union with God as a means of recovering our primal, prelapsarian nature. At the same time, he sees mystical experience as a means of enriching our ethical response to ourselves, our neighbors, and God. This primarily affective and ethical understanding of mysticism is the chief note of Cistercian spirituality.

Victorines

Like the Cistercians, the canons of the house of St. Victor just outside Paris rang a change on an institution in place for centuries. Canons were priests typically attached to a cathedral. They ministered to the congregation and helped the bishop administer his diocese, receiving individual stipends for their support. In the twelfth century, the rise in urban population and need for more priests led to the idea that economies of scale as well as spiritual benefits would result if canons pooled their resources and lived in community, engaging in a life of common prayer as much as their pastoral duties allowed. Those canons whose lives were reorganized in this way were called Augustinian because their rule was based on the association of clerics with whom Augustine lived when he became a bishop and a letter of advice he had written to a woman seeking to found a community of nuns. A number of orders of Augustinian canons emerged in this period. What was special about St. Victor was its establishment by William of Champeaux (*c.* 1070–1121), a former master at the cathedral school of Notre Dame, and its swift acquisition of royal patronage. The Victorines took as their pastoral charge the ministry to the many students who flocked to the schools of Paris. These circumstances enabled St. Victor itself to become a leading school until the last quarter of the twelfth century, attracting or producing masters in the liberal arts, systematic theology, liturgical poetry, biblical exegesis, and philosophy. The broad educational mission of Hugh of St. Victor also informed the distinctive Victorine approach to mysticism reflected by Hugh and by his disciple, Richard of St. Victor (d. 1173).

While Hugh does not ignore the ethical dimensions of the contemplative life and while he agrees with Bernard on free will, he aligns himself, and Victorine mysticism, with the view that mysticism is a source of suprarational knowledge. He places this subject in the context of a Neoplatonic understanding of the creation of all things by God and their return to God. Hugh explains how contemplation is related to the other ways we can know this procession and return. We have scientific or philosophical knowledge of created nature through our senses and reason, enabling us to know God as the first cause through His effects in creation. We also have discursive theological knowledge, first in biblical revelation and then in our logical organization of the data of revelation. Theological knowledge thus involves a combination of grace and reason: through it we can know God as our redeemer as well as our creator. Next comes contemplation. It also requires both reason and grace and it enables us to know God in Himself and creation from God's perspective, and to experience His transforming power and love. For Hugh, contemplation imparts knowledge as well as moral renewal. Unlike some mystics who regard the knowledge provided by visionary experience as a foretaste of the beatific vision, Hugh distinguishes contemplative knowledge in this life, which, in nuptial imagery, is analogous to an engagement ring, from posthumous beatitude, which he analogizes to the consummation of a marriage. Another way Hugh positions contemplation is by distinguishing it from thinking and meditation. When we think, our minds operate discursively on things made available to them by our physical senses or memory. Meditation is also discursive. It deals with data we already have in mind, but in a complex or obscure state. By judicious and concentrated rumination, we seek to clarify and understand them. But, when we contemplate, we experience a spontaneous, intuitive grasp of our object of knowledge, understanding it immediately and as a whole.

Having located contemplation in his larger epistemological scheme, Hugh treats it more specifically in three works, *On the Vanity of the Things of This World*, *Noah's Ark Morally Understood*, and *Noah's Ark Mystically Understood*. In style and substance, the first treatise owes much to Augustine. Reviewing earthly goods, Hugh accents their mutability and finitude. Given our longing for an infinite good that can never be lost, they are bound to yield disappointment. This conclusion turns us toward the love of God as the only enduring good, an ordering of our love that brings us to the beginning of the contemplative journey outlined in Hugh's *Noah's Ark* treatises.

But why Noah? Here Hugh reflects a characteristic Victorine tendency to base contemplative theology on a moral and allegorical reading of the Old Testament. Reprising our restless, unsatisfied quest for the true good among the transient goods of this world, he notes that these goods are swept away, as the world was in Noah's flood. Our only refuge is the ark of Noah we can build within the soul, with God as our helmsman. This image draws Hugh into a protracted discussion of Noah's ark, its parts, and its construction, subjected to the fourfold method of biblical exegesis. Once on board the ark within, we can understand the creation as a manifestation of its creator and we can contemplate God Himself. In moving from the world to God, Hugh explores two biblical metaphors of Christ as mediator, the tree and the book of life. Christ is like a tree because He shelters and feeds us; He is like the book of life because He teaches and chastises us. Hugh concludes by noting that our building of the ark within the soul as well as the contemplative activities that take place there require the active collaboration of free will with God. He joins Bernard in rejecting the late Augustine on free will despite the heavily Augustinian coloration of his contemplative doctrine in other respects.

Richard of St. Victor takes for granted Hugh's broad approach to education, his situation of contemplation in a larger epistemological framework, his combination of cognitive and affective mysticism, and his use of the Old Testament as a springboard for contemplative doctrine, and goes on from there. Like Hugh, he wrote discursive as well as mystical theology. From a contemplative standpoint, *On the Trinity* is his most important work. Richard borrows from Augustine the idea of the lover, the beloved, and the love that unites them as an analogy of the triune God Who is love. Since we are made in God's image, our chief resemblance to Him lies in our affective faculty, lodged pre-eminently in the will. But our will has been weakened by original sin. Still, with the aid of grace, it can regain its purity and return us to God. For Richard, this return requires a threefold process, the purgative, illuminative, and unitive ways of the Pseudo-Dionysius. Richard spells them out, respectively, in his *Benjamin Minor*, *Benjamin Major*, and *The Four Degrees of Violent Charity*.

Benjamin Minor outlines the purgative way. Taking a cue from Gregory the Great, Richard treats Leah as a type of the active life, standing for practicality and prudence, while Rachel typifies the contemplative life, standing for pure intelligence and wisdom. Rachel is the more beloved of Jacob's two wives. But he must work for and wed Leah before he can work for and wed Rachel. Leah's seven children signify the affections leading to the virtues; for Richard, as for Plato and Aristotle, the affective faculty, rightly ordered, contributes to virtue. Rachel's son Joseph stands for discretion. This is the faculty that governs the affections and orients them to virtue. Rachel's son Benjamin, Jacob's best-loved child, stands for contemplation, the highest form of understanding, which leads to self-knowledge and the knowledge of God. Thus far, we can see Richard including the affections and the virtues and at the same time privileging cognition. As he points out, in the biblical account Rachel dies giving birth to Benjamin. Thus, while contemplation is the child of reason, it eclipses reason, moving beyond it to ecstatic experience that yields suprarational knowledge.

Reprising Hugh's definitions of thinking, meditation, and contemplation, Richard outlines the illuminative way in *Benjamin Major*. He divides it into six stages, the first two involving imagination, the second two reason, and the last two transcending reason. Imagination calls on the physical senses to understand the natural world and uses it to venerate God as its first cause. Reason moves us from things visible to things invisible, understanding the visible world as a reflection of eternal truths and also perceiving angels and human souls and their relationship to

God. In the suprarational stages of illumination we enjoy the direct contemplation of spiritual truths and mysteries of Christian doctrine that are revealed in the Bible and acquired by faith. They require grace collaborating with reason. With Hugh, Richard holds that the benefits of this process are moral as well as cognitive. And, as the soul is illuminated, it begins to experience God's sweetness.

Richard reserves his fullest exposition of the unitive way to the *Four Degrees*, and sweetness does not characterize all its phases. He calls the love described in this treatise violent because it draws us forcibly from our normal psychic states into ecstasy. Richard uses many sensory images to describe mystical union. Among them are the soul compared with fire ardently flaming upward, wax liquefying, or iron growing white-hot and melting with the application of heat. He combines such metaphors with nuptial imagery. The concreteness and psychological precision with which he analyzes the four stages of mystical union constitute a landmark in the history of Christian mysticism. In Richard's first stage, the love that wounds, God's love penetrates the soul, leaving it in a state of fervent suffering, like an intermittent fever, because of its desire to possess God fully. The affective faculty is concentrated on God, Who gives the mystic débutant a consolation analogous to the betrothal, in nuptial terms. In the second stage, the love that binds, the cognitive faculty is taken captive, especially the memory. The mind receives a suprarational understanding beyond what Richard describes in *Benjamin Major*. He compares this stage to the wedding. In the third stage, the love that languishes, the soul is gripped by an even greater yearning for God, Who becomes its only desire. All other goods cease to appeal. The soul feels the pain of separation from its object of longing, Whose absence reduces it to intellectual and affective paralysis, devoid of all joy. This terrifying psychic state, the seedbed of the 'dark night of the soul' in later mystics, continues until God relieves it with the union the mystic craves. Richard's nuptial analogy is the consummation of the marriage. His last stage is the love that unmakes and remakes the soul. Mystic union engenders moral rebirth, returning the soul to its prelapsarian state, even as it provides a suprarational knowledge and a love beyond all earthly loves. Richard shares Bernard's view that the key virtue in the reborn soul is humility. For Richard, the exemplar of this virtue is the human Christ, identifying His will at all times with the will of God the Father. In Richard's nuptial imagery, this final stage of mysticism is analogous to the bearing of offspring by the married couple. The vision and joy of the earlier stages of contemplation lead to moral fruitfulness; the reclamation of our primal nature is also a restoration of the right moral relationship between the soul and God, its neighbor, and itself.

No Christian mystic before Richard of St. Victor and few after him described and analyzed the upper reaches of the mystic's ascent in such elaborate, architectonic, and electrifying detail. As an incisive taxonomist of the states of soul in the itinerary he presents, he combines schematic with reportorial mysticism to a high degree. His achievement in this field earned him Dante's accolade, 'In contemplation he was more than man.'[1] Richard unites his brilliant experiential gifts with the systematic and synthetic Victorine spirit, always keeping before the reader's eyes the place of each psychic stage in the overall picture and the place of contemplation in the larger epistemological landscape. His equally Victorine manipulation of Old Testament allegory is consistent with Hugh's practice, as is his accent on cognitive mysticism even as he makes its moral rewards and effects the conclusion of the mystic's quest. In all these ways, Richard is as much a virtuoso in articulating the specifics of Victorine mysticism as Bernard is in doing the same for the Cistercians. Both Victorine and Cistercian mysticism proved influential in the later Middle Ages. But both found some stiff, if friendly, competitors in the mystics of the Franciscan and Dominican schools.

CHAPTER 17

Franciscans, Dominicans, and Later Medieval Mystics

The mysticism considered in this chapter owes much to the practitioners of a new ecclesiastical reform, the friars, who emerged in the early thirteenth century to fill a perceived gap in the pastoral ministry not addressed by parish priests, monks, or canons. The founders of the earliest orders of friars, Francis of Assisi (1182–1226) and Dominic de Guzmán (c. 1170–1234), simultaneously concluded that the church needed clerics who were mobile, not tied to a cloister or a territorial parish, free to take the church into the streets, to preach, hear confessions, and minister to the people where the people were. Both orders saw their calling as the imitation of Christ, in their preaching mission and in their practice of voluntary poverty as mendicants. From the outset, the Dominicans, and after temporizing, the Franciscans, adopted rules that made their religious orders more highly structured than earlier ones. The friars were organized in regional and national provinces with superiors at each level who met regularly, governed at the top by a single head. Both orders were immensely popular. They drew enthusiastic financial support from the laity and a wide membership, including some of the most outstanding speculative thinkers of the high Middle Ages. Both orders swiftly adapted their calling for women. Dominican nuns played an active role in the education of girls, while Franciscan nuns, or Poor Clares, exemplified radical poverty. In addition, both launched another innovation, the third orders. Tertiaries were lay people earning their livings in secular occupations, who associated themselves with the spirituality of each order, sometimes living in community and sometimes in their own families, without taking monastic vows. Both orders of friars, as well, developed distinctive approaches to devotion and mysticism. Coupled with the friars' commitment to vernacular preaching and pastoral work, their structural innovations made these styles of religious experience available to an increasingly large number of people whether formally affiliated with the orders or not.

Franciscans

It is no surprise that Franciscans developed their own approach to devotion and mysticism, since their founder was one of the most gifted and original mystics in the Christian tradition. Francis left practically no writings. But, whatever their other differences, his followers who told and retold his story in the thirteenth century agree on the keynotes of Franciscan mysticism as exemplified in his life.

These keynotes reflect Francis' personality and the traits he brought with him from the lay state to his new calling. Two of these were courtesy and cheerfulness. As a youth, the son of a wealthy cloth merchant, Francis led a carefree life, known and admired for his graciousness and good manners. He loved French lyric poetry; indeed, 'Francis' is actually the nickname he was given because of his literary tastes. Francis underwent a conversion experience in which his personality and literary interests played a role. He met a leper on the road. We must appreciate the fear and loathing that leprosy inspired in medieval people, partly because of the horrible appearance of its victims in the terminal stage of illness and partly because they thought it was extremely communicable. There was no cure for leprosy, and lepers were segregated from the rest of society. If it was necessary for a leper to leave the leper-house he was required to carry a bell and ring it when approaching a healthy person, who could then give him a wide berth. When Francis met the leper, he was moved to embrace him instead of shrinking from him. Then, looking back before continuing on his way, he found no one there. As Francis interpreted this event, it had been Christ Who had appeared to him in the form of a leper, the least of His brethren, and it had been Christ Who had converted loathing into brotherly love. Francis' first response to this experience was to minister to the lepers. Then he decided to rebuild a ruined church. When his father found Francis abstracting funds from the family business for this purpose, he chastised him to no avail. So his father asked the bishop of Assisi to bring Francis to his senses. In the public square, in front of the bishop, his family, and the populace of Assisi, Francis proclaimed his new calling by divesting himself of his clothes and with them his family's wealth and status. Henceforth, he declared, he would serve Lady Poverty. The courtly motif of service to a lady derived from the love poets he admired and the genial, cheerful, outgoing personality of Francis transmuted themselves into a religious leadership of unprecedented magnetism, the accent on poverty as the central Christian virtue, and the notion that the chief motivation in the Christian life should be love and joy, not fear and sadness.

Francis certainly put to use the endowment he brought to his religious mission. He had a good, and multilingual, literary education. But he was in no sense a trained theologian. Nor did he value book-learning in that field. His own theology came largely from the Bible and from his personal religious experience. Francis did not promote intellectual pursuits: he thought that a Christian teaches best by the force of moral example. Yet he was an eloquent preacher. His message was love of neighbor, peace, the practice of corporeal as well as spiritual works of mercy, and conversion. By the latter he meant both inspiring Christians to act on their convictions and missionary activity, which he personally undertook in Egypt as a pointed criticism of the Crusades and of the spread of Christianity by force.

Francis preached not only to his human neighbors but also to animals, reflecting his major religious innovation, nature mysticism. He regarded all created beings, animate and inanimate, as his family. With them and through them he could offer praise to God. His relationship to the natural world was not scientific but affective, in some cases shaped by the natural metaphors for Christ in the New Testament. Aside from the rapport with the natural world which all his biographers relate, Francis himself voices this distinctive outlook in his celebratory *Canticle of the Creatures*, glorifying God in such phenomena as Brother Sun, Sister Moon, Brothers Wind, Air, Cloud, Fair Weather and Rain, Sister Water, Brother Fire, Mother Earth, and even Sister Bodily Death, to be appreciated as part of the God-given life cycle.

Another characteristic feature of Franciscan spirituality manifested in the founder's life is Christocentric devotion. While in no sense unique to Franciscans, this practice received its own stamp from the order. Along with the Dominicans, they saw themselves as following in Christ's footsteps by bringing the gospel to the people and by imitating His poor and itinerant life. They also venerated Christ in the Eucharist. The specifically Franciscan approach to this extremely popular devotion, which led to the establishment of the feast of Corpus Christi in the thirteenth century, was to see themselves as imitators of Christ when, as priests, they consecrated and distributed the Eucharist. On more than one occasion, this action is reported as triggering the mystic transports of Francis and his followers. Another important aspect of Franciscan devotion to Christ was the love of the human Christ. This theme is on the same trajectory as Cistercian devotion to Christ and the Franciscans likewise geared it more to the mobilization of the believer's affections than to theological reflection. The Franciscans promoted the veneration of the infant Jesus and invented the Christmas crèche as an adjunct to the celebration of that feast. Another note they struck was the veneration of Christ as the man of sorrows: by empathetically participating in His passion, they believed, they could give a redemptive meaning to human suffering.

Virtually all these themes converged in the mystic experience Francis underwent on Mount Alverno in 1224. Both he and his followers saw it as the crowning moment of his life. After a number of preliminary visions and many days spent in prayer, Francis offered his poverty, chastity, and obedience to God and was vouchsafed knowledge of God. Nature was involved in the event. A falcon awakened Francis every day and other birds surrounded him with song. After a fast of forty days and nights imitating the fast undertaken by Christ before beginning His public ministry, Francis then faced and overcame the last and most subtle of temptations, the feeling that he was worthy of imitating Christ to the end. Having mastered it, he received the final vision. Christ appeared to him in the form of a seraph with six wings, two over His head, two over His body, and two over His outstretched arms, describing the image of Christ crucified. And, in a new departure in the Christian tradition, in receiving this vision Francis also received the stigmata, the physical wounds of the crucified Christ. These marks were held to be authentic, and miraculous, by Francis, his followers, and other medieval Christians. His reception of them was seen as direct divine proof that he was a saint. Despite the elaborate procedures to verify sanctity that existed by the early thirteenth century, Francis was canonized within two years of his death, a world record in church history.

Aside from organizational problems, Francis having been rather vague in that area, the question confronting Franciscans after 1226 was the sense in which the founder's charismatic aptitudes and personal experience could be made normative for an order that soon had hundreds of thousands of members, few of whom were mystics, and tasks ranging from the education of university theologians to the staffing of foreign missions in lands as remote as China. This question paralleled the debate on whether to insist on mendicancy or to use the vast resources donated and bequeathed to the order to finance its activities, letting lay coadjutors manage them. Two ways of addressing the issue of Franciscan spirituality emerged. One was to reformulate it philosophically, making it accessible to intellectuals. The second was to popularize it, making it available to lay people, whether learned or unlearned and whether mystics or not.

The first path was taken by Bonaventure (1217–74). Devoted to Francis from his youth, Bonaventure was a student of theology at the university of Paris when his master, Alexander of Hales (1170/85–1245) joined the Franciscan order. The notion that this calling could be combined with scholastic theology propelled Bonaventure into making the same decision and qualified him to occupy the Franciscan chair of theology before being elected head of the order in 1257. In his writings from the 1250s to 1263, Bonaventure recast what he regarded as the essentials of Franciscan spirituality in scholastic terms. This effort led him to de-emphasize some features of the original Franciscan message. Bonaventure dropped Francis' accent on cheerfulness, along with his distrust of higher education. At the same time, Bonaventure retained the idea that the goal of learning was service and that the purpose of theology was to mobilize the heart and not merely to inform and convince the intellect.

A major Franciscan theme that Bonaventure reformulates is the love of nature and the feeling of communion with it. Combining this idea with Franciscan Christocentricity, he rephrases it in Neoplatonic terms in the first part of his *Breviloquium*, one of his major scholastic treatises, where he describes the creation, viewed as an emanation from God, as a chain of being whose links serve as mirrors of the creator and as means by which we can reascend to Him. Christ functions as the *logos* or supreme archetype of the world order, linking us to God cosmologically as well as personally. Here, Bonaventure takes the nature mysticism and affection for Christ that were spontaneous and intuitive for Francis and articulates them in systematic scholastic form.

Bonaventure also produced spiritual writings that reworked Franciscan mysticism. He unites the Franciscan theme of identification with Christ's passion with ideas from the Neoplatonic, Augustinian, and Victorine traditions. Bonaventure wrote a *Soliloquy* modeled on an early Augustinian work with the same title as well as on a similar work by Hugh of St. Victor. Where Augustine's interlocutors are himself and his reason, Bonaventure's are the soul and the conscience. The conscience tries to impress on the soul a personal awareness of Christ's saving work. Bonaventure divides the text into four parts, in each of which he invokes an event in Christ's life to instruct and motivate the soul. Two treatises that are companion pieces and that use biblical metaphors of Christ in a Victorine way are his *Tree of*

Life and *Mystical Vine*. Both are meditations on Christ's passion and exercises in visual as well as emotional imagination. The reader is asked to visualize the tree of the cross, with flowers, leaves, and fruit stemming from it, and a vine with its leaves and bunches of grapes. Each of these images symbolizes a mystery of the faith exemplified by a particular moment in Christ's passion. The biblical metaphors Bonaventure chooses and subdivides so elaborately are designed to catalyze the reader's conversion as he contemplates and internalizes Christ's passion.

Another important spiritual work of Bonaventure and one that reinterprets a traditional approach to Christian mysticism is his *Three-Fold Way*. The title refers to the Pseudo-Areopagite's purgative, illuminative, and unitive ways, which Bonaventure alters in two respects. First, he treats the three ways as simultaneous, not as successive. Second, each way uses a different mental faculty; each engenders a different moral state; each is symbolized by a different kind of angelic being. The purgative way works through meditation by means of the conscience. It engenders peace and is symbolized by the thrones. The illuminative way works through prayer by means of the intellect. It engenders truth and is symbolized by the cherubim. The unitive way works through contemplation by means of wisdom. It engenders love and is symbolized by the seraphim. Here, Bonaventure applies the Victorine distinction between meditation and contemplation. But, in true Franciscan form, he privileges affective over cognitive spirituality and his work provides guidance to non-mystics and mystics alike.

Equally indicative of Bonaventure's reworking of Franciscan spirituality is his *Six Wings of the Seraph*. The title evokes Francis' most exalted mystical experience. But, what Bonaventure presents here is not a scholastic road map helping the reader to induce a vision of Christ or receive the stigmata. Rather, he uses the image of the seraph to discuss six virtues that he thinks religious superiors should have: zeal for justice, kindness, patience, exemplary moral character, discernment, and devotion to God. These virtues do not include the personal charisma that Francis had. Nor do they include visionary aptitude. What they do require are administrative skill and the ability to lead and inspire a large and heterogeneous organization of the type that the Franciscan order had become by Bonaventure's day. These were qualities that enabled him to keep the order together despite the dissension in its ranks, even as his scholasticized spiritual writings updated Franciscan mysticism and made it more widely available.

The Franciscan message was also imparted and applied widely on quite another register of high medieval religious culture, the register of lay piety. Indeed, the leading Franciscan mystic of the late thirteenth and early fourteenth centuries was a laywoman, Angela of Foligno (1248–1309). She illustrates well how relatively unlearned people, including women, could gain a good theological education and an education in the spiritual life through vernacular preaching. In Angela's case, her sex and lay status were not impediments to her acquisition of considerable religious authority as well as religious knowledge. A comfortable middle-class wife and mother for most of her life, Angela was freed from family responsibilities in middle age by the death of her husband and children. She used her free time for religious pursuits. Instructed by Franciscan preaching, she became a Franciscan tertiary, joining a community of them in her city. As a contemplative, Angela combines descriptive mysticism with analytical language, sophisticated theological concepts, and a schematic series of steps outlining the stages in the mystic's preparation for visionary experience. She also followed the active life, ministering to the poor and sick in Foligno and, perhaps more surprisingly, serving her fellow citizens as a spiritual director. A group of followers assembled around her, seeking her counsel. She showed great insight, skill, and wisdom in advising them and in guiding their spiritual development. Angela was regarded as a holy woman, and the saint's lives devoted to her document her religious experiences and activities, as do her own writings.

Dominicans and Later Medieval Mystics

The fact that mystics and spiritual writers attached to the Franciscan order dominate the field in the thirteenth century is predictable, given the example of Francis, the writings of Bonaventure, and the wide attraction of the Franciscan order. What is more surprising is the entry of Dominicans into the mystic arena and their massive influence in the fourteenth century, given the fact that their founder did not have a mystical bone in his body. Dominic was an organizer and an intellectual, an educated man who had been a priest and canon of his local cathedral until a preaching mission against heresy in southern France inspired him to found an order with the express purpose of fighting fire with fire. Both to attack heresies with sophisticated philosophical and theological foundations and to help the faithful avoid them, he thought it necessary for Dominicans to be learned. Their convents were houses of study from the outset. This intellectualism carried over into Dominican spirituality, which emphasized meditation on theological truths to extract their dogmatic meanings and interrelations rather than to stir the emotions. Dominicans were among the most rationalistic of the high medieval scholastics. Yet, this order produced the most influential mystics of the fourteenth century.

The single most important was Meister Eckhart (1260–1327). He and his immediate followers share a strongly analytical approach to mysticism. They were all friars, priests, and pastors, men with university educations. Their advocacy of the union of action and contemplation is as typical of them as it is of the Cistercians and Franciscans. Eckhart entered the order after receiving his education from the Dominicans at Cologne and Paris. He himself taught philosophy and theology at Paris, professing the order's Christian Aristotelianism. He then held administrative posts, heading the order's school at Cologne and its Saxon province, becoming its vicar in Bohemia, and eventually heading the order for all of Germany. Wherever his assignments in Germany took him, he preached to the laity and provided them with spiritual direction. Eckhart's mystical teachings are found in his German sermons and treatises. In the last years of his life, questions were raised about his orthodoxy, but the accusations, coming from Paris and motivated by philosophical partisanship, had nothing to do with ideas in his German works. Some of Eckhart's mystical teachings also provoked debate. The difficulties may stem from the contemporary imprecision of German as a language in which to express subtle theological ideas. In any case, his followers were careful to restate Eckhartian mysticism in orthodox terms on just those points.

As a Christian Aristotelian and as an essentially cognitive and analytic mystic, Eckhart sees mysticism as consummating our innate desire for knowledge. This knowledge begins with our understanding of the natural world through the senses and reason. Once the data are assembled, we can organize them into a scientific whole, connecting causes logically with effects. This type of knowledge, available to all, is conceptual and discursive. Beyond it lies mystical knowledge, which requires divine grace as well as reason and which moves from the knowledge of how things work to a direct grasp of their essences, and, beyond that, to their ground of being, without the need for a ratiocinative process. Eckhart thinks we can go beyond even the mystic knowledge just described. True, as mystics we can contemplate beings and their essences and we can contemplate the supreme being, God. But, in so doing, we are still treating God as a being Who acts in relation to other beings. For Eckhart, and here John Scottus joins his account, the highest type of mystical knowledge is the knowledge of God as the One beyond being, the Godhead perfectly at rest, not interacting with anything else. This God transcends the normal mystic categories. He can be approached only by negative theology and negative psychology. Eckhart brings this Neoplatonic agenda to bear on a God also conceived as Aristotle's unmoved mover. He states that, in the created order, he loves best those things that most resemble God, and for this reason, he prefers stillness above all.

Despite his intellectualistic bent, Eckhart does not see mysticism as involving or affecting the intellect alone. As with most earlier mystics, he regards the practice of virtue, involving the heart and will as well as the intellect, as a necessary preparation for mysticism. He does not counsel rigorous asceticism, which in any case would have been impossible for the lay people he directed, but the imitation of Christ in the sense of submitting one's will obediently to the will of God in ways suitable to one's calling in life. Eckhart highlights correct inner intentions over external acts and sees a perverse spiritual temptation lurking in extreme self-discipline. It is preferable, and sufficient, to follow the Beatitudes in a spirit of modesty. Eckhart also advocates faithful liturgical observance and frequent communion. Unlike the Franciscans and the earlier Rhineland Benedictine nuns, he does not see the Eucharist as triggering mystical experience but as a source of grace and spiritual refreshment. The practice of the social virtues, a mandatory preparation for mysticism, is also, for Eckhart, its consequence. He regards active service of others as essential, before, during, and after contemplation.

While the will, which points us toward the good and which is the seat of virtue, is thus by no means ignored in Eckhart's teaching, he is still primarily a cognitive mystic. This fact emerges from Eckhart's lexicon and imagery. He does not use nuptial language to refer to the soul's union with God; nor does he describe it in terms of other kinds of human love. He does not speak of union with the human Christ but of union with the Godhead, divinity in its most abstract sense. Indeed,

Eckhart criticizes affective mysticism as self-centered. He describes his own intel-lectualistic approach, by contrast, as disinterested.

Having practiced preparatory virtue, discursive philosophy, normal mysticism, and negative theology, the mystic must finally engage in negative psychology before uniting with the Godhead. Drawing here on Richard of St. Victor but giving his own account of the process, Eckhart describes the soul emptied of all knowledge and self-concern, retreating into the interior castle; or, in another of his images, he speaks of breaking the soul's nutshell to extract the kernel. He defines this kernel as a spark of the divine and as the seed of eternal life. It is here that Eckhart's ter-minology fails to clarify whether he sees the human soul as consubstantial with God or as made in His image and as capable of beatitude. Eckhart compares mystic union with the merging of a drop of water into the sea. This too could be read as sug-gesting that the mystic's individual identity is absorbed by the divine nature. These were the points that Eckhart's Dominican disciples, John Tauler (1306–61) and Henry Suso (1295–1336), took pains to present in lucid and unexceptionable terms. But despite his problematic language, Eckhart's mysticism achieved an original fusion of Christian Aristotelianism with Christian Neoplatonism, giving each its full weight in its own sphere. He unites them by placing them in a clear hierar-chical relationship and by specifying the different conditions of labor that each requires.

Among Eckhart's immediate disciples, Tauler makes his contribution by analyz-ing in great psychological detail the penultimate stage of the soul when it has with-drawn into the interior castle and awaits its union with God. He describes this stage as one of silence and passivity, in which the mind is beyond speech, beyond con-cepts, beyond images, beyond action, waiting in a state of pure openness and recep-tivity to God. Tauler speaks of a special disposition of the soul that enables it to move into this frightening suspension of its accustomed modes of operation, reach-ing a point where it can do nothing at all, for as long as God wills, until He comes to the mystic's rescue. This is his version of the 'dark night of the soul' first put on the mystic agenda by Richard of St. Victor. Along with Eckhart's interior castle, it continued to supply grist for the mills of mystics like Teresa of Avila (1515–82) and John of the Cross (1542–91) in early modern times.

For his part, Suso's re-expression of Eckhartian mysticism is interesting for his integration of Franciscan imagery into it. This bow to a rival school of mystics is a token of things to come, the tendency toward eclecticism in late medieval mystics, especially those not associated with particular religious orders. Suso borrows from the Franciscans the understanding of mystic union as an interpersonal love rela-tionship and empathy with Christ's sufferings as inspiring the ethical preparation for it. This notion leads him to prescribe a moral regime more ascetic than Eckhart's, even though he also addressed a lay audience. Suso takes the conversion of Francis as the model for his own, expressing it likewise as loving service to a lady. But he shows his Dominican colors by choosing Lady Wisdom as his mentor and beloved. He also draws on Eckhart's Neoplatonism in understanding the effects of meditating on the crucifixion. For Suso, more is involved than stimulating compunction and internalizing the moral meaning of redemption through suffering. He adds the intellectual experience of escape from nothingness to being. By 'nothingness' Suso means the created order, with its vast metaphysical inferiority to God. Suso also shares Eckhart's negative theology and his understanding of God as the One beyond being. He is careful to insist that the distinction between divine and human natures is not obliterated when they unite mystically.

The profound and widespread influence of Dominican mysticism, often in combination with themes from other schools of spirituality, was expressed in various registers of the late medieval religious culture. Like the Franciscans, the Dominicans produced a leading mystic in this period who was a tertiary, Catherine of Siena (1347–80). With Angela of Foligno, she reflects the vernacularization of the friars' teaching and the popularity of mysticism among laywomen. Catherine never married, living at home with her family. A mystic from her youth, she had won acclaim for her visionary gifts by the age of twenty-three. Capitalizing on the account of the conversion of her saintly namesake, Catherine of Alexandria (d. early fourth century), she describes the most climactic vision of her youth as a mystical marriage with the infant Jesus. In other respects her theology and spirituality are solidly Dominican. Illiterate, Catherine acquired a thorough theological education from Dominican preachers; like Angela, she then became a recognized theologian and spiritual leader in her own right. What are regarded as her 'writings' were oral dictations to her confessor, who redacted them. Along with other clerics and lay people, male and female, he was an enthusiastic member of the group who flocked to Catherine for spiritual counsel.

Like all mystics associated with the friars, she combined the active and the contemplative lives. Like Angela, she first ministered to the poor and the sick in her city before becoming a spiritual director. But, from about 1370 onward, Catherine took on a broader mission, focusing on ecclesiastical problems at the highest level. Since the early fourteenth century, the popes had resided at Avignon, a fact deplored by Catherine, along with many other Italians. Even more reprehensible was the corruption at the papal court and the hierarchy's inattention to the spiritual needs of Christians. Catherine directed many letters to popes and other high officials of church and state, expressing her concerns and urging remedies. She travelled extensively to win support for her cause, not hesitating to go to Avignon to criticize the pope in person. Even more than Angela's, Catherine's career illustrates how the spiritual gifts and insights and the perceived sanctity of a female mystic could win authority, enabling her to transcend the limitations of sex, education, and lay status that would otherwise have confined her.

Yet another lifestyle followed by people of both sexes who made important contributions to late medieval mysticism was anchorism. Mystical anchorites and anchoresses are best documented in fourteenth-century England. Although the name of their calling bespeaks the solitary life, it is to some extent a misnomer; for these figures had social functions ranging from spiritual direction to the arbitration of conflicts to the collection of bridge tolls. The community supported them generously from the royal family on down; a city with an anchorite or anchoress in its midst regarded itself as blessed. The late medieval English mystics who followed this lifestyle were heavily influenced by Dominican mysticism, although selectivity and the creation of individual perspectives on the basis of relevant sources are also strongly evident. Both the sources and the writings of these mystics were increasingly vernacular; the *Ladder of Perfection* of Walter Hilton (d. 1396) is the only major mystical text of his time and place written in Latin.

Hilton and the anonymous author of the *Cloud of Unknowing* (*c.* 1370) are the two English mystics most deeply in the debt of the Dominicans. As the titles of their treatises suggest, they are analytical mystics presenting schematic accounts of their subject. Both draw on Eckhart. Although Hilton began his career as an Oxford scholar and ended it as a canon, he was an anchorite when he wrote the *Ladder* and he dedicated it to a friend who was an anchoress. He reprises Eckhart's itinerary, moving from philosophical to mystic knowledge to negative theology and psychology. He calls the soul's state of suspension in the stage immediately preceding union with the Godhead the 'night of murk.' Elsewhere, he is quite faithful to Eckhart's language, likewise eschewing erotic imagery and downgrading sensuous metaphors. The author of the *Cloud* is less inclusive than Hilton. He takes for granted the earlier parts of Eckhart's program and confines himself to the negative theology and psychology stage. In his terms, the cloud of unknowing describes the soul's divesting itself of its normal intellectual activities. Unlike Hilton, the author preserves the combination of action and contemplation important to Eckhart, seeing the harvest of rapture as service to others.

The two other English mystics considered here were both solitaries. Unlike Hilton and the author of the *Cloud*, they are descriptive mystics and authors who ring notable changes on their sources. Richard Rolle (*c.* 1300–49), an anchorite from his youth, makes heavy use of sensuous imagery of all kinds in his *Living Flame of Love*. He describes mystic union in terms of warmth, song, and sweetness, reporting an experience essentially affective, for him, not cognitive. As a means of arousing religious feeling Rolle promotes the Jesus prayer, the repetition of the name of Jesus. This technique takes the Cistercian and Franciscan devotion to the human Christ in a new direction. Also reportorial and affective is Julian of Norwich (1343–1413), who took her name from the patron saint of the church next to which she built her anchorhold. We have no external evidence about her education, but her *Showings* or *Revelations of Divine Love* indicates that Julian was well read, knowing the Christian Neoplatonists, the Dominicans, the Franciscans, and Bernard of Clairvaux. A major Franciscan theme on which she draws is devotion to the suffering Christ. Julian reports her visions of His passion in vivid sensuous detail, her imagery tactile and olfactory more than visual. Julian's most distinctive contribution to Christian mysticism is her understanding of the affective bond between the mystic and God in terms of maternal love. Apart from having had a loving and supportive mother in her own life, Julian attaches this idea to the veneration of the Virgin as the universal mother of Christians. Also, picking up on a theme in Matthew 23:37 first articulated by Augustine and Bernard, and one on which she expands, Julian describes Jesus as mother. She chooses motherhood to describe God's love because she regards it as the purest, most selfless, and most moving form of human love.

A final expression of the individuality with which late medieval mystics put together their own spiritual doctrine from diverse sources is found in John Ruysbroeck (1293–1384), a priest educated in Brussels who wrote his spiritual works in Flemish. Ruysbroeck organized a group of secular priests into a community like St. Victor, committed to study and contemplation along with pastoral work. His group also placed a Benedictine stress on liturgical prayer. Like contemporary Dominicans and Richard of St. Victor, Ruysbroeck is extremely analytical, spelling out the stages of mysticism in great detail. Like Eckhart's followers, he notes with care that the divine and human natures are not confused in mystical union. Ruysbroeck was also familiar with Bonaventure's spiritual writings and makes use of his *Three-Fold Way*, likewise presenting the purgative, illuminative, and unitive ways as simultaneous. He agrees with Bonaventure that the created universe, resembling its creator, is a sign of Christ, its prime exemplar, and that contemplating nature can lead us back to God. With Augustine and Richard of St. Victor, he sees the supreme created analogy of the Trinity as the human soul. With Bernard and other followers of Origen, Ruysbroeck appeals to the Song of Songs tradition, using nuptial imagery extensively in his descriptions of mystic union. But his greatest achievement is the well-tempered balance he holds among all these sources and between the cognitive and affective dimensions of mystical experience and the active and contemplative lives.

Whether inclusive and synthetic, like Ruysbroeck, or interested only in some of the themes and emphases of their predecessors, the late medieval mystics as a group reflect the wide appeal of mysticism to large numbers of people of all kinds. They also indicate the growing production of mystical literature in the vernacular and the mystics' increasing confidence, as they choose what they want from their sources. The earliest mystical writers of the high Middle Ages, Benedictine, Cistercian, and Victorine, presuppose the monastic life or the ordered life of Augustinian canons as the obvious and necessary social context in which mysticism can take place. With the Franciscans and Dominicans, we see mystics who are friars themselves. But, thanks to their ministry and the new forms of religious life for lay people they created, we also see as associates of the friars an expanding number of mystics who are lay, female, and educated through vernacular preaching. By the late Middle Ages, the wide availability of mystical literature in the vernacular made it possible for mystics to put the pieces together on their own. Throughout the period Christians irrespective of status could find self-validation and the respect of contemporaries through their religious experience, making the Christian tradition their own in new and diverse ways and finding thereby their own voices, whether with official support or independently. In some cases, their approaches to mysticism endured well beyond the Middle Ages, providing themes of continuing appeal to later Christians. But there were others in the same period whose desire to internalize and articulate their religious beliefs and values earned them not the esteem of their society but anathematization and persecution. Their story is also part of the history of high medieval Christianity.

CHAPTER 18

Heresy in the Twelfth and Thirteenth Centuries

Ecclesiastical reform was a major dimension of cultural revival in the high Middle Ages. Led by successive waves of monastic reform generating a host of new orders and approaches to the spiritual life, reform was also applied to the secular clergy and to the institutional church. In the second half of the eleventh century, several popes mounted concerted efforts to free the church hierarchy from political manipulation by lay rulers. In 1059, the College of Cardinals was created as a mechanism for electing popes by clerics alone. The ban on lay investiture of bishops and other church leaders launched by Pope Gregory VII (*c.* 1020–85) met with fierce resistance from European kings, provoking a conflict that was not settled until 1107 in France and England and 1122 in Germany. The popes won a moral victory but the kings retained effective control over the appointment of prelates. Along with structural reforms, some more successful than others, came programs designed to upgrade the moral and educational qualifications of clerics and to impose mandatory clerical celibacy.

Improvements there were. But the demand for good pastors continued to outrun supply. Despite new orders and reforms, lay criticism of the clergy was pervasive and reflected ongoing problems. It sometimes took the form of orthodox cries for reform. But it also took shape as heresy. On one level, the proliferation of heresy in the twelfth and thirteenth centuries can be seen as a manifestation of the desire to personalize religion and to express and institutionalize it in new ways. Heresy was on the same trajectory as orthodox reform movements and targeted many of the same concerns. On another level, despite the variety of heresies that emerged, in one way or another most of them criticized an institutional church seen as worldly and corrupt and clerics who were seen as unable to perform their pastoral duties. Just as the heresies of the early church highlighted the contemporary problems of Christian leaders in evangelizing philosophically trained pagans who balked at the paradoxes embedded in central Christian doctrines, so the heresies of this period, for the most part, were reactions against a rich and worldly clerical establishment, itself made possible by the expansion of commerce. Attacks on that establishment were acute enough to take some critics out of the orthodox fold altogether.

Another source of heresy, if less significant statistically in the twelfth and thirteenth centuries, was the rise of speculative thought. Already in the eleventh century, the application of semantics and logic to theology by such figures as Berengarius of Tours and Roscellinus had led to conclusions deemed heterodox. Academic heresies continued to appear in the twelfth and thirteenth centuries. In some cases, like that of Gilbert of Poitiers (1079–1154), the problem lay less with heterodox teaching than with his rebarbative vocabulary and unfortunate formulae, which were misunderstood by his critics. Although Gilbert was questioned at the council of Rheims in 1148, no verdict of heresy was returned and he went back to Poitiers to live out his remaining years as its bishop. Another academic, Abelard, also faced criticism and fared less well. He is important enough to warrant more extended treatment in a later chapter.

Aside from reflecting the suspicion that philosophy might lead academics astray, these two cases display another dimension of high medieval heresy found in popular heresy as well. We might call it accidental heresy. Some groups and individuals had powerful allies or made a better defense than others who were more vulnerable for circumstantial reasons. A good example of the differential outcomes faced by a popular movement whose participants believed and did essentially the same thing involves the Beghards and Beguines. These groups of laymen and laywomen, respectively, lived in community, following lives of prayer and voluntary poverty. They did not join existing monastic orders or seek to have themselves recognized as a new order. In some dioceses, bishops and the wider community hailed them as persons of exemplary piety, while in other dioceses they were regarded as heretics.

Yet another motive inspiring the condemnation of heretics, especially among academics, was the rise of universities and their collective quest for legal and scholarly autonomy. In seeking it, professors had to show their willingness and capacity to police their own ranks. It is no accident that the leading academic heresies of the thirteenth century arose and were banned at Paris, which housed the first and greatest theological faculty in medieval Europe. The year 1210 saw the posthumous condemnation of two academic heretics, David of Dinant (*fl.* second half of the twelfth century) and Amalric of Bena (d. 1206/7). As with many heresies of this period, it is difficult to reconstruct all the arguments of David and Amalric, since they have come down to us in fragmentary form through hostile witnesses. It seems clear, however, that David was inspired by the *Periphyseon* of John Scottus. His own major work, *On the Divisions*, likewise subdivides all being into several categories. Instead of John's four divisions, David posits three: matter, mind, and separate substances. By the third term he means suprahuman intelligences, a class headed by God. Having made these distinctions, David proceeds to argue that mind and matter can be identified with each other and with God. He offers two reasons in support of this claim. First, matter, mind, and God can all be classified as beings. As subcategories of being, they are all logically subordinate to the idea of being in general. David's second argument has two parts, one equating God with matter and the other equating Him with mind. Matter, viewed in its undifferentiated state before forms are imposed upon it, evades all categories. God likewise evades all categories. This conclusion does not square with David's first claim that God, like matter and mind, is a sub-category of being. In any event, he also argues that God can be equated with mind since mind and God are both immaterial. The rubric under which David was condemned was pantheism. The label may be inexact, but it is safe to say that he fails to preserve a distinction between God and creatures sufficient to satisfy orthodox Christians or, for that matter, philosophers who regard God as transcendent.

We know more about the career of Amalric, who taught both logic and theology at Paris and in whose case the designation of pantheism is more apposite, since he pressed the doctrine of divine ubiquity to its ultimate conclusions. Amalric applied this notion to Christ and to the Holy Spirit, but not to God the Father. In his view, Christ is present in the physical universe, really and corporeally, in the same way that He is present in the consecrated bread and wine of the Eucharist. The Holy Spirit dwells fully in human souls, so that all human beings are divine and perfect; anything they do is *ipso facto* good. It is easy to see why orthodox Christians would object to these conclusions on both metaphysical and moral grounds. Unlike most academic heretics of his age, Amalric developed a popular following and there is an organic connection between his anthropology and that of the Free Spirit heretics who emerged later in the thirteenth century. Another connection between Amalric and popular heresy, although it is not clear how or whether it is related to his pantheism, is his rejection of the veneration of the saints and their relics and the orthodox doctrines of heaven, hell, and the resurrection of the body.

There were other heretics who were not academics and who also objected to certain popular devotions. A good case in point is Peter of Bruys (*fl.* 1117/29–35/6), a renegade cleric and unlicensed preacher in southern France. He reverted to a heresy held by more than one group in the early church, the notion that Christ's humanity was not real but illusory. For Peter, Christ had never been born in the flesh and had never truly suffered and died. Hence, he thought it improper to venerate the crucifix. He expressed this view by lighting a bonfire of crucifixes in front of the abbey church of St. Gilles one Good Friday, which led to his lynching by the enraged citizens. His disciple, Henry of Lausanne (*fl.* 1116–48), continued Peter's preaching, which also included the rejection of the sacraments and the need for a clergy to administer them.

Another contemporary heresy that is even more of a throwback and one that raises unanswered questions about the relations between Jews and Christians in late twelfth-century Italy is the Passagian movement. In essence, the Passagians rejected Christianity in favor of Judaism. Denying the divinity of Christ and the doctrine of the Trinity, they held that the Messiah was still to come and that the Mosaic covenant and the laws of the Old Testament, including circumcision, dietary restrictions, and the observance of the sabbath on Saturdays, were still normative.

It was much more typical for heretics who used the Bible to validate their ideas to turn to the New Testament. Those who did so fall into two categories, appealing either to a myth of the past, the golden age of apostolic Christianity, or a myth of the future, a millennial age when pure Christianity would be practiced. Either way, the church of the present, measured against such a past or future, was inadequate. Those heretics advocating a return to apostolic Christianity have much in common with orthodox reform movements. Like the friars, they preached voluntary poverty and criticized the wealth and worldly power of the church. But they sometimes attached to these doctrines the complete rejection of private property and the idea that ordination and ecclesiastical authorization were not needed by ministers.

A version of this approach highly specific to Italy is the heresy of Arnold of Brescia (*c*. 1100–55). The main New Testament value he wanted to restore was a church without wealth and political power. In particular, he objected to the political reality of the papal states, which he sought to abolish, leading an attack on the pope and the Roman curia in a revolt that aimed at overthrowing papal jurisdiction and restoring the ancient Roman republic. Arnold was the first of many Italian revolutionaries who appealed to ancient Rome as the solution to contemporary ills. He saw no chronological disjunction in his linking of republican institutions to an apostolic pattern of life that postdated them. Arnold's revolt was crushed not by ecclesiastical authority but by the army of Emperor Frederick I (*c*. 1123–90) in 1155.

The single most important and popular heretical expression of the desire to return to the apostolic age was the Waldensian movement, named after its founder, Peter Waldo (*fl*. 1170–84). A wealthy merchant from Lyons, he had a conversion experience in *c*. 1173, after which he distributed his property, living and teaching a simple life marked by voluntary poverty, celibacy, and lay preaching. It was the third part of his program that invited official opposition, leading to Waldo's ejection from Lyons. Having been cast out by the orthodox church, he radicalized his views, arguing that moral uprightness, not ordination or theological expertise, was what qualified a person to preach and to administer the sacraments, regardless of sex or status. Here, we may note that in contrast to some contemporary heretics, Waldo did not abandon the sacraments, except for holy orders, but revised the criteria for their valid administration. His movement spread southward to Spain and eastward to Italy. By the early thirteenth century, the Italian Waldensians, calling themselves the Poor Lombards, had developed their own interpretation of Waldensianism. In 1205 a formal schism occurred between the French and Italian Waldensians over the propriety of accepting sacraments from the hands of ordained priests, even if they were morally worthy. To this proposition the French said yes, the Italians no. Later in the thirteenth century the Poor Lombards spread northward into Switzerland and Germany. At that point, both divisions of the Waldensians grew more highly organized. Paradoxically, they developed institutions that mirrored the Catholic ecclesiastical hierarchy that Waldo had originally opposed, with a supreme head and a clergy separated from the laity by ordination and special vows, uniquely entitled to preach and administer the sacraments. The Waldensians continued to insist that moral uprightness was also needed to validate the ministry. Secure in their mountain fastnesses, they survived repeated efforts to extirpate them in the later Middle Ages. Eventually, most of them were absorbed into one Protestant movement or another; although Waldensian congregations exist to this day in Italy.

The leading example of a biblically based heresy informed by a myth of the future is the movement launched by Joachim of Fiore (*c*. 1135–1202), derived largely from his interpretation of the Book of Revelation. Joachim began as a Cistercian abbot in southern Italy who then founded his own order. He advocated a millenarian doctrine that in some respects can be seen as a recrudescence of the third-age eschatology of the Montanists. Joachim shares the view that there are three ages, presided over by God the Father, God the Son, and God the Holy Spirit respectively, during which the Old Testament, the New Testament, and a spiritual, eternal gospel will be in force, along with the Jews, the Christians, and a new, spiritual church as God's covenanted people. Joachim adds subdivisions within each age and the notion that they can be identified with certain kinds of people, the married and old people in the first age, clerics and youths in the second, and monks and infants in the third. This last point suggests the idea that monasticism is the most perfect Christian lifestyle and that entrance into it constitutes a second baptism. While Joachim was something of an embarrassment to the Cistercians and while orthodox as well as heterodox applications of his teachings were made, it was the heretical use of his ideas after his death that made him notorious. In the 1250s, despite Bonaventure's efforts, tensions increased between the conventual Franciscans, wanting to modify the rule of radical poverty, and the spiritual Franciscans, wanting to preserve it. A member of the latter group, Gerard of Borgo San Donino (*fl.* 1250s), wrote a work, the *Eternal Gospel*, based on Joachim's ideas, showing that he had grasped the revolutionary implications of the idea that the coming reign of the Holy Spirit would sweep away the current ecclesiastical order. Gerard was also convinced that the third age would begin in 1260. As with the ancient Montanists, he argued that the spiritual Franciscans, who would usher it in, had to live lives of exemplary purity, thus connecting Joachite chiliasm with the defense of the spirituals' position on poverty. The passing of the year 1260 without incident cleared the air somewhat and in the early fourteenth century the spiritual Franciscans were condemned. Joachite ideas remained in circulation in the later Middle Ages, part of a climate of opinion in which millenarianism was far from abnormal. The notion of a purely spiritual church survived to inform some later medieval heretics and some radical Protestants of the sixteenth century.

Different as they are, the heresies of Arnold, the Waldensians, and Gerard were all efforts to replace the existing institutional church with a different kind of religious organization validated, in some sense, by the New Testament. To a greater or lesser degree, these heresies also have moral components. But there is another category of heresy in the twelfth and thirteenth centuries that made personal ethics and individual salvation its centerpiece. Two movements illustrating different approaches to that common goal are the Flagellants and the heresy of the Free Spirit. Both arose in the thirteenth century and were even more popular in the fourteenth.

The Flagellants can be regarded as Christians who, from the perspective of orthodoxy, read the part for the whole. The discipline of the flesh certainly played a role in some orthodox ascetic regimes, and connecting this practice with the desire to participate in the passion of Christ tapped into a major high medieval popular devotion. The Flagellants, however, saw these two points as the sum total of the Christian life, believing that self-mortification alone was salvific, excluding

participation in the liturgy, the sacraments, and the personal and social virtues. The
Flagellants adopted a formulaic procedure for their activities. They began by pro-
cessing into a town, assembling in the public square, and offering a prayer to the
Virgin. Then, they removed their outer garments, prostrated themselves in a circle,
and flagellated themselves until the blood flowed, while their leader prayed and
preached over them. The Flagellants first appeared in 1260, the year when the Joachite third age was supposed to begin. They tended to resurface at moments of
crisis. One was the year 1291, when the Muslims defeated the Christians in the
Near East with the conquest of Acre, the last Crusader stronghold. In the fourteenth century they re-emerged in the plague year of 1349 and at other dates
marked by plague, famine, and other calamities. Also in that century, the Flagellants' association of their program with Christ's passion sometimes led them to
turn against the Jews and to participate in pogroms. Throughout their history, they
connected their activities with the belief in the impending apocalypse. Eventually,
in the fifteenth century, they were declared heretics and suppressed. This outcome
might be cited as another example of accidental heresy, reflecting a change in Christian public opinion as to what was acceptable.

The heresy of the Free Spirit, which was not an organized sect but a theology
drawing an assortment of individuals and small groups, arose earlier in the thirteenth century than the Flagellant movement. Its first known exponent was Ortlieb,
a citizen and magistrate of Strassburg, who was condemned for his beliefs in 1216.
The Free Spirit movement flourished in towns and drew adherents from all levels
of urban society. Pantheistic and anti-clerical, its members shared Amalric's view
that the Holy Spirit dwelt fully within their souls, that they were perfect, and that
they, or at least their leaders, could do no wrong. In the case of some Free Spirit
heretics, their beliefs led to libertine behavior. In other cases, its members absorbed
third-age eschatology and led lives of great moral austerity as befitted the heralds
of the reign of the Holy Spirit.

Of all the heresies of the twelfth and thirteenth centuries, the most popular and
most solidly entrenched and the one that addressed virtually all the concerns manifested in other heretical movements of the day was the Catharist or Albigensian
heresy. The first name derives from the Greek term for purity, reflecting the moral
desiderata of the movement. The second refers to its location, southern France,
where a major stronghold of the heresy was the fortified town of Albi. Catharism
has marked parallels with Manicheism. Although its version of cosmogenesis is not
exactly the same, it is also based on metaphysical dualism, the belief that matter is
intrinsically evil, spirit is intrinsically good, and that there are two divine principles responsible for the creation of these two kinds of being. The logical neatness
of this solution to the problem of evil continued to appeal, which kept dualism alive
after the age of the early church, largely in the Balkans. It was from there that the
doctrine was brought to France and then to northern Italy by Mediterranean
traders. It would be a mistake, however, to attribute the popularity of Catharism to
its metaphysics alone. For the Cathars drew institutional as well as ethical corollaries from their first principles. They saw life in the body as the imprisonment
of the human soul, the intrinsically good locus of human identity, in the evil,

material, charnel-house of the body. Marriage and sexual behavior that could lead to procreation, or the entrapment of other good souls in evil bodies, were to be avoided. So was the eating of foods derived from creatures that reproduce sexually. This dietary principle led the Cathars to rule out meat and eggs. The limitations of their zoological and botanical knowledge permitted them to eat fish and vegetables. The surest and swiftest way to liberate the soul from the body was the *endura*, or ritual suicide performed by self-starvation. Cathars rarely took that route except as an act of martyrdom in the face of persecution, otherwise the movement would soon have exterminated itself. Next best was the practice of rigorous asceticism. This was the path followed by the Perfects, the leaders of the sect. For other adherents, it did not matter what one did with one's body, so long as the sexual and dietary laws were observed, since the body was not seen as part of one's personal identity. Antinomianism was acceptable to Cathars and was sometimes practiced.

The Cathars also felt free to reject Christian moral laws because the institutional correlative of their theology was the rejection of the Christian church, some books of the Old Testament, and the sacraments. In their place, they created their own para-ecclesiastical organization, their own substitute for penance, and their own entrance rite as a substitute for baptism. In understanding why the Cathars did so, it must be recognized that more was at stake for them than the anti-clericalism and the critique of the established church found in so many other heresies. For the social, economic, and political history of Catharism indicates that the movement was deeply embedded in the secular struggles of its time and place. The region's leading noble, the count of Toulouse, used Catharism as a tactic of opposition to his suzerain, the king of France. Other nobles used it to oppose the count or the bishops of southern France, with whom they competed for lordship. Townsmen used it against bishops for the same reason, and some townsmen used it against other townsmen whose wealth they wanted to expropriate. The complexity of the cross-hatching interests involved explains both the broad social appeal of Catharism and the stubborn resistance of its members to all efforts at theological persuasion. Wave after wave of orthodox churchmen went to southern France to preach and debate, to no avail. Nor was ecclesiastical repression in the form of the papal inquisition, created in the first instance to attack the Cathars in the early thirteenth century, effective either. What finally wiped them out was the Albigensian Crusade begun by King Philip II of France (1163–1223) and completed by his grandson, Louis IX (1214–70). Their military victory also had the political effect of annexing this region of France to the royal domain and of redefining Crusades as battles against heretics within Europe's borders. Another extension of the concept of Crusade was made by former Crusading orders, like the Teutonic Knights, who turned missions to the pagan peoples on Europe's northeastern frontier into wars of conquest and forced conversion.

The presence of so many heresies in the twelfth and thirteenth centuries and the large number of supporters that some of them drew thus has to be placed on a continuum that includes the contemporary battles between Christians and Muslims and the perceived threat of Jews and pagans that led to the sharpening of high medieval Europe's understanding of itself as the Christian commonwealth. On the one hand, the conception of Europe as Christendom spurred church leaders to clean house, to found reformed monastic orders, and to promote new and inspiring articulations of Christian belief and religious practice. On the other hand, the threat of heresy and the challenge of non-Christian religions led to crisper, and hence more restrictive, definitions of orthodoxy, to the creation of institutional mechanisms for identifying and punishing heterodoxy, to the ghettoization, expulsion, or massacre of Jews, and to the substitution of armed force for the spreading of Christianity by peaceful means. The growth of religious intolerance, extending even to the view that the Greek church was not a part of Christendom, was the dark underside of these developments. Yet, it was in the name of Europe as the Christian commonwealth that both orthodox and heterodox thinkers of the twelfth and thirteenth centuries understood their religious mission. That situation was to change in the next two centuries.

CHAPTER 19

The Christian Commonwealth Reconfigured: Wycliff and Huss

John Wycliff (*c.* 1330–84) and John Huss (1372/3–1415) were the major heretics of the fourteenth and fifteenth centuries. In relation to earlier medieval heretics, two facts about them emerge clearly. First, they addressed many of the same issues as had agitated earlier critics and reformers, both orthodox and heterodox. But the social, political, and ecclesiastical conditions of their age were markedly different. One notable feature of this new environment was the increasing vernacularization of Christian doctrine. This phenomenon reflects the increasing laicization of religious life and the growing sense that it should be organized in national churches, whose bonds with the European Christian commonwealth were fraying. This attitude was intensified by developments in the institutional church itself. The heresies of the twelfth and thirteenth centuries had arisen in a period of church reform. But in the fourteenth and early fifteenth centuries no new monastic orders were founded and no church councils sought to upgrade the qualifications of clerics. Nor were there any papal initiatives in these directions. This in no sense reflected the lack of a need for reform. The need for a more competent clergy actually increased in this period thanks to the numerous crises afflicting European Christendom, including war, plague, famine, economic depression, depopulation, and social change and dislocation on a wide scale.

The main reason why church leaders promoted no reforms in the later Middle Ages is both a symptom and a cause of the problem, the residency of the popes at Avignon, under French auspices, between 1304 and 1378. Losing much of their freedom of action, popes and members of the ecclesiastical hierarchy grew increasingly bankrupt, morally, as a consequence of this Babylonian Captivity of the church. Enemies of France, like England and Germany, saw the Avignonese popes as puppets manipulated by their arch-rival and lost confidence in them. And, in 1378, the Great Schism occurred. Disputed papal elections led to the seating of two rival popes, one in Rome and the other in Avignon. The cardinals supporting each pontiff saw the others' pope as illegitimate and the split continued, plunging the church into a state of acute crisis, a double papacy lasting for forty years, compounded in 1409, when, in desperation, the two sets of cardinals convened a council at Pisa that sought to unify the papacy and that resulted in the election of a third pope. The papal schism was ended only in 1417 at the council of Constance.

Calls for reform of the church in head and members were frequent reactions to these conditions. But, while reform in the previous two centuries was as likely to come from orthodox leaders promoting ideas and institutions that could be plowed back into the general life of the church as it was from heretics, it was now being expressed in terms that were more radical and likely to fragment European Christendom. The careers and teachings of Wycliff and Huss reflect this fact unmistakably.

Another notable difference between them and earlier heretics is the role of political theory in their teachings. Both Wycliff and Huss appealed to their kings to assume a larger role in church life. Apart from the Cathars and Arnold of Brescia, earlier heretics had not concerned themselves with politics, except in so far as they tried to avoid political persecution. But the extension of royal jurisdiction over the church is central to Wycliff and Huss. In part, they advocated this idea because kings were the only rulers strong enough to wrest power from a corrupt church hierarchy for the purpose of church reform. In part, they did so because they saw a royally led national church as a means of asserting political and ecclesiastical independence from the papacy and, in Huss' case, from the Holy Roman Empire as well. With these thinkers, then, we move into an age of national separatism, the quest for national churches that eventually led to the Protestant and Catholic Reformations.

John Wycliff

A professor of theology at Merton College, Oxford, Wycliff was one of the leading speculative minds in England in his day. His forum was his lecture hall and his technique was reasoned argument, the application of logic and metaphysics to theology. Wycliff was also a propagandist paid by the English royal family to write anti-papal tracts. Two things moved him from reform to heresy. One was his tendency toward intellectual extremism. Wycliff always asserted the most radical form of any position he maintained: he had a temperamental urge to push his reasoning to its ultimate logical conclusions, even when this process took him to a point beyond which it could shed light or yield serviceable results. A second, equally important reason why Wycliff became a heretic lies in ecclesiastical politics. The Great Schism radicalized him. Instead of merely criticizing the papacy, he developed a heterodox theology and ecclesiology that lost him his government backing. By that time he had taken the irrevocable steps on the path to heresy that drew his followers, the Lollards, into open revolt and that led the state eventually to persecute them.

Most of Wycliff's major theological works were written in a brief span of years just before and after the outbreak of the Great Schism. During this period his ideas developed rapidly. His haste led to some inconsistencies and left some unanswered questions. Although a sharp enough critic of the papacy before 1378 to provoke English church leaders to impugn his orthodoxy, attempts forestalled by his royal patronage, Wycliff also acquired several parishes, none of which he lived in, a moral blind spot in an opponent of clerical irresponsibility. Starting in 1378, Wycliff began to publish heretical ideas on the church and the sacraments. His university invited him to resign from his chair and banned his preaching in Oxford. Wycliff retired to Lutterworth, one of his parishes, where he died unmolested in 1384, receiving the last rites of the church he had attacked so vigorously.

This attack is characterized by Wycliff's application of philosophical principles to theology. Of key importance is his position on universals. A defender of the logical priority of universals, he takes the extreme view that they signify abstract entities that are metaphysically prior to their concrete manifestations. Had he stopped there, Wycliff would have been no more than a Platonist. But he goes farther. It is not enough to say that abstractions or the ideal essences of things have a higher degree of being than their concrete manifestations. Wycliff goes on to say that natural phenomena can and should be reduced to their ideal essences. These essences constitute their real being for him. The essences of things are autonomous; they exist pre-eminently, independent of whether or not they are reified phenomenally. From this perspective, the contingent world of nature, time, and change is incidental and can be ignored. What really counts is the world of timeless and necessary essences.

This radical doctrine raises several important questions. What is the relationship between the essential archetypes and God? Wycliff regards them as ideas in the mind of God, a view faithful to Augustine's understanding of them. But Wycliff holds that they share the perfection, eternity, immutability, and necessity of God Himself. Like God, they cannot be envisioned as non-existent or as being any different than they are. But they are the models for God's creation of natural phenomena. If the archetypes are necessary, so is the natural order, meaning that God was constrained to create it the way it is and did not create freely. At the same time, since Wycliff sees the archetypes as the true realities, the natural world is non-essential and accidental. It is difficult to see why God should have bothered to create it at all.

Although Wycliff's metaphysics is problematic in these respects, he does not hesitate to apply it to theology. A good example is his doctrine of the Eucharist. Wycliff rejects the orthodox view that the bread and wine on the altar change into the body and blood of Christ when the celebrant says the words of consecration. His reason is that bread and wine, like everything else, are reducible to their essential, archetypical natures, natures not subject to change. Thus, no substances, Eucharistic bread and wine included, can change into other substances, under any circumstances whatever.

Wycliff's tendency toward metaphysical reductionism can also be seen in his positions on the Bible, church, and state. He has an utterly fundamentalistic view of the Bible, seeing it as the sole source of religious authority and accepting its literal sense alone. The revealed truth it contains is valid always and everywhere; it is in no sense conditioned by the cultural, rhetorical, or historical contexts in which its authors wrote or in which later audiences read or hear it. Wycliff takes this stand both because it is compatible with his essentialist philosophy and because the Bible, as a timeless norm, can be used as a criterion by which the contemporary church and its theology can be judged and found wanting. As such, it is important, for Wycliff, that the Bible be freshly translated into the vernacular and widely preached.

With respect to the church, and its relation to the state, Wycliff's ideas developed swiftly. Three stages in his teaching can be detected and dated precisely. In works written before 1376, Wycliff agrees with earlier reformers. He regards the church of the apostolic age documented by the New Testament as a timeless ideal, to be reconstituted in the present. The church must divest itself of wealth and temporal power. The second stage of Wycliff's teaching is found in his *On Civil Dominion* and *On Divine Dominion*, published in 1378. In each work Wycliff considers how to enforce reform on a recalcitrant church in the context of a general analysis of dominion. Dominion over all things, in both church and state, is God's, Wycliff begins. God delegates authority to human rulers, but on the model of feudalism. As God's vassals, rulers hold authority conditionally. If they fail to fulfill their contract with God by disobeying His moral law, they forfeit legitimate authority. Wycliff concludes that only rulers in a state of grace govern the church or state legitimately. The goal of this argument is to nullify the authority of immoral popes and clerics. Since they can easily be shown to be corrupt, they have no valid right to rule the church. Wycliff adds the not incidental point that secular rulers have the right to determine their guilt and to deprive immoral clerics of authority and property. But there is an unresolved problem in this theory. As Wycliff sees it, the state is authorized to judge the church and to punish its leaders if necessary. But his argument also applies to secular dominion. Who judges secular rulers and penalizes them if necessary? And, what if immoral leaders are governing both church and state? Wycliff answers neither question.

These issues were far from hypothetical. It was child's play to demonstrate that church leaders had placed European Christendom in a state of moral crisis. But it would have been equally easy to demonstrate the incompetence of the current English government. Edward III (1314–77), who had been king since 1327, was so senile that he could not control crown officials, leading Parliament to create the procedure of impeachment in 1376 in order to remove Edward's chancellor for his egregious abuse of power. Edward's successor was his grandson, Richard II (1367–99), a boy of ten. The government was in the hands of a factionalized regency council composed of ambitious, power–hungry nobles, the wicked uncles of Shakespeare's history plays. They reopened the Hundred Years War with France, in which England was faring badly, and imposed domestic policies such as the poll tax that provoked the Peasants' Revolt of 1381. No contemporary would have regarded England's rulers as upright, or even as particularly intelligent, during these years. It is easy to see why the royal family stopped supporting Wycliff in 1378.

Wycliff then developed a third and even more extreme position on church and state in *On the Church*, *On the Office of King*, and *On Papal Power* of 1379. In these treatises he took as his theme, stated earlier, the idea that secular rulers have authority over the clergy, and expanded it, yoking it to the late Augustine's doctrine of predestination while omitting the anti-Donatism Augustine associates with it.

Wycliff defines the church, in this life and in the next, as composed exclusively of the elect, predestined to salvation from all eternity. The reprobate have no part in the church. Augustine had said that, in this life, the elect and the reprobate are mixed together in the church; God alone knows who the elect are and He will separate the sheep from the goats in the last judgment. Wycliff is more radical. As he sees it, we human beings can know who the elect are. The sign of their election is their upright life. Sinners testify to their own reprobation. They must be ejected from the church. Now, the ecclesiastical hierarchy, especially the popes, he continues, lead lives of scandalous immorality. Thus, they prove their reprobation and must be banished from the church. Secular rulers should cast them out. The effect of that action is to cast out most ecclesiastical institutions as well. What is left is a largely invisible, spiritual church. In the absence of upright priests, its spiritual functions—preaching, catechesis, the administration of the sacraments, and pastoral counsel—can be carried out by upright laymen. Moral purity, not ordination, is what authorizes people to exercise the ministry. Such vestigial functions of a visible church as remain, such as poor relief and the maintenance of church buildings, can be administered by the state. From this argument, it follows that an institutional church as a distinct sub-corporation within civil society ceases to exist.

If there are problems with Wycliff's ecclesiology and political theory in the second stage of his development, additional problems mark his position in its third stage. In his desire to make moral purity, as a sign of election, the only basis for church office and membership, he has, in effect, provided a rationale for a Donatist-type elitist and sectarian church. Yet his goal is to find a rationale for a national church, embracing the English people and governed by their kings, who are not necessarily or ex officio members of the elect. Wycliff does not succeed in reconciling this basic discrepancy in his theory.

Despite its potential utility against the papacy, Wycliff's ecclesiology and political theory made the English government nervous for all too evident reasons. But, in the generation after his death, some of his ideas were put to use by discontented groups and individuals who mounted revolts under a Wycliffite banner. The first Lollard revolt was led by John Oldcastle (*c.* 1378–1417) in 1414. A member of the royal household and of the House of Lords, he had been knighted personally by the king. Sympathetic to Lollardy from his youth, he appointed Lollard preachers as his domestic chaplains. The clergy and king tried to change his mind, to no avail. He was tried for heresy, convicted, and imprisoned in the Tower of London. Effecting his escape, Oldcastle organized a revolt in which he was joined by other noble leaders. They raised an army and prepared to march on London. Oldcastle's goal was to overthrow the monarchy and to assassinate the king, as well as to kill all prelates and members of religious orders and to destroy all church buildings. He offered no constructive alternative as a substitute for the current arrangements once they were demolished; total anarchy was the idea. Oldcastle's plot was uncovered and he and its other leaders caught and put to death. But other Lollard revolts cropped up later, the last significant one led by William Perkins in 1431. Perkins recapitulated Oldcastle's program, but instead of the anarchy Oldcastle proposed he wanted to replace the discarded kings and prelates with 'certain poor men' not identified more specifically. The participants in Perkins' revolt were mostly artisans, but some peers of the realm were among its leaders. After this revolt was put down, the Lollards stopped being a political problem; although there is evidence that Lollardy remained a religious movement, largely underground, later in the fifteenth century. One fact revealed by the Lollard revolts is that the association of heresy with political or economic protest in late medieval England did not typically appeal to the impoverished or dispossessed. These revolts drew no support from the peasants or the poorest urban classes and they were all led by socially prominent men. The English government could not support Wycliffism after 1378 because it was just as dangerous to the state as to the church. But, in one of history's delicious ironies, to the extent that it adopted any of his ideas, the one it singled out was the state's right to jurisdiction over religion. In the early fifteenth century, Parliament passed several statutes institutionalizing that idea. A statute of 1401 empowered the state to burn heretics at the stake. Another, of 1414, allowed civic officials to try heretics in secular courts. These statutes are ironic for two reasons. First, they were the legal weapons used against Wycliff's own followers. Second, they were acts of Parliament, an institution never mentioned in Wycliff's political theory. This notable omission suggests that his taste for abstract, absolutist positions was what ultimately prevented him from devising a theory attractive and applicable to a political community committed to the less pure and crystalline institutions of corporatism and limited monarchy. The reduction of things to their essences, which haunts Wycliff's speculation from beginning to end, was also what made it incapable of addressing itself constructively to the real, phenomenal, concrete world of historical fact and political reality.

John Huss

The leading heretic of the fifteenth century, Huss was branded a follower of Wycliff, a label accurate only in part. His views were less extreme and grounded in ethics rather than metaphysics, and his place in the history of his homeland was as different from Wycliff's as his intellectual temperament. Where Wycliff conceived radical ideas used by rebels crushed after his death by the English government, Huss was a moderate working in a context of reformist theology, popular preaching, and mass action, one that existed before, during, and after his lifetime with the support of the kings of his native Bohemia. Huss specified the direction that this pre-existing movement would take and supplied it with symbols and grievances through his martyrdom. Where Wycliff's speculative extremism led him to live in a world of pure ideas, insensitive to political realities, Huss had his finger on the pulse of his own community. These are the principal reasons why the Hussite movement succeeded where the Wycliffites failed, in establishing a new national church separate from Rome.

Like Wycliff, Huss was an academic heretic, a professor of theology at the university of Prague. He was also the rector of the Bethlehem Chapel, founded in 1391 by a wealthy merchant to support preaching in Czech on reformist themes. Its congregation included people of all classes, up to the queen, whose confessor Huss became. Huss voiced many of the standard attacks on clerical immorality and papal interference in temporal affairs. Preachers like him had received royal patronage in Bohemia since 1360. Throughout, his stress was on moral reform. He urged repeatedly that clergy and laity had to renew themselves from within through piety, the practice of evangelical virtue, and the sacraments. He had little to say on the restructuring of the church as a means of reforming it. The Prague theologians were certainly conversant with Wycliff's writings. Indeed, Huss made personal copies of three of them. But, at the start of his career, he confined himself to Wycliff's critique of ecclesiastical abuses and bypassed his other teachings.

In order to grasp how Huss came to be identified as a Wycliffite and persecuted as a heretic, we need to consider the political, ecclesiastical, and academic circumstances that explain these developments. Bohemia was a principality in the Holy Roman Empire. Like other parts of the empire, it sought greater autonomy in the later Middle Ages. Its rulers managed to elevate themselves into monarchs, three of whom succeeded in challenging the Austrian Habsburgs in elections for the imperial title in the late fourteenth and early fifteenth centuries. The separatist urge that Bohemia shared with other German principalities was religious and intellectual as well as political. Although it was located in the easternmost part of Germany, Bohemia had entered the church as a colony of the archbishopric of Mainz, in the Rhineland on the opposite side of the country. The archbishop of Prague, the primate of Bohemia, had been freed from this demeaning subordination only since 1347. National jurisdiction over the Bohemian church, so recently won, was jealously guarded. Another source of friction lay in the university. Founded in 1348 as the first university east of the Rhine and an immediate magnet for the intellectual life of central and eastern Europe, the university, like the archbishopric, reflected its German origins. Although Czech masters greatly outnumbered their German colleagues in the early fifteeenth century, the university statutes gave the Germans majority voting rights. At the beginning of Huss' career, the Bohemian king, Wenzel IV (1360–1419), was also Holy Roman Emperor elect. But, putting Bohemia first, he supported all policies that would free Bohemia, its government, its church, and its intellectual life, from Germans, from the empire, and from the papacy.

Huss faced opponents both as a professor and as a preacher. Within the university, most of the German masters were nominalists. The Czech masters, including Huss, defended realism. As realists, the Czechs were less extreme than Wycliff and their position was as much an expression of ethnic conflict as a matter of philosophical conviction. The upshot of this controversy, which first associated Huss with Wycliff's thought, was a Czech victory. In 1409, Wenzel reorganized the university, banished the Germans, and gave the Czech masters complete control. The disgruntled Germans founded a new university at Leipzig or joined existing faculties as far west as Paris, also moving south to Rome where they loudly proclaimed that they had fled Prague because the university was a nest of Wycliffite heretics, chief among whom was Huss. At the same time, Huss' preaching came under fire from the archbishop and other churchmen threatened by his attacks on clerical immorality. In 1409, the archbishop persuaded the local inquisitor to examine Huss on suspicion of heresy, but the inquisitor found none of his ideas heterodox.

What, then, moved Huss into heresy? If the Great Schism of 1378 was the turning point in Wycliff's career, 1409 marked a turning point for Huss. What radicalized him was the council of Pisa and its election of a third pope. Aside from compounding the agony of the church in general, this event complicated affairs in Bohemia. For the archbishop backed the Roman pope, who had supported his appointment, while the king was a partisan of the Pisan pope. The resulting tension between king and archbishop polarized the situation. The archbishop hardened his opposition to reform and his hostility toward Huss, while the king strengthened his advocacy of reform and his defense of Huss. In 1410, the archbishop banned Wycliffism at the university and withdrew Huss' license to preach. The faculty of theology protested, staging a marathon disputation on Wycliff's Trinitarian doctrine, designed to show that, since it was fully orthodox, the archbishop's ban on all his teachings was misinformed. Huss took part in this debate. As a result, he and his colleagues emerged from it looking more Wycliffite than they really were. Huss also continued to preach at the Bethlehem Chapel despite his lack of authorization. It was this decision that first set him at variance with ecclesiastical authority. Wenzel then took action against the archbishop by seizing his property. The archbishop retaliated by placing an interdict on Prague, suspending all church services. Wenzel responded by refusing to enforce the interdict and by deposing the archbishop. These events had two important consequences for Huss. First, before his deposition, the archbishop excommunicated Huss. When the king and the university masters wrote to the Roman pope urging him to overrule this action, the archbishop assembled a dossier of Huss' public statements and sent it to Rome. The result was that Huss was cited to appear in Rome for questioning. He refused, and was excommunicated by the cardinal in charge of the hearing, on grounds of disobedience. Second, when Wenzel forbade the observance of the interdict, Huss wrote a justification of his stand, drawing on Wycliff's *On the Office of King*. In it he states that the king has the right to the obedience of all his subjects, prelates included, and the right to supervise religious life. This justification marks Huss' first step into substantive heresy and his first association of himself with Wycliff's views on church–state relations.

Events immediately thereafter moved Huss to develop a more radical position. In 1411, the Roman pope authorized a sale of indulgences. The idea that participation in a good cause, initially the Crusades, could shorten the purgatorial stay of a repentant sinner who had confessed and received absolution, had been part of church doctrine since the eleventh century. In the high Middle Ages, indulgences were granted to people performing other pious works and popes began to sell them. By the fifteenth century, the sale of indulgences had become a regular technique of papal fund-raising. Many reformers put it on a par with simony, the sale of church offices. Huss was not opposed to indulgences as such or to their sale; he had purchased one for himself in 1393. But he did object to the essentially political purpose of the indulgence campaign of 1411, the financing of a papal war against Naples.

The acrimony this issue raised led Huss to write *On the Church* in 1412, in which he puts forth an unequivocally heretical ecclesiology.

The main point Huss makes in this work is that priests can preach without the authorization of bishops or popes. The church, he argues, has no right to silence a preacher by excommunication. For it is not ordination, or communion with the pope, that legitimizes a priest's office or his exercise of it. Huss offers a Wycliffian rationale for this claim, although he does not go as far as Wycliff does in his treatises of 1379. Huss agrees that the current Roman pope is not the head of the church, but not on the canonical grounds given by supporters of the Avignonese and Pisan popes. Rather, he argues on moral grounds and on the basis of Augustine's doctrine of predestination. With Wycliff, he asserts that moral uprightness is the criterion of legitimate ecclesiastical office. On this basis, the pope and the hierarchy stand condemned. With Wycliff, Huss also argues that we can identify the elect by their upright life. However, he rejects Wycliff's idea that the church on earth is confined to the elect and he does not reduce the church to an invisible, largely spiritual body. Huss draws a distinction not made by Wycliff between prelates and ordinary parish priests. Prelates lose their spiritual authority if they are immoral. But, according to Huss, the personal moral failings of parish priests do not destroy their capacity to preach and to administer the sacraments efficaciously. Clearly, Huss does not seek to make holy orders superfluous or to laicize the church as drastically as Wycliff does. Instead, his goal in this treatise is to delegitimize clerics at the top of the ecclesiastical hierarchy and to argue that secular rulers are competent to judge their behavior, to enforce their obedience, and to reform the church by means of the civil law. While Huss avoids many of Wycliff's difficulties, *On the Church* still leaves two questions open. If immorality disqualifies a prelate, why should it not disqualify any priest? If sacerdotal authority resides in the office, not the man, why should this rule apply to some priests and not others? Second, if a sinful person forfeits dominion in the spiritual order, at least at its highest levels, why should this condition not apply to civil dominion as well? It is a index of Huss as a theologian that he refrains from raising these questions. He is not interested in pushing his argument to its logical conclusions: he takes it only as far as he thinks it needs to go to deal with the problems at hand.

Huss' conclusions, none the less, were far enough from orthodoxy to give the church grounds for taking action against him as a heretic. During the two years following his publication of *On the Church*, Huss concentrated on expounding his ideas in the vernacular. What altered his situation terminally was the succession of Wenzel's brother Sigismund (1368–1437) as Holy Roman Emperor elect in 1410, after the brief tenure of Rupert of the Palatinate (ruled 1400–10). Sigismund decisively reversed Wenzel's policies, seeking to strengthen the empire at the expense of its principalities, including his own. He withdrew royal support from Huss, using his influence to persuade delegates to the council of Constance, which he forced the Roman pope to convene, to try Huss as a heretic. This they did and Huss was convicted and executed in 1415. Many Bohemians were outraged by these events, and with good reason. Sigismund had been duplicitous, offering Huss safe conduct to Constance for an open hearing on his views, only to withdraw the safe conduct, arrest Huss, and subject him to a kangaroo court. Many Bohemians feared that Sigismund would try to thwart the Bohemian national movement politically as well as ecclesiastically, and that he would do so by stigmatizing the whole Bohemian nation as heretical. They were right on both counts. The result was a Hussite revolution that lasted until the late 1430s. After defeating Sigismund's forces, the Hussites were willing to negotiate, but failed to win from the Catholic church the theological concessions they demanded as a condition of remaining in its fold. They formally severed connections with the orthodox church and made Hussite doctrine the official theology of a Bohemian national church separated from Rome for the rest of the fifteenth century, with the support of the Bohemian kings after Sigismund. In the next century, the Hussites joined forces with the Lutherans, although without renouncing their own theology and, as a consequence of Bohemia's defeat by the Habsburgs in the Thirty Years War (1618–48) that ended the age of religious wars unleashed by the Reformation, it was forcibly re-Catholicized. Some Hussites managed to survive underground into modern times. In the long run, the Hussite movement was not an enduring success. But, from a medieval standpoint, it was a remarkable success, a Reformation before the Reformation possessing the two requirements enabling Protestants to found established churches in the sixteenth century. One necessary factor was the ruler's political support, which the Hussites enjoyed, Sigismund excepted. The second was a doctrine that was a real departure from Catholicism but one that stopped short of Wycliffian extremism, laying the theological foundations for an inclusive national church rather than for an exclusive sect. The Hussite movement thus crossed the border dividing late medieval heresy from the Reformation. Along with Wycliff and Wycliff's England, it highlights the differences between these successive chapters of European church history. And, coupled with the history of mysticism and devotion, the history of medieval heresy helps us to distinguish those aspects of medieval Europe's religious culture in which the Reformation boundary stone is a meaningful one from those in which it is not.

PART VI

HIGH AND LATE MEDIEVAL
SPECULATIVE THOUGHT

CHAPTER 20

Scholasticism and the Rise of Universities

The emergence of the scholastic method and the rise of the university as the culminating institutional setting in which scholarship flourished in the high and late Middle Ages is an important subject in its own right, and one that also serves to introduce the period's speculative thought. There are continuities linking the revival of speculation in the eleventh century with the interests and methods of masters at cathedral schools and universities in the twelfth century and after, especially the confidence that reason could shed light on many subjects and the increasing use of a logic and semantics that was to take medieval philosophy well beyond its classical roots. At the same time, using Anselm of Canterbury as a benchmark, there are marked differences between Anselm and the speculative thinkers of the age that follows. The interlarding of speculative theology with prayer, as Anselm does in his *Proslogion*, goes by the board. So does the appeal of rational reflection as an adjunct to monastic meditation. Also superseded is the tendency to address a series of theological or philosophical themes in individual treatises and the notion that they should be treated by reasoned argument alone. Instead, early and high medieval scholasticism is marked by synthetic and systematic thought in all disciplines, the creation of general syllabuses including everything a student needed to know, organized in coherent form. The goal of pedagogy was now to train professional, full-time scholars with a substantive and methodological grasp of entire fields of knowledge, enabling them to push back frontiers and to defend their own positions against rival views. Debate with other interpretations, articulated by proponents both living and dead, was expected to take place as a normal condition of intellectual labor. In all fields, the expression of a range of competing views within the boundaries of acceptable teaching was seen as a natural outgrowth of scholarship and was regarded as invigorating and healthy, not threatening. The twelfth-century maxim, 'diverse but not adverse,' sums up this attitude. In positioning their own opinions in the context of other views, scholastics did not rely on reason alone. They also had to show their mastery of past authorities and to demonstrate their ability to winnow out those that were irrelevant, inconsistent, or addressed to outdated conditions, to harvest those that illuminated their subject, and to offer principled reasons for agreeing or disagreeing with their sources.

This set of scholarly and pedagogical priorities, launched in the twelfth century, led to the emergence of new genres of scholastic literature and new ways of approaching existing genres. In several fields, works called sentence collections or *summae* appear. Their goal was to present a complete curriculum in their subject and to show how its individual subdivisions fitted together. They also reviewed past authorities and current opinions, giving the author's analysis of them and his reasons for rejecting some and accepting others. Altogether, the methodology already in place by the early twelfth century shows the scholastics' willingness, and readiness, to criticize the foundation documents in their respective fields. More than simply receiving and expanding on the classical and Christian traditions, they set aside ideas from those traditions deemed to have outlived their usefulness. They also freely realigned the authorities they retained to defend positions that those authorities might well have thought strange and novel. Older genres, such as commentaries, were now rarely mere summaries and explications of their authors' views. Scholastic commentators were much more likely to take issue with their chosen author or to bring to bear on his work ideas from emerging schools of thought or the scholastic's own opinions.

These pedagogical methods and approaches were developed initially in the cathedral schools of northern Europe in the early twelfth century, especially in Paris and its environs. The locus of speculative creativity shifted decisively from monastic to cathedral schools at this time. The twelfth-century cathedral schools in the vanguard of these developments had an increasingly international draw, reflecting the mobility of students and teachers and the larger number of laymen being educated for careers and learned professions in a society of growing wealth and complexity. Students in the liberal arts, law, and theology could find important posts in ecclesiastical and secular government, while scientific and medical studies prepared them for both practical and theoretical applications of their expertise. In striking contrast with Byzantium and Islam, all of these subjects flourished and were supported in the same schools. Basic education in the trivium and quadrivium ensured that scholars in law, medicine, and theology had a command of logic and the other verbal disciplines as well as mathematics and science. The fact that scientists and philosophers studied in faculties adjacent to theologians trained to raise questions about ultimate values, and that theologians interacted with colleagues in fields not informed by religious criteria, forced all involved to take account of the perspectives and ground rules of other disciplines as well as the disagreements within their own. The scholastics who created this heady educational environment rapidly outpaced monastic scholars as speculative thinkers. Monastic leaders, like Bernard of Clairvaux, who tried to thwart approaches different from their own, might create temporary setbacks in the careers of scholastics, but they were no longer in the vanguard of medieval speculation.

The organization of learning in the twelfth-century cathedral schools involved not only the licensing of masters by bishops or their chancellors and the recruitment and training of masters by cathedral chapters but also the rise of independent masters, whose authority was based on non-episcopal licenses or on their recognized expertise. Masters illustrating all these models can be found in the schools of Paris and its environs. The cathedral school of Notre Dame became a major center of early scholasticism, as did those of Laon, Soissons, and Melun. The royal abbey of Ste. Geneviève just outside Paris was much favored by avant-garde thinkers because its abbot licensed teaching on his premises without scrutinizing its content. Independent masters taught on the Mont Ste. Geneviève until the middle of the thirteenth century. St. Victor was another important school in this vicinity, welcoming externs and recruits until the death of Richard of St. Victor. And there were completely independent scholars, like the logician Adam of Balsham (*fl.* 1132–before 1159), also called Adam du Petit-Pont because he set up his own school at the foot of the bridge connecting the Île de la Cité with the left bank of the Seine.

In the second half of the twelfth century, the schools and masters of Paris coalesced to form the university of Paris. Along with Oxford, Montpellier, Salerno, and Bologna, Paris was one of the first European universities. These early universities share common features as well as having distinctive organizational traits and academic specialties. Like the schools in monastic communities and the cathedral schools out of which many of them grew, universities were legal corporations, associations of students and teachers with collective legal rights usually guaranteed by charters issued by princes, prelates, or the towns where they were located. The university corporation contained sub-corporations, its individual faculties. It might also have sub-corporations such as nations, associations of foreign students who banded together for mutual protection and to act as pressure groups in the local urban economy, and colleges, in universities that had colleges, endowed to provide housing, instruction, libraries, and other facilities for the students benefactors wished to support. An important feature of the status conveyed by membership in a university corporation was exemption from the civil law. All students and masters, whether or not they were clerics or had any intention of becoming clerics, had benefit of clergy. They were judged under canon law, a decided advantage, since it was more lenient than civil codes and could not impose the death penalty. In these respects, universities resembled chartered towns, which likewise guaranteed collective rights, privileges, and exemptions to their citizens. And, like towns, when the early universities acquired their first charters, they gained recognition that they were institutions already in place and forces to be reckoned with.

On another level, universities resembled a different kind of medieval corporation, the craft guilds that arose to organize high medieval industries. Like guilds, universities were self-regulating. They determined their own rules for membership and for marking the levels of competence required for advancement to higher grades of activity. The main reason why universities sought, and gained, legal independence was to ensure that promotion was based on academic competence, as verified by masters with the requisite expertise. This principle was sometimes won peaceably but at times was the result of litigation, university shut-downs, and all-out warfare. The resultant liberties gave medieval universities far more academic freedom than parallel institutions in Byzantium and Islam. They enabled faculties, whoever endowed them, to set their own standards and to modify and update curricula in the light of new intellectual developments and materials. Universities also took seriously the responsibility of enforcing their own rules and policing their own ranks. There were no supra-university accrediting agencies to provide norms and guidelines.

On the model of the craft guild, the undergraduate was analogous to the apprentice. He was put through a preparatory course in the seven liberal arts. If he completed this course of study—and he could attend classes without having to matriculate as a degree candidate—he acquired the bachelor of arts degree, which entitled him to teach the liberal arts if he so desired. If the student sought advanced education, he enrolled in the faculty of law, medicine, or theology. His initial postgraduate degree typically required him to do some teaching in the arts faculty. Theology, the longest course of study, had more academic hurdles to be overcome than law or medicine before students acquired the terminal doctorate. At the master's level, the student was analogous to the journeyman in the guild; to gain recognition as a doctor, he had to present a 'masterpiece' in the form of final examinations and the defense of a doctoral thesis. The successful candidate was immediately granted full status and voting rights in his faculty. He gave an inaugural lecture and was expected to teach for a period, even if his goal was practice or administration rather than a teaching career. His doctorate also made him eligible for a chair as a regent master in his faculty, if one was vacant. Medieval university degrees authorized their holders to teach anywhere in Europe, and university men were quite mobile. Degrees were marks of competence, not indices of the accumulation of a specified number of course credits or the meeting of residence requirements. This fact is dramatically illustrated by the careers of two women who received doctorates in law and who taught at Bologna, although women were not allowed to matriculate at the universities. Daughters of law professors who educated them at home, they presented themselves as doctoral candidates, passed their examinations and defended their theses with flying colors, were duly awarded their degrees, and joined the faculty.

While the sequence of subjects studied in the higher faculties and the textbooks used in the liberal arts might vary over time or from one university to another, corporate status and degree requirements mandated by the faculty were common to all universities. Where they differed was in their organization and academic specialties. There were two basic types of university organization in the Middle Ages, well illustrated by Paris and Bologna. They were found most prominently in northern and southern Europe, respectively. Paris is the classic example of a professor-run university. Nations existed here but colleges were more prominent, reflecting an academic demography whose largest subdivision comprised students in the arts faculty, which they entered as early as the age of thirteen or fourteen. Parisian colleges may well have been founded as a result of a perceived need to supervise these young scholars. If the arts students predominated numerically, the academic jewel in the university's crown was theology. Paris had medieval Europe's first chartered and most eminent theological faculty. As the queen of the sciences and the discipline drawing the best minds and the greatest institutional support, and also as the most high-risk discipline, theology at Paris was frequently the field in which the most acrimonious debates within the university took place. Defense of the autonomy of this faculty above all was the goal of its hard-won but successful achievement of corporate independence. Paris also had a medical faculty, eclipsed by those of other universities, and a faculty of law limited to the study of canon law. The other standard subject, Roman law, was not taught there because the legal system of northern France was based on feudal law, so Roman law would have had little utility to a native of that region hoping to practice there. The undergraduate faculty and each of the higher faculties at Paris elected a dean from among its ranks. The dean of the arts faculty served as rector of the whole university. Most of the regulations legislated by the Paris professors were designed to control the studies and lives of the students.

For its part, Bologna could easily have been an institute for advanced study, a graduate research establishment without undergraduates at all, given its foundation as Europe's first and most distinguished law school and the lavish support its jurists received from both church and state. Bologna's fame derived from the rediscovery of the *Corpus of Civil Law* there in the late eleventh century, at a moment when popes and secular rulers were locked in the investiture controversy. Matilda of Tuscany (1045–1115), ruler of this part of Italy, who supported the papacy in this dispute, saw immediately that precedents from Roman and canon law could be used to defend papal claims. She therefore endowed a law school at Bologna whose generous stipends drew the most distinguished legal scholars. Rulers taking the opposite position on lay investiture were equally quick to perceive that these studies could also lend support to their side of the debate and added their own endowments. Scholars eager to gain credentials in Roman and canon law, whose utility to secular and ecclesiastical administration was no less obvious than its applicability to political theory, flocked to Bologna. The law professors, who could easily have supported themselves with their stipends, their research grants, and their consultancies, did not need the students' tuition fees. Bologna never developed a theological faculty and its medical school emerged later. At the beginning of its history, most of its students were postgraduates in law. At Bologna, unlike Paris, the average age of students was older and they were vocationally oriented. Students came from all over Europe, eager to acquire the degrees qualifying them for prestigious and lucrative careers. The Bolognese students first organized in nations. There were no colleges to house or supervise them. They then organized against the professors. Their goal was to guarantee the delivery of pedagogical services. The university statutes, legislated in 1317, placed restrictions on the professors. They were not to leave town without depositing a fee with the student government to ensure their return. They were required to teach for the whole class period, not arriving late or dismissing the class early. They had to cover topics in their syllabuses fully and systematically, not omitting anything or leaving the hard parts until the end of the term and skimping them. If a professor drew five or fewer students to a lecture, he would be fined as if he had cancelled the class. In all these ways, the students at Bologna saw to it that they got their money's worth.

Other early universities display their own organizational and academic emphases. Salerno was the oldest European university. It was essentially a medical school, a specialty developed owing to its southern Italian location and its proximity to Muslim medicine. Like Bologna, Salerno was primarily a postgraduate institution and did not develop a full range of faculties. Salernitan medical education won high marks for the cure rate of its practitioners, who taught common sense and preventative medicine, stressing balanced diet, fresh air, and exercise. Montpellier, in southern France, emphasized medicine as well as law. Its location close to Muslim Spain also explains its medical eminence. Being in a part of France whose institutions were shaped by Roman rather than feudal law, Montpellier taught that subject as well as canon law and was the place to go in France to study it. Oxford is unique among the earliest universities since it was not located in a cathedral town, Oxford having no bishop in the Middle Ages. Initially, it was under the jurisdiction of the bishop of Lincoln, some 120 miles away. Oxford gained more independence from its bishop than was typical; for, when it emerged, its bishop was Robert Grosseteste (*c.* 1175–1253), a distinguished Oxford theologian and scientist himself before accepting ecclesiastical preferment. Grosseteste was a bishop on whose understanding and support the Oxford masters could rely. In this case it was not the bishop but the town that tried to block the university's acquisition of legal autonomy. Oxford won its independence only after subjugating the town militarily, depriving its citizens of representation in Parliament until well into modern times. Oxford was renowned for the study of theology, logic and, above all, natural science, chiefly at Merton College. Like Paris, Oxford had many colleges and did not teach Roman law, for the same reasons. English common law was studied at the Inns of Court in London, originally hostelries for lawyers during sessions of the London courts. They developed into law schools by the high Middle Ages.

The universities already discussed were not expressly founded; they just grew. But, from the thirteenth century onward, rulers deliberately founded universities. The first of these was the university of Naples chartered by Emperor Frederick II (1194–1250). Universities proliferated on this basis east of the Rhine, starting with Prague in 1348; between then and the late fifteenth century over a dozen universities opened their doors in the German lands. Cambridge split off from Oxford; Orléans and Bourges emerged to rival Montpellier as Roman law faculties in France, and the increasing rollback of the Muslims by Christian kings in Spain led to the founding of universities there as well, of which Salamanca was the flagship. The multiplication of universities in the later Middle Ages sometimes brought with it the princely requirement that subjects study in their own homeland, as was the case with Frederick's Naples. Rulers sometimes required professors to support their policies as a condition of employment, occasioning academic career shifts. While professors continued to pursue highly mobile careers that could take them from Paris to Vienna or from Prague to Paris, the expansion of university education at the regional level, the growth of regional and national consciousness, and wars making it impossible for kings to protect their subjects at universities in enemy lands all tended to reduce the international character of student bodies in the later Middle Ages.

The university is one of the main contributions of the Middle Ages to the western intellectual tradition. Some of its degrees and programs and even the colors of academic regalia signifying different fields of study are still with us today. At the same time, if an academic time-traveler could go from a modern to a medieval university, he would be struck by the differences between them. One of the first things our hypothetical visitor would notice, outside of an extremely lean administrative staff, would be the relative absence of buildings and grounds. Apart from college buildings, in those universities that had them, and libraries, medieval universities had no campus to speak of, no dormitories, gymnasiums, student unions, faculty clubs, infirmaries, laboratories, administration buildings, convocation halls, or classroom buildings. Our visitor would find no offices housing development or alumni relations either. To the extent that colleges offered residences for students, it was by gift of the donors endowing colleges. The university itself felt no obligation to provide for students' residential, physical, medical, moral, or recreational needs. Most students rented rooms on their own. No organized athletics or extracurricular activities existed as a means by which students could discharge youthful high spirits. They generally let off steam in unsanctioned ways: crime, gambling, women, and drinking were their standard pursuits. Tavern brawls in university towns were frequent, bitter, and sometimes fatal. The tension between town and gown based on the economic dependence of merchants on students who were frequently foreigners and who enjoyed legal privileges often exploded into violence. Students could also get into trouble by violating university statutes, attacking each other in class with cutlasses, making illegal loans, and trafficking in textbooks in defiance of the university's regulation of the book trade. University authorities contented themselves with applying damage control after the fact in sermons preached in university churches berating student misdeeds. Nor did universities supply facilities for professors. If their own houses were too small to accommodate their classes, professors hired halls or arranged for the use of local churches at their own expense. No bursar ensured that students paid their tuition bills or issued salaries to the masters; they had to make their own arrangements directly with students, often collecting fees with great difficulty, as their complaints attest. For such general university functions as convocations and commencement exercises, faculties or the whole university would have to hire a large church or meeting hall.

Other differences from modern universities would emerge if our visitor attended classes or read a medieval university's curricular requirements. All instruction, and, indeed, all conversation within university precincts, was in Latin. In each school or faculty there was a single, prescribed course of study. Everyone studying for the same degree took the same courses in the same sequence. There were no electives. But students could always choose among professors: there were always several professors teaching the same courses, each with his own interpretation of the material. Students usually audited a few classes at the beginning of the term and decided which professor to study with depending on whose approach they found the most authoritative or interesting. When the friars arrived at the universities their students were educated by masters from their own orders. But freedom of choice among professors, and among points of view, was the rule for everyone else.

University courses were not courses on a theme but courses on a book, the *Institutes* from the *Corpus of Civil Law* in law, for instance, the Pauline Epistles in theology, or Aristotle's *Categories* in elementary logic. Professors used three modes of instruction to impart information and to develop mental skills. In the morning, the professor lectured on the text. He began by reading a portion of the text; if all students had a copy, he might give only the first few words before surveying previous interpretations of the passage, or of individual words and phrases, noting opinions he found erroneous and unhelpful, and why, as well as those he agreed with, and why, before giving his own opinion and showing its relationship to the previous tradition of scholarship. These discussions of short passages, words, and phrases, called glosses, were the building blocks out of which the professor constructed a commentary on the whole work or a major part of it. In the afternoon, the professor held a drill session in which students discussed and could ask questions on the material covered by the lecture. They were also quizzed and required to argue pro and con all the positions the lecture had presented.

On the more formal level of the disputation, debate also figured as a major pedagogical method and as the means by which professors interacted with their colleagues and publicized their views. Disputations, culminating in those at which candidates defended the theses admitting them to degrees, followed the same form as those conducted by professors, reminding us of the importance of the oral exchange of information even in the most highly literate segment of medieval society. What have come down to us as scholastic texts are often the redactions of live disputations or of class lectures. After the master had checked the redaction for accuracy, the work was placed in the hands of the booksellers whom the universities closely regulated. To expedite the production of books, they divided texts into small parts so that several scribes could work on a manuscript simultaneously. Like lecturers, disputants always framed issues in terms of the questions on which they undertook debate, with any member of their faculty. The questions were announced ahead of time; redactions of disputations of this type are called *quaestiones disputatae*, or disputed questions. Sometimes the disputant would agree to take on any questions that his opponents might care to raise, without prior notice of what they might be, resulting in *quaestiones quodlibetales*, or questions 'on whatever you want.' Either way, the disputant entertained objections from colleagues who opposed his views. Then, after a brief statement of his own position, he sought to refute each objection in turn, by showing that it was irrelevant or illogically framed, or that it invoked authorities inappositely, or both. The same structure of argument is found in the *summae* or systematic works of high medieval scholastics, although the tendency to combine debated questions into a synthetic whole is more typical of thinkers in the twelfth and thirteenth centuries than in the fourteenth century.

The impact of this mode of education, applied to all subjects, first at cathedral schools and then at universities, was to elevate logic over literary studies as the pre-eminent preparatory discipline in the liberal arts. Another consequence of scholastic method was to guarantee a thorough knowledge of past and current interpretations of one's subject and the ability to analyze tradition with a keen and ruthless eye, giving no quarter to fallacies, irrelevancies, and outmoded views, however august the source. Medieval scholastics brought to the task of dissecting traditional ideas and relating their own solutions to the questions they raised both a high degree of virtuosity and a strong sense that it was their right and duty to adapt tradition to contemporary uses. The essential techniques, as well as the willingness to make innovative and critical use of their materials, were already in place well before the arrival of the Greco-Arabic and Greco-Jewish translations that enabled high medieval scholastics to appropriate their classical heritage more fully. Before, during, and after the reception of these new materials, scholastic controversialists showed not only their substantive disagreements with each other and the centrality of open debate in their methods of learning and teaching but also their simultaneous ability to engage with and to disengage from tradition.

CHAPTER 21

The Twelfth Century: The Logica Modernorum *and Systematic Theology*

As we move from the institutional setting and the educational methods that informed scholastics between the twelfth and fourteenth centuries to their contributions to philosophy and theology, and then to other fields of thought, two issues need to be kept in mind in contextualizing the thinkers encountered. The first is the reception of Greco-Arabic and Greco-Jewish philosophy and science, translated into Latin from the second half of the twelfth century and absorbed as fully as medieval thinkers were going to absorb them by the end of the thirteenth. Of the scholastics discussed in the next three chapters, some lived before, some during, and some after that process. A question vital to placing their work is how much of this new material was available to them. A second question, integrally related to the first, is how they chose to use the material at hand, whether old or new, and the problems to which they applied it. Some scholastics stressed methodology over substance. Others worked at developing new ideas. Still others sought to integrate everything they knew into an organized whole. For those aiming at synthesis, however, there was more than one way to achieve it. But some scholastics rejected synthesis in favor of analysis, treating the topics they considered one by one. Reasons for avoiding system-building varied from one thinker to another, as did the themes they singled out for attention. In this sense, scholasticism as an intellectual movement is marked less by adherence to common doctrines or by agreement on a common agenda than by the common status of scholastics as professional scholars and the common educational experience and methodology that shaped their outlook.

In twelfth-century scholasticism, the most important contributions were made by thinkers who lived before 1160. All worked prior to the Greco-Arabic and Greco-Jewish translations. With one exception, a Latin translation of the theology of John of Damascus known first to Peter Lombard (*c.* 1100–60), they used sources that had been available for centuries. Yet, as with Anselm of Canterbury, they made striking and innovative applications of these materials. Their most notable advances were in the fields of logic and systematic theology.

The Logica Modernorum

The logicians called 'modern' launched a project in the early twelfth century that was to make logic the fastest growing and most creative area of medieval philosophy. The modernity of their logic lies in its post-Aristotelianism. Well before the advanced logic of Aristotle was available in Latin, they addressed aspects of logic that they thought Aristotle and Boethius had ignored or treated inadequately. Even more than Anselm of Canterbury, they read across Boethius to his Stoic sources, appropriating from them the idea of formal logic, whose goal is not to structure the data of extra-mental reality and to test them empirically but to order the world of concepts and to verify conclusions intra-mentally. The excitement engendered by this kind of logic drew thinkers who often disagreed in other respects. A case in point is twelfth-century nominalism. The twelfth-century definition of this term differs from its later medieval meaning as a position on universals opposed to that of the realists. Twelfth-century nominalism was a semantic theory arguing for the univocal signification of nouns and verbs. Nouns in inflected languages like the Latin used by medieval thinkers have varied case endings, depending on their syntactical functions in particular sentences. Verbs denote actions in the past and future as well as in the present, and do so in different tenses and moods. The nominalists held that nouns and verbs none the less have a unitary significance. They consignify the same things and actions in oblique or inflected forms as they do in the nominative or present indicative. Some proponents of this doctrine used it to argue that what was true once is always true. Thinkers defending the reality of historical change or future contingents attacked the nominalist position. Peter Abelard applies the nominalist principle to the argument that God cannot do different, or better, than He does. He defends this thesis by asserting that verbs in propositions stating the goodness of God are univocal with verbs in propositions describing the goodness of His creative activity. On the other hand, Peter Lombard observes that Abelard has left God's freedom and omnipotence out of the equation. He argues that God's freedom and power always transcend any particular application of them He may make. It is at the level of divine freedom and omnipotence that the Lombard applies the nominalist theory of the unitary significance of verbs in propositions referring to God's absolute power and to His ongoing capacity to make choices, including better creative choices, than the ones He actually made.

Another logical theme, attracting attention in the eleventh century and flowing into the twelfth, was the debate on universals. Some proponents of both the logical priority or posteriority of universals follow Roscellinus, applying their theories to ontology as well as logic. Extreme defenders of the priority of universals claim that universal entities exist and are more real than individual beings as well as being known first. Extremists supporting the opposite position argue that individual things are not only known first but also that they are either more real than the classes of which they are members or that they alone are real.

It was Abelard who put this debate on a new footing. He makes two important points in so doing. First, he insists that the problem of universals is a strictly logical one. It deals with the priority and posteriority of different kinds of concepts. It is not, and it should not be treated as, a debate about the degrees of being possessed by the things concepts signify. Logic is about logic, Abelard insists. Its function is to clarify the relations between concepts and the propositions in which we use them. Logic is not designed to inform us about beings and their properties. Abelard's clear definition of the scope of logic, and of what lies outside it, is a major statement of the 'modern' desire to create a post-Aristotelian and purely formal logic. Although he could not prevent some later medieval thinkers from making what he would have regarded as an unwarranted leap from logic to metaphysics, Abelard did much to advance the conception of logic as a discipline in its own right.

Abelard made a second contribution to the debate on universals, his substantive conclusion regarding their status. He develops a position between extremes, conceptualism, or 'non-realism' as recent scholars call it. Abelard begins by observing that, as concepts, ideas signifying individual things and ideas signifying universals are both less real than the things to which they refer. For the things would be there, whether or not we conceptualize them. But concepts, of whatever sort, only come into being because we formulate them. All concepts, then, are derivative. But some are more derivative than others. Here, Abelard aligns himself with those who think we acquire ideas of individual things first. The example he gives in his *Beginners' Logic* is a rose. Once we have gained knowledge of the rose and have formed a concept of it and given it a name, we can use that name in logical propositions referring to the rose long after it has faded and died. It is the name of the rose and its significance in particular propositions that are the logician's proper concerns, not the nature of the rose and its existence as an extra-mental phenomenon. Repeating the same process with other roses, we can abstract common traits from our concept of each rose, eventually arriving at a universal concept signifying roses in general. While he sees the universal as posterior to the concepts representing individual roses in the order of knowledge, Abelard holds that 'rose' can have both an abstract and a concrete significance, depending on how the term is used in the propositions in which we use it. Many later thinkers found Abelard's treatment of the problem of universals persuasive. Whether they accepted it or not, many took his larger point that logic is a terminological science dealing with concepts and propositions, whose conclusions we can verify intra-mentally, not a science whose conclusions deal with or are verifiable in terms of the extra-mental realities from which concepts ultimately derive.

The 'moderns' introduced other new logical themes that proved equally durable. Some of them have excited the interest of philosophers as anticipations of recent logic. Central to all these innovations is an interest in semantics and in how terms signify in different propositional contexts, which has given the name 'terminist' to this kind of logic. One major contribution made by the 'moderns' was the distinction between signification and supposition. Signification refers simply to a verbal sign that stands for an object of knowledge and brings it to mind. Supposition involves a more multifaceted naming of the thing known by means of the sign. It includes the connotations as well as the denotations of terms. It includes terms referring to the classes things belong to as well as to the individual members of a class. Supposited terms can refer to things in the past and future as well as those in the present. Supposition also has several subheadings, such as copulation, ampliation, restriction, and appellation. Copulation refers to the particular connections between the predicates of logical propositions. Ampliation extends the denotations of supposited terms; restriction limits their denotations. The 'modern' concept of appellation, more specific than Anselm of Canterbury's, can be seen as a restriction of supposition. It confines itself to designating things that are currently in existence. Another major 'modern' innovation was the distinction between categorematic and syncategorematic terms. Categoremata are words like nouns and verbs. They signify the things and actions they stand for by themselves, in addition to gaining a range of more precise denotations when they are used in particular propositions or when one or another of the modes of supposition conditions their semantic force. Syncategoremata are parts of speech like prepositions, conjunctions, and adjectives. They have no signification standing alone and acquire meaning only within propositions, where they modify categoremata or specify the relations between other terms in the proposition. The 'moderns' also developed rules for inferring logical consequences, or relations between propositions, and for framing both simple and complex statements in propositional form. Other topics they added to the logical curriculum were insolubles, or logical antinomies, and obligations, or rules governing the arguments of both attackers and defenders. These innovations continued to attract attention and further elaboration in the thirteenth and fourteenth centuries. Thanks to the corporate freedom of arts masters at cathedral schools and universities, they could and did add these advances to their logical curricula. And, thanks to the logical education that thinkers in all fields received, they were well informed about these developments before as well as after the reception of Aristotle's advanced logic in the second half of the twelfth century. This fact is amply visible in the field of systematic theology.

Systematic Theology

The theology of Abelard is a clear case of a scholastic's effort to bring philosophy to bear on his work. Having won acclaim as a logician, he decided to take up theology. Abelard studied briefly with Anselm of Laon, whose largely biblical approach he found conservative and boring. Entering the field himself, he soon attracted students. Abelard's hasty preparation for his new career may be partly to blame for the questionable positions he sometimes takes and the poorly defended conclusions he sometimes draws. In any case, he soon became an extremely controversial figure. While it was monastic critics like Bernard of Clairvaux and William of St. Thierry (c. 1085–1145) who made him notorious with their allegations of heresy, Abelard's scholastic colleagues offered better-informed criticisms and constructive adaptations of his views.

Aside from the question of whether God can do different, or better, than He does, there were three other areas in which Abelard's theology provoked debate: his Trinitarian doctrine, his view of Christ's saving work, and his ethics. On another level, Abelard's general approach in the three unfinished systematic theologies he essayed was seen as in need of modification. Organized under the headings of faith, sacraments, and charity, these treatises are notable for the large number of topics they omit or treat cursorily, topics that other contemporary scholastics thought systematic theology should cover. In these works Abelard ignores last things altogether. He discusses only three sacraments, without giving a definition of sacrament in general. He reserves his treatment of creation, the fall, the redemption, and ethics to separate treatises or exegetical works. In this sense, Abelard does not truly make the transition from topical to systematic theology. The Trinity and the divine nature are the main themes he addresses in his general theologies under the heading of faith.

Abelard makes three claims about the Trinity that provoked his critics. First, he asserts that the terms power, wisdom, and goodness are attributable pre-eminently to the Father, Son, and Holy Spirit as proper names. This argument was denounced at the council of Soissons in 1121. For, despite the biblical texts Abelard uses to buttress his position, it presents real problems. If Abelard were correct, we would have to say that the Father does not have wisdom and goodness, the Son does not have power and goodness, and the Holy Spirit does not have power and wisdom. Problematic as this doctrine is with respect to God's external manifestations of Himself, it presents even greater embarrassment when applied to the unmanifested Trinity. From that perspective, Abelard's names for the Trinitarian persons cannot clarify the respects in which They are one and the respects in which They differ. Abelard tries to address this last objection with a second Trinitarian argument in one of his most regrettable formulae and one that only compounds his woes. He analogizes the Trinity to bronze, a seal made of bronze, and the impression in wax made by the seal. This analogy scarcely succeeds in showing that the Trinitarian persons, although personally distinct, are consubstantial and coeternal.

Even more troublesome is Abelard's description of the Trinity as the One, Mind, and World Soul of the Platonists. William of St. Thierry thought that Abelard understood this idea as the Chartrains did, thereby confusing the issue on two counts. First, in contrast with the Chartrains, Abelard does not make this point in the context of cosmogenesis. Second, his reading of Platonic texts differs from theirs. Where the Chartrains seize on passages where Plato presents doctrines allegorically, from which they seek to extract his literal philosophical teachings, Abelard reads passages where the Platonists present their theology literally as allegorical references to the God of Christian faith. It was certainly a standard apologetic argument that pagan philosophy foreshadows Christian truth. But Abelard moves from the Platonists' adumbration of the doctrine of the Trinity to the claim that they had held and taught that doctrine in all essential respects. This position, which was also attacked at Soissons, yields two unacceptable conclusions. First, it proposes a hierarchical and emanationist relationship among the Trinitarian persons, which fails to square with the orthodox belief in their equality and coeternity. Second, in arguing that the Platonists had discovered the doctrine of the Trinity by reason alone, Abelard strikes it from the list of revealed mysteries that orthodox Christians held were knowable only by faith. In the third of his theologies, Abelard tries to meet his critics by arguing that the Platonists were vouchsafed a special revelation of the Trinity before and outside the Christian dispensation. Thus, they had actually been believers. This fancy still leaves unaddressed the issue of subordination and emanation within the Trinity. It has to be said that if Abelard's monastic critics were inaccurate and tendentious in reporting his teachings, his Trinitarian theology left him wide open to them.

Abelard and his critics were less far apart than either realized when it came to his doctrine of Christ's saving work. On this subject, Abelard entered a field dominated by the rights of the devil theory recently challenged by Anselm of Canterbury. Abelard rejects both approaches as too externalistic and as making the same error, the idea that Christ's role is to change God's mind about mankind, persuading the Father to accept our restored allegiance to Him or to impute to us Christ's merits. In Abelard's view, God does not need to change His mind. His attitude toward mankind has always been one of constant love. It is our minds that need changing. Christ accomplishes this change, by His teaching, by His example, and above all by the love He displays in His self-sacrifice for our sake, which mobilizes our minds and hearts, enabling us to respond in love to God and neighbor. Although neither Abelard nor Bernard acknowledges the fact, their teachings on Christ's saving work are almost identical. Both accent our internalizing of God's love and its subjective efficacy, rather than viewing the redemption in purely objective, political, or forensic terms. The critique of Abelard's position as exclusively subjective, then and later, is off the mark.

The same desire to interiorize the lived experience of Christians is visible in Abelard's ethics. In this area he shares a concern not only with Bernard but also with other scholastic theologians, canon and civil lawyers, and writers of romance, although he takes their common stress on intentionality farther than most contemporaries were willing to go. Abelard defines sin as the attitude of the sinner, his voluntary and deliberate decision to act in contravention of God's will. God's will constitutes an objective norm here. At the same time, what is determinative, in Abelard's analysis, is the sinner's understanding of God's will. The sinner may suffer from error or self-delusion, but it is his estimation of God's will that counts in his decision to act in spite of it. The locus of sin is not the sinner's passions or his misdirected love but his intellect, the seat of the judgment informing his moral choice, his free will, and his understanding of God's will. Abelard draws two corollaries from this analysis that raised orthodox hackles. One is that the people who put Christ to death committed no sin. For, according to their best lights, He was a blasphemer or rebel Who deserved execution. Second, Abelard applies the same conception of sin to all sins without exception. He thereby obliterates the distinction between original sin and sins committed with the sinner's knowledge and consent. A further objectionable corollary of this last idea is that baptism, as a universal remedy for original sin, is unnecessary.

What abruptly terminated Abelard's teaching career, thanks to the machinations of Bernard and William at the council of Sens in 1140, were not only these abrasive teachings but also his general conception of the role of philosophy in theology. On this score, more was at stake than the troubling inferences he draws from theological premises or his idea that the doctrine of the Trinity is knowable by reason alone. Also at issue were positions he stakes out in his *Dialogue* and *Yes and No*, unexcepti' nable to scholastics, but deeply disturbing to his monastic critics. Abelard's *Dialogue* treats a theme interesting to contemporaries both monastic and scholastic, the awareness that Christianity coexists and competes with other faiths, which inspired actual or purely literary debates among Christians, Jews, and Muslims and the translation of the Koran into Latin as a weapon for Christian polemicists. Abelard's *Dialogue* features a Christian, a Jew, and a philosopher. The philosopher attacks both the Jew and the Christian as relying on religious authority alone and as unable to defend their beliefs rationally. Even when they appeal to the same authority, the Old Testament, they interpret it differently. He enjoins each religionist to develop a philosophical rationale for his faith and offers to show them how. It is true that Abelard is not evenhanded in the *Dialogue*, presenting Judaism as more difficult to rationalize than Christianity. Still, it is impossible to miss his larger point that faith must be explained and supported by rational argument. It is an index of the scholastics' capture of the field mapped by Anselm of Canterbury and the retreat of monastic theology into exhortation and devotion that Bernard and William found the *Dialogue* a threatening expression of intellectual pride on Abelard's part.

They applied the same adverse judgment to his *Yes and No*, a work codifying an important aspect of current scholastic method, the analysis and criticism of conflicting authorities. Abelard begins by summarizing the understood ground rules. Be sure, he counsels, that your text has not been corrupted by scribal error or interpolation. Be sure that the opinion of your authority is his own opinion, not his reprise of someone else's. If your authority argues one way in one context and another in another, take these rhetorical circumstances into account. If your authority changed his mind over time, take his last opinion as his final one. If your authority is a papal or conciliar ruling, ask if its intention was to legislate for the church always and everywhere or to resolve a local and transitory problem. If the latter, its binding force can be relativized by historical criticism. After this excellent advice, Abelard presents 158 debated questions and the conflicting opinions of the authorities on each of them. Since the *Yes and No* was written as a workbook for use in class, where he would show students how to analyze the authorities and arrive at reasoned conclusions, Abelard does not resolve these questions in the text. To his monastic critics, *Yes and No* looked like an effort to undermine the Christian tradition altogether by exposing the authorities' conflicting views. Their censure of Abelard was a passing victory. They could not stop the scholastic tide or its program of clarifying, defending, and making contemporary applications of the Christian faith through critical intelligence and rational analysis.

There were other scholastics writing systematic theology at the time who succeeded much better than Abelard in advancing the methodological objectives they shared with him. They also offered approaches to systematic theology that were far more inclusive and thematically cogent than Abelard's. The two most important were Hugh of St. Victor and Peter Lombard.

In his *On the Sacraments of the Christian Faith*, Hugh's model is the Neoplatonic procession of all things from God and their return to God. He describes these divine manifestations as God's work of institution and His work of restitution. Placing his theme in the context of the different kinds of human knowledge, Hugh observes that both modes of divine action can be known through biblical revelation, accessible by faith. They can also be known through our understanding of the natural world, accessible by reason. Discursive theology, the enterprise at hand, combines faith and reason. The theologian draws on God's revelation of Himself in history, related in the Bible, and orders it rationally, combining it with the knowledge of God obtainable from the natural world. Athough there are some redundancies in *On the Sacraments*, Hugh's scheme yields an organization and coverage beginning in Book 1 with the creation, the knowledge of God it affords, the fall, and its consequences, moving to Christology, the redemption, ethics, sacraments, and last things in Book 2. He entitles the work as he does because he views as sacramental all the ways that God manifests Himself to us and redeems us.

Several features of Hugh's account of the work of institution stand out as specific to his interpretation of Christianity. His treatment of creation follows the account in Genesis. Hugh wants to discuss the creation of angels, their nature, and their fall. He has understandable trouble fitting them into the hexaemeral story, since it does not mention them. Hugh has a Neoplatonic understanding of human nature. He sees the human person as the soul making use of a body. As such, mankind before the fall is a subject of interest to him, despite its current unavailability for observation. Hugh takes his own line on whether Eve or Adam sinned more grievously and on what temptations led to their downfall, questions vigorously debated in his day. Reflecting anti-feminist assumptions, many contemporaries saw Eve as less intelligent than Adam and as succumbing to her passions, while Adam's temptation was rational. They saw Eve as the guiltier party because she fell first and implicated Adam in her fall. Hugh sweeps aside these arguments. In his view, the issue of who fell first is irrelevant. Adam and Eve were equally sinful. Eve's temptation was a rational one, doubt concerning the correctness of God's rules governing life in Eden. Adam's temptation was emotional, his elevation of his love for Eve over his love of God. Rather than treating these two temptations as paradigmatic of feminine and masculine psychologies or as a rationale for female subordination, Hugh sees them as twin human weaknesses leading to a single fall, viewed as a psychodrama that can take place in any human soul.

In the section of *On the Sacraments* dealing with God's work of restitution, Hugh staunchly defends the rights of the devil theory of the redemption and makes his most original contribution to the Christian tradition in his definition of the sacraments. Marriage is the sacrament on which he offers the freshest insight. It is true that Hugh's broad conception of 'sacrament' complicates the task of distinguishing between baptism, confirmation, the Eucharist, penance, unction, holy orders, and marriage and their Old Testament antecedents or parallels, on the one hand, and other Christian rituals, such as the sign of the cross or the use of holy water, on the other. Still, and influentially so, he adds a new note to the definition of sacrament inherited from Augustine, the sign of a sacred thing or the visible sign of invisible grace. Hugh holds that sacraments also contain, transmit, and effect in the recipient's soul the grace they signify. Hugh's definition of sacraments as efficacious signs won instant approval from other orthodox theologians. It articulated an emerging consensus position, one also reflecting a perceived need to exalt the sacraments in an age of anti-sacramental heresy.

Some individual sacraments also inspired debate within the orthodox fold. Of them, marriage drew the most attention. Hugh makes a distinctive contribution to this subject. Contemporary orthodox opinion was divided. The Italian school maintained that, while the spouses' consent was needed, a sacramental and indissoluble marriage did not come into being until it was consummated. The French school maintained that the spouses' present consent when they exchanged wedding vows was what made the marriage, not the future consent given at the betrothal or the consummation following the wedding. Hugh strongly defends the French school's position. Reflecting the cross-fertilization between popular devotion and scholastic theology, he offers an argument informed by Mariology. Medieval Christians agreed that the marriage of the Virgin Mary and St. Joseph had been celibate. Consent, not sexual consummation, must be the essence of a marriage, Hugh asserts, otherwise the marriage of Mary and Joseph would not have been a real and sacramental union, a view unacceptable to twelfth-century sensibilities. Hugh paints a glowing picture of their marriage, marked by a union of minds and hearts and by mutual affection and support in all their joys and sorrows. He holds up this marriage as a model for Christian spouses to emulate, no doubt a counsel of perfection. But the effect of Hugh's argument is to enhance the dignity of marriage and to emphasize the free consent of spouses and the moral and emotional character of their union, not just its legal and sexual aspects.

Even more influential than Hugh as a systematic theologian was Peter Lombard. It was his work that proved the most durable, serving as the basis for systematic theological education in the cathedral schools from an early date and as the required introduction to that subject in university theological faculties from the next century onwards. For centuries thereafter, incipients based their first essays in systematic theology on Peter's *Four Books of Sentences.* Its shelf-life was remarkable considering the influx of new materials just after its completion and the move of scholastics to new themes and problems. Yet Peter develops a scheme, a methodology, and an address to particular questions that gave his work its impressive and lasting utility.

An arrival from northern Italy to France, and an eclectic thoroughly grounded in the work of scholastics of the past two generations, the Lombard learned much from Hugh of St. Victor and from Abelard, both of whom he also criticizes. He agrees with Hugh that systematic theology should be inclusive and that it should have thematic as well as logical coherence. His own theme is the distinction between signs and things, use and enjoyment found in Augustine's *On Christian Doctrine.* For Peter, these distinctions apply not only to biblical exegesis and preaching; they also describe the theological enterprise as such and are a key to reality. God is the supreme 'thing' that alone merits enjoyment. He provides signs of Himself in the Bible and the natural world to help us acquire the knowledge and love of God. Peter reads the New Testament and the natural order literally in extracting the information they yield. The sacraments and the witness of moral example are other useful signs drawing us to God. So is the understanding provided by theological study. In the end, all these media will be superseded by the God to Whom they lead, a God Who dwells beyond the signs of Himself available to us in this life.

For Peter, God is not a Neoplatonic deity, the One beyond being, but being itself. He is not a deity with an internal hierarchy or one Who creates by emanation. He can be known not by negative theology but by positive metaphysical reflection. Peter expresses this idea at the beginning of Book 1 of the *Sentences* by offering several proofs of God's existence. While he starts with observable natural phenomena, he quickly moves to the intrinsic nature of finite and mutable beings and their need of an immutable, infinite being as a metaphysical foundation.

This note, which Peter strikes early in the *Sentences*, underlies his doctrine of God. It informs his criticism of all current versions of Platonizing Christianity, be they Chartrain, Abelardian, or Victorine. Peter accents God's transcendence. The most exalted object of knowledge is God in His unmanifested state. This God is in no sense consumed, circumscribed, or exhausted by His manifestations of Himself in the cosmological and charismatic orders. In both orders, He could have made arrangements different from those He ordained. So insistent is Peter on this point, which adds substantially to the distinction between God's absolute and ordained power, that he states that although Christ was born, suffered, and died in the flesh once for all, God, if He willed it, could replicate these events. Just as Peter's God is totally free and omnipotent, so God's transcendence means that He does not constantly intervene in the created universe. Rather, He creates beings capable of carrying out their own natural functions independently. God does not communicate the divine essence to creatures when He creates them; He endows them with the freedom and power to function as secondary causes. This doctrine preserves God's transcendence while at the same time opening a zone in which the operations of creatures can be understood by natural philosophy, in its own terms. In comparison with Hugh, Peter desacramentalizes nature. In the charismatic order, Peter's understanding of the relations between God and human beings preserves and enhances human free will. Working concurrently with divine grace, it enables us to develop virtues and merits that then become part of our own personalities. Peter's stress on divine transcendence also conditions his approach to Trinitarian theology. In sharp opposition to Abelard, he thinks that the entire Trinity acts in any of God's external self-manifestations. Of even greater interest is the unmanifested Trinity. The properties distinguishing its members must be understood in their relationships to each other, not to other beings. Thus, for Peter, the only terms properly attributable to the Trinitarian persons as persons are unbegotten, begotten, and proceeding. They alone denote correctly and exclusively the relationships structured eternally into the Trinitarian family.

After devoting fully one quarter of the *Sentences* to these all-important points about the deity, Peter moves to the creation, human nature before the fall, and the fall and its consequences in Book 2. He avoids one of Hugh's difficulties, the placement of angels in the creation account, by arguing that angels and primordial matter were both created first, and simultaneously, before God produced the rest of creation according to the hexaemeral order. Peter is even more interested than Hugh in human nature before the fall, despite its necessarily speculative character. Unlike Hugh, he regards human nature as an integral union of body and soul. He therefore gives more attention to the physical side of life in Eden, treating such activities as the enjoyment of food, sex, rest after work, and productive work itself as fully natural. This perspective opens another region in which reflection on human nature as such could be extended philosophically. Peter also parts company with Hugh on the fall, holding that both Adam and Eve succumbed to intellectual temptation. They abused wisdom and science, respectively.

Book 3 of the *Sentences* deals with Christology, the redemption, and the virtues. Peter insists on the full humanity of Christ and on its integral union with His divinity in the incarnation, even during the three days He lay in the tomb between His death and resurrection. Peter reviews the three orthodox descriptions of the hypostatic union current in his day. He shows that they all have authoritative foundations and that they are all, none the less, problematic. They may use confusing terminology in denoting either Christ's divinity, His humanity, or its constituent body and soul. They may divinize the human Christ or treat His human nature as accidental and as partible from His divine nature. In making these assessments, Peter freely departs from major authorities such as Augustine and Boethius when he thinks they confuse the issue rather than clarify it. This whole subject is a remarkable indication of Peter's ability not only to deal critically and incisively with authorities but also to apply the general idea that there can be more than one position within the orthodox consensus, even on fundamental questions. Also noteworthy is his advice against the premature foreclosure of debate on the hypostatic union. He urges that the matter be left open, pending further reflection.

The full humanity of Christ is essential not only to a correct grasp of His nature, for Peter; it also plays a central role in His saving work, which redeems us in body as well as soul. Peter's view of the redemption draws positively on Abelard and Bernard of Clairvaux. With them, he sees the chief effect of the human Christ's love for mankind and the obedience of His human will at all times to the Father as the conversion and liberation of the human heart, enabling us to love God and neighbor. To the extent that the devil remains in this account of redemption, Peter radically psychologizes him. The devil becomes our own internal inclination to sin. If the tempter is internalized, so is our yearning for the good. Reintroducing this topic into Christian ethics for the first time since Jerome, Peter agrees that we have a conscience, a spark of reason not extinguished even in the worst of sinners, that motivates us toward the good.

The major difficulty in Peter's theology, both substantively and organizationally, is his handling of ethics. He describes the psychogenesis of sin in treating the fall in Book 2 of the *Sentences*. He describes the conditions under which virtue is acquired in Book 3. Aside from the repetition which this plan involves, it also creates a lack of symmetry. For Peter analyzes virtue under the heading of Christ's human attributes. Yet, Christ had a human nature freed from original sin and united to the Word from the moment of His conception. By grace, the human Christ had a knowledge beyond that which any mortal can possess. His moral psychology is perforce radically different from that of other mortals, and the sense in which He can truly be a moral exemplar for us is an issue that Peter does not adequately resolve.

The final book of the *Sentences* treats the sacraments and last things. Peter agrees with Hugh's definition of sacraments as efficacious signs. He uses it to draw a clearer distinction between sacraments and other Christian rites as well as their Old Testament precursors. Peter's organization of his treatise on the sacraments avoids redundancies found in Hugh's. Hugh takes up holy orders first, since priests are needed to administer other sacraments, and then discusses marriage, as the only sacrament God ordained before the fall; he then repeats himself on these two sacraments later. Peter's scheme proved more influential. He begins with the sacraments received by all Christians, in the order in which they are received, and then treats holy orders and marriage as sacraments received only by some Christians. Consistent with his stress on divine transcendence, Peter presents the sacraments as the normal channels of God's grace. But—and he makes this point in his discussion of baptism, generally regarded as a sacrament of necessity—God is just as free in the order of grace as He is in the order of nature to suspend the laws He lays down for creatures. He has the power to save whomever He wills, baptized or not. Peter is heavily influenced by Hugh on marriage. His chief contribution here is to incorporate the canonists' analysis of this topic and to use their dossier of authorities, whether he agrees with their conclusions or not. He borrows from the canonists an idea that they in turn take from Roman law, the concept of marital affection, to describe the union of minds and hearts of spouses married by present consent. With the jurists, Peter means by marital affection the honor, dignity, and respect accorded to one's lawful spouse. He sees it as a more attainable model for ordinary Christians than the marriage of Mary and Joseph. Further, since celibate marriage is abnormal, if acceptable, he regards as sacramental both the union of minds and hearts and the union of bodies in the typical marriage. It was basically the Lombard's version of the French school's teaching on marriage that became the consensus position stated in the decretals of Pope Alexander III (*c.* 1105–81).

In comparison with Hugh and with most other systematic theologians of his day, Peter gives an extremely abbreviated account of last things. He is unique in omitting all reference to the Antichrist in the *Sentences*, although he had developed a theology of the Antichrist in his Pauline exegesis. Peter limits assertions on last things to those supported by reliable and unfrivolous authorities. No names are named, but he clearly wants to repress wild-eyed millenarian speculation of the type later associated with Joachism. What Peter accents is the justice of God's posthumous arrangements. The damned, he agrees, are punished harshly and eternally. But they are punished less than they deserve, and they retain their malice and continue to will evil. Hence, they continue to merit their damnation. The blessed continue to will the good and continue to merit and rejoice in it eternally. The joy they experience is greater than anything they could have hoped for or imagined. Above all, they enjoy the knowledge and love of the God Whom they can now encounter face to face, beyond signs and beyond all forms of utilitarian mediation.

The exaltation of the saints with which Peter concludes the *Sentences* thus integrates these posthumous outcomes of the Christian life with the central theme he articulates at the beginning and orchestrates throughout the work.

The guidance Peter provides in criticizing conflicting positions, the broad learning, and the overall coherence of the Lombard's *Sentences* do much to explain his continuing appeal. So does the elbow room he leaves at various points in his work, opening areas for philosophical speculation for which there is little space in the work of his competitors. Thinkers with a philosophical bent thus found the *Sentences* hospitable to their reflections. During the generation after 1160, the translation of Greco-Arabic and Greco-Jewish thought began to make philosophical material widely available. Some scholastics seized on these materials, using them to develop topics that the Lombard had put on the agenda but had discussed only briefly. The most notable areas in which these developments occurred in the second half of the twelfth century are logic, semantics, and ethics.

The expansion of logic and semantics was partly a continuation of the 'modern' logic of the first half of the century and partly a response to Aristotle's advanced logic, the earliest of the new materials to be translated into Latin. Having been trained in Aristotle's elementary logic, scholastics found it easy to assimilate the rest of his logical corpus. Among Parisian theologians who were particularly keen to do so were disciples of the Lombard, such as Peter of Poitiers (1130–1205), Peter of Capua (*fl.* 1201/2), Stephen Langton (d. 1228) and Prepositinus of Cremona (1130–1210). They applied state-of-the-art semantic and logical analysis to areas of the Lombard's theology where the problem of theological language is central, and to debatable and open questions. Themes that drew their attention were the senses in which particular names or terms can be attributed properly to God in general, to the Trinitarian persons, and to the human Christ.

Symptomatic of these interests is the debate on the hypostatic union in the second half of the twelfth century. Some theologians of the day argued that the incarnate Christ possessed a single person, His divine person. Since He lacked a human person, they concluded, He was nothing, in so far as He was a man. This position was called Christological nihilianism. Other theologians, agreeing that the incarnate Christ lacked a human person, rejected the view that He was nothing in so far as He was a man, since He had a human nature composed of body and soul. The debate came to turn on whether one phrased the humanity of Christ in terms of nominal or adjectival propositions, given the different semantic force accorded to nouns and adjectives. This controversy inspired Alexander III to issue bans on Christological nihilianism in 1170 and 1177, neither of which halted the debate or the growing semantic refinement of the arguments on both sides. Since the Lombard had left open the explanation of the hypostatic union, scholastics deemed it eminently debatable. Peter of Poitiers goes so far as to limit the task of professional theologians to discussing doubtful matters, which reason can clarify. He sees no point in rehashing consensus positions. A similar outlook characterizes many other scholastic theologians of the later twelfth century. Although Stephen Langton wrote a magisterial commentary on the *Sentences*, he in no sense feels obliged to comment on every chapter. He confines himself to topics he finds interesting or problematic and to areas where he thinks he can amplify the Lombard's position.

Another major subject on which such amplification seemed necessary was ethics. Seeking to eliminate the overlaps and asymmetries in the Lombard's ethics, Peter of Poitiers consolidates his master's teachings, develops them, and puts everything he wants to say on ethics in a single place, a book situated between sacraments and last things in his own *Sentences*. Logical as his five-part scheme may have been, it had no takers. A Lombardian theme that Peter of Poitiers and other theologians of his generation expand on greatly is conscience, developing several alternative theories about its psychological underpinnings and operations.

Also of great interest was the sacrament of penance, because of its intimate connection with the moral lives of Christians. In the Lombard's day, penance was almost as controversial as marriage. In deciding when during the three-part process of contrition, confession, and satisfaction the penitent's moral state is altered by God, theologians and canonists divided into contritionists and confessionists, paralleling the French and Italian schools on marriage and recruiting supporters for similar reasons. Like thinkers who highlighted consent as the principle of marriage formation, contritionists see the inner intentions of penitents as determinative. Like those stressing the importance of sexual consummation, confessionists accent the need for a physical expression of penitential intention and also the need for formal, ecclesiastical intervention. While the contritionist–confessionist debate was not settled in favor of the view that the penitent's state was changed through priestly absolution after confession until the thirteenth century, the later twelfth century saw increasing support for the confessionism that fed into that new consensus. The mission of the friars as confessors, the promotion of frequent confession for the laity, and the proliferation of manuals for confessors assisting them in this pastoral duty are all signs of the times, as is the requirement of at least annual confession legislated by the Fourth Lateran council in 1215.

In this context, theological discussion of penance and its place in the moral lives of Christians attracted wide attention. Among those contributing to this development were Victorines, now writing in conscious opposition to speculative thought. Others were scholastics who united a concern with ethics and pastoral theology with a speculative turn of mind. They were men conversant and comfortable with the logic of the day. The Notre Dame theologian Peter the Chanter (d. 1197) well illustrates this second group. And, while some authors of ethical or sacramental treatises or manuals for confessors reflect traditional conceptions of the sins we are heir to, others, like Alan of Lille, sharpen their attack on homoerotic and non-procreative sexual behavior, informed by the newly available Aristotelian notion that the final cause of copulation, for human beings as for other animals, is reproduction. This notion soon found a hearing as well in vernacular authors like Jean de Meun.

Another ethical concern of the late twelfth century was the analysis of the virtues. Taking the four cardinal virtues inherited from authors like Cicero, sometimes as reprised by Ambrose or Augustine, a number of contemporary theologians wrote treatises on them, calling them the political virtues, since Aristotle orients them to civic life. They analyze and subdivide these virtues in great detail. Theologians like Peter of Poitiers, Alan of Lille, Simon of Tournai (d. *c*. 1201), and Peter the Chanter are interested in how these virtues can be turned into Christian virtues, enabling their possessor to acquire merit leading to salvation. But the anonymous author of the *Teachings of the Moral Philosophers* contents himself with the cardinal virtues and their divisions, suggesting that he thinks it possible, and desirable, to cultivate natural virtue as such.

In these assorted ways, the speculative thought of the twelfth century, launched with such flair by logicians and theologians active before the new translations arrived, reflects the capacity of early scholastics to make notable contributions to the intellectual life of their day on the basis of materials already to hand. The educational institutions and methods they created made it easy for scholastics to understand and make use of the philosophical heritage increasingly available in the second half of the century. Late twelfth-century speculative thinkers indicate which aspects of that legacy they find most interesting and most helpful in addressing their practical and theoretical concerns. The Victorines after Richard of St. Victor reflect the countervailing tendency to theologize in detachment from the more innovative ideas of the day. An analogous range of options faced thinkers in the thirteenth century. But in their case, the accessibility of the entire corpus of Greco-Arabic and Greco-Jewish thought raised the stakes. The question was no longer whether or how to use this or that piece of philosophical thought. The question was now whether to accept, or not, the world view of the ancient Greeks, a vision of the universe that, for the first time, presented them with a holistic, self-consistent, and comprehensible rational alternative to Christian revelation.

CHAPTER 22

The Thirteenth Century: Modism and Terminism, Latin Averroism, Bonaventure, and Thomas Aquinas

The thirteenth century saw both the continuing development of post-Aristotelian logic and the reception of Greco-Arabic and Greco-Jewish thought that made Aristotelianism available along with the scientific and philosophical advances of Muslim and Jewish thinkers. Some scholastics in the first half of the century eyed these materials with suspicion and hesitation, or used them piecemeal. Others embraced them warmly. Attitudes differed at different universities. Natural philosophers at Oxford absorbed Aristotelianism swiftly, although Oxford theologians made scant use of it. But Aristotle's natural philosophy and metaphysics were banned at Paris in 1210 and again in 1215, the second prohibition showing that the first had not been observed. In 1231, a committee of theologians was charged with scrutinizing Aristotle's works and purging them of error. In 1255, university statutes placed them on the list of required reading for the master's degree. In the second half of the century, then, all scholastics knew both Aristotelian and 'modern' logic and those in higher faculties had studied Aristotle's other works as well. They made notable use of them in both philosophy and theology. But, just as Aristotelianism gave them a common philosophical vocabulary, it also divided scholastics, who disagreed on how to respond to the challenge it represented.

Modism and Terminism

In the long run, the reception of Aristotle had less impact on logic than on other subjects, thanks to twelfth-century developments in this field. In the thirteenth century, terminists continued to develop supposition theory on the basis of their predecessors' work, sometimes ringing their own changes on it. Peter of Spain (1210/20–77), the Paris logician whose *Summary of Logic* was the standard account of terminism for his time and place, agrees that supposited terms refer both to individual beings and to the classes to which they belong, in the past, present, and future. For Peter, suppositions are natural when they are based on simple signs corresponding to the things they signify. Suppositions are conventional when the meanings of the terms derive from common agreements about their denotations, which do not have to be grounded in extra-mental reality. Peter holds that supposited terms are meaningful only in grammatical contexts but that these contexts can be sub-propositional as well as full propositions. Thus, 'the king' refers to the ruler of the country we are in, without further specification. The English terminist, William of Sherwood (1200/10–66/71), limits the contexts in which supposited terms gain meaning to propositions more strictly, if not exclusively. He calls Peter's natural supposition habitual supposition and agrees that the same supposited terms can refer to individual things and the classes to which they belong. But he departs from Peter and joins Roger Bacon (*c.* 1220–92) in limiting the reference of supposited terms to currently existing things. He adds that they can stand for their referents both substantially and accidentally.

In about 1250 the terminists were joined by modist logicians, sharing the field with them for the next twenty-five years. Modism appealed particularly to the friars, who had now joined university faculties, sometimes after heated struggle. The emergence of modism reflects the wish, in some quarters, to Aristotelianize logic and to apply it across the curriculum. With terminists, modists see semantics as the chief area in which Aristotelian logic is deficient and needs amplification. They likewise distinguish between the natural significance of words and the meanings they acquire in grammatical contexts. But modists posit less of a gap than terminists between signification and supposition. Modist logic treats words and concepts as authentic signs of real beings. Language and thought are isomorphic with the world outside the mind. Logic can thus be used to understand and to structure a world made up of beings with fixed essences, whose intelligible aspects can be conceptualized on the basis of empirical data. Abstractions can then be built on the foundation of concepts representing individual beings. Modist logic also makes possible rigorous thought about cause–effect relationships and metaphysical and theological objects of knowledge that are not empirical. For these reasons, modism appealed to some theologians and natural philosophers, especially those most eager to Aristotelianize their work.

The modists begin with the idea that the function of words is to signify real beings. Once we have ascertained the properties of these beings, we impose names on them. At this stage, names stop being mere words and become signs. For the modists, signs are specifically vocal. They are not merely ideas but ideas articulated, whose meanings can vary, depending on the modes of signification we impose on them when we place them in propositions and use them as different parts of speech. Verbal signs can refer both to individual things and to the common natures shared by members of a group. Thus far, the modes of signification theory resembles the theory of supposition. But, for modists, verbal signs also acquire fixed meanings along with their varying grammatical meanings in particular propositions. These fixed meanings are derived from the fixed essences of the things they represent, whether individually or in groups. On either the individual or the universal level, the fixed significance is real, accurate, and verifiable, extra-mentally as well as intra-mentally. These meanings are also immutable, since the essences of the things signified do not change.

Both the modist idea that, once given their real semantic assignments, terms do not change their basic meanings, and their view that language and thought are authentic indices of extra-mental reality, were attacked by terminists as a retrograde lapse into the Aristotelian logic they had left behind for over a century. Their criticism of modist logic reflects their own increasing impatience with Aristotelianism. Not without cause, terminists charged that modist logic was semantically rigid and that it lacked the flexibility of terminist logic, which is better adapted to explain analogous, equivocal, and synonymous terms, circumlocutions, complex meanings, and counterfactual ideas that can nevertheless be thought and stated. The inability of modism to respond convincingly to these objections accounts for its decline in the last quarter of the thirteenth century and its eclipse by terminism in the next century. Still, at its point of arrival, the appeal of modism was the very Aristotelianism that made it simultaneously untenable to terminists and attractive to scholastics drawn to Aristotle for other reasons.

Latin Averroism

One group of Paris scholastics, all masters in the arts faculty, whose enthusiasm for Aristotle sometimes inclined them toward modism, were the Latin Averroists. Chief among them were Siger of Brabant (1240–84) and Boethius of Dacia (*fl.* 1260–77). Their teaching drew supporters up through the time of John of Jandun (*c.* 1286–1328) despite heavy opposition, after which Averroism moved to the universities of Bologna and Padua. As the movement's name indicates, the Latin Averroists' embrace of Aristotle included Averroes' interpretation of him. This position entailed two conclusions for them. First, they shared Averroes' conviction that it was possible, and appropriate, to study philosophy as an end in itself, ignoring any theological issues that this enterprise might provoke. Second, they adhered to Averroes' reading of Aristotle in all particulars, including the agent intellect and eternity of matter doctrines. These proved fully as vexatious to the Latin Averroists' Christian colleagues as they had to Averroes' Muslim critics, and for the same reasons. For the first of these doctrines denies the immortality of the individual soul, while the second opposes divine creation out of nothing. Part of the animus the Latin Averroists inspired stemmed from the theologians' view that, since Aristotelianism has theological implications, they should control its teaching. Interfaculty no less than intellectual rivalries were at issue. For some theologians, it was insufficient just to refute Averroism. One also had to show how one could make Aristotle one's own without it. This process began in the early thirteenth century. Its most creative exponents were Bonaventure and Thomas Aquinas.

Bonaventure

In some ways, Bonaventure is more representative of thirteenth-century scholasticism, for his thought is connected organically both with the Neoplatonic and Augustinian traditions and with the Aristotelianizing theologians of the first half of the century. He moves both enterprises forward, integrating and expanding on his sources. Bonaventure learned much from Parisian scholastics of the previous generation who drew freely, if unsystematically, on Aristotle's metaphysics and psychology. Invoking Aristotle's definition of science, William of Auxerre (*c.* 1150–1231) defines theology as a science. In his view, its first principles, the articles of faith, are axiomatic. Known immediately as such, they can be used as premises in demonstrative syllogisms that yield scientifically valid conclusions. Philip the Chancellor (*c.* 1160/85–1236/7) agrees that theologians should start with first principles. His are the transcendentals—being, the one, the good, and the true. He argues that they are mutually convertible and identifiable with God; we can deduce the rest of theology from them. Philip is the first European medieval thinker since Boethius to discuss the transcendentals. He reflects both the influence of Avicenna and Averroes and the wish to assert the unity of the supreme being against the Cathars. Bonaventure's own master, Alexander of Hales, joins William and other scholastics of his day in internalizing Aristotle's concept of being. They agree that creatures are substances made up of matter and form, in contrast with God, seen as pure form. This being the case, Alexander and William find angels the most difficult creatures to explain. Unlike twelfth-century theologians, who were interested in how angels fit into the creation account and in their exercise of intellect and will, they devote extended attention to the metaphysical anomaly angels present, from an Aristotelian perspective. Bonaventure's Franciscan predecessor, John of la Rochelle (*c.* 1190–1245), was one of the first scholastics to assimilate Aristotle's psychology. Bonaventure reflects all these interests in the theology he wrote before administrative duties and mystical theology claimed his attention.

Typical of mid-thirteenth-century scholasticism, Bonaventure's works have an architectonic and synthetic character. In addition to their clear logical structure, with subdivisions carefully marked, they also have great thematic unity. There are three major themes visible throughout his thought: his metaphysical bias, his use of light imagery, and his view of the theologian's conditions of labor. In each case he draws on earlier thinkers and puts his own stamp on his borrowings from them.

Like Avicenna and Philip the Chancellor, Bonaventure starts with being as such, which he thinks we can know as the first object of the mind. Indeed, we need to grasp the nature of being as such before we can understand how being inheres in particular substances. This orientation inclines Bonaventure to use deductive logic. He infers conclusions from first principles and refers things back to their sources or models.

At the same time, his metaphysical bias combines with his use of light imagery to make induction possible as well. Bonaventure's light imagery comes from Augustine and the Neoplatonists and from the Gospel of St. John, where Christ is described as the light of the world. Bonaventure analogizes light to God. As such, light functions as an epistemological, a metaphysical, and a moral principle. Epistemologically, God the light must exist so that we can know Him and so that we can know, and verify our knowledge of, other things. In addition to guaranteeing the truth of our concepts, the divine light also activates the process of concept formation. This is Bonaventure's rejoinder to the Averroist and other Muslim accounts of the agent intellect. As a metaphysical principle, God the light is the supreme being. Bonaventure develops this idea in two ways. First, he shares the Neoplatonic conception of the creation as a great chain of being emanating from God. As Bonaventure reworks this theme, the links in this chain reflect the Triune God visually. They are luminous, translucent, or opaque, in terms of their decreasing spirituality. Creation, in an image he takes from Alan of Lille, is a book we can 'read' to discover God's nature in creatures that all resemble Him more or less clearly. Bonaventure's exemplarism is a second way he treats the divine light as a metaphysical principle. He joins Augustine in viewing the archetypes, or exemplars of created beings, as ideas in the mind of God, the father of lights. When God creates He imposes these uncreated forms on created matter to produce individual beings. Bonaventure expands this theory by describing Christ as the supreme archetype. In cosmological terms, He is the *logos* or rational principle of creation.

Bonaventure also understands God the light as the good. The chain of being is also a chain of goodness; each being's value is directly correlative to its degree of being. We can thus use the creation, with its lesser and greater lights, as a ladder of reascent to the supreme good. This doctrine recasts Franciscan nature mysticism in philosophical terms while retaining its contemplative and Christocentric character. For the reascent to God involves more than a scientific understanding of created beings and created goods. It also involves love and moral purity and the mediation of Christ as the nodal link reintegrating us with God. Bonaventure adds that his research includes 'experimental' knowledge. By this he means the data of religious experience, which is on the same trajectory as the charisms leading to salvation.

These perspectives inform Bonaventure's three most important discursive theological works, the *Breviloquium*, the *Mind's Road to God*, and the *Reduction of the Arts to Theology*. The organization of the *Breviloquium* follows Peter Lombard's *Sentences*. At the beginning, Bonaventure asserts that theology is a practical discipline. Its aim is the salvation of the theologian and the people he serves. It is not an abstract science to be studied objectively. Rather, it should be approached devoutly, for its personal value to the practitioner. As Bonaventure presents it, the content of theology derives from biblical revelation, knowable by a faith armed with the literary training that equips us to interpret the text. We then apply logic to the truths of faith, the better to understand them and their interrelations. As an exercise of faith seeking understanding, Bonaventure's theology departs from Anselm of Canterbury's in two ways. First, with other scholastics, he thinks that past authorities should be criticized, analyzed, and used to anchor theological conclusions in addition to rational arguments. Second, he is a systematic thinker concerned with the interconnections among articles of faith; he freely uses the norm of theological appropriateness to test his conclusions.

This essay on method in place, Bonaventure describes the creation and redemption of beings in the body of the *Breviloquium*. While his model of procession and return is Neoplatonic, he uses Aristotelianism in describing the nature and functions of creatures. With early thirteenth-century scholastics, he finds angels extremely problematic. In this area, he fudges his Aristotelianism, calling angels substantial forms, an oxymoron in Aristotle's lexicon, to indicate that they are creatures although they lack matter. Bonaventure shows his Neoplatonic colors in viewing human nature essentially as the soul, ignoring the body as part of the human constitution. But his analysis of the human mind and the passions is thoroughly Aristotelian. He agrees that we have a vegetative faculty, shared with plants, that controls nutrition, growth, and reproduction; a sensitive or animate faculty, shared with animals, that controls sensation, imagination, memory, and self-propelled motion; and an intellectual faculty specific to human beings, that controls cognition and affection. Cognition is lodged in the intellect and inclines us toward practical and speculative knowledge; affection is lodged in the will and the instincts and inclines us toward the good. As this last point indicates, Bonaventure shares with Plato, Aristotle, and the Victorines the idea that our infrarational faculties can contribute to virtue, if guided by reason. He recapitulates Aristotle's distinction between the concupiscible passions, oriented to objects of immediate gratification, and the irascible passions, also oriented to the assuaging of our wants and needs but able to defer gratification and to engage in long-range planning. The virtues which the rational use of our mental faculties and passions makes possible are, like the sacraments, means of accomplishing our return to God. But, in tune with his cosmology, with its opaque, translucent, and luminous beings reflecting the Trinity as a trace, an image, and a likeness, it is largely through the Neoplatonized Franciscan contemplation of nature that Bonaventure thinks we return to God.

He describes this mental ascent in more detail in the *Mind's Road to God*. Here, he turns around the pattern of creation and uses it as an itinerary for the return trip. With a sexpartite subdivision of each stage based on the mental functions involved, he pilots the reader from the vestiges of God in nature to the image of God in the human soul to suprarational realities and at length to God Himself. The final stages of this journey require mystical experience and the traveler cannot embark on it unless, like the prophet Daniel, he is a 'man of desires,' joining love with knowledge, and virtue and grace with intellectual study.

Bonaventure presents another version of the return to God in the *Reduction of the Arts to Theology*. By 'arts' he means all human knowledge; by 'reduction' he means its reintegration in God through Christ as a moral and epistemological mediator. In this work, Bonaventure extends Augustine's doctrine of illumination to everything we know. The exterior light enables us to master the mechanical arts. The inferior light activates our sense perception. The interior light empowers our reason to grasp philosophical truths, logical, moral, physical, and metaphysical. Finally, the superior light, the light of grace, enables us to grasp the revealed truths of faith. A central Bonaventurian conviction is that our minds require divine illumination in order to function at all, whatever our objects of knowledge. Another idea governing his conclusion in the *Reduction* is that all the lesser illuminations can be reduced to the superior light, since the same God illuminates us in all cases.

In assessing Bonaventure's personal synthesis, it is clear that, despite his description of theology in the *Breviloquium*, he does more than just order logically the data of revelation. In addition to this instrumental use of logic, he draws on philosophy for his subject matter in many areas. From the Platonic and Neoplatonic traditions he takes his metaphysical bias, his exemplarism, his emanationism with its cosmology of procession and return, and his conception of human nature as identifiable with the soul. From Aristotelianism he takes the structure of created being, angels excepted, his analysis of our mental faculties and passions, and the ethical options this analysis entails. To this mix he adds much material from the Bible and from previous Christian thinkers, ranging from Augustine to the Pseudo-Dionysius to Anselm of Canterbury to Richard of St. Victor to Francis of Assisi and to earlier scholastics, adding his personal experience as a contemplative. Although Bonaventure uses large amounts of philosophy and applies logic painstakingly to the subdivision of topics in his works, it cannot be said that he really imbibes the spirit of Greek philosophy or the rationalism of its leading Muslim and Jewish exponents. Bonaventure lacks Aristotle's common-sense empiricism and his interest in the world in its own right. Nor does he share the Platonic view that the material world must be abandoned if we are to be saved. For him, the material world is a manifestation of God's superabundant goodness and love, created through Christ. It is not to be cast aside but redeemed through Christ and used as a means of salvation. This overarching vision of reality and the illuminationist and ultimately mystical epistemology that gives access to it are the chief keynotes of Bonaventure's theology.

Thomas Aquinas

Bonaventure's leading scholastic opponent and the contemporary theologian who inspired almost as much controversy as the Latin Averroists was Thomas Aquinas. In rushing to his defense, his Dominican confrères stressed his originality. The adjective they applied most frequently to him is 'new.' The aspects of Thomas' contribution highlighted here are those his colleagues thought the most innovative.

One major new dimension of Thomas' thought is that he used a better text of Aristotle than was available to his predecessors, thanks to his studies with Albert the Great (1206/7–80). Albert taught him at the Dominican convent in Cologne and at the university of Paris, where Thomas completed his education and taught for most of the rest of his life. Albert made major contributions in many fields of natural science and developed his own version of Dominican theology, which Thomas did not follow. But one area of Albert's teaching that caught and held was the view that the problems many contemporaries found in Aristotelianism derived from interpolation and misinterpretation. Many teachings that passed for Aristotle's, Albert held, were actually opinions of his ancient commentators or his Arabic translators. Albert knew Greek. He set for himself, and for other Dominicans like William of Moerbeke (*c.* 1215–*c.* 1286), the task of retrieving a purified text of Aristotle from the Greek manuscripts. Just as Averroes had provided the best access to Aristotle available in the twelfth century, so Albert and his collaborators produced a still more accurate reading of Aristotle, which they passed on to Thomas. Among other things, Albert's text made it possible to reprove Averroes for his own departures from Aristotle. Thomas embraced this newly corrected Aristotelian philosophy wholeheartedly. While he takes ideas from other philosophical schools, notably Neoplatonism and Stoicism, it is his thoroughgoing synthesis of Aristotelianism, as a system, with Christianity, that gives his thought its new look and special flavor.

There are other traits that distinguish his work. Thomas shares with other scholastics the analysis and criticism of authorities, using them, along with rational arguments, to attack opponents and defend his own positions. In comparison with earlier scholastics, he is less interested in contextualizing authorities rhetorically and historically. He judges their opinions in terms of whether he finds them correct, or helpful in shedding light on the question at hand. His goal is to discover the truth. Authorities can be witnesses to the truth whether they are pagans, Jews, Muslims, or Christians. But the accuracy of an authority on one point, or his general reputation, is no guarantee that he is correct on another point. On each issue a fresh, objective, and independent assay of authorities must be made.

Thomas extends the same critical yet open-minded attitude to contemporary opponents. Whether or not he agrees with an opinion, he presents it as forcefully and accurately as possible. He takes its author seriously as a fellow seeker after truth. He listens to the author, hears what he has to say, and argues with him on grounds they share. Thomas is also sensitive to an opponent's point of departure. For this reason, he sometimes treats the same material differently in different works, depending on his audience and specific objectives. While Thomas handles authorities and opposing views with all the seriousness and respect indicated, in comparison with contemporaries he relies less on authorities than on reasoned argument. He thinks it particularly important to teach students how to reason things out for themselves, and finds the closing off of debate by citing a proof-text a stultifying technique.

Another striking feature of Thomas' work, especially if one comes to it after reading Bonaventure, is his literary style. Where Bonaventure uses effusive language, appeals to the reader's emotions, and refers to his own religious experience, Thomas deliberately adopts an emotionally neutral, rational, and impersonal style. He purges symbolic language, figures of speech, and terms with multiple connotations from his lexicon. Instead, his vocabulary is spare, precise, and economical. He often uses technical terms in contexts where they convey his exact meaning. His aim is clarity, the avoidance of ambiguity, and the elimination of idiosyncrasy. Aside from Thomas' liturgical poetry, an excellent gauge of his rationalistic and ruminative mentality, there are only two points in his vast *oeuvre* where Thomas the man intrudes. Both occur in the largest synthesis of his mature thought, the *Summary of Theology*. At one point he asks how far the duty of filial obedience extends. Recalling his own resistance when his noble family opposed his entrance into the newfangled mendicant Dominican order, he concludes that disobedience is permissible if parents try to thwart a child's religious calling. At another point he raises the question of whether theologians should debate in public. In responding he draws a distinction. If the audience is uneducated, he answers no, lest their minds be confused and their faith shaken. But if the audience is learned, we should by all means debate theology. For this is how we deepen our understanding of doctrine and refute error. Besides, he adds, it is fun.

Thomas is well aware of the alternative logics available in his day and, as a convinced Aristotelian, chooses modism. The same allegiance informs his position in the realist–nominalist debate, as the debate on universals was now called. He combines Abelard's conceptualism with a richer Aristotelian epistemology. We begin, he says, with the data impressed on our senses, from which we obtain a sensible image, or phantasm, from which we extract intelligible species, out of which we form concepts that accurately represent the individual beings they signify and that we can cross-check empirically against their referata. We then abstract traits shared by concepts representing individuals, working up to universals and cause–effect relationships. Thomas holds that universals, although they are posterior in the order of knowledge, are just as meaningful and verifiable as ideas standing for individual things. Likewise, classes of being are just as real as their individual members.

This conviction reflects Thomas' acceptance of Aristotle's natural philosophy 'both in substance and in spirit. His logic is designed to provide scientific knowledge of the natural world, as well as to apply logical rigor to metaphysical objects of knowledge. Thomas embraces Aristotle's epistemological method, and a logic compatible with it, convinced that they will give us a fully natural knowledge of the created world, in general and in particular. In this respect he shares the outlook of the Muslim and Jewish Aristotelians. At the same time, in explaining the process of concept formation, Thomas rejects Aristotle, Averroes, and all previous doctrines of the agent intellect, offering one of his own that proved extremely controversial. Thomas holds that the agent intellect is not a separate intelligence, on loan to individual human minds. Rather, the capacity to form concepts and abstract ideas is intrinsic to human nature. Thomas agrees that human nature is made up of body and soul. The soul is the substantial form of the human person. It dies with the body. But, he argues, we also have another form, likewise integral to human nature, called the active form. It is this form that functions as the agent intellect. It survives the death of the body, preserving our knowledge until it is joined with the resurrected body in the next life. In union with the resurrected body, the active form enables us to enjoy personal immortality.

In expanding the range of objects we can know naturally and scientifically, Thomas can be contrasted with Avicenna, William of Auxerre, Philip the Chancellor, and Bonaventure. His point of departure is not metaphysical concepts or being as such. Rather, he begins with natural philosophy, working empirically from physical phenomena to their causes by inductive reason. The range of topics Thomas covers in his natural philosophy is much broader than Bonaventure's and his approach is rational, not contemplative. With the Lombard, he rejects the idea of creation by emanation as limiting God's freedom and as requiring Him to share His creative efficacy with subordinate intelligences. Further, God engenders out of nothing both the forms and the matter He unites with them to produce created beings. Here, while Thomas agrees with Aristotle's view that created substances contain their own principles of explanation, he rejects the eternity of matter, no less than the eternity of forms, and replaces Aristotle's unmoved mover with a God seen as supremely active.

Thomas coordinates this natural philosophy with supernature, clarifying what we can know in each subdivision, how we can know it, and how these areas are related. Embracing the entire physical world under the heading of nature, Thomas thinks that Aristotle's explanation of it is basically correct. In this area, demonstrative and categorical syllogisms whose premises are based on empirical facts provide conclusive, and testable, scientific knowledge. He agrees with Aristotle that the world is structured intelligibly and that the human mind is naturally capable of knowing it, a knowledge available to any human being. The fact that a pagan philosopher could arrive at these conclusions, without revelation and faith, is Thomas' empirical rationale for rejecting Bonaventure's pan-illuminationism. In the realm of nature, reason alone is sufficient.

In the realm of supernature, however, reason, while important, is subordinate to faith. Here, our starting point is revelation, not metaphysical first principles. Thomas' line on theology as a science differs from William of Auxerre's and Maimonides'. The articles of faith are not self-evident. This conclusion, like Thomas' rejection of illumination in natural knowledge, is empirical. If the truths of the Christian faith were self-evident, he notes, everyone would be a Christian, which is not the case. Not only are there non-believers; there are also believers of other revealed religions whose convictions differ from those of Christians. Thus, he concludes, we need grace in order to accept as true the creed specific to Christianity. Once we receive that grace, the articles of faith can serve as first principles in the realm of supernature.

With them in hand, we work by deductive reason, coordinating one doctrine with another and inferring their implications. While reason can structure the data of revelation, and while theology can thus be viewed as a science, Thomas restricts this notion more than William of Auxerre and Maimonides. Adverting to Aristotle's definition of science, he notes that all sciences begin with axioms that are not demonstrable. They are held because they are self-evident or because of their explanatory power. But, as he has shown, the first principles of theology are not self-evident. Also, not all the articles of faith can be rationalized. Thomas contrasts the demonstrative syllogisms used in natural philosophy, which compel assent, with dialectical syllogisms whose premises refer to probabilities or non-empirical realities not subject to empirical tests. Dialectical syllogisms yield probable, not necessary, conclusions. They may invite consent but they do not compel it. This type of reasoning prevails in the realm of supernature. While, through faith, we hold the revealed first principles of theology with certitude, neither they nor the conclusions we can infer from them provide scientific knowledge in Aristotle's sense.

There is, however, an area where nature and supernature overlap, their different methods yielding the same conclusions. Thomas thinks we can prove rationally God's existence, which we also know by faith, by examining His effects in the natural world. While Thomas limits the scientific character of theological knowledge more stringently than either William of Auxerre or Maimonides, he also criticizes theologians who claim that God's existence cannot be proved. Against them he offers five proofs. None is original to Thomas and this is exactly his point. They are proofs found in the philosophical literature familiar to all contemporary theologians. It is absurd, and obscurantist, to say that God's existence cannot be proved when this has already been done. Not only is it possible; it is desirable. The proofs extrinsically support the convictions of believers and they can show non-believers that theism is not irrational. It is in this spirit that Thomas offers his proofs from motion to a prime mover, from cause–effect relationships to a first cause, from possible or contingent beings to a necessary being, from degrees of goodness to a supreme good, and from the order of the universe to a supreme and intelligent orderer. Of the five, two are based on the analysis of metaphysical concepts and three are based on observable natural phenomena. The balance, for Thomas, weighs more heavily on the side of natural theology. He calls the conclusions yielded by these proofs preambles of faith. They do not impart saving truth, for which faith is necessary; although they can point non-believers in that direction.

Thomas' views on the relations between faith and reason and his innovative alternative to Averroistic psychology evoked more debate than any of his teachings, but his positions on other subjects also gave his theology a new look. While he criticizes Averroes on the agent intellect and on the eternity of matter, in many areas Thomas follows his lead, agreeing that Aristotle is the best corrective for Neoplatonic errors. Likewise, the philosophical workhorses in his stable are the doctrines of substance, essence and existence, and potency and act.

Aside from allowing him to dispense with creation by emanation, eternal exemplars as the forms of created beings, and the eternity of matter, the doctrine of substance enables Thomas to locate the principle of individuation of each being within it. Where a Platonist would see a being's pre-existing exemplary form as its explanation and its matter as what reifies it phenomenally, Thomas sees its created form, integrated with its matter, as what differentiates it from other beings with the same material composition. The forms of physical beings also yield the intelligible species that enable us to grasp their essences. Form and matter are also two of the Aristotelian causes that empower creatures to carry out their natural functions independently and to act as secondary causes, without the intervention of God or subordinate intelligences. Since created substances are composites of matter and form, they can be contrasted handily with God as pure form.

This account leaves open the vexing question of angels. In understanding their nature and in finding an adequate distinction between them and God without fudging Aristotle's metaphysics, Thomas invokes the essence–existence distinction, which he applies to other creatures as well. As purely spiritual beings, angels are an exception to Aristotle's definition of created being. They resemble the deity in their constitution, but as creatures they are not entirely simple. For, in God, essence and existence are identical. But a created being's existence can differ from its essence. While Thomas disagrees with thinkers who see this distinction as metaphysical and not as purely logical, he uses the essence–existence distinction to explain how creatures can act in ways that fail to square with their essential definitions or best selves. This is particularly true of creatures possessing free will. The fact that angels and human beings choose to depart from their essences when they sin accounts for the angels' fall, an event inexplicable in Neoplatonizing theologies that place angels in a fixed location in the chain of being. The very ability of creatures to act as physical efficient causes also enables rational creatures to exist in sub-essential ways, to act out of character, and to swerve from their ends.

The distinction between potency and act also supports this conclusion. For Thomas, God alone is pure act and always has been; He has not undergone any process of self-realization. God brings creatures into being and endows them with the capacity to attain their natural ends. Rational creatures also have supernatural ends and supernatural capacities activated by the collaboration of nature and grace. However well endowed, creatures in this life are in constant motion. They are engaged in actualizing their potentialities. Even when fully actualized, with their ends attained, they will still be distinguishable from God since they will have had to undergo change and development in so doing.

This combination of doctrines enables Thomas to argue for a creation both dependent on and independent from a deity Who radically differs from it. He acts freely as its first cause, as its metaphysical efficient cause in Avicenna's sense, and as its final cause. His nature as pure act is the model creatures emulate in actualizing their own potentialities. They do so through their own agencies. This world, a world in a dynamic state of change, is fully real and it is a positive source of scientific information about the God Who transcends it. This vision of reality, while it certainly acknowledges the supernatural ends of rational creatures, also makes possible a serious consideration and validation of their natural ends, physical, intellectual, and moral. Combined with Thomas' Aristotelian conception of human nature as an integral union of body and soul, this position informs his treatment of ethics and the workings of grace.

Thomas goes farther than any Christian theologian before his time in developing a natural ethics. Reprising the same Aristotelian distinctions between the passions and the faculties of the soul as Bonaventure, and rejecting his identification of human nature with the soul alone, Thomas lays the foundation for a non-ascetic, natural ethics in which reason and the golden mean rule our use of our physical, emotional, and mental endowments. Virtue can bear fruit in all these aspects of our nature. In attaining our natural ends, Thomas holds that we actualize our potentialities naturally. He adds to this generally Aristotelian account the Stoic notion of natural law as right reason, an ethical norm that all human beings can apprehend on their own. From it we derive rationally our natural ethical obligations. In moving to the supernatural ends that can be attained only with grace, Thomas makes three characteristic points. First, in providing supernatural grace through the sacraments, God takes account of human nature as He created and redeemed it. Since we are integral units of body and soul, both of which are saved, sacramental grace is given to us through physical media. Here, Thomas provides a philosophical rationale for the consensus position on the sacraments. His influence as a sacramental theologian was massive, even in quarters where his thought received sharp criticism. Second, Thomas agrees with the Lombard that, through the collaboration of free will and grace, we can develop virtues that become part of our personality structures. He adds that these virtues become connatural, making it easier for us to resist temptation and grow in virtue. Finally, although the order of grace is different from the order of nature, since the gifts of nature are universal while grace is possessed only by those to whom God grants it, the pursuit of our supernatural ends does not require us to stop being natural human beings. As Thomas puts it, grace does not destroy nature. It presupposes nature and perfects it.

It is largely Thomas' commitment to Aristotelianism and his critique of Neo-platonizing theologies that produced the innovations his contemporaries found so striking, and, in some cases, so offensive. At the head of the list are the role he grants to reason in the theological enterprise and in our knowledge of the creation, his doctrine of the active form, and the naturalism of his anthropology and ethics. In part, Thomas' positions on these and other matters reflect his strongly rationalistic bent. In part, they reflect his wish to defend Christianity against other faiths and against heresies like Catharism, as well as to stake out his own theology against that of other orthodox Christians.

In 1270 and again in 1277, conservatives at his university asked the bishop of Paris to condemn a series of propositions, including some ascribed to Thomas. This move is startling from professors whose collective goal was to free the academy from episcopal authority and to initiate their own open debates against masters thought to be out of line. The fact that these scholastics took such an uncharacteristic step indicates how troubled some of them were by the innovations of their more avant-garde colleagues. Although he was a Dominican, the archbishop of Canterbury also issued a list of condemned propositions, likewise including Thomistic positions along with those of Latin Averroists. These episcopal interventions had little effect on the development of speculative thought in the period after Thomas and Bonaventure. While the Dominicans closed ranks in 1279 in the effort to make Thomism obligatory, the more Neoplatonic theology of Albert attracted some members of the order. Secular masters not committed to either order of friars freely drew on, or criticized, their work and put the pieces together in their own way. Change is most visible among Franciscans, who in some respects objected to Bonaventure as much as to Thomas. They sought, with considerable success, to put Franciscan philosophy and theology on a new footing on the basis of their own new ideas.

CHAPTER 23

Later Medieval Scholasticism: The Triumph of Terminism, Henry of Ghent, John Duns Scotus, and William of Ockham

The late thirteenth and fourteenth centuries experienced growing restiveness with the same Aristotelianism that was the scholastics' common coin. The synthetic drive of earlier scholasticism waned. Terminist logic decisively supplanted modism. The broad Christian Aristotelianism developed by Aquinas and defended by most Dominicans faced growing competition both from Franciscans and from secular masters drawing on a range of old and new positions. The period's logicians are in the vanguard of post–Aristotelianism. But the leading speculative thinkers of the day, Henry of Ghent (*c.* 1217–93), John Duns Scotus (1265/6–1308), and William of Ockham (*c.* 1285–1347), show an increasing tendency to depart from Aristotle in their metaphysics, physics, ethics, and epistemology as well. Motivated partly by the desire to criticize contemporary and recent thinkers and to assert their own ideas, these figures, especially Scotus and Ockham, also reflect the felt need of Franciscans to take a hard look at Bonaventure and to rethink or replace his legacy altogether. While, as Franciscans, Scotus and Ockham share this concern, they also disagree sharply with each other. Their positions played a major role in shaping scholastic debate for the rest of the Middle Ages and drew more support than those of any other high or late medieval thinkers.

The Triumph of Terminism

In the fourteenth century, terminism succeeded in defeating modism. Reviving the agenda informing their approach since the twelfth century, the terminists moved it forward. They agreed on the questions logic should ask and provided a range of answers to them. So pervasive was terminism that it could transcend the debate between realists and nominalists, enlisting thinkers from both camps. The central conviction uniting late medieval terminists was the view that the only grammatical contexts in which supposited terms are meaningful are full propositions. They rejected the sub-propositional phrases accepted by Peter of Spain. However named by his successors, Peter's natural suppositions also came increasingly under fire. Whether they were realists, like Walter Burleigh (*c.* 1275–1345), John Wycliff, and Vincent Ferrer (1350–1419), or nominalists, like Ockham, Albert of Saxony (*c.*

1316–90), and Marsilius of Inghien (d. 1396), logicians now drew a much sharper distinction between signification and supposition than their thirteenth-century predecessors. Since the realists granted universals an extra-mental reference, they had less difficulty explaining universal terms and accounting for their significance than nominalists. The standard terminist doctrine that supposited terms refer to individuals and to the classes to which they belong, whether past, present, or future, was not problematic for realists. Nor did they have difficulty defining beings in terms of their essences. Since the nominalists saw universals as mental constructs with no extra-mental referents, they found it harder to explain the meaning of supposited abstract terms and were more likely to argue that such terms have meaning only when individual beings manifesting their attributes actually exist. From this standpoint, it follows that categorical statements referring to members of species past, present, and future are false, unless the subject terms refer to concrete phenomena in existence at the moment the proposition is stated. While it did not rule out generalizations altogether, the effect of nominalism was to restrict the occasions on which they can be made and to limit their semantic force.

This position left nominalists with the problem of assessing the premises and conclusions of categorical and demonstrative syllogisms, held to be true always, such as the production of the same effects by the same causes under the same circumstances. One way to address this issue was to treat the propositions stating scientific findings of this type as non-demonstrative and non-categorical. Ockham takes this route, reframing them as hypothetical syllogisms. This tactic enables him to draw conclusions verifiable in formal logic, whatever may be the case in the extra-mental world. Other nominalists rejected Ockham's strategy precisely because hypothetical syllogisms do not draw conclusions about actual beings or facts. The chief alternative to Ockham's was developed by John Buridan (1300–58), who contrasts nouns, whose significance he regards as omnitemporal, with verbs, which designate particular times. In Buridan's view, scientific statements are also omnitemporal. Since nature makes no leaps, such statements refer to events that always take place under the same conditions. In order to validate scientific statements Buridan revives natural supposition. He holds that a term has a natural supposition when the proposition in which it is stated accurately depicts a concrete individual example of that term, whether in the past, present, or future. While future cases cannot be validated, the meaning of the term and the truth of the proposition are stable, given their conformity with concrete, actual beings. It is not necessary to posit a level of metaphysical reality higher than individual beings, as the realists do, to achieve this validation. Thus, for Buridan, one can be a nominalist, and a terminist, and one can also accept categorical and demonstrative reasoning of a scientific nature. The positions of Ockham and Buridan were the poles around which debates on supposition raged among fourteenth-century nominalists. Despite their differences, they agree in rejecting the realists' understanding of supposited universal terms as referring to generic and transtemporal extra-mental realities. No consensus on these issues was achieved in the Middle Ages despite the conviction of most logicians, since the late eleventh century, that semantic theory was central both to logic and to scientific thought, and that logic exists primarily to structure the world of thought. It can refer to real beings, but has to be able to account for counterfactual ideas and for possibilities that are logical if not actual.

Henry of Ghent

Movement away from Aristotelianism and back to it at some points can also be seen in the thought of Henry of Ghent, the most influential Parisian scholastic in the 1280s and 1290s. His ideas inspired debate both because he changed his mind as an epistemologist and because in that area, as well as in metaphysics, he maintains conflicting claims. As a metaphysician, Henry asserts that the concept of being is analogous. We know being immediately, either as contingent or as necessary. The only necessary being is God, Who cannot be conceived not to exist. Henry posits three kinds of contingent being. One is exclusively intra-mental. Concepts standing for intra-mental entities, such as our internal states of mind, may have no extra-mental reference. Henry nevertheless accords metaphysical status to pure mental constructs. The second type of contingent being is possible being. By this Henry means beings God contemplates in His mind before deciding to create them. He contrasts possible beings with actual beings, those God does create. Actual beings are still contingent, since God is under no constraint to create them or to make them as they are. This distinction between possible and actual beings recalls Anselm of Canterbury's distinction between contingent and necessary possibility, with less emphasis on things as they are and more on things as they might be. Another metaphysical distinction Henry applies to actual beings is the distinction between substantial and accidental being. In a highly idiosyncratic reading of Aristotle on substance and accidents, he holds that some actual beings are substances and that others are accidents that modify other, substantial beings. An additional metaphysical idea specific to Henry is that essence and existence apply not to creatures but to God's relationship to creatures. Essential creatures are those God contemplates before He decides whether to create them; existential creatures are those God actually creates. Essence and existence are thus synonymous with possible and actual being in Henry's lexicon. Henry also has his own position on the principle of individuation. It is neither matter nor form but the indivisibility of a being and the fact that God has made it different from all other beings.

In arriving at these conclusions, Henry sees no need to inspect the world of nature. As with Avicenna and scholastics influenced by him, Henry's approach is basically metaphysical. He offers three proofs of God's existence, from causality, supereminence, and exemplarity, all of which are based on his analysis of the metaphysical concepts and requirements involved. Henry thinks we can grasp directly the idea of being and of concepts like necessity and contingency, without the need for empirical information. But, in maintaining this position, he distances himself from Avicenna and from all proponents of creation by emanation, to preserve God's freedom and transcendence. For the same reason, he distinguishes clearly between the exemplars of possible or essential beings in the mind of God and the created forms He unites with their created matter when He actualizes them.

Henry's metaphysics contains a problem he does not resolve. He asserts that the concept of being is analogical. At the same time, he excludes a notion of being more general than necessary and contingent being, of which they are manifestations. And the modes of being he describes are so different from each other that it is hard to see in what sense they are analogous. What Henry really proposes is an equivocal conception of being.

If there are contradictions in Henry's metaphysics, problems abound even more in his epistemology. Here, his difficulties stem from the fact that his teaching underwent three distinct stages. Within each stage he tries to fuse positions informed by conflicting assumptions. Henry's initial position dates to before 1276. At that point, his chief concern, realized imperfectly, was to criticize Bonaventure's pan-illuminationism, which was receiving enthusiastic support from Franciscans such as Matthew of Acquasparta (*c.* 1237–1303), John Peckham (*c.* 1225–92), and Roger Marston (*c.* 1250–1303). It is true that Aquinas gives a trenchant critique of Bonaventure's epistemology, noting that the ability of pagans to discover the truths of natural philosophy disproves the claim that we need divine illumination in all kinds of knowledge. Henry does not follow his lead. His argument is not based on empirical evidence. Rather, it reflects the metaphysical bent found elsewhere in his thought. Henry begins by asserting that we can possess knowledge with certitude in a purely natural way. The criteria of truth are intellectual, not empirical. The mind validates the sense data we receive and also its own operations. It enables us to grasp the essences of things as well as the truth of abstract ideas and of the scientific propositions we frame. At each level of intellection, Henry invokes the Avicennan norm of truth as the adequation of our ideas to their objects. The objective norm he proposes is twofold. On one level, it is the intelligible species of the class to which an individual belongs, which we acquire when we apprehend the individual at the start of the cognitive process. On another level, the intellectual criterion is the being's exemplar in the mind of God. Thinkers with access to God's mind can have full and infallible certitude about their objects of knowledge. But, not everyone has this access: it requires the grace of illumination granted to a few saints and visionaries, and only briefly and intermittently. Henry sees illumination functioning, for them, as the agent intellect. It enables them to form totally accurate concepts and to attain greater scientific certitude than is possible for other mortals. This theory is at odds with Henry's initial claim that we can acquire true and certain knowledge with our natural rational endowment. This discrepancy aside, the most striking feature of Henry's initial epistemology is the view that the indices of our concepts of phenomena are not the phenomena themselves but universals and exemplars of them in the mind of God.

In the epistemology he taught between 1277 and 1280, Henry adds more Aristotelianism to his theory, while continuing to argue that the essences of things are the true objects of the mind and that our knowledge of individual beings, in the first instance, includes a knowledge of how they participate in the essences of the groups to which they belong. He yokes this notion to a thoroughly realist view of universals. At the same time, at this juncture he removes divine action from his analysis of concept formation, substituting potency and act. Our minds, he holds, have an intrinsic potential ability to know their objects truly and to form accurate concepts of them. We can actualize this potentiality naturally. At this point in Henry's development, he argues that the essences of extra-mental things are the criteria of the adequacy of our concepts of them and agrees with Aquinas that we perform a conscious mental act in testing our ideas against their referents. But he continues to hold that these reference points are not their empirically observable features. Henry's account of concept formation in this phase of his teaching is also somewhat more Aristotelian. He sees the senses as receiving data out of which we construct a phantasm, from which we derive intelligible species and form concepts. We then form concepts of greater abstraction until we arrive at universals. Confusingly, however, he continues to argue that, as objects of knowledge, universals are presented to the mind at the same time as individuals and that we know their essences directly. He uses Averroes' analysis of our mental functions in the production of the abstract ideas on which scientific knowledge depends, but does not consider what effect this agent intellect doctrine has on personal immortality.

Henry revised his epistemology yet again after 1280. At this point, he wanted to integrate the two earlier phases of his thinking, combining Aristotelianism with illuminationism. He now teaches that ordinary mortals, not just saints and mystics, need illumination to grasp the essences of things, to form concepts, to validate their truth, and to acquire scientific knowledge based on universals. Illumination is also required by the few privileged to test the correspondence of their ideas with ideas in the mind of God. Henry now dismisses the notion of intelligible species. Either our minds grasp the essences of things directly, or phantasms turn into concepts more or less automatically. Henry tries to inject such Aristotelianism as he retains into his illuminationism by treating the two theories as describing successive stages of cognition. So far as he accepts it, Aristotelianism accounts for the knowledge of the essences of things we derive from sense data. But the verification of our concepts of those essences, and concept formation itself, are governed by illumination, which functions as the agent intellect in all human minds in Henry's final position.

Altogether, the permutations of Henry's epistemology show him maintaining practically all accounts of cognition available in his day, short of pan-illuminationism and Thomism. Despite his desire to criticize Bonaventure, he reflects the appeal of the idea of illumination, especially to a thinker with a metaphysical bent looking for non-empirical guarantees of truth. Yet despite these proclivities, Henry also shows how difficult it was for a contemporary scholastic to reject Aristotle completely. His changing views and the problems in his account at any stage along the way gave scholastics who took issue with Henry a wealth of points to attack. In so doing, some of them move even farther from Aristotle than Henry, while rejecting his illuminationism as well.

John Duns Scotus

This description certainly fits John Duns Scotus, although he shares Henry's emphasis on metaphysics and his interest in non-empirical knowledge. A master at

Oxford, Cambridge, and Paris before moving to the Franciscan house of studies in Cologne in the year of his death, Scotus was as brilliant and subtle as he was original. His ideas attracted interest, and controversy. His frequent transfers required him to redefend his basic ideas in the light of objections they drew locally. This circumstance, as well as his early death, prevented him from developing a range of views on all subjects. His accounts of creation, of the structure of created being, and of our knowledge of it, are particularly lean. What interest him most are metaphysical realities, spiritual beings, and how we know them. Scotus is especially concerned with developing an epistemology that can explain our knowledge of spiritual beings in the next life as well as in this. Another of his central emphases is God's freedom, power, and transcendence. Scotus sees Bonaventurian emanationism as compromising these divine attributes. He also thinks that the Christian Aristotelianism professed by Aquinas chains the deity to the laws He creates for the natural world. Scotus therefore rejects both Bonaventure's quasi-mystical contemplation of the Trinity in the book of nature and Thomistic natural theology. In his estimation, neither approach contributes to our knowledge of God. Although logic is of considerable help, the chief branch of philosophy that sheds light on theology is metaphysics. Scotus shares the metaphysical bias of thinkers like Avicenna, Henry of Ghent, and Bonaventure. But, to the extent that he takes Franciscan themes from the latter, he forcibly reshapes them and gives them a distinctly personal look.

Epistemology is decidedly one of these themes. Scotus rejects Bonaventure's notion that we need illumination to know created beings, physical or spiritual, or philosophical ideas. We can grasp all these objects of cognition naturally, and with certitude, and use them to gain scientific knowledge. Scotus joins Henry of Ghent in replacing empirical criteria of truth with intellectual ones. But he departs from Henry's notion that ideas in the mind of God are available for that purpose. His own agent intellect doctrine opposes both Thomas' and all Muslim versions of the theory. He thinks that human substances have two forms, their substantial form and the Avicennan form of corporeity they share with other corporeal beings. The form of corporeity, intrinsic to the human constitution, is the agent intellect. According to Scotus, no philosopher has demonstrated the immortality of the individual soul. He supports that position but thinks we can do so on the basis of religious faith. Scotus agrees with Henry that we can know both the essences of individual things and the essences of the classes to which they belong, and that concepts standing for both essences have an extra-mental reference. But, in Scotus' epistemology, we apprehend the generic concepts first. We then discover how an individual member of a class participates in it. In describing intellection, Scotus distinguishes the apprehension of objects of knowledge from abstraction. He also draws a sharp distinction between our apprehension of physical beings, on the one hand, and spiritual beings and purely intellectual objects of knowledge, on the other. In the first case, his account is approximately as Aristotelian as Henry's. It involves the reception of sense data, the formation of a phantasm, the extraction of intelligible species, and the formation of a concept. Like Henry, he is disinclined to refer the concept back to its empirical source in order to validate it. A telling index of Scotus' approach is his handling of the traditional empiricists' argument about a straight stick partially immersed in water that appears to be bent because air and water refract light differently. The stick can be proved to be straight by removing it from the water and looking at or feeling it; the senses supply the remedies for their own defects. As Scotus argues, the stick can be proved to be straight on the basis of the intrinsic nature of wood and water. Wood is hard; water is soft. Soft water cannot bend hard wood. This argument may not persuade. Consider the softness of water in a tidal wave. But it reflects Scotus' unwillingness to place confidence in empirical arguments, even in the case of empirical realities.

In explaining our knowledge of non-empirical realities, Scotus presents one of his major innovations, the theory of intuition. When he and other late medieval scholastics speak of intuition they do not mean mystic contemplation, psychological acuity, or a vague oceanic feeling. The term has a precise cognitive sense. For Scotus, it is the mind's direct, unmediated grasp of the existence and nature of a non-empirical object of knowledge. No sense data are involved, since the object of knowledge is immaterial. There are no intelligible species. Nor is there a ratiocinative process. By intuition we apprehend a spiritual object of knowledge with certitude. We first grasp the essence of the class of beings to which it belongs and then the way the essence inheres in individual members of the class. Scotus develops this theory to account for the knowledge possessed by the soul after death and in the next life. Scotus posits two kinds of intuitions. There are perfect intuitions, which involve objects of knowledge currently available and currently apprehended. There are also imperfect intuitions of two kinds. When we remember a spiritual object of knowledge, our present memory is an imperfect intuition, even though we may have intuited the object perfectly when we first apprehended it. Scotus does not think we can intuit non-existents. But he argues that prophets and people with second sight can have imperfect intuitions about the future. Unlike perfect intuition, imperfect intuition requires intelligible species. While, in this life, intuitive cognition is limited to purely spiritual and intellectual objects of knowledge, Scotus thinks that the blessed in heaven will be able to know all creatures intuitively.

Whether our apprehensions derive from sense data processed to form concepts or from immediate intuitions that we conceptualize, once we arrive at concepts we can engage in the abstract intellection that produces scientific knowledge. The criteria Scotus develops for validating scientific knowledge go beyond the Aristotelian idea of categorical or demonstrative syllogisms whose conclusions compel assent. This departure from Aristotle is consistent with the metaphysical emphasis of his epistemology in general. For Scotus, the syllogisms that yield scientific certitude do not have premises or conclusions we can test empirically. As he sees it, scientific propositions state necessary truths. These truths cannot be derived from the fluctuating world of natural phenomena. Nor are they immediately self-evident. Rather, they are derived from ontological first principles or from the principles of a higher mode of scientific knowledge. When we deduce conclusions from these principles, we gain a scientific understanding of their effects, including events in the phenomenal world. In cross-checking these conclusions, the reference points, for Scotus, are the metaphysical foundations or causes that account for them. Through this deductive process we acquire scientific knowledge that is evident and full.

One motivation for this definition of scientific knowledge is Scotus' wish to depart from other thinkers' conceptions of theology as a science. In his view, theological data are not derived from the natural world or its resemblance to God. Nor are theological data self-evident. Nor are they derived from some higher science. Nor, he adds, are they fully known. Rather, they are derived from revelation and faith, and they are known in part, through a glass darkly. In no sense can the deductions we make from the data of faith be validated empirically. This exclusion applies to Bonaventure's 'experimental' knowledge. At the same time, Scotus rejects Thomas' view that the arguments we make in theology yield only a probable truth. He thinks that we can prove God's existence metaphysically using arguments that meet his own criteria for scientific knowledge. But, while we can prove God's existence conclusively and infer major divine attributes once we have done so, we can never know the divine nature evidently and fully.

Scotus' proof is heavily indebted to Avicenna and to Henry of Ghent. He replaces possibility or contingency and necessity with finitude and infinity, but maintains, as they do, that these concepts are immediately available to the mind and that they enable us to infer the necessary existence of God as an infinite being, causing and sustaining finite, contingent beings. The main difference between his argument and theirs, outside of his substitution of metaphysical concepts that are functional equivalents of contingency and necessity and that include them, is that Scotus holds that we know the metaphysical concepts at issue intuitively. He also folds into the initial concept of God proved by his argument the transcendentals of unity, goodness, truth, and being, agreeing with Philip the Chancellor that they are mutually convertible and identifiable with God. In ruling out natural theology as relevant to the proof of God's existence, Scotus rejects the Aristotelian argument from motion to a prime mover as both counterintuitive and counterfactual. For the human will can move without an external mover. He also rules out arguments based on formal, material, and efficient causation in the natural order because each of them requires the co-causality of another cause. His own proof, on the other hand, yields a first efficient cause, an Avicennan metaphysical efficient cause, and a final cause that is supereminent and acts alone.

In inferring other divine attributes from those intrinsic to his proof of God's existence, Scotus invokes another principle for which other scholastics gave him the credit, the formal distinction, which he uses elsewhere as well. For Scotus, a formal distinction is less real than a metaphysical distinction but more real than a logical one. He does not regard divine attributes like omnipotence and omniscience as identical with the divine nature in the same way as infinity and unity. Scotus distinguishes them from the divine nature formally. He also uses the formal distinction to differentiate the Trinitarian persons from the divine nature they equally share. Scotus applies the formal distinction to created beings too: he thinks it can work for them as well because, unlike Henry, his view of being is univocal. Scotus distinguishes the faculties in the human soul from the subsistent soul in which they inhere formally. He also uses this principle to reframe the essence–existence distinction in creatures as formal rather than metaphysical or merely logical.

Another area in which Scotus uses the formal distinction is the realism–nominalism debate, which yields his extremely original principle of individuation. Scotus' epistemology is certainly hospitable to realism, since he thinks that we grasp first the essences of the classes to which individuals belong and grants universals an extra-mental reference. At the same time, he refrains from saying that the referata of universals are more real than those of concepts standing for individuals. The difference between the individual and the class to which it belongs is neither metaphysical nor purely logical but formal, irrespective of which we know first. In understanding how the essence of the class inheres in one of its individual members, Scotus defines the principle of individuation as *haecceitas*. This Latin neologism, which translates as 'thisness,' denotes a mode of individuation utterly specific and exclusive, found only in the particular being it informs. We might compare it to the way that 'dogness' or 'collieness' inhere in Lassie, in contrast with the way they inhere in Lad and other collies, including those in Lassie's immediate gene pool. One of the reasons why *haecceitas* appeals to Scotus as the principle of individuation is that it applies just as well to spiritual as to material and composite beings. Also, it explains our posthumous as well as current grasp of individuals.

While, as his use of the formal distinction and of metaphysical arguments indicates, Scotus sees philosophy as playing a wider role in theology than just the structuring of revealed data, he removes natural theology from that enterprise completely. As he sees it, the only knowledge of God we can derive from inspecting the creation is that He willed to create it and to make it as it is. Scotus aligns himself with thinkers who draw a clear distinction between God's absolute and ordained power, a distinction he strengthens. He insists on God's freedom in creating our world, from among any number of possible worlds He could have created. The existence of our world and the particular natural laws that govern it are in no sense necessary. They are both contingent on an act of divine will. Having made His choices, God retains the power to do otherwise. There is no condition at all, including God's own intelligence and benevolence, that required Him to create the present world order. Scotus emphasizes this point heavily against both emanationists and Christian and other Aristotelians. The former, he thinks, bind God to the inner necessities of His own nature; the latter bind God to the natural laws He transcends. Both positions are thus unacceptable.

Scotus also emphasizes will in his ethics. He firmly rejects natural law ethics. In the charismatic no less than the cosmological order, we are connected to God primarily in terms of will. The moral law we follow must be obeyed because it is God's revealed will. Scotus distinguishes between the inclination toward a good that is to our advantage and the love of justice, which inclines us toward a good because it is intrinsically good. The only acceptable motivation in the moral life is the love of justice, which moves us to obey God's law because it is God's will. Doing so, for that reason alone, is the only way to acquire the merit leading to salvation. Scotus acknowledges that some divine commands coincide with obligations we can derive rationally. Such concurrence is irrelevant. In the moral life, we must obey God's will because it is God's will and not because we find His injunctions reasonable.

Will is critical on the human side of the moral transaction as well. Our obedience must be a free exercise of will. Scotus shares the medieval consensus view that free will and grace must collaborate in the moral life. With Peter Lombard, he sees their interaction as concurrent, not sequential. A major concession he makes to Neoplatonism is to view sin and evil as non-being. But, more generally, he supports, while recasting, the Franciscan stress on will over reason in the moral life. This is because the will is the seat of love while the intellect is the seat of knowledge. While the intellect can be constrained by demonstrations that compel assent, the will remains free. Yet, for Scotus, it is not only the primacy of love over knowledge that informs his ethics but also the normative nature of the act of will by which we accept God's will. Scotus' voluntarism in this area moves the focus from our affective response to God's love to our free acknowledgment that God has the right to ordain moral laws we are obliged to obey whether we find them reasonable or not. This conclusion raises a question that Scotus is fully prepared to answer. Why is it that God has changed His moral law over time, suspending it on occasion or commanding some people to do things otherwise forbidden? Scotus' response, one that locates his ethics in the larger context of his doctrine of God, is that God transcends human understanding as well as the manifestations of Himself He has chosen to make. Ultimately, His decisions on what rules to legislate, His alteration of His rules, and His suspension of them, lie in an absolute divine will that frees Him from His actual ordinance. We cannot compass it, but must revere and obey, in a universe governed by a God far less accessible than the God of Bonaventure or Thomas.

William of Ockham

While Scotus' thought marks a notable break with some of his thirteenth-century predecessors, with William of Ockham we enter an intellectual environment whose change of climate is far more palpable. If Scotus' peregrinations forced him to re-enter debates addressed earlier and impeded his development of positions in all areas, Ockham's career had a similar effect. Contingencies aside, synthesis was not to his taste. An Oxford theologian, Ockham was cited to appear at the papal court on heresy charges inspired by the animus of the arch-Thomist John Lutterell (*fl.* 1317–35). Thomism had never been popular at Oxford and Lutterell was so widely loathed for his intemperate attacks on non-Thomists that he had been deposed as the university's chancellor by petition of the entire faculty. His accusation distorted Ockham's views. Still, Ockham went to Avignon for a hearing. Papal justice could be dilatory and four years passed before his case was heard. In the meantime, he befriended Michael of Cesena (*fl.* 1316–42), head of the Franciscan order, who had been accused of spiritual Franciscanism, which had recently been banned. In 1328 Michael was convicted and so was Ockham, on a guilt by association charge, not for his own views or those Lutterell ascribed to him. Without waiting for the verdict, Michael and Ockham decided to flee. The German emperor, Louis IV (*c.* 1283–1347), came to their rescue, spiriting them away to his court in Munich.

Ockham remained in Germany for the rest of his life, writing political propaganda in Louis' support. He sought reconciliation with his order and with the church but it is not known if his excommunication was lifted before he died. Nor is it known if he returned to academic life in Germany. His major works all date from his years in England. They include his commentary on the *Sentences*, commentaries on Aristotle's physics and logic, and the *Golden Exposition* and *Summary of Logic* which give Ockham's position on logic and the realism–nominalism debate.

Ockham's chief interests, and certainly his greatest innovations, lay in logic and epistemology. His teachings in these fields inform his positions in other areas. As noted, he made a major contribution to both nominalism and terminism. His logic is heavily colored by his account of cognition. Ockham holds that there are three kinds of human knowledge: intuition, abstraction, and faith. The first two require only our natural rational endowment. The third requires revelation and grace. Each uses a different method and affords a different type and degree of certitude. The boundaries Ockham draws among them are extremely sharp.

In contrast with Henry of Ghent and Scotus, Ockham is an empiricist, deeply interested in our knowledge of physical beings. Where Scotus confines intuition to non-empirical objects of cognition and thinks that intelligible species play a role in all forms of knowledge except perfect intuition, Ockham discards intelligible species altogether and applies intuition to our knowledge of phenomenal beings. We apprehend empirical objects of knowledge immediately, both sensibly and intellectually. These apprehensions are full and direct; they involve no ratiocinative process and they provide a certain knowledge of their objects' existence and nature. Our intuitions of physical beings are verifiable empirically. Also, intuitions apprehend simple, individual beings, one at a time. Intuition gives us full and certain knowledge of their characteristics as individuals. It does not encompass characteristics these individuals share with other, similar beings. Ockham also thinks we can intuit non-existents, but only with the help of grace. Otherwise, intuitive cognition is entirely natural.

We can then proceed to the second type of rational knowledge, abstraction, and pursue it in great detail, conceiving generalizations, cause–effect relationships, and universals. As a logician, Ockham gives abstract knowledge, and the propositions and syllogisms in which we use it, extended attention. But he defines all concepts in this realm as mental constructs, derivative to a greater or lesser degree. None is a sign of a being apprehended by intuition. Once we have converted intuitions into concepts, we cannot verify the concepts empirically. They no longer have referents in the real world. As we then convert initial concepts into more abstract ones, they become, increasingly, mental signs of other mental signs. We can validate propositions containing them logically. But the fact that formal logic can do so does not authorize us to regard concepts as indices of real beings. In any event, universal concepts have no extra-mental reference, for Ockham. This analysis is perfectly congruent with his reformulation of the categorical or demonstrative syllogisms that yield scientifically certain conclusions in more Aristotelian systems of logic into hypothetical syllogisms. In Ockham's thought, and this constitutes a major departure from Aristotle, we can know only individuals with certitude, by intuition.

We cannot have scientific certitude about the interrelations of individual beings, about cause–effect relationships, about the laws of nature. We cannot demonstrate scientifically that a world order exists at all. Abstract knowledge, composed as it is of mental constructs, provides at best probable conclusions about the world outside the mind.

This analysis of rational knowledge, which heightens the criteria for certitude in intuitive cognition while it renders uncertain the conclusions of abstraction, also informs Ockham's treatment of faith and his estimate of whether either kind of rational knowledge can clarify it. Going well beyond Scotus' rejection of natural philosophy as relevant to theology, Ockham also dismisses metaphysics. Intuition has nothing to do with faith, as he sees it. For intuition apprehends physical beings. Neither God nor the spiritual truths contained in articles of faith can be known empirically. As for abstract knowledge, it has a purely intra-mental nature and reference. It cannot provide information about theological realities that exist outside and above the mind. In theology, then, we are dependent entirely on faith. Ockham regards the knowledge we have by faith as certain. But its certitude is guaranteed by the authority of revelation and by the grace that enables us to accept it as true. While faith is certain, it cannot provide full knowledge of its objects. God's nature and the mysteries of faith transcend our comprehension. While logic helps us make coherent inferences from the data of faith, Ockham reduces appreciably the utility of reason to theology, in comparison with Scotus and earlier medieval thinkers.

Ockham makes obsolete a number of ideas in natural philosophy and epistemology that had linked other scholastics with Aristotle, if with increasing tenuousness. He relegates to the epistemological dustbin intelligible species of any kind. As he sees it, no one has ever proved their existence. Instead of regarding sensation and intellection as sequential, his theory of intuition presents them as simultaneous. In rejecting the extra-mental reference of universals, he takes an extreme nominalist position, reducing scientific knowledge of nature to probability. In understanding what makes the world operate, Ockham replaces the multiple causes of Aristotle with the immediate efficient causes of phenomena. This principle of economy, 'Ockham's razor,' the unwillingness to invoke more causes or explanations than are needed to account for the immediate behavior of phenomena, removes from the agenda the need to account for their existence, nature, and purpose in larger terms. Ockham also rejects Aristotle's quintessence as constituting the heavenly bodies. He argues that they are materially the same as earthly bodies although they have superior forms. Two other determinations of creatures that Ockham abandons are substance and accident and essence and existence. Since the beings we apprehend intuitively are simple individuals, they cannot be entities with distinguishable aspects or components. The distinctions between matter and form and between essence and existence are not metaphysical, for Ockham. Nor are they logical. They are merely terminological.

In theology, Ockham's conception of what can be known and proved with certainty limits considerably the role of reason in the theological enterprise. His principle of economy leads him to abandon ideas in the mind of God as agencies through which He acts. When God acts, for Ockham, He acts directly, without exemplars or secondary causes. Since neither natural philosophy nor metaphysics provides proofs of God's existence, we can know God only by faith. In any event, Ockham notes that all proofs of God's existence assume that the infinite regress of causes is absurd, in order to arrive at a first cause. He himself is perfectly comfortable with the idea of infinite regress. If we accept its possibility, we cannot prove that the world is finite and that it is not eternal. We cannot prove that any cause is the first cause. We cannot even prove that our world is the only world currently in existence. And, Ockham concludes, to the extent that we can prove the existence of a first efficient cause as the ground of being of all other efficient causes, we still cannot prove that this cause is the same being as the God of the Bible.

What we know about the God of the Bible, as creator and redeemer, is derived from religious faith. Where Scotus accents will as the chief attribute God manifests, cosmologically and morally, what Ockham finds chiefly revealed is God's power. He sharpens appreciably the distinction between God's absolute and ordained power, bringing his epistemology to bear on this doctrine. God's ordained power embraces His ordinance for the natural world and His ordinance for our salvation. Our inability to grasp the laws of nature with scientific certitude, because they involve abstractions that are pure mental constructs that we cannot verify extra-mentally, makes the natural order radically contingent on God. It is contingent for its existence and for the fact that it remains in being. It is contingent as the home where God has decided to lodge us, instead of one of the other possible worlds that might exist concurrently. It is contingent in the exercise of natural functions that are directly dependent on Him. God also ordains an order of salvation. He lays down moral laws and religious observances, like sacraments, as means of grace. In this area, we are totally dependent on God's power, since we cannot save ourselves and we cannot discover how He wants us to behave on our own. Having revealed Himself, God has covenanted Himself to His people. Ockham thinks that God will remain faithful to that commitment. Yet and still, God has absolute power, which frees Him from His own ordinances in the natural order and in the order of grace alike. In the natural order, He can suspend His own laws, and does so when He performs miracles. Further, He could annihilate our world and create a different one, with arrangements we cannot imagine. And, He could destroy our world and not create another. While we are bound by the rules for human salvation that God lays down, He is not. He can save people who do not follow His rules. The fact that we do follow them gives us no claim on salvation. Ockham agrees with Scotus that it is God's decision to accept our obedience that counts. While we are more likely to find favor in God's sight if we obey Him, in the final analysis God's absolute power leaves him just as free in the order of grace as it does in the order of nature.

These theological conclusions, in addition to the conclusions Ockham draws in natural philosophy, epistemology, and logic, made him the most widely discussed scholastic of his day. Years of controversy ensued before Ockhamism was deemed teachable at Paris. He became the single most influential scholastic of the later Middle Ages, not only at Paris, but also at German and English universities. Supporters and opponents agreed that he had established the terms of debate. His followers did not always receive the same message from their master. In theology, some Ockhamists used him to defend radical fideism, to the point of complete anti-intellectualism in religion. They sometimes associated that position with biblical fundamentalism. Others, confronted with the idea that God has the absolute power to overturn His own charismatic order, found Ockham's deity too arbitrary and became religious skeptics. In natural philosophy, the idea that natural laws cannot be discovered with certitude led, in some quarters, to scientific skepticism or to occasionalism, the view that events in the natural order occur randomly and by chance. There were also less extreme applications of Ockhamism in the late Middle Ages and beyond. For some Ockhamists, the theological lesson he taught was that God's covenant is reliable and that we should elevate the authority of theological first principles known by faith above conclusions human ingenuity may deduce from them. Some followers of Ockham in the natural sciences pushed forward his questioning of Aristotle and saw the clear distinction he draws between reason and revelation as a charter of liberties, authorizing them to study nature free from extrinsic theological and metaphysical concerns. The multiform legacy of Ockham, as well as that of the scholastics preceding him, was thus applied to other fields of speculation. Some of these developments flowed on into early modern thought while others remained markers of a purely medieval outlook.

PART VII

THE LEGACY OF
SCHOLASTICISM

CHAPTER 24

The Natural Sciences: Reception and Criticism

Natural science provides a particularly vivid illustration of the impact of scholastic philosophy and theology on other subjects. Its practitioners were themselves scholastics, trained to evaluate ancient and recent authorities and comfortable with the idea that they could be criticized. Interest in science before and outside of the reception of Greco-Arabic and Greco-Jewish thought did exist, as Bede, Gerbert, and Hildegard of Bingen attest. But, aside from the efforts of thinkers associated with Chartrain Platonism to develop a naturalistic cosmogenesis, scientific studies were fitful at best before the twelfth and thirteenth centuries, confined largely to the data and outlook of the Roman encyclopedists, the quadrivium authors, the transmitters, and those who commented on them. It was the reappropriation of the Greek scientific tradition as amplified by medieval scientists writing in Arabic that launched high medieval science in the Latin west. Scientific study was institutionalized at the medieval universities. Medical faculties added Galen (129–after 210) and Hippocrites (*c.* 460–*c.* 370 BC) as well as Aristotle and Avicenna to their curricula. Aristotle's works were also studied in the arts and theological faculties. It was the Aristotelian scientific corpus that generated the most interest, whether for his summations of ancient Greek consensus positions, as in astronomy, or for his own methods and findings.

There were two main stages in the medieval reaction to this material. They paralleled, and were influenced by, contemporary developments in other fields of speculative thought. The first, in the thirteenth century, was the reception of scientific texts translated from Arabic and Greek. This reception was anything but passive; for leaders in the movement added to what they received, both substantively and methodologically. Then a shift, analogous to the move away from Bonaventure and Aquinas in the thought of Scotus and Ockham, occurred in fourteenth-century science, in which thinkers made notable departures from Aristotelianism, sometimes in the name of Aristotle's own critics within the classical tradition and sometimes as a result of the innovations of medieval philosophy and science themselves.

In the first, or reception, stage, the most important and influential scientist was Robert Grosseteste. He is a good example of a thinker who combined Neoplatonism and Christianity with science. Grosseteste professed both light metaphysics and a doctrine of divine illumination similar to Bonaventure's teaching a generation later. These views were one reason why he chose optics as the branch of science to study. They also affected his interpretation of Aristotle's scientific method. Aside from a period spent studying theology at Paris (1209–14), Grosseteste made his academic career at Oxford, serving as its chancellor in 1234, the year before he became bishop of Lincoln, which enabled him to keep the university under his purview and to encourage the studies he had launched. Grosseteste's knowledge of Greek enabled him to participate in the translation of Aristotelian science and he also translated Aristotle's ethics and some of the Greek church fathers. While this translation program shows his desire to connect theology and values with science, Grosseteste did not seek to synthesize everything he knew. He was content with a Neoplatonically based theology derived largely from Augustine and did not try to Aristotelianize Christianity. His interest in Aristotle was primarily scientific. Still, his view that divine illumination is needed for every act of human intellection limits Grosseteste's acceptance of Aristotle's epistemology. Simultaneously, he goes beyond Aristotelian science by investigating phenomena that can be measured mathematically as well as tested empirically.

These tastes pointed Grosseteste toward phenomena he could manipulate and control in a laboratory setting. He studied the rainbow and concluded that it is caused by the refraction of light through a cloud composed of drops of water acting as lenses. This conclusion derived from experiments with spherical lenses. Also typical of Grosseteste's interest in optical phenomena susceptible of measurement was his analysis of double refraction, basic to the understanding of the function of a burning glass. Grosseteste measured the refraction of light rays as they enter a spherical or convex lens and also as they exit. He found that the angle of refraction of the exiting rays was much more acute, producing the concentration of heat at their focal point that ignites tinder. Grosseteste combines a fascination with the explanation of natural phenomena as knowledge valuable in itself with a concern for the technological applications of science. His work with lenses made him the first Latin author to realize that they could magnify objects and correct deficiencies in human eyesight. His breakthrough later led to the invention of the telescope and, by the end of his century, eyeglasses.

In the area of scientific methodology, Grosseteste can be described as simultaneously Aristotelian, para-Aristotelian, and post-Aristotelian. He agrees with Aristotle that there are four causes involved in natural phenomena, the material and formal causes constituting substances, the final cause, and the efficient cause. He also agrees that scientists begin with empirical observation, collecting sense data and using inductive logic to discover the essential natures of substances and the causes of effects. Grosseteste also thinks, with Aristotle, that scientists then reverse the process as a means of cross-checking their conclusions using deductive logic, analyzing whether effects do follow from causes and enabling them to predict similar outcomes in similar situations. But Grosseteste has qualifications of his own that he adds to Aristotle's scientific method. The first is the controlled experiment. Although he thinks that the combination of inductive and deductive logic should confirm the accuracy of scientific conclusions, the controlled experiment provides greater certitude. Ideally, experiments should involve data that can be measured, quantified, and assessed mathematically as well as observed empirically, as was the case with his lenses. The controlled experiment is a genuine innovation. At the same time, the fact that many natural phenomena cannot be manipulated and measured in a laboratory setting limits its applicability, in Grosseteste's view, and forces us to acknowledge that many scientific conclusions regarded by Aristotle as fully certain lack the complete certitude uniquely afforded by mathematical demonstrations.

Grosseteste's insistence on this point makes normative mathematically measurable scientific proofs more rigorous than Aristotle's, while it denies that Aristotle's demonstrative syllogisms, whose terms and conclusions refer to empirically verifiable facts, yield the scientific certitude that Aristotle claims for them. Another limit Grosseteste places on the certitude of conclusions based purely on Aristotle's methodology stems from the variety of causes at work in phenomenal events. Of the Aristotelian four causes, some may be involved to a greater, others to a lesser, degree. Also, not all these causes may be fully knowable, and other, instrumental or intermediary causes, of which we are unaware, may also play a role. Some of these causes may not be amenable to controlled experiments. And so, Grosseteste concludes, scientific explanations in many areas must be regarded as merely probable, but not absolutely certain.

In Grosseteste we meet a genuinely creative scientist, in both his methodology and his actual discoveries. He is the first scientific thinker in any of the sister medieval societies to see that the Aristotelian causal system can limit what we know with certitude about natural events. His insistence that the logic we join to observation must have the rigor of mathematics undergirds his critique of Aristotle's demonstrative logic as insufficient. He deliberately confines himself to the study of phenomena that meet his own stringent criteria. Still, Grosseteste leaves unanswered the question of how the replicability of controlled experiments, which presupposes the accessibility of scientific knowledge to anyone, squares with his illuminationist epistemology, which would limit scientific knowledge to theists.

Both the mathematization of science and the notion that it should be studied as part of a complex of knowledge that includes theology and ethics were important legacies Grosseteste left to his Oxford followers. His most immediate disciple was Roger Bacon. Bacon also had a Parisian stage in his career (1240–7), being the first master to lecture on Aristotle after the initial relaxation of the ban on Aristotelian studies there. Bacon followed Grosseteste in studying theology as well as science, continuing in the same conservative Neoplatonic-Christian vein as his master. In addition to criticizing the Aristotelianizing of theology, he swam against the current by objecting to the commentary on Peter Lombard's *Sentences* as a way to teach theology. Instead, he urged the study of the Bible in its original languages. These views led contemporaries to regard Bacon as something of a crank. His entry into the Franciscan order in 1257 after he was already an established master may have reflected a desire for institutional support for his research. For, as a scientist, he continued Grosseteste's investigation of optics in a laboratory setting, and his experiments were expensive. Bacon established the focal lengths of various kinds of lenses and mirrors and concluded, correctly, that much could be learned about the physiology of the human eye by dissecting the eyes of cattle and pigs. He also offered some new hypotheses regarding light: the idea that the sun's rays coming to earth can be treated as parallel lines and the idea that the speed of light, although enormous, is finite. Like Grosseteste, Bacon assimilates natural science to mathematics. But he assimilates more of it to mathematics and thus enlarges the range of phenomena we can know with certitude.

Bacon's unpopular theological views and his dissatisfaction with the level of funding his order provided led him to seek patronage from a cardinal and to defy a rule the Franciscans instituted in 1260 requiring that works by members of the order be approved by their superiors before publication. The Franciscans prevented Bacon's writings from reaching his would-be patron, causing an uproar that led to his official censure by his confrères in 1277. This event limited Bacon's subsequent mobility but not his research and writing. His falling-out with his order is paradoxical. For Bacon shared, and expanded, Grosseteste's notion that the moral and theological ends of scientific study are important and that science should be put to the service of mankind and the glorification of God, an attitude compatible with the friars' view that the purpose of knowledge is service.

In the following century, Grosseteste's influence is visible mainly in the group of scientists at Merton College collectively called the 'Oxford calculators.' Leading members of this group were Richard Swineshead (*fl.* 1344–54), John Dumbleton (*fl.* 1331–49), and William of Heytsbury (*c.* 1313–72) and the movement was in its heyday between 1325 and 1350. They too were interested in the mathematization of science but they took this theme in a different direction, the analysis of qualities that inhere in beings and the analysis of motion, which was also receiving sustained attention at Paris and Padua. The very idea of treating qualities quantitatively was a move away from Aristotle, who held that quality and quantity are essentially different. One thing these thinkers shared, whatever their university, was a lack of interest in connecting theology with science and a disinclination to study phenomena testable in laboratory conditions. Rather, they viewed scientific speculation as pure theory. The calculators' main goal was to recast the logic in which propositions concerning qualities and motion are expressed into mathematical formulae. In this sense, their main contribution lay in pushing forward the project of making mathematics, and not Aristotelian logic, the language of science.

Their contemporaries who theorized on the physics of local motion took issue with the substance of Aristotle's explanations as well as with his logic. What attracted them to this subject was Aristotle's failure to describe phenomena as they observably occur. They were also informed by the rejection of Aristotelian multiple causation. Wielding Ockham's razor, they thought that the only cause of motion they needed to explain was the efficient cause. The ultimate reasons for motion and its role in actualizing a moving body's potentialities they found either irrelevant, unknowable, or both. This position, as much a departure from Grosseteste and Bacon as from Aristotle, derives from Ockham's epistemology and its limitation of scientific thought to subjects yielding secure or likely conclusions. Only one of the physical theorists of the fourteenth century, Thomas Bradwardine (d. 1399), also wrote theology, and it does not overlap with his science. John Buridan and Nicholas Oresme (*c.* 1320–82), the other leading physical theorists, did not.

In studying the local motion of bodies on earth, the aim of these theorists was to criticize Aristotle's explanation of their behavior and to substitute their own account. Representing the ancient consensus view, Aristotle held that each of the four elements has an innate density. If they existed in a pure state, earth, the heaviest, would be at the center of the universe, surrounded by water, air, and fire. Since substances usually combine two or more elements in their material composition, the predominant element determines how they move, unless deflected by an unnatural force. Heavier bodies move downward, toward the earth; lighter bodies move upward, away from the earth. Another central Aristotelian premise is that motion is what needs explaining. The state of rest is an ideal or normative state, not requiring explanation. Inertia applies only to rest. Left to their own devices or when set in motion by an external force, bodies move because of their desire to return to their natural homes in the universe. If we hold a stone, predominantly made up of earth, and release it, it will descend to earth in a straight line. If we throw the stone instead of dropping it, it will remain in the air for a time and then descend to earth in a straight line. The unnatural extension of its trajectory after leaving the thrower's hand is caused by the intervention of the thrower's action. But, once the effect of that unnatural intervention subsides, the stone will seek its natural home, moving downward to the earth. Assuming that the resistance of the medium through which the stone moves remains constant, the speed of the stone, in Aristotle's account, depends on how much force the thrower exerts on it. Given a constant motive force through a constant medium over a constant length of time, the stone will move at a constant velocity. It will neither accelerate nor decelerate unless the resistance of the medium changes, the other factors remaining constant.

Now, Aristotle did notice that falling bodies accelerate as they fall. He explained this anomaly by invoking the qualitative understanding of matter connected to the theory that elements have natural homes and are eager to return to them. The stone, thus, accelerates as it nears the earth because it is happy to arrive at its natural home, as a horse or a dog would be. This 'psychologizing' of matter reflects the belief that elements act in accordance with their innate dispositions.

The fourteenth-century physicists criticized two aspects of this Aristotelian theory, the shape of the trajectory described by a projectile in motion and Aristotle's explanation for its acceleration. First, they noted, Aristotle had been just plain wrong in stating that, once the propulsive force becomes inactive, the projectile sinks to the earth in a straight line. Observation shows that the projectile forms an arc, not a straight line. Why does the stone continue to move in the air after we have thrown it and why does it return to earth gradually, in an arc-shaped trajectory? In place of Aristotle's theory, they propose the theory of impetus. They view impetus as a new quality, a form of energy acquired by the stone after it leaves the thrower's hand. This impetus gives the stone additional thrust after it has been thrown. But, the stone's acquired impetus eventually wears off, and it wears off gradually. This is why the stone descends to earth in an arc, not in a straight line. The fourteenth-century physicists also substitute the theory of accidental gravity for Aristotle's explanation of the acceleration of falling bodies. They see accidental gravity, like impetus, as a quality added to the stone in the course of its motion. It provides additional weight that increases as the stone moves. Combined with the stone's original weight, this added weight creates a constantly increasing heaviness, causing the stone to fall to earth at a constant rate of acceleration.

These new physical theories did solve certain problems not soluble in Aristotelian physics. But while they criticize Aristotle's physics of local motion, they share some of his physical assumptions. Like Aristotle, the impetus theorists think that bodies naturally move in a straight line and that curved motion is somehow unnatural and requires explanation. Like Aristotle, they do not conceive of inertia as applying to bodies in motion as well as to bodies at rest. Like Aristotle, they have a qualitative conception of matter. For them, impetus and accidental gravity are qualities, like heat and sound, that can be added to a body and that then wear off, as with a poker heated in a fire that cools when removed from the fire or a bell that starts reverberating when struck and eventually stops reverberating. These theorists do not go as far as Ockham in obliterating the difference between the matter and motion of bodies on earth and the matter and motion of heavenly bodies. They content themselves with the notion that the heavenly bodies have an impetus that never wears off. At the same time, Ockham must be viewed as the source of their basic assumptions and agenda. The work of these physical theorists is as unthinkable without him as is that of the calculators without Grosseteste and Bacon.

The increasing willingness to criticize Aristotle in many other quarters of high and late medieval scholasticism had further effects on scientific thought, especially astronomy and geography. In the background were two conditions. First, even with the naked eye as one's sole instrument, the ancient astronomy summarized by Aristotle and illustrated in Dante's *Paradiso* did not square with astronomical phenomena actually observed. Second, medieval logicians and theologians had made widely thinkable the concept of possible worlds, different from ours, and had made rigorous thinking about counterfactuals possible. The concept of possible worlds, existing simultaneously with ours, had inspired some proponents of this corollary of divine omnipotence to reject the widely held ancient view of the universe as finite. Empty space must exist, they reasoned. The universe must be unbounded, since there must be a void beyond our world to accommodate the other, possible worlds that may exist concurrently. The combination of the discrepancies between Aristotelian astronomical theory and astronomical occurrences led late medieval astronomers not only to envision an infinite universe unlike Aristotle's but also to take Ptolemy's effort to correct Aristotelian astronomy more seriously than had their Muslim predecessors. Starting with Bacon in the 1260s, they refined the system of epicycles attached to the planetary orbits much further. And the revisions of ancient geography that made the discovery of the Americas conceivable in the late fifteenth century were in place in the work of the Parisian scholastic Pierre d'Ailly (1350–1420).

In this connection, it is worth keeping in mind that medieval learned opinion in the field of astronomy, from the time of Martianus Capella onward, had cut its teeth on Ptolemy, well before the Aristotelian alternative became available. In the high Middle Ages, the fact that Ptolemaic astronomy approached its subject mathematically enhanced its appeal, over Aristotelian astronomy, for scientific thinkers eager to mathematize their subject. The Ptolemaic system, with its added epicycles, was able to 'save the phenomena' better than Aristotelian astronomy could, making it easier to predict with accuracy the changes in the movements of heavenly bodies. It thus recommended itself to thinkers of an empirical bent as well.

As for geography, medieval thinkers from the beginning of the period held that the earth was spherical. By the high Middle Ages another consensus view was that there were three continents, Europe, Asia, and Africa, separated by oceans. Geographers divided the world into five climatic zones. The two antipodes at the Arctic and Antarctic were held to house frigid zones; immediately adjacent to them were two temperate zones; while a torrid zone was located at the equator. Europe was viewed as lying in the northern temperate zone. By the fourteenth century, some scientific thinkers, such as Buridan and Oresme, had added the view that the earth rotates on its axis. In thinking about medieval geography, it is worth noting that scholastic texts provide the best sources of information, not maps. Medieval cartographers were not interested in displaying the period's geographical knowledge with scientific precision or to scale. Maps, for them, had a didactic and spiritual value; they placed Jerusalem at the center of the earth's surface because of its perceived spiritual centrality.

In considering the ways in which medieval scientists came to criticize the Aristotelian legacy, in the name of alternative classical theories or in the light of their own discoveries and criteria, we cannot say that late medieval scientists achieved a paradigm shift as massive as the one associated with the scientific revolution of the seventeenth century. What these developments do indicate is that the willingness to look critically at foundation documents and received authorities and to reject their basic assumptions and conclusions if they failed to square with observable facts or more rigorous standards of proof is a key aspect of high medieval science, of a piece with the scientists' scholastic education. Habits of mind first nurtured in other parts of the academy had an important effect in creating a climate of opinion in the scientific community that made it possible for scientists to do more than make discoveries along the lines of their Muslim and Greek predecessors. In addition to doing so, they questioned fundamental axioms and offered alternative theories. The continuities that may be seen between particular quarters of the high and late medieval scientific enterprise and the new science of the seventeenth century are, ultimately, less central in making it a foundation of the western intellectual tradition than the ability of medieval scientists to compass a world order as well as an account of particular phenomena different from those of the ancients.

CHAPTER 25

Economic Theory:
Poverty, the Just Price, and Usury

The thinkers contributing to economic theory in the Middle Ages were primarily theologians and canonists. Patristic thought on the subject was reinforced between the twelfth and fourteenth centuries by arguments derived from Roman law and Aristotelian philosophy. The chief hallmark of medieval economic theory is that it is framed in essentially ethical terms. The theorists' concern is the correct moral use of wealth and the correct moral attitude to take to persons lacking it. Theologians participating in this enterprise were influential only to the extent that their arguments persuaded others and motivated their behavior. Canonists had a wider sphere of influence. The legislation of the church, which they codified and commented on, provided the rules and precedents used by judges in ecclesiastical courts. The views of canonists did shape the administration of justice in these courts, but church courts were typically limited in their jurisdiction to clerical personnel and matters like the sacraments. Also, unlike secular courts, they could not invoke political sanctions on persons they convicted. The penalties they imposed were spiritual, the most serious being excommunication. In the area of economic theory, secular jurisprudence was rarely informed by canon law. Thus, although canonists and theologians might agree consistently on certain economic theories, their views often had little or no impact on the policies of secular governments or the attitudes of medieval Christians. The major subdivisions of economic theory differ sharply in their effect on medieval behavior patterns, indicating that Christians at that time felt free to decide what to accept and what to reject in the economic teachings of church leaders.

Poverty

Theorists on poor law considered what attitude should be taken toward poverty and poor people and how the poor should be treated. A striking feature of medieval views of poverty is that, despite the positive revaluation of work found above all in Benedictine monasticism, the work ethic did not entail the glorification of wealth or the idea that poverty is a sign of vice. Work, to be sure, was praised by monastic writers as a source of moral discipline, breeding humility in the individual and community spirit. A means of supporting the abbey and of serving its extra-mural neighbors with its surplus, work was also seen as an offering to God and a form of prayer. At the same time, throughout the Middle Ages, theologians and canonists agreed with monastic writers that poverty can have a positive moral value. What determines whether it has this value is whether poverty is embraced voluntarily. Voluntary poverty was one of the central vows taken by monks and nuns and the friars gave it still more emphasis as an aspect of the imitation of Christ. All agreed that the value of voluntary poverty is that it frees those embracing it from worldly cares, the better to serve God and neighbor. On the other hand, when poverty is involuntary, either because one is born into that state or because of economic reverses, poverty is neither a virtue nor a vice but a misfortune. All medieval thinkers concurred that it is wrong to punish an involuntarily poor person on either count. The appropriate moral response is to help the poor, making special provisions for them not extended to others.

Particularly with the revival of canon law launched by Gratian (*fl.* 1130–40), whose *Decretum* played a role in the education of university canonists analogous to that of Peter Lombard's *Sentences* in theology, canonists devoted much attention to poor relief, especially in the courtroom. They took sharp issue here with Roman law, which discriminated between rich and poor, giving harsher sentences to the latter for the same crimes and disadvantaging them in litigation. In contrast, the canonists made a point of declaring litigants equal before the law in church courts, regardless of wealth. While granting the poor equal rights, they also sought to mitigate practical disadvantages the poor might suffer in court. The views of canonists were consistent here, and they were reinforced by papal edicts. Eugenius III (ruled 1145–53), for instance, decreed that church courts would not subpoena the poor as witnesses if it was financially burdensome for them to appear in person. In that event, the court would authorize someone to go to the witnesses and receive their testimony, presenting it in court for them, to save them the cost of the trip and the loss of wages. Thirteenth-century canonists add that the poor could be excused from appearing in person if they had once been rich but had lost their wealth through misfortune, to spare them embarrassment. In the fourteenth century, canonists refined this doctrine, now proposing that the court should bear the expense of bringing witnesses whom a poor litigant could not afford to bring to testify on his behalf. Another source of legal relief extended to the poor by canon law was the rule, instituted by Pope Honorius III (before 1160–1227), that litigants unable to pay for legal counsel would be provided with an attorney at the court's expense.

These rules applied only to ecclesiastical courts. Secular courts were not sensitive to the needs of the poor and there is little sign of canonical influence on their practice, whether their jurisprudence was based on Roman, feudal, or some other local system of law. For secular governments, the poor were 'invisible men.' In jurisdictions with representative assemblies, the poor did not have the vote. If they were convicted of crimes, it was difficult to extract judicial fines from them. Poor people naturally preferred to plead their cases in church courts, if they could, since they alone felt a responsibility to protect the interests of a class of people, 'wretched persons,' that included the poor along with widows and orphans. With respect to the wretched, after some controversy, the church and secular governments agreed to distinguish between widows and orphans wealthy enough to hire counsel to defend their own interests and persons really in need. The former were to plead their cases in secular courts but had recourse to appellate justice in church courts if they were unsatisfied with the first verdict. The genuinely poor could plead immediately in church courts. This was the sole concession made by secular jurisprudence to canonical theories on the legal rights of the poor. The evidence from canonical jurisprudence in practice indicates that church courts did apply the canonists' theories and rules to a great extent.

The second major topic theorists addressed under the heading of poor law was property rights and the duty of charity. This subject drew considerable discussion owing to the conflicting principles found in the Bible, in Roman law, in the church fathers, and in high medieval political institutions. The most important Latin church father to treat property rights in any detail was Augustine. His position became standard, dominating early medieval theory on the issue. Gratian reprises Augustine, agreeing that all things were held in common in Eden. Private property is a consequence of original sin, since postlapsarian mankind, subject to the vice of greed, finds it difficult if not impossible to function without mine and thine. The sharing of all things is an ideal for which we should strive, and which is institutionalized, in the post-apostolic age, in monasticism, as the more perfect way. Since most people are not called to live the monastic life and are not given the divine grace needed to do so, private property rights are plausible and practical. Gratian fuses Augustine's doctrine of original sin, the idea of a fall from a golden age in classical thought, and property rights as they existed both in the Roman law of Augustine's time and in the secular legal systems of his own. Both thinkers agree that private property is legitimate given our fallen state and what we can reasonably expect about human behavior. But neither sees private property as an ideal situation or a natural right reflecting normative human nature. Rather, it is a concession to human weakness that should be tolerated even as we seek to transcend it. This position found no dissenters up until Gratian's day, whether from canonists, scholastic theologians, or monastic writers.

As we move beyond Gratian into the later twelfth and thirteenth centuries, both canonists and theologians combine Augustine's teaching with other ideas, developing the notion that people have the right to own and enjoy their own property, up to what they need to support themselves and their dependants and up to what is fitting to their social status. But the right to private property, they agree, is not absolute. It requires justification and it is conditional. Even the strongest proponents of private property rights limit them in some way. Some thinkers, influenced by Aristotle directly or by way of Cicero, argue that private property is a natural right possessed by all rational human beings as such. Still, its use is limited by the requirements of the common good and of needy individuals. Superfluous wealth, they insist, should be given to the needy. This is a personal and social duty demanded by justice, for the well-being of the needy and for the good of society as a whole. Some proponents of the natural law position, like Aquinas, add a psychological rationale for private property. People, he argues, are more likely to take good care of their own property than of property belonging to everyone. Even the use of wealth that is not superfluous came under the judgment of some economic theorists, reflecting the influence of secular political institutions like feudalism. In feudal tenure, property is not held outright but conditionally, according to the contract binding lord and vassal. If the vassal fails to meet his contractual obligations, he risks legal forfeiture of his property. Even in the case of property owned outright, the theorists stress that the owner will always be called to account for his stewardship morally. Although theorists continue to discuss these positions in increasingly juridical language, the fact remains that they are describing moral rights and duties that are enforceable only by moral suasion. No form of action existed in church courts through which a person could be tried and penalized for failing to give superfluous wealth to the poor.

Still, both canonists and theologians treat in detail the moral obligations of charity, analyzing its characteristics and effects on donor and recipient alike. They emphasize the importance of correct moral intention on the donor's part as well as the giving of alms with discretion, so as to benefit the recipient as much as possible without embarrassment. The prevailing scheme for this analysis was provided by Peter Lombard and adopted by Aquinas. It stresses both correct intention and its issue in appropriate action. This topic drew an impressive amount of analysis. The *Ordinary Gloss* (*c.* 1250), the legal compendium which replaced Gratian's *Decretum* as the standard text for educating canonists in its century and after, states that it is sinful to give alms to a beggar out of motives of vanity, the desire to gain praise, or to rid oneself of his importuning. The canonists also analyze the moral position of recipients of charity. Recipients, they argue, play a positive moral role because they help donors practice the virtues of charity and justice. Accepting help graciously also enables recipients to develop the virtue of humility.

The final topic taken up by theorists on poverty was whom to aid and in what order of priority. While some twelfth-century scholastics make need the global index of priority, the Lombard states what became the consensus view. One's first responsibility is to one's parents. Next come children, then spouses, then other relatives, then members of one's household, then fellow citizens, and finally strangers. Among strangers, people needy because of age or illness head the list, followed by those otherwise poor through no fault of their own. As between two people equally needy, one a Christian and the other not, the Christian comes first. Other things being equal with respect to strangers, the degree of need is determinative. The canonists add another category of person who, they think, should not receive alms, the able-bodied beggar, poor because he is idle out of laziness. Although medieval thinkers do not regard poverty as such as vicious, they do see willful idleness as a vice. In this connection it is worth noting that unemployment was not a real problem in the Middle Ages. Typically, jobs were available to people seeking work. The canonists therefore assume that people capable of working who remain idle do so deliberately. Medieval economic theorists also assume that poor people and beggars who might capitalize on other people's charity or misuse alms are the exception, not the rule. In doubtful cases, they think it better to err on the side of generosity.

Given that the church had no way of enforcing these principles, to what extent were they implemented in practice by medieval Christians? Here, in contrast with the indifference of secular governments to canonical theories of the rights of the poor in court, there is considerable evidence to show that the teaching of canonists and theologians on poor relief found a hearing and informed medieval consciences and activities. This evidence is found in wills, guild records, donation and endowment charters, the enactments of urban governments, royal and ducal statutes, and episcopal registers. A wide range of entities from individual donors and testators to religious confraternities and guilds to urban administrations, dioceses, regional, and national governments felt a duty to provide for the needy and did so with direct gifts, appropriations, and bequests to individuals, the founding and support of hospitals, leprosaria, orphanages, homes for the rehabilitation of former prostitutes, schools and colleges, and old age homes, assisting members of their own groups and others. Sometimes charitable donations were funneled through religious orders that staffed institutions of these kinds. Increasing laicization of the administration of poor relief marks the later medieval centuries. If the evidence for charitable activities is widespread, it is also uneven. The best documentation comes from cities; we know far less about the alleviation of rural poverty. Also, strong evidence of charitable activity can be countered with evidence of persistent and endemic poverty on the one hand and conspicuous consumption and waste on the other. In the fourteenth century, earlier strategies for poor relief seemed to work less well, as the needs triggered by plague, famine, and massive economic depression increased dramatically. The assertion of secular control reflects the fact that governments alone had the resources to deal with these problems, which were often combined with vagrancy and population movements. Another reason for that outcome, which parallels the desire of lay people to take over the organization of their own devotional lives and forms of literary expression in the later Middle Ages, is that poor law theorizing was far less vigorous and imaginative in the fourteenth century than it had been earlier. The theorists seem to have run out of ideas for addressing the escalating needs brought on by current crises.

The Just Price

The theory of the just price is often regarded as a typically medieval economic concept. But the notion of the just price and the term itself derive from Roman law, perpetuated in the early Middle Ages by Carolingian legislation. The Roman-Carolingian position informed theory on this topic until the legal and Aristotelian revivals of the twelfth and thirteenth centuries gave scholastics new ways of approaching it.

According to the Romans and Carolingians, goods and services do not have an objective or intrinsic value. Their value is subjective, reflecting the price sellers are willing to accept and buyers are willing to pay. The just price is the market price actually asked and paid. It indicates agreement between buyer and seller as to what a fair price is. In coming to their common estimation of what commodities are worth, they take account of market factors like supply and demand. The only shift in emphasis between the Roman and Carolingian conceptions of the just price is that Roman law stresses the convergence of the opinions of buyer and seller as a condition making the sale legally binding, while the Carolingians emphasize the market price definition as a way of determining the basis on which price levels should be set.

The high medieval changes in just price theory reflect the revived study of Roman law, the availability of Aristotle, and the speculation on other economic issues engaged in by just price theorists. A new stress on human need is added to the earlier conditions defining the just price. Albert the Great and Aquinas use Aristotle's *Nicomachean Ethics* as the basis for their positions; as Aquinas puts it, '[The] one standard which truly measures all things is demand. This includes all commutable things inasmuch as everything has reference to human need.'[1] This conclusion reinforces the earlier view that commodities do not have objective value. The main force of the principle enunciated by Aquinas is to emphasize demand over supply as a price determinant. Thirteenth-century theorists do continue to take supply into account, agreeing that the just price of strawberries should be higher in January than it is in June. But, for them, demand becomes the primary factor. Human wants and needs should determine what things cost. At the same time, the theorists agree that any just market price must satisfy seller and buyer alike.

A final shift in just price theory marks the fourteenth and fifteenth centuries. At that time, all scholastics writing on this topic include the idea that the seller has a right to set a price that enables him to pay for his costs and labor and that gives him a reasonable profit, so that he can provide for himself and his family. This principle acknowledges the subjective needs of the producer or seller, making them as important as the subjective needs of the consumer. Theorists in the later Middle Ages continue to think that, despite the conflicting interests of producers and consumers, the market will sort things out and create a consensus on the just price. They staunchly condemn any artificial manipulation of the market.

As to the influence of just price theory on economic attitudes visible in practice, it compares more with the secular courts' indifference to canonical teachings on the legal rights of the poor than with the charitable behavior of medieval Christians. All jurisdictions in medieval Europe with the legal authority to do so fixed prices and regulated many other aspects of economic life, especially in the fourteenth century, when governmental reactions to the current depression followed the lead taken centuries earlier by guilds and urban governments. Records of guilds and towns, the richest sources for price controls both before and during the fourteenth century, show the desire of these agencies to balance the interests of producers and consumers well before economic theorists started to consider the topic. The same records also reveal a far less optimistic view of the ability of the marketplace to generate consensus on the just price by itself. For they apply vigorous controls on prices. The just price, then, was a *de facto* reality in the minds of guild and urban legislators, and later of other governments, but they conceived of it as a means of guarding and generating prosperity within their own corporate communities as a whole. These legislators share with the just price theorists the idea that commodities do not have an objective value. But in place of the subjective values of buyers and sellers, and of them alone, in a free-floating context of supply and demand, they determined a conventional value, agreed on by political authorities as the one best for the community at large, and enforced that value by law.

Usury

Like the just price, usury theory spells 'Middle Ages' in common parlance. Yet, the roots of the theory are likewise pre-medieval. And, in comparison with other aspects of medieval economic thought, usury theory inspired both the greatest unanimity among theorists and the greatest disparity between theoretical teachings and the attitudes and behavior of medieval people. Usury is the profit obtained from interest on a loan. With one exception, an exception who proves the rule, all medieval thinkers regard usury as sinful. The chief authority on which they rest their case is the biblical condemnation of usury. Between the fourth and sixth centuries, a number of theologians and church councils repeat the point, although without explaining why they think usury is intrinsically evil. This was the situation inherited by Gratian, the first thinker to give extended attention to usury. His main contribution was to sum up earlier condemnations, including the recent prohibition of usury by the Second Lateran council (1139), and to reopen discussion on the subject.

Gratian's work was the point of departure for canonical usury theorists for the next century. They were confronted by the discrepancies between two authoritative traditions. The Christian tradition, from the Bible onward, opposed usury. But Roman law permitted the lending of money at interest. After essaying various intellectual contortions designed to square these opposing positions, canonists by the early thirteenth century decided to abandon that effort and split into two groups, the rigorists and the moderates. The rigorists asserted the primacy of religious authority over Roman law, maintaining that usury is a sin whatever the *Corpus of Civil Law* says. The moderates, reasoning that Justinian was a Christian emperor, sought to mitigate the sinfulness of usury, invoking a lesser-of-the-two-evils argument. It is permissible to lend money at interest, they hold, if the borrower might otherwise perish.

As we move deeper into the thirteenth century, theologians also enter the conversation, treating usury under the heading of moral theology. They generally adhere to the rigorist position, which they strengthen considerably. Most canonists, at this point, support the moderate line. The refinement and elaboration of the examples usury theorists cite in developing their arguments attest to the growing sophistication of European economic life and the fact that no one active in it was paying attention to ecclesiastical strictures against usury. Another thirteenth-century trend is the incorporation of ideas from Roman law and Aristotelian philosophy into the subject, along with natural law theory. Rigorists use these ideas to provide rational support for their religious objections to usury. Another shift is the tendency of rigorists to discuss usury under the rubric of justice, while moderates place it under the rubric of charity. This choice reflects their respective orientations. For, it was held, sins against charity can be forgiven if the penitent has the sincere intention of abandoning sin. But sins against justice can be forgiven only if the penitent also makes restitution. Viewing usury as a sin against justice thus gives more teeth to anti-usury teaching.

The single most influential usury theorist, not only in his own century but for the rest of the Middle Ages, was Aquinas. His authority on this subject was massive, swamping the cause of the moderate canonists and convincing other scholastics however opposed they might be to Thomism in other respects. Aquinas is a rigorist who calls on natural law, Roman law, and Aristotle alike, using them as sources for arguments against a practice which neither Roman law nor Aristotle found problematic. Aquinas on usury is thus a good example of the medieval recycling of authorities to achieve the desired conclusions. As Aristotle says, he notes, all things have final causes. For its part, money is not an end but a means to the end of securing the goods we need. Usurers, Aquinas argues, confuse ends and means. They make money for the sake of making money. He thus enlists Aristotelian teleology as a weapon against the profit motive.

Aquinas has two other arguments against usury based on natural law theory, one invoking Aristotle and the other Roman law. By nature, he asserts, money bears no fruit. Its function is to measure the fruits derived from economic activity. In making money out of money, usurers thus commit a crime against nature. Money, moreover, is a substance, possessing matter and form. The fluctuations of the economy and the correlative changes in the purchasing power of money are material. The formal attribute of money is the face value stamped on coins. Now, if money itself were sold, Aquinas continues, its formal character, which is its changeless, essential, and intelligible principle, would be submerged into its material character, since its price would fluctuate along with the market. This outcome would annihilate money as a substance. Money, he concludes, is a non-vendible commodity, the measure of things sold but not saleable itself. This argument, a highly original one, is also a triumph of Aristotelian metaphysics over economic reality. Aquinas offers a final argument based on the idea that usury conflicts with the nature of money. In it he calls on a Roman legal distinction between goods consumptible in use and goods not consumptible in use. Payment in kind is an example of goods consumptible in use. After the goods are eaten or used their value is no longer available to the payee. A plot of land on which crops are grown is a good not consumptible in use. The owner can profit, repeatedly, from the crops grown on the land without diminishing the land's value. With this distinction in place, Aquinas states that money is a form of goods consumptible in use. He does not demonstrate this claim but merely asserts it, an assertion only one later medieval thinker on usury challenged. Since money is consumptible in use, the use of money cannot be distinguished logically from the substance of money. Therefore, a usurer who loans both money and the use of money and receives back the money loaned and a fee for its use is guilty of selling the same thing twice, the money and its use. He sins against natural justice. Like Aquinas' other arguments, this one is grounded on the idea that money by nature bears no fruit.

Strange as these arguments would have sounded to Aristotle and the Roman lawyers, they convinced all usury theorists for the next two centuries except Duns Scotus. Scotus' rejection of the Thomistic equation of money with its use cut no ice. It was, and was perceived to be, a polemical position taken to defend the conventual Franciscans' claim that it is acceptable to use money so long as one does not own it. Analyses of usury grow ever more detailed in the fourteenth and fifteenth centuries. They all reach the same anti-usury conclusions, although there are shades of opinion on technical details. This pattern continued until the late fifteenth and early sixteenth centuries, when the revisionism of some scholastic theorists, who at last realized that their confrères had been talking to nobody but each other for centuries, was made official by papal mandate.

The history of the enforcement of the canonical rules against usury shows that usury was practiced with impunity by everyone active in the high medieval economy, from the popes and their bankers on down, despite the remarkably strong consensus of thinkers against its acceptability. The severity of canonical penalties against usurers was no deterrent and the efforts of church leaders to persuade or exhort secular authorities to penalize it were unavailing. Indeed, if Christians had followed the teachings of their ecclesiastical leaders in this area, Europe would not have developed into a commercial society with many features of incipient capitalism in place by the end of the period. Both usury theory and the other areas of economic thought considered in this chapter highlight the gaps between theory and practice in medieval Christendom, the areas where theological trickle-down did not occur, and the selectivity and independence of medieval people in deciding which authorities to take seriously and which to set aside as irrelevant to an economy in which bank loans were used as venture capital that expanded wealth and employment opportunities. This subject shows the carry-over to economic theory of habits of mind first developed in other areas of scholasticism. It also shows that lay Christians shared the critical outlook of the academicians and that they applied it for their own ends, which frequently differed from those of the theorists. Medieval economic theory, and its impact or lack of impact on economic practice, thus includes both markers of medieval values and sensibilities that differ from those of later ages and some clear points of continuity with them.

CHAPTER 26

Political Theory: Regnum and Sacerdotum, Conciliarism, and Feudal Monarchy

The three major issues in medieval political theory addressed in this chapter have two things in common with each other and with economic theory. In all cases, they reflect the legacy of scholasticism, applying ideas produced by the revival of legal, philosophical, and, in one case, scientific study to political questions. They also involve responses to actual events, enabling us to track beliefs and tolerances in political behavior as well as in theory. Each area of political thought also contains ideas specific to medieval thought that do not survive the period, or, if they do, not for long; ideas already abandoned by the period's close; and ideas carried over into early modern thought, to receive resolution, when they do, only in the sixteenth or seventeenth century. We begin with church–state relations, the topic drawing the most attention from political theorists. Assumptions supporting that subject also informed conciliar theory. And, while feudal monarchy was not the only political system governing medieval Europeans and while its post-medieval outcomes varied in different countries, it joins the other topics in this chapter in receiving the impress of scholasticism and in moving political theory from an international to a national stage.

Regnum and Sacerdotum

In thinking about what we would call church and state, medieval political theorists do not see themselves considering institutions that are fundamentally distinct. They regard the European political and religious community as a single international Christian commonwealth with two complementary kinds of ruler, ecclesiastical and secular. All secular rulers claimed to rule by divine right, whatever other sanctions they might invoke. They held themselves responsible for the religious life of their people. Ecclesiastical rulers, after the creation of the papal states and the feudalization and manorialization of bishops, abbots, and abbesses, had rights and duties in secular politics. Thus, the functions as well as the sanctions empowering spiritual and temporal rulers overlapped, a fact impossible to ignore for theorists treating their appropriate relations. For most of the Middle Ages, debate centered on the relations of popes and Holy Roman emperors, seen as the highest officials in their respective subdivisions of the international Christian commonwealth. Starting in the thirteenth century, and broadening in the fourteenth, the relations between popes and the rulers of national or regional monarchies joined the discussion. This development reflects the shift of the political center of gravity away from the German empire toward its own constituent principalities in central Europe and to other national monarchies, above all France. Still, the bulk of the political theory, even in the later Middle Ages, centered on papal–imperial relations, with theorists scholasticizing arguments first articulated in other terms in the early Middle Ages.

While these issues were controversial, there were assumptions shared by all involved. First, and despite the evidence that could be cited to the contrary, was the belief that the Christian commonwealth existed and that it defined European civilization. The second assumption was that its secular and religious leaders had positive and necessary functions. However much high papalists might advocate theocracy, they never regarded the office of king or emperor as expendable and never urged the church to govern civil society. And, however Caesaropapistic emperors and kings might be, they always sought coronation from the appropriate prelate and they did not seek to exercise the clergy's sacerdotal functions.

The basic source for this perceived complementarity of church and state was Augustine's *City of God*. Augustine sees Christian society as having both physical and spiritual needs and as thus requiring secular and ecclesiastical institutions to minister to them. The love of God that distinguishes the city of God from the city of man naturally expresses itself in these two kinds of institution, although neither of them, in this life, can be identified fully with the city of God. Also, although he regards both church and state as rooted in human nature as well as divinely ordained, Augustine sees them both as limited. One limit is their purely temporal character. When time ends, at the last judgment, neither church nor state will endure. Persons judged to be members of the city of God will enter the eternal community of the blessed and their opposite numbers will form the anti-community of the damned. Since the states of souls in these posthumous abodes are unalterable and since the resurrected bodies to which they are joined lack the needs of the earthly body, the ministrations of church and state are no longer required. Aside from temporality, another limit Augustine places on church and state concerns their functions. Each ministers to one aspect of human nature and neither performs the other's functions; although we should recall Augustine's anti-Donatist brief for the political enforcement of religious orthodoxy.

In so far as a theory of the good state can be extrapolated from Augustine's teachings, two marked differences from classical political theory are evident. First, he defines the good society in terms of its loves and values, not in constitutional terms. Second, there is no such thing as 'pure politics' in Augustine despite his recognition of mankind's natural needs as a positive sanction for political life. A well-run commonwealth, as he sees it, is marked by the worship of God and an upright moral life, traits found only in communion with the orthodox church. The ideal state would maintain correct religious doctrine and practice and would be guided by the norm of justice. Policies promoting these goals cannot be divorced from those that promote salvation. And, since all power comes from God, ecclesiastical and secular dominion, however organized, have a divine as well as a natural sanction.

Augustine also considers political life in states that do not promote justice and salvation. If Christians have the misfortune to live in them, they must obey the government unless it orders them to contravene God's law. For, even bad states are divinely ordained. Given the sinful propensities of fallen mankind, God permits such states to exert coercive power to deter and punish sinners. In this context, Augustine offers a negative divine sanction, along with the natural and positive divine sanctions he proposes for good states.

Virtually all medieval political theorists shared these Augustinian views. They deployed them selectively, and in opposing ways, and in combination with ideas drawn from other sources. Political circumstances as well as the legal and philosophical vocabulary available and the theorist's own propensities all played a role in the shifting patterns of theory on the Christian commonwealth. The earliest to enter the debate after Augustine was Pope Gelasius I, strongly motivated by his opposition to the Caesaropapism of the Byzantines who were currently trying to reconquer the western Roman empire. His formula, later called 'Gelasian dualism,' recapitulates Augustine's point that emperors and popes are required to minister to our physical and spiritual needs. To this he adds that, since the soul, with its eternal destiny, is more important than the body, the pope is superior to the emperor. Anti-Byzantine sentiment also informs the interpretations of Charlemagne's imperial coronation in 800. Charlemagne and Pope Leo III (d. 816) agreed that the Byzantine throne was vacant *de jure* in 797 and that Charlemagne could assume the imperial title. But conflicting views of his coronation yielded a royalist alternative, in which Leo had played a purely ceremonial role, and a papalist one, in which the pope had exercised his authority to transfer the title.

The next stage of the debate began with the dramatic clash between Pope Gregory VII and Emperor Henry IV (1054–1106), part of the papal attack on lay investiture. Gregory's opening salvo in 1075 and Henry's prompt reply laid down classic positions which later publicists on each side made their point of departure. In his own modification of Augustine, Gregory argues that the negative divine sanction alone applies to secular rulers, good or bad. He also explains, in his 'Two Swords Theory,' how coercive power is granted to them. God initially places both the spiritual and the temporal swords in the pope's hands. The pope then delegates secular authority to the emperor. Gregory adds that the pope can judge how rulers wield the temporal sword. If they do so badly, he can recoup it and grant it to another ruler. Popes, according to this theory, can do more than admonish emperors. They can do more even than excommunicate them, as Ambrose had done. They can actually depose emperors, freeing their subjects from their allegiance. Henry's subjects grasped this point. He retaliated with his own theory. He agrees on the need for temporal and spiritual institutions headed by emperors and popes, respectively. He agrees that each office is sanctioned by God. But he argues that the divine sanction of temporal rule is as positive as it is for ecclesiastical rule

and that God gives each sword to the apposite ruler directly. In the immediate political outcome of this debate, Gregory scored a symbolic victory but the emperors
stuck to their guns.

In the thirteenth century, while both sides follow the main lines of argument
established by Gregory and Henry, new analyses and metaphors enter the discussion, reflecting scholastic developments, and theorizing is extended from emperors
to kings. Pope Innocent III (1160/1–1216) updates Gregory's position in his 'Sun
and Moon Theory,' testifying to the appeal of astronomical symbolism in an age of
revived scientific study. Just as the moon shines with light reflected from the sun,
so, he concludes, temporal rulers, be they emperors or kings, acquire their divine
right indirectly, from the papacy. Innocent succeeded in translating this theory into
practice, granting diplomatic recognition to emerging Christian kingdoms on the
Iberian peninsula as the leader of European Christendom, and forcing the English
king, if briefly, to accept the status of a papal vassal.

If kings were in the news in the thirteenth century, this was even more the case
in the fourteenth. It was Philip IV of France (1267/8–1314) whose mettle Boniface VIII (*c*. 1235–1303) tested when he made the most global statement of papal
supremacy ever enunciated in a document addressed to that monarch in 1302. The
upshot was Boniface's arrest at Anagni by Philip's agents, his sudden death, and
the beginning of the Avignonese papacy. Boniface's theory was one he had no hope
of enforcing. But, while he is sometimes viewed as out on a limb, it is worth noting
that there were other contemporary high papalist birds on the same limb, such as
Giles of Rome (*c*. 1245–1346), who advocated similar ideas. Giles had been tutor
to the young Philip IV, who clearly rejected his position. The publicist for his own
countervailing theory was John of Paris (d. 1306), a Dominican and university theologian. John adds his own twist to the traditional imperialist position. In arguing
that the king of France gets his authority directly from God, not the pope, he
observes that the popes do not crown French kings, as they crown the German
emperors. John uses this political fact to bolster his conclusion that Boniface's
claims, with respect to France, are irrelevant as well as pretentious. Another of
John's additions, deriving from his Thomism, is to recast Augustine's natural sanction for political authority in terms of natural law theory.

As the fourteenth century continued, other arguments were yoked to the imperialist or royalist side of the debate. One, encountered already as a heresy, was
Wycliff's theory of civil dominion. Three thinkers regarded as orthodox illustrate
the range of positions available and their increasing radicalization. Dante annexes
Aristotelianism and a historical argument to the imperialist tradition, developing
his theory most fully in *On Monarchy*. His point of departure is Innocent's 'Sun
and Moon Theory.' Actually, he states, to denote the true parity of the divine sanctions of church and state one would have to argue for two suns, making his point
with this astronomical anomaly. Next, equating the current Holy Roman Empire
with the ancient Roman empire, he observes that the empire existed before the rise
of Christianity. It is thus absurd to claim that the pope is the immediate source of
imperial authority. Finally, with John of Paris, Dante unites positive divine right
with the Aristotelian view that we are by nature political animals. Further, we need

a society with sufficient tranquillity if we are to attain our intellectual and spiritual ends. While the church, which ministers to our spiritual needs, is ultimately more important than the state, it is the state alone that provides the peace needed for the church's ministry. Dante also proposes a single, universal emperor as the provider of that peace. If one ruler held all temporal dominion, he argues, wars would cease. The universal emperor achieves peace by political means, a secular outcome that is a precondition of the church' successful labor.

Our second example, Marsilio of Padua (1275/80–1342), takes a leaf from Dante's book in his *Defender of the Peace*, since the emperor is the ruler his title describes. Marsilio also borrows from both the republican and imperial chapters of Roman law. He uses the latter in arguing for the subjection of the church to the state. Ecclesiastics, for him, have no benefit of clergy, no exemptions from the civil law. The role of the church is spiritual only, and if clerics trespass into temporal affairs, the emperor has the right to judge and to punish them under the civil law with political sanctions, up to the pope himself. In other areas of his theory, Marsilio combines the principle of modified popular sovereignty derived from Roman republican law with the representative theories informing current political institutions such as self-governing cities and parliaments. He applies the resultant amalgam to the sanctions of papal and imperial power and to the operations of existing rulers. Marsilio retains the divine right principle but argues that God grants power directly to the political community and to the faithful, which is the political community at prayer. In the case of both church and state, the community then delegates power to a leadership group: bishops, cardinals, and general councils in the church and officials called the 'weightier part' in the state. These leaders then elect and work in tandem with popes and emperors. Marsilio's popular sovereignty principle is thus not egalitarian, and he is more concerned with defining the political functions essential to governance than with prescribing their institutional forms and procedures. This functionalism, along with his combination of populism, divine right, and imperial freedom from and jurisdiction over the church, are distinctive of his theory.

It might seem that Wycliff's expansion of the latter idea would make him his century's most radical theorist on church and state, but Ockham, if earlier, goes even farther. Although he frames his theory in terms of the Holy Roman Empire as a result of his role as an imperial propagandist, his ideas are even more corrosive of the international Christian commonwealth than Wycliff's. As with Thomists who bring their Aristotelianism and natural law theory to bear on politics, so Ockham draws on his own philosophy, especially his epistemology. We recall his crisp distinction between supernatural truths known only by faith and rational knowledge in which we can have certitude only of sensible individual things known by intuition, in contrast with abstract ideas, mere mental constructs that yield probability at best. When Ockham switched to imperialist political theory, he inherited a traditional vocabulary including notions like natural law and the empire and papacy as universal institutions. In his terms these concepts were abstractions with no demonstrable extra-mental existence. He had, perforce, to use them. But he does so as restrictively as possible. Ockham applies his separation of reason from revelation to an argument against papalist claims that is as original as it is elegant. Divine law certainly exists, he notes, and it is the pope's task to administer it. But, since this law is revealed, it cannot be discussed rationally. Likewise, it is implausible for popes to conceive of their jurisdiction in rational terms. Since it extends only to matters of faith, papal authority has no role in temporal politics and cannot use political means. Popes can resort to moral suasion only, unlike secular rulers who can resort to force.

Having thus disposed of the temporal power of popes, Ockham next considers how church and empire conduct their internal business. Here, his application of Ockham's razor undermines the universalistic claims of both institutions. As abstractions, a universal church and empire are not fully real. What are fully real are local political and ecclesiastical communities, on a national, princely, or urban level, and the concrete positive laws they enact for themselves. One can only go beyond this level to the extent that international, inter-princely, inter-urban, or inter-diocesan agreements are made, since they are enacted by these local bodies and are part of the positive law that binds them.

With Ockham, his position as an imperial publicist notwithstanding, medieval political thought goes beyond universalism and even beyond the later reconfiguration of the Christian commonwealth on a national basis to a still more localistic understanding of political and ecclesiastical life. If Wycliff puts the Christian commonwealth on the cusp of the sixteenth-century state churches, Ockham puts it on the cusp of the still more local political and ecclesiastical sovereignties of early modern Europe. Despite the imperialist position he ostensibly defends, he reveals, even more than Wycliff, the situation at the end of the Middle Ages, when the concept of the pan-European Christian commonwealth, with spiritual and secular governance guided by single rulers in church and state, first launched by Augustine, was growing daily more untenable.

Conciliarism

Conciliar theory, or reflection on the place of general councils in the constitution of the church, has many parallels with theorizing on church–state relations. Like Marsilio, many thinkers have positions on both issues. This topic was also profoundly affected by the revival of legal and philosophical study. Similarly, whatever positions they espouse, ecclesiologists shared basic assumptions. Their thinking was also influenced by events and crises in church history. And implicit conciliar theory, or attitudes on what was deemed acceptable and authoritative, are visible in the ways participants in church councils behaved and in how they and later churchmen regarded conciliar decrees.

For the first millennium of church history, conciliar theory was largely implicit. From the first ecumenical council convened at Nicaea in 325 until the schism between the Greek and the Roman churches in 1054, most councils were held in Byzantine territory. Attendance was often patchy. Although, in principle, the five patriarchal sees of Jerusalem, Alexandria, Antioch, Rome, and Constantinople were supposed to be represented for a council to be regarded as valid, on some occasions, popes or their legates and other western prelates were absent. Representation from more than one major region sufficed to make such councils general, in the eyes of churchmen. Sometimes the convener and presiding officer was the Byzantine emperor. When a cleric played that role, he was usually one of metropolitan or archiepiscopal rank, although not necessarily. The chief concern of the early general councils was the definition of doctrine, the statement and reaffirmation of creeds or dogmatic formulae, and the anathematization of heresy. Three points important for the later development of western conciliarism emerge from the implicit conciliar theory yielded by early conciliar history. First, ecumenical councils were regarded as the locus of the church's highest magisterial authority; it was they that defined Christian orthodoxy. Second—irrespective of the breadth of actual attendance, papal presence, papal confirmation of conciliar acts, or the status of the convener and presider—conciliar decrees were authoritative because they were treated as authoritative and used as precedents in later theology, canon law, and ecclesiastical jurisprudence. Third, one of these precedents, and one certainly compatible with Byzantine Caesaropapism, was the idea that the emperor could call and preside over general councils of the church.

The next stage of conciliar history in western Europe begins with the First Lateran council of 1123. The schism with the Greek church, combined with changes in the constitution of the Roman church, gave the popes far more prominence in general councils than had been the case earlier. Since neither the Roman nor the Greek church now recognized the other's jurisdiction, general councils of the Roman church rarely included major delegations from the Greek church; the exceptions that prove the rule are Lyons II (1274) and the council of Ferrara-Florence (1435–9), which tried, but failed, to reunify the two churches. Lateran I was called just after the resolution of the investiture controversy. While the settlement left control of episcopal appointments in the hands of lay rulers, the popes succeeded in freeing papal elections from lay intervention by creating the College of Cardinals in the mid-eleventh century. This constitutional innovation, ensuring that clerics alone elected the pope, had administrative implications as well. For the cardinals functioned collectively as a court, advising the pope and helping him govern the church. But their existence and activities raised a major question for conciliarists. Since the cardinals elected the pope, could they also depose him in the name of the Christian community? Or, since they were associated with the pope in his governance, were they identifiable with the pope and unable to act against him? Latent at the time of Lateran I, this issue surfaced overtly in both theory and practice later in the Middle Ages.

Along with papal presidency, another shift in conciliar history in the twelfth century and after lay in the competence of councils. In sharp contrast with early councils, which saw doctrinal definition as their key task, councils in the high Middle Ages stressed disciplinary legislation. Only one, Lateran IV (1215), defined doctrine, in this case transubstantiation, the formula denoting how the consecrated bread and wine of the Eucharist change into the substance of Christ's body and blood while retaining the accidents, or sensible attributes, of bread and wine. Given the growth of theological faculties at universities, especially Paris, the church's magisterium tended to move to them, to the extent that university theologians achieved doctrinal consensus. For their part, councils concentrated on decrees mandating standards of behavior and religious practice for clergy and laity and the creation of the administrative instrumentalities for enforcing them. They also recognized, and controlled, the proliferation of new religious orders. Thus, the scope of conciliar authority widened to include discipline and tactics, along with doctrinal definition.

Simultaneously, thinkers began theorizing expressly on the role of councils in the church, their relation to the faithful, the bishops, the popes, and even to the Holy Spirit, the Trinitarian person believed to oversee the church. Explicit conciliar theory can be divided into two periods, the eleventh to the thirteenth century, with most of the action in the latter century, and the fourteenth and fifteenth centuries. Most of the essential ideas, on all sides, were articulated during the first period, and most theorists were papalists who saw councils as a means of strengthening the pope's governance of the church. In the second stage, while the papalists by no means vanished, the vast majority of theorists elevated the authority of councils over papal authority, a move directly related to the crisis of authority resulting from the Avignonese papacy and Great Schism.

Notwithstanding that momentous change, conciliarists and papalists shared some common assumptions, as did conciliarists who advocated different applications of their own version of these assumptions. The central idea uniting all conciliarists is that the whole church, the community of the faithful, is distinguishable from the Roman church, or the pope, his court, and the College of Cardinals governing at the center. For conciliarists, the whole church has greater authority than the Roman church. The whole church possesses sovereignty and delegates power to the ecclesiastical hierarchy. This agreement on the delegated authority of the Roman church was elaborated in several ways. Its most popular expression involved the application of Roman corporation law to the church. According to this view, the pope is the chief executive officer of a collective body made up of the faithful, who delegate power to popes through general councils. Councils and popes represent the faithful, who legally empower both to act on their behalf. Papal actions are subject to scrutiny by the faithful, to whom popes are responsible, through the agency of councils. A second application of the conciliarists' core assumptions focuses on the cardinals as the chief mechanism through which the sovereignty of the whole church is expressed and delegated. Proponents of this variant note that, unlike general councils, the cardinals actually elect popes and collaborate with them in governing the church. Thus, they are better situated to serve the interests of the faithful than councils, which are not always in session. The cardinal-based theory also extends to papal government the feudal principle that rulers are limited, acting lawfully only with the counsel and consent of their vassals. Yoking that idea to Roman corporation law, the second subdivision of conciliarists sees the College of Cardinals as the group legally entitled to call an errant pope to account, and to convene a general council if he refuses to do so.

Just as conciliarists share fundamental assumptions while disagreeing on their best implementation, so conciliarists of all stripes share a basic assumption with their papalist opponents. Their major point of agreement is the indefectibility of the church. Before ascending to heaven, Christ had sent the Holy Spirit to remain with and guide the church. Agreeing on that point, conciliarists and papalists disagree on the locus of this indefectibility. Papalists argue that Christ lodged the church's inerrancy in the papacy primarily, or, if they are very high papalists, in the pope alone. Conciliarists argue that the church's inerrancy is lodged partly in the papacy but more fully and perfectly in other institutions, such as general councils. Over time, however, conciliarists apply this notion differently. Until the end of the thirteenth century, they view inerrancy as a negative quality preventing the church from going off the rails. In the fourteenth and fifteenth centuries, as a result of contemporary problems, they treat inerrancy as a positive quality, inhering in the body of the faithful and manifested in councils, which could be turned against popes if necessary, correcting and even deposing them.

By the end of the thirteenth century, ecclesiologists had elaborated the corporation theory and had extended it to abbots and bishops and their relations with their abbeys and diocesan clergy. In both cases, they develop mechanisms for deposing heretical, sinful, or incompetent leaders, with the abbey's brethren or the diocesan clergy taking over the deposed leader's functions until a new one is installed, saving, in the latter case, functions that canon law reserved to bishops, such as administering the sacraments of confirmation and ordination. Starting with Gratian, theorists also assert that popes are also subject to judgment. By the late thirteenth century, the list of papal crimes inviting judgment included heresy, fornication, robbery, and sacrilege. Yet, by that point no enforcement mechanism had been found; unlike bishops, whose cases could be taken to the courts of their archbishops or the papal court, the pope could not be sued in his own court.

It is here that the conciliarists, at the turn of the fourteenth century, introduce the notion that an errant pope can be tried, and deposed, by a general council of the church. But, even with agreement on that point, practical and theoretical problems remained. Who would call and preside over such a council? Although popes had called and presided over all the general councils in the west since 1123, the convener and presider could not be the incumbent pope. For, if so, he would be judge and defendant at the same time. And, practically speaking, what pope would call a council whose express purpose was to try and depose him? If the pope is ruled out, conciliarists consider two alternatives, the cardinals and a secular ruler like the emperor. There were, indeed, notable precedents for the idea of imperial convocation and presidency in the first millennium of church history, but not lately, and not in western Europe. As for the cardinals, they had been in existence only since the mid-eleventh century. But conciliarists disagree on their possible role here, some saying that they do express the sovereignty of the faithful while others, viewing papal governance as a collegial activity of pope and cardinals combined, think that, if the cardinals convened such a council, they would be putting themselves, collectively, in the place of the defendant.

The crisis of the Great Schism enlarged the flow of theorizing and prompted conciliarists to translate theory into practice. Between 1409 and the 1430s, several general councils were held. In establishing clear outcomes, the most important were the councils of Pisa (1409) and Constance (1414–18). As noted earlier, the cardinals of the Roman and Avignonese popes called the council of Pisa. Neither pope recognized its legitimacy. For, despite the theorizing about the role of cardinals already in place, there was no historical precedent for their action in 1409. Compounding the problem that this council was called to resolve with the election of a third pope, the consequence of Pisa was to destroy definitively the idea that cardinals had the authority to call a valid general council and that a council they convened had the authority to depose a pope. For its part, the council of Constance made the clearest and most far-reaching statement ever made in the Middle Ages of the conciliarist position, effectively putting it into practice. As we recall from the story of John Huss, the emperor elect Sigismund pressured the Pisan pope into convening the council, which, as he had hoped, was used to declare Huss a heretic. We might say that Constance was called by a pope *de jure*, and by the emperor *de facto*. Once the delegates convened, the Pisan pope fled from Constance. He was captured, tried, and deposed as an illegal office-holder, thus leaving the council without a presiding officer. Sigismund assumed that function and the council continued its deliberations. On the heels of that fact, the Roman pope, seeing the handwriting on the wall, abdicated and the Avignonese pope was deposed. The council continued in session, with no pope in office. It proceeded to elect a new pope whom all recognized, ending the schism.

Thus, in practice, the council of Constance did demonstrate the superiority of a council over the papacy. Yet, later in the fifteenth century, popes regained initiative and control over councils and their exact place in the constitution of the church received no final answer by the end of the Middle Ages. Two broad reasons may be suggested for that outcome, or lack of one. In addition to ending the Great Schism, councils of the early fifteenth century placed on their agenda complex and intractable items, such as the reform of the church in head and members and reunion with the Greek church, problems that were both extremely difficult and incapable of swift resolution. These councils promised more than they could deliver. Another reason for conciliar inefficacy was the way conciliar delegations deliberated and voted in the fifteenth century. The system was tried informally at the council of Pisa and institutionalized at Constance. Members were seated, debated, and voted in national delegations. This mode of operation reflects a fact already noted, the increasing appeal of the idea of national churches, whether within the orthodox consensus or not. National interests frequently impeded the resolution of issues affecting Christendom at large. The tension between the international Christian commonwealth, as a definition of European civilization, and its religious reconfiguration at smaller local or national levels, is visible in sharp focus in these councils. Above all, it is symptomatic of that tension that Sigismund, whose theory of imperial office depended on an internationalist conception of European Christendom in which he was the paramount temporal ruler, sought to use the council of Constance, the supreme organ of international Christendom, to quell the breakaway Hussite movement toward a national church and failed to achieve that goal. The national church, Catholic or Protestant, was to triumph in the sixteenth century. The precise role of general councils in the governance of the Catholic church and in the articulation of its magisterium, despite Romanist claims to the contrary, has never been settled, an ambiguity that medieval conciliarism bequeathed to modern Catholicism. At the same time, the ecclesiological tensions between advice and consent, representation and consent, and the initiatives and prerogatives of rulers, which can also be read as an application of the doctrine of God's ordained and absolute power to human institutions, are features of medieval political thought more generally. Similar tensions and ambiguities, likewise driven by political crises, can be found in feudal monarchy.

Feudal Monarchy

Along with economic ideas like the just price, feudal monarchy is a hallmark of the Middle Ages, although it has partial analogies in other times and places, it varied from one medieval setting to another, and it was not the only form of medieval government. These limitations notwithstanding, it is a fitting conclusion to our consideration of medieval political thought because it clearly displays political beliefs and tolerances specific to medieval Europeans as well as contributions they made to later constitutional thought. As with ecclesiastical and economic theory, we can discover the operative assumptions of major players by observing what they said and did—and refrained from saying and doing—in contexts taking us beyond formal treatises to public documents, political rituals, and political behavior in times of crisis. For purposes of convenience, we will confine ourselves to medieval England, for the richness of its available sources and the abundance of its political crises, although many of the same ideas and outcomes could be documented in other feudal monarchies.

By definition, feudal monarchy is limited monarchy and it was Europe's first venture into the terrain of government by contract. In such monarchies, the king, as suzerain, is bound to each of his vassals by a feudal contract specifying reciprocal rights and duties. The suzerain grants political protection, guardianship of the vassal's children if they are minors when he dies, a court in which cases between vassals are heard, and counsel and consent, the duty to ask for and obtain the vassal's advice and approval for legislation and major policy decisions. The king also grants the vassal a fief, usually land, giving him the income that enables him to uphold his side of the contract, along with jurisdiction over any people living on the land. The vassal owes the king loyalty, a stipulated amount of military service, availability on call for consultative purposes, financial dues collected to defray specific expenses, such as the marriage of the suzerain's eldest daughter, the knighting of his eldest son, and ransom, should he be captured. The vassal also has the duty of hospitality, if the king chooses to visit him, and owes an unspecified feudal aid, an emergency contribution in extraordinary circumstances. Key features of feudal monarchy are this bilateral contract binding rulers and the ruled and government understood as mixed sovereignty. If the vassal fails to perform his duties, the king has the legal right to escheat his fief, to take back his land, terminating their relationship. If the suzerain is remiss, the vassal can formally remove himself from his lord's allegiance, returning the fief and severing their relationship. Normally, however, when tensions occurred between kings and their vassals, they tried to restore the contract to correct working order rather than end it. In this relationship, the king has some of the ultimate authority to make political decisions, while some of that authority lies in his vassals' consent. Despite the theoretical and practical requirement of baronial consent, all acknowledged that kings had royal prerogatives. These included the right to take governmental initiatives, the right to choose men for appointive offices, the right to judge and to delegate that function to judges of the king's choice, the right—and duty—to enforce the law, and to suspend it in times of emergency. To the sanctions of counsel and consent medieval feudal monarchies added the sanctions of divine right, hereditary right, and tradition or precedent, both substantive and procedural. Over the course of the high Middle Ages, the counsel and consent principle was expanded to include persons who were not royal vassals. In England they were knights of the shire, or lower nobles, and burgesses, or townsmen, representing their communities in Parliament. The social groups participating varied in their organization in countries with such representative bodies; in England the Parliament was bicameral, with lay and ecclesiastical vassals of the crown sitting in the House of Lords and the knights and burgesses sitting in the House of Commons. Along with the reframing of limited monarchy in parliamentary terms came the application of ideas from theology, Roman and canon law, and classical political theory to feudal and common law concepts.

We can divide the theorizing, implicit and explicit, into two stages of English history, the pre-parliamentary and the parliamentary. The first, beginning with the Norman conquest and extending to the late thirteenth century, provides considerable evidence of the understood duty of kings to act with their vassals' consent. Even when adverting to their divine right, kings from William the Conqueror onward preface royal decrees, charters, and writs with the statement that they have made decisions with counsel and consent; to these documents are appended the signatures of vassals who witnessed the transaction as well as the king's. And royal coronation ceremonies and coronation charters issued by kings, notwithstanding their liturgical character, stress the sanction of the vassals' consent to the king's accession.

The earliest English political theorists also reflect the combination of royal authority devolving both from God and from the king's vassals. *On the Laws and Customs of the Kingdom of England*, attributed to the justiciar Ranulf de Glanvill (1130–90), a crown officer supervising the courts and acting as viceroy in the king's absence, while largely a description of the forms of action available in land tenure cases in English common law, shows some traces of Roman law and some effort to specify the powers and limits of royal authority. Sometimes Glanvill contrasts English and Roman law. When they conflict, the law of the land prevails. Sometimes he adopts Roman legal concepts; he accepts the Roman rule that, if someone encroaches on royal land and erects a building thereon, the building becomes royal property. And he states that the criteria used in decision-making in the king's court are equity, discretion, practicality, and common sense; it would be hard to imagine guidelines more prototypical of the Roman legal mind. In defining the king's functions, Glanvill cites the two medieval necessities: the king must fight and judge, defending his people, keeping the peace, and administering justice impartially. Some of the law he enforces, Glanvill notes, is unwritten or customary. Since the law is generally known, that fact does not impair its authority. Customary law is legitimate because it rests on four sanctions: reason, tradition, the counsel and consent of royal vassals, and the king's will. Apropos of the last sanction, Glanvill states, 'What pleases the prince has the force of law.'[1] The context in which Glanvill places this tag from the imperial phase of Roman law indicates that he sees princely will as one sanction among others. Yet—and this targets the central ambiguity of the mixed sovereignty characteristic of feudal monarchy—Glanvill does not clarify how royal authority is related to the other three sanctions. And, although the bulk of his treatise outlines the substance and procedure of the land law, which he expects the king and his judges to observe and enforce, Glanvill does not consider whether subjects have any recourse if they fail to do so.

This latter issue is raised by John of Salisbury in his *Policraticus*, a work altogether more classicizing than Glanvill's. There are some startling contradictions in the *Policraticus*. John argues that there are two sanctions of royal authority: feudal right, or the vassals' homage and consent, and divine right. Under the latter heading he invokes the negative Augustinian sanction, the coercive power rulers need to punish evildoers. John does not indicate whether either of these sanctions overrides the other. He then lists two additional sanctions: right of inheritance and Roman corporation law as applied to the kingdom, viewing the king as the head of a corporate body that delegates authority to him. On the model of divine right and inheritance right, a king obtaining his office legitimately would have to be endured even if he ruled tyrannically. On the model of feudal right and corporation law, a king could be called to account by his vassals, and, if remiss, deposed. John does not resolve these inconsistencies. Some readers think his problem stems from a mélange of conflicting classical sources poorly digested in his mind. This may well be true. Yet the paradoxes in the *Policraticus* mirror those of feudal monarchy itself.

The clearest, and most problematic, articulation of the mixed sovereignty position in the pre-parliamentary stage of English history is Magna Carta (1215), the document seeking to end a civil war between King John (1167–1216) and vassals rightly alarmed by his violations of lawful procedure and feudal custom as well as his political losses in confrontations with the pope and the French king. The charter states many principles of feudal law, including the requisite of counsel and consent and the king's need to adhere to the usual and reasonable in assessing feudal aids. It stresses his duty not to act arbitrarily. In all these ways it is an effort to restore the feudal contract between John and his vassals to good working order. At the same time, the charter proposes something new, a mechanism for enforcing the king's feudal obligations. Clause 61 outlines this procedure. If the king breaks the charter, a watchdog committee of barons will call the matter to his attention. If he fails to rectify the situation within forty days, the barons will force him to do so, making war on him—saving the persons of the king, the queen, and their children—and, when redress has been obtained, they will obey him as before. Innovative as it is, this clause was never put to the test. Magna Carta was broken almost immediately after it was signed. But it was the barons who breached it, not John. Although Magna Carta was reconfirmed early in the reign of John's successor, Henry III (1207–72), and repeatedly in the later Middle Ages, the enforcement clause was omitted. The fundamental problem of how to enforce the feudal contract against the king, without the vassals' breaking it themselves by armed revolt, was not resolved by Magna Carta.

A similarly nugatory outcome resulted from Henry III's conflicts with his barons. Henry did violate the feudal contract by making major decisions without baronial consent, in addition to evoking other, more personal and political, grievances. Civil war ensued and twice the barons defeated the king, each time replacing him and royal initiative with government by baronial committee. Although each baronial government was legislated into being, with king and barons both assenting, neither was effective and both stirred complaints from other social groups. Henry regained the initiative and won the third and last round of civil war, unseating the barons and restoring the status quo ante, again by legislation to which both sides agreed. If Henry had violated the constitution of his feudal monarchy by ignoring the need for baronial consent, his rebellious vassals did likewise, not only in the act of rebellion itself but also by governing, when in power, without royal consent.

Written in the midst of the barons' war against Henry, *On the Laws and Customs of England* by Henry de Bracton (d. 1268) conceptualizes the issues raised by the crises of his reign and the preceding one. Bracton, a man with considerable experience as a judge, knew the English legal system intimately. He uses concepts drawn from both the republican and imperial phases of Roman law to clarify the rights and duties of kings. Following the *Digest* and *Institutes*, he divides his subject into the law of things, persons, and actions. Bracton begins by asserting, with Cicero, that law is the common agreement of the commonwealth. The king's coronation oath confers authority on him and also limits him. Both counsel and consent and 'what pleases the prince' legitimize his decisions. Bracton also states that 'the king must not be under man but under God and under the law.'[2] Although he is subject to the rule of law, no human agency can enforce it upon him. As Bracton further notes, royal power can be subdivided into governance and jurisdiction. Governance is the king's coercive power as the enforcer of law. It also covers royal prerogative and discretionary rights. In this area, the king has no peer and shares his power with no one. Jurisdiction is the activity of legislation and policy-making. Here, the king is limited. He must act with counsel and consent, following lawful procedures. What if a king, under the heading of jurisdiction, violates these norms, as Henry III and John had done? Bracton takes account of this possibility and answers that, while subjects can ascertain when kings act illegally, no legal procedure exists for bringing them to book. No writ runs against the king. With Bracton, the mixed sovereignty constitution of feudal England remains in force. His treatise describes this contemporary situation accurately.

The problem stated so crisply by Bracton continued to exist as feudalism developed into parliamentary government. The range of subjects whose counsel and consent was now deemed necessary for royal legislation and policy-making widened but the basic relationship between ruler and ruled remained similar. Parliaments assembled when kings called them and sat until kings dissolved them, or until they were automatically dissolved by the termination of the incumbent's reign. In writs to local officials ordering the selection of knights of the shire and burgesses, kings from the late thirteenth century onward stress both the representative principle and the principle of consent in noting that these members of the House of Commons are to come with full power of attorney to speak and act for their communities. In a writ to Robert, archbishop of Canterbury, for the Parliament of 1295, asking him to produce representatives from the lower clergy, a group not usually called, Edward I (1239–1307) bolsters his request with a tag from Roman private law, 'for what affects all, by all should be approved.'[3] Here, a rule first developed to ensure that all members of a business partnership agreed to any change in the partnership's terms is converted into a constitutional principle.

The English Parliament acquired many important powers and prerogatives in the later Middle Ages, including the right to define the qualifications of voters for members of the House of Commons, control of tax legislation, freedom from arrest for members during parliamentary sessions as well as freedom of speech on the floor of Parliament. A major reason for these gains was the crown's fiscal need, given its military commitments in the British Isles and France and the growing bureaucratization of royal government, with ever more officials on the payroll in an age of economic depression. None the less, the theoretical and practical advances of Parliament, including the development of the impeachment process to use against crown officials who abused their trust, did not give Parliament control of royal appointments and royal initiatives. And, although Parliament was the highest court in the land, it did not develop a mechanism for trying kings when they violated the law.

The inability of the institutional and legal system of later medieval England to attain these goals is revealed dramatically in the depositions of two fourteenth-century kings, Edward II (1289–1327) and Richard II (1367–1400). Each did, indeed, overstep the limits of the law in addition to inspiring opposition for other reasons. In both cases, rebel barons made war on the king, defeated him in battle, and imprisoned him, thus deposing him politically. In both cases, however, the rebels wanted to make this *de facto* situation look legitimate by using bodies they called Parliaments. The assemblies in question did not have parliamentary status *de jure*. In calling the 'Parliament' of 1327, the rebel leaders wrested from Edward the Great Seal used to authenticate royal documents and claimed that he had issued the writs of summons. In 1399, Henry of Lancaster (1366–1413), the leader of the revolt who succeeded Richard as Henry IV, did the same. Since both kings had to surrender the seal under duress and neither wished to call a Parliament, the legal status of the writs in both cases was null and so was the parliamentary status of the resulting assemblies. Further, neither body tried the king. In Edward's case, a list of charges against him was read before the assembly in his absence, and accepted. Then, a delegation took the charges to him in prison and told him that his son would be passed over as his heir unless he abdicated. He did so. In Richard's case, the delegation asking him to abdicate went to him the day before the assembly met.

Even if that assembly had been a legal Parliament, the termination of Richard's reign the day before would have dissolved it automatically. Key to both deposition scenarios is the understanding of all involved that the only people with legal authority to end the reigns of Edward and Richard before their deaths were Edward and Richard themselves.

Another telling expression of that common understanding occurred in Henry IV's first Parliament, held a week after the assembly that had met the day after Richard's abdication. Exactly the same people were present in both conclaves. Henry opened proceedings with a speech stating that he was king by divine right, by right of inheritance, and by the help of his friends. On the second point, he ignored Richard's legal heir, a cousin related more closely to Richard than he was, but a child to whose defense no one rose. Next, Henry recognized the archbishop of Canterbury, who made a speech purporting to describe the last days of the reign of Richard II which all present knew was historically false. In this version of events, Richard had called a Parliament voluntarily before abdicating; he had named Henry as his heir, and he had abdicated willingly and happily. The archbishop made this speech so that the false version of events would be enrolled in the rolls of Parliament and made the official record. The fact that it was deemed necessary to seek retroactive legitimation of acts that had not been legitimate when they had occurred a few days earlier indicates the group's recognition that they had been illegitimate and that Richard alone had had the legal authority to end his reign.

These depositions, then, reflect the understood limits of the English medieval Parliament as the institution in which counsel and consent and the observance of lawful procedure constrained royal government and as the vehicle for enforcing these principles on kings who ignored them. They show that Parliaments, or bodies calling themselves Parliaments, could not and did not remove Edward and Richard from office, and that subjects knew they could not do so without breaking the law. This same dilemma, characteristic of medieval limited monarchy in both its feudal and its parliamentary stages, finds voice in England's last medieval political theorist, John Fortescue (*c.* 1394–1474). Like Bracton and Glanvill, Fortescue had a hands-on knowledge of English law, serving as chief justice of the court of King's Bench, the branch of the royal judicial system handling criminal cases. Like these predecessors, he is descriptive. But Fortescue is also prescriptive, advocating institutional reforms, as well as polemical; he reflects the anti-French bias of an England engaged in the Hundred Years War. Fortescue formulates his own principle for distinguishing between absolute and limited monarchy in his *Praise of the Laws of England*, attributing the former, erroneously and tendentiously, to France. What Fortescue calls royal rule is absolute monarchy, in which the king is the sole source of power, legislation, and administration, limited by no legal or institutional constraints. He, and he alone, has sovereignty. What Fortescue calls political rule is limited monarchy, in which the king acts with counsel and consent expressed in Parliament, along with other institutions through which consent is expressed, like the king's council when Parliament is not in session. In this type of monarchy, the governed have sovereignty and are represented by these institutions, to which they delegate it. Fortescue then describes England as a country with royal and political rule. Its king is absolute in some areas and limited in others. Aside from his framing of his definition of political rule in terms of popular sovereignty and his incorporation of Parliament into his analysis, signs of the times, Fortescue essentially restates Bracton's position. And, with Bracton, he sees no legal way to enforce the law against royal abuse of it, or to control royal prerogatives or royal appointments before the fact.

The theme of mixed sovereignty that runs through this story, in express theory as well as in the common understanding of the powers and limits of law revealed in political behavior, is a legacy feudal monarchy bequeathed to parliamentary monarchy and which parliamentary monarchy bequeathed to early modern Europe. The ability to live with the ambiguities basic to this theory is a distinctly medieval political tolerance. In the event, Europeans did not discard it until the seventeenth century, when most parliamentary monarchies absolutized the autocratic element in the mix while England and Sweden absolutized the limited monarchy element, vesting sovereignty in Parliament. In this area of political thought, medieval arrangements and sensibilities were better able to weather the Renaissance and Reformation than were conciliarism and theories of church–state relations, despite their clear parallels. The time–lag was shorter for the latter two topics because they both assumed the existence of universalistic institutions like the Holy Roman Empire and the papacy, which were already victims of declining universalism in the later medieval centuries and which became politically irrelevant in the sixteenth century. This was not true of constitutional theories emerging out of national monarchies that, in many cases, did not settle the crises stemming from the reconfiguration of the Christian commonwealth along national lines until the seventeenth century. High and late medieval political theory offers both ideas that did not survive the Middle Ages, ideas already criticized and rejected within that period, and ideas that were foundational in immediately succeeding centuries, some remaining of durable interest and utility even more recently. The interplay of varied sources, from Roman law to canon law to classical political philosophy to patristic and scholastic theology to common law traditions and to feudalism, an institution created in the Middle Ages, makes political theory a good example of the wider tendency of medieval thought to engage in crossover, to put old wine into new bottles, and to make free with all its traditions, ancient and recent, to resolve current problems, and to juxtapose, whether in equipoise or tension, ideas that post-medieval thinkers would find impossible contradictions.

Conclusion

In drawing together the threads pursued thematically in this book, especially in Parts IV to VII, this conclusion will highlight areas of discontinuity, markers of medieval modes of thought and sensibility that end with the period, and areas of continuity, markers of ideas and attitudes that make the Middle Ages the first chapter of the western intellectual tradition. We will track these issues under the four major subdivisions of medieval thought treated above: literature; the religious culture; theological, philosophical, and scientific speculation; and political and economic theory. We will also consider the dynamics at work in these branches of intellectual activity.

In the field of literature, language, style, form, subject matter, and sensibility all offer their own answers to the relations between discontinuity and continuity. The history of the various vernaculars differs, and a complicating factor is that old ideas can be expressed in a new idiom, and vice versa. Langland and Chaucer can be called the last major medieval authors in English. But the last medieval authors in Italian are Dante and Boccaccio, who lived decades earlier, and between those figures stands Francesco Petrarch (1304–74). The Italian of Petrarch's cycle of love lyrics is not that different from Dante's. But, although his organization of the cycle has him discovering his lady in church on Good Friday, the day when the action in the *Divine Comedy* begins, with one poem for each day in the liturgical calendar of the following year, Petrarch is universally seen as expressing a post-medieval attitude to love and a post-medieval sensibility in his vernacular no less than his Latin works. If the date-line for Italian is thus problematized by Petrarch, we would have to say that the Middle Ages did not end in German until the early sixteenth-century use of that language by Martin Luther (1483–1546), above all in his translation of the Bible.

Style, form, and subject matter do not provide readily visible turning points either. Literary devices popular in the Middle Ages, like allegory, first arose in classical literature and had long and healthy careers ahead of them in early modern and more recent literature. In any case, allegory does not define medieval literature; major genres, such as Norse sagas, Irish epics, and fabliaux, dispense with it altogether. As for literary forms created in the Middle Ages, like stressed and accented poetic meters with rhyme and alliteration, the short story, the novel, and comic drama as revue, they remain with us today. The same applies to history as chronicle and to universal history subordinating vast stretches of material to a single theme or idea. To be sure, the conflict between Augustine's two cities has given way to secular ideologies, social and economic forces, or political paradigms of rise and fall, but the didactic and metahistorical intent remains intact.

Subject matter is just as elusive in demarcating medieval literature from the literature of successive ages. The recycling of classical and medieval materials in updated settings and new genres can be tracked across modern European literature as well. Indeed this western propensity for reusing ancient sources in fresh ways distinguishes the Middle Ages, as part of the western intellectual tradition in literature, from the Byzantine veneration of the classics, preserving them in amber rather than using them as inspiration for literary creativity. This hallmark of European literature, launched by authors who recast Aeneas or Alexander the Great as heroes of romance or as knights of the Round Table, has resonances as recent as the *Omeros* of Derek Walcott (b. 1930), in which classical epic is the vehicle for defining personal and national identity in a post-colonial Caribbean island republic. The same can be said for the reuse of themes, plots, and characters of medieval provenance. The revamping of Arthurian materials characteristic of the Middle Ages continued after that period up until *Camelot* (the play, 1961; the film, 1967), both as drama and as political metaphor. The same applies to Roland and company, who inspired post-medieval writers from Ludovico Ariosto (1474–1533) to Virginia Woolf (1882–1941). More than one character from the *Divine Comedy* became the subject of modern opera, not to mention the use of Norse and continental Germanic epics by Richard Wagner (1818–83) in his *Ring* cycle and his use of medieval romance in his *Parzifal*, yoking them to political agendas that would have been incomprehensible to the redactors and authors of those texts.

The durable appeal of these approaches and literary subjects makes medieval literature the beginning of many modern vernacular traditions, as does the increasing use of vernaculars themselves as media for the expression of ideas in all areas, classical and Christian, sacred and profane. A genre in which this trend is especially visible is drama. The self-definition of Francophone writers in relation to their own medieval vernacular literature in the early fifteenth century is an important theoretical statement of this development, as is Dante's treatise on the vernacular, matched in practice by his literary masterpiece and those of Boccaccio and Chaucer and the expansion of vernacular preaching and devotional writing. In estimating the widening functions and audiences of vernacular texts, we must take account not only of the artistry of the writers and the perennial appeal of certain themes. There is also the fact that literature, in western Europe, has enjoyed a wider variety of patronage sources than any other form of intellectual or artistic expression, and a wider range of consumers. Lack of literacy was no bar to audiences for literature performed orally, as medieval literature was. The best tales are often the twice-told or thrice-told tales. Literature arising in one milieu was quick to find acceptance in others, as well as in different genres and languages, driven by market demand and the ability of writers and booksellers to meet it. In the Middle Ages, and later, literature, more than any other form of culture, has illustrated the dictum of Alan of Lille, 'Authority has a nose of wax; it can be twisted in different ways for various reasons.'[1] It has also been better able than some other forms of culture to be driven by its own internal dynamics as well as responding to external issues.

As for Latin literature, it has a much clearer cut-off point, but it is a post-medieval one, the fifteenth and early sixteenth centuries. Paradoxically, it was the efforts of Renaissance humanists to insist on the imitation of authors from the golden age of Roman literature that turned Latin into a dead language for purposes of literary creation. Latin did remain in use as a medium of scientific and technical interchange for some time after that; medievalists today still encounter doctoral theses in their fields published in Latin in the late nineteenth and early twentieth centuries. And, until the 1960s, Latin remained the liturgical language of the Catholic church and of papal encyclicals, providing those who drafted such documents with the challenge of inventing neologisms with which to discuss contemporary subjects. But the use of Latin as a literary language ends with the Renaissance.

If most aspects of literature point to continuities with post-medieval Europe, there are several other areas of medieval literary culture that bear closer scrutiny as possible markers of medieval values that do not survive the period. They are the phenomenon of crossover, the free borrowings from Christian, classical, and medieval materials, the conjoining of attitudes or modes of sensibility from diverse ideological, generic, and cultural registers, and the willingness to satirize and subvert literary authorities, old and new, including the subversion of the genres in which authors write as well as the use of alternative genres for that purpose. The flexibility of medieval writers, patrons, and audiences, their capacity to live in more than one world at the same time, their adaptiveness, their playfulness, and their willingness to take a critical or subversive stance, whether expressed seriously or humorously, are all distinctive qualities of the medieval literary imagination that were passed on to later European literature. A society in which the same patrons supported the goliardic *Gambler's Mass*, devout liturgical poetry, and philosophy, or *chansons de geste* side by side with courtly romances and saints' lives, also felt comfortable producing biblical rewrites that altered the biblical account, adding topical and non-biblical material to religious drama, and donating vast sums to monasteries even as the lecherous cleric became a stock character in more than one literary genre. This medieval outlook continued to inform a European literary sensibility tolerant of works that parody or criticize cherished traditions, including religious ones. Here, the contrast with medieval and modern Islam is striking. On the other hand, a marker tending to separate medieval literary sensibilities from those of later periods is the combination of sacred and secular materials and attitudes in the same work. A lyric poet's praise of his lady-love in rhetoric drawn from hymns to the Virgin Mary, or a Franciscan scribe's dedication of his copy of Ovid's *Remedy of Love* to the Virgin raised no eyebrows in the Middle Ages, but they did tend to provoke unease in later Europeans and the view that disparate literary or musical materials and attitudes should be treated in discrete literary or musical forms.

In sum, literature is an area in which it is relatively difficult to locate and to date a chronological end of the Middle Ages. Subject matter, stylistic devices, and linguistic history aside, the two most important sectors in which medieval literature can be seen as foundational for later European literature are its ability to use canonical texts, whether classical, Christian, or medieval, as springboards for innovation and creativity, reaching across literary genres and registers in so doing, and its vernacularizing of literary production, consumption, and self-understanding, enabling the vernaculars to guarantee the perdurance and continuing transformations of classical and Christian literature as well as of medieval literature itself.

Turning next to medieval religious culture, the period's approach to the Christian tradition, it must be said at once that Christianity existed before, during, and after the Middle Ages. Our task here is to ascertain whether there were distinctly medieval ways of practicing and thinking about Christianity as well as notes struck by medieval Christianity that had post-medieval reverberations. Some medieval religious movements, to be sure, simply mark perennial options in the Christian tradition or continuing problems in theism or in the church as a social institution. The dualism of the Manichees has much in common with that of the Cathars; the third-age eschatology and spiritual church doctrines of the Joachites and the Free Spirit heretics have antecedents in Montanism and later parallels in some radical Protestant movements of the sixteenth century. In other cases there are real continuities. In spiritual doctrine and mysticism, in the desire to make a personal appropriation of the Christian message, medieval Christianity informed Protestant and Catholic lay piety and the experience and doctrine of mystics and contemplatives in later ages. Scholastic theology also made its post-medieval contributions. The thought of Thomas Aquinas, revived in the fifteenth and sixteenth centuries, was given more attention then, and in the nineteenth and early twentieth centuries, than it ever received in the Middle Ages, even if its partisans failed to make it the only orthodox option for Catholics. Ideas of the later scholastics that resonated with magisterial Protestant theologians include the stress on divine omnipotence and on God's direct action in the charismatic order, our inability to guarantee our salvation by following His law, and the shift from natural causality as the perceived relationship between God and the creation to the notions of will and covenant as the connections between God and the cosmos and God and humankind. Protestant scholasticism, born in the later sixteenth century out of the need to provide seminarians with systematic theological education, drew on the methods and structures of its medieval precursors. These ideas of orthodox medieval theologians were joined by ideas deemed heterodox in the Middle Ages, such as double predestination, the Bible as the sole norm of belief and practice, anti-sacramentalism, and anti-clericalism in the thought of many Protestant divines.

There are, at the same time, some distinctive medieval approaches to Christianity that did not continue into successive ages. The 'diverse but not adverse' outlook that enabled medieval theological schooling to embrace different interpretations of Christianity as equally capable of dwelling within the orthodox consensus and as equally deserving of official support proved frightening rather than stimulating to many theologians in the early sixteenth century. Whether the break-up of Christian unity put them in the Catholic or the Protestant camp, it coincided with the tendency, on the part of all confessions, to select some elements that had coexisted in the medieval orthodox consensus at the expense of others. The resultant new creedal formulae cut off access to the broader range of opinions with which medieval Christians felt comfortable. Even within Catholicism, although other alternatives remained available in the face of efforts of neo-Thomists to promote their position as normative, the conception of the orthodox consensus narrowed, became more rigid, and was enforced by new institutional mechanisms for imposing censorship and repressing theological deviance. While there are more continuities between medieval Christianity and early modern Catholicism than between medieval and Protestant thought, the effort to limit theological options gave counter-Reformation Catholicism a different texture. Perhaps most striking is the abandonment of the Ockhamism that had been the single most popular movement in high and late medieval theology.

The most visible and significant markers of medieval religious attitudes that ended with the period are the concept of Europe as an international Christian commonwealth, the notion that this commonwealth's two chief leaders are the pope and the Holy Roman Emperor, and that its highest loci of authority are ecumenical councils of the church. As a viable center of power, the empire began to self-destruct in the second half of the thirteenth century. While, in theory, the imperial office was open to any European candidate, the Germans rejected that idea. Their Golden Bull of 1356, a major piece of constitutional legislation, stipulates that the contest is open to German candidates only and renames the imperial title Holy Roman Emperor of the German Nation. Ecclesiastical universalism was also on the wane, helped along by the seating of participants in general councils in national delegations in the fifteenth century and by the polarization of national allegiances based on whether rulers were pro-French or anti-French during the Avignonese phase of papal history and then the Great Schism. In these respects, the viability of the notion of a pan-European church whose unity was guaranteed by a pope recognized by all European Christians was endangered from within, well before the Middle Ages ended. These conditions set the stage for the reconfiguration of the Christian commonwealth along national, princely, or urban lines in the sixteenth century, whether or not that move meant the rejection of the pope's spiritual authority. Here, the Hussite movement marks the end of medieval Christianity. With a theology different from that of Rome and the support of fifteenth-century Bohemian kings except Sigismund, it possessed all the attributes of a Protestant state church. The fact that Sigismund tried to use his imperial office and the council of Constance, in theory and practice European Christendom's highest authority, to crush Huss and his followers, and the fact that he failed, points up vividly the demise of the universalism to which Sigismund appealed and the birth of the national church movement that replaced it. In this area, medieval Christianity created both an internationalist self-conception and also the anti-universalist tendencies that were to undermine it decisively.

A distinctive quality of medieval thought that is a major foundational attitude in religion, theology, law, philosophy, and science is the boldness and rigor with which thinkers interrogated their foundation documents and traditions. Religious leaders and thinkers criticized and contextualized biblical and patristic authority, naturalized their religion repeatedly in Roman, Germanic, Celtic, and feudal terms, and reinvented monasticism again and again, adapting it to meet current needs. The fact that theology was seen as the queen of the sciences drew the best and most creative minds and the most institutional support to this subject. The critical attitude to authorities is also visible in the work of canon lawyers and it informed philosophy as well, since much philosophy was done by theologians. Theologians and canonists saw that the price of survival was adaptation and the explication and defense of religious ideas in language and arguments comprehensible and persuasive to intellectuals in other fields. In contrast with their opposite numbers in Byzantium and Islam, their preparatory education perforce acquainted them with philosophy and science and they taught in universities cheek by jowl with colleagues in other disciplines, which put them on their mettle to do just that. They also recognized the importance of preaching and spiritual direction in the vernacular to a widening circle of lay people, who were thereby empowered to make their own contributions to religious life, theology, and mysticism. Percolation up and trickledown both describe the interactions of the learned and the less learned in pursuit of holiness. There is a real parallel here with the vernacularization and laicization of literature. There were also some subjects, notably sex and money, on which medieval Christians followed their own lights, in opposition to their ecclesiastical leaders. Philosophy made its single most important collective statement in the logicians' decision that Aristotelianism was inadequate and in their striking innovations from Anselm of Canterbury to the late medieval terminists. Their supplanting of revered authorities with new philosophical ideas and the ability to think rigorously about counterfactuals and to imagine possible worlds created an outlook that had a destabilizing effect on authority and on received ideas as such. In some cases, the specifics of medieval philosophy, theology, and science had a significant post-medieval impact, as with the controlled experiment, the mathematicization of science, the development of formal logic, and the rejection of Aristotle's explanation of local motion or his doctrines of intelligible species and quintessence. More important as a foundational contribution is the habit of mind and the attitude toward authority that made these positions possible for high and late medieval scholastics. Similar attitudes made possible the scientific revolution of the seventeenth century, whose effect was also to overthrow those aspects of the classical world view, as modified by medieval Jewish, Muslim, and Latin thinkers, that continued to inform European science and philosophy after the Middle Ages.

Economic theory also offers clear lines of demarcation. We can certainly say that the distinctive medieval theories of the just price and the sinfulness of usury were abandoned well before the end of the Middle Ages by governments that fixed prices for reasons notably different from those of the theorists, and by all involved in commerce and banking, even if we have to wait until the late fifteenth and early sixteenth centuries to see the usury theory abandoned by Catholics and Protestants alike. The distinctive medieval view of poverty as a misfortune, not a vice, and the period's understanding of who deserved support did not inform secular jurisprudence in the Middle Ages itself. Medieval poverty theory was retained after the

Middle Ages in canon law courts and in the poor relief systems of early modern Catholic jurisdictions and abandoned in those where the Puritan equation of poverty and vice held sway. The most formative legacy of the Middle Ages in this area was the laicization of the agencies for administering poor relief as a response to the economic and demographic crises of the fourteenth century, a secularizing trend that continued to define practice in early modern Europe in every confessional environment.

Political theorists, including ecclesiologists, were likewise responsive to crises and, throughout the high and late Middle Ages, were increasingly informed by a common fund of ideas from Roman and canon law, from classical political philosophy, and from philosophical and theological ideas of medieval derivation. Whether focusing on church–state relations, the relations between popes and general councils, or the relations of kings and barons or kings and parliaments, thinkers in all these fields display similarities. They all drew on Roman corporation law, applying a private law concept to constitutional theory, the idea of counsel and consent and representation and consent, and the notion that secular authority extends over a ruler's clerical subjects. Feudal monarchy theorists added the idea of government by contract. Theorists in these areas and people engaged in politics saw as complementary institutions that were actually at loggerheads. However much they weighted one side of a complementary pairing against the other, they agreed that, ideally, popes and lay rulers, popes and councils, kings and barons, kings and parliaments ought to cooperate. Aside from a thinker like Wycliff, who thereby placed himself outside the medieval consensus, they did not think that if one side got out of hand it was acceptable for the other side in the pairing to subsume it. Both papalists and imperialists and papalists and conciliarists believed that a unitary Christian commonwealth existed in which both institutions were necessary, however power might be allotted between them. Constitutionalists believed that both kings and barons and kings and parliaments were needed, however much they might want to alter the balance of authority between them. What makes these thinkers medieval is their tolerance of mixed sovereignties of these kinds. And, with the exception of conciliarism, whose role in the constitutional theory of the Catholic church received no definitive answer in the Middle Ages or later, this medieval tolerance of mixed sovereignty proved unacceptable to early modern Europeans. With respect to church and state, all medieval views on their relations fragmented in the sixteenth century, coalescing again in a new symbiotic relationship in both Catholic and Protestant confessions, with the state at every level domesticating the church. The issue of the location of sovereignty within the state was not settled for early modern Europe until the seventeenth century in most countries, with royal absolutism triumphing on the continent except in Sweden, and parliamentary sovereignty triumphing in England. These early modern arrangements, departures from medieval political theory at its most basic, sometimes made use of medieval thought, from the conciliarists to Marsilio of Padua to Aquinas to Magna Carta to the theological distinction between God's absolute and ordained power. Still, the discontinuities are clearer here than elsewhere.

In sum, the points in time when the Middle Ages ended differ markedly in different aspects of medieval intellectual history. The variable extent to which medieval tastes, tolerances, modes of thought, methods, and concrete ideas were superseded in some areas and endured as foundations of early modern or more recent European thought in others reminds us, as we conclude, that diversity, inconsistency, and contradiction, and the ability to live with them and to thrive on them, are features of medieval culture that militate against any monolithic, schematic, or simplistic understanding of it. Developments in some fields were affected profoundly by political, economic, or ecclesiastical crises or developments in adjacent scholarly fields; other movements marched to their own drummers. The staying power, appeal, or perceived utility of medieval culture to post-medieval Europeans differed from field to field. But the central lesson every field conveyed to later ages is that it is possible, and desirable, to invent and to reinvent ideas and aesthetic forms of expression, maintaining an organic connection with tradition while using it critically to fuel a continuous process of intellectual self-fashioning.

Notes

The following abbreviations will be used:

CCCM = Corpus Christianorum, Continuatio Medievalis
CCSL = Corpus Christianorum, Series Latina
PL = *Patrologia latina cursus completus*, ed. J. P. Migne

Translations are my own when other translators are not cited.

CHAPTER 1   *From Apology to the Constantinian Establishment*

1.   Tertullian, *Apologeticum* 50.13, ed. E. Dekkers, CCSL (Turnhout, 1954), 1: 171.
2.   Vincent of Lérins, *Commonitorium* 2.3, ed. R. S. Moxon (Cambridge, 1910), p. 10.
3.   Tertullian, *De carne Christi* 5.1.4, ed. Aem. Kroymann, CCSL (Turnhout, 1954), 1: 881.
4.   Tertullian, *De praescriptio haereticorum* 7.9, ed. F. R. Refoulé, CCSL (Turnhout, 1954), 1: 193.

CHAPTER 2   *The Latin Church Fathers, I: Ambrose and Jerome*

1.   Ambrose, to Emperor Valentinianus, *Epistula* 18.7, *PL* 16: 974A.
2.   Ambrose, *De officiis ministrorum* 3.4.28, ibid., 153B.
3.   Jerome, to Eustochium, *Epistula* 22.29, in Jerome, *Select Letters*, ed. F. A. Wright (Cambridge, MA, 1963), p. 124.
4.   Jerome, to Marcella, *Epistula* 127.5, ibid., p. 450.

CHAPTER 3   *The Latin Church Fathers, II:*
Augustine and Gregory the Great

1.   Augustine, *Confessiones* 8.17, ed. Lucas Verheijen, CCSL (Turnhout, 1981), 27: 124.
2.   Ibid. 8.29, 27: 131.
3.   Plotinus, *Enneads* 6.9.11, ed. and trans. A. H. Armstrong (Cambridge, MA, 1988), 7: 344

CHAPTER 4 *Hanging by a Thread: The Transmitters and Monasticism*

1. Cassiodorus, *Institutes* 1.27.2, trans. Leslie Webber Jones (New York, 1966), p. 127.

CHAPTER 7 *Celtic and Old French Literature*

1. Brigid [?], 'The Heavenly Banquet,' trans. Seán O'Faoláin, in *The Silver Branch*, ed. Seán O'Faoláin (New York, 1938), p. 31. I have altered the translator's punctuation slightly here and in the next two quotations.
2. 'May Day,' trans. T. W. Rolleston, ibid., pp. 42–3.
3. 'The Monk and His Cat,' trans. Seán O'Faoláin, ibid., pp. 40–1.

CHAPTER 8 *Varieties of Germanic Literature: Old Norse, Old High German, and Old English*

1. *The Lay of Atli*, trans. Bertha Phillpotts, in *Edda and Saga* (London, 1931), p. 60.
2. *Njal's Saga*, ch. 70, trans. Magnus Magnusson and Hermann Palsson (Harmondsworth, 1960), p. 159.
3. *The Saga of Grettir the Strong*, ch. 40, trans. George Ainslie Hight (London, 1913), p. 112.
4. Ibid., ch. 83, p. 216.
5. *Njal's Saga*, ch. 1, p. 39.
6. Ibid., ch. 77, p. 171.
7. *The Nibelungenlied*, trans. A. T. Hatto (Harmondsworth, 1965), p. 291.
8. 'Elene,' trans. Charles W. Kennedy, in *Early English Christian Poetry* (New York, 1963), p. 185. I have omitted the spacing the translator places in each line to indicate the caesura here and in the quotation cited in n. 10.
9. 'Wulf and Eadwacer,' as trans. and quoted by George K. Anderson in *The Literature of the Anglo-Saxons*, revised edn. (Princeton, NJ, 1966), p. 164. I have altered slightly the translation of the last line quoted.
10. 'The Dream of the Rood,' trans. Kennedy, in *Early English Christian Poetry*, pp. 93–4.

CHAPTER 10 *Peoples of the Book: Muslim and Jewish Thought*

1. Trans. Edward Westermark, in *Anthology of Islamic Literature from the Rise of Islam to Modern Times*, ed. James Kritzeck (New York, 1964), p. 67.
2. Trans. L. P. Elwell-Sutton, ibid., p. 68.
3. Ibn Sara, 'Pool with Turtles,' trans. Harold Moreland, ibid., p. 137.
4. Ibn Wahbun, 'On Hearing Al-Mutanabbi Praised,' trans. Moreland, ibid.

CHAPTER 11 *Western European Thought in the Tenth and Eleventh Centuries*

1. Anselm of Canterbury, *Proslogion* 2, in *Opera omnia*, ed. Franciscus Salesius Schmitt, 6 vols. (Edinburgh, 1940–61), 1: 101.

CHAPTER 12 *The Renaissance of the Twelfth Century*

1. John of Salisbury, *Metalogicon* 3.4, ed. J. B. Hall and K. S. B. Keats-Rohan, CCCM (Turnhout, 1991), 98: 117.
2. John of Garland, *De triumphis ecclesiae*, ed. T. Wright (London, 1856), p. 14.

CHAPTER 13 *Courtly Love Literature*

1. William of Aquitaine, 'Ab la dolchor del temps novel,' trans. James J. Wilhelm, in *Seven Troubadours: Creators of Modern Verse* (University Park, PA, 1970), p. 48.
2. Beatrice of Dia, 'A chantar m'er de so qu'ieu no volria,' trans. Wilhelm, ibid., p. 140.

CHAPTER 14 *Goliardic Poetry, Fabliaux, Satire, and Drama*

1. 'Sir Penny,' trans. George F. Whicher, in *The Goliard Poets* (New York, 1949), p. 147.
2. 'Spring,' trans. Helen Waddell, in *Medieval Latin Lyrics*, 5th edn. (London, 1951), pp. 207–9.
3. 'Let's Away with Study,' trans. Waddell, ibid., p. 203.

CHAPTER 15 *Later Medieval Literature*

1. Dante Alighieri, *Convivio* 2.1.2–6, in *Opere*, ed. Fredi Chiapelli (Milano, 1966), p. 153.
2. Dante Alighieri, *Paradiso* 33.145, ibid., p. 808.

CHAPTER 16 *Cistercians and Victorines*

1. Dante Alighieri, *Paradiso* 10.132, in *Opere*, ed. Fredi Chiapelli (Milano, 1966), p. 727.

CHAPTER 25 *Economic Theory: Poverty, the Just Price, and Usury*

1. Thomas Aquinas, *Commentary on the Nicomachean Ethics* 5. lect. 9.981, trans. C. I. Litzinger, 2 vols. (Chicago, 1964), 1: 426.

CHAPTER 26 *Political Theory:* Regnum *and* Sacerdotum, *Conciliarism, and Feudal Monarchy*

1. Ranulf de Glanvill, *Tractatus de legibus et consuetudinibus regni Angliae*, ed. and trans. G. D. G. Hall (London, 1965), p. 2.

2. Henry de Bracton, *On the Laws and Customs of England*, trans. Samuel E. Thorne, 4 vols. (Cambridge, MA, 1968–77), 2: 33.

3. Edward I, to Robert, archbishop of Canterbury, 30 September 1295, trans. B. Wilkinson, in *Constitutional History of Medieval England, 1216–1399*, 3 vols. (London, 1961), 3: 331.

CONCLUSION

1. Alan of Lille, *Contra haereticos* 1.30, *PL* 210: 333A. I would like to thank Winthrop Wetherbee for this reference.

Bibliographical Note

For further bibliography, with titles published up until April 1993, see Marcia L. Colish, ed., 'Medieval Europe: Church and Intellectual History,' in *The American Historical Association's Guide to Historical Literature*, 3rd edn., ed. Mary Beth Norton and Pamela Gerardi, 2 vols. (New York, 1995), 1: 676–703, with a historiographical orientation, 1: 621–4. The *Guide*'s sections on Byzantine, Islamic, and Jewish history and history of science also provide further titles and historiographical assessments of recent changes in those fields in their introductions. The publication dates given for titles in this note will be those of the most recent editions, rather than copyright dates, in cases where they differ.

We will proceed both topically and chronologically, starting with classical and Latin Christian learning. Although dated and reflecting a classical bias, Edward Kennard Rand, *Founders of the Middle Ages* (New York, 1928) provides a lively introduction to the apologists, church fathers, early Latin Christian writers, and Boethius. L. D. Reynolds and N. G. Wilson, *Scribes and Scholars: A Guide to the Transmission of Greek and Latin Literature*, 3rd edn. (Oxford, 1991) survey schools and scriptoria where classical manuscripts were copied, edited, and transmitted. The best introduction to pre-Carolingian Latin culture is Pierre Riché, *Education and Culture in the Barbarian West from the Sixth through the Eighth Century*, trans. John J. Contreni (Columbia, SC, 1978). The best recent overview of its subject is John J. Contreni, 'The Carolingian Renaissance: Education and Literary Culture,' in *The New Cambridge Medieval History*, vol. 2, ed. Rosamond McKitterick (Cambridge, 1995), pp. 709–57. For the speculative thought of the Carolingian period Contreni can be supplemented by M. L. W. Laistner, *Thought and Letters in Western Europe, AD 500–900*, revised edn. (Ithaca, NY, 1966). The contributors to Rosamund McKitterick, ed., *Carolingian Culture: Emulation and Innovation* (New York, 1994) present current assessments of the topics covered. Eleanor Shipley Duckett, *Death and Life in the Tenth Century* (Ann Arbor, MI, 1971) charts the highs and lows of Latin culture, treating monasticism, literature, and art as well as education. The seminal interpretation of twelfth-century Latin culture, classically biased yet fundamental, is Charles Homer Haskins, *The Renaissance of the Twelfth Century*, first published in 1927 (Cambridge, MA, 1976); for views on how his thesis has held up after fifty years, see the papers in Robert L. Benson, Giles Constable, and Carol A. Lanham, eds., *Renaissance and Renewal in the Twelfth Century* (Toronto, 1991). The best one-volume treatment of medieval universities is Alan B. Cobban, *The Medieval Universities: Their Development and Organization* (Berkeley, CA, 1988), covering institutions and curricula in various countries. Charles Homer Haskins, *The Rise of Universities* (Ithaca, NY, 1979) offers a highly readable introduction to student life and professorial working conditions. The essays in David L. Wagner, ed., *The Seven Liberal Arts* (Bloomington, IN, 1986), explain how each discipline was taught and understood throughout the Middle Ages.

A topic of central importance for understanding the dissemination of vernacular as well as Latin culture and one receiving increasing attention in recent scholarship is literacy, both in itself and in relation to orality. Rosamond McKitterick, *The Carolingians and the Written Word* (Cambridge, 1989) argues convincingly for wider lay literacy than was hitherto suspected; the essays she has edited in *The Uses of Literacy in Early Medieval Europe* (Cambridge, 1990) do the same, for both Byzantium and western Europe. A seminal and wide-ranging study of the changing relations between literacy and orality is Brian Stock, *The Implications of Literacy: Written Language and Models of Interpretation in the Eleventh and Twelfth Century* (Princeton, NJ, 1983). Charting the impact of growing literacy on politics and ecclesiastical life as well as literature, the findings of M. T. Clanchy, *From Memory to Written Record: England 1066–1307*, 2nd edn. (Oxford, 1993) could well be extended to other countries.

A basic introduction to medieval literature from the seventh to the sixteenth century, W. T. H. Jackson, *Medieval Literature: A History and Guide* (New York, 1966) is compact, readable, and covers Latin and the vernaculars. C. S. Lewis, *The Discarded Image: An Introduction to Medieval and Renaissance Literature* (Cambridge, 1994) provides essential background on the beliefs and world views, pagan and Christian, that informed medieval authors and their audiences. Peter Dronke, *Poetic Individuality in the Middle Ages: New Departures in Poetry, 1000–1050*, 2nd edn. (London, 1986) offers an important reinterpretation of the place of medieval poetry in the western literary tradition that can be applied to prose as well. His *Women Writers of the Middle Ages: A Critical Study of Texts from Perpetua (d. 203) to Marguerite Porete (d. 1310)* (New York, 1984), is equally path-breaking. The best guides to major vernacular literatures are Michel Zink, *Medieval French Literature: An Introduction*, trans. Jeff Rider (Binghamton, NY, 1994), a comprehensive survey of all genres with a history of the French language; George K. Anderson, *Literature of the Anglo–Saxons*, revised edn. (Princeton, NJ, 1966), which translates texts cited into modern English; J. A. Burrow, *Medieval Writers and Their Work: Middle English Literature and Its Background, 1100–1500* (Oxford, 1982), which locates authors in their social and educational contexts; Bertha S. Phillpotts, *Edda and Saga* (London, 1931), which introduces readers to the literary conventions specific to Old Norse; J. E. Caerwyn Williams, *The Irish Literary Tradition*, trans. Patrick K. Ford (Cardiff, 1992), chs. 1–4, which provides generous samples of texts in translation; Maurice O'Connell Walshe, *Medieval German Literature: A Survey* (Cambridge, MA, 1962), an overview of all genres; and the relevant chapters of Ernest Hatch Wilkins, *A History of Italian Literature* (Cambridge, MA, 1954) and Gerald E. Brenan, *The Literature of the Spanish People from Roman Times to the Present Day*, 2nd edn. (Cambridge, 1953). The best one-volume survey of medieval Latin literature is Frederick A. Wright and Thomas A. Sinclair, *A History of Later Latin Literature* (New York, 1931).

Three wide-ranging introductions to the medieval church and religious culture are Jeffrey Burton Russell, *A History of Medieval Christianity: Prophecy and Order* (New York, 1968), whose theme is the creative tension between the church's reforming mission and its accommodations to secular society; David Knowles and Dmitri Obolensky, *The Christian Centuries*, vol. 2 (New York, 1968), covering the evangelization of Europe and the development of Christian institutions and doctrines; and Joseph H.

Lynch, *The Medieval Church: A Brief History* (London, 1992), which combines narrative church history with analysis of institutions, theology, religious orders, sacraments, heresy, and women in religion. The best guide to the latter subject, dealing both with laywomen and those in religious orders, is John A. Nicholas and Lillian Shank, eds., *Medieval Religious Women*, 3 vols. (Kalamazoo, MI, 1984–92). The single best introduction to medieval monasticism is C. H. Lawrence, *Medieval Monasticism: Forms of Religious Life in the Middle Ages*, 2nd edn. (New York, 1989). A classic evocation of monastic culture is Jean Leclercq, *The Love of Learning and the Desire for God*, 3rd edn., trans. Catherine Misrahi (New York, 1982).

Of the works surveying popular religious devotion, wide-angle views are provided by Bernard McGinn, John Meyendorff, and Jean Leclercq, eds., *Christian Spirituality: Origins to the Twelfth Century* (New York, 1992) and Jill Raitt, Bernard McGinn, and John Meyendorff, eds., *Christian Spirituality: The High Middle Ages and the Reformation* (New York, 1989). Contributors to the first volume treat liturgy, theology, mysticism, religious art, clergy, laity, and women in religion east and west; the second volume also charts continuities and discontinuities with post-medieval Christianity. The classic one-volume study is Herbert Grundmann, *Religious Movements in the Middle Ages*, trans. Steven Rowan (Notre Dame, IN, 1995), covering heterodox as well as orthodox movements. Fine treatments of important popular devotions, beliefs, and practices include Peter Brown, *The Cult of the Saints: Its Rise and Function in Latin Christianity* (Chicago, 1981), which contextualizes this cult socially as well as spiritually; Brown's *The Body and Society: Men, Women, and Sexual Renunciation in Early Christianity* (New York, 1988), a finely nuanced study of the development of Christian sexual asceticism against the backdrop of pagan asceticism; Marina Warner, *Alone of All Her Sex: The Myth and Cult of the Virgin Mary* (New York, 1983) treats both theological and popular approaches to Mariology; Jonathan Sumption, *Pilgrimage: An Image of Medieval Religion* (Totowa, NJ, 1976) focuses on France; Jeffrey Burton Russell, *Witchcraft in the Middle Ages* (Ithaca, NY, 1972) provides the best introduction to that subject; Richard Kieckhefer, *Magic in the Middle Ages* (Cambridge, 1989) covers white and black magic; and Caroline Walker Bynum, *Holy Feast and Holy Fast: The Religious Significance of Food to Medieval Women* (Berkeley, CA, 1987) is an insightful study of fasting and Eucharistic devotion among women and of how medieval notions of gender affected their religious practice.

The best treatment of theology as an aspect of high culture is Jaroslav Pelikan, *The Christian Tradition: A History of the Development of Doctrine*, vols. 1–4 (Chicago, 1971–89). Thematically organized, these volumes trace the emergence of consensus Christianity in the early church and its permutations up through the Reformation, also delineating continuities and discontinuities with post-medieval confessions in vol. 4. Vol. 2 treats the theology of the Greek church and its Slavic daughter churches to the fifteenth century. The approach, while magisterial, is accessible and ecumenical. For the initial emergence of scholastic theology, see Gillian R. Evans, *Old Arts and New Theology: The Beginnings of Theology as an Academic Discipline* (Oxford, 1980), which accents the interplay of theology and the liberal arts in the twelfth century; and Marcia L. Colish, *Peter Lombard*, 2 vols. (Leiden, 1994), which provides an in-depth study of the most influential figure in scholastic theological education and also reconstructs the theologies of masters in his milieu in the first half of the twelfth century. Another major dimension of medieval theology is treated by the contributors to G. W. H. Lampe, ed., *The Cambridge History of the Bible*, vol. 3 (Cambridge, 1969), who cover all aspects of Bible study, Latin and vernacular; and Beryl Smalley, *The Study of the Bible in the*

Middle Ages, 3rd edn. (Oxford, 1983), a seminal work accenting the rise of literal exegesis in the twelfth century.

Philosophy is a field in which it is harder to recommend titles with unconditional enthusiasm. Recent scholarship, particularly on the fourteenth and twelfth centuries and on logic and semantics, has moved very swiftly in the past three decades. No single work in English summarizes this new material in a manner accessible to non-specialists, integrating it with previous knowledge. Reservations, therefore, attach to all the titles mentioned here. An initial effort to bring new findings on medieval logic together with other aspects of medieval philosophy is David Luscombe, *Medieval Thought* (Oxford, 1997). But its explanations are often unclear and sketchy and its treatment of Muslim and Jewish figures is inadequate. The most balanced general introduction is Frederick C. Copelston, *A History of Philosophy*, vols. 2–3 (New York, 1950–3), although its date means that recent new editions and discoveries are, perforce, not noted. John Marenbon, in *Early Medieval Philosophy: An Introduction* (London, 1983) and *Later Medieval Philosophy (1050–1350): An Introduction* (London, 1991), highlights the relations between the liberal arts and philosophy in the first volume and overemphasizes psychology in the second, at the expense of other equally important topics. Uneven in the quality of its contributions, Peter Dronke, ed., *A History of Twelfth-Century Philosophy* (Cambridge, 1988) is strongest on Abelard and Chartrain Platonism. While the contributors to Norman Kretzmann, Anthony Kenny, and Jan Pinborg, eds., *The Cambridge History of Later Medieval Philosophy* (New York, 1988) display more uniform expertise and touch on most aspects of philosophy from the reception of Aristotle onward, the editors allow the history of logic, important as it is, to elbow aside other subjects.

Readers seeking additional information on political, economic, and legal theory fare better. All aspects of political, ecclesiastical, and legal thought receive fine treatment by contributors to J. H. Burns, ed., *The Cambridge History of Medieval Political Thought, c. 350–c. 1450* (Cambridge, 1988). Paul Vinogradoff, *Roman Law in Medieval Europe* (New York, 1968), long the classic treatment of its subject, is now happily joined by James A. Brundage, *Medieval Canon Law* (New York, 1995), the only one-volume survey in English and an extremely valuable contribution. Brian Tierney, *Religion, Law, and the Growth of Constitutional Thought, 1150–1650* (Cambridge, 1982) is an outstanding study of the impact of theology, Roman law, and canon law on political theory, secular and ecclesiastical, by the leading scholar in the field; his *Foundations of Conciliar Theory: The Contributions of the Medieval Canonists from Gratian to the Great Schism* (Cambridge, 1968) is the single most important work on conciliarism. John T. Gilchrist, *The Church and Economic Activity in the Middle Ages* (London, 1969) provides a solid survey of canonical thought on the just price, usury, and poor law. Karl F. Morrison, *Tradition and Authority in the Western Church* (Princeton, NJ, 1969), shows the growth of multiple authoritative traditions in canonical thought to the twelfth century. Frederick H. Russell, *The Just War in the Middle Ages* (Cambridge, 1975) is a classic analysis of the reversal of the Christian turn-the-other-cheek doctrine through Aquinas. Antony Black, *Political Thought in Europe, 1250–1450* (Cambridge, 1992) covers secular and ecclesiastical theories, their varied sources and local applications, with a valuable comparison between European political theory and that of Byzantium and Islam. Finally, Denys Hay, *Europe: The Emergence of an Idea* (Edinburgh, 1957) shows how the medieval idea of Europe as the Christian commonwealth gave way to other conceptions of European civilization.

Moving to science, art, and music, David C. Lindberg, *The Beginnings of Western*

Science: The European Scientific Tradition in Philosophical, Religious, and Institutional Context, 800 BC to AD 1450 (Chicago, 1992), is an outstanding and accessible introduction. The subtitle accurately reflects Lindberg's emphasis and he also acquaints non-specialists with debates in the field, especially the relation of medieval science to later chapters of its history. His edited collection of essays, *Science in the Middle Ages* (Chicago, 1978) brings together papers by leading experts on a wide range of scientific subjects. Edward Grant, *The Foundations of Modern Science in the Middle Ages: Their Religious, Institutional, and Intellectual Contexts* (Cambridge, 1996), a masterful synthesis by a leading scholar, sees the Middle Ages as foundational in science in much the same way as this book does. The single best introduction to medieval medicine is Nancy Siraisi, *Medieval and Early Renaissance Medicine: An Introduction to Knowledge and Practice* (Chicago, 1990), which treats the social and educational status of practitioners as well as their theories. The most recent and best introduction to medicine in medieval Islam, although densely written, is Manfred Ullmann, *Islamic Medicine*, trans. Jean Watts (Edinburgh, 1978). George Molland, *Mathematics and the Medieval Ancestry of Physics* (London, 1995) is the most recent synthesis of research on the Oxford 'calculators' and the mathematization of science in the high Middle Ages. The single best one-volume introduction to medieval art is Marilyn Stokstad, *Medieval Art* (New York, 1986), covering all periods, regions, and genres. For Byzantine art, a comparable survey, equally well balanced, is provided by David Talbot Rice, *Art of the Byzantine Era* (New York, 1963). Jeremy Yudkin, *Music in Medieval Europe* (Englewood Cliffs, NJ, 1989) is an outstanding introduction, covering ecclesiastical and secular music, musical instruments and musical patronage, with melodies cited in modern notation and accompanying texts translated into English. Each chapter ends with a discography and bibliography. The standard authority on Byzantine music is Egon Wellesz, *A History of Byzantine Music and Hymnography*, 2nd edn. (Oxford, 1962), a thorough survey integrating music into the history of the Byzantine liturgy; many texts cited are translated.

On Byzantium more widely, all aspects of its intellectual, spiritual, and artistic history are treated by contributors to Alexander P. Kazhdan et al., eds., *The Oxford Dictionary of Byzantium*, 3 vols. (New York, 1991), a standard reference work. Kazhdan and Giles Constable, eds., *People and Power in Byzantium: An Introduction to Modern Byzantine Studies* (Washington, 1982) include essays surveying art, religion, and literature. N. G. Wilson, *Scholars of Byzantium*, 2nd edn. (Baltimore, MD, 1996) provides the only overview in English of Byzantine classical philology. Paul Lemerle, *Byzantine Humanism: The First Phase*, trans. Helen Lindsay and Ann Moffat (Cambridge, 1986) is broader in range, covering schools, learning, and literature to the end of the tenth century. Alexander P. Kazhdan and Ann Wharton Epstein, in *Change in Byzantine Culture in the Eleventh and Twelfth Centuries* (Berkeley, CA, 1975), while presenting a dated, Marxist, view of culture as an epiphenomenon of society's material concerns and while overstating the case for change, none the less provide a valuable survey of Byzantine culture in the centuries indicated, although art, theology, and jurisprudence are omitted. John Meyendorff, *Byzantine Theology: Historical Trends and Doctrinal Themes*, 2nd edn. (New York, 1987) is a lucid and concise introduction by a renowned authority.

For Muslim intellectual history and for Jewish thinkers writing in Arabic, the standard reference work is Peter Malcolm Holt, Ann K. S. Lambton, and Bernard Lewis, eds., *The Cambridge History of Islam*, 2 vols. (Cambridge, 1970), with contributions on all pertinent topics. Richard Walzer, *Greek into Arabic: Essays on Islamic Philosophy* (Columbia, SC, 1982) provides a basic account of the translation and absorption of

Greek science and philosophy. Charles M. Stanton, *Higher Learning in Islam: The Classical Period, AD 700–1300* (Savage, MD, 1990) treats religious and legal education and the parallel schooling in science and philosophy, while it lasted, with an overview of Muslim philosophy and science. M. L. J. Young, ed., *Religion, Learning, and Science in the 'Abbasid Period* (New York, 1990) contains up-to-date essays on the topics indicated. Ignaz Goldziher, *Introduction to Islamic Theology and Law*, trans. Andras Hamori and Ruth Hamori (Princeton, NJ, 1981), is the most authoritative and influential study of its subject. Reynolds A. Nicholson, *A Literary History of the Arabs* (London, 1992) is now the standard survey of that field. Majid Fakhry, *A History of Islamic Philosophy*, 2nd edn. (New York, 1983) offers a balanced introduction to philosophy, accenting the increasing Aristotelianism of thinkers through the age of Averroes. A. J. Arberry, *Sufism: An Account of the Mystics of Islam* (London, 1979) is the standard introduction to Sufism, which it treats evenhandedly. The leading authority on medieval Jewish speculative thought is Colette Sirat, *A History of Jewish Philosophy in the Middle Ages* (Cambridge, 1985), covering its subject comprehensively. Joseph L. Blau, *The Story of Jewish Philosophy* (New York, 1962) places Jewish thought in its social context, a perspective that needs more attention. Gerschom G. Scholem, *On the Kabbalah and its Symbolism*, trans. Ralph Manheim (New York, 1972) is the best introduction to Jewish mysticism by the authority chiefly responsible for launching interest in this subject in recent scholarship.

Index